FOOTBALL is an unrelentingly punishing sport, and every NFL team prepares constantly for the likelihood — the certainty — that even franchise players can go down at any time. Someone new must always be ready, trained, and primed to step in at a moment's notice.

In the NFL there is only one sure thing: every day, someone will have to be the Next Man Up.

NEXT MAN UP

ALSO BY JOHN FEINSTEIN

Last Dance

Let Me Tell You a Story
(with Red Auerbach)

Caddy for Life

Open

The Punch

The Last Amateurs

The Majors

A March to Madness

A Civil War

A Good Walk Spoiled

Play Ball

Hard Courts

Forever's Team

A Season Inside

A Season on the Brink

Last Shot
(A Final Four Mystery)

Running Mates
(A Mystery)

Winter Games
(A Mystery)

NEXT MAN UP

A Year Behind the Lines in Today's NFL

JOHN FEINSTEIN

BACK BAY BOOKS
Little, Brown and Company
New York   Boston   London

Back Bay Books / Little, Brown and Company
Hachette Book Group
237 Park Avenue, New York, NY 10017
www.hachettebookgroup.com

Originally published in hardcover by Little, Brown and Company, October 2005
First Back Bay paperback edition, October 2006

Back Bay Books is an imprint of Little, Brown and Company. The Back Bay
Books name and logo are trademarks of Hachette Book Group, Inc.

The publisher is not responsible for websites (or their content) that are
not owned by the publisher.

Library of Congress Cataloging-in-Publication Data

Feinstein, John.
  Next man up : a year behind the lines in today's NFL / John Feinstein.
    p. cm.
  Includes index.
  HC ISBN 978-0-316-00964-5
  PB ISBN 978-0-316-01328-4
  1. Baltimore Ravens (Football team)   I. Title.
GV956.B35F45 2005
796.332'64'097526 — dc22   2005017217

10 9 8 7 6

RRD-H

Printed in the United States of America

*This is for Martin Feinstein, my dad,
who has always read what I have written —
even when the subject isn't opera.*

Contents

NEXT
MAN
UP

Introduction

FOR AS LONG AS I CAN REMEMBER, the National Football League has had an aura around it.

When I was a boy in New York, tickets to see the New York Giants play in Yankee Stadium were as coveted as a seat on the New York Stock Exchange. No one I knew could remember when Giants tickets had been sold to the general public. What's more, if you lived in New York, there was no way to see Giants home games on television because Commissioner Pete Rozelle's blackout rules forbade broadcast of games within a seventy-five-mile radius of the stadium where they were played. I knew New Yorkers who drove to Connecticut on Sundays so they could watch the Giants game on the CBS affiliate in Hartford. Even then, in the 1960s, every NFL game was a big deal.

I grew up listening to Marty Glickman, Al DeRogatis, and Chip Cipolla broadcast the home games on WNEW radio. In that sense, I was fortunate, because Glickman was a genius and I loved listening to him say, "Take it, DeRo," when it was time to break down a play. At the same time, I became a fan of the New York Jets, who had a flashy young quarterback named Joe Namath and, most important, tickets available. My friends and I would buy $3 standing-room tickets and almost always find empty seats in the corporate boxes in the downstairs sections of Shea Stadium, especially late in the season when the weather got cold. I still remember my dad getting tickets from a friend to see the Jets play the Houston Oilers in 1965, two days after I'd had eight teeth taken out in preparation for orthodonture.

I couldn't eat much at the game, but Namath threw four touchdown passes and the Jets won, 41–14.

On the day that the Jets played the Baltimore Colts in Super Bowl III — January 12, 1969, a date I never have to look up — I paced up and down in front of the television set as the game began. That had become my superstition. When I paced, the Jets won. By the fourth quarter the Jets were leading, 16–0, and my father came home from a concert, walked in, and asked me the score. When I told him, he was shocked and sat down to watch. "Stop pacing," he said. "You're making me dizzy."

The lead seemed comfortable enough. I sat down. Don Shula put Johnny Unitas into the game and he immediately took the Colts the length of the field to cut the margin to 16–7. "Go ahead and pace," my father said, knowing I would never forgive him if the Colts somehow pulled the game out. They didn't, of course, and history was made. The Jets haven't been back to the Super Bowl since. Maybe I should have kept pacing.

I always knew pro football was a big deal when I was a kid. After all, there were only fourteen regular season games, so they all mattered. But it wasn't until my parents moved to Washington during my senior year of high school that I understood how it can become an entire town's obsession. My parents' move coincided with George Allen's second season as coach of the Redskins. I was finishing high school in New York, but I went to Washington most weekends and I was amazed by the Redskins' hold on the entire city. As I watched television, listened to the radio, read the sports section of the *Washington Post* and the *Washington Star*, it was as if nothing else existed. I still remember going to the Safeway one Sunday afternoon during a Redskins game and feeling as if I had wandered into a ghost town. The guy behind the counter looked at me strangely, as if to say, "If you don't *have* to be out, why are you?" He had a radio tuned to the game, naturally.

When the Redskins went to the Super Bowl that season, the story seemed only slightly more important than the impending end of the Vietnam War. Richard Nixon was sending plays to Allen from the White House. When the Redskins lost the Super Bowl to the Miami Dolphins, the entire city went into an extended state of depression.

I wasn't a Redskins fan by any stretch of the imagination, but I loved reading the *Post*'s saturation coverage of the team. Leonard Shapiro, the *Post*'s Redskins beat writer, became one of my first heroes in journalism, as did Ken Denlinger, their primary Redskins columnist. When I joined the *Post* after college, I got a close-up look at how important the Redskins were to the newspaper, to the local media in Washington, and to the entire city. During my first year at the paper, I was sitting at my desk on the first day of the NFL draft — this was so long ago, it was before the draft was on TV — when Ben Bradlee, the *Post's* legendary executive editor, came bouncing back to the sports section.

"Hey, George," he yelled at sports editor George Solomon, "who'd we get?"

I was twenty-one and even more of a wise guy than I am now. "Jeez, Ben," I said, "I didn't realize the *Post* had a pick in the NFL draft."

Bradlee whirled around, pointed a finger at me, and said, "Listen, Feinstein, if you don't like the Redskins, you can get the f—— out of town right now."

Those of you who have read or seen *All the President's Men* know I'm not exaggerating about the profanity. What's more, he wasn't smiling when he said it.

I learned my lesson: don't joke about the Redskins around the brass.

Twenty-five years later, little has changed in Washington or any other NFL city. The NFL team is the big news in town almost year-round. Those of us who still try to make the claim that baseball is the national pastime get laughed down in most quarters. Not only does the NFL have its own network — so does the NBA — people actually watch it. As I'm writing this paragraph, the NFL Network is providing in-depth coverage of the NFL combine. Think about this: people are sitting glued to their television sets, listening to scouts and general managers analyze the 40-yard-sprint times of wide receivers, the bench press of offensive linemen, and the arm strength of quarterbacks. Washington finally had a baseball team to cheer for in 2005 after thirty-three years without the sport, but there was far less speculation around town about the Nationals' starting rotation than about the Redskins' number one draft pick. A few miles up I-95, the acquisition of a solid wide receiver named Derrick Mason by the Ravens was at least as important to most people in Baltimore as the trade that brought Hall of Fame home run hitter Sammy Sosa to the Orioles.

I was never an NFL beat writer during my years at the *Post*, but I was assigned early on to write sidebars at Redskins games, then to cover big games in other cities. I always wanted to write a book about the NFL. What fascinated me about the league was that aura, the ability to do things that no other professional league can do. For instance, most professional sports make their players available to the press often. Almost every NFL team severely limits access to its players. There are limited times each week when the locker room is open to journalists, but most players simply stay out of the locker room during that time. Most practices are off-limits, except perhaps for a few minutes of stretching at the start of the day. Coaches are paranoid and secretive about everything. During his first stint in Washington, Coach Joe Gibbs once accused a friend of mine of writing a story about the weaknesses of an 0-5 Eagles team in order to get the Eagles fired up to beat the Redskins. He was completely serious.

And the NFL has clout with television far beyond other sports. NFL commissioner Paul Tagliabue, who had the good fortune to follow Pete Rozelle, undoubtedly the greatest commissioner in the history of sports, is professional sports' Last Don. Two years ago, when ESPN began airing a fictional show called *Playmakers,* based on the off-field lives of NFL players that depicted virtually all of them as womanizers, drug users, liars, and all-night partiers, Don Tags was horrified. He informed the ESPN people that he wasn't at all happy with the content of the show. It is worth remembering there may be no organization in sports that fancies itself more omnipotent than ESPN. The assumption among ESPN executives is that they are the most important people in sports. In fact, the *Sporting News* last year dubbed ESPN president George Bodenheimer number one on its list of the 100 most powerful people in sports.

They were wrong. Don Tags offered Bodenheimer and ESPN a deal they couldn't refuse: get the show gone, or we might just take our Sunday night games (and the Monday night games that air on corporate sister ABC) elsewhere. ESPN couldn't afford to take a chance on ending up with network TV's version of a horse head in the bed: no NFL football. Even though the show's ratings were very good and the reviews better than most of ESPN's so-called original entertainment offerings, they canceled the show. Pure coincidence, everyone on both sides said. The NFL would *never* tell ESPN what to do. Of course it wouldn't. It didn't have to. The message was clear.

Last year, with ABC's *Monday Night Football* ratings reaching record lows in part because of weak games that are placed on the schedule months before the season begins, Tagliabue decided it was time to strengthen the prime-time package — or packages, since the league has talked about possible Thursday and Saturday night games when its new TV deal begins in 2006 — by cherry-picking key games late in the season and moving them from Sunday afternoon to Monday night. Such a move couldn't possibly make Fox and CBS, who carry the Sunday games, very happy. And yet both willingly signed new deals in November of 2004 in which they agreed to pay more money — a total of $8 billion between the two of them, as opposed to $4.2 billion under terms of the current contract — in return for a weaker schedule. Only the NFL could sit at a negotiating table with two powerful networks and say with a straight face, we're giving you less and in return we want more.

Then this spring the NFL renegotiated its prime-time packages. ESPN took over *Monday Night Football,* paying $1.1 billion a year, about double what ABC paid for a package that had been absolutely bleeding money the past few years. NBC, desperate to get back into the NFL after a few years of the XFL and Arena football, paid $600 million for the Sunday night deal — the same money ESPN had been paying for Sunday night games. At these prices it is almost impossible for any of the networks to actually make money on the NFL. They don't care. They just want to have the NFL on their air.

I had several thoughts on how to go about writing an NFL book. One way was to use an approach I had enjoyed in writing about the pro golf tour, the pro tennis tours, and Major League baseball: just follow the sport for one season, from the draft through the Super Bowl. Certainly it would have been interesting to watch different teams, players, and coaches at critical times during the course of a season. But I knew doing such a book on the NFL wouldn't be at all like golf or tennis, because those sports are covered year-round by only a handful of people and are in the consciousness of most of the public only during those few weeks a year when their major championships are being played. Baseball is covered like a blanket, but unlike football, there is constant access to the players, coaches, and managers, allowing someone like me to develop relationships and follow stories. I knew I wouldn't get that opportunity in football, working with nothing more than a media credential.

The better route, I decided, was to find one team that could serve as an example of what life in the NFL is like. Each of the thirty-two teams is entirely different, of course, run by different people with different personalities and stories to tell. But the pressures are the same: the violent nature of the sport makes every game and, to a lesser degree, every practice an adventure. Every football team suffers serious injuries during the course of a season. No one knows when those injuries will occur or who will be hurt, just that someone will. There are no guaranteed contracts in the NFL. There may be no phrase in sports more meaningless than "Joe Smith signed a seven-year contract today" with an NFL team. The only thing the player is guaranteed is his signing bonus. A team can cut him five minutes later if it wants to and not pay him another cent. That's why, every spring, star players are cut or have their contracts restructured for less money. Almost anyone can get cut if a team doesn't think he is living up to the money he is being paid or if he is injured and not able to perform at the level expected when he was signed.

What's more, the NFL season is seventeen weeks (including the bye) of intense pressure and scrutiny, and I thought following one team, up close, through the highs and lows of their season would be infinitely more dramatic than following an entire league or conference. Because there are only sixteen games, each one is viewed as something just short of life-and-death by everyone involved. One loss in football is the equivalent of a ten-game losing streak in baseball. There are few places on Earth more miserable than an NFL team's training facility on the Monday morning after a loss. People talk in whispers, no one dares tell a joke or laugh out loud. Is that over the top? Sure. But livelihoods are at stake. Just look at how frequently coaches change jobs. Last year, when Brian Billick completed only his sixth season as coach of the Baltimore Ravens, he was tied for *fourth* place in longevity among NFL head coaches, behind only Bill Cowher (thirteen years in Pittsburgh), Jeff Fisher (ten years in Tennessee), and Mike Shanahan (ten years in Denver). The résumé of most NFL assistants reads like that of a career military man. Consider Mike Nolan, who left the Ravens at the end of last season to become the head coach in San Francisco. Nolan's travelogue goes like this: Oregon; Stanford; Rice; LSU; Denver Broncos; New York Giants; Washington Redskins; New York Jets; Ravens. That means the move to San Francisco will be the tenth for his wife, Kathy, and their four children. Of course, Nolan's a grizzled coaching veteran — he turned forty-six this past March.

In essence, I was looking for one team that would lift the NFL's cloak of secrecy and let me inside. The Baltimore Ravens struck me as ideal for a number of reasons — one of them, in the interest of full disclosure, being that their training facility is only an hour from my home, so I could spend a lot of time there easily. But there was far more than that. The franchise has a fascinating history, first as the Cleveland Browns of legend, then as the controversial Ravens, their first controversial moment coming on November 6, 1995, when owner Art Modell announced his intention to move the team to Baltimore. In Brian Billick and Ray Lewis and Jamal Lewis they have a coach and players who have climbed the heights of the game and dealt with serious issues along the way — Billick's being how he dealt with the murder charges against Ray Lewis following a horrific incident in Atlanta on Super Bowl Sunday night in 2000. The Ravens have been a very good team under Billick and Ozzie Newsome. They won the Super Bowl in January 2001, then went through a salary cap purge during the 2002 season that forced them to start almost back at square one as a franchise. They recovered quickly to win a division title in 2003 and entered 2004 with high hopes, believing they had the ingredients to be a Super Bowl team in February 2005. Why that didn't happen makes for, I believe, a compelling story of dealing with injury and letdowns, controversy and dashed hopes. When I first approached the Ravens with the idea of making them the focus of a book about the NFL, I had no idea that I would get Deion Sanders as a bonus.

What also drew me to the Ravens was their reputation for stepping outside the box where media access is concerned. In 2001 they allowed HBO and NFL films total access to their training camp for the series *Hard Knocks.* Interestingly, Billick's willingness to allow camera crews complete freedom in areas normally off-limits to any media was his belief that going through the experience might *help* his team. "We were the Super Bowl champions, so we were going to spend the entire season under the microscope," he said. "Plus, we were Super Bowl champions who attracted a lot of off-field attention whether we wanted it or not, because of Ray, because of me getting the media upset at the Super Bowl when I defended Ray, because we were considered a team with a lot of bad boys and swagger. I figured if the guys spent training camp being trailed by cameras and microphones everywhere they turned, it would be easier for them to handle whatever came after that during the season."

Of course, what I was asking was different. Allowing access behind the scenes during camp and exhibition games is one thing. Giving an outsider complete access when the real games start — not to mention during the draft — is quite another. Ravens owner Steve Bisciotti was comfortable with the idea right away, but he set up a meeting with general manager Ozzie Newsome and Coach Brian Billick because, as we both agreed, there was absolutely no point in starting the project if the general manager and coach resisted it.

The first question Ozzie Newsome asked during my initial meeting with the Ravens was "Why would I let you [a complete stranger] into my draft room when I won't let ESPN [an NFL business partner] in there?"

It was a good question. The answer is this: live television, even a cut-up, taped segment, is essentially unfiltered. A book has the advantage of context, setting up why something happened as opposed to merely showing *what* happened.

The other question raised during the meeting was the one I had most expected: "Are you looking to write the book version of *Playmakers*?" (It wasn't phrased just that way, but that's what the question was.) The answer was no. As I pointed out, if a Raven got into serious trouble, all of that was going to be reported in the newspapers. If anything, by earning the trust of the players, I might be able to provide readers with — again — context on what actually happened. There's no more perfect example than Jamal Lewis. Within a week of my initial meeting with the Ravens, the story broke about his arrest on drug-trafficking charges. It has since been adjudicated, and as I write this, Lewis is spending four months in jail as part of a plea bargain. There are people who will always believe that Ray Lewis is a murderer, and many of those will always also believe that Jamal Lewis is either a junkie or a drug dealer. The fact is that he's neither. He made, by his own admission, a stupid mistake as a twenty-year-old, taken in by a good-looking woman. He was guilty of being twenty and naive as much as anything. The fact that the judge who handed down his sentence after the plea bargain said to him in open court that he was convinced there was almost no way Lewis would have been found guilty had the case gone to trial is fairly compelling evidence of that.

Some will no doubt say that makes me an apologist for Jamal Lewis. I understand. One of the perks of being a star athlete is that your fans will think you innocent of just about anything as long as you are performing (exhibit A: Barry Bonds in San Francisco). The flip side is that some fans of the opposition will consider you guilty, regardless of any evidence to the contrary. I have a tendency to deal in facts.

Maybe that's why the Ravens said yes. They knew when they let me into their world that if one of their players was found guilty of a crime or acted like a jerk, I would report it. The Ravens aren't perfect. As team owner Steve Bisciotti says, "If you have fifty-three rich young guys, they're going to make mistakes." Every team in the NFL is evidence of that. But they had enough confidence in the people in their organization to open it up to me. Billick was comfortable with my involvement, but all of Newsome's football-player and general-manager instincts told him that you simply can't let an outsider inside the secret society that is the NFL. Still, he gritted his teeth and agreed to go ahead, and for that I'm grateful. I think this book proves that they knew what they were doing.

My access, as you will read, was pretty much complete. Billick never once asked me to leave a room, and the players, who weren't quite sure who I was or why I was there — many referred to me early on as "the book guy"— became, I believe, comfortable with my presence. Deion Sanders even took the trouble to pull my jacket collar up while we were standing in the tunnel in Pittsburgh, saying, "Man, you have to at least *try* to look good on the sideline."

Steve Bisciotti's role in this book cannot be overstated. He was my first contact with the Ravens because of our mutual friendship with Maryland basketball coach Gary Williams. Bisciotti is one of the more remarkable people I've ever met. As Kevin Byrne, the Ravens public relations honcho pointed out, "When you spend a little time with Steve, you understand that his success was not an accident." Bisciotti is one of those very rich and successful people who feels no need to explain why he's rich and successful. My friend Rob Ades, a lawyer who represents a lot of college basketball coaches, tells a story about playing golf with Bisciotti a couple of years ago and asking him what he did. "I'm with the Ravens," Bisciotti answered.

"I thought he was in marketing," Ades said. "We got along very well, so a couple months later I called and asked him if he wanted to go to a Maryland game because I had pretty good seats. He thanked me and said he actually had tickets of his own. I get to the game and I look across and he's sitting in the front row at center court. I asked someone how he had gotten those seats because they seemed a little bit expensive. The answer I got was 'Don't you know who he is? He *owns* the Ravens.'"

At the time Bisciotti owned a mere 49 percent of the team. Now he owns 99 percent — former owner Art Modell retained a 1 percent stake when the final deal was cut on April 9 of 2004. At that first meeting back on February 10, 2004, I walked into the Ravens complex in Owings Mills a couple of minutes early and was explaining to Vernon Holley at the security desk that I had a ten o'clock appointment. Just as Holley picked up the phone to let someone know I had arrived, the door opened. Holley put down the phone and pointed behind me. "Here's Steve now," he said as Bisciotti walked up.

Think about those three words: "Here's Steve now." In how many NFL offices do you think the employees routinely refer to the owner by his first name? (I guarantee not in Washington, the one place where the NFL team owner is actually younger than Bisciotti, who is forty-five — four years older than the man his close friends and family call *Mister* Snyder).

My hope when I first approached Steve Bisciotti was to come away with a deeper understanding of what an NFL season is like. Certainly a 9-7 season was not what the Ravens had in mind when they planned that year. But the ups and downs the Ravens experienced certainly provided a fascinating story, full of more nuance and emotion than any amount of television commentary and capsule biography could deliver. There were great highs — a come-from-behind victory against the Jets — and great lows — a blown 20–3 lead at home against Cincinnati that ultimately cost the team a spot in the playoffs. There were conflicts, within the team and within the coaching staff, but as I came to understand, such disagreements are inevitable, especially on a team enduring a rocky season. I was asked often during the season if anything really surprised me. The answer was (and is) yes: the constant tension. The NFL is the most insecure world there is in professional sports because the season is so short, leaving little margin for error — injuries can occur quickly and in devastating fashion and today's star can be tomorrow's cut. Just check the small print in your newspaper's sports section every March and every June.

I also got a better understanding of the hold the NFL has on people's lives. The passion of the fans in every NFL city is a tribute to the quality of the game, to the league's marketing, and to the fact that over the past forty years the league has become a cultural monolith. The hardest thing for everyone in the NFL to do, I think, is not to take themselves as seriously as the fans and the media do. That's not easy. When you are treated as though you are special everywhere you go, it is easy to forget that it is the uniform you wear, not you, that makes people think you're special. Just ask ex-players who were not stars how quickly those perks disappear.

Which is why I have to give Brian Billick credit. Many find him arrogant. Certainly he has the extreme self-assurance that virtually anyone who is very good at something has. But he also has a self-deprecating sense of humor that many people miss. On the last Sunday of the season, with the Ravens almost certain to miss the playoffs after a loss at Pittsburgh the previous week, Billick made his traditional walk from the team hotel in downtown Baltimore to the stadium. As he and Vernon Holley approached the entrance to the stadium, most of the fans waiting in line to be patted down by security moved aside for them, as they do every week.

One yellow-jacketed security guard planted himself between Billick and the entrance. "Sir, I need to pat you down," he said.

Before Billick could say anything, three other security people jumped in and pointed out that the coach of the home team didn't need to be patted down. Billick walked away, smiling.

"See what happens when you're 8-7," he said. "Everyone wants to pat you down."

Everyone may not want to pat you down. But they certainly want to second-guess you at best, fire you at worst. To play, coach, or work in the NFL is to breathe rarefied air. But it can be very thin air at times, and breathing can be very difficult.

Which is what makes each week in an NFL season such a compelling story. The Ravens' season in 2004 was a roller-coaster ride, filled with both chills and spills. This is the story of that ride.

1

Unexpected Good-byes

January 3, 2005

FROM A DISTANCE, it looked like any other football Monday in Owings Mills, Maryland. The coaches arrived early at the spectacular, brand-new $32 million facility located at the optimistic address of 1 Winning Drive. They grabbed quick cups of coffee from the first-floor cafeteria and headed up to their offices to begin their day by preparing for their morning meeting. The players came later. Like the coaches, they stopped in the cafeteria, but they sat at the round tables in groups of three and four, eating lunch before gathering in the posh auditorium that served as the meeting room when the entire team was together.

But this was a Monday like no other in the nine-year history of the Baltimore Ravens. There wasn't a soul in the organization who had thought before the season began that this would be the day when everyone said good-bye. In his first meeting with the entire team, on the morning that the veterans' mandatory minicamp began in early June, Coach Brian Billick had made his expectations clear: "We have a two-, perhaps three-year window to win the Super Bowl," he said. "In this room, we have the talent, the experience, and the understanding of what it takes to win to get to the Super Bowl and to win it. We can do it this year, we can do it again next year, and perhaps the year after, the way we're structured. We've built to this the last two years. We're ready for it."

Billick had repeated that message at training camp and on the eve of the first game in Cleveland. He had clung to it throughout the fall as the team sputtered and the dream began to fade before it finally teetered like an aging Christmas tree and collapsed with a crash on the day after New Year's. There would be no Super Bowl; there wouldn't even be a playoff game. Instead of being one of twelve teams preparing for the National Football League playoffs, the Ravens were one of twenty teams making plans for next season.

That wasn't just a cliché, either. When football coaches say next season begins on the last day of this season, they mean it. In fact, Billick had been meeting with team owner Steve Bisciotti, team president Dick Cass, and general manager Ozzie Newsome since early December to discuss the team's future. By the time the coaches met at 11 A.M. that morning, two coaches — long-embattled offensive coordinator Matt Cavanaugh and defensive assistant Phil Zacharias — were gone. One office over from where the coaches sat with schedules Billick had handed them for 2005, Cavanaugh was starting to clear out his office. Two phone calls had already come in from teams interested in talking to him about a job.

For everyone involved, this was a difficult day. The hallways in the building were quiet, no one knowing quite what to say to one another. In the locker room, players went through the ritual of putting their things in boxes to carry to their cars while saying good-bye to one another. Deion Sanders, the future Hall of Fame defensive back, limped around on a foot that would need surgery for a torn tendon and paused to sign autographs for younger teammates who thought there was at least a 50-50 chance he would not be back when veteran minicamps began again in June.

It had been less than twenty-four hours since the 2004 season had ended with a too-little, too-late 30–23 win over the Miami Dolphins. The victory had left the team with a 9-7 record. Had they been part of the National Football Conference, those nine victories would have easily put them into the playoffs. But in the American Football Conference, it left them a win short of the 10-6 record required to earn a playoff spot. "Only one team finishes the season satisfied," Billick told his players when they gathered for their final meeting before heading to their homes to begin an off-season full of questions. "But we all know we're sitting here because some of us didn't do our jobs as well as we could have or should have. We're all emotionally spent because of the energy we've put into the last twenty-five weeks.

"That's why I'm not here to put a lot on you right now. I appreciate the fact that a lot of you have played in a lot of pain these last few weeks. You're tired and you're hurt and I admire you for doing what you did. But we have to take a good, hard look at ourselves." He held up a spiral notebook. "I've got about ninety pages of notes in here about things that need to be looked at and improved upon before next season starts. About five of them are for the coaches; another five are for you guys. The rest are for me.

"The simple fact, though, is this: we didn't reach our expectations. I think we have a Super Bowl–caliber team in this room. There are any number of reasons why we're sitting here today having this talk instead of getting ready for a playoff game. What we have to think about going forward is this: how do we get from 9-7 to being an elite team, I don't mean a 10-6 team like last year, but a 13-3, 14-2 kind of team. That's the kind of team we all think we can be. But we have a lot to do to finish the job. That's our challenge for next year — finish what we began this season."

Billick had been far more blunt when he met with his coaches that morning. The mood of the meeting had been somber, almost glum. Everyone in the room knew what had happened already to Cavanaugh and Zacharias.

"A good man is going out that door because of what we and I haven't done," Billick said, referring to Cavanaugh. "There are also additional changes I need to make, and we'll talk about them starting tomorrow." He paused. "Don't get me wrong. This is a good room. There are good people in here. I don't like what happened today with Matt or what we're going to have to do. It's what will drive me out of this business eventually."

The coaches looked at one another. Each was scheduled to meet individually with Billick the next morning. The message was clear: others would be going out the door, too. In front of them, in addition to a schedule that told them their responsibilities from now until the first day of training camp, was the team's roster. On the right-hand side was a list of fifteen players who would be free agents. Some would not be back. The coaches would meet on January 17 along with Newsome and his staff to talk about every single player who had played for the Ravens the previous season.

Newsome and Billick had already reached the conclusion that they had not been aggressive enough the previous season. "The question we need to ask," Newsome said, "is, did we take the safe route last year by bringing back twenty-one of twenty-two starters? Did we allow continuity to become more important than upsetting the applecart and bringing someone else in who might be better than what we have?"

The questions were rhetorical. Newsome and Billick had won a Super Bowl together following the 2000 season and they wanted to win another one. Both now believed that they had overestimated some of their players based on what they had accomplished in 2003. "The biggest mistake I made was thinking that the experiences we had last year, winning the division and going to the playoffs, made us a more mature team than our collective age would have indicated," Billick told his coaches. "We were still a young team this season and we didn't handle some things that came at us very well. That's why we have to take a hard look at ourselves and at our players. I want you guys to tell me *exactly* what you need at each position to get better. You want a better player, find him, tell us who he is and why he's better than what we've got, and we'll go get him. We're in great cap shape. We're going to attack in free agency."

The Ravens have never been a team that makes headlines in March with big-name free-agent signings. They probably weren't going to make any major headlines in March of 2005, either, but Billick's message was clear: we need to get better. It didn't take a football genius to know that the Ravens were lacking at the wide receiver spot or that the offensive line had been through a disappointing season. The defense would be reconfigured to try to make life easier for Ray Lewis, the heart and soul of not only the defense but the entire team. Hard decisions had to be made on good players who were about to become free agents and might not be worth the money they could command on the open market. There were a number of older players, men who had been solid contributors throughout distinguished careers but simply couldn't perform at the same level anymore.

There are no guaranteed contracts in the NFL. The only money a player is guaranteed is the money in his signing bonus. From the moment that check is cashed, contracts go in one direction: the team's. A player who signs a seven-year contract is committed to that team for seven years. Once the bonus check is paid, the team isn't committed to the player for seven years, seven months, seven weeks, or seven days. That's one reason why there is no job in professional team sports as insecure as that of an NFL player. Players frequently go from starting to cut in one year because a team decides he isn't worth what he will be paid for the next season or because a team has to off-load salary because of the salary cap. Often players are asked to restructure contracts for less money. When that happens, most players are given two options: take a cut or be cut.

That was why the mood was somber when Billick met with his players that day. "We want you all back," Billick said. "But we know that won't happen. We all know the realities of this business. We talk about them all the time. We didn't reach expectations, and we now have to figure out why. We have a lot of work to do before we know about who we're going to want back. Some of you have to make decisions about whether you want to come back here.

"I have faith in the talent and the emotional makeup in this room. But this was a disappointing year. There's no getting around that. Everything we're going to try to do next year starts with the unfulfilled feelings we all have right now. Think about that in the off-season. Get rested. Get healthy. Come back here ready to finish the job we didn't get done this year."

Two weeks later, when Billick and his staff met with Newsome and his staff to go through the roster player by player and begin making decisions for the 2005 season, there were a number of missing faces. Cavanaugh had been named the offensive coordinator at the University of Pittsburgh, his alma mater. Jim Fassel, the former New York Giants coach, sat in his seat. Chris Foerster sat in what had been offensive line coach Jim Colletto's seat. Colletto had been with Billick for six years, but Billick believed he needed to bring in a fresh face to coach an aging offensive line. Mike Nolan, the defensive coordinator, was also gone, but for happier reasons: he would be introduced the next day as the new coach of the San Francisco 49ers. Newsome's top scout, personnel director Phil Savage, was also absent: he had become general manager of the Cleveland Browns.

As the coaches went through each player, there were some whose reports were read strictly as a courtesy to the coach who had written it. "You wrote it," Newsome said. "We should at least listen to it."

So they listened. In some cases the end of the report said simply: "We need to improve at this position for 2005."

In the case of one longtime veteran, linebacker Cornell Brown, Billick said quietly, "All I can say is God bless him."

In the NFL, that is what passes for a eulogy. Next Man Up.

2

Meet the New Boss

THE YEAR 2004 HAD STARTED very differently for the Ravens from how it ended. In fact, exactly one year to the day prior to the breakup meetings for the 2004 season, the Ravens had hosted a playoff game in a sold-out stadium. With the third-youngest roster in the National Football League, they had won the AFC's North Division with a 10-6 record. That made them the home team for a first-round playoff game against their onetime bitter division rival, the Tennessee Titans. The game had swung back and forth all evening until a critical personal foul penalty just prior to a Ravens punt gave Tennessee field position just good enough that quarterback Steve McNair was able to maneuver his team to the Baltimore 28-yard line in the final seconds. From there, forty-four-year-old placekicker Gary Anderson converted a 46-yard field goal that barely sneaked over the crossbar to give the Titans a 20–17 victory.

The irony of Anderson's kick wasn't lost on Brian Billick. Five years earlier, in what had turned out to be Billick's last game as the Minnesota Vikings' offensive coordinator, Anderson had lined up a 37-yard kick with under two minutes remaining in the NFC Championship Game against the Atlanta Falcons. The Vikings, who had gone 15-1 during the regular season, breaking all sorts of offensive records to make Billick a hot head-coaching candidate, led, 17–10. Anderson had not missed a single field goal all season, and the 37-yarder was considered nothing more than a chip shot. In fact, Vikings coach Dennis Green had told Billick to keep the ball on the ground once the offense had driven inside the 25. A field goal would put the game out of reach, and Anderson was automatic.

Not this time. He missed the kick; the Falcons drove the length of the field for the tying score and won in overtime. They went to the Super Bowl. The Vikings went home. Two days later Billick was introduced as the new head coach of the Ravens. When Anderson's kick cleared the crossbar, dooming the Ravens, Billick's first comment to his coaches was concise: "*Now* he makes it."

The loss to Tennessee marked the end of Art Modell's forty-two years as owner of the franchise. Technically, Steve Bisciotti would not become the Ravens' new owner until April 9, 2004, but in a practical sense, the transfer of power began the moment the game ended. At halftime, Modell had become the first person associated with the Ravens to be inducted into M&T Bank Stadium's "Ring of Honor." Even if the Ravens had won, the game would have been their last home game under Modell's ownership. The ceremony was his farewell.

Bisciotti was new to the team only in the sense of becoming the man in charge. He had been around the franchise for four years, dating back to December 17, 1999, when he had agreed to pay Modell $275 million in exchange for 49 percent minority ownership in the franchise and the option to buy out Modell for a total price of $600 million in four years. There was never any doubt that Bisciotti would exercise the option. The only reason for the four-year delay was to give Modell and his family time to adjust to the notion of no longer running the team. Modell had purchased the Cleveland Browns in 1961 at the age of thirty-five, and the team and the National Football League had been the centerpiece of his life ever since. He had moved the team from Cleveland to Baltimore in 1996 in a franchise shift that left emotional scars on almost everyone involved. Modell believed he had no choice at the time. He had negotiated with the city of Cleveland for several years, trying to get a new stadium to replace antiquated Municipal Stadium, better known throughout the sports world as the Mistake by the Lake. When the city came up with funding for both a new baseball stadium and a new basketball/hockey arena but did not agree to build Modell a new luxury-suite-laden building, Modell began considering a move.

"There wasn't any choice," he said years later. "There was no way we could survive financially if we continued to play in the old stadium. And it was clear to me that the city wasn't going to budge."

Unlike some team owners, Modell didn't have the money to build a new stadium for himself. In fact, he was in very poor shape financially. So when the city of Baltimore offered him a sweetheart deal that included a brand-new stadium, Modell accepted the offer. He didn't want to sell the team. He wanted to pass it on to his family's next generation, notably his son David, whom he had named team president. The only way to keep the team in the family was to accept Baltimore's offer.

There was a sad irony in the fabled Cleveland Browns, one of the NFL's signature franchises, leaving Cleveland for Baltimore. Twelve years earlier Baltimore had been the victim of a franchise shift when Colts owner Robert Irsay backed moving trucks up to the team's facility in Owings Mills, Maryland, and moved the team, lock, stock, barrel, and team name to Indianapolis. Modell wasn't nearly as sneaky or ruthless. He announced the move on November 6, 1995, with several weeks left in the season, forcing the Browns to finish the season as a lame-duck team in a stunned city. He also agreed to leave behind the Browns name and all the team records so that the NFL could put an expansion franchise in Cleveland if the city ever agreed to build a new stadium (which it did, bringing the new Browns into existence in 1999).

People in Baltimore were shocked by the sudden turn in their football fortunes, but many had mixed emotions about the arrival of the new team. The departure of the Colts had scarred the city's soul because the Colts had been an emotionally important part of Baltimore. Many of the players lived in the neighborhoods around Memorial Stadium, and the team was filled with great players and great characters, none more revered than legendary quarterback Johnny Unitas. Baltimore and Cleveland are similar towns in many ways, working-class cities with now-outdated reputations as tough places with grimy downtowns. Both have been revitalized in recent years, but the character of those who live in the two cities has changed little. Each still harbors something of an inferiority complex. Losing the Colts had fed that feeling in Baltimore, and many in Baltimore, knowing how they had felt about the Colts' departure, could not help but empathize with those now going through the same trauma in Cleveland.

One Baltimorean who felt little of that was Steve Bisciotti. A self-made billionaire who had started his own company supplying temporary engineers to aerospace and technology companies out of his basement in 1983, Bisciotti had been a lifelong Colts fan and a football fan for as long as he could remember. "I wasn't crushed when the Colts left town because at the time they were awful," he said. "I didn't like it, but I also felt if the city had been willing to renovate Memorial Stadium for Irsay, he wouldn't have left. It might have cost ten million dollars to do it, and they didn't do it. So I didn't hate Irsay the way some people did. When the Browns came here because Cleveland wouldn't do anything for Art Modell, I understood. I also believed that Cleveland would get a new team as soon as it agreed to build a stadium. I didn't think people there would go twelve years without a team the way we had."

Bisciotti probably would have been more upset about the Colts' departure if he hadn't been completely immersed in building his business when the Colts left. He had grown up in Severna Park, the youngest of Bernie and Pat Bisciotti's three children. His memories of boyhood are happy: he grew up in a close, loving family and had friends who to this day remain close to him. It is remarkable that his memories are as happy as they are, given that his father died of leukemia when Steve was eight.

"We knew he was sick because there were long stays in the hospital," he said. "But it was one of those things where we were just told that Dad was sick, he needed to get better, and then he would come home and it would seem as if he was better. I honestly don't think the thought that he was dying crossed my mind until the morning when he died."

That was on a Saturday. Steve was spending the night with a friend across the street. He was surprised when his friend's dad came in early and told him that his mom wanted him to come home. When he walked across the street and saw a strange car parked outside, he knew something was up. "Once I got inside I saw my uncle Joe, Dad's brother," he said. "That's when I found out."

Later that day after lunch, the local parish priest sat Steve and his sister, Cathy, and brother, Mike, down to read them a letter that their father had written to them shortly before he died. It was a four-page, handwritten note that was meant not only to say good-bye but to tell his children his hopes and dreams for them.

"The easiest way for me to start a letter like this is to say I love you," it began. "You collectively have brought more joy and happiness and fulfillment to my life than I will ever express in a full lifetime of trying. You truly have given me as a parent so much more than I've given you. Your very existence has been a source of satisfaction that only when you become parents will you be able to understand what I'm trying to express.

"Your dad finds writing this awfully hard because there are so many things in my heart that I want to say to you, but just don't know where or how to go about doing it."

Bernie Bisciotti went on to talk about his love for his wife and about his deep Catholic faith. "Your mother also has her job cut out for her because now she will have to be both father and mother. By doing this she has her chance to prove to God how much she loves and understands what he planned for us. You also get a chance by carrying heavier responsibility to show God your love and understanding. . . . I will pray for you always and want you also to pray to God for guidance in growing into fine decent people. (Remember, God gives us the chance to make up your own minds as to what kind of people we are going to be.)"

Later, when he would go back and read the letter, Bisciotti starred the sentence in parentheses to remind himself of that message. His father concluded with a request and with his final wishes: "Love your mother always. She needs you so very much. Never — never — do anything to hurt her, because she truly is a wonderful God-like person and doesn't ever deserve to feel the pain that unloving acts of her children could cause her.

"I know how good you all are — I truthfully never met children I was ever more impressed with than you. Of course I'm terribly prejudiced and filled with love for you.

"As a selfish man, I hope you will remember me with love and I hope that in some way I have been important in helping form your character and outlook on life. The love and affection you have given me is beyond my ability to describe, but somehow I'm sure you'll find out what I mean. . . . Your Loving Dad."

Bisciotti keeps his father's letter in the desk he works at in his house. Thirty-seven years after it was written, he still pulls it out frequently to remind himself what his father wanted him and his siblings to become. It has clearly influenced him because, even with all the success and all the money he has made, he seems to make a point every day of reminding himself how fortunate he has been and goes out of his way to make it clear that he doesn't think being wealthy makes him any better or smarter than anyone else.

"I was never a good student," he said. "I got Bs and Cs and worked for them. I have a feeling if I was a kid today, I'd have been diagnosed as ADD, but back then no one did that. My mother never berated me for not doing better in school, because I think she knew I was trying. She always said to me, 'Stephen, you're going to do fine in life because people like you and you're a nice person.'"

As it turned out, he was also a born salesman. He went to Salisbury State on Maryland's Eastern Shore and helped pay for his education by working numerous jobs: pier-building in the summertime, bartending during the winter. When he graduated he went to work for a firm that supplied high-tech temporary engineers to companies, a relatively new but growing business. Less than a year into the job, he got caught on the wrong side of a power struggle between the two men who owned the company and got fired. This was in the fall of 1983. Bisciotti was engaged (he had first met Renee Foote in high school but hadn't dated her until just after he graduated from college) and didn't want to leave Baltimore. But he had a no-compete clause in his contract that said he couldn't take a job in the Baltimore area with a firm that did similar work. It was his future father-in-law, a land developer, who suggested he start his own company.

"His point was that the guy couldn't really impose a no-compete when he had fired me without cause," Bisciotti said. "He told me to start my own company, the thought being he would take me to court and that I'd have a really good chance to win on the no-cause basis. The main reason for doing it was so I could get a job that would allow me to stay in Baltimore."

By the time his former employer got around to taking him to court nine months later, Bisciotti had four employees and a growing business. Early on, he persuaded Jim Davis, his cousin and best friend growing up, to come into the company with him. Davis had a good job at Price Waterhouse but decided to make the jump anyway. He handled the books, Bisciotti handled the sales side: persuading high-tech companies to use them rather than competitors to find trained engineers quickly for short-term jobs that they didn't have enough staff for.

"I think we just outworked people," Bisciotti said. "If a company needed fifty engineers for a project, our competitors would work the phones until six o'clock, looking for guys, and then go home. We'd work until six, send out for pizza and beer, and then keep going until eleven, tracking guys down on the West Coast. If we got a potential job on a Thursday, we'd be back to the company with a list of names and résumés on Friday. Our competitors might call on Monday or Tuesday and they'd hear, 'Sorry, we've already got all the people we need.'"

Bisciotti and Davis were pretty certain they would win the court case based on the no-cause firing and based on the fact that it had taken nine months for his ex-boss to file suit. Rather than take a chance, though, they offered a settlement: $11,000 cash on the spot and an agreement not to call on certain clients for a year. The deal was made. "That next year was a little bit tough because we were limited in people we could go after," Bisciotti said. "But after that, we started to take off."

To put it mildly. The company — Aerotek — went from sales of $10 million in 1987 to $3.4 billion in 2001. "Then the economy nose-dived and our sales went down," Bisciotti said. "But in those fourteen years our business went up markedly every year."

By the time business slacked off in 2001, Bisciotti was semi-retired. In 1997 he had decided to turn a lot of the business over to his partners. His sons, Jack and Jason, were ten and eight at the time, close to the same age Bisciotti had been when his father died. "I wanted that time to be with them," he said. "I was lucky that I could make the choice at the age of thirty-seven to give up the seventy-hour weeks and spend more time at home."

By then, Bisciotti was a Ravens season ticket holder. He had put down a $5,000 deposit on season tickets when the city was a candidate for an NFL expansion team in 1993. Those teams ended up going to Jacksonville and Charlotte. Those who had put down the deposits were asked by city officials to leave their money in escrow in the event that another team became available in the future. "I figured, what the hell, it was five thousand dollars and if we ever got a team, I'd have the jump on the best seats in the house."

When the Browns came to Baltimore — they were christened the Ravens in honor of local Baltimore poet Edgar Allan Poe's most famous work — Bisciotti bought twelve season tickets — four prime seats in the club area, four in the upper deck, and four in the end zone. "I figured I'd use four for myself or close friends, four for company executives, and four for employees," he said. "The first week I took my wife and sons and spent most of the game either waiting in line for beer or soda [they were separate lines] or to take one of the boys [then nine and seven] to the bathroom. After that we decided we'd take the kids when they were a little older."

The Ravens played two seasons in Memorial Stadium, waiting for their new stadium to be built. They also moved into the Colts' old facility in Owings Mills, which had been used as a police academy by the city of Baltimore, and found it as antiquated and outdated as the old stadium. That problem would have to wait, though. The immediate focus was on getting into the new stadium.

The new place finally opened in September of 1998, a gorgeous, modern stadium right across the street from Camden Yards, the jewel of a baseball stadium that had opened in 1992. By then, Bisciotti was furious with Ravens management. When the time had come to select his club seats in the new stadium, he had been informed that he was being given the best available seats — on the 30-yard line.

"I blew up," Bisciotti said. "I said, 'Wait a minute, I put my money up in 1993 and the best I get is the thirty-yard line? They told me that the suite holders had the option to buy club seats and they got first crack. I told them that I was going to go and look at my seats and if I didn't like them, I wanted my money back. The contract said nothing about it, but I threatened to go to the *Sun*. So they said, 'Okay, we'll let you do it that way and call it the Bisciotti Rule.'"

Bisciotti eventually decided his seats were acceptable. That same year, he had been contacted by Bank of America, which had been hired by Florida Marlins owner Wayne Huizenga to identify possible buyers for his team. Because he had been a Baltimore Orioles season ticket holder and appeared to have the kind of capital needed to buy a franchise, Bisciotti was asked if he wanted to take a look at the confidential prospectus being sent to potential buyers.

"I was intrigued," he said. "I already had a home in South Florida and I figured as I got older I'd be spending more time there. I liked the fact that the team was in the National League because I wouldn't have been comfortable competing on a regular basis with the Orioles. But when I read the prospectus, it turned out that John Henry had already been designated as the managing partner in any deal and was just looking for investors who wouldn't have any real input in running the team. I wasn't interested in that."

A year later Bank of America came back to Bisciotti with another potential deal: the Minnesota Vikings. "I was certainly interested in the possibility of owning an NFL team," he said. "But when I talked to Renee about it, she asked me if I intended to move to Minneapolis. The answer, of course, was no. So were we then going to fly to every game? No. The deal was good enough that I might be able to buy the team and sell it for a good profit, but that wasn't the point of buying a team to me. I wasn't looking for a business deal, I was looking to get involved in something that would be fun to do."

Having let the Vikings deal go, Bisciotti settled into the role of season ticket holder. In the meantime, things were not going so well for the Ravens or the Modells. Soon after deciding to move the team, Modell had decided to shake up the team's leadership. He had fired Coach Bill Belichick, who had also been the team's de facto general manager since he had final say on all personnel matters. In his place, Modell named Ozzie Newsome, an all-time Browns great as a tight end, the team's personnel director and Ted Marchibroda, who had been the last man to coach the Colts in Baltimore, the new coach.

The team began its new existence on September 1, 1996, with a victory, but things spiraled downward after that and the Ravens finished their first season 4-12. A year later they improved to 6-9-1 and began the 1998 season in the new stadium with legitimate hopes — or so Modell and Newsome believed — of making the playoffs. "Everything went wrong right from the beginning that year," Newsome remembered. "First play of our first game in the new stadium, Matt Stover kicks the ball out of bounds. We go on and lose [to archrival Pittsburgh] and it was downhill from there." Before season's end, it had been decided that Marchibroda would not be asked back. Newsome and David Modell were put in charge of the search committee to find a new coach.

In the meantime, even with the infusion of money from the move to Baltimore, the Modells continued to struggle financially. There were cost overruns on the new stadium that the Modells had to help finance. The profit levels for the Ravens were not enough to make up the losses suffered in Cleveland and in some of the other investments made by the Modells. By the time the 1998 season ended, the Modells were over the NFL's debt limit for owners. During the owners' meetings that winter, Art Modell was politely told by his fellow owners that he needed to find new money for his team, that he could not be allowed to continue to operate over the debt limit because of the precedent it would set. Modell began searching for minority ownership.

Midway through the 1999 season, with Brian Billick now coaching the team, it was apparent that no one was going to step forward with the kind of money the Modells needed in return for nothing. "What is a minority ownership?" Bisciotti asked rhetorically. "Essentially, it is an interest-free loan to an owner in return for a suite and a parking spot. No one is going to give someone a hundred and fifty million dollars for that. The only way the Modells were going to get anyone interested was with an option to buy."

Shortly after Thanksgiving in 1999, Bisciotti and his business partner Jim Davis were approached by John Moag, the man who had brokered the Browns/Ravens deal on behalf of the Maryland Stadium Authority. Moag had been less than happy when the Modells had hired Alex. Brown, a Baltimore-based investment firm, to try to find a minority owner. He had set out on his own looking for an investor, figuring, according to Bisciotti, that if he couldn't get in on the Modells' side of the deal, maybe he and his company, Legg Mason, could get involved on the other side.

Moag explained to Bisciotti and Davis that, according to his NFL sources, the Modells were running out of time. If they weren't able to come up with financing to cover their debts by the time the NFL owners met after the season, the league might very well put the team for sale by auction. That would mean the Modells would have no control over the amount the team would be sold for, who it would be sold to, or how quickly — most likely right away — the new owners would take control. Because of all that, Moag believed the Modells might be willing to make a deal that would include an option to buy at some point in the future.

"If there's an option, I'm interested," Bisciotti said. "Otherwise, forget it."

Moag asked if he could approach the Modells to set up a meeting. Bisciotti and Davis agreed. Within a week, the two men had been invited to Owings Mills for a get-to-know-you visit. They watched the end of a practice one afternoon, met Billick and Newsome, and were then introduced to Art Modell, who was sitting, as he did every day, on his golf cart, watching his team practice. When practice was over, Modell took Bisciotti and Davis upstairs to his office, introduced them to David, and then left the room.

"You have to understand," David Modell explained to his surprised visitors. "This is very hard for him. Even being in the room discussing turning the franchise over to anyone else is difficult."

Bisciotti and Davis said they understood. The barest parameters of a possible sale were discussed. David Modell explained that if an option to buy was to be included in the deal, then the up-front money had to be more than the $150 million that Moag had talked about. Something close to double that was what they were looking for. A meeting was set up for Friday, December 17, to try to hammer out an agreement.

"This was really moving fast," Bisciotti said. "When David started talking about three hundred million dollars, I had to get Bank of America moving fast to figure out if I could come up with that kind of liquidity and to put everything in place before the meeting. John Moag wasn't happy because he thought he should be doing all that. I made him part of the negotiation but told him I needed Bank of America. He wasn't happy. I told Bank of America he had to be in the deal because he had brought it to us. They weren't happy. So, by the time we got to the meeting, the guys negotiating for me were already unhappy."

On Bank of America's recommendation, Bisciotti had hired Dick Cass to head his negotiation team — even though Cass's work for and friendship with Cowboys maverick owner Jerry Jones made him nervous.

When Bisciotti walked into the meeting on the morning of December 17 at the downtown law offices of Hogan & Hartson, the first thing he did was tell everyone in the room that this would be a one-day negotiation, that he was prepared to stay as late as necessary, but that if there was no deal by day's end, there would be no deal. "I had made a point of staying under the radar my entire adult life," he said. "If I was going to become a public figure, it was going to be for a deal I *made*, not for one that didn't get made. I knew if we dragged on, eventually the negotiation would leak and I'd be in the papers, working on a deal that might not happen. Was there a little bit of negotiating ploy there? Probably. Because if they'd come back two weeks later and said, 'Okay, we acquiesce, we'll give you what you asked for or close to it,' I'm not gonna tell you I'd have said no. But my basic approach going in was it was today or never."

By the time the two sides broke for a late lunch, Bisciotti was convinced there would be no deal. The Modells had started at $700 million for the team, with the option kicking in after five years. Bisciotti wanted to pay $500 million and have an option to buy after three years. By midafternoon, they had closed the gap from $200 million to about $100 million but had made no progress on the option or on other crucial terms — like how much interest the Modells would pay on the money Bisciotti would be, in effect, loaning them prior to the option. Bisciotti went home briefly, told Renee he didn't think there was going to be a deal and suggested she have the limousine they had hired for the evening pick her up shortly before six o'clock and then come get him at the law office so they could go to Washington to meet ten other couples for their annual pre-Christmas dinner.

Shortly before six, he called Renee back and told her to delay the limo driver for a while. A deal might get done.

"We were willing to go to six hundred million, and my sense was so were they," he said. "But we were far apart on the terms, so far there really didn't seem room for compromise. I finally said to my guys, 'I want to talk to Art alone.' They thought that was a bad idea, but I said, 'What have we got to lose? Right now, the way we're going, this isn't going to happen.' They agreed. When the two groups were back in the room together, Bisciotti asked to speak to Modell one-on-one. Modell agreed. They went down the hall to a small conference room. It was the first time they had been alone.

"I remember when we started talking I instantly liked him," Bisciotti said. "There was a warmth to him. He wasn't hardballing; this was difficult for him. He told me there was no way his people would let him make the deal for less than six hundred million dollars. I said I understood, but if we were going to six hundred million, it had to be our terms — interest rate, three-year option, things like that. I suggested he go back and tell his group that and we agree that in the next fifteen minutes we either have a deal or walk away. We shook hands on it. Fifteen minutes later they came back in and said if we would compromise at four years on the option, we had a deal."

Two hours later, with the lawyers still hammering out details, Bisciotti slid into the limo next to Renee and whispered, as much in shock as in glee, "We got it. We got the Ravens."

The final deal was actually for $580 million, plus a commitment by Bisciotti to spend at least $20 million on a desperately needed new practice facility.

Twenty-four hours after the paperwork was signed, Keith Mills, the weekend sports anchor at Channel 2 in Baltimore, broke the story that the new owner of the Ravens would be Steve Bisciotti, a thirty-nine-year-old local businessman. Very few people knew who Bisciotti was, except perhaps those who regularly attended University of Maryland basketball games and couldn't help but notice the casually dressed guy with the slicked-back brown hair who sat in the front row at midcourt and kept up a running commentary on the work being done by the officials. That was intentional. Once he became wealthy, Bisciotti had no desire to become famous. Now, though, he would have little choice. He was about to become a member of one of the world's most exclusive clubs: NFL owner.

"I did a couple of interviews on the weekend of the sale," he said. "Ron Shapiro [a prominent Baltimore lawyer who represented, among others, Cal Ripken Jr.] told me I should get it over with, let a photographer take some pictures of me [none though of his family], and that would keep them from stalking me. So I did that. Once that was over, though, I was determined to go underground for the next four years. It was still Art's team and I didn't want anyone to think different for a minute until it was time for me to take over."

Now that time had come. While the public still didn't know much about Bisciotti, those who worked in the Ravens complex felt as if they did. He was the friendly guy with the wide smile who insisted on being called Steve. He came to know everyone in the building by name, sat in on the draft and other meetings, but offered input only when asked and didn't even ask for office space. If he needed to talk to someone, he went to that person's office.

"I was learning," he said. "Let's face it, what I knew about an NFL team was no more, no less than any other fan. I had opinions, but they certainly weren't based on expertise. I wanted to come in and be someone who could help the people running the team, not be a burden to them."

The Ravens' fortunes changed radically during 2000, Bisciotti's first year as a minority owner. After finishing 8-8 in their first season under Billick, they upgraded their defense radically during the off-season — notably with the predraft signing of free-agent defensive tackle Sam Adams — and emerged as a defensive powerhouse. They improved the offense by adding future Hall of Fame tight end Shannon Sharpe. After a 12-4 regular season, they swept through the playoffs, winning road games at Tennessee and Oakland to reach the Super Bowl before routing the New York Giants, 34–7, to win their first championship. They became known as a swaggering, cocky team, that attitude personified by Billick and by Ray Lewis, the brilliant linebacker who had been involved in a bizarre stabbing incident a year earlier during the Super Bowl in Atlanta that had landed him in jail, accused of a double murder. The murder charge was eventually dropped and Lewis pleaded guilty to an obstruction-of-justice charge, based on his initial conversations with police on the night of the murders. When Billick began Super Bowl week by lecturing the media to leave Lewis alone and not ask questions about what had happened in Atlanta, he made himself the media's target for the week.

Which was exactly what he wanted. The Ravens won the game easily and earned the enmity of most of America in the process. They didn't much care in Baltimore. The championship was the city's first in any sport since the Orioles won the World Series in 1983 and first in football since the Colts had beaten the Cowboys in 1971 in Super Bowl V.

The Ravens returned to the playoffs a year later, winning a game before losing to the Pittsburgh Steelers. Then, like many NFL teams, they were forced to purge a number of veteran players because of the salary cap and they began the 2002 season almost back at square one again. "We had some great players on the team," Billick said. "We still had Ray, we still had [All-Pro left tackle] Jonathan Ogden, and some other very solid guys. But not many. When I looked at the roster that spring, I couldn't have told you twenty guys who would be on the team for sure. I remember thinking, 'Please, God, don't let me be the first coach to win a Super Bowl and then go 0-16 two years later.'"

The Ravens did considerably better than that. Even though Ray Lewis suffered a season-ending back injury in the fifth week of the season, they were 7-7 with two weeks to play and still in contention for a playoff berth. Those hopes ended when the new Browns — then in their fourth season — drove the length of the field in the final two minutes to pull out a 14–13 victory in Baltimore. That victory helped the Browns make the playoffs. The Ravens lost their finale, 34–31, at Pittsburgh and finished 7-9.

In all, though, it had been an encouraging season, considering that the Ravens were the youngest team in NFL history. Newsome and Billick and their scouts believed they needed to strengthen the quarterback position, an Achilles' heel throughout Billick's regime, in order to make a playoff run. After some major draft-day maneuvering, they traded their number one pick in 2004 to New England for the Patriots' pick — the nineteenth in the draft — and used it on Kyle Boller, a strong-armed kid from the University of California–Berkeley who had blossomed as a senior under a new coach. Most people, the Ravens included, figured the team would at least begin the season with Chris Redman, a four-year veteran from Louisville, at quarterback to allow Boller to learn from the bench before being thrown into the fire.

It didn't work out that way. Billick decided during training camp that Boller had progressed so quickly that it was pointless to let Redman start the season, and named him his starter, almost unheard-of in the modern NFL. Boller and the Ravens took a licking on opening day in Pittsburgh, but with running back Jamal Lewis putting up record numbers, they took a 5-3 record into St. Louis. Late in the first half, Boller took a hard shot in the thigh, damaging his right quadriceps muscle.

After Redman played a miserable second half in Boller's place that day, Billick made another radical decision, deciding to hand the quarterback job to third-stringer Anthony Wright in Boller's absence. It was a difficult decision because he liked Redman but was convinced that Wright was more capable of getting the team to the playoffs. He was correct. Wright led a miraculous fourth-quarter comeback from 17 points down against Seattle, and the Ravens ended up 10-6, winning the AFC North Division by two games over the Cincinnati Bengals and four over the Steelers, who stumbled to a surprising 6-10 finish.

Even after the loss to Tennessee, the sense was that 2003 had been just a beginning. The Ravens were still the third-youngest team in football and would bring back almost all of their starters — including a healthy Boller, whom Billick named as his starter the day after the season ended to make sure there would be no Boller-Wright controversy during the off-season or in training camp. The team would also search for a big-play wide receiver to help balance the offense, which had become almost entirely dependent on Lewis's running during 2003.

Before the playoffs began, Bisciotti, Newsome, and Billick made plans to get together the week after the season ended — whenever it ended — to begin making plans for the future. They all knew that there would be a lot of general talk about how they would proceed with Bisciotti now the boss, as opposed to Art and David Modell. But they also knew there were a number of specific issues that needed to be addressed — most notably, the offense, with an emphasis on the future of one man: offensive coordinator Matt Cavanaugh.

"I'll see you Thursday," Bisciotti said to Billick after the Tennessee game ended the 2003 season. He would be flying to Florida to unwind for a few days.

"Looking forward to it," Billick said, meaning it.

He knew Bisciotti was going to want to talk about Cavanaugh. That was fine with him.

Bisciotti was still in Florida when someone in his office faxed him a story written by Mike Preston in the *Baltimore Sun* two days after the Tennessee loss. Preston is the most outspoken member of the Baltimore media when it comes to the Ravens. A former beat writer turned columnist, he can be sharply critical of Billick and the team. Billick is very good at disarming the media. Those who know him well understand his sometimes prickly sense of humor and know that the best way to deal with his occasional antimedia tirades is to go right back at him. Those who don't know him frequently find him intimidating or annoying.

Preston knows Billick and is willing to trade barbs with him, both in print and in person. Billick has no problem with that even though he is often angered by what Preston writes. Now Preston was campaigning for Cavanaugh's firing, saying that Bisciotti's first act as owner should be to insist that Billick fire the offensive coordinator. When Preston asked Billick if he expected to address the issue with Bisciotti, Billick's answer was direct: "There is no issue. Matt's the coordinator. End of discussion."

When Bisciotti read Billick's comments to Preston, he blew up. "I do have a temper," he said. "I've always been aware of the fact that there are times when I need to rein it in because I'll say things I don't want to say when I'm angry. But when I read this I was *really* angry. Brian knew that Matt was one of the issues I wanted to discuss with him when we sat down. When he makes that comment, it comes across to me as 'I don't want or need input from anyone, and anyone who doesn't agree with my position doesn't know what he's talking about.' By the time we sat down on Thursday, I was still hot."

Billick and Newsome arrived at Bisciotti's house, which looks down on the Severn River, prepared for a long day of discussions about personnel — both on and off the field. They already knew that Dick Cass, the Washington lawyer who had worked on Bisciotti's purchase of the team and had also worked on the sale of the Washington Redskins from the Jack Kent Cooke estate to Dan Snyder, was going to replace David Modell as team president. As part of the deal, Modell would remain on the payroll for another year at a salary of $1 million as a consultant. Beyond that, they had no idea what changes — if any — Bisciotti was contemplating.

Bisciotti wasn't planning any major changes. He didn't see any reason to tinker with success. The Ravens had been in the playoffs three years out of four, had won a Super Bowl, and gone through a salary purge, coming out on the other end as a playoff team two seasons later. He was very happy with the direction of the team. But he was angry at his coach.

When he confronted Billick on the Cavanaugh issue, Billick was repentant about his comments to Preston but not about his belief that Cavanaugh should remain on the job. "I told him that Mike had backed me into a corner," Billick said later. "I wasn't going to sound as if I was on the fence on the issue, because I wasn't. If I had said, 'That's something Ozzie and I will discuss with Steve,' it would have sounded as if I was hedging publicly on Matt. I didn't want to do that. But my intent was not to make it sound as if I didn't want to hear what Steve had to say."

That explanation softened Bisciotti . . . a little. "I had decided this was the time to kind of lay everything out for Brian, not just on Cavanaugh. I didn't want him to think for a second that he wasn't the guy I wanted to be my coach for the next ten years, because he absolutely was. But there were some issues that related to the way he dealt with people that I wanted to get out in the open right away, and the Cavanaugh thing crystallized them for me in many ways."

When Bisciotti talks, on almost any issue, he does so with great passion. His voice is almost always scratchy because he speaks so rapidly and so intently once he gets on a roll. When he is upset about something, the words come tumbling out and can take people by surprise because most of the time he is a hail-fellow-well-met. Now there was no sign of the outgoing, gregarious guy who had been hanging around the Owings Mills facility for the past four years.

"You have some bad habits," he said to Billick. "For example, you always address me as 'young man' when you see me, and my wife as 'young lady.' First of all, I'm five years younger than you, I'm not some kid and neither is my wife. Second, I'm about to become the owner of this team — *your boss* — and you greet me the same way you greet some kid coming up to you for an autograph. That's disrespectful."

Billick was rocked. Who had kidnapped the smiling, friendly guy in the blue jeans and replaced him with this suddenly in-your-face new boss? "I don't mean it as a sign of disrespect," he said. "It's just a habit."

"I know you don't," Bisciotti said. "Because you aren't really that way. But that's the way it comes across. It's a bad habit."

He wasn't finished. "Another thing you do is you don't show our scouts enough respect. To begin with, you're always getting right up in their face when you talk to them. You're six foot five, most of them are about five-eight. That's uncomfortable and intimidating. One of the first things I teach my salesmen is to give someone they're talking to a full arm's length of room, especially if you're taller than the other guy. Do not ever look straight down at someone. It's not fair. And you need to make a point of telling them how much you respect the work they do because they work thousands of hours trying to get you the best players they can and then you act as if they don't even exist half the time you're with them. Half the time when [personnel director] Phil Savage is trying to talk, you don't let him finish a sentence."

Now it was Billick's turn to be angry. He didn't think Bisciotti understood the natural — and healthy — scrimmaging that went on between the personnel and coaching staffs. He was, in fact, proud of the fact that he and Newsome could often disagree without ever getting personal about it. The same went for the two staffs. "I've always liked the fact that we can sit in a room, really go at it, motherfuck one another at times, and then come out of it understanding we all want the same thing. I didn't think Steve understood that was the way the building worked, in some ways it was what *made* the building work."

Billick also believed that Bisciotti tended to have warmer feelings for Newsome and the personnel people than for him and his coaches. "It was only natural," he said. "When Steve came to practice, the coaches were working, Ozzie and the scouts were watching. So he spent more time with them. It was understandable that he would see their point of view more than ours."

When Billick made that point, Bisciotti didn't disagree. The meeting filled the entire afternoon. They hadn't even really gotten to the Cavanaugh issue. The next morning Billick called Bisciotti. He wanted him to know he understood where he was coming from but sensed the new boss still had more to talk about. Bisciotti agreed. They decided to meet on Saturday morning at the facility, knowing it would be virtually empty since the staff was away on brief postseason vacations. When the two men arrived the next morning, Billick couldn't find a key to his office — usually the offices in the building were left unlocked — so the two men ended up sitting down in Cavanaugh's office (which wasn't locked) to discuss Cavanaugh.

By his own admission, Bisciotti was looking at the offense from a fan's point of view. The passing game was pathetic — last in the league — and had never been good in the six years Billick had been the coach and Cavanaugh the coordinator. "Sometimes you just have to make hard decisions, that's what you get paid for," Bisciotti told Billick.

"Steve, don't you see, the easy decision for me would be to fire Matt," Billick shot back. "I'd make you happy, I'd make the media happy, I'd make the fans happy. It's almost like a magic trick. Fire one guy, make thousands, including your boss, happy. But it wouldn't be right or fair. The reasons for our failures on offense go beyond Matt. For one thing, I'm the one who decides what our offensive strengths are. This year it was the run, so we ran the ball and we ran it very well. For another, we had a rookie quarterback for half the season and an ex–third stringer for the second half. For another, we're not real strong at wide receiver. Firing Matt would be easy, not hard. But it wouldn't be right."

Bisciotti is, if nothing else, a good listener. He can be tough, as Billick had learned, but he's also fair. They continued talking until Bisciotti had to leave to go to a basketball game one of his sons was playing in. They agreed to meet one more time, the next day back at Bisciotti's house. "I was feeling better about things by then," Bisciotti said. "And I was pretty close to convinced Brian was right about Cavanaugh. But I'm not sure Brian was feeling better. That's why we needed to meet again."

Bisciotti was right about Billick. The two meetings had shaken him. The last thing he had expected was an owner who got right in his face when he disagreed with him. "It occurred to me that Steve reminded me of somebody," he said. "Me. He came right at you, told you what he thought, and if you didn't like it, tough. I certainly respected that; I'd be a hypocrite if I didn't. But it unnerved me. I honestly wondered if the two of us were going to be able to work together."

Bisciotti had no such qualms. He knew he had shaken Billick up, and that was okay. But he also knew that, one way or the other, he was going to make Billick understand that even if they disagreed at times, they could work together and that he was going to do everything he could to provide Billick with what he needed to win another Super Bowl. "As a boss, if someone's good at what they do, you might shake them up every now and then to try to make them better, but you make it clear to them that you support them and want them to be there."

Uncertain what to do next, Billick called his old boss and mentor Denny Green. "Don't bother trying to change," Green told Billick. "For one thing, you can't do it. For another, if you win, that's the ultimate answer. If you don't win, you can do everything the guy wants you to do and you're going to get fired anyway."

In short: Just win, baby.

The Sunday meeting was the most relaxed of the three. Bisciotti felt he had made the points he needed to make to Billick, and Billick was relieved and pleased that Bisciotti had come around to his way of thinking on Cavanaugh. Even though Billick's contract specifically said that he had complete control over the hiring and firing of coaches, the last thing he wanted was to begin the new owner's regime with a confrontation. Bisciotti told Billick that he had won him over on the subject of Cavanaugh and that he planned to tell Cavanaugh just that when he returned from vacation.

The two men shook hands at the door. Bisciotti told Billick he felt a lot better than he had three days earlier. Billick said he felt better, too.

They both meant what they said. Or, at the very least, they *hoped* they did.

3

Ozzie Transcends Us All

WHILE BRIAN BILLICK WAS HAVING a difficult first week dealing with his new boss, Ozzie Newsome had no such problems. Bisciotti had asked only one thing of him during the transfer of power: "If you're going to do something that will make news, let me know before you do it so I don't hear about it from one of my friends."

An NFL general manager could hardly ask for greater carte blanche from an owner. That was pretty much the way it was for Newsome in the Ravens' organization. Years earlier Kevin Byrne, the team's vice president for public relations, had half-jokingly said, "Ozzie transcends us all." Billick repeated the line so often that newcomers thought it was his. What Byrne meant and others understood was that no one who worked for the Ravens questioned Newsome. Not the old owner, who viewed him as an adopted son; not the new owner, who respected and trusted him completely; not the head coach, who was almost awed by his lack of ego; and not anyone else who worked in the building.

Much of that respect centered on Newsome having been part of the organization for his entire adult life: He had been drafted by the Cleveland Browns in 1978 as a first-round pick out of the University of Alabama. He had played for the team for thirteen years and had retired having caught more passes (662) than any tight end in NFL history. He was a beloved figure in Cleveland, and Art Modell asked him to stay on as a scout, an assistant coach, or both — whatever he wanted. He eventually chose scouting, and when the team moved to Baltimore and Modell fired Bill Belichick, Newsome was put in charge of personnel decisions.

If there was any doubt about his ability to run a team, it was put to rest only a couple of months after he had taken over, during his first draft. Almost everyone in football was convinced that the Ravens, with the fourth pick, were going to take the supremely talented but supremely troubled Lawrence Phillips, the controversial running back from Nebraska. Modell thought Phillips was worth the risk and told Newsome so. Newsome and his scouts thought Jonathan Ogden, the mammoth left tackle from UCLA, was a better player who came with less risk. Over Modell's objections, he took Ogden.

"Looking back on it, the reason I'm still here today is because I took Ogden and not Phillips with that pick," he said, laughing. "I knew what Mr. Modell wanted but I also knew what I thought was the best thing for us to do. I figured if I was going to fail, I was going to fail doing what I thought was right."

Later in the first round Newsome, with a pick the team had acquired the year before from San Francisco, took Ray Lewis, a ferocious linebacker out of Miami, considered too small by a lot of scouts and too much of a trouble-maker by some others. Three linebackers — Kevin Hardy, John Mobley, and Reggie Brown — had already been selected before Newsome took Lewis with the twenty-sixth pick of the first round.

Nine years later Ogden and Lewis are the centerpieces of the Ravens and lock Hall of Famers when their careers are over. One draft, two Hall of Famers. A pretty good start for anyone. In 1999 Newsome was elected to the Pro Football Hall of Fame. A year later the Ravens won the Super Bowl. In 2002 Modell made official what had been fact for six years and named Newsome general manager. That made Newsome the first African American to hold that title with an NFL team.

"To be honest, I didn't think much about it at the time, because I'd been doing the job for six years," he said. "So, while it was nice to have the title, it didn't change my life on a day-to-day basis at all. But then I was on a radio show with [former Georgetown basketball coach] John Thompson and he said to me, 'What's important about this is that African American kids can now look at you and say, "Why can't I be an NFL general manager, too?"' That was when it seemed like a big deal to me."

What makes Newsome transcendent is that very few things are a big deal to him. He grew up in Alabama, born in the town of Muscle Shoals, which is part of a quadrangle of four midsize towns in the northwestern corner of the state. His father, Ozzie Sr., was an entrepreneur. He operated restaurants and a cab company and sold bootleg alcohol at different times during his life. His mother, Ethel Mae, worked on occasion to make sure her five children (Ozzie was the third) had whatever they wanted, but she spent the majority of her time making sure the children stayed on the straight and narrow — did well in school, made it to church every Sunday — at the very least.

"If the sun was up and something was going on at church, we were there," Newsome said. "Most Sundays, we showed up at nine in the morning and didn't get out until midafternoon. Every Sunday it was shoutin' and praisin' and preachin' and prayin' and we held hands and then we prayed some more. The church was an important part of life for blacks in the South because it was one place we could go where we felt we had some control of our lives. The sanctuary in the church was ours, no one else's. There was still a good deal of segregation when I was young, and then when integration did start, there was a lot of tension. But in our church [Cave Springs Missionary Baptist Church] there was no tension. It made you feel grounded in life no matter what else was going on. It wasn't just about religion or about God, it was about learning discipline and how to conduct yourself and do the right things."

It was natural for Newsome to be drawn to sports. His grandfather was a huge fan of the Atlanta Braves, who moved to the South when Newsome was ten. His dad had been a renowned catcher as a semi-pro player in the Negro Leagues. "My dad was five-six and probably weighed about two-ninety," Newsome said. "He was a big man. When I was a kid, people always told me about how he could throw runners out from the sitting position. He never stood up, just whipped the ball from the sitting position and threw people out."

At the age of ten, Newsome was presented with an unusual opportunity by his mother. Segregation was slowly going away in the South. Newsome can still remember going as a young boy to Sheffield, the largest town in the area, and seeing separate entrances for whites and "coloreds," separate drinking fountains and bathrooms, too. Now, with schools becoming integrated, Ethel Mae Newsome asked her son if he wanted to go to the same school he had been attending, which was more than 90 percent black, or go to sixth grade down the road at a school that was 90 percent white.

"I was always a reader," Newsome said. "I would read anything I could get my hands on, especially if it was about sports. I had read in the local newspapers about how the white school had better facilities, better equipment, better classrooms, all of that. I told my mom I wanted to go to school there and see how I did."

Predictably, the first year wasn't easy. Newsome and the handful of black students entering the school understood that their presence was resented by some. Plus there were all the normal headaches of being a new kid. "First day on the schoolyard we chose up sides for baseball," he said. "I was the last guy picked because no one knew me. First time I came up I was going to show them, I was going to hit the ball farther than anyone had ever hit a ball. I struck out."

Things soon got better. Newsome was a good athlete and a good student. In eighth grade he played organized football for the first time and became a wide receiver on the first day of practice because he arrived late, and as he was running to get onto the field, the first group of players he came to were the receivers. His ascension was rapid. By his junior year, he was being recruited by all the major football powers. By then, he had grown to six foot two and 175 pounds, with soft hands and excellent speed. And he was one of the better students at Colbert County High School.

"For a long time my mom wanted me to go to Vanderbilt," he said. "Academics. Bill Parcells was on the staff at the time and he was recruiting me hard. But I'd played basketball with Leon Douglas. He was a year ahead of me and he went to Alabama. He kept talking to me about how it was important for an Alabama boy to stay in Alabama. In the end, it came down to Auburn and Alabama, and both my mom and I were pretty much convinced I should go to Auburn. I had teammates there, including my quarterback, and it just seemed right. So, the day before the signing date, I committed to Auburn."

A day later he signed with Alabama. The reason, according to Newsome, was John Mitchell, who had been the first African American to play at Alabama under Bear Bryant. "He came up the day before the signing date and I told him I'd decided to go to Auburn. He asked if he could take me to dinner. In those days [1974] there were no rules about what alumni could and could not do. I said okay. During dinner, he convinced me. He just said Alabama was *the* place and that Coach Bryant was completely color-blind. He won me over. So I went home and told my mom I'd decided to go to Alabama.

"She was furious. She started screaming at John that her son was going to Auburn, that the decision had been made. I said to her, 'Mama, the Lord told me I should go to Alabama.' Then she really got mad. She said, 'Don't you start putting the Lord into this!' She ordered John to get out of her house. John pulled me aside and said, 'Ozzie, I've got to stay here tonight because Coach Bryant told me not to come back without you.' Somehow I got my mother to let him stay the night, and the next day I went and hid out from all the other recruiters and signed with Alabama."

Newsome thrived at Alabama from the start. Perhaps because he had been in predominantly white schools since the sixth grade, the lack of black faces didn't bother him. He couldn't help but notice that each recruiting class had an even number of blacks in it —"Roommates," he said. "They weren't quite ready to mix blacks and whites in the same room yet." But as a football player, he never felt any serious prejudice. "At Alabama, if you played football, you were on a pedestal, regardless of color," he said. "And Coach Bryant, he really didn't care about color. He just cared about making everyone better, whatever it took."

Newsome became a starter by the end of his freshman season and began his senior year as a highly touted pro prospect. By then, he was a Big Man on Campus and, apparently, acting like it. "Coach Bryant called me into his office before the season started and said, 'Ozzie, I'm getting that senior strut vibe from you as if you think you're bigger than the program. I don't like the way you're acting. I think I'm gonna call your mama and tell her how you're acting.'

"Now, by then, my mom was the biggest Alabama fan on earth. She had learned that if your son played football at Alabama, everyone knew about it and it was a really big deal. She adored Coach Bryant. If he told her I was misbehaving, I'd be in big trouble. So I said, 'Please, Coach, don't call my mom, I'll be okay.'"

He graduated —"I did enough to get by and that was about it"— with a degree in recreation administration the following spring and was drafted by the Browns with the twenty-third pick. To this day, Newsome tries as hard as he can to be straight with potential draft picks about what his team's interest or non-interest is, because he remembers his own draft day so vividly.

"It was torture," he said. "In those days there was no combine [the annual NFL meat market held in Indianapolis that most draft hopefuls attend], and teams only came to work you out if they were really interested. The Packers came down and they worked me out for two hours. I was exhausted. Then the Browns came down and I said, no way am I going through that again. They were there to see [close friend, running back] Johnny Davis, too, and they had him call me and ask me to come over just for ten minutes. The guy who came was Rich Kotite [who later coached the Eagles and Jets] and he just tossed a few balls to me and that was it. I found out later he really just wanted to look me over, specifically, he wanted to get a look at my butt to see if I had the potential to get bigger than two-twenty."

On draft day — the draft wasn't on TV in those days — Newsome sat by the phone. Word came that the Packers had taken wide receiver James Lofton with the sixth pick. Then, at number twelve, the Browns took Clay Matthews. "I'm not happy, but I'm not panicked because Cleveland had another pick. But then they traded the pick to Minnesota. Now I'm really getting bummed. Who's going to take me? Anyone? A little while later the phone rings and a voice says, 'Ozzie, this is Art Modell, are you ready to become a Cleveland Brown?' They had traded with someone to get the twenty-third pick. I went from frustrated and worried to overjoyed in about a minute."

Newsome got a $75,000 signing bonus from the Browns and a three-year contract that paid him $50,000, $57,500, and $65,000. He also got a shock when Coach Sam Rutigliano told him at the end of the first mini-camp that he was being moved to tight end. "I'd never played anything but wide receiver my entire life," he said. "But Sam said not to worry, I'd still catch plenty of balls."

The first time he touched the ball in a real NFL game, Newsome ran 40 yards for a touchdown on an end-around play against the San Francisco 49ers. He was so excited, scoring right in front of Cleveland's infamous "Dog Pound" that he spiked the ball. Then he thought about what Bryant always told his players: "When you get in the end zone, act as if you've been there before." Or when a player really hotdogged he might say, "If you want to be in the circus, there's one you can join down the street. We're here to play football."

Concerned that Bryant would see a replay of the spike, he called several friends back home and told them if Bryant did happen to see it, to tell him it was an accident, a heat-of-the-moment thing. He never heard from Bryant all season. "Then when I went home at the end of the year, I went to see him," he said. "First thing he said was 'I saw you spike that ball.' I told him that I forgot myself because I was so excited. He just nodded and said, 'You didn't do it again, did you?' I said, 'No, sir.' He said, 'You ever going to do it again?' I said, 'No, sir.' He just nodded and smiled and moved to another topic."

The only blemish in an otherwise sterling career was the Browns' inability to get to the Super Bowl. The Browns were good during most of Newsome's thirteen-year career — they made the playoffs seven times — but always found a way to come up just short of the ultimate game. In 1980, playing at home against the Oakland Raiders, the Browns trailed, 14–12, when they drove to the Raiders 13-yard line in the final minute. A field goal would win the game, but with the wind swirling inside the Mistake by the Lake and Don Cockroft having already missed two field goals at that end of the stadium, Sam Rutigliano decided to try for the end zone once more, giving quarterback Brian Sipe orders to "throw it in Lake Erie" if someone wasn't wide-open. Newsome was wide-open — or so Sipe thought. At the last possible second, cornerback Mike Davis jumped in front of Newsome and intercepted the ball. The Raiders went on to win the Super Bowl.

In 1985 the Browns led the Miami Dolphins, 21–3, in the third quarter in the opening round of the playoffs — and lost. If they had won, they would have hosted the AFC Championship Game the next week. A year later they *did* host the AFC Championship Game, against the Denver Broncos. That game produced the famous (or, in Cleveland, infamous) John Elway–led 98-yard march to tie the score with 37 seconds left that became known simply as "the Drive." A year later it was "the Fumble," Earnest Byner fumbling on the goal line in Denver when he was about to tie the game late in the fourth quarter. Again, the Broncos went to the

Super Bowl. They went again in 1989, this time beating the Browns soundly in their third championship game matchup in four years.

"There was the Drive, the Fumble, and the Rout," Newsome said, remembering all three games. "The one that hurt the most was the Drive. Usually, when the defense was on the field, I didn't watch. I'd sit on the bench and rest. But in that game, we're less than two minutes from the Super Bowl, I'm watching. They have a third-and-seventeen. They make it. Then they score. Even in the overtime, we got the ball first and didn't do anything with it. I can still remember at the start of the Drive, thinking, 'I'm finally going to a Super Bowl,' because I'd always said I wasn't going until I played in one."

Following the Rout in 1989, Newsome flew home with the team, walked into his house, and could tell by the look on his wife Gloria's face that something was wrong that had nothing to do with the game. "Your dad died a couple of hours after the game," she told him. It wasn't a shock — Ozzie Newsome Sr. had liver and kidney problems and was extremely overweight, but it was still a shock because it was his dad. "Last time we talked had been Friday," he said. "Dad said to me, 'Ozzie, you've got to do something about that Elway.' I told him not to worry, that we had a plan for him this time. He was skeptical. I think the last thing he ever said to me was 'Watch out for Elway.'"

Newsome thought he was ready to quit at that point. He'd played twelve years and his body had taken a pounding and he sensed that the team's time as a Super Bowl contender had come and gone. But Modell persuaded him to come back. "If we sign [cornerback] Raymond Clayborne and you come back, I think we can make another run at it," he said.

Newsome came back. The last game was in Cincinnati. By then, Coach Bud Carson had pretty much told Newsome he could put himself in the game or take himself out as he saw fit. In the second half, even with teammates encouraging him to go back in to catch a few more balls, he stayed on the sideline. "I knew it was time," he said. "I called my mother and said, 'The fire's out. I'm done.'"

Newsome and Modell had always had an unspoken understanding that he would stay with the team when he retired. They had become close through the years to the point where, during the 1987 strike, Modell had called Newsome personally when the strike was about to end, and pleaded with him to come in and play in the final scab game against Cincinnati because he believed the game was critical to the Browns' playoff chances. Newsome — and many other stars — came back that weekend. The Browns won and made the playoffs, but the locker room was split because some players had crossed the picket line, others had not.

The plan was for Newsome to learn scouting. But Bill Belichick, the newly hired head coach, wanted him to work on the field, too. Newsome eventually became a hybrid — part coach, part scout — working on the field during the season, scouting during the off-season. "At one point I think I had the longest title in the history of the NFL," he said. "I was the 'head coach offense/pro personnel director,'" he said. "By then, I think I knew I wanted to be on the personnel side, but Bill kept pushing me to keep coaching."

Newsome was learning as he went. He still remembers vividly the Sunday night in 1993 when Belichick decided to cut quarterback Bernie Kosar, who had been just about as popular in Cleveland as Newsome. "I came in Monday morning and it was done," he said. "It was a mistake. It happened because people were angry and frustrated. The lesson I learned from that was never make a decision, a big decision, right after a game. Look at the tape, calm down, and then if you think it is time to make a move, make it. But never while you're still emotionally wound up from the battle."

Newsome was among a small handful of people to whom Modell revealed his moving plans early in the 1995 season. He was stunned. Cleveland had become his home; he knew everyone in town and they knew him. Modell wanted to be sure Ozzie would go with him to Baltimore, and Newsome agreed to go. Soon after the move, Belichick was fired and Marchibroda was hired in his place. Mike Lombardi, the vice president in charge of football personnel, was also let go. It was Jim Bailey, the team's executive vice president on the business side, who recommended to Modell that he put Newsome in charge of personnel. In one of his first conversations with Marchibroda, the two of them agreed that if they ever had a disagreement they couldn't resolve, they would go to Modell to discuss it together. It is a policy Newsome has continued to this day in his relationship with Billick and Bisciotti. "The best thing about my relationship with Brian," Newsome said, "is that it never comes to that. We always figure something out between ourselves."

* * *

The move to Baltimore was chaotic. On April 1 — four weeks before the draft — a skeleton crew of Cleveland refugees moved into the Colts' old facility. The building had almost no furniture; there was dust everywhere and there was no place to file anything. "All of our scouting reports and tapes were lined up in the hallway outside our offices," Phil Savage, who had come with Newsome as the newly minted director of college personnel, remembered. "It was hard to believe you were working in the NFL."

The team had to purge some salaries to get under the cap in order to have a chance to sign the two first-round draft picks they were entitled to. Key veterans, such as linebacker Pepper Johnson, wide receiver Andre Rison, and cornerback Donnie Griffin, had to be cut. "We had fifty-one players under contract and no practice squad," Newsome said. "It was all we could afford."

And yet the Ravens came up with that historic draft, taking Ogden and Lewis in the first round, working from that shell of a building. Certainly there was some luck involved. The Ravens were convinced that Arizona was going to take Ogden with the third pick, but the Cardinals ended up taking Simeon Rice. "They actually tried to bluff us," Newsome said. "They thought we wanted Phillips, so Mr. [Cardinals owner Bill] Bidwill had his people write a card in New York that our guys could see that said, 'Lawrence Phillips,' on it to try to get us into trading up with them. Oldest trick in the book. Plus, I didn't want Phillips anyway."

Modell did. He kept pointing out that the team needed a running back. Everyone in the room said the same thing. Newsome was determined to "stay true to the board," meaning that he was going to take the highest-ranked player on the Ravens draft board when it came his turn to pick — regardless of position. Even though he had two experienced tackles, he believed Ogden could play guard for a year and then become a great tackle. So he took Ogden, and Phillips ended up going to the St. Louis Rams, where he became a complete bust.

The Ravens also needed a linebacker. A lot of teams were wary of Ray Lewis. He had refused to go through workouts at the combine — as did many players — and had interviewed there with only a few teams. The Ravens had been one of them. Even the Ravens had a Z, by his name on the board because he was "height deficient," being just a shade over six feet tall. "What we saw was a little linebacker who was immature and, some people thought, pretty arrogant. But [assistant coach and former Pro Bowl linebacker] Maxie Baughn had gone down and worked him out and he came back and said, 'The guy's a competitor, a real competitor. And he can really shoot his gun.'"

In English that meant Lewis made plays — lots of plays. The Ravens took him. Even so, the rebuilding process was a slow one. By the third season, with the team in the new stadium and two more drafts in place, the team appeared ready to make a playoff run. Then came the opening-day debacle against Pittsburgh. That loss, as it turned out, was the beginning of the end for Marchibroda.

"I remember David [Modell] was ballistic after that game," Newsome said, laughing. "I mean, he was mad at me, he was mad at Ted, he was mad at everybody. We had everything exactly right except for the way we played. After that, the pressure just kept building until it popped. It was almost inevitable."

The final pop came on November 1, following a 45–19 home loss to Jacksonville, the team's fourth straight loss. That dropped their record to 2-6. Those few fans who remained in the fourth quarter filled the stadium with chants of "Ted Must Go."

One of the chanters may have been Art Modell. As soon as the game was over, Newsome got a call from Sam Miller, Modell's assistant. Modell wanted a meeting — *now*. "I knew exactly what we were going to talk about," Newsome said.

The meeting was in Modell's box and included Art and David Modell, Jim Bailey, James Harris (Newsome's head of pro scouting and confidant), and Newsome. The Modells wanted to fire Marchibroda on the spot. Newsome, remembering his vow not to make important decisions in the aftermath of a bad loss, counseled caution. "I said, 'Who are you going to make coach if you fire Ted?'" he remembered. "'If you name one of the assistants as an interim, what good does that do? Is there anyone on the staff or out there you want to commit to right now, give a long-term contract to, because if you want to hire someone permanently, you have to give them that contract and make that commitment.'"

Newsome won the debate. Marchibroda would be allowed to finish the season if only so that potential coaches wouldn't see the Ravens as an organization in chaos. Modell asked Newsome and his son to head the search committee for a new coach and to begin their work immediately. Newsome liked that idea. "I never understood why, when you were making the decision that was probably going to make or break your team for the next few years — picking a coach — owners would do it by picking up a phone and asking a buddy, 'Who do you like?' or taking a recommendation from a friend. It was almost casual and it was so important. There's no one more important in the organization than your coach, and you hire him just because your buddy said he's a good guy?

"My idea was to mirror the approach we take in the draft. Put together a list with everyone on it and then winnow it down from there. David and I would meet almost every night at his house and all of us put in long hours, going down lists of names. We would usually have a bowl of macaroni and cheese that Art's chef would make for dinner and then get Popeyes chicken when it got late. We started with every NFL coordinator and every major college coach on our list.

"We checked to make sure people weren't interested. Shack [James Harris, whose nickname as a kid was "Sugarshack"] called Joe Gibbs to see if he was interested. No. We checked Steve Spurrier to see if he was interested. No. Eventually, we narrowed the list to people who were gettable and, we thought, good."

The best-known name on the short list was Mike Holmgren, who was as hot as any coach in the NFL because he had just been to back-to-back Super Bowls in Green Bay. Holmgren was looking to leave Green Bay because he wanted to go someplace where he had total control. Newsome and Modell decided if Holmgren could be had, they should do whatever had to be done to get him. "We did our due diligence," he said. "His wife was a Christian Scientist, so we found the one Christian Scientist church in the area for her. I had told the Modells that if Mike Holmgren needs absolute power to come, give it to him, I'll relinquish mine if that's what is best for the team and, to tell the truth, I thought it might very well be. We were looking at George Seifert, too, but then Jerry Richardson [Carolina's owner] snapped him up.

"Turned out we never got the chance to interview Holmgren. We had a plane waiting in Seattle to bring him here after he talked to Paul Allen, but he never got on it because Allen offered him total control and so much money that he couldn't turn it down."

They ended up with four coordinators as finalists: Brian Billick, Chris Palmer, Jim Haslett, and Emmitt Thomas. The hot name was Billick because the Vikings had just set a handful of offensive records. Palmer was also an offensive coordinator and the other two were defensive coordinators, not a bad thing in Newsome's mind since the Ravens were building a very strong defense. He was a little concerned that Palmer kept talking about how his old boss, Bill Parcells, would do things. "I always remember Coach Bryant telling all of us that if we got into coaching, not to try to emulate him because you have to be your own guy. You can learn from Coach Bryant or Parcells, but you can't be them.

"Brian was impressive for several reasons. First, I talked to a lot of people about him and so did David. Cris Carter [the Vikings wide receiver] told me they had hated each other at first, but that had changed and they got along well. I asked him if he would come and play for him if he had the chance and he said absolutely. Warren Moon said the same thing. Bill Walsh [Billick's first mentor] said we couldn't go wrong if we hired him.

"But what sold me was when we talked to him. There just wasn't any of the same old rhetoric you hear from guys when they're trying to get a job. He was above the curve. I could tell he was a risk taker. At one point I asked him how we would resolve differences we might have on the draft and the roster, did he think we would be able to compromise? And he just said, 'No, Ozzie, I don't believe in compromise. Because if we compromise, then neither of us is responsible for the final decision.' I liked that. Then he said that either I would convince him or he would convince me. I liked that, too. I also liked the fact that he was up front about feeling that way."

By the Friday before the NFC Championship Game between Atlanta and Minnesota, the Ravens had decided that Billick was their choice. They couldn't formally offer him the job while his team was still in the playoffs, but they made it known to him that the job was his if he wanted it. The word that came back was: I'll get back to you. The reason: the new Cleveland Browns were also making a big play for Billick.

"Art was furious," Newsome said. "Especially since it was Cleveland. He said, 'If he doesn't want it, forget it, let's go hire Chris Palmer.' We convinced him, let's wait and see. I think David and I both thought he was really the guy. When the Vikings lost that Sunday, Dwight Clark [Cleveland's general manager] was up there with a plane and orders to bring Brian to Cleveland to make a deal and sign him. But David got the deal done by phone. He and Brian talked numbers, we talked about those numbers, and then made a deal. We flew him in and introduced him the next day. Then we got on a plane together to go to the Senior Bowl [in Mobile, Alabama], and Brian showed me on his computer some of his plans for the off-season. I was amazed. He had done, in a few hours, things we used to spend days charting and planning. I can remember thinking, 'We've got the right guy now. Let's go to work.'"

4

The T.O. Caper . . .
and Other Adventures

THEIR WORK PRODUCED remarkable results remarkably quickly. In 1999 the Ravens were 8-8, winning five of their last seven games. A year later they stumbled to a 5-4 start, going five straight games without scoring a touchdown. Brian Billick made the decision at that point to bench quarterback Tony Banks and go with veteran Trent Dilfer. The offense's marching orders under Dilfer were simple: don't lose the game. The defense was evolving into one of the most dominating in the history of the NFL, led by two huge defensive tackles — Tony Siragusa and Sam Adams — a superb defensive backfield, and a young linebacker who seemed to be in on every play: Ray Lewis.

The Ravens ripped off seven straight victories to end the regular season and made the playoffs for the first time in their four-year history, as a wild-card team. They beat Denver at home and Tennessee and Oakland on the road to reach the Super Bowl against the New York Giants. Reaching the Super Bowl for the first time is always a defining moment for a team, for a coach, and for a team's star players. Never was that more true than for the Ravens team that went to Tampa in January of 2001.

Ray Lewis had emerged that season as the heart and soul of the defense, which was also the heart and soul of the team. The Ravens had given up 165 points during the regular season, an NFL record for fewest points allowed since the expansion to a sixteen-game schedule in 1978. Lewis had played, however, with an undeniable cloud hanging over him: the incident in Atlanta a year earlier on the night of the Super Bowl, which had left two men dead and a plethora of questions that simply would not go away.

When police had questioned Lewis after the two murders, he had been, according to them, uncooperative and unwilling to tell them what he knew — or what they thought he knew. Lewis was arrested and spent fifteen days in jail, charged, along with two of his friends, Joseph Sweeting and Reginald Oakley, with the two murders. He was released on bail — a changed man, he would say later — and went to trial two months later. Midway through the trial, according to Lewis's attorney, Ed Garland, the prosecutor came to his house on a Sunday morning to tell him he was planning to drop the charges against Lewis because he did not believe there was any way to get a guilty verdict. In return, he told Garland he wanted Lewis to testify as to what he had seen that night. Garland agreed because he knew that Lewis *wanted* to tell his version of the story. The prosecutor had one condition under which he would agree to call Lewis: he would have to admit under oath that he had lied to the police on the night of the incident. That would lead to a misdemeanor conviction for obstruction of justice. There would be no jail time. Lewis, through Garland, agreed. Even with Lewis's testimony, Sweeting and Oakley were acquitted. No one was ever convicted of committing the murders.

Lewis was sentenced to one year of probation for his obstruction conviction and fined $250,000 by the NFL.

From the beginning, the Ravens, while saying they knew the judicial system had to run its course, defended Lewis. The public stance adopted by the franchise was simple: we know Ray Lewis, we believe in Ray Lewis, and we do not believe Ray Lewis did what he has been accused of doing. When Lewis returned to the team for preseason minicamp, he was greeted with open arms by everyone in the organization. He agreed to answer questions about what had happened — not at the scene that night in Atlanta, but in the aftermath — and then the team made it clear that, as far as they and Ray were concerned, the issue was closed. Lewis had answered the questions once, and now he was entitled to move on with his life.

"You have to remember that none of us had ever dealt with anything like this before," Billick said. "It wasn't as if I could call some other coach and say, 'Hey, when this happened to you, what did you do?' We were sort of flying blind. But the one thing we kept coming back to was that we all believed, truly believed, that Ray just wasn't capable of doing something like that. Was he in the wrong place at the wrong time? Absolutely. Did he handle the situation badly with the police that first night? You bet. But that's a long way from being a murderer or any of the other things he has been accused of being."

Opening Lewis up to the media at minicamp and then saying he was through dealing with the issue wasn't about to prevent the story from coming up wherever the Ravens went on the road that season. It didn't prevent fans from screaming, "Murderer!" at Lewis whenever he walked out of a tunnel away from home. "We all knew that was the way it was going to be," Billick said. "Ray knew it, too. In a way, it became a rallying point for all of us. Here was our leader, dealing with this, and we were all going to be there to stand behind him because we believed in him."

Now the Ravens were walking into the hottest media crucible in sports. No event draws more media attention than the Super Bowl. It is one solid week of more than 3,500 media members (that's about a 35:1 ratio of media to players) looking for something to write about because there is no real story — the game — until Sunday and they all have to justify being in the city where the game is being held by writing something. One story stood out in Ravens vs. Giants for anyone who had ever picked up a notebook or a microphone: Ray Lewis. One year after he had landed in jail on a murder charge in the immediate aftermath of the Super Bowl, he was likely to star in the Super Bowl. No self-respecting reporter could be expected to ignore that story.

Billick, who had started his post-football-playing career as a public relations assistant for the San Francisco 49ers, understood that. So did Kevin Byrne, who had been the Browns/Ravens public relations honcho for twenty-two years after starting out on the other side of the fence as a college journalist. Both men knew that the minute the Ravens' plane landed in Tampa, Ray Lewis's name was going to be on everyone's lips. They needed a plan.

"Basically we decided that the best thing to do was make me the target," Billick said. "I knew I could handle it and, to be honest, it was more important that Ray not be distracted or bothered than it was that I not be distracted or bothered, because I knew I wouldn't lose sleep over it."

On the plane ride down on the Monday before the game, Billick and Byrne went over a number of bullet points that Byrne had put together. This is standard procedure every week between the two men. Byrne will suggest subjects Billick wants to cover in his Monday press conference, and while Billick may not hit them all, he will certainly use them as a guide. Byrne's points on Lewis were clear: Ray has already addressed this. You have the right to ask what you want, but he may not answer any questions on this subject while he is preparing for the biggest game of his life. . . . The facts speak for themselves. . . . Ray pleaded guilty to a misdemeanor, the murder charges were dropped. . . . He has already been penalized by the NFL. . . . He has had to live with the incident all year when the team has played on the road and no doubt will continue to have to live with it. . . . This has been discussed within the team, and no one on the team is likely to respond to questions on the subject, either.

Byrne thought that if Billick laid that out briefly during his opening statement, it would undoubtedly anger some writers, especially those who didn't cover football regularly and saw the Lewis story as fresh. That's one thing that makes the Super Bowl unique: many who cover it don't really cover football. What Byrne didn't count on was Billick's temper. The night before, ESPN (which does cover football regularly) had aired a lengthy piece during which reporter Jeremy Schaap had interviewed relatives of Richard Lollar and Jacinth Baker, the two victims. One of them said on camera that he believed Ray Lewis was a murderer. Others talked about how much they missed the two men and how shocking it was to have them go out for a night on the town and never come home.

To Billick, this was piling on. It was especially surprising since ESPN has such a cozy relationship with NFL teams 99 percent of the time. This was far from cozy. If ESPN was beginning the week with this sort of piece, Billick could imagine what was going to come next. "I thought the piece was unfair," he said. "The prosecutor dropped the charges against Ray because there was no evidence he committed the murders. Then they let this poor kid, whose grief I completely understand, call Ray a murderer. That's just wrong."

Most coaches begin press conferences with a brief statement before taking questions. Billick frequently goes longer than most because there are certain questions he can anticipate, so he gets them out of the way. Usually they involve an injured player's status or a move the team has made involving the acquisition or the departure of a player. This was entirely different. Billick talked for ten solid minutes, essentially lecturing the media, not something most people in the profession take well to.

"We are not going to retry this," he said, bringing up Lewis and the case almost immediately. "It's inappropriate and you're not qualified. . . . Those who wish to embellish it, not to crystallize it, not to shed new information, but to sensationalize it for your purposes — this is my personal observation, it is reprehensible. I don't like it. It's unprofessional.

"I've seen some reports that are embellishing on it and embarking on an area that I just see no productivity. I don't think it's in the best interest of the families, I don't think it's in the best interests of the league, I don't think it's in the best interests of Ray Lewis, and, quite frankly, I don't think it's in your best interests, because I don't think you-all, when you do that, come across real well."

He had made his point by then, but he didn't stop: "I'm a little disturbed with the focus that is being brought to it for the reasons it is being brought. I equate it to an ambulance-chasing mode. You decided you wanted to take on a sensational aspect to it. Nothing you hear or find is going to crystallize the situation or unearth anything that hasn't already been brought forth. So your preoccupation with it is something I'll address one time only.

"All charges were dropped against Ray Lewis. There was no plea bargaining. It became very apparent to the district attorney and anybody who witnessed the proceedings that Ray's involvement did not warrant the accusations or the charges. Ray, after the charges were dropped, offered to testify and admitted readily to not having handled the situation the way he wished he had in not dealing with the police in a forthright manner. You can stir it up, but it's not going to change the facts."

Many of the questions that followed were contentious, including one reporter asking Billick what right he had to tell the assembled media members how to do their jobs. "I have the podium," Billick replied. "And you-all are here to listen to me."

They listened. And then they reacted — angrily. Billick knew while he was still on the podium that he had pushed the envelope a little too hard.

As he walked away, he looked at Byrne and said, "I think I may have gone too far."

"No kidding," Byrne answered.

Anyone who knew Brian Billick at all would not have been the least bit surprised by his performance that day in Tampa. He had grown up in a family where dinner was often a forum for heated debate. He was the fourth of Don and Mildred Billick's five children. Mike, his eldest brother, wanted to follow in his father's footsteps and be a pilot. He was in the ROTC program at Cal-Riverside and then in the air force. His vision prevented him from becoming a pilot, meaning he ended up becoming a navigator when he graduated. Don Billick had grown up in Toledo, Ohio, and had gone into the air force as a mechanic. He became a pilot when his superiors noticed that he knew more about the planes than anyone, and suggested he get into the test pilot program. During World War II he met Mildred Bale at a USO party. They fell in love, got married, and moved to Dayton after the war because that's where the test pilot program was located. Brian was born outside Dayton in February of 1954, following Mike and two sisters. His brother Gary was born sixteen months later. By then, the Billicks were living in Redlands, California, having moved there along with the test pilot program.

As it turned out, Brian was the family jock. He went from short and round in junior high school to tall and less round in high school. As a freshman at Redlands High School he became a starter at safety and had eight interceptions. "I was like Paul Krause," he said, referring to the Minnesota Vikings Hall of Fame safety. "I just sat back and played center field, roamed wherever I thought the ball was going."

It is not surprising that Billick would use Krause as a reference point, because he was a Vikings fan as a kid. "Not sure why," he said. "Maybe it was the colors, maybe it was the helmets, maybe it was all those playoff games in freezing cold weather. I liked [Fran] Tarkenton a lot, too, liked to watch him scramble."

Billick became a quarterback his sophomore year, although he continued to play both ways throughout his high school career. By the time he was a senior he was six foot five and was the California state record holder for interceptions and an all-state quarterback. It was while he was in high school that Mike went to Vietnam. By then, his sisters, Barbara and Donna, were in college and had taken part in antiwar marches and were very much against the war. When they were home for dinner, Brian would watch in amazement while they shouted at his father about the war and he shouted back.

"It was very intense and very emotional," he said. "They were saying that the war was morally wrong, that their brother was a baby-killer like everyone else over there, and that we should be ashamed that he was involved in this thing. To my father, doing what Mike was doing was an automatic, a given, something you should be very proud of. This was about God and country. As far as he was concerned, there was no debate."

Only there was debate, most of it at extremely high decibel levels. Brian was torn: the two people he admired most in the world were his father and his brother. And yet what his sisters were saying seemed to make sense because the war didn't make much sense to him. "I kept wanting to know why we were over there," he said. "I'm not sure I ever got an answer that really worked for me."

Vietnam was winding down when it came time for Brian to make a decision on where to go to college. His father wanted him to go to the Air Force Academy. He considered UCLA but dropped that idea after a less-than-ideal meeting with Coach Pepper Rodgers. "Pepper spent the whole time we were in there swinging at imaginary tennis balls with his tennis racquet," Billick said. "I know now that was just Pepper being Pepper, but my father was really upset. He said, 'Brian, I'm not telling you where to go, but you are not going to play for that man.'"

Navy recruited Billick. He even got a call from Roger Staubach. "That was thrilling," he said. "But when I said the word 'Navy' to my dad, he looked as if he was going to get sick. I really ended up going to Air Force by default. It just seemed like the right thing to do."

Right from the start, Billick struggled at Air Force. On the first day he was there he had to fill out a form asking — among other things — what his religious affiliation was. "Back then, you were going to church someplace on Sunday, no ifs, ands, or buts," he said. Billick's mother and father had raised their children in the Episcopal Church. There was just one problem: "I didn't know how to spell *Episcopalian*," he said. "I had to write down Catholic, which meant I had to go to Catholic services every Sunday the entire time I was there."

He never felt comfortable at the school. "Very early on, they sent all the plebes out on one of those field missions, out in the middle of nowhere with a compass and a backpack and just about nothing else," he said. "We were in a place called *Jack's Valley*. I remember it was pouring down rain and I was sitting with my back against a tree, wet, cold, hungry, exhausted, and I looked up at the sky and saw a few stars and had an epiphany: this place ain't for me. I knew right at that moment that I'd never graduate."

If there was anything that might have rescued him, it would have been football. But that was a disappointment, too: he never saw the field the entire season, relegated to playing on the junior varsity as a linebacker. When the semester was over he went home and told his parents he had tried, but the academy just wasn't for him. "They were disappointed," he said. "But they understood."

He decided to transfer to Brigham Young, even though he knew he would be very much in the minority as a Catholic or even if he learned to spell *Episcopalian*. He had figured his best position as a college player was going to be tight end, and LaVell Edwards had a reputation as a coach who liked to throw the ball. So he transferred to Brigham Young, where religion again brought him to grief quickly.

"I went in the weight room to work out," he said. "Now, I knew it was a Mormon school but I noticed some of the guys were wearing shirts that had a cross on them and said, LDS. I figured there must be two branches of their church — the Mormons and the LDS."

Armed with his new understanding of the religion, Billick found himself in the cafeteria one day when he spotted a very attractive young woman eating by herself. "Red-blooded American boy, I walked over, sat down, and looking for an opening, I said, 'So, tell me, are you Mormon or LDS?'

"She gave me this disgusted look and said, 'Let me guess, you're a football player, right?'"

He was, in fact, a football player and he became a good one. He even learned that the Mormon Church was also known as the Church of Jesus Christ of Latter-Day Saints (LDS) and managed to avoid marriage while an undergraduate — no small feat. "As a sophomore, they want to take you to meet Mom and Dad on the third date," he said. "As a junior, it's the second date. By the time you're a senior, they're getting desperate. They want to go straight to Mom and Dad and get the ball rolling."

Billick was one of only a handful of senior football players who weren't married in the fall of 1975. He had a good year as a tight end, earning Honorable Mention All-American status. The team went to the Tangerine Bowl and he was drafted in the eleventh round by the San Francisco 49ers. He went to camp thinking he might have a chance to make the team. Those thoughts disappeared after the third exhibition game.

"I started," Billick said, "because they wanted to take a good look at me. We were playing the Houston Oilers. They had a linebacker named Robert Brazile, who was an All-Pro. First play of the game he lined up across from me. It was hot, so he had no sleeves on his shirt and his arms were bigger than most offensive linemen's legs. He was making these strange sounds. I remember thinking, 'Maybe if I don't move at all, he won't eat me.'"

Brazile didn't eat him, just flattened him. Billick was cut soon after that.

He went back home to Redlands and spent the fall helping out his old high school coach while also coaching at the University of Redlands. "It was like doing an internship in coaching," he said. "I loved it."

He wanted one more shot to play, though, so he accepted a free-agent contract after the season was over with the Dallas Cowboys. As it turned out, he had no chance to make the team —"I wasn't much more than a camp slapdick," he said — but the time he spent with Dallas turned out to be important. Soon after he was cut, he was hired in San Francisco as a public relations assistant. His boss was George Heddleston, who had worked previously for the Cowboys. That summer Heddleston had a pool party at his house. Billick was invited. So was Kim Gooch, a young Texan visiting town who had also worked for the Cowboys, as team president Tex Schramm's assistant. "First time I saw her I decided I was going to marry her," he said. "Don't ask me why or how I figured I'd have any chance with her, but I just knew."

Perhaps because he didn't ask her if she was Mormon or LDS, Billick was able to persuade Kim to date him. Less than a year later they were married. Billick spent two years in San Francisco, focusing a lot more on what Bill Walsh was teaching him about coaching than on requests for interviews with Walsh or any of the 49er players. Walsh became a mentor and, to this day, remains someone Billick talks to and relies on for advice and guidance. His career in San Francisco did not, however, get off to a roaring start.

As low man on the totem pole, he was charged with preparing everything for the coaches on the morning of the 1979 draft. This was before the draft was on TV and it began at 9 A.M. in New York — 6 A.M. in San Francisco. That meant the staff had to be in at 4:30 A.M. to start getting ready. Billick was more than ready when they arrived. "My dad was great at breakfasts," he said. "He knew what the best bagels were, pastries, breads, juices — you name it. I had one of the all-time great spreads waiting for those guys when they came in."

There was one small problem. Billick had never been a coffee drinker as a kid. Then he had gone to a Mormon school, where caffeine was banned. It had never occurred to him that a group of bleary-eyed coaches arriving for work at 4:30 in the morning might want coffee.

"No one noticed the bagels or the pastries or anything else," he said. "They were just screaming, 'Where the hell is the coffee!'"

Billick had earned his first NFL nickname: Coffee Boy.

After two years in San Francisco, Billick jumped on the coaching merry-go-round. San Diego State led to Utah State, which led to Stanford, which led to Minnesota. He had first met Denny Green when Green had worked for Walsh in San Francisco, and it was Green who brought him to the NFL, first as his tight ends coach and then, a little more than a year later, as his offensive coordinator. It was there that Billick emerged as a coaching star, leading to his hiring in Baltimore. He had always been considered a media-friendly guy, articulate and accessible, two huge assets in the eyes of any reporter.

A lot of that changed soon after he stepped off the plane in Tampa on that Monday afternoon in January.

Where Billick had, in Kevin Byrne's words, "stepped off the cliff," was with the comment about ambulance chasing. He was thinking of the Schaap piece, but he was generalizing, lumping everyone together. His tone didn't help either: "You aren't qualified." Not qualified to do what? Even so, Billick had clearly accomplished his mission to make himself the media's target. While Lewis had to deal with the questions the next morning —

which he dodged by saying repeatedly that the incident was in the past, that he felt bad that it had happened, and did anyone have a football question? — it was Billick who was pilloried all week. To this day there are a number of national football columnists who have not forgiven him for his lecture, including one — Len Pasquarelli of ESPN.com — who not only refuses to speak to Billick but won't set foot inside the Ravens' training camp — even though he annually writes a training camp report on all thirty-two teams.

Those in the media who know Billick like him. He is probably as accessible, if not more so, than any coach in the NFL. Beat writers know that if they walk down the hall to Billick's office, the door is likely to be open and they will be waved in if they need a few minutes of his time. Billick is smart and quotable — and occasionally arrogant, which he now considers part of his persona — but most reporters would much rather deal with Billick than with most of the secretive, paranoid, make-sure-to-say-nothing coaches who populate the NFL. But to many national media members, Billick's reputation as a pompous, self-righteous know-it-all was sealed forever that day in Tampa.

Billick is, essentially, unrepentant. "Okay, I probably went a little overboard," he said. "*Ambulance chaser* is a very strong term, but I was reacting to ESPN and Schaap. I was angry. But what about all the guys who wrote that I had it wrong when I said there was no plea bargain. Did they do their homework? No. There was no plea bargain."

To this day, there are writers who insist that what occurred was a modified version of a plea bargain. It comes up often enough that Byrne carries with him a newspaper clipping in which Garland explains in detail the sequence of events, pointing out that in many ways, the prosecutor coming to him to drop the charges was even more of an exoneration than a not guilty verdict or even a directed verdict would have been.

The rest of that Super Bowl week went about as well for the Ravens as was possible. David Modell had given instructions to the staff to bring no problems of any kind to Billick. "He told them if the building across the street burned down, just to tell me there was a barbecue going on there," Billick remembered. "I was able to focus completely and totally on getting ready for the game."

The Ravens turned the game into a rout in the second half and won,

34–7. The Giants' only touchdown came on a kickoff return. In two short years, the Ravens had gone from laughingstock to Super Bowl champions. They had gone from being regarded by some in Baltimore with suspicion to being a part of the town's fabric. For Billick, the suddenness of the rise was almost overwhelming. To him, becoming an NFL head coach had been a seminal moment in his life. At the press conference on the day he was introduced, he had thought about his father, who had died suddenly on Brian's fortieth birthday, and had almost been too choked up to speak. "I knew my dad would have looked at that day as an indication that I was okay, that I was, for lack of a better term, taken care of. He didn't need to worry anymore about what Brian would do or what Brian would become. The thought that I would coach a Super Bowl champion wasn't really tangible at that moment even though it was clearly the goal and what I'd been hired to do."

Billick went through the postgame rituals, accepting the trophy, the lengthy press conference, and the celebrations — first at the stadium, then at the team hotel afterward. At some point in the wee hours of the morning it occurred to him that he had to attend an 8 A.M. post–Super Bowl press conference that the NFL requires the winning coach to be present for. He went up to his room and sank into a shower to try to give himself an energy burst before meeting the media. It was there that he was seized by a brief moment of panic.

"It was something of a Peggy Lee moment," he said, referring to the famous song, "Is That All There Is?" — a thought that crosses almost every successful person's mind at some point after a momentous ultimate triumph. "But it was more than that. I'd known a lot of great coaches who never won a Super Bowl: Denny Green, Bud Grant, Marv Levy, Bill Cowher — just to name a few. Now, here I am, forty-six years old, in my second year as a head coach, and I've won one. The question was, what now? Can I stay motivated the way you need to, having done that? I thought about it for a few minutes and the answer was, yes, I could. I loved doing what I did, I didn't just do it to win a Super Bowl, I did it because I loved it. And now I was in a position where I could, essentially, make my own legacy. If we never won again, there would be people who'd say I was a one-shot wonder. Fine. I could handle that. But it was in my hands now, because I figured I was going to have a chance to do this for a while."

They had a chance to repeat the next year — or so they thought — after the decision was made to pay the money it would require to keep the team together for another season. Elvis Grbac was brought in to play quarterback in what was supposed to be an upgrade from Trent Dilfer. But the team never jelled the way it had the year before. Jamal Lewis, who had been superb at running back in his rookie season, tore up his knee in training camp. Grbac never seemed to get comfortable quarterbacking a team with lofty expectations. The defense was still very good, but not as dominant. The team made the playoffs again and won a first-round game against the Miami Dolphins before being beaten handily in Pittsburgh. That loss was painful, in part because everyone had believed the game winnable but also because the opponent was Pittsburgh. Mostly, though, it was painful because everyone knew it was an ending. As in 1996, when the team first arrived from Cleveland, salaries had to be purged to get under the cap. Siragusa was gone; Adams was gone; Grbac retired rather than restructure his contract; Rod Woodson, the Hall of Fame safety, was gone. The team went from experienced to inexperienced in the blink of an eye.

"Most years when we go to camp, I can tell you anywhere from forty to fifty of the guys who will be on the fifty-three [man roster] when we start the season," Billick said. "In '02, there weren't twenty. That's how young we were." Which was why the next two seasons were so encouraging. First the 7-9 and then the 10-6 that included a division title and a trip to the playoffs. After the Tennessee loss came that hectic first week in which Bisciotti and Billick had to hash out the Cavanaugh situation and establish ground rules for their relationship that each man would feel comfortable with. Once that was done, the Ravens turned to the question every NFL team begins to address each February: how do we get better?

While Newsome and his scouts prepared for the 2004 draft as they always did — although without a first-round pick because of the Boller trade — there was one name that was on the lips of almost everyone working in the old building on Owings Mills Boulevard: Terrell Owens.

Everyone in football knew that Terrell Owens wasn't going to be a San Francisco 49er again in 2004. Brilliant as he was, he had more or less worn out his welcome in San Francisco with his showboating and his battles with teammates and coaches. He was about to become a free agent and there was no question that a number of teams would be willing to pay him a lot of money — baggage and all — to wear their uniform.

The Ravens were right at the top of the list of potential suitors. With good reason. If the team needed one thing more than anything, it was a receiver who could, in the vernacular, "go vertical," or "stretch the field." In English, they needed someone with the speed to get open. The Ravens' best receiver was their tight end, third-year Pro Bowler Todd Heap, a wonderful talent with soft hands and excellent speed for someone who was six foot five and 250 pounds. None of their wide receivers — Marcus Robinson, Frank Sanders, or Travis Taylor — had shown a consistent ability to "create separation," which is football-speak for getting open. Taylor and Robinson were not without ability. Taylor, who had been a Ravens first-round pick in 2000 (the tenth pick overall) showed flashes of great talent. But he was as apt to drop an easy pass as he was to catch one spectacularly. Robinson had moments, too, and was, in fact, a solid receiver. But he wasn't the game breaker Owens was. Few people in the game were.

The question for the Ravens was whether they could come up with the money to pay Owens. There was no salary cap issue, just the matter of how much Owens was worth and how his signing would affect the cap in the long term. "Traditionally T.O. is the kind of free agent we don't sign," Billick said. "We don't usually make big splashes in March [which is when most free agents sign]. It hasn't been the Ravens' way."

But this was different. The need was obvious. The other question was Owens's personality. He was right at the top of the selfish self-absorption list in a league filled with self-absorbed people. Under the wrong circumstances he could become a serious problem in what was, for the most part, a problem-free locker room. The Ravens knew all of this. They were not about to make a move that would change the nature of their team and their locker room without a lot of discussion, a lot of homework, and a lot of thought.

Newsome spearheaded the research team. He put together a T.O. tape — not a highlight tape, but one that showed Owens at his best and his worst to present to the team's decision makers, a group that included Bisciotti, Cass, the scouts, Billick, and the offensive coaches. Newsome showed everyone the tape on a February afternoon, showing a T.O. who made great plays but also made not-so-great plays, at times not running routes to their finish, occasionally backing off from tough catches. This was typical Newsome. Before he asked for input, he wanted everyone in the room to have all the information that was available.

The consensus when all was said and done was that T.O. was worth the risk. Billick was confident that the leaders on the team — Lewis, Jonathan Ogden, Ed Reed — would handle Owens's foibles and eccentricities. Lewis had publicly campaigned for the Ravens to try and sign Owens. That endorsement was not lost on the team's leadership. Billick was convinced that Owens could fit in to the locker room and would make a huge, tangible difference on the field, especially in an offense that would be run by a second-year quarterback who had started nine NFL games. A decision was made: go after him. If it became a bidding war and the price got out of control, they would probably back off. But they would, at the very least, make a run at Owens. Billick half-jokingly told Newsome he didn't believe the Ravens would get Owens because someone would make an off-the-charts offer and the Ravens would be out of the running.

Newsome knew that was a possibility. He also knew that a lot of teams would shy away from Owens because of his reputation. Newsome is, if nothing else, thorough. He had checked to see if Owens had any problems off the field (no) and if he there were any skeletons (like drinking or family problems) that hadn't come out publicly (no again). He talked on the phone to both Owens and his agent to gauge their interest in the Ravens (considerable, he believed) and to let Owens know why he believed Baltimore would be an ideal place for him. The more he did his homework and the more he talked to Owens, the more convinced Newsome became that the Ravens had a chance to get him. Billick continued to be skeptical.

That thinking changed suddenly and surprisingly on February 26. Somehow, David Joseph, Owens's agent, had failed to file with the league by the February 21 deadline the proper paperwork declaring his client to be a free agent. Under league rules, that meant he still belonged to the 49ers and was not free to negotiate with anyone but them. The response to this news in the Ravens' offices was one of disbelief. How could Joseph have possibly made such a mistake? How could he possibly keep his job, given that the oversight could cost Owens millions of dollars? Far more important to the Ravens was the question of whether the ruling would actually stand. Newsome began calling everyone in the league — the management council, the union, the league office — to find out if this was a technicality that would ultimately be overturned or if it was real. Categorically, he was told the same thing by everyone: it's real. He still belongs to the 49ers.

"Which means," Newsome told everyone, "that Terry Donahue is now driving this bus."

Donahue was the 49ers' general manager. Since the 49ers were in a major rebuilding process, there was no way they wanted Owens and his salary and baggage back. That meant they would try to trade him. Whomever Owens was traded to would need to sign him to a new contract, but it would not be as burdensome as a free-agent contract since there would be no competition. Owens would have a choice: sign with his new team or not play.

The T.O. caper was now being played out on two separate playing fields with four teams in the competition: the Ravens, Eagles, Jets, and Dolphins. On one field, Newsome and the other three general managers were negotiating with Joseph to establish contract parameters that would make Owens happy if and when a trade was made. On the other, the four GMs were talking to Donahue about what it would take to make the trade. If any of the teams were willing to offer a first-round draft pick for Owens, the Ravens were eliminated because their 2004 number one was in New England as a result of the Kyle Boller trade the previous April. But Newsome was fairly certain — correctly, as it turned out — that no one was going to trade a first-round pick to a team that had to make a deal. General managers generally look at first-round picks the way fathers look at their eldest daughter: just as almost no one is good enough to marry your daughter, almost no one is good enough to trade a first pick for.

It quickly became apparent that the deal would turn on a number two going to San Francisco for Owens. The Dolphins had no second-round pick, so they dropped out, not willing to give up their number one, knowing that a three would not be good enough. The Jets appeared to be a threat because they had the forty-first pick in the draft — ten spots ahead of the Ravens' first pick. But Newsome was making major progress with Joseph. The message coming back to him was: T.O. likes what you're offering; we want him to come to Baltimore. That was great, except, as Newsome kept saying, "Terry Donahue is still driving the bus."

Donahue, naturally, wanted to get as much as he possibly could for Owens. The Eagles wanted him, but their second-round pick came seven spots after the Ravens'. To counter that, they were offering a fifth-round pick and a player, described in Billickese as "some slapdick." Anyone who is anything less than brilliant at his or her job is, in the world according to Billick, a "slapdick"— or "a slappy," for short. Billick isn't sure where he first picked up the phrase but he thinks it may have been from Rick Smith, the longtime public relations guru for the San Diego Chargers and, more recently, the St. Louis Rams. Players who get cut early in training camp are "slapdicks." Writers (and there are many) who Billick doesn't approve of are "slappies," as are mediocre coaches, movies, and restaurants. If you take Billick to dinner, it had better be a high-class place, not some "slapdick joint."

With the Jets unable or unwilling to come up with the kind of money Owens was looking for and with the Eagles offering a fifth-rounder and a slapdick, Donahue wanted his bus to land in Baltimore. He told Newsome late on the afternoon of March 3 that he was almost certain he would trade Owens to the Ravens the next day for the fifty-first pick overall. "Unless something better comes up tonight, I think we can close this tomorrow," Donahue told Newsome.

Billick was still skeptical. "Close it tonight," he told Newsome impatiently. "Write it up, let's get this done before something happens."

One of the reasons Newsome and Billick work so well together is that each understands the other's temperament. Newsome knows that Billick wants everything done *now*, and he doesn't get upset when Billick starts pacing the halls, wanting to know why lunch can't be delivered right after breakfast. Billick, on the other hand, knows that Newsome isn't going to rush into anything. He can be in the middle of a heated negotiation and when it comes time for him to leave for his daily workout, he goes to his workout, then picks up where he left off. On Fridays after lunch, he goes to get his haircut. If Paul Tagliabue really needed to see Newsome on a Friday, Newsome would make time for him: after his haircut.

Newsome is never rushed into a decision. To him, the process — talking to his scouts, getting input from the coaches looking at tape, discussing a player with people around the league, finding people who might know what a player is like off the field — must be followed, regardless of Billick's wanting something decided yesterday. "It's one of Ozzie's great strengths,"

Billick said. "The process is inviolate. I understand that, but it doesn't prevent me from occasionally walking in and saying, 'Come on, Ozz, this is a no-brainer, let's do it.'"

At those moments, Newsome will nod, tell Billick he's right, and say he'll get back to him as soon as something happens. In the old Colts facility, Newsome's office was at one end of a hallway, Billick's at the other. Those with offices in between could always tell when something big was occurring because the two men would take turns wearing a path between each other's office.

The next day — March 4 — Newsome's patience paid off. Donahue called back to say that the 49ers were accepting the Ravens' offer. Elated, Newsome called Owens to welcome him to the Ravens. Owens's response was a bit baffling and a little disturbing: "Talk to my agent," he said.

That wasn't what Newsome had expected to hear. He knew he still had to close the deal with Joseph, but with the trade done, those conversations should be little more than a formality. "Call my agent," Owens repeated when Newsome tried to explain to him that the contract was all but done and he was going to be a Raven. Billick, who was in the room, was stunned.

"At the very least, players don't talk that way to Ozzie, simply because he's Ozzie Newsome, Hall of Famer," he said.

Newsome put in a call to Joseph. There's no deal, Joseph was insisting. Philadelphia is offering more money than you guys, so we want to go to Philly. Newsome tried to explain as patiently as he could that Owens had been traded to the Ravens. The only team that could sign him was the Ravens. Before finalizing the deal, he had again checked with the league, the management council, and the union to be absolutely certain there weren't any loopholes that would allow Owens to escape the contract he was now bound to with the 49ers. There was nothing. Joseph didn't seem to get it — or want to get it. T.O., he said, wanted to go to Philadelphia.

Billick was now officially bouncing off the walls. He was calling Joseph names far worse than slapdick. Even the usually unflappable Newsome was a bit unnerved. When the trade was announced, the Ravens wanted Owens to come to Baltimore for an introductory press conference. No way, Owens told them, I'll never play for the Ravens. Again, the league was contacted. If Owens tried to contest the trade, was there any way it could be overturned? Bisciotti told Newsome to tell the people in the office that he didn't want an answer from anyone but Commissioner Tagliabue. The word came back: "It's a slam dunk."

One reason the Ravens wanted to be absolutely certain they were going to get Owens was that Marcus Robinson was pressuring them for a decision on his status. If Owens became a Raven, then Robinson was a luxury item the team didn't need. Without Owens, the team would probably want to re-sign him, the belief being there were no wide receivers available other than T.O. who were better. Two days after the Owens trade, Robinson called wide receivers coach David Shaw. The Minnesota Vikings were about to make his agent an offer. If Shaw thought the Owens deal was going to happen, then Robinson might as well sign with the Vikings. Vikings coach Mike Tice, whom Billick had worked with while in Minnesota, called Billick to ask the same question. The Vikings didn't want to waste time putting an offer on the table to Robinson if he was going to end up re-signing with Baltimore. The Ravens were still being told that when all the smoke cleared, Owens would be playing for them in 2004. Billick told Tice, and Shaw told Robinson: T.O.'s coming to Baltimore. Robinson signed with the Vikings on March 8.

"Essentially we were taken out of the free-agent market for receivers," Bisciotti said later. "If we hadn't been involved with T.O., we might very well have brought Marcus back. Or we might have gone after someone else; obviously there was no one out there at T.O.'s level, but there were some guys we could have signed. But as long as we thought we were getting T.O. we wouldn't — really couldn't — move on anyone else. And we had every assurance that in the end, when the dust cleared, T.O. would be a Raven."

In fact, Newsome and Billick made a conscious decision to keep Billick out of the ongoing controversy. Newsome would be the out-front guy in a situation like this under any circumstances, but it was only natural for reporters to go to the loquacious Billick for comment. Billick was convinced that Joseph was a slapdick and angered by the entire episode. But, for once, he made a point of keeping his mouth shut. "At the end of the day, when

T.O. became a Raven, I was the one who was going to be dealing with him day to day. It was important I be the good guy in the whole thing, that I be able to say to him, 'Yeah, the business side wasn't pretty, but you and I need to work together now so that we all end up rich and happy.'"

So, as the battle unfolded in the papers and on TV, Billick lay low.

Joseph and Owens were now claiming that Owens should have the right to make a deal with any team, that he had clearly declared his intent to become a free agent and the lack of paperwork was nothing more than a technicality. The players union, which had initially told the Ravens that it agreed with the 49ers' contention that Owens was not a free agent, had now made an about-face and was siding with Owens. A hearing before a special master who was a law professor at the University of Pennsylvania was scheduled for Sunday, March 15, in Philadelphia.

Technically, the Ravens were not a part of the hearing. Joseph and Owens were claiming that the league had done Owens wrong by denying him free agency based on a changed rule — the deadline had been moved up — for which Joseph had not received official notification. The league had faxed the new deadline date to agents, and Joseph — now through the union — was claiming that did not constitute official notice.

The Ravens were not part of the hearing, but they were clearly an interested party. Bisciotti dispatched Dick Cass, whom he was going to hire as team president as soon as the official transfer of power took place in April, to represent the Ravens in New York. Cass was a logical choice. He was a lawyer — Princeton undergrad and Yale Law, where he had been a year ahead of Hillary Clinton and two ahead of her future husband — and had done lots of NFL-related legal work before getting to know Bisciotti. He was leaving an extremely successful practice at Wilmer Cutler Pickering in Washington after thirty-two years to join the Ravens.

What Cass heard when he got to Philadelphia was shocking. The union presented a case that made it clear — at least to Cass — that the league had not done everything it was supposed to in order to make the new deadline clear to agents. The league had very little response. As the day wore on, Cass knew the Ravens were in trouble. His concerns were confirmed at the end of the day when the special master looked at the NFL's lawyers and said something along the lines of "Please tell me this isn't all you have."

He went on to suggest that, before he ruled the next day, the league and the Ravens might want to cut some kind of deal to salvage something, because the ruling wasn't going to come back in their favor. The next day the league asked the Eagles if they would give the Ravens a fifth-round draft pick, to compensate them for being innocent bystanders in what was quite clearly a screwup on the part of the league and the management council. The Eagles readily agreed. Thus, the master never had to actually make a ruling, because the parties reached a "compromise": Owens was free to sign with the Eagles. The Ravens would get back the second-round pick they had traded to the 49ers and the Eagles' fifth-round pick.

The Ravens were furious. Bisciotti, not even officially an owner yet, was angry with the management council, but angrier with Tagliabue — who had personally assured him that the trade would stand. Cass, having heard the case in person, was almost disbelieving. Billick was also furious. "It's one thing to let me down or even to let Steve down, but how could they let Ozzie Newsome down this way?" he asked. "All he's ever done is follow all the rules the league has — he's on the competition committee, for crying out loud — and they do *this* to him?"

Newsome, for his part, was the calmest member of the group. "Stuff happens," he said. "Is it upsetting? Of course it is. But there wasn't any malice involved. They miscalculated. The unfortunate thing is, we got hurt by their miscalculation."

The media had a field day with their miscalculation. Ray Lewis criticized Owens for his behavior and said he couldn't wait for the Ravens to play the Eagles, not so much in preseason in August, but on Halloween in Philadelphia. More important than any of that, the Ravens' less-than-sterling receiving corps now had one less dependable receiver, with only a handful of borderline free agents still available and a draft coming up in which the team didn't pick until the second half of the second round.

It was turning out to be a long winter in Baltimore.

5

The Draft

THE T.O. CAPER was not the only cloud hanging over Owings Mills as the snow began to thaw in March. A month earlier, shortly after the Super Bowl and before the Owens non-free-agency saga started to unfold, the Ravens had received an out-of-the-blue phone call from Atlanta with news that rocked everyone in the organization: Jamal Lewis had been arrested. Federal prosecutors were alleging that he had been involved in a conspiracy to sell drugs in July of 2000 — a little more than two months after he had been drafted by the Ravens and a few weeks before he had signed his first contract with them.

Just when it seemed the Ravens were putting Ray Lewis and Atlanta behind them for good came charges that their star running back, coming off the second-greatest season any back had ever had in NFL history (2,066 yards), was a drug dealer. Lewis had hired Ed Garland, the same lawyer who had defended Ray Lewis, and was maintaining that he had been set up. Dick Cass, who was doing a lot of work for someone not officially on the job yet, talked to Garland at length to find out exactly what the team was dealing with. In the meantime, headlines screamed all over the country and the Ravens found themselves dealing once again with their image as a thug team.

Beyond that, it was apparent from the moment the team learned of the charges that this story would continue well into the season. The 2003 season had ended, even after the loss to Tennessee, with a feeling of optimism. The rebuilding was ahead of schedule. There were only a few truly significant free agents the team had to worry about re-signing: Marcus Robinson (gone to Minnesota), linebacker/special teams star Adalius Thomas (signed), center Mike Flynn (signed), placekicker Matt Stover (signed) and backup quarterback Anthony Wright (signed). In all, twenty-three or twenty-four starters — including Stover and punter Dave Zastudil — were returning, an unheard-of number in the salary-cap era of the NFL. The off-season goal was to upgrade in a couple of key areas, pick up depth through the draft, and come back ready to make a run at the Super Bowl. Everyone in the building believed it was possible.

But the early signs weren't good. Owens had been lost, and now one of the two men who would appear on the cover of the media guide was likely to spend the season with drug charges and possible jail time hanging over his head.

The Ravens knew that Lewis had been around drugs growing up in inner-city Atlanta and they knew he had used marijuana, having been suspended in 2001 for testing positive a second time. They also knew that since then he had been in the very stringent NFL drug-testing program, in which a player can be tested up to ten times a month, year-round, and had been clean in every test. "I've smoked marijuana," Lewis admitted. "I never smoked it like Ricky Williams [the Miami Dolphins running back who would walk away from the game in July rather than give up marijuana] but I smoked it. That's it, though. Nothing else."

In fact, the charges against Lewis did not allege that he had used drugs of any kind. When Cass began to gather information, he came away convinced —"albeit through biased eyes," he said — that Lewis had been set up by a good-looking woman. The woman was named Michelle Smith and she had a rap sheet slightly longer than one of Yao Ming's arms. She had been in federal prison when she made a deal with the FBI to act as bait in a sting the agency wanted to run in Atlanta designed to catch college athletes who had taken money from sports agents while still in school. The targets of the sting were the agents more than the athletes. Smith was able to find no evidence that Lewis had taken money from any of the targeted agents, but she did glean that some of his boyhood friends and acquaintances were familiar with the drug scene in Atlanta. That hardly made Lewis different from anyone else who had grown up in his neighborhood.

"Where I grew up was like a lot of places," he said. "You had a choice — drugs or sports. I chose sports. I was never into the drug scene. But, of course, I knew people who were."

After Smith had become "romantically" involved with Lewis — or so he thought — she asked him if he could help her get some drugs. He called a friend on his cell phone to set up a meeting for her. It was that phone call that made him, according to the prosecutors, an accomplice in a drug deal even though he never received any money and never purchased any drugs.

The Ravens were baffled and angered by the charges. Why now, three and a half years after the event had taken place? The answer, according to the prosecutors, was that Lewis was a small piece in a massive case that was just now coming together. The Ravens were convinced that his celebrity had a lot to do with it, especially after his record-breaking season had made him a national figure. "Part of it may have been publicity seeking," Cass said. "But I also think, to be fair, that part of it was concern that if someone came across Jamal's name in the files, which was entirely possible, and it came out that they had him on a cell phone setting up a deal and never prosecuted him, that they'd get nailed for *not* charging him."

Regardless of the reasoning and regardless of the fact that Lewis was twenty when the incident occurred and not even technically a Raven yet, the news was another blow to a franchise constantly dealing with image questions. In the NFL world according to Paul Tagliabue, every player is supposed to come across like those who appear on the carefully crafted United Way commercials: men whose hearts are as big as their bodies, men who give back to their communities, men who spend their free time helping those in need. That image crafting was one of the reasons Tagliabue had gone ballistic over the ESPN series *Playmakers,* which fictionalized a dark side of pro football life: players doing drugs, hitting their wives, staying out until all hours every night, lying and cheating at every turn.

It was a measure of the power of Tagliabue and the NFL that ESPN canceled the show after one season rather than risk the wrath of the commissioner and the league in the next round of TV rights negotiations, which were scheduled to begin late in 2004. When Tagliabue and company screamed, ESPN backed down in less time than it takes to tape a United Way spot.

In truth, the *Playmakers* portrayal of life in the NFL is no more accurate than the United Way portrayals. Football players do get into trouble. But there are also football players who are as charitable as the Tagliabue-created United Way bits make them out to be. The majority fall someplace in the middle. In the Ravens' media guide, every player bio contains a note in unmissable block letters about some charitable act performed by the player.

Jamal Lewis's arrest would not make the media guide. But it would make a lot of headlines and take up a lot of time around Owings Mills in the months ahead.

With Owens headed to Philadelphia and free agency essentially a nonstarter for the Ravens, they turned their full attention to the draft. For years, this had been the strength of the franchise, beginning with the historic 1996 draft that had brought them Jonathan Ogden and Ray Lewis. Newsome was justifiably proud of the work he and his scouts had done through the years, not just in the first round, where teams are expected to find good players, but in the later rounds and with undrafted free agents.

The two key men for Newsome in preparing for the draft were Phil Savage and Eric DeCosta, neither of whom looked like, sounded like, or had the background of a typical NFL scout. Savage was thirty-nine, a graduate of the University of the South in Sewanee, Tennessee, where he had played both football and baseball in Division 3. He had joined the organization in 1991 as an assistant coach, the same year Newsome had retired as a player, and had started to learn the ropes of coaching and scouting. He and Savage had worked together almost daily in Cleveland and Baltimore for fourteen years. When Newsome had been promoted to personnel director after the team's move in 1996, one of his first decisions had been to promote Savage to director of college scouting.

Seven years later, when James Harris, who had been the team's director of pro scouting, left to become personnel director in Jacksonville, Newsome promoted Savage to director of player personnel. By then, Modell had made Newsome general manager. When Savage moved up, DeCosta was given his job, making him, at the age of thirty-one, the youngest scouting director in the NFL. He had also played college football, at Colby

College in Maine, another school with outstanding academics but hardly a proving ground for future NFL players or scouts. George Kokinis, who was the Ravens' director of pro scouting, had graduated from Hobart — *another* Division 3 school known more for academics and lacrosse, not football.

What the three had in common was a hunger to succeed. Each had started on a bottom rung of the business, Savage as a graduate assistant coach at Alabama, DeCosta as a graduate assistant at Trinity College, and Kokinis as an intern with the Browns. Newsome had trained them, nurtured them, and promoted them, and all of them believed they formed the nucleus of the best scouting staff in the NFL.

There was ego in that, but there was also a track record. Going into 2004, seven of the eleven first-round draft picks selected by the Ravens had been Pro Bowlers at least once. Ten of the eleven were still with the team, and two of the Pro Bowlers — Ed Reed and Todd Heap had been late first-rounders (twenty-fourth and thirty-first) who had gone on to make the Pro Bowl in their second seasons. In all, fifty-four of the sixty-four players the Ravens had picked in the draft had made opening-day rosters, an uncommonly high number. What's more, they could point to several success stories in free agency, notably Priest Holmes, who had become a Pro Bowl running back as an undrafted free agent before moving to Kansas City, and Mike Flynn and Will Demps, who were currently the team's starting center and starting strong safety. Newsome was as respected as any general manager in the game, and Savage was considered a GM-in-waiting. He had almost become the general manager in Philadelphia three years earlier and had almost gone to Jacksonville in 2003. Everyone in the organization believed it was only a matter of time before he was given his own team to build.

Even so, this draft would be different from others because there was no first-round pick. That pick was already on the team in the form of Boller, a decision they had made a year earlier that he was not only the best quarterback they could get in that draft but better than any quarterback they would be able to get in this draft. "We would have been drafting twenty-first," Newsome said on the morning of the 2004 draft. "There are two quarterbacks [Eli Manning from Mississippi and Ben Roethlisberger from Miami of Ohio] who graded a tiny bit higher than Kyle and one quarterback [Philip Rivers from N.C. State] who graded the same as Kyle. They'll all be gone long before we draft. So I think we did very well getting Kyle when we did."

So it was going to be a long wait during the first round. The NFL draft has somehow become a major sports event in the United States. Every minute of the draft, from noon on a Saturday in late April until about 6 P.M. on Sunday evening, is televised by ESPN. The draft dominates sports pages and sports telecasts and sports talk radio for weeks, before and after it takes place. Mock drafts are held all over the country, and a number of people have made themselves into cult figures by becoming draft experts. Mel Kiper Jr., the ESPN draft guru, isn't even a cult figure — he's a celebrity, period. Not only is the draft heavily attended by "draftniks" in New York City, it is watched for hours on end by people who really and truly want to know who Baltimore will take in the seventh round. In all, there would be 255 picks in the 2004 draft, and each one would be analyzed at length. After all, Tom Brady, the New England quarterback who might be the league's most important player, had been taken with the 199th pick of the draft four years earlier. One never knew where the next Brady lurked.

The week of the draft, with the Ravens as with all teams, is one of great excitement and speculation — not only among fans but within the team. Assistant coaches spend large chunks of time campaigning with Newsome and the scouts to get certain players chosen. Position coaches point out their needs and how a certain player might fill those needs if the chance to draft him were to arise. When Marvin Lewis was the Ravens' defensive coordinator, he would often set up a chair outside Newsome's office and wait for him to break from his meetings with scouts so he could tell him what he wanted and why he wanted it. Every coach had a list of players at his position and an idea of when they might be drafted and which of them might be available when the Ravens had a chance to draft.

The entire staff gathered on the morning of April 24, a bright, clear day, to go through the process that the NFL officially calls its "Annual Selection Meeting." The Ravens' draft room was just barely big enough to fit everyone involved. A long conference table sat in the middle of the room, with Newsome, wearing a blue shirt, khaki pants, and loafers with no socks (in fact, none of the three major personnel decision makers on the Ravens —

Newsome, Billick, or Bisciotti — wore socks on draft weekend), seated at one end with two telephones in front of him. His staff fanned out around him: Phil Savage and Eric DeCosta were to his right; Pat Moriarty, the capologist, to his left. Dick Cass sat midway down on the right, and George Kokinis was across from him. Daniel Jeremiah, one of the team's younger scouts, was on a phone hookup to New York, where another scout, T. J. McCreight, sat relaying the names of the players being selected a few seconds before Tagliabue actually announced them.

About an hour before the draft began, Newsome briefed the room on what he expected from the day. The Ravens had approached the draft, he said, no differently than in the past, even though they had no first-round pick. They had ranked 150 players and expected that the ten picks they had — one second, one third, one fourth, two fifths, two sixths, and three sevenths — would come from that list. A trade into the first round was highly unlikely. Newsome had talked to some general managers about swapping second-round picks and might try to move up in the second round if that meant getting a player he wanted. He had also spent a good deal of time during the week shopping for a wide receiver. Several veterans would be available, he thought, once teams had drafted a wide receiver. There were four realistic possibilities: Joe Horn from New Orleans, Dennis Northcutt from Cleveland, Jabar Gaffney from Houston, and Kevin Johnson from Jacksonville. Keenan McCardell of Tampa Bay was also a possibility, but Tampa Bay GM Bruce Allen wanted a first-day pick (the first three rounds are conducted the first day) in return. "I've only got two of them," Newsome said. "I don't think I want to give one up." The other four could probably be had for mid-round draft picks because of age, salary, baggage, or a combination of all three. Newsome thought the deal most likely to happen was a deal with Jacksonville, which would bring Johnson for either a fourth this year or a third-round pick in next year's draft.

Directly behind where Newsome sat was a board with a five-by-seven card for each of the Ravens' top two hundred prospects. They were listed by position with the top-rated player at the position at the top of the board and the others lined up below him. To Newsome's left was a second board with cards for every other player the Ravens had scouted or had a scouting report on. There were more than four hundred cards on the side board, which Billick jokingly called "the leper board." Good players came off the leper board in virtually every draft. Will Demps and Mike Flynn, both now starters, had once been on the Ravens' leper board. Billick traditionally put up $100 for the person on staff who picked the name of the first player chosen (by anyone) from the leper board. He also put up $300 to go to the person who picked the most players chosen between the tenth and twenty-fifth picks. (The first nine were considered too easy.) To Newsome's right was an empty board, with a helmet logo for each of the thirty-two teams. As players were drafted, their cards were moved from the draft board to the drafted board. The fourth wall of the room consisted of an empty greaseboard, a screen used to look at tape and, in the corner, a cabinet behind which Billick kept the names of the fifty-three players he expected to be on the roster in September. That was, of course, subject to constant change. Some of the players drafted would go right onto that list.

The draft boards represented months and months of work by the scouts; thousands and thousands of hours of traveling, making reports, and breaking down tape. The total cost for putting the board together was about $2 million. Each player's card was filled with information. It had his name and uniform number, his exact height down to a hundredth of an inch, weight, and 40-yard-dash time. It also had his college, the number of years he had started, and his score on the Wunderlik test. The Wunderlik is the NFL's version of an IQ test. Virtually every player takes it, most at the weeklong combine (the term comes from combining all NFL teams in one place) in Indianapolis, where all thirty-two teams gather to meet and greet (and test and retest) most draft prospects. Some teams put great emphasis on the Wunderlik; others virtually ignore it. The Ravens probably fall somewhere in between: a high Wunderlik doesn't mean they are going to draft someone and a low one doesn't mean they won't, but they factor the score in along with the other information they gather. In 1996 Jonathan Ogden had the highest Wunderlik score of anyone on the draft board. That was nice. The fact that he was six foot nine, 345 pounds, and quick was nicer.

Each player was given a number grade by the scouts after adding up all factors. The highest you could grade was 8.0, and that had happened twice: to O. J. Simpson and Bo Jackson. A player who was 6.5 or higher was considered a surefire NFL starter. Anyone over 6.0 would play in the league. Anyone in the 5.5–6.0 range had a chance to make a roster. Anything lower than that was a long shot. In scoutese, Manning and Roethlisberger were "sixty-sevens"— 6.7s — as was Iowa's massive tackle, Robert Gallery. A player considered an "eighty" — an 8.0 — was the football equivalent of a perfect ten. There were no Bo Dereks in this draft.

The back of each card contained even more details: a player's 10-yard-dash time, his "box score" (an agility test), his hand size, and any other notes that might be pertinent. Some of the cards contained black dots. That meant that someone on the scouting staff had raised a serious concern about a player for one reason or another. In some cases, it was because of an injury. In others it was drug use or an arrest record. The NFL's security staff kept teams apprised of any arrests that it was aware of involving players. There was also a Web site that tracked any alleged drug use, positive drug tests, or arrests involving players. One significant player, Michigan running back Chris Perry, had been black-dotted by the Ravens because scout Joe Douglas had seen him dislocate a shoulder during a workout. Another player had been black-dotted because the Ravens had learned in their background research that he was a witch doctor, meaning he did not take conventional medicines. A light brown dot indicated that a player might be a medical question mark. A blue dot meant he was a punt/kickoff returner. A dark brown dot meant he was a long snapper.

Newsome began the day holding out long-shot hopes that one of three receivers — Lee Evans of Wisconsin, Michael Clayton of LSU, or Rashaun Woods of Oklahoma State — might fall into the second round. "If one of them is still there, we'll try to trade up to get them," he explained to Bisciotti and Art Modell, who sat at the far end of the table next to Bisciotti.

This was the first draft in which Bisciotti had been the majority owner and Modell a minority owner. Everyone in the room knew this was not going to be an easy day for Modell. Bisciotti was supremely conscious of that and peppered Modell with questions about drafts past, knowing that Modell loved to tell stories. "One year there were two guys named Brian Lawrence in the draft," he said. "One was a defensive lineman, the other a wide receiver. We drafted the receiver. We call him and I get on the phone, introduce myself, and say, 'We were very impressed with your forty time.' He says to me, 'Forty time? What kind of scouts do you guys have up there in Cleveland?' Turns out we'd called the defensive lineman."

Everyone involved in the draft has a story about something good or bad that happened on draft day. Jim Fassel, the former New York Giants coach who had just been hired by Billick as an "offensive consultant," remembered the year the Giants wanted to draft Miami tight end Jeremy Shockey. "Tennessee was just ahead of us on the board, Cleveland just behind," Fassel said. "[Tennessee coach] Jeff Fisher calls and says Cleveland wants to trade with them so they can jump ahead of us to get Shockey. He says, 'Give me a third,' and I won't do it. I told him I'd give him a fourth and if they made the trade with Cleveland, I'd take the defensive lineman I knew he wanted. He took the fourth. Of course I have no idea if he was really ready to deal with Cleveland and I wasn't about to take that lineman, but this is one time when you can tell a lie and it's accepted as part of the business."

The draft began a few minutes late after an awkward ceremony in which Tagliabue attempted to honor Pat Tillman, the former Arizona Cardinals defensive back who had been killed that week (by friendly fire as it turned out) in Afghanistan. The league had gone out and found several marines to stand behind Tagliabue for the moment of silence he was asking everyone to join in. The only problem was that Tillman had been in the army. Perhaps no one from the army could be rounded up on short notice. Or perhaps Tagliabue just liked the idea of a marine honor guard. Tagliabue mouthed the usual platitudes about Tillman's death, giving everyone a different perspective on sports. Then the San Diego Chargers announced that they had taken Eli Manning with the number one pick, and all the New York Giants fans in the audience, thinking they were now not getting Manning, booed him heartily when he came onstage.

So much for perspective.

The afternoon crept along very slowly in Baltimore. "It's going to take an awful lot to convince me to ever trade a number one again," Newsome said at one point as ESPN showed a Coors Light commercial for perhaps the thousandth time of the day. Calls came in to Newsome occasionally. James Harris called so often that Bisciotti suggested at one point that Newsome put him on speaker so everyone in the room could yell, "SHACK!" like the shout-out to Norm on the sitcom *Cheers*.

The hot news of the day turned out to be that the Giants did finally trade with the Chargers to get Manning, giving up their first pick (fourth in the draft), Philip Rivers, and next year's number one, three, and five picks. Most in the Ravens' draft room were surprised they would give up that much to swap two quarterbacks rated by most people as just about equal. Soon after the trade, Manning was taken across the river to Giants Stadium for a press conference. ESPN's Sal Paolantonio asked him, "When you got out of the car and you saw Giants Stadium and [Coach] Tom Coughlin, what did you think?"

Before Manning could answer, George Kokinis answered for him: "I thought, 'Oh shit!' " Everyone in the room, aware of Coughlin's dour manner and autocratic ways, cracked up.

Newsome, Savage, and DeCosta had known it was a long shot for any of the three receivers they sought to fall into the second round. They were right: Evans was the fourth wide receiver taken, going at thirteen to Buffalo. Clayton went to Tampa Bay three picks later, and Woods went to San Francisco at thirty-one. That hope gone, they began to focus on two defensive players: Travis LaBoy, an outside linebacker from Hawaii, and Bob Sanders, a defensive back from Iowa. Some might be surprised that a team so strong on defense would draft a defensive player first. But the Ravens' philosophy in the early rounds has always been "stay true to the board," meaning you draft whoever is your highest-ranked player on the board when your turn comes, regardless of position. That was why linebacker Terrell Suggs had been taken with the tenth pick overall a year earlier even though the team desperately needed a quarterback. He was ranked fifth on the Ravens' board; Kyle Boller, the highest-ranked quarterback available at that moment, was ranked tenth. In the later rounds, the Ravens would sometimes draft for a specific need. They were planning to take a kick returner and a backup quarterback in the sixth and seventh rounds already.

The other reason to take LaBoy was that there was serious concern in the organization about the status of Peter Boulware's knee. The All-Pro linebacker had been injured in the second-to-last game of the season and had undergone surgery. It was almost a certainty that he would miss the start of the season and there was some thought he might not play all year long. LaBoy went to Tennessee early in the second round, nine picks before the Ravens had a chance to get him. The room groaned when Jeremiah announced the pick. Billick snapped his fingers in frustration. "They needed a pass rusher," Newsome said, shaking his head. Newsome was already working the phones, seeing if it was possible to move up to get Sanders. San Francisco, which was at forty-six, was interested in swapping if the Ravens would give up a fourth-round pick in return. Newsome wanted to give up a fifth, but Moriarty, keeper of the "trade chart," which tells teams what makes an equitable swap of picks, said that San Francisco was entitled to a fourth.

"That's too much," DeCosta said. "I wouldn't do it."

The phone rang again. It was New Orleans, which had the forty-eighth pick. The Saints would take a fifth to move down three spots. Before Newsome could respond to the offer, he heard Jeremiah's voice: "Indy [at forty-four] is taking Sanders."

"They just took my guy," Newsome said, hanging up the phone with a sigh.

It was 7:25 in the evening, more than seven hours into the draft, before the Ravens finally went "on the clock," meaning it was their turn to make a pick. In the first round, teams are allotted fifteen minutes (which is why the first round drags on for more than five hours). In the second and third, they get five minutes. By the time the Ravens were on the clock there was no question about whom they were going to take. In fact, as soon as New Orleans — which had traded down with Minnesota — had taken Devery Henderson, a wide receiver from LSU, with the fiftieth pick, a distinctive *Whooee!* could be heard from the room across the hall because defensive line coach Rex Ryan knew he was getting his man.

That man was Dwan Edwards, a six foot three, 315-pound defensive tackle from Oregon State, who was number thirty on the Ravens' list and the next man up once LaBoy and Sanders were gone. Edwards was a player Ryan was convinced could help the D line right away. The act of finally drafting a player energized the room. Instead of wondering and hoping they might get a player, they actually had a player, one they believed could make the team better.

Just before the Ravens' pick was announced, ESPN tossed the telecast to a set hosted by Andrea Kremer, where four young NFL players, including Kyle Boller, had been gathered to talk through the weekend about various aspects of the draft.

"No one needs a wide receiver more than the Ravens," Kremer said, turning to Boller for insight on whom his team might be taking.

"You're right," Boller said. "The only established receiver we've got right now is Travis Taylor. We could use some help there."

The room groaned. "That's a great lead into announcing we're drafting a defensive lineman, huh?" Billick said.

While everyone was wondering if Boller could be reached by cell phone before he made any more pronouncements on his team's needs, Newsome was dialing Dwan Edwards's cell phone number. Whenever the Ravens select a player, they go through a preset ritual: Newsome calls the player and opens the conversation by saying, "It's Ozzie Newsome, are you ready to become a Baltimore Raven?" (To this day no one has ever said no.) Newsome chats briefly with the player, then hands the phone to Billick, who welcomes him, tells him there is a minicamp for rookies the next week, and asks what his academic status is at that moment. In 2004 there was one major change to the ritual. Instead of Modell taking the phone, Bisciotti did. "You're my first pick as a full owner," Bisciotti said to Edwards. Then he quickly added, "Are you ready to play on the same defense with Ray Lewis?"

As Bisciotti chatted with Edwards, Newsome used his other phone to call New York and say, "Put the card in." Within two minutes, Dwan Edwards was a Raven.

With the pick made, the room took a break. Newsome, Billick, Savage, and DeCosta went downstairs to the meeting room that the team used as an interview room to talk to the media about the pick and what might happen the rest of the weekend. Bisciotti did not go downstairs. Unlike some owners who want their picture taken every time a player is acquired, Bisciotti had no interest in putting his face in front of a camera or a microphone. He had reluctantly agreed to Kevin Byrne's request to do a round of interviews with local media once he had become the majority owner, but he did not want to be quoted regularly or follow the lead of Dan Snyder, his counterpart in Washington, who made a point of claiming he didn't speak to the media in-season and then called favored members of the media to whisper his side of every story to them on an off-the-record or background basis. Anyone who read the *Washington Post* knew exactly who the paper's reporters were talking about when they quoted "sources close to Redskins owner Daniel M. Snyder." Bisciotti would not go that route.

The Ravens *did* take a wide receiver on the third round, Devard

Darling, from Washington State. Darling might have gone higher, but there were some medical concerns about him because his twin brother, Devaughn, had died suddenly of a heart attack during off-season drills while the brothers were at Florida State. Devard Darling had been through thorough testing and had been cleared to play football by every doctor he had seen, but any risk factor — no matter how small it might appear — got the attention of NFL scouts.

That was it for day one. The Ravens had added two players. There was still a lot more work to do before the long weekend was over.

On Sunday morning Newsome and the scouts gathered before the draft began again — with the start of the fourth round — at 10 A.M. They went through their lists of who was left on the board and decided the two players they would really like to get in the fourth round — they were picking twenty-fourth in the round, which was the 120th pick in the draft — were defensive players. One was linebacker Reggie Torbor of Auburn, since they were still looking for help there because of Boulware's cloudy status. The other was cornerback Nathan Vasher of Texas. "If we can't get either of those guys," Newsome said, "I'll trade the pick to Shack [Jacksonville] for Kevin Johnson."

If Torbor or Vasher were available, Newsome would offer Jacksonville the Ravens' third-round pick in the 2005 draft. "I think that's what Shack wants anyway," he said.

One person who was hoping that scenario would not play out was Phil Savage. He was far less sold on Johnson than was Newsome. "Ozz, I think he's an ordinary player," Savage said. "I think we can do better."

"He's caught more than sixty balls a year since he's been in the league," Newsome said. "He's a pro. And he's not yet thirty. The other guys we've been talking about are all in their thirties."

Savage was unconvinced. But he knew arguing further was pointless. Newsome had made up his mind, and his mind was changed only on rare occasions. Which was one of his strengths. During Billick's first draft with the Ravens (1999) Newsome had gotten a call from the Atlanta Falcons just before the Ravens were going to draft in the second round. The Falcons had a player targeted that they wanted to take in the second round.

The Ravens had the fifth pick of the round, and Atlanta called to offer its first pick the next season in return for that pick.

Billick was against the deal. "We were talking about a pick in the mid-thirties, against what I figured would be a pick the next year in the mid-twenties, since they had just been to the Super Bowl and figured to be good the next year and drafting late in the first round. I thought we needed players *now*. There were a couple guys we had targeted."

Billick told Newsome he was against the deal and why. Newsome listened and then made the deal. Billick stalked off angrily to his office. Only later did he understand that Newsome knew exactly what he was doing. The players the Ravens wanted — Edwin Mulitalo and receiver Brandon Stokley — were still there when they drafted in the fourth round. The Falcons proceeded to fall flat the next season and the pick became the fifth pick overall in the 2000 draft. The Ravens used it to pick Jamal Lewis. Billick never seriously challenged Newsome's wisdom in the draft room again. "I'll still raise things and I might point out something about a player or a need," he said. "But that deal taught me that Ozzie knew exactly what he was doing — both long-term and short-term."

About thirty seconds after the draft had reopened, the New York Giants began the fourth round by drafting Reggie Torbor.

"Nice start," DeCosta murmured.

One of their targets was already off the board.

As the round proceeded, Newsome became convinced that Vasher would not last until the Ravens picked. He began calling teams to see if anyone was willing to move down, offering either a fifth-round pick or both his sixth and seventh picks to move up. No one was interested. Everyone had someone they wanted to pick. Newsome finally got Bruce Allen from Tampa Bay on the phone. Allen had the fifteenth pick in the round, nine spots ahead of the Ravens. Savage was trying to reach the Bears, who were on the clock at that moment with the fourteenth pick, to see if they would make a last-second switch.

While Newsome was talking and Savage was holding, word came from New York: Chicago was picking Vasher. Savage hung up his phone; Newsome sighed and told Allen, "Chicago just took our guy."

Turning to Savage and DeCosta, he said, "I had a feeling we were going to get wiped out in this round."

There was some discussion about trying to pick up an extra pick in a later round by now trading back from where they stood in the fourth round. "There still may be someone we like at one-twenty," DeCosta said.

"Yeah," Newsome said, "except they're all guys we just decided we like in the last fifteen minutes."

Thoughts then turned to going back to the original plan to trade the pick for Kevin Johnson. But Harris was balking. A fourth this year or a third next year wasn't enough. Newsome shrugged and began looking at who was next on his list. The next name was Roderick Green, another pass-rushing linebacker from Central Missouri State. Green was considered a raw talent with, in scoutese, "great upside" — as in potential. The Ravens would have had him higher on their board except that he had done very poorly on the Wunderlik. That grade was mitigated by his having a learning disability that caused him to test poorly. He came across well in person, which was why he was worth taking a chance on in the fourth round.

Two picks before the Ravens' turn, Jacksonville took Anthony Maddox, a defensive tackle from Delta State. He was the first player taken off the leper board.

"Jessie wins the hundred," DeCosta said, referring to Newsome's assistant Jessica Markison.

Moments later, as soon as Minnesota had taken Mewelde Moore, a running back from Tulane, Newsome placed the phone call to Green since the Ravens were on the clock. He gave him the "Are you ready to be a Raven?" speech and handed the phone to Billick, who did his normal song and dance. Then it was Bisciotti's turn. The owner had gone past the Ray Lewis segment of his monologue and was asking Green if he had any brothers and sisters, when Newsome's second phone rang. It was James Harris. He now wanted to accept the deal Newsome thought dead: Kevin Johnson for the Ravens' fourth-round pick. The Ravens had two minutes left to make their pick.

"I'll do it," Newsome said, hanging up the phone. He immediately instructed Jeremiah to tell T. J. McCreight in New York not to turn in the card with Green's name on it, which would have gone in as soon as Bisciotti finished speaking to Green. Turning to Bisciotti, who was telling Green what a great role model he was going to be for his younger siblings, Newsome said, "Tell him you have to go, we just traded the pick."

Bisciotti turned white. "Roderick, um, we'll call you back," he said, and handed the phone to Savage.

"Something has come up," Savage explained to Green.

"What just happened?" Bisciotti asked.

"Tell you in a minute," Newsome said. He was dialing New York to inform the league about the trade, which had to be done in the now less than sixty seconds before the Ravens were off the clock. When "latest pick — Jacksonville from Baltimore . . . Ernest Wilford, WR, Virginia Tech" flashed across the screen, everyone breathed a sigh of relief.

Except Bisciotti. "I just cut that poor kid off in mid-sentence," he said. "I feel awful."

Newsome, who was now trying to track down Kevin Johnson because he had to take a physical as soon as possible to make the deal official, had Savage call Green back. Savage asked Green if he had heard from any other teams. He hadn't. He apologized for what had happened and told him the team would take him in the fifth round if he hadn't been picked already.

"If we pick him again, let Art talk to him," Bisciotti said, recovering his sense of humor.

The Ravens had the twenty-eighth pick — the 160th overall — in the fifth round. This was the pick they had gotten from Philadelphia in the wake of the T.O. debacle. Newsome now really wanted Green, in part because he, too, felt bad about what had happened but also because he thought he had a lot of potential as a fifth-rounder. He began calling teams ahead of him to make a swap to move up so he could take Green. He started with Cleveland — seventeen picks before the Ravens — and, as he got turned down, kept working his way down. At one point, talking to Jerry Jones in Dallas, Newsome said, "we're at one-sixty-one, seventeen spots below you. No wait, we're at one-sixty. I was looking at Cleveland at one-sixty-one." He smiled. "I reverted back there for a minute."

Jones said no to either Baltimore's or Cleveland's pick. Finally, Newsome found a taker, Washington at 151. Vinny Cerrato was willing to take the Ravens' seventh-round pick to move back nine spots. "We'll call you when we're on the clock," Cerrato said. A few minutes later, Cerrato called back. "Sorry," he said. "We decided to go ahead and pick." Newsome said nothing. Clearly someone in the Redskins' draft room had overruled Cerrato. Finally, Miami, picking at 153, agreed to the deal — the Ravens first seventh-round pick (number 222) for pick 153. An hour after not becoming a Raven, Roderick Green became a Raven.

"Welcome to the team, part two," Billick said when it was his turn on the phone. Bisciotti passed on the chance to learn more about Green's family.

Harris was on the phone again. "I'm sorry I took so long on KJ," he said. "I had some disagreement in the room here."

"You put me into a pretty deep corner there for a while," Newsome said, half-joking with his friend.

There was one final glitch before the draft was over. In the sixth round, picking at 187, Newsome wanted to take Clarence Moore, a rangy six foot six wide receiver from Northern Arizona, considered a project with potential, probably someone who would spend the season on the developmental squad. He called Moore and a woman answered the phone. When he asked for Clarence Moore, the woman said he wasn't there and didn't know where he was. Newsome tried a second number and got no answer. Time was running out. Newsome sighed, took out the card for Josh Harris, a quarterback from Bowling Green, and dialed his number. He answered on the first ring.

"Put the card in for Josh Harris," he instructed New York. He had planned to draft his young backup quarterback later, but not reaching Moore, he had to change plans on the fly.

"Where in the world can the kid be, today of all days?" Bisciotti said.

"One time I couldn't find a kid because he was at the movies," Newsome said. "His mother finally ran down there and got him out of there so he could call me back."

"You won't take a kid if you can't reach him?" Bisciotti asked.

"No way," Newsome said, shaking his head. "He might be in jail, he might be in the hospital, he might be dead, for all I know. I need to talk to him, know where he is, before I draft him."

This is not nearly as far-fetched as it might sound. One year the Oakland Raiders drafted a player named Don Mosebar in the first round even though they couldn't find him when it was their turn to pick. The next day they found him — in the hospital, where he had undergone back surgery over the weekend, thus explaining his failure to answer the phone.

"I got a better one for you," Jim Fassel said. "Few years back, a CFL team drafted a guy they couldn't find. The reason they couldn't find him was because he had died."

The Ravens had another sixth-round pick twelve spots after taking Harris. By then, Savage had run down another number for Moore. "We had the wrong number," he said. Newsome decided to give him one more try. This time he reached Moore. "I'm glad I found you," he said. Moore said he'd been getting a lot of phone calls, most recently, he said, from the Redskins, Titans, and Panthers. "Have you heard anything from Pittsburgh?" Newsome asked, since the Steelers were on the clock at that moment. No, Moore said, he hadn't. Newsome instructed Moore to stay on the phone. The Steelers took a center from Stanford. The 49ers then took a safety. Newsome breathed a sigh of relief and told Moore he was a Baltimore Raven.

"I think that one is going to need some babysitting," Billick said. He turned to Chad Steele, the Ravens' public relations manager. "You may need to play big brother with him."

Steele nodded. He was the son of Gary Steele, the first African American to be a football letterman at Army, and had played college basketball at Winthrop. He was twenty-nine and was close to several of the team's younger African American players.

The final round was the spot where it had been predetermined the team would draft a kick returner. The Ravens were not happy with Lamont Brightful, their incumbent returner. He had lost confidence somewhere along the way and had started to have trouble hanging on to the ball. The team had scouted about a dozen potential returners prior to the draft. The scouts liked Derek Abney, a bright-eyed kid from Kentucky who had speed and could be a spot player at wide receiver. That opinion was not shared by Gary Zauner, the special teams coordinator.

Zauner was a special teams savant. Unlike other coaches who saw coaching special teams as a stepping-stone to another job, Zauner had always coached special teams and had no desire to do anything except coach special teams. He had been the first full-time special teams coach ever when LaVell Edwards hired him to do that job in 1979 at Brigham Young. He had been both a punter and a placekicker in college and had been in NFL training camps as a punter, though he had never made a team. He understood everything about special teams play. He had studied it for years, spending hours and hours looking at special teams tape and working on the practice field with special teams players. Practice periods devoted to special teams work were known as "the Zauner hour." All the other coaches — except for Zauner's assistant, Bennie Thompson — simply cleared the stage for Zauner to work.

Zauner and Billick had worked together in Minnesota for five seasons. In 2002 Billick had brought Zauner to Baltimore as special teams coordinator. Billick had absolute faith in Zauner's understanding of special teams play and special teams players, a faith that was occasionally disturbing to the scouting staff, since Billick was apt to take Zauner's word over theirs if there was a conflict.

Now there was a conflict. Zauner liked Abney, too, but he liked a kid named B. J. Sams better. Sams had played at McNeese State, a 1-AA school in Louisiana. He had been spotted by Ron Marciniak, the wise old head on the Ravens' scouting staff. At seventy-one, Marciniak was decades older than almost everyone else on the staff but, after twenty-five years in the league, still kept his hand in doing some scouting for the Ravens. He had recommended that Zauner take a look at Sams. "What I liked about him," Zauner said, "was he caught every ball. A lot of return guys have speed, not all of them can catch every single ball. He seemed to do that."

Newsome wasn't about to defer to Zauner on a draft pick. Abney got the nod. A few minutes later Brian Rimpf, an offensive lineman from East Carolina, became the Ravens' final pick. When Newsome called him, whoever answered the phone told him that Rimpf was on the phone with Tampa Bay. "Tell him to hang up," Newsome said. "They're behind us. There's nothing they can do for him."

At 5:05 the card for Rimpf went in and everyone took a deep breath. The end of the draft did not, by any means, mean the end of the day. Every NFL team keeps a list of potential free agents — undrafted players — and a wild scramble to get some of those players begins as soon as the final draft pick has been made. Some teams spend a decent-size chunk of money to entice free agents. In 2003 the Cowboys spent close to $120,000 in bonuses to attract free agents, including giving one player $25,000. That was more than the Ravens' entire budget for free-agent bonuses. Rarely did they offer more than $2,500.

What the Ravens sold was opportunity. The sheet that the scouts and assistant coaches worked off of while calling free agents reminded them to bring up names like Priest Holmes and Mike Flynn and Will Demps and Bart Scott, all Ravens free-agent signees who had become successful NFL players. In fact, 50 of the 150 free agents signed by the Ravens since 1996 had made NFL rosters, and nine of the fifty-five Ravens under contract at that moment had been free agents.

Zauner was pushing Newsome to bring Sams into minicamp for a look. Newsome wasn't eager to do it. He had Abney and he had Brightful. In his mind, the two would compete for the job. "Just give him a shot," Zauner said. "It won't cost you anything."

Newsome threw up his hands, exasperated because Zauner wouldn't let the argument go. "Tell you what, Gary," he said. "I'll bring him in here to make you happy. In fact, if he makes our opening-day roster, I'll give you two thousand dollars."

"Deal," Zauner said, delighted that his nudging had paid off.

By the time the staff went home that night, twenty-seven players had agreed to come to rookie minicamp as free agents. Some got small bonuses. Some got nothing. And some would have to come in before minicamp for what amounted to a tryout to see if they were worthy of a minicamp uniform. "The *Gong Show*," Savage called it.

The rookies would report on Friday. The draft was over. The scouts could take a deep breath. Now it was time for the coaches to go to work.

6

Camps and More Camps

YEARS AGO, THE END OF THE FOOTBALL SEASON meant a lengthy break for NFL players. Most would return to their homes, take off several months, and perhaps do a little bit of conditioning work before reporting to training camp in July. Once they reported for two-a-days, they began working to get into shape for the start of the season. Those days are long gone. Most players take almost no break now from some kind of conditioning, and all are expected to take part in an off-season training program, whether one prescribed by the team or one put together by a personal trainer, frequently with the approval of the team.

The Ravens' best-known veteran players — Jonathan Ogden, Ray Lewis, Jamal Lewis — all left town during the off-season. Many veterans had homes in Baltimore and worked out at the team's facility under the watchful eye of strength coaches Jeff Friday and Paul Ricci throughout the winter and spring months. Players who had just finished their first NFL season — especially those who had been on either the developmental squad or injured reserve — were expected to be back in Baltimore by the end of March for more formal workouts. Their arrival marked the beginning of a gradual return of the entire team. Rookies first came at the end of April for a three-day rookie minicamp. During May there were two "passing camps" for all quarterbacks, running backs, and receivers, with some special teamers and a handful of linemen also present. Then, in the first week of June, came the first of two veteran minicamps. One was mandatory; the other, "voluntary." As in "you better volunteer to be there." "Making the team is also voluntary," Billick liked to say. Only one person was not expected to be back for those two weeks — cornerback Chris McAlister, whom the Ravens had designated as their "franchise player," meaning he could not negotiate with other teams and would not sign a new contract at a locked-in price ($7.1 million) until the end of training camp.

Like the team, Brian Billick's staff had experienced relatively little turnover. The most significant loss had been defensive backs coach Donnie Henderson, who had been hired by the New York Jets as their defensive coordinator. In Henderson's place was Johnnie Lynn, who had been the defensive coordinator on Jim Fassel's New York Giants staff for the past two years but who had been purged after Fassel's departure. This was the way of the NFL: position coaches become coordinators, fired coordinators become position coaches, just as coordinators become head coaches, and fired head coaches become coordinators once again.

Lynn was one of four new coaches on staff. Jeff FitzGerald, who had worked with defensive coordinator Mike Nolan in Washington, had been rescued after four seasons in purgatory with the Arizona Cardinals and would coach the outside linebackers. Jedd Fisch would work with the offense, breaking down tape, putting together scouting reports, and offering his computer expertise to some of the less-computer-literate coaches.

Most notable in that group was the fourth — and most prominent — new name on the staff: Jim Fassel. Technically, the former Giants coach was not an assistant coach, he was a senior consultant. In reality he was in Baltimore to coach one player: Kyle Boller. The idea to hire a personal tutor for Boller was Billick's. Fassel and Billick had known each other for more than twenty years, dating back to Fassel's days as an assistant at Stanford (where he had coached John Elway), which had coincided with Billick's tenure with the San Francisco 49ers as a public relations assistant/unofficial assistant coach. Each man had come under the influence of Bill Walsh — Fassel during Walsh's last two years at Stanford, Billick during Walsh's first two years with the 49ers. They had remained good friends as their paths crossed through the years.

Fassel had become a head coach in 1997 in New York, Billick two years later in Baltimore. They began a tradition of getting together for dinner each year at the scouting combine in Indianapolis. If their teams played each other, the winning coach bought. If not, whoever had the better record bought. In 2001 their dinner came a month after Billick's Ravens had hammered Fassel's Giants, 34–7, in the Super Bowl. "I walked in and told the manager I wanted the most expensive wine he had on the menu and to keep it coming," Fassel said. "Brian was more than happy to pay."

The two men would talk long into the night, the subjects ranging from preparing for a Super Bowl to negotiating a contract to hiring assistants to what it was like to get cut in training camp without ever playing in an NFL game to raising girls (Billick) and raising boys (Fassel). "I think it is fair to say that I've had as many discussions with Brian on as many different topics as I've had with any friend of mine through the years," Fassel said. "I think we're completely comfortable with one another."

Fassel had announced his resignation as Giants coach with two weeks left in the season in order to save the Mara family the pain of having to fire him. He'd had a good seven-year run in New York — three playoff teams, two division titles, one Super Bowl trip — but the Giants had never completely recovered from a devastating playoff loss in San Francisco at the end of the 2002 season and, decimated by injuries, had lost their last eight games in 2003, to finish 4-12. Most football people believed Fassel would be snapped up for another head coaching job before the Super Bowl had been played. He was interviewed by the Buffalo Bills, Arizona Cardinals, Atlanta Falcons, and Washington Redskins. At one point, it appeared likely that Dan Snyder was going to hire him to coach the Redskins. But Snyder ended up shocking the football world by bringing Joe Gibbs back instead.

"I certainly couldn't blame him for hiring Joe Gibbs, could I?" Fassel said. "I mean that's a no-brainer, a slam dunk. I didn't know it at the time, but I think I was lucky not to get a job. I was burned-out, more burned-out than I knew. Seven years as a head coach in the NFL, especially in New York, wears on you. How many head coaches are there in the league right now who have been in their jobs for double-digit years?" (There are three: Bill Cowher in Pittsburgh, Mike Shanahan in Denver, and Jeff Fisher in Tennessee. Billick, going into his sixth year, was tied for fourth in tenure with his current team.) "When I didn't get a job, I realized I was relieved. I needed a break."

The plan then was to take the year off. The Giants still had to pay him his $3 million annual salary for another season. That left Fassel free to spend time watching John, his elder son, coach his team at New Mexico Highlands and Mike, his younger son, kick at Boston College. The rest of his time would be spent relaxing, watching some games, and putting together a coaching plan to present to prospective employers at the end of the 2004 season. Then Billick called.

"Basically, I wanted Jim to put together a schedule he would be comfortable with," Billick said. "Do as much or as little as he wanted. Everyone knows how great he has been with quarterbacks through the years, and I knew Kyle would benefit from any time he spent with him. We eventually decided he would come down a couple days a week, be with us in camp, and come to any games that didn't conflict with one of his sons' games. It was also a way to keep his name out there a little during the season. I thought it was a good deal for everyone."

Fassel liked the idea. The commute from his home in New Jersey would be a relatively simple one and he would be gone for only a couple of days at a time most of the season. He and Billick came up with the notion of making him a "senior consultant" rather than a coach because it meant he could sign a contract that would expire December 31 — two days before the end of the regular season. That meant that any team wanting to interview Fassel for a head coaching vacancy at the end of the regular season would not be restricted by the NFL's rules on contact with assistant coaches should the Ravens be in the playoffs. It was a dream deal for everyone: Fassel got to keep his hand in without being taxed by the hours most assistant coaches have to put in. Boller got a tutor who had worked with Elway and Phil Simms and Boomer Esiason and Kerry Collins. The Ravens got a former head coach for almost nothing, because anything the Ravens paid Fassel cut into how much the Giants had to pay him. Only one person might have had a complaint about the hiring: offensive coordinator Matt Cavanaugh.

"The only person this isn't fair to is Matt," Billick said. "If our passing game gets better and Kyle improves, Jim will get the credit. If we don't get better, Matt will get blamed anyway. In a sense, he can't win."

Matt Cavanaugh smiled when Billick's no-way-Matt-can-win theory was put to him. "There's one way I can win very easily," he said. "If we win games, go to the playoffs, make the Super Bowl, I win. If people don't want to give me credit, that's fine. Just as long as we win games. That's always the best answer."

Or so it would seem. In 2000 the Ravens had won a Super Bowl and people talked about an offense that managed not to lose games. In 2003 the Ravens had their best season on offense under Billick and Cavanaugh and people were screaming for Cavanaugh's head. "When Steve [Bisciotti] came in to tell me about his conversations with Brian, he said to me, 'I know you're going to be under a lot of pressure this coming season.' I told him that wasn't really true. Look, I've been cut, I've been traded, I've been injured, I've had things thrown at me, and I've had people screaming for my head around here the last few years. I'm really okay with it. I enjoy doing what I do. If I'm not doing it here next year, I feel confident I'll be doing it someplace else. I know I can coach."

Cavanaugh's "I can handle whatever comes" approach probably dates back to his upbringing. He grew up in the working-class town of Youngstown, Ohio. His dad was a salesman, the prototypical tough-love dad, a disciplinarian whose four kids knew the difference between right and wrong from a very young age. Dan Cavanaugh was a two-pack-a-day Lucky Strike man and someone who liked to drink with his buddies after work and was, according to his son, "always the life of the party." It was only later, when he was an adult, that Matt Cavanaugh realized that his dad was an alcoholic. "It wasn't anything I thought about when I was a kid," he said. "Where I came from, people drank after work. It didn't seem to me to be anything that unusual until I was much older."

Matt was a good athlete as a kid, a baseball player first —"probably my favorite sport even after I started playing football really well" — but eventually he blossomed into a football star. He was widely recruited but opted for Pittsburgh, where Johnny Majors was building a powerhouse led by a freshman running back named Tony Dorsett. Cavanaugh became a star at quarterback in his junior season, the year the Panthers went 12-0 and won the national championship, led by Dorsett, who won the Heisman Trophy. Cavanaugh had an outstanding year, good enough that he went into his senior year as one of the favorites to succeed Dorsett as the Heisman Trophy winner. That bubble burst in the opener against Notre Dame, when Cavanaugh broke his wrist trying to break a fall while scrambling. He came back at midseason to lead Pitt to a 10-2 record and was drafted in the second round by the New England Patriots. His first coach there was Chuck Fairbanks, who walked into his first meeting with the rookies, lit a cigarette, and said, "There's not one of you in here that we need." He was a part-time starter during his career with the Patriots before being traded to the 49ers in 1983, where he backed up Joe Montana for three years, including 1984, when the 49ers won the Super Bowl. "The first day I was there Bill Walsh greeted me and told me how thrilled they were to have me, how he thought they were a better team because they had me," Cavanaugh said. "I learned a lesson right there: it isn't that hard to make a player feel good about playing for you. He was the complete opposite of Fairbanks."

In 1986 he was traded to the Eagles and spent four seasons in Philadelphia before being cut by Buddy Ryan during training camp in 1990. "Buddy had told the front office to offer me a ten percent pay cut to come back," Cavanaugh remembered, laughing. "Somehow, they got confused and offered me a ten percent raise. Naturally, I took it. Buddy said to me, 'How the hell did this happen?' I told him, they offered and I took. Not long after that he cut me.

"It wasn't a shock when it happened, but it *was* a shock, especially since I thought I'd had a really good camp. My wife and kids had stayed back in Rhode Island during camp because I knew there was a chance I'd get cut. I'd played twelve years, that's a long time. But even so, it's an awful feeling. I remember making that drive back home just feeling worthless. I mean, I knew better, but that's the way you feel when you get cut."

Players call the trip home after getting cut "the drive of shame." The feeling didn't last long for Cavanaugh. About an hour after he walked into the house, the phone rang. The person on the other end was whispering. "You know who this is, right?" Cavanaugh was pretty sure he knew. "Okay, I can't really talk to you until you clear waivers tomorrow, but I want you down here. I need a number three quarterback with some experience because I lost Jeff Rutledge to Washington and I've got a kid as my backup. Officially, we haven't talked. Unofficially, you interested?"

Cavanaugh hung up the phone. When his wife asked him what the call was about, he shrugged and said, "Officially, that was no one. Unofficially, I'm pretty sure it was Bill Parcells and he wants me to come to New York and back up Phil Simms and Jeff Hostetler."

The money was the same as he would have been paid as a backup in Philadelphia. Cavanaugh had made no plans for the 1990 season, so he said yes. As it turned out, Simms went down late in the season and Hostetler ended up leading the Giants to a Super Bowl win over the Buffalo Bills. Cavanaugh got into the Super Bowl for several plays when Hostetler got nicked during the game. He played one more year in New York and then retired after fourteen NFL seasons.

"The two years in New York were like a bonus," he said. "I ended up getting another Super Bowl ring, which I certainly didn't count on, and I met Jim Fassel, because he came on staff in '91. I was really lucky."

During the 1991 season Pitt coach Paul Hackett, whom he had played for while with the 49ers, called him. He knew Cavanaugh was coming to the end and he thought he should be a coach. Specifically, Hackett wanted him to come back to his alma mater as the offensive coordinator at the end of the season. Once, Cavanaugh would have laughed at such an offer. "When I first got out of college, I thought I would end up doing something involving criminal justice. That's what my degree was in. What I really wanted to do was be in the FBI. I even took some night classes my first few years in the league to prepare for applying. But as time went on, I realized it wasn't going to happen. I hadn't planned to play for as long as I did. Starting in a new profession at thirty-six with no experience wouldn't be easy. So, when Paul suggested coaching, I thought it made sense."

There was only one problem: Hackett got fired at the end of the season. The good news was that his replacement was Majors, rehired by Pitt (after being forced out at Tennessee) to try to re-create the Panthers' glory of the '70s. "I figured I was a lock to get hired by Coach Majors," Cavanaugh said. "I thought I'd be offensive coordinator, quarterbacks coach worst-case scenario.

Which is why he was stunned when Majors called to say he had one job left: tight ends coach. Cavanaugh took it. "Probably the best thing that ever happened to me," he said. "It forced me to look at the game differently, to learn to understand blocking schemes and to see the game through the eyes of someone other than a quarterback."

A year later he had a chance to become the quarterbacks coach for Tom Coughlin at Boston College. He was preparing to go to Boston to finalize the deal when Buddy Ryan called. Ryan had apparently forgiven Cavanaugh for getting a 10 percent raise in 1990. He was now in Arizona and wanted Cavanaugh to join him as his quarterbacks coach. "I felt badly, because I had said yes to Tom," Cavanaugh said. "But I thought coaching in the NFL would be more of a pure coaching experience. No recruiting. No classes to worry about. No limits on practice time."

He was in Arizona for two years, then spent a year in San Francisco before getting hired as the offensive coordinator by Dave Wannstedt (another Pitt grad) in Chicago. Two years later Wannstedt was fired and Cavanaugh was out of work involuntarily for the first time in his life — except for those six hours between the time he was cut in Philadelphia and the unofficial Parcells phone call. There was nothing to do except wait for the phone to ring, and Cavanaugh decided not to wait around for that to happen. He and his wife went on a winter vacation to see friends in Wisconsin. "The kids tracked me down out there and said some guy named Brian Billick had called."

Cavanaugh and Billick had never met. Billick was riding high as the coordinator of the record-breaking Minnesota Vikings offense. His name was being mentioned as the next head coach in several places. "All I knew about Brian was secondhand, from being on the opposite sideline," Cavanaugh said. "I thought he was very good at what he did, very arrogant and extremely cocky."

Cavanaugh called Billick back. "I think I'm going to get a job whenever we're finished playing," Billick said. "I'd just like to have a chance to talk to you whenever I land someplace. If you get an offer before then, I'd appreciate it if you'd at least give me a chance to talk to you first. Obviously, I can't take a job until we're done."

Cavanaugh was surprised and flattered. "I decided he was pretty smart for someone who was arrogant and cocky," he said, laughing. "I told him I wouldn't take a job, if I was offered one, until I had a chance to talk to him."

As it turned out, Cavanaugh *was* offered a job before Billick was hired in Baltimore — by Tom Coughlin, who was now coaching in Jacksonville. Apparently, Coughlin hadn't held a grudge against Cavanaugh for turning him down at the last moment five years earlier. Cavanaugh told Coughlin he had given his word to Billick to wait until he landed before taking another job. Coughlin pushed for a decision. Cavanaugh decided to wait. The day after he was named the Ravens coach, Billick flew to Mobile, Alabama, for the Senior Bowl. Senior Bowl week is one of the NFL's conventions. Entire coaching staffs make the trip, as do scouting staffs, to look at top senior players but also to network and socialize. It is almost a tradition for newly minted coaches to set up in a hotel room in Mobile and interview candidates for their staff. That was where Billick and Cavanaugh sat down.

"When he showed me what he was doing on his computer, I was blown away," Cavanaugh said. "He was way ahead of the curve in terms of using the computer to make the job more efficient. He had spreadsheets on practice schedules, breakdowns of practices, game planning, the works. I felt like I had a chance to get on board something that was going to be different and fun, plus a learning experience for me."

The only hard part was calling Coughlin — again — to turn him down. "When Tom got the Giants job [in 2004] I'm guessing I wasn't on his list of guys to call," Cavanaugh said, laughing.

Billick told Cavanaugh that his plan was to start the season calling plays and gradually turn that job over to Cavanaugh. That was okay with Cavanaugh, who was learning a new offense and understood Billick's reluctance to give up the offensive reins altogether upon starting a new job. Seven weeks into the season, the Ravens were 2-5 and struggling to score points. The old Browns were headed to Cleveland for the first time back there, to the new stadium that had not been built for Art Modell. Modell wasn't going to make the trip, but his team was. Which made it a very big deal. To make things even better for the Ravens, Billick began the week by saying at his press conference that it would be tough enough dealing with the fans, but he was also pretty certain there was no way his team was going to get any calls from the referees, either.

The next day Billick went into Cavanaugh's office and told him he would be calling the plays on Sunday. "Between preparing for the game and going into Cleveland with the firestorm I created yesterday, I've got enough to do this week," he told Cavanaugh. "You call the game."

Cavanaugh called the game, the Ravens won, 41–9 — the refs were apparently not a factor — and Cavanaugh was the play caller after that. A year later the Ravens went five weeks without an offensive touchdown. Cavanaugh went to see Billick to ask him if he wanted to make any changes — including Billick's calling plays again. "He told me, 'Matt, if I thought the play calling was the problem, believe me, you'd know. Just keep doing what you're doing until I tell you not to.'"

That was the first time Cavanaugh came under fire. It ebbed when the Ravens won eleven straight games and the Super Bowl but never really went away, even with another trip to the playoffs the next year and through the rebuilding years of 2002 and 2003 — the division title notwithstanding. Cavanaugh never blinked. "When I watch a game on TV I second-guess the offensive play calling, too," he said. "The way football is, it is a lot easier to question the offense than the defense. When something goes wrong on defense, you can't really be sure why. Was it a blown call or a blown coverage? Did someone use the wrong technique? It's just tougher to tell. On offense, if you throw the ball and it doesn't work, you should have run. If you run and it doesn't work, you should have passed. It's simple. Anyone can second-guess."

Cavanaugh and Billick had decided that Cavanaugh would move up to the press box for the 2004 season to call the game from there. This was done in part because a coach can see the whole field better from upstairs but also because both men felt that with Fassel on the field with Boller, it was okay for Cavanaugh to be upstairs. What's more, Cavanaugh would be less of a target for the fans upstairs than he would be downstairs. That, however, was the least of Cavanaugh's worries.

"I told Steve [Bisciotti] when he came in to talk to me that if we don't produce on offense this year, he won't have to fire me," he said. "I'll quit just like [Kansas City Chiefs defensive coordinator] Greg Robinson did and Brian can cry at the press conference. Or they can fly Dick Vermeil in to cry." Vermeil, the Chiefs' coach, was famous for tearful press conferences, the most recent having come when Robinson had stepped down amid screams for his head in Kansas City.

Cavanaugh's approach to the season may have been best summed up when wide receiver Travis Taylor came to see him one day before mini-camp began. Taylor was on the last year of his contract and, as a onetime number one pick, was viewed by most in Baltimore as Ozzie Newsome's one failed top draft pick. "Travis, it's you and me together this year," Cavanaugh told him. "Either we're going to fly together or we're going out the door together."

He was smiling when he said it. He was also completely serious.

*   *

The surprise of the rookie minicamp (except to Gary Zauner) was B. J. Sams, the dimunitive (five foot ten, 185 pounds) kick returner from McNeese State. As soon as the coaches saw him, they understood why Zauner had been so high on him. He had speed, he had the ability to make defenders miss, and he caught the ball — most notably on punts with defenders running straight at him — without fear. Every day at the end of special teams drills, Zauner would line up his returners — there were six or seven different players being asked to return kicks — and ask them how many balls they had dropped. Every day Sams's answer was the same. "None, Coach."

Like most rookies in a new, somewhat frightening environment, Sams was quiet, even around the other rookies. He was the youngest of his mother's four children and the youngest of his father's *twenty-six* children. "He started young," Sams said. "And he finished old."

Samuel Sams made a career in the air force, flying as a pilot in World War II. By the time he retired and moved to Mandeville, Louisiana, he had been through several marriages and divorces and had twenty-two children. He moved to Mandeville because he had relatives there and met Marian Smith — who was twenty-eight years his junior. They were married and had four children, the youngest of them named Bradley Jamar — B.J. to everyone in his family right from the start. B.J. was always small, but he loved to follow his brother Andrew to football practice. By the time he was eleven, Andrew's friends had noticed that little B.J. could run and catch as well as the bigger kids, so he began playing with them.

"Problem was, I was still tiny when I got to high school," he said. "I played on the freshman team at four-eleven and eighty-seven pounds. All they let me do was run down on kickoffs and punts because I was fast."

A year later he had grown enough to play cornerback, and by the time he was a junior, he was five-nine and 150 pounds and was playing all over the field. "My coach felt like if they got the ball in my hands, good things were going to happen."

His speed and elusiveness attracted a lot of attention from college recruiters, but the fact that he hadn't taken the ACT turned a lot of them off. "I procrastinated taking the test," he said. "I think I was just nervous about it. Then when I took it, I did fine — passed it with flying colors. But by then, McNeese was the only one that still had a scholarship for me."

The blow of ending up at a 1-AA school instead of a 1-A school was softened by the presence of Andrew, who was a backup fullback on the team. As in high school, Sams needed a full year to get the attention of the coaching staff and to grow a little bit more. He was a starting wide receiver as a sophomore and returned all kicks. By the end of his junior year, he was thinking he had a shot at playing pro ball. But when the pro scouts came to town that spring to look at some of his senior teammates and asked him to run a 40, his time was 4.51. "For someone my size, they thought that was slow," he remembered. "My coach [Tommy Tate] told me I had to get bigger and faster if I wanted to play in the NFL."

He worked out almost maniacally as a senior and did everything for a team that was 10-2. His 40 time that winter improved to 4.41 — still not blazingly fast, but enough to earn him some predraft attention from the Ravens, Colts, Eagles, and Titans. The only team to bring him in for an interview was the Ravens. "When I met with Mr. Newsome, he said they really liked me but he was worried I was too slow," Sams said. "I didn't know if he was joking or not. But then he told me if he called me on draft day, he wanted me to say, 'Mr. Newsome, when people watch *Monday Night Football* this year they aren't going to remember who Dante Hall [the Chiefs' Pro Bowl kick returner] is, they're going to remember B. J. Sams.' I told him, 'Yes, sir, I can do that.'"

Newsome didn't call on draft day, Zauner did — about five minutes after the draft ended (and about sixty seconds after talking Newsome into letting him make the call). He offered a free-agent contract with no bonus. Sams jumped at it. Two other teams — the Colts and Saints — called later, but Sams had already committed to Baltimore.

"All I want is a chance to show what I can do," he said. "That's all I've ever asked for in football and whenever I've gotten it, I've done well."

Like the other rookies, Sams was living in the Hilton Garden Inn, which was about a mile down Owings Mills Boulevard from the Ravens' practice facility. He had no car and was making $460 a week, all the while dreaming he would be one of the chosen few who would sign a $235,000-a-year rookie contract at the end of training camp. When the team wasn't in a minicamp or a passing camp, his life consisted of hitching rides to the facility to lift weights and then go to a nearby mall. "I've seen every movie they have there," he said. "My favorite day is Friday because the movies change and we get to see something new.

"I know the coaches are saying nice things about me. The other day I heard Coach Cavanaugh say to one of the other coaches, 'I think we've found a secret weapon.' That made me feel good. But I'm not getting too excited. It's a long way from here to opening day."

The notion of a free agent who had received no bonus at all making the team wasn't new to the Ravens. Will Demps, who was penciled in to be the starting safety, had made the team in 2002 as an undrafted free agent. What was even more remarkable about Demps was that he had made his college team at San Diego State as a walk-on after not being offered any Division 1 scholarships as a high school senior.

Like Sams, Demps had been discovered by Zauner, who had worked him out as a senior and then talked the team into giving him a shot as an undrafted free agent. He had gone from making the team as a special teamer to becoming the starter at safety. A year earlier he had appeared on several billboards around Baltimore as part of a promotional campaign for one of the Ravens' clothing sponsors. "I'm the guy who they always think they can replace every year," Demps liked to say. "They're always going to think they can bring in someone better than me. All I know is, I'm still here."

Sams was now hoping to join him.

While the coaches were searching for diamonds in the free-agent rough during the passing camps and the minicamps, the player being watched by the most people most of the time was Kyle Boller. There was still considerable debate in and around Baltimore about whether the trade that had allowed the Ravens to draft Boller had been a good idea. To some, Boller had won the quarterback job in 2003 by default and then had been protected during his nine-game stint as the starter by the running of Jamal Lewis and the play of the defense. Already some people were putting him on the list of quarterbacks who had come and gone in Baltimore since Billick's arrival: Scott Mitchell, Tony Banks, Trent Dilfer (given an asterisk since he had won a Super Bowl), Elvis Grbac, Jeff Blake, and Chris Redman. To others he was a work in progress, but one with great potential.

Since Billick allows the media to watch practice from start to finish throughout the preseason, Boller's progress in both the passing camps and the minicamps was monitored locally with an intensity similar to that of the returns from Ohio on election night. In his case, the voters weren't leaning blue or red, they were leaning failure or future star. One day during a passing camp, Boller threw two interceptions late in practice. The local TV stations did everything but live cut-ins to report the disaster.

The subject of all this scrutiny was a baby-faced twenty-three-year-old (even in his second season he would be the youngest starting quarterback in the league) who had an easy smile and the kind of laid-back approach to things that seemed to fit his image as a surfer dude who had grown up in Southern California (in Boller-speak: So-Cali) and had gone to college in northern California (you guessed it, No-Cali) at Berkeley. Boller was handsome enough to draw sighs from young girls and had briefly dated actress Tara Reid during the off-season. This was big news in Baltimore, which wasn't used to having sports stars making gossip headlines in Hollywood.

What was funny about Boller was that he was almost nothing like his image. Sure, he could sound like a hip kid, referring to his father as "being real cool for an old dude" (his dad was forty-seven) and could shrug his shoulders as if to say, "No biggie," when asked about the pressures of being the quarterback of a team with Super Bowl ambitions in just his second season. But underneath the smile, Boller was both a lot tougher and a lot more vulnerable than he appeared.

For one thing, he was from a family of firefighters. His dad was a firefighter, his grandfather and great-grandfather had been firefighters, and three of his uncles were firefighters. For a long time, growing up in Valencia, Kyle had thought he would follow in their footsteps and become a firefighter, too. The first clue he got that maybe he wasn't destined to go in that direction came when he spent a day with his father at the fire station doing a ride-along at the age of sixteen. "I loved it," he said. "Although the reality of it was a lot different than what I had seen in the movies. I mean, you have no idea what you're walking into. I remember we went into one home on a call and it was a really old man and he was just lying there, dead. They tried to bring him back, but it was too late. By the end of the day, I was wiped out. At about four o'clock in the morning they got a call to go on another run and I just slept through it. Alarms going off and everything, but I'm such a heavy sleeper I missed it and, of course, they didn't wake me. If I'd been a real firefighter, it would have been different."

The other thing that led Boller away from his dad's career was football, which he decided at a young age was his sport, in large part because he enjoyed hitting. "I was a linebacker when I first started to play," he said. "I was always big — like eleven pounds, twelve ounces when I was born — and then kind of a bulky kid. Then when I was in eighth grade, my height hadn't caught up with the rest of my body. I had the hands and feet of someone who was six-three and I was about five-six. My nickname was Monkey Boy. My parents took me to the doctor, and he said my growth plates were wide open — it was just a matter of time until I grew. But it took a while."

In fact, Boller didn't become the starting quarterback at Hart High School until he was a senior. Hart was a powerhouse program that churned out quarterbacks and Division 1 players. Even so, he dreamed of going to UCLA and being the starting quarterback because the school was near his home and beautiful. "I went to camp there after my junior season and J. P. Losman was there, too," he said. "At the end of the camp, they offered J.P. a scholarship. I hadn't really done anything yet, so I understood, but I was disappointed. Then my senior year, I blew up."

Playing on a dominant team, Boller had superb statistics and all of a sudden had colleges from all over the country chasing him. He ended up making visits to Florida State, Oregon, Southern California, and Cal. "If my SATs had been higher, I think Stanford might have recruited me harder and I might have ended up there," he said. "But I had really good grades [3.89 GPA] and not-so-hot SATs [under 1,000], so they backed off. I wanted to go someplace I could play right away. I didn't want to redshirt. USC had Carson [Palmer] and Oregon had [Joey] Harrington. Florida State was just too far."

That left Cal. Not only was Boller expected to start right away, he was expected to save the program. Shortly after he arrived on campus he picked up the student newspaper and saw a headline that read, JESUS IN CLEATS. Underneath the headline was his picture. "I thought to myself, 'Whoa, people, slow down. I'm a seventeen-year-old kid who started for one year in high school,'" he said, laughing.

Boller made his college debut in the second half of Cal's second game, a one-sided loss at Nebraska. He still remembers one of the Nebraska line-backers pointing at him as he came to the line of scrimmage and snapping his fingers as if breaking a twig in half. "I started laughing," he said. "I thought it was sweet, me, playing in Nebraska's stadium, and this guy saying he's gonna kill me. I loved it."

A week later he got his first start and led the Golden Bears to a fourth-quarter comeback win over Arizona State. Maybe the headline had been right. "Not exactly," he said. "We ended up 3-8. I think I got sacked about ninety times." It didn't get any better the next two years. Cal was 4-7 and 1-10 and, if that wasn't enough, under NCAA investigation for grade fixing on the football team. By the time his junior year was over, Boller was ready to walk away from football.

"I was thinking, I'll get my degree, go home, and get a job," he said. "I was beaten up, mentally and physically. But then they hired Jeff Tedford and everything changed. I thought we had a chance again."

Tedford had been the offensive coordinator at Oregon when Boller visited there and Boller had been impressed by him. He came to Cal with a mandate to clean up the program and point it in another direction. Cal was 6-5 in Boller's senior year, finishing with a win over archrival Stanford for the first time in Boller's career, and as in high school, he was suddenly drawing major attention from coaches and scouts at the next level. In this case, that meant the NFL. Boller was part of a highly touted quarterback class that included Carson Palmer, who had won the Heisman Trophy at USC; Marshall's Byron Leftwich; and Florida's Rex Grossman.

He went to the combine in Indianapolis and, like most players, was horrified by the whole thing. "It's such a cattle call," he said. "I mean, the idea that you walk out there on a stage wearing just your shorts and they all look you over like it's a beauty pageant or something. Then you take the Wunderlik test. My agent actually had me study for it. Everybody's got sample copies of the test, so you go through it that way. Here I am, after four years at Cal, looking at questions like 'If you can get a dozen lemon drops for forty cents, how many can you get for two dollars?' Then there's the Giants test. Must be three hundred questions. I still remember there was a question that said, 'If you find a wallet lying in the gutter, what do you do with it?' By that point I was so fed up, I wanted to write, 'Pocket the money and run like hell.'"

The one part of the combine Boller didn't mind was the personal interviews. He liked it when teams asked him to go to a board and explain Cal's protection schemes and asked him questions about adjustments that could be made. Even more, he liked the give-and-take with the coaches and scouts — most notably, his meeting with the Ravens. Billick asked him why the Ravens should take him, given the chance, over Palmer or Leftwich. "I remember hesitating for a minute," he said. "I didn't want to put those guys down in any way and I didn't want to sound cocky, either. But then I just pointed out that Carson had played on great teams at USC, had great offensive lines, great receivers. I felt I'd only had one year where we'd had our act together and I had done really well. I said, 'I think Carson and Byron are great football players, but I honestly believe I can throw with them and play with them. I'll go out there with them right now and show you.'

"Then they asked me how I would become the kind of leader a quarterback has to be when they had a leader like Ray on defense. I told them I thought leadership was earned, that I hoped I would learn how to lead [by] watching Ray, and at some point I'd become the leader of the offense because, if I'm the quarterback, it has to be my offense for the team to be successful."

The Ravens were impressed with Boller. So were the Bears, Cardinals, and Steelers. The Bengals liked him, too, but everyone knew they were going to take Palmer with the number one pick. Boller went into the draft thinking he might get taken by the Ravens at ten or the Bears at twelve. "I was hoping for the Ravens, not so much because they were picking a little higher but because I liked them, I thought I clicked with Brian and Ozzie and Matt. I also thought I could play right away there."

As with many players hoping to go high in the first round, draft day was torture. When the Ravens came up at number ten, Boller held his breath — and heard Terrell Suggs's name called. "That was a bummer," he said. "Then Chicago didn't take me at number twelve. Now I'm thinking it might be Arizona, and I didn't want to go there. They passed on me, too. Now I was thinking it was going to end up being Chicago at number twenty-two because they had another pick and still hadn't taken a quarterback."

Boller was still thinking Bears when he saw a trade flash on the screen while the Patriots were on the clock with the nineteenth pick: "New

England trades its pick to Baltimore. . . ." He was still digesting that news when the phone rang. It was Newsome. "We wanted you and we got you," Newsome told him.

Even though he held out for a few days when camp started — much to Billick's annoyance — Boller won the starting job over Redman, the closest thing the Ravens had to an incumbent. He picked up the offense with remarkable speed. "I remember thinking, 'This kid is learning amazingly fast,'" said Anthony Wright, who was scheduled to go into 2004 as Boller's backup. "He almost never made the same mistake twice."

Boller took his licks during the first eight games, but the Ravens reached the midway point of the season at 5-3. Late in the second quarter of the ninth game, against the Rams in St. Louis, Boller took a shot to his right thigh and crumpled in agony. When the doctors looked at him at halftime, they told him there was no way he could go back and play and they suspected he was going to be out for several weeks. They reported this to Billick.

"The next thing I know, Kyle's there, telling me, 'Coach, I'm okay, I can play, it isn't that bad,'" Billick remembered. "I told him he was hurt and he wasn't playing. He was really angry about it. I finally had to tell him in no uncertain terms I wasn't risking him or the team by putting him back on the field. I told the trainers to keep him in the locker room for a while until he calmed down."

Even though he had to talk sharply to Boller at that moment, Billick was impressed by the toughness his rookie quarterback had showed. His teammates noticed, too. Underneath the baby face, Boller had the heart of a firefighter's son. He wasn't afraid to run into a burning building or play on one leg.

Now, though, anointed as the starter again the day after the season had ended — even though Wright had stepped in and played well — Boller knew all eyes were going to be on him all day, every day.

"We have everything else in place here to be a championship team," he said. "I know it's on me now to get the job done. If I don't, I'll get the blame and that's the way it should be. I'm not a rookie anymore, I'm in my second year. I know I'm gonna have ups and downs, I understand that. I remember talking to John Elway at a party last year and he said the most important thing about being a quarterback is keeping your equilibrium. Because when you play well, people are going to put you on a pedestal you don't belong on. When you play badly, they're going to bury you. You're never that good or that bad. I have to try to remember that."

When Boller arrived in Baltimore, Redman had been wearing number 7 — Elway's number. With Redman gone, Boller had asked to change his uniform from number 8 to number 7. Actually, it didn't really matter much what number Boller wore. Whether it was 8 or 7 or anything else he might pick, whatever uniform he wore was going to have a large glowing target on it. On a team with eight returning Pro Bowlers and two cinch Hall of Famers, no one was going to be scrutinized more during the 2004 season in Baltimore than the firefighter's kid from So-Cali.

The first really significant date on the Ravens' calendar was June 7. That would be the first day the entire team — minus Chris McAlister — would be together. Ray Lewis would be back in town from Florida; Jonathan Ogden would fly in from Las Vegas. And Jamal Lewis would be in from Atlanta and would meet with the media to discuss the drug-dealing allegations made against him.

Even before the start of the first veterans' minicamp, the Ravens had suffered their first crucial injury of the season. On May 24, during the second passing camp, they had learned that Anthony Wright had a torn labrum in his throwing shoulder that would require surgery. Wright had actually suffered the injury during the 2003 season, but the doctors initially thought the muscles were just worn down from the rigors of becoming a starter. When he continued to have soreness, they examined him again and the tear was discovered. The prognosis was a four-month recovery period, meaning Wright would probably miss the first six weeks of the season.

There is no position in football where the backup is as important to the team as at quarterback. Everything a team does begins with the quarterback, and quarterbacks are always vulnerable since they are frequently hit while throwing even on plays when they aren't sacked. No team wants to be put in a position where an injury to its starting quarterback puts the entire season in jeopardy. The Ravens had been fortunate in 2003 that Wright had filled in as capably as he had when Boller was injured. Now they found themselves looking at a preseason roster that had three quarterbacks: a starter with nine games of NFL experience and two rookies — one a sixth-round draft pick (Josh Harris), the other a free-agent rookie (Brian Gaither). That was unacceptable.

Ozzie Newsome and Brian Billick called a meeting on the afternoon of May 24 to tell the coaches and scouts about Wright's injury and to discuss a replacement. "Whoever it is, we're going to pay the minimum [salary], and that's it," Newsome said. "So let's keep that in mind."

Names were thrown out from around the table: Jim Fassel was close to Kerry Collins, the Giants quarterback who had asked for (and received) his release after the team drafted Eli Manning. In fact, Collins had called Fassel the day after the draft, looking for a pep talk. Rumor had it that Collins was getting ready to sign with the Raiders for a lot more than the minimum. There was a good chance he could start there since Rich Gannon was considered a question mark because of age and injuries.

Other names came up: Kordell Stewart, the onetime starter in Pittsburgh who had spent an unproductive season in Chicago. There was a rumor that Gannon might be cut in Oakland if Collins signed and might land back with John Gruden, his old coach, in Tampa Bay. In that case, Brad Johnson, who had played for Billick in Minnesota, might become available. Or what if Gannon ended up on the open market? It was Phil Savage who cut to the chase after everyone had thrown out different names. "The best guy out there is Collins," he said. "The guy we're probably going to end up with is Stewart."

Newsome asked Fassel if he thought there was any chance Collins might come to Baltimore. "Don't really know," Fassel said. "I did tell him when he called me in April that he might be better going someplace on a one-year deal where he'd be a backup and then have the whole off-season next year to pick and choose a place where he could start. I wasn't thinking about us at the time, but now we kind of fit that bill."

The decision was made: Fassel would call Collins to gauge his interest. If Collins wasn't interested, they would wait to see if there were any surprises on June 1, the day teams had to cut veteran players or be responsible for their full (salary) cap number for the season. If Collins wasn't interested and no one else of note became available, they would probably sign Stewart. The question then would be how Stewart, who had been a starter most of his career, would deal with being a backup. "Let's remember one thing,"

Fassel said. "Kyle Boller is this team's future. We don't want to bring anyone in here who is going to cast any kind of shadow that leaves any doubt in anyone's mind who the starter is."

"Amen to that," Billick said.

Fassel made the call to Collins. Much to his surprise, Collins expressed interest in coming to Baltimore. Two days later he signed with the Raiders for more money than the Ravens had been told was on the table. "I think, at the very least, we made Kerry some money," Fassel said.

On the second day of minicamp, Kordell Stewart was signed to back up Boller. Leigh Steinberg, his agent, kept telling Newsome that there were several other teams interested in Stewart and that Newsome needed to up the money ($760,000 for a ten-year veteran) if he expected to sign Stewart. Newsome always knows when an agent is bluffing, because he works the general manager's grapevine as well as anybody. He told Steinberg to call him back when Stewart was ready to sign for the minimum. On June 7 Steinberg called. The next day Stewart was on the field in uniform.

7

Ray and Jamal

BEFORE THE RAVENS TOOK the field for their first day of mini-camp, Jamal Lewis had to face the music. Or, more accurately, he had to face the cameras and notebooks and tape recorders.

Which meant that Kevin Byrne had to put together a list of bullet points. Byrne had been with the Cleveland/Baltimore organization for twenty-four years, and everyone — from Art Modell to Steve Bisciotti to Ozzie Newsome and Brian Billick — always looked to him for guidance with any kind of public relations, whether it was the announcement of a new Ravens charity, the hiring of an assistant coach, the cutting of a veteran player, or a star player dealing with felony charges.

The Ravens had first dealt with the issue of a star player being charged with a serious crime in 2000, when Ray Lewis had been accused of the Atlanta Super Bowl murders. When Lewis made his first appearance in Baltimore for minicamp that year, five days after the charges against him had been dropped and he had pleaded guilty to obstruction of justice, he was immediately made available to the media with the caveat that he would talk once — and once only — about the events of Atlanta and their aftermath.

Jamal Lewis's situation was different because the case was ongoing. Ray Lewis had been able to talk about his case in the past tense and his lawyer, Ed Garland, had been able to begin the press conference by quoting the prosecutor who had dropped the murder charges, saying, "I have concluded Ray Lewis is innocent of these charges and I am going to dismiss these charges."

Jamal Lewis couldn't make that claim. He could say that he was innocent and that he believed he would be exonerated. But he also had to be
careful not to say anything that might anger the prosecution, because there
was no way of knowing at that point what direction the case was going to
go. No trial date had been set. There was speculation that the trial might
come during the season, or it might not come until the season was over.

The specter of another star Raven facing felony charges was disturbing
to the entire organization. Dick Cass had talked to Lewis's lawyers at
length about the charges and their circumstances and had come to the conclusion that Lewis had essentially been suckered by the FBI's female plant
and that the crime he was accused of was a technical one: by using a cell
phone to set up a meeting that eventually led to the sale of drugs, he had
broken federal law. What was concerning to Cass the lawyer was that while
the government might have a case only on that one technical point, conviction on that point meant a ten-year jail sentence, minimum. A conviction
would end Lewis's NFL career.

The other concern was a more general one about the image of the team.
Dating back to the Atlanta incident and the swagger of the team that had
won the Super Bowl a year later, the Ravens had been labeled thugs and
criminals by many in the media. Billick was still viewed by many as arrogant and overbearing, in large part because of that first press conference in
Tampa.

For the past two years, the team had been slowly shedding that image.
Many of the veteran players responsible for that swagger were gone, most
of them leaving in the salary-cap purge of 2002. Ray Lewis had done a remarkable job of resurrecting his public image. He was an absolute icon in
Baltimore, beloved because he was a truly great player, respected as the absolute leader of the Ravens, and revered because he did a great deal of charity work in the area. Even nationally he had been redeemed in many, if not
most, eyes. He was both a corporate and an NFL spokesman, someone
looked up to by most connected with the sport.

But, of course, there were always going to be pockets of people who still
called him a murderer, others who would talk about his plea bargain, even
though there hadn't actually been one. The charges against Jamal Lewis
brought all the old Ray Lewis stories bubbling to the surface. Additionally,
Ray Lewis's close friend defensive back Corey Fuller had been charged

with felony gambling during the off-season for running an illegal card game out of his home in Tallahassee. Shortly before that, Fuller had been involved in a bizarre shooting incident outside his house in which he had been shot at — and returned fire — by two men he believed were trying to rob him. Throw in a year-old assault charge against linebacker Terrell Suggs for his role in a fight outside a bar in Phoenix and a lot of people were having a lot of fun depicting the Ravens as the NFL's answer to the team Burt Reynolds had quarterbacked in *The Longest Yard.*

Publicly, the Ravens dealt with each situation matter-of-factly, saying in each case that when the facts came out, people would understand that Jamal Lewis, Fuller, and Suggs were good men who had not committed any serious crimes. There was, however, a good deal of concern about Lewis, Fuller, and Suggs — or, more specifically, about the team's image — inside the Ravens facility. Cass had talked to the lawyers in each of the three cases and reported back that he believed none of the three players had done anything seriously wrong and might, especially in the cases of Fuller and Suggs, be completely innocent. Even so, everyone agreed that those facts weren't going to make the issue go away. The concern was how much of a distraction all the questions about the cases and the team's image were going to be as the season approached.

That concern was crystallized on the first day of minicamp when an ESPN crew showed up, ostensibly to talk to players about the upcoming season and their hopes that they could build on their successes of 2003. Byrne, who was friends with the director assigned to the shoot, made it clear that the team felt it had dealt with all the Jamal Lewis questions earlier in the day at Lewis's prepractice press conference and that all the players had been told the subject was off-limits except perhaps to express empathy and support for their teammate. Billick never told his players what to say to the media, he just informed them what the team's public position was and let them go from there.

Normally when ESPN shows up, NFL teams roll out the red carpet. ESPN is one of four networks — along with CBS, Fox, and ESPN's corporate sister, ABC — that pays the league hundreds of millions of dollars for broadcast rights. What's more, ESPN televises the draft and devotes hours and hours of coverage to the NFL, which amounts to invaluable free advertising for the league. If ESPN wants something from an NFL team, it almost always gets it. In this case, the director wanted Byrne to bring players in one at a time to the trailer the Ravens used as a media workroom so he could set up cameras and talk to them in a private environment, away from the locker room. Byrne was happy to cooperate.

Not surprisingly, the first player he sent in was Jonathan Ogden. There were several reasons for this, one of them being that Ogden was just as much a lock Hall of Famer as Ray Lewis. He was also very smart, very articulate, and more than able to deal with any question that might be thrown at him. When Ogden came out of the trailer, he went straight to Byrne. "I don't think you should send anyone else in there," he said. "They aren't here to talk about football."

ESPN had pulled the old bait-and-switch: start out with football questions, then shift into questions about "distractions," specifically distractions such as Jamal's impending trial. Ogden knew right away what was going on. He danced around the questions and then went straight to Byrne. At that point Byrne told the ESPN director that the locker room was open to ESPN, as it was to anyone else in the media, but the Ravens wouldn't be providing any more players that day.

When Billick heard what had happened, he decided it was time for him to sit down and talk the whole situation through with the key people in the organization — starting with the new owner and working from there to the players. Billick had never believed in any kind of formal player council, as some teams have, in part because he didn't feel it was needed but also because he knew he ran the risk of offending certain players who might think they belonged on it and weren't asked. Now, though, he called two meetings for the next day: one with Bisciotti, Cass, Newsome, and Byrne, to be held in Billick's office in the afternoon; the second to be held at night at Billick's house, the invitees being Ray Lewis, Jamal Lewis, Jonathan Ogden, Todd Heap, Ed Reed, and Matt Stover. The first five had been Pro Bowlers the year before. Stover had been the team's placekicker since 1991 and was a respected elder even in a sport where placekickers are usually sneered at by "real" players. Billick thought about asking Boller to the meeting for the simple reason that he was the team's starting quarterback and had to be one of the team's leaders in order for it to succeed. He decided against it for the same reason he generally didn't call these meetings in the first place: there were other, more established players on the team who might resent Boller's presence after a total of nine NFL starts.

"Looking back, I probably erred on the side of caution," Billick said. "In all probability, everyone would have understood why I asked Kyle to be there."

Both meetings were essentially the same. Billick wanted to sit down with Bisciotti and Cass to make sure that everyone was on the same page. Billick was still feeling edgy about his relationship with the new owner. Some tension still simmered from their January meetings. Was Bisciotti bothered, he wondered, by all the negative publicity floating around the team? Did he think he had bought a team populated by thugs? Billick was pretty sure he knew the answers, but he wanted to hear them from Bisciotti and wanted to be sure that he was conscious of the fact that the team was fighting an image problem in a league that is nothing if not image-conscious.

"If I thought it was a question of character, I'd be concerned," Bisciotti said. "If I thought we had bad guys, I'd be concerned. But I don't. I tell my kids all the time that I know they're going to make mistakes. I've made mistakes and I still make mistakes. But if you make mistakes, serious mistakes, repeatedly, then it becomes a question of character. Right now I don't think it's a question of character. I think we've got some guys who have made mistakes or in some cases been unlucky. But that's where I think it ends."

They talked about the need to keep the pending court cases — especially Lewis's — from becoming a distraction once training camp began at the end of July. The Ravens would go into the season as a team given a shot to get to the Super Bowl. The favorites would be the defending champion New England Patriots in the AFC and the Philadelphia Eagles in the NFC; but the Indianapolis Colts, Kansas City Chiefs, and the Ravens would be mentioned in the AFC, and the Green Bay Packers, Seattle Seahawks, and Carolina Panthers would be seen as contenders in the NFC. That meant there would be a fair number of national media members in training camp. The same questions put to Jonathan Ogden by ESPN would no doubt be put to players then.

"I think we have to be clear, just like we were with Ray, that this is a non-issue for us as a team right now," Billick said. "We respect the system; we will let the case play out, however it plays out. But right now our focus is on football, and the chances are good that our guys aren't going to want to answer questions about Jamal except if they are about his abilities as a running back. And Jamal has addressed it in his press conference. If you weren't here, the transcript is available. That's where it ends."

Billick's message was similar that night, but he wanted to be sure the players were comfortable with handling it that way. Reed and Heap hadn't been around during the post–Ray Lewis arrest period, so Billick wanted to get a sense from them about how those on the team who hadn't lived through that felt. He also wanted to see if there were any other issues on his players' minds. At one point he turned to Ogden and asked him how he felt about Lewis being such an iconic figure in Baltimore. "You've been in the Pro Bowl for seven years," he said. "You know how much you mean to this team. Yet, when people talk about us, it's always 'Ray, Ray, Ray.' Does that ever bother you?"

Ogden, who would be just as happy never to be recognized by anyone — difficult when you are six-nine and 345 pounds — laughed. "Doesn't bother me at all," he said. "I know what Ray means to the team and how important his leadership is. That's who he is. Who I am is different, and I'm very comfortable with that."

Billick is a big believer in attacking issues directly. He had become even more of a believer in that approach when he had attended the Black Coaches Association convention earlier in the spring. He had been asked there as a speaker but had remained after he finished to hear the speaker who followed him, a female psychologist. "She talked about something she called 'stacking,'" Billick said. "Stacking is something we all do. Something is bothering me at work, so I get really upset because some SOB cuts me off in traffic. Then I get home and one of my kids is doing something mildly annoying and I go off on them because I'm already upset about work and about the guy who cut me off. Then I go back into work the next day in a bad mood to begin with because I'm stacking one thing on top of the other.

"It can get to be a cycle. I wanted to make sure, right at the start, that we didn't start doing any stacking. I thought with everything that was floating around, everything the guys were no doubt hearing, with a new owner, getting ready to move into a new facility — which I knew would be great ultimately but would also involve a lot of work — we could get into stacking very easily. I wanted to try and cut that off before it got started."

Not surprisingly, the cover of the Ravens' 2004 media guide featured a photo of Ray Lewis congratulating Jamal Lewis as he came off the field. Equally unsurprising was the photo itself: Ray, helmet off, eyes full of intensity; Jamal, back to the camera, helmet on, the only thing identifying him his number and the name above the number. Ray and Jamal Lewis were by far the biggest stars on the Ravens. As great as Ogden was, the combination of his personality and the fact that he played a position that really got noticed only if he made a mistake made him almost invisible to the fans.

Not Ray and Jamal — although Jamal would probably have been just as happy living in near anonymity, much the way Jonathan Ogden did.

Ray Lewis loved the spotlight, even if it had caused him a fair amount of discomfort at times. His attitude toward being a public figure and the anointed leader of a pro football team may have been summed up best two years earlier when he had injured a shoulder in Cleveland, an injury that ended up costing him the last eleven games of that season. When he went to have the shoulder examined, he had to fill out the forms people fill out when they go to a doctor's office. Under occupation, he had written, "Entertainer."

He had been that way for as long as he could remember. The eldest of Sunseria Keith's five children, Ray Lewis never knew his father. "Knew of him, but never knew him," he said. He had three younger sisters and a younger brother (who is now a running back at the University of Maryland). By the time he was six, like most kids growing up in Lakeland, Florida, Ray wanted to play football. But his mother, who worked three jobs to support her children, couldn't spare the $15 it would cost to sign her son up for Pop Warner football. In 1985, the year Ray turned ten, the Chicago Bears were the NFL's dominant team, going 15-1 and beating the New England Patriots, 46-10, in the Super Bowl. Lewis remembered watching that team with his grandfather, who loved football and loved watching the NFL. "I was transfixed watching," he said. "I loved Mike Singletary and I loved Walter Payton. I just loved the passion of the whole thing. I knew watching them that I wanted to be that way someday."

Lewis went to his mother to plead with her to let him play football. "I said to her, 'Mama, someday you're never going to work again. I promise. Just let me play.'" Sunseria Keith was torn. She was afraid her eldest son might get hurt playing football. There was also still the money issue. "I went out to practice one day, just practice," Ray said. "I was running around out there, and the coach asked me if I was signed up to play. I said, no, that my mother wasn't sure she wanted to let me or if we could afford it. He went to my mom and offered to pay half the fee. I begged her to do it. I said, 'Mama, just give me once chance to do it. One chance.' She said okay. First play of my first game we ran a reverse on the kickoff and I went eighty yards for a touchdown. After that I was completely hooked."

Lewis is a believer that drive and desire are something one is born with but that they can be nurtured through experience. He always believed he was his family's leader, its father figure, since there was no adult father figure around. "I mourned not having a father," he said. "My mother gave me everything she possibly could. Everything I am today is because of her. But she couldn't be my father. I wanted to do everything I could to give my siblings a father figure. My mother was out of the house so early in the morning by the time I was in junior high school that I would get my sisters and brothers out of the house and off to school. I would walk them to the bus stop, then go to school myself. I always told my friends if they wanted to play football after school, they had to do it at my house because I had to look out for my family. I liked that kind of responsibility. It made me a man at a young age, I think. I always felt I could deal with whatever came my way."

If his mother is the person he looks up to most, the church is the place he cares about the most. For as long as he can remember, Lewis has gone to church every Sunday, often on Saturdays as well, and to Bible study at least once a week. He sang in the choir at Greater Faith Missionary Baptist Church and was a junior deacon. Like many raised in the Southern Baptist Church, he frequently makes references to God's plan for him. When the Ravens hold chapel services on Saturday night, the loudest respondent in the room is always Lewis, who frequently chimes in during the sermon with cries of "Oh my God!" and "Yes, absolutely, so true, so true!"

"I've learned two things in life," he often says. "Put your absolute trust only in God and not in any man. And no man can curse what God has blessed." When he talks about the church and his relationship with God, he frequently quotes the Bible and speaks with at least the same intensity that people hear so often when he is miked during a football game.

Once Lewis began playing football, the only issue was his size. He had great speed, an uncanny ability to find the ball and the ballcarrier, and a will that couldn't be measured. As a high school sophomore, he was five-nine and 160 pounds. By his senior year he had grown to six feet and 190 pounds — bigger, but still small for a college linebacker. "I wanted to go to Florida State in the worst way," he said. "I was a lifelong Seminole fan and I had a cousin who was there playing wide receiver. I went up for my visit and I met with Chuck Amato [now the head coach at N.C. State], who I think was the defensive coordinator at the time. He says to me, 'Ray, we love you, we want you here at Florida State.' I'm thrilled, I'm just jumping up and down inside, thinking I'm going to Florida State. Then he says, 'We'll redshirt you for a year, give you a chance to get in the weight room, get bigger and stronger. Then you'll back up Derrick Brooks for a year and when you're a sophomore, you'll be ready to start. I stood up and said, 'Coach, what makes you think I'm not better than Derrick Brooks right now?'" Lewis had no intention of watching other people play football for two years.

He knew he was ready to play big-time college football right *now*. But he had visited only two other schools: Auburn (his first trip on an airplane) and Florida A&M. In the state playoffs that fall (1992) his team — Kathleen High School — played Fort Myers. Miami coach Dennis Erickson came to the game to scout one of Fort Myers's wide receivers. He came away wanting to know how to get in touch with Ray Lewis. "I think I rushed for a hundred and eighty-seven yards and I made twenty-five tackles," he said. "Two days before the national deadline, Miami offered me their last scholarship. I had never seen the school, but it *was* Miami. I said, 'Let's go.'"

The coaches whispered something about redshirting, but Lewis was hearing none of it. "Once they saw me on the practice field, that was over," he said. "I started the season behind a senior, Robert Bass, but then he got hurt in the opener against Virginia Tech. I came in and made eighteen tackles. The next week we played at Colorado and I had fifteen tackles, a sack, a pick, and started a fight. I still remember Warren Sapp and some of the older guys grabbing me, saying, 'No, Ray, no, Ray, stop, we can't afford to lose you!'"

By his sophomore season, Lewis was co–Big East defensive player of the year along with Sapp, who left school that year to become the first draft pick of the Tampa Bay Buccaneers. He was picked as a preseason All-American prior to his junior year and flew to Las Vegas to be part of a photo shoot for the All-American team. It was there that he met a huge tackle from UCLA named Jonathan Ogden. Each still remembers the other: "All I thought was, 'Little linebacker, big mouth,'" Ogden said. "I mean he never shut up."

"He kept giving me these looks like I was the class clown," Lewis said. "Which I was. Everyone was so tight. I just wanted to have fun."

He had a good deal of fun that season, making every All-America team and being voted the Big East's defensive player of the year. "That's when I knew it was time to go," he said. "I was pretty sure before my junior year, certain afterwards. College football had become too easy for me by that point. I was ready for the NFL and I knew it."

The NFL wasn't quite as sure. Ozzie Newsome still believes some teams were scared off by Lewis's bluntness, his tattoos, and his outspokenness. Lewis is convinced it was all about size. "Same as high school," he said. "People didn't think I was big enough. I'll never forget going to the combine. They stand you up there in front of everyone and measure you. I was six feet zero, zero seven inches — just a tad over six feet even. I can still hear Bill Cowher's voice saying, 'Is he really that small?' I can remember thinking, 'Small? You think I'm small? Have you ever seen me run to the football?'"

There was at least one person who was completely convinced that Lewis wasn't too small to play in the NFL — Ravens' linebackers coach Maxie Baughn. He visited Lewis to work him out and talked to him on several occasions. Every time he saw Lewis, he came back to Newsome and told him, "Everything I give him to do, he asks for more. No matter what you give him, he goes and gets it and then asks for more."

Knowing about the doubts scouts had about his size, Lewis went into draft day simply hoping to get taken in the first round. Even so, as he watched one linebacker after another being taken before him, Lewis was dismayed. Kevin Hardy went to Jacksonville with the second pick; John Mobley went to Denver with the fifteenth; Reggie Brown went to Detroit with the seventeenth. "I knew I was better than they were," he said. He heard ESPN's draft expert Mel Kiper Jr. saying that he had great speed and talent but was simply too small to be a star in the NFL. Finally, late in the first round, the phone rang. It was the Packers. They had the twenty-seventh pick and, as soon as Baltimore got through making its pick at twenty-six, they were planning to take him. Lewis was fine with that. He wondered if Maxie Baughn would be disappointed that the Ravens had decided not to take him. Another phone rang. It was Newsome. He would not, as it turned out, be going to Green Bay.

The first day he showed up at the Ravens' training facility, he went into the weight room and asked what the team record for pull-ups was. "Forty-six," he was told. He promptly took off his shirt, did forty-seven, and put his shirt back on. It didn't take long for the Ravens to figure out they had found a special player. Lewis was so fast and had such a nose for the football and a drive to make every tackle that he quickly became a star. By his second year he was chosen as the AFC's best linebacker. He became a perennial Pro Bowler. By the end of the 1999 season, he was clearly one of the elite players in the game.

All of which led him to Atlanta.

The Super Bowl has become an annual sports convention. People flock to the city where the game is being played to party, to see and be seen, to hawk products, to get their picture in the paper and their faces on TV. Lewis went to have a good time with some friends and then was planning to fly to Hawaii for the Pro Bowl. "My mother begged me not to go," he said. "She knew something. She pleaded with me to skip it. Three times she said to me, 'Junior, don't go there.' I told her I had made commitments — to my friends, to make appearances. I thought I had the whole thing under control. My kids were there; my girl was there. We were going to Hawaii the day after the game. But that last night my friends all wanted to go out. I made a mistake. I went outside the structure I had set up for myself while I was there."

He was out with those friends after the game on Sunday night, hanging out at a club in the chic Buckhead district. Outside the bar, there was a fight. It escalated, and before it was over, two men were lying in the street with fatal knife wounds. Lewis later testified that as the fight escalated he got into the limousine he had rented for the weekend and began urging his friends to get into the limo. In the early hours of the morning, when police came to question Lewis, he was, by his own admission, less than forthcoming. Before the day was over he was in jail, charged with a double murder.

He was there for fifteen long days. "It was awful," he said. "It was awful because jail is awful. But it was also awful because it had nothing to do with me. This was not a place where I belonged. It was painful."

Lewis can still remember the lowest moment of his time in jail, about five days after he had been there. Before he went to bed each night, he did sit-ups and push-ups to get himself to a point of exhaustion where he could sleep. That night, though, it didn't work. "I lay there on the bed and I cried," he said. "I just cried and cried. I sat up and I looked at the tears in my hands and I said, 'Okay, Lord, now I understand. You're up to something. You've got a plan. I'm not going to worry anymore, I'm not going to cry anymore. I'm going to wait and see what your plan for me is going to be.' From that moment on, I was okay. I really was okay."

When he got out of jail, Lewis had to deal with the fact that he had now become the symbol of the thug football player — actually, beyond thug because now there were people who were saying he was a murderer. "People who never met me were saying and writing this was part of a pattern," he said. "I said, really, what pattern? When have I ever been in trouble? Never. Not once. But they knew. They knew Ray Lewis. Of course, there were others [most of them in Baltimore] who loved me and knew I was innocent. They didn't know me, either, but they did have faith in me. That's the part of it I'll never forget. I'll never forget the way Art Modell and Ozzie Newsome and Brian Billick and my teammates stood behind me then."

When the prosecutor dropped the charges in June and Lewis admitted on the stand that he had lied to police when first approached, he was given a year of probation on the obstruction-of-justice charge. At the press conference in Baltimore a few days later, Ed Garland was adamant when he explained that there was no plea bargain and that the charges had been dropped because the prosecution had reached the conclusion that Lewis was innocent. Garland clearly went too far when he likened the obstruction charge to being "no worse than a speeding ticket." That comment understandably angered a lot of people, since the police had been seeking answers to questions about a double murder when they spoke to Lewis that morning.

Almost exactly one year after the Atlanta incident, Lewis stood on a podium in Tampa, holding the Super Bowl MVP trophy. It was then, he says, that he knew God's plan. "He wanted me to see everything," he said. "He wanted me to see that hands and feet that were once shackled could carry me to that podium and to that trophy and to sharing the feeling of winning the Super Bowl. I know that's what it was all about now."

Perhaps even more remarkable than coming back to win the Super Bowl MVP was the respect Lewis now engendered from people not just on the field but off. At twenty-nine, he was generally considered the best defensive player in the NFL. He talked proudly about his six children — three he'd had with his longtime college girlfriend, three who had come from later relationships — and had all of them living close to him in Baltimore. His mother was also in Baltimore and he had fulfilled his promise to her in the spring when he graduated from the University of Maryland with a degree in business administration. Lewis's arrival for minicamp was, in many ways, the official signal that the football season was under way. Four and a half years after he had cried in his prison cell, Ray Lewis was an iconic figure in the city of Baltimore and, at the very least, a respected one around the country.

And what about those people who would always see him as a murderer who had gone free because he was a rich and famous football player? "They can't hurt me," he said. "They can only hurt themselves."

Jamal Lewis hadn't spent any time in jail . . . yet. The specter of the trial and how that might affect his and the Ravens' season was something he knew he was going to have to deal with for a while.

"What pisses me off is, if I don't rush for two thousand yards last year, they probably don't even bother charging me," he said. "I think the prosecutor saw my name in a file and said, 'Wait a minute, we can't let this go, this is a famous guy.'"

Lewis was a very small part of the FBI sting. But once the charges had been filed, his role became far more important than that of anyone else. He understood how that worked. Bumps in the road weren't anything new to Lewis. Unlike Ray Lewis, who had never been in trouble before Atlanta and never had a serious injury until his seventh year in the NFL, Jamal Lewis had dealt with both injuries and controversy even before he arrived in Baltimore.

He grew up in Atlanta, where his father worked as a railroad engineer and his mother as a corrections officer. Although they lived in the inner city, the Lewises were a middle-class family. "We lived in a nice house and my parents both made pretty good money," he said. "That wasn't true of some of my friends. I was like a lot of kids. I had a choice: trouble or sports. Most of the time I chose sports."

He first played football when he was eight and was told to play center. Midway through that season he announced to his mother that he was retiring from the game. "Being a lineman wasn't for me."

He played on and off until high school, when he began to grow into his body. By his sophomore year he was five foot ten and 195 pounds and a battering-ram running back. His father, John Lewis, was retired by then, thanks to a disability settlement resulting from an accident, and he was at every practice and every game Jamal played in. "Between my father being at practice all the time, my mom being in corrections, and my coach [Michael Simms] watching me all the time, I couldn't have gotten into trouble if I had tried," he said. "I had to get pretty good grades — or else. The only problem I had was the SAT. I must have taken it six times before I passed."

Once he had the minimum score on the SAT that he needed, every football school in the country wanted him. Like so many kids — including Ray Lewis — he thought he wanted to go to Florida State. "Everyone wanted to go to Florida State back then," he said. "But they wanted me to play fullback because they like those little running backs. I didn't want to be a blocker. So I started looking other places."

Georgia might have been a factor, but the school wasn't that interested in kids from the inner city with borderline SATs. "They came in late after everyone else had recruited me for a while," Lewis said. "By then it was too late."

He thought he wanted to go to Nebraska even though it was ten degrees when he got off the plane for his visit. He was impressed by Tom Osborne, and Lawrence Phillips — the man who made Ozzie Newsome's career by not becoming a Raven — was his hero and role model as a running back. For a while he thought he would go there. "Coach Osborne was calling me all the time, saying things like 'I'm just leaving Hawaii, I signed two big offensive linemen to block for you.' I really liked him. My mom, though, she liked Michigan — great school and all. But then I went to Tennessee. Great program, great stadium. Peyton [Manning] was telling me he was gonna come back and be there as a senior. In the end, it was Tennessee — three hours away — or Nebraska — fourteen hours away. I went with the three hours."

His biggest problem as a Tennessee freshman was his first pregame meal. "I'd never seen so much food in my life," he said with a laugh. "I didn't think I was going to play, so I sat there and ate steak, spaghetti, chicken — everything. Second half, we're killing them and Coach turns around and says, 'Jamal, you're in.' I'm like, 'Me? Look how fat I am right now.' But I got through it. Next week we played UCLA. I didn't eat very much at the pregame meal that day. Or anytime after that."

By the time Tennessee went to Georgia midway through the season, Lewis was the starter. He had a huge day at Georgia, only to come home and find that a story had broken in the Atlanta papers about a shoplifting incident he had been involved in during his senior year in high school. "It wasn't like I went in and started stashing things in my clothes and walked out," he said. "I knew the girl at the register and she gave me a bunch of stuff half price. It was dumb. Week after the Georgia game, it becomes a story."

Lewis never went to court. He was fined and did some community service. A year later he really broke out as a star the first four weeks of the season as the heart of an offense rebuilt after Manning's graduation. But in the fifth week of the season, he tore up his knee. Surgery. End of season. He ended up watching on the sidelines while his teammates won the national championship. "That was tough," he said. "I was happy we won, but not playing hurt. I just said to myself, 'I'm gonna rehab and come back better than ever.'"

His junior year was also up and down. He ended up splitting time with Travis Henry, at least in part — he believes — because he publicly criticized the play calling after a loss to Florida. There were injuries (a high ankle sprain) and general unhappiness with the coaching staff. He decided to turn pro, even though he didn't have any scintillating numbers to overwhelm NFL scouts with. Until the scouts came to watch him run. He was now five-eleven, 235 pounds, and he ran a 4.38 40. That meant more to the scouts than 2,000 yards rushing would have. The Ravens took him with the fifth pick of the draft. It was while he was waiting to sign and go to training camp that he met Michelle Smith and made the phone call that would lead him to grief four years later.

He had an excellent rookie year — complete with a Super Bowl ring — but in keeping with the pattern of his life, that was followed by trouble: first another knee injury in training camp, then a positive drug test (marijuana) that led to a four-game suspension. He came back to play well in 2002 and then had the monster year in 2003 that he was convinced led to the prosecutors' deciding to charge him in the drug sting.

"Some coincidence, huh?" he said. "I rush for two thousand yards and all of a sudden something that happened four years ago is a big deal. They say everything's a learning experience. I'm twenty-five years old. I've already learned a lot."

8

The Love Boat

AS MUCH AS FOOTBALL PLAYERS TALK about dreading training camp and the torture of two-a-days in the hot sun, the modern-day NFL camp is actually a mere shadow of what it once was. Back in those legendary days, training camps were longer and tougher and led to the kind of hijinks that are inevitable when testosterone-driven young men are cooped up in a monastic existence for six weeks. Back then, players often had to lose twenty, thirty, or forty pounds to get into shape for the start of the season. Coaches sometimes withheld water on hot days to toughen up the players.

Nowadays, most players arrive in camp physically ready to play and to deal with two-a-days. They have learned a lot of the plays during the mini-camps. Players are closely monitored on hot days and given frequent water breaks. Most training camps start at the end of July, rather than in early July, and last no more than four weeks. The exhibition season — or in the euphemistic world of the NFL, "preseason" — is four games long, as opposed to twenty-five years ago, when all teams played six exhibition games and the lucky twosome selected for the Hall of Fame Game played *seven* meaningless games.

There may be no training camp in football that is easier on the players than the one Brian Billick runs. Around the NFL, Camp Billick is jokingly referred to as "the Love Boat" or "Club Med." Which is exactly what Billick wants it to be. He subscribes to the theory that players react best to a coach who treats them like men and asks them to behave like men in return. He is also a believer that a team that doesn't beat itself up in July and August is likely to have more left in the tank in December and January, when the games mean the most and many teams are running on fumes.

No one appreciates the Billick approach more than the Ravens' veterans who vividly remember the three training camps run by Ted Marchibroda. Marchibroda was an old-school coach, one who believed in full pads twice a day, every day, and all-out hitting to separate the men from the boys. "It was brutal," Ray Lewis, probably the best-conditioned of the Ravens, remembered. "We wore ourselves out. Check our record in close games those three years. We'd get to the fourth quarter and be worn out because we'd left so much on the practice field. Check our record under Billick in the fourth quarter and in December and January. That tells you all you need to know."

Under Marchibroda, the Ravens went 1-3, 2-2, and 1-3 in their final four games of each season. Under Billick, they were a combined 13-7, and 5-2 in postseason, meaning they were 18-9 overall in late-season and post-season games. Perhaps coincidence. Neither Billick nor the players think so. "Whatever you may think of Brian Billick, and I know a lot of people have a lot of different opinions about him, the man knows what he's doing," said Corey Fuller, the eleventh-year defensive back who has played on Billick-coached teams in both Minnesota and Baltimore. "Players want to play for Billick. They know he won't kill them, they know he'll be fair, and they know he's as well organized as anyone. You can't really ask for anything more."

Training camp 2004 began on Thursday, July 29, a predictably hot and breezy day in Westminster, Maryland. The Ravens had trained in Westminster since their first season, on the campus of what had once been Western Maryland College, now renamed McDaniel College. The small, tree-lined campus was almost perfect for an NFL team. There were two football fields: one down the hill from the field house, in the 10,000-seat stadium where McDaniel played its Division 3 games during the fall, and a second one located right outside the locker rooms, where makeshift stands were set up on the shady side of the field so that fans could watch. On most days, the team would practice in the morning on the stadium field, which had the same kind of artificial turf on it that the Ravens played on in M&T Bank Stadium. In the afternoon, mostly to save the players' legs, they practiced on the upper field, which had a natural grass surface.

The team had just re-upped with McDaniel for six years. There had been some pressure to move from Michael Busch, the speaker of the Maryland House of Delegates, who was pushing Frostburg State (which was in his district), and from John Moag, the man who had helped broker the sale of the team. He wanted the Ravens to consider his alma mater, Washington College, which was on the Eastern Shore. Bob Eller, the team's operations director, was a Towson graduate, so that school got a look, too. In the end, McDaniel had everything the team needed logistically and aesthetically, so they returned there.

Training camp got off to a mixed beginning as far as Billick was concerned. The good news was that he and Bisciotti had agreed on a new contract extension that guaranteed Billick would coach the Ravens through the 2007 season and raised his pay to about $4.5 million a year, making him one of the highest-paid coaches in the NFL. What made the new deal important to both men was that it was evidence that their rocky start was nothing more than that. Both men recognized that their similarities might cause them to clash at times. But they also both recognized that they liked and respected each other and wanted to work together.

"I told Brian and Ozzie the same thing," Bisciotti said. "You guys need to shape *me* as an owner. I'm new at this, you're not. They know I'll listen to them. I think they also understand that I'd like them to listen to me." What Bisciotti liked about the contract was that it sent a clear sign to Billick that he meant what he had said about wanting him around for the long haul. "Now when I yell at you about something, you have no reason to think I'm thinking of getting rid of you," he told Billick. Billick understood. The contract was about more than money to him — it was about feeling secure with the new boss.

The new contract was good. Getting stopped for speeding by a cop on Route 140 just outside Westminster en route to camp was not. During training camp, the local police line Route 140 — the road that most people take from Baltimore to Westminster — to pick up those speeding to and from the Ravens' camp. The players are warned on the first day of camp to beware. Billick had been stopped for speeding a few times during his years in Baltimore but usually got off when the cop realized who he was. Not this time. "The guy wasn't wrong," he said. "I was going too fast."

The ticket was annoying. Far worse was the news Billick had gotten a couple of days earlier that the team had suffered its first key loss before a snap was taken in camp. It wasn't an injury, it was an illness. The Ravens had signed Dale Carter just prior to minicamp to be their nickel (third cornerback). Carter was thirty-four and had been a Pro Bowler four times. He also had been suspended twice by the league for violating its substance-abuse policy — which meant he had to have tested positive for drugs at least three times, since a player isn't suspended until the second positive test. At his best, Carter had been a shutdown cornerback, someone other teams rarely tested. At his worst, he had a drug problem. The Ravens didn't expect Carter to be what he had been at his peak, but they didn't need him to be since he would be expected to play only between fifteen and twenty-five snaps a game and come in only in passing situations. They had signed him to an incentive-laden contract that allowed them to release him with very little financial risk at the first sign of trouble or if he didn't have the skills necessary to succeed anymore in the NFL.

Minicamp had been encouraging. It was clear that Carter could still play. He was saying all the right things about being given another chance and how grateful he was to have it. But Carter's pre–training camp physical had turned up a blood clot in his lungs. The doctors recommended that he not play football, it was just too risky. The day before camp began, the Ravens announced that Carter wouldn't be with the team. Even though they didn't have to pay Carter anything, the Ravens gave him an injury settlement, paying a small portion of what he would have earned had he stayed on the team all season. "He came to us in good faith and tried hard," Newsome said. "It wasn't as if he did anything wrong. He just caught a bad break."

Carter's bad break meant the Ravens didn't have anyone in camp who filled the bill as a third cornerback behind starters Chris McAlister and Gary Baxter. Corey Fuller had been an effective cornerback for most of his career, but at thirty-three, everyone — including Fuller — agreed he was better off playing safety. Chad Williams had become a solid dime back (number three safety) but might be overmatched at times moving up to the third spot at corner. The same would be true for Raymond Walls, another young defensive back who was far better suited to playing safety.

Even without Carter, the Ravens arrived in camp with high hopes. They would be headquartered for four weeks at the Best Western Westminster, which sits right off Route 140, about half a mile down a back road from the

McDaniel campus and the practice fields. For the Ravens this was an ideal setup. The team rented the entire hotel, all 160 rooms, throughout camp. They used the rooms as offices for the coaches and front office people, as workrooms and film rooms, and as rooms for the players. The sign out front read simply, NO VACANCIES UNTIL AUGUST 24TH. Security patrolled to keep any unauthorized vehicles out of the parking lot, and anyone without ID either as a player, Ravens staff, or media could not enter the hotel. The hotel had a small convention center, complete with meeting rooms, a banquet room that served as the team's cafeteria, and a hallway filled with video games that the players frequented. The drive from the hotel to the field-house parking lot took anywhere from one to three minutes, depending on whether you made the light at the bottom of the hill.

The veteran players wouldn't spend all that much time there. After the first four nights of camp, the veterans were not required to spend nights at the hotel. Most of them lived no more than forty-five minutes from Westminster, so once the evening meetings were over, they jumped in their cars and drove home. Only the rookies and players who had not spent a full season on the active roster had to stay in the hotel overnight once those first few days were out of the way. There was no bed check for those who did stay. Lights-out was eleven o'clock, and Billick expected it to be adhered to without having to check rooms. The Ravens did not eat the hotel's food. The Classic Catering People, the same caterer that provided the team's food at the Owings Mills facility, supplied the food for camp.

Billick's first-night speech to his players wasn't very different from the one he had given on the first morning of minicamp. This was a team that had a chance to go to the Super Bowl. It had the talent and the experience to play with anyone in the league. The only starter not back was wide receiver Marcus Robinson, and the team believed that he could easily be replaced by the combination of veteran Kevin Johnson and the drafted rookies, Devard Darling and Clarence Moore. Knowing that the players were aware of his new contract, Billick used it to make a point:

"The only person in this room who has exactly what he wants right now is me," he said. "I've got the job I want and the contract I want. As much as I respect Ozzie, there's no amount of money in the world you could pay me to have his job and deal with all of your agents all the time. You rookies, you want to make this team, draw an NFL salary. Special teams guys and backups, you want a chance to start. Starters, you want to get to the Pro Bowl level, get that big contract that sets you up forever. Pro Bowlers, you want to be All-Pro, take that next step toward the Hall of Fame. Hall of Famers, you want one more big contract. Position coaches, you want to be coordinators. Coordinators, you want to be a head coach. So, all of you have something to play for, something to reach for, something to work for. It starts tomorrow."

The players liked Billick's direct approach. He would not have stood in front of the 2002 team and talked about the Super Bowl. He was very straight with them about expectations, trying not to set the bar too high or too low. He honestly believed this team had a chance to reach the top. Everyone else in the room believed it, too.

Even before the first horn had blown to start the first workout of training camp, it was apparent that the players and coaches weren't the only ones who thought the Ravens would be playing deep into the postseason. Long before the scheduled 8:45 A.M. start of the first practice, cars were snaking down Route 140 and the back roads leading into Westminster, many of them adorned with purple Ravens flags or Ravens bumper stickers. Spectators poured into the parking lots of McDaniel and surrounded the lower practice field, some sitting in the bleachers right below the giant RAVENSTOWN sign. Others ringed the field, sitting on the grassy hills below the orange-brick dorm buildings and on the hillside at the end of the field where the players entered. Just below the parking lots were the school's tennis courts, which had been converted into the "Ravens Experience," complete with games and contests and concessions and souvenirs. Corporate signs could be seen all around the complex. There was no charge to watch practice or to park. But training camp, like everything else associated with the NFL, was an opportunity to make a few extra dollars. The Ravens could have made more if they wanted to — some teams charged people to park their cars — but they opted to make spending any money voluntary.

Every training-camp practice was open to the public. Some teams open parts of practice or close certain practices entirely. The Washington Redskins, under returning Hall of Fame coach Joe Gibbs, would actually hold several practices at undisclosed locations.

There were almost five thousand people on hand for the Ravens' opening practice. They cheered the players as they came onto the field. They cheered any time Jamal Lewis broke through the line carrying the ball or when Ray Lewis chased someone down or when Kyle Boller completed a long pass. The conditions on the first morning were perfect — warm but not humid, with enough breeze to keep everybody comfortable. Billick was pleased with what he saw until the last fifteen minutes. Perhaps getting a little bit ahead of themselves, the players got sloppy those last few minutes: a missed tackle, a poor throw, a fumble after a catch. Billick wasn't happy with what he saw but he also knew the carelessness gave him an opportunity to make a point. When the team gathered at midfield after the two-hour-and-fifteen-minute workout, Billick let the players have it.

"Fifteen minutes ago I was ready to kiss your ass," he said. "Then you started dropping balls and making mental errors at the end. That's no good. I can get any slapdick sitting on this hill to come out here and drop passes, fumble the ball, and miss cuts. You can't afford to play well for an entire game or practice and then piss down your leg at the end. Vince Lombardi once said that he didn't develop character, he just takes eighty guys and finds the fifty-three with the most character. Don't think you can't get cut, you can. I know a lot about getting cut, I went through it twice myself. Okay? So let's come out here this afternoon and be sharp the *whole* practice."

One message delivered, he had another one of an entirely different nature. "I want you guys to take a few minutes signing autographs coming out of here," he said. "You've got staff waiting down there with Sharpies you can use. Just keep moving along the rope, but give these people some time. They're the ones who pay your salary, they're the ones who pay my salary." He paused. "Well, there probably aren't enough of them here today to pay *all* of my salary."

They all got a laugh out of that line. Then they headed for the locker room. To get there, they had to walk up a hill that had been roped on each side, much the way a golf course is roped so that players can walk from green to tee. On both sides, fans pressed against the ropes, pleading for autographs. Following Billick's instructions, most of the players moved slowly along the rope, signing and walking, signing and walking. Billick and his assistants also signed as they made their way up the hill. Once they reached the top of the hill, most sprinted across the upper practice field so they could grab a shower, get back to the hotel for lunch, and then take a nap before the afternoon meetings began.

Training camp is all about ritual. A typical Ravens day began about seven o'clock with breakfast, followed by morning meetings, getting taped, and morning practice. Lunch, a rest period, afternoon meetings, and afternoon practice followed. Then came dinner and evening meetings. Two days a week, afternoon practice was special teams only, meaning some of the regulars got a breather. The morning meetings were usually devoted to going over the plays that would be used in practice that day. The afternoon meeting was a review of morning practice and a brief primer on the afternoon. The evening meetings were another review.

While the players were resting, the coaches were usually meeting, going over tape, discussing player performance, deciding which players were surprising them, which were disappointing. There were eighty-five players in camp on the first day, down from the eighty-seven who had been on the roster at the end of minicamp. Carter's illness had cut the roster to eighty-six, and Mike Solwold had been cut a couple of hours prior to the first meeting.

Solwold was an example of why life in the NFL is a lot harder than it appears. He was a long snapper who had come into the league out of Wisconsin as an undrafted free agent in 2001. In three seasons he had been waived or cut a total of six times by four teams. He had been activated by the Ravens late in the 2003 season as insurance because Joe Maese, their regular long snapper, had chronic back problems. Now Maese was healthy, the Ravens had a rookie long snapper named Don Muhlbach in camp, and Solwold's leg injury, suffered in minicamp, had healed. If he had still been injured, the Ravens would have had to give Solwold an injury settlement in order to cut him. Since he had the misfortune to be completely healthy, they owed him nothing.

Solwold was twenty-six, bright and engaging, a college graduate who had spent time during the off-season working as an intern at the Smithsonian Institution's National Museum of American History. He understood how the NFL worked and took the news in stride even though he admitted to being a little surprised to make the drive to Westminster and *then* get cut. "I thought maybe I slept on the wrong side of the bed," he said. When Billick gave him the "we might bring you back" portion of his exit speech, Solwold shook his head emphatically. "No way, Coach," he said. "I'm not coming back here unless you let me play quarterback."

It was one of the few times in his coaching career Billick could remember laughing while cutting a player.

It was en route to dinner after the first day's afternoon practice that Corey Fuller had an idea. He had spent the off-season preparing to be a safety. Now, with Dale Carter gone, the Ravens were telling him to think of himself as a cornerback again. Fuller knew that wouldn't be the best thing for him or for the team. He had spent a good portion of the day thinking about who might be available to come in and be the Ravens' third cornerback. Just before he walked in the doorway that led to the cafeteria, he had a brainstorm.

Deion.

"I knew he was in shape, because he played basketball all the time," Fuller said. "I knew he didn't have the game completely out of his system. And I knew — I mean, *knew* — that he could come back and be a nickel corner. I mean, come on, we're not talking about your average player here, we're talking about Deion Sanders."

Deion Sanders — Prime Time to anyone who had ever paid attention to football — was not by any stretch of the imagination your average player. During his twelve seasons in the NFL, he had redefined the cornerback position, playing it so well and so aggressively that offensive coordinators drew up game plans that, for all intents and purposes, removed Sanders's half of the field from consideration. Throwing in his direction wasn't just pointless, it was foolish.

Sanders had made himself into one of the best-known personalities in sports not just by being perhaps the best cornerback ever but by becoming a solid Major League baseball player and a luminous, if at times controversial, personality. He had been dubbed "Prime Time" coming out of Florida State because of his penchant for making spectacular plays at key moments — or in prime time — and had ridden his talent and that persona to millions on and off the field. He had retired from football just prior to the start of the 2001 season after deciding he didn't want to play for newly hired Washington Redskins coach Marty Schottenheimer. He had worked out a deal with Redskins owner Dan Snyder and then played one more year of baseball before retiring in 2002.

He had been hired to do CBS's pregame show and had been very good on the air. He was smart, he was funny, he had presence, he knew the game, and, perhaps most important, he knew the players. "I could call just about anyone in the game," he said. "If someone speculated on how the Ravens' defense might attack the Steelers' offense, I could say, 'I talked to Ray Lewis last night, and here's *exactly* what they're planning to do.'"

Sanders had decided not to return to CBS in 2004 after the network had turned down his request to double his salary from $1 million to $2 million. Most people saw that decision as another example of an athlete (or ex-athlete) trying to bleed every dollar he could out of an employer. It wasn't quite that simple. Sanders had never been comfortable working with Boomer Esiason, the ex-quarterback on the CBS pregame set. The two men argued frequently on the air. Most people thought the arguments were schtick. Sanders said they weren't.

"Boomer and I just disagreed on a lot of things," he said. "It wasn't an act and it wasn't fun. To me, retirement is supposed to be something you enjoy. I wasn't really enjoying myself that much. I felt like if I was going to go back and do that again, I wanted to be paid the way the top guys in those jobs are being paid. CBS made a business decision not to pay that much. Their show is number two [behind Fox] and they didn't think it was worth that much money when the show was number two. I understood. Business is business. I'm still cool with those guys, I like almost all of them. But I decided to take a break, go home for a while, and spend time with my family."

Sanders was home on his 112-acre ranch in Prosper, Texas (a Dallas suburb), when his cell phone rang. It was Fuller, who had pulled out his cell phone and called Sanders almost as soon as the idea crossed his mind. Fuller had chosen to attend Florida State because Sanders had played there. The two had become close friends, and Sanders referred to Fuller and Ray Lewis — whom he had met years earlier because they had the same agent — as his "little brothers." Now Sanders answered the phone and heard one of his little brothers jabbering on about him coming back to play football because the Ravens needed a cornerback and he could still play cornerback.

"You're crazy," Sanders told Fuller. "I'm done. I'm coaching my son and spending time with my kids. I'm not playing football."

He hung up the phone. His wife, Pilar, asked him what that had been about. "It was Corey with some wild idea about me going back to play," he said.

"You tell Corey to leave you alone," Pilar Sanders said. "You're staying right here."

"I know," Sanders answered. "I know."

A few hours later the phone rang again. This time it was both Fuller and Lewis. Fuller had talked to Lewis during dinner, and once the evening meetings were over, they called back to double-team him.

"You know you can do it," Lewis said. "You'll be with us. We can have a great team. We can go to the Super Bowl. Come on, man, we need you."

In the background, Lewis and Fuller could hear Pilar Sanders yelling, "Leave my man alone!"

She was too late. The seed had been planted.

"Let me think about it," Sanders said finally.

The next day Fuller and Lewis approached Billick. They had an idea, they told him. Billick was accustomed to Lewis and Fuller making suggestions, something he accepted because Lewis was the team's leader and Fuller was someone he had known for many years. They had never had an idea quite like this one before. "What makes you think he'd do it?" he asked. They told him about their conversation with Sanders. Billick was intrigued. "I'll talk to Ozzie," he told them.

Most nights in camp, Newsome would have dinner in the players' dining room along with his scouts at the one table in the room marked RESERVED. The rest of the tables were used by players, while coaches and staff usually ate in the adjoining room. The setup had a purpose, giving the players some room to breathe away from the coaches at the end of the day. Most nights one or more of the rookies would be required to stand on a chair, announce his name, his college, and how much his signing bonus was for — the range in 2004 went from second-round pick Dwan Edwards at $1 million down to most of the undrafted free agents at zero — and then sing a song. Unlike the old days, when rookies were required to sing their college fight songs, they could sing any song they wanted to, knowing that if their rendition was not done with gusto, they would be booed heartily. If they did well, the veterans were apt to join in, or at least clap rhythmically as the performance reached a crescendo.

Billick ate in the players' dining room only if his family was in town or if there were corporate sponsors around whom Dennis Mannion, the team's senior vice president of business ventures, had asked him to entertain. One had to be a major sponsor to eat a training-camp meal with Billick. Most days Billick's lunch and dinner routines were identical: at lunch he would make himself a multi-fruit-flavored smoothie and then take it back to the room that served as his office. "This way I feel like I'm watching what I eat," he said. "Then at dinner, I go crazy." Normally he took dinner back to his office, too. On this night, though, after the second day of two-a-days, he walked his tray into the players' eating area and sat down with Newsome.

"Ray and Corey have come up with an idea," he said. Newsome smiled, figuring something wild was coming. He wasn't wrong.

"They think Deion might be willing to come and play for us."

Newsome's eyebrows went up. Sanders is one of those athletes who can be identified by his first name only. Even when people use his nickname, they frequently call him "Prime" and everyone knows who they are talking about.

"Are they serious?" he asked. "More important, is *he* serious?"

Billick shrugged. "Don't know. They say he is."

The two men decided on a two-pronged strategy: Billick would call Sanders and feel him out. Newsome would call Eugene Parker, Deion's longtime agent. After that, they would have a better idea of whether this was a Lewis/Fuller fantasy.

"You couldn't ignore it because of the man's talent," Newsome said later. "We are talking about a lock Hall of Famer. What kind of player he would be three years after he last played was hard to know. But my guess was he wouldn't put himself out there if he didn't honestly think he could still do the job. It was definitely worth investigating."

That night Lewis and Fuller gave Sanders's phone number to Billick, who called him. Billick's notion was that if this was going to happen, it needed to happen fast. He wanted to get Sanders into camp, give him a physical, sign him to a contract, and find out what he could do. "The sooner you get here, the better," he told Sanders.

Sanders didn't want to go quite that fast. "I wanted to find out what kind of shape I was in before I actually showed at camp," he said. "I knew the minute I got there it was going to be a media circus and I didn't want to just walk into that, cold. At that moment, my foot was actually in a boot because I'd rolled my ankle badly playing in my basketball league a few days earlier. There was no point in my coming in at that point or in them making any financial commitment. I told Brian to give me some time."

Billick didn't feel as if he had that much time. The first exhibition game was in twelve days, and opening day in Cleveland was six weeks off. If he was going to count on a thirty-seven-year-old retired cornerback, he wanted to know as soon as possible what the man could do. He reported his conversation to Newsome, who called Parker. Parker told him he thought Sanders wanted to do it but had to find out what kind of shape he was in first. They agreed to talk again after Sanders had a chance to test himself once his ankle was healed.

While the Ravens moved on with camp, Sanders began working out on his own. Parker found three wide receivers who had been cut early in training camps and sent them down to Prosper to work with him. Sanders was soon convinced he could still cover people. Then, one afternoon in the blazing heat, he did two sprint sets. The first was 10x100 yards with ten seconds' rest in between. After that he did 10x40, all-out, same rest. He felt great. "That was when I decided, 'I can do this.'"

He called Parker and told him to try to make a deal with the Ravens. By that time, word had spread among the players that Deion might be joining the team and, naturally, the story had leaked. Jamison Hensley broke it in the *Baltimore Sun* on the Sunday before the opening exhibition game. "Whether it happens or not," he said, "if they're even talking to Deion Sanders, it's a story."

While the Deion buzz spread, the rituals of camp continued. The first circled date on the calendar was Friday, August 6, the eighth day of camp. That was when the team would hold its annual scrimmage. For the veterans, the scrimmage was something to get through. They would play a series or two, then stand on the sideline and watch the younger players try to kill one another in order to get the attention of the coaches. The attitude of most of the vets was summed up best when offensive line coach Jim Colletto announced during a meeting with his players on the morning of the scrimmage that the starters would play two series that night. "*Two* series?" Jonathan Ogden said, sounding aghast. "That's a lot of work, isn't it?"

It surprised absolutely no one that Ogden wouldn't want to be on the field for a single play more than was absolutely necessary. He had long ago figured out exactly how much work he needed to do and he had no desire to do anything more than *exactly* that. "I understand that there are times when we have to do things I don't think I need to be doing," he said. "But the other guys need it. So I don't say anything about it."

That wasn't exactly true. If not saying anything meant he didn't argue or debate, that was accurate. But if not saying anything included sighs or the occasional groan or rolling of the eyes, then it could be argued that Ogden always made his position clear. Of course, nobody minded much. That was just J.O. being J.O. "The guy's a freak of nature," starting center Mike Flynn said. "He just doesn't need to do all the things the rest of us need to do in order to be great."

Ogden had been charged with giving up one sack in 2003, and he was still upset about it. "Kyle went the wrong way," he said. "He was supposed to go left and he went right. I blocked the guy right and ran him right into Kyle — who wasn't supposed to be there."

He had forgiven Boller for the mistake. Sort of.

There was no doubting Ogden's greatness. He was the prototypical left tackle, the position considered by many in the NFL to be second only to quarterback in terms of importance because it is the left tackle who protects every right-handed quarterback's blind side. Ogden was six foot nine and weighed 345 pounds. And yet he didn't look that big. His body was almost sleek. He had speed and quickness belying his size, perfect technique, and a streak of competitiveness that was actually a lot different than the laid-back persona he presented in public.

"I think the thing that drives me the most is fear of failure," he said. "I've never given much thought to the notion that I might be in the Hall of Fame someday or that people say I'm one of the great left tackles. I just don't want to get beaten, I don't want a guy to get by me, and I don't want to walk away from any game feeling I was outplayed."

There had not been many times in Ogden's life when he had been outplayed at anything. He had grown up in Washington, D.C., the eldest son of Shirrel, an investment banker, and Cassandra Ogden, a lawyer who worked for a group that provided counseling and recruitment services to young men and women from disadvantaged homes who wanted to go to law school. He was always a good athlete and a good student, but he began to focus on football when he arrived at the prestigious St. Albans School (alma mater of, among others, Al Gore) in Northwest Washington. Soon after he started high school, his parents separated. Like many kids watching their parents go through a divorce, Ogden found escape from what was going on at home in athletics.

"Part of it, I'm sure, was just because I was pretty good," he said. "But the other part was that the football field became a place I could go and not think about the upheaval in my life. My friends on the team became people I could talk to about things that had nothing to do with all that. As I got bigger and better, football became more and more important and I realized it was going to be a part of my future, at least in terms of getting me into college."

By the time he was a junior, Ogden was so big and so fast and so good that the St. Albans coaches just lined him up wherever the other team's best defensive player was, and that pretty much ended that player's day. Because he had excellent grades and good SATs, Ogden was sought after by every football-playing school in the country. "Actually I only made in the eleven hundreds when I took the SATs," he said. "My mother freaked out. She said, 'You have to take them again.' My dad said, 'The boy's a football player. He's going to get in anyplace he wants with that score.' Of course, he was right."

Ogden visited Notre Dame but found it "too Notre Damish." He liked Florida and Steve Spurrier and he also liked Virginia, a place where a number of St. Albans players, including Jesse Jackson's son Yusef, had gone and become successful players. But when he got off the plane in Los Angeles to visit UCLA, he was sold pretty quickly. "They drove me up the Pacific Highway, then they showed me Bel-Air and Beverly Hills and the campus. They played good football, if not great football. They were also good in track. [Ogden was also a shot-putter.] It was a good school. It was gorgeous. I was sold."

He became a starter five games into his freshman season. By the end of his junior year he knew he could turn pro and almost certainly be a first-round draft pick. But his future agent counseled him to wait a year (rare advice from an agent) on the grounds that the class of '95 was filled with stud offensive linemen and he might drop to late in the first round. A year later he would almost certainly be the first lineman drafted. He waited. Sure enough, when people started putting together mock drafts a year later, he was in everybody's top five.

He was interviewed by all six teams picking at the top of the first round: the New York Jets, Jacksonville Jaguars, Arizona Cardinals, Baltimore Ravens, Washington Redskins, and St. Louis Rams. The one team he was fairly certain wouldn't be taking him was Baltimore. "I knew the Jets were taking Keyshawn [Johnson] and I had heard that Kevin Hardy or I would go next, but that if the Jaguars or Cardinals didn't take me, the Ravens were going to take Lawrence Phillips. Worst case, I'd go five to Washington or maybe six to St. Louis. The one place I thought I didn't want to go was Baltimore. They had just moved, their facility was absolutely brutal, and everything was in upheaval. But I knew I wasn't going there anyway, especially since they had two experienced tackles, so I didn't worry about it."

On draft day, he sat in the green room in New York and heard the Jets announce they were taking Johnson. Fine. Jacksonville took Hardy. Ogden wasn't 100 percent sold on the idea of going to Arizona. The organization wasn't exactly the Packers of the '60s, but the location was great and Ogden thought he would help the team improve. He sat and waited to hear his name. Paul Tagliabue walked to the microphone and, in his well-practiced monotone, said, "With the third pick in the 1996 NFL draft, the Arizona Cardinals select . . . Simeon Rice from the University of Illinois."

Ogden did a double-take. He hadn't even heard Rice's name in the early mix. He was surprised. He sat back and waited for Baltimore to take Phillips so he could find out if he was going to Washington or St. Louis. The phone in the green room rang. It was Ozzie Newsome calling him: "Jonathan, are you ready to be the first draft pick in Baltimore Ravens history?"

Stunned, Ogden said something like "Yeah, sure."

A few minutes later he was standing onstage with Tagliabue, putting on a white cap with a black bill and the word RAVENS printed across it. The team still didn't have a logo yet. Little did he know that Newsome had gone against the wishes of his owner and most of his scouts by taking him over Phillips. Before making the pick, Newsome had asked offensive line coach Kirk Ferentz one question: "Are you absolutely certain he can play guard?" since the Ravens had Orlando Brown and Tony Jones, both quality offensive tackles. "Absolutely," Ferentz had answered, sealing the deal.

Ogden quickly decided he would be fine in Baltimore. It was only forty-five minutes from home, but not right on top of all his family and friends the way he would have been if he had been drafted by Washington. It was still the NFL. Playing guard wasn't a problem, especially on the left side, where he was comfortable. "It actually would have been tougher to adjust to right tackle at that point since it was an entirely different stance," he said. "Left guard was just fine."

The Ravens knew almost right away — even before Phillips became a complete bust — they had made the right pick. Ogden was so smart, he picked things up almost instantly and was mature beyond his years. Most O linemen need two or three years to adapt to the NFL from college. Even changing positions, Ogden had no such trouble. A year later he was moved back to tackle and immediately became an All-Pro. He had quickly become the most respected offensive lineman in the game. He had become the team's quiet leader, someone everyone looked up to, even though his next pregame speech would be his first.

Ogden had turned thirty on the second day of two-a-days and was in the process of negotiating what he hoped would be his last contract. It would be for huge money — the signing bonus would be in the neighborhood of $15–$20 million. He was very much the leader of the offensive line even though he was legendarily thrifty. Most of his teammates were convinced he had yet to spend his rookie signing bonus.

There was also the Bern's story.

Bern's is a famous steak house in Tampa, the one place every tourist goes at some point while in town. It looks like a brothel on the inside and is most famous for the fact that customers don't eat dessert at their tables, they go instead to a separate dessert room. Bern's is, if nothing else, a unique dining experience. When the Ravens arrived in Tampa for the Super Bowl in January of 2001, Ogden announced — to the shock of his linemates — that he was taking the entire O line to Bern's to celebrate their presence in the Super Bowl.

Off they all went to Bern's, where, as you might expect, each of them ordered a huge steak. Ogden took two bites of his and pronounced it unacceptable. He sent it back (much to the horror of the waiter) and demanded another one. Needless to say, he was pilloried for being spoiled and inflexible and for being the one person in the party whose steak wasn't judged superb. Ogden sat quietly while everyone else ate and waited for his new steak. The barbs continued. Finally, the check came. Ogden grabbed it and announced that each of them owed $100.

"What happened to you buying?" they demanded to know.

"It ended when you guys killed me about sending the steak back," Ogden said. "Haven't you ever heard the old saying, 'never bite the hand that is feeding you?'"

Four years later the story was still told and retold. Ogden's defense was simple and to the point: "Come on guys, it was four years ago. Get over it."

While Ogden and the veterans viewed the scrimmage as an evening they would have to endure, the rookies and free agents in camp saw it as an opportunity to get the attention of their coaches. The rookies dressed in a separate locker room from the veterans in the McDaniel Field House, and the atmosphere at their end of the hall on the night of the scrimmage was entirely different from that in the veterans' locker room. While the older players told jokes, played loud music, and made plans for the weekend, the rookies dressed quietly, eyeing one another, taking deep breaths, and glancing constantly at the clock, hoping that staring at it would make it move faster.

"I just want to do something out there that convinces them not to cut me right away," said Matt Zielinski, a free agent from Duke who had received a $1,000 bonus to sign.

Zielinski wasn't going to get cut based on the results of the scrimmage. The Ravens didn't need to make a cut until after the third exhibition game, when the roster had to be trimmed from eighty-five players to sixty-five. That meant everyone would get a chance to show what he could do under game conditions on four occasions — the scrimmage and the three exhibitions. In some cases, that chance would be a series or two. Just as Ogden wanted to play as little as possible, the rookies wanted to play as much as possible.

Some knew they had virtually no chance to make the team. Punter Clint

Greathouse, a rookie from Texas Tech, was thrilled just to be in a training camp. He knew he wasn't going to beat out Dave Zastudil for the job, in part because the team was committed contractually to Zastudil but more so because he could see on the practice field each day that Zastudil was better than he was. All Greathouse wanted from camp was to learn from Gary Zauner and Zastudil and, just as important, get into a game or two so his agent would have game tape to show to other teams in the future.

Many of the rookies in camp knew they weren't going to make the Ravens. Don Muhlbach, the long snapper from Texas A&M, wasn't going to beat out Joe Maese. But he might play well enough to get another team to take a look at him, if not now, then later in the season. If not, then next season. Brian Gaither, the free-agent quarterback from Western Carolina, knew the Ravens had four quarterbacks under contract: Kyle Boller, Kordell Stewart, sixth-round draft pick Josh Harris, and the injured Anthony Wright. Only another injury would give him any chance to make the team. If he was cut, though, it wouldn't mean the end of his career. Football players rarely go home and look for a job these days when they get cut. They continue to train, they might take a part-time job, but they all check their phone messages every day, hoping it will be someone from an NFL team calling to tell them someone has been injured and can they please fly in for a tryout. When Billick cuts players, he reminds them of the violent nature of the game and tells them that someone, somewhere, is going to get hurt and that's when their next chance may come.

The evening of the scrimmage was as close to perfect as one could hope for on an early August night. The temperature was in the mid-seventies, the humidity was low, and the little campus sparkled in the sun as thousands and thousands of cars descended on Westminster. The scrimmage would start at six o'clock. By four o'clock, all the roads leading to town were choked with cars. The Ravens would announce the attendance for the scrimmage at 16,820, a number that again proved the power of the NFL. This was not a real game, it wasn't even a fake game like the exhibitions, it was a scrimmage, Ravens vs. Ravens. And yet the number of people willing to fight the traffic on a Friday night to get to and from the game was the same as a good crowd for an NBA basketball game or an NHL hockey game.

The presence of the crowd — and the team's cheerleaders and band — was what made the scrimmage different from a normal practice. There would be officials, and the team would go through its normal pregame routines, except that Billick would be on the field answering questions from the fans instead of pacing the locker room getting ready for a pregame talk.

The players walked to the field through the ropes that led down the hill to the little stadium. Fans pressed against the ropes, screaming players' names, hoping for a smile or a nod or a high five. Many of the players had not yet put on their helmets, so they put out their hands as they walked by, smiled, nodded, perhaps pointed at someone they knew. Being this close to the players was a big deal for many of these people, which was why they had made the effort to come to the scrimmage. The player whose name was screamed the most already had his helmet on: Ray Lewis. There were more "52" jerseys sold in Baltimore by far than any other, although "31" (Jamal Lewis) was becoming more and more popular. There were hardly any "75" jerseys to be found. Left tackles, even ones going to the Hall of Fame, were rarely seen as heroes.

Ray Lewis walked down the hill, eyes straight ahead, looking neither left nor right, even as Corey Fuller screamed, "It's a rock concert, starring Raaaaay Lewis!" He was wearing a football uniform and he was about to perform in public — even if for only a couple of series. Lewis took every opportunity he had to play football very seriously. Still, as he reached the bottom of the hill, he noticed two kids in wheelchairs seated at the end of the rope. They had ear-to-ear grins on their faces as different players came by and shook their hands or patted them on the head. Lewis stopped, took his helmet off, and crouched in front of each of them to shake their hands and pat them on the back. The kids couldn't stop smiling.

The scrimmage was played under a scoring system that had been handed down from Bill Walsh to Denny Green to Billick. The defense scored by causing a three-and-out, by getting an interception, or by recovering a fumble. The offense got points for first downs and for touchdowns. There would be no field goal attempts, except at halftime, when kickers Matt Stover and Wade Richey would have a field goal kicking contest. Stover had already checked the wind and told the coaches that he and Richey should kick toward the end of the stadium opposite the locker rooms because they'd have the wind at their back.

Stover was the last of the old Cleveland Browns. He was entering his fourteenth season as a Brown/Raven and his fifteenth in the NFL. He was thirty-six and had just signed a new five-year contract. He believed he could kick until he was forty and he worked tirelessly all year long to keep himself in shape. He had jet-black hair and could easily pass for a defensive back or a youthful Republican congressman. (Being a professional athlete, the chances of Stover being a Democrat were about one in a hundred.) He was one of the most consistent kickers in NFL history and one of the most popular Ravens. He was friendly and articulate, with an easy smile that hid a manic competitiveness. He was already dreading that Richey, who was the team's kickoff specialist, would probably beat him in the kicking contest.

"Wade's got as strong a leg as anyone in the league," he said.

Richey had a strong but inconsistent leg. He had kicked a 53-yard field goal in 2003, but inside 50 yards no one was more consistent than Stover. With no rush and no pressure, Richey would probably win. But Stover would definitely go down kicking.

Just before kickoff, a number of the veterans jokingly tried to pick the rookie or free agent who would have the best scrimmage. Every year one player would get himself noticed in the scrimmage with a big play or two. Stover announced he had number 44.

"That," said Trent Smith, standing a few feet away, "is probably a good pick."

Smith was in good position to know. Number 44 was Daniel Wilcox, a free-agent tight end the Ravens had signed in June after the minicamps. The reason Wilcox had been signed was Smith. Specifically, the condition of Smith's left leg, which had been shattered a year earlier in the Ravens' first exhibition game. A rookie drafted in the seventh round out of Oklahoma, Smith had the team made when he was injured. He had impressed the coaches with his speed and his hands. He was six-five, 245, but could explode off the line and get open. He had just caught a pass for 39 yards when he broke his leg.

"For some reason, as they were carrying me off, I remember thinking, 'I just lost a hundred and fifteen grand,'" he said, a reference to the fact that on injured reserve he would be paid 50 percent of the rookie minimum, which was $230,000 in 2003. "I'm not sure why I thought that. I think I was in shock. I remember looking up in the stands for my mom and knowing from the way guys were acting that I was hurt bad."

The Ravens had hoped that Smith would be ready for the 2004 season, but the leg had broken in multiple places and was healing slowly. By the end of minicamp, Newsome and Billick were convinced he wouldn't be ready for the start of the season and might not play the entire year. Wilcox had played in NFL Europe, the developmental league. He had been in and out of the NFL for three years, having been cut seven different times by the New York Jets and Tampa Bay Buccaneers. He had been recommended by Daniel Jeremiah, one of the team's young scouts. Jeremiah and Wilcox had been teammates at Appalachian State — Jeremiah a quarterback, Wilcox a receiver — and Jeremiah was convinced that even though he was under-sized for a tight end at six-two and 230 pounds, Wilcox would thrive in the Ravens' multiple-tight-end sets, in which one tight end was offset from the line of scrimmage.

Wilcox had already impressed everyone in camp. He was a good route runner and an accomplished special teams player. Stover proved prescient. Wilcox made four catches in the scrimmage, including one from Josh Harris on the last play of the night for a 19-yard touchdown that gave the offense a come-from-behind 19–18 victory. He had clearly been the star of the evening, along with Richey, who had won the kicking contest by making a 61-yarder after both he and Stover had made every kick out to 56 yards. "Got under the last one," Stover said, smiling, but still clearly not happy to lose.

The smile on Wilcox's face as the backup players he had been on the field with celebrated in the end zone was quite real. He knew he had taken a giant step toward making the team with his performance. Trent Smith watched it all and felt his stomach churning. He liked Wilcox and knew he was a talented player who could help the team. But that should have been his catch and his celebration out there. Except his leg wouldn't let him do it. Smith was the first player to leave that night, not hanging around for any postscrimmage rehashing or going out for a drink with his friends. He got in his truck and drove, wanting to drive a lot faster than he knew he should.

"I had to get ahold of myself," he said. "It was such a helpless feeling. I know I'm a good football player. I knew I could make the plays Daniel was out there making. And there I was, standing and watching, standing and watching. I went right home. If I hadn't, I might have wrapped my damn car around a tree."

9

The Games Begin

THE ONLY GOOD NEWS for Trent Smith was that he didn't have to worry about being cut. If he wasn't healthy enough to play, the team would put him on injured reserve again, meaning he could not be activated for the entire season. Injured reserve is the Twilight Zone of the NFL. For a marginal player, being placed on IR can be a boon because a player cannot be cut when he is injured. If a player is deemed to have a season-ending injury, he must be placed on IR even if he was going to be cut. That means he makes 50 percent of whatever salary he is due for the season — more than players on the developmental squad make. The developmental (or practice) squad consists of eight players who did not make the fifty-three-man roster but are kept by the team to take part in practice, be available to move up to the fifty-three if someone is hurt, or have a chance to make the team the following season. In 2004 a player on IR would make no less than $117,500 for the season. A practice squad player would make $4,350 a week, or $73,950 for the season if he remained there for all seventeen weeks. Few players spend the entire season on the practice squad. Some move up, some are moved out as other players become available that the team thinks more useful, and some go to other teams when offered the chance to be activated.

Injuries are a dicey issue in the NFL. If a player suffers a relatively minor injury and a team wants to cut him, an injury settlement must be reached. The way it usually works is the team gets a medical report that says the player has a two-week injury and therefore should be paid for two weeks.

The player's agent then finds a doctor who insists the injury will take six weeks to heal. Everyone then agrees that the player should be paid for four weeks. One of the reasons that the league requires every team to tape every single practice is so that a player cannot claim he was cut while injured. That occurs several times a year. A player is cut, he files a grievance claiming he was cut while injured, and the team is then asked to provide tape showing he was practicing the day before he was cut. Of course, that doesn't necessarily resolve the issue, because the player can still claim he was hurt that day.

Matt Zielinski, the rookie defensive lineman who had worried about being an early cut, clinched a spot on the Ravens' payroll during the scrimmage. In a pileup in the second half, someone rolled onto his right knee. At first, Zielinski didn't think he was hurt that badly, but by the end of the night, he had considerable swelling. The next day he found out he had torn his anterior cruciate ligament (the big one) and would need surgery. Welcome to the NFL. Zielinski would spend the season on IR and then be given a chance to make the team in 2005.

"It wasn't exactly what I had in mind," he said with a wan smile. "I came here because I thought I had a chance to make the team. I was nervous every day, but the coaches seemed to think I was doing pretty well until this happened."

The coaches did think he was doing well. Rex Ryan, the defensive line coach, was impressed with his strength, and Mike Nolan, the coordinator, liked his attitude. Now it would be another year before Zielinski would find out if he had what it took to play in the NFL. In the meantime, he would be making more money than most of those he had graduated with from Duke in the spring.

There were a lot of players in camp who knew that the first three exhibition games would decide a lot about their future. Billick had told the players early on that he thought he knew fifty of the fifty-three names that would be on the final roster, but that was subject to change. "You can play your way onto this team, or you can play your way off," he said. "People will get hurt and spots will open up. We all know that. If your chance comes, you better be ready."

The two rookies in camp who were absolutely going to get a chance were the rookie kick returners, B. J. Sams and Derek Abney. Sams had been the one wowing people early, but he broke a bone in his hand in the scrimmage. That meant Abney and Lamont Brightful, the incumbent, would be given chances to show themselves in at least the first two exhibition games, against Atlanta (at home) and Philadelphia (on the road). Billick had penciled in Sams as the returner after minicamps but was now worried about throwing him in for the regular-season opener if he didn't get back in time to play in at least one exhibition game.

There weren't that many other slots open for new people. Kyle Boller and Kordell Stewart would start the season as the active quarterbacks, with Josh Harris, the rookie, as the third quarterback, meaning (by rule) he would get into a game only if the other two were injured. Once Anthony Wright returned, a decision would have to be made on whether to keep the veteran Stewart or the rookie Harris. Jamal Lewis, Chester Taylor, and Musa Smith were set at the running back spot. Alan Ricard was going to be the fullback, backed up by backup tight end Terry Jones, who could play both positions. The offensive line had five starters back — Ogden and Orlando Brown at tackle, Edwin Mulitalo and Bennie Anderson at guard, and Mike Flynn at center. Casey Rabach and Ethan Brooks were experienced backups: Rabach at center and guard, Brooks at tackle. That left three-year veteran Damion Cook to battle with free-agent pickup Tony Pashos and rookies Brian Rimpf and Lenny Vandermade for the remaining spots. Tight end was the team's deepest position, led by Pro Bowler Todd Heap with Jones and Wilcox backing him up. Rookie Brett Pierce could make a lot of teams (he would eventually land in Dallas), but not the Ravens. The most fluid position on offense was wide receiver. Travis Taylor and Kevin Johnson were set. Behind them it was wide-open, with Randy Hymes, a converted Grambling quarterback who had been on IR a year earlier; third-year veteran Ron Johnson; second-year player Kareem Kelly; and the rookies, Devard Darling and Clarence Moore all in the mix. Only four would suit up most weeks; no more than five would make the fifty-three.

The defense was almost as set: The line was led by Kelly Gregg, Anthony Weaver, Marques Douglas, and Jarret Johnson, all proven veterans. Dwan Edwards had caused some concern when he reported to minicamp weighing 320 pounds, but he was down to 308 by the start of camp and Ryan was convinced he would be in the rotation in the team's 3-4 set.

Third-year player Maake Kemoeatu was huge (six-five, 340) and improving. He would make the team. In all likelihood, Aubrayo Franklin would, too. Linebacker was more set than any position on the team: Ray Lewis was the star, and Edgerton Hartwell would start next to him on the inside. They would be backed up by Bart Scott and T. J. Slaughter, who were both ferocious special teams players. On the outside, Terrell Suggs, who had shown so much potential as a rookie, appeared ready to be a star. Adalius Thomas, who had made the Pro Bowl as a special teams player a year earlier, would start opposite Suggs until Peter Boulware was healthy enough to return or, more accurately, *if* Boulware was healthy enough to return, a major concern given that Boulware was a four-time Pro Bowler who had been having his best year in 2003 until he had torn up his right knee in the second-to-last week of the regular season. A couple of the young linebackers in camp, Brandon Barnes and John Garrett, had impressed the coaches, but, barring injury, there wasn't going to be a roster spot for either. The secondary was the team's other great strength: Chris McAlister had made his first Pro Bowl at cornerback the year before and many people thought Gary Baxter, entering the walk year of his contract, had almost as much potential. Ed Reed was a rising star in his third season at safety, and Will Demps, the other starter, was one of those guys the team kept looking to replace — except he continued to be better than those brought in to replace him. There was experienced depth here with Corey Fuller (who had been a starter his entire NFL career), Chad Williams, and Ray Walls, not to mention the looming specter of Deion Sanders. Javin Hunter, who had been converted from wide receiver to cornerback, Gerome Sapp — another excellent special teams player — and rookie Lance Frazier were essentially competing for one spot. Sapp, because of his special teams skills, was the favorite, although Nolan and secondary coach Johnnie Lynn had been impressed by Frazier.

Everyone else in camp was hoping to get someone's attention — if not in Baltimore, then somewhere else. There were experienced players who were going to lose their jobs by the end of camp, and everyone knew it. One early candidate was Ron Johnson, a player who knew he was on the bubble — perhaps. Johnson had been a fourth-round pick two years earlier and had flashed potential at times. But he was flighty, picked up a lot of penalties, and seemed to think that he was a far bigger star than anyone else saw him as. Walking off the practice field one day, he had yelled at a staffer who wasn't moving quickly enough to give him a pen so he could sign some autographs. The Sharpie was delivered. Johnson signed for a few people, tossed the pen on the ground, and walked into the locker room. He would have to be considerably better than his competition to retain his spot on the team. The scouts were already quietly campaigning with Billick and Newsome to make him an early cut.

Each night, while the players were winding up their position meetings, Newsome and his staff would meet to look at tape. They would go through every play of both practices, all of them making notes without comment. Only after the tape had been looked at thoroughly was there any discussion of what they had seen or about specific players. Newsome encouraged bluntness and disagreement, usually saying nothing himself because he didn't want to influence the opinions of the scouts. When the coaches and scouts met together, he rarely said anything unless he thought an absolute mistake — keeping a player who shouldn't be kept or cutting one he liked — was about to be made.

The scrimmage had for the most part confirmed what the coaches had thought about the players. With each passing day they were more and more sold on the tight end Daniel Wilcox. "The thing that makes you wonder is, how come he's never caught on before now," Billick said. "He can really play. I keep waiting to see the Achilles' heel, but so far there hasn't been one."

Jamal Lewis appeared unbothered by his pending legal troubles, but Billick still ran practice long a couple of times to get extra carries for Chester Taylor and Musa Smith. The team had to be prepared if Lewis, who had now been told his trial date would be November 1, was away from the team for any extended period. The wide receivers weren't going to blow anyone away, but the coaches were intrigued by Moore, the six-six rookie from Northern Arizona whom Newsome had had so much trouble finding on draft day. Billick liked tall receivers, and Moore could give the offense a dimension it lacked. He had been drafted initially with the notion that he would spend the season on the developmental squad, but that was no longer a certainty.

The most pleasant surprise of the camp, though, wasn't a rookie or a wandering free agent. It wasn't even someone the team expected — or wanted — to be a major contributor. It was Kordell Stewart. The Ravens had signed Stewart after Wright's injury because he was available, because he was cheap ($760,000 as a ten-year veteran), and because they wanted to bring someone in whom the fans would not start screaming for the first time Boller threw back-to-back incomplete passes. The major concern in deciding to sign him had been how Stewart would respond to being a backup who had no chance to start, barring injury. Would he pout? Would he make life difficult for Boller?

The answer, as it turned out, was absolutely not. In fact, right from the start, no one on the team was a bigger supporter of Boller than Stewart. "I remember how some of my backups treated me in Pittsburgh," he said. "I want to be the backup that I never had."

The argument could be made that few players in NFL history had seen the highs and lows that Stewart had seen, especially during his eight turbulent seasons with the Steelers. Stewart had come into the league in 1995, having played on excellent teams at Colorado. Growing up in New Orleans, he had lived in projects that were directly across the highway from the Saints' practice facility. His first football memories were of lying flat on his stomach along with his friends so he could see under the padded fence and watch the Saints practice.

"I thought it was the coolest thing I'd ever seen," he said. "I could lie there for as long as they practiced and watch. I just loved it. In the back of my mind, I said, 'Someday, I'll be inside and people will be trying to watch me.'"

He was a tagalong little brother who learned football — and all sports — playing with older kids. Even though his parents split when he was young, his father was always nearby. After his mother died when he was eleven, he and his brother and sister moved back in with their dad. "Needless to say, that was a tough time," he said. "My dad did a great job of keeping the family together after my mom died. I can remember, when I was little, when they were still together, every night we'd get together as a family around their bed and read the Bible together. When we were older, after mom was gone, we did the same thing."

Stewart was a running back when he first played football, but by the time he was in high school, his arm strength was such that he was moved to quarterback. This was in the late 1980s, when it was just coming into vogue not to convert talented African American athletes to running backs or wide receivers or cornerbacks. Doug Williams had won a Super Bowl playing for the Redskins at the end of the 1987 season, and Stewart was part of the first generation of young quarterbacks who did not have "black" attached to their name every time they were referenced in print, as in "Black quarterback Kordell Stewart . . ."

He was just talented quarterback Kordell Stewart when he opted to go to Colorado, which was coming off a controversial co–national championship (the Buffaloes won one game because they were given a fifth down by officials, and the Orange Bowl on a shaky clipping call that negated a Notre Dame touchdown) and had a controversial coach in Bill McCartney, who would eventually leave coaching to form Promise Keepers, the evangelical Christian group that preached (among other things) that men had to be in charge of their families at all times.

Stewart liked McCartney as a coach and as a person. When Rick Neuheisel was hired during his junior year to be the offensive coordinator and coach the quarterbacks, Stewart blossomed. The Steelers took him in the second round of the draft, and he arrived in Pittsburgh as a promising backup behind the veteran quarterback Neil O'Donnell. It quickly became apparent to Steelers coach Bill Cowher that Stewart was much too talented to wield a clipboard every week. He began experimenting with him, putting him in as a running quarterback in goal-line situations and then using him on occasion as both a running back and a wide receiver. When Cowher was asked to describe Stewart's role, he shrugged and said, "I guess he's a quarterback slash running back slash wide receiver." Thus, Stewart's nickname was born: Slash.

He was an All-Pro in the slash role the next year, backing up Mike Tomczak while playing the other two positions. In the final game of the regular season he started at quarterback and had an 80-yard touchdown run, the longest run from scrimmage by a quarterback in NFL history. A year later he became the starting quarterback and appeared destined to be a big star for years to come. He passed for more than 3,000 yards and rushed for almost 500 more and was a Pro Bowl alternate. But the following season, his star faded: he threw more interceptions than touchdowns, the team struggled, and Stewart was booed. There were even whispers around town that he was gay. Six years after the fact, Stewart laughed when the subject of that season came up. Back then, it wasn't even a little bit funny.

"There are always going to be people who are ignorant," he said. "There were people who didn't want me to succeed because I was a black quarterback, but I honestly think by 1998, they were a distinct minority. To tell you the truth, I feel sorry for people like that. It's their problem, not mine. I sincerely doubt that any rumors would have started if we had kept winning. But when you don't win the way people think you are supposed to win, people come up with all sorts of wild ideas."

The next three years were a roller coaster for Stewart. He was benched the last five games of '99 and moved back to wide receiver. He became the starter again in 2000 and then had a Pro Bowl season in 2001, leading the Steelers into the conference final. But the Steelers lost that game at home to the New England Patriots, and a lot of people blamed Stewart for the loss. A year later he was benched after three games in favor of Tommy Maddox and, with his contract up at the end of the season, he knew his days in Pittsburgh were numbered. Stewart insisted there were no hard feelings about those final days in Pittsburgh, but when he talked about them, it was evident that there was still some bitterness.

"I'll never forget the game in Tennessee when Tommy got hurt," Stewart said. "I have to go in and I look over at the sidelines, and Cowher has taken off his headset. To me, the message was crystal-clear: Kordell's in the game, why bother? I couldn't believe what I was seeing. Then we score twice, we get back in the game, and, what do you know, the headset's back on. I knew that day it was over, if there was any doubt before then."

Stewart thought about signing with the Ravens that off-season but landed eventually in Chicago for the simple reason that the money was better and he thought he would have a chance to start. He did start — seven games — but the team was bad, and understandably, they decided to go with rookie quarterback Rex Grossman at the end of the season. On March 1 Stewart found himself looking for a job for the second time in twelve months. There was some irony in landing in Baltimore. Not only were the Ravens and Steelers bitter rivals, but Stewart had often tortured the Ravens, having some of his best games against them even in years when he was struggling. "These colors do feel a little bit funny," he said his first day in minicamp, eyeing the purple uniform he had on. "But I'll get used to it."

That he fit in well was evident at the end of training camp when the players held their annual vote for "the ugliest man in camp." This was another ritual — a bonding one, really, because the "award" never went to the ugliest man in camp. It went to someone who was popular, who was being accepted into the group, who everyone knew could take the ribbing and laugh about it. Billick had won it one year; Corey Fuller had won it a year earlier, his first full year with the team. The winner in 2004 was Stewart, who accepted the robe (a purple towel) and scepter (a plunger) with great joy and thanked everyone in the room for allowing him to flourish with the team. "You have allowed me," he said, "to bring out my true ugliness."

The wild cheers made it clear that the Ravens were very pleased to have Stewart, and all that came with his presence, among them.

After two weeks of near-perfect weather, the morning of the exhibition opener against the Atlanta Falcons dawned rainy and ugly. It was one of those August days when being outside is miserable. It was warm and humid and the rain just kept coming down all day and all night. If the Baltimore Orioles had been scheduled to play across the street in Camden Yards that night, the game would have been postponed by noon. But neither rain nor snow nor dark of night stops football games — lightning can, but that's it — so the two teams arrived at M&T Bank Stadium to play before a crowd announced as a sellout (69,299) even though the number of fans disguised as empty seats grew throughout the evening.

Very few coaches make a big deal of exhibition games. Most have a set plan on exactly how much their starters will play and then how much time the veteran reserves will play before getting a look at the players fighting for roster spots. Billick's goal for his starters is for them to play at least one full game over the course of the four exhibition games: a series or two in the opener, perhaps a quarter in the second game, a full half in the third, and then back to a series or two in the finale. The first two games are really an opportunity for the players trying to get noticed to get on the field for a long period of time.

The opener did not start auspiciously. After Falcons quarterback Mike

Vick, who was going to play exactly one series, was sacked on his team's first possession, the Falcons punted and Lamont Brightful fumbled the punt. The fact that the Falcons got the ball back wasn't all that important, but Brightful's having trouble catching the ball — albeit a wet one — was a disturbing continuation of the previous season. It was another step toward cementing his fate. When the Ravens did get the ball, Boller was sacked on two of the first three plays. Offensive line coach Jim Colletto was screaming at the offensive line, Billick was demanding to know what in the world was going on, and the stadium was silent, except for a few scattered boos.

It got better after that. Falcons rookie quarterback Matt Schaub simply had no chance against the Ravens' defense — starters, backups, third-stringers. Billick kept the offense on the field for an extra series in the second quarter, and Boller completed a 12-yard touchdown pass to Dan Wilcox to finish off a 95-yard drive. Stewart then led a 74-yard drive in the third quarter, and the final was 24–0. The Ravens had just dominated a team that would end up in the NFC Championship Game.

The defense appeared to be everything they thought it would be. The offense had showed signs of being effective. Billick always tells his players to enjoy wins — any win — and he told them just that. But he also told them there was a lot of work to do. He was concerned about Brightful's fumble and about Stewart's taking a sack at the end of the first half that denied the team a field goal opportunity inside the 10-yard line. He wasn't thrilled when Wilcox was penalized for unsportsmanlike conduct after an overly enthusiastic spike following his second touchdown catch of the game.

Billick had mixed emotions about the mistakes. On the one hand, they concerned him, especially since two of them were mental errors. Brightful's fumble was especially worrisome since Derek Abney, who had handled punts in the second half, had separated his right shoulder in the fourth quarter and was headed for IR. That meant he had Brightful and Sams — who still hadn't caught a kick in a game and wasn't yet ready to play — as his returners. He was certain now that he didn't want Brightful returning kicks for another season. But it made him nervous to think about throwing a rookie in without any preseason play.

The good news about the mistakes was that they gave him a chance to keep after his players, who he knew, exhibition or no exhibition, would be feeling just a little bit cocky after winning so easily. Billick waited until the end of the following Monday's practice, the team's first full workout in pads after the exhibition opener, to make his points about what he didn't like. After each full workout, Billick always gathered the team in a circle at midfield. Sometimes he did nothing more than remind them about the schedule for the rest of the day. Other times he would make a joke or tell a story, frequently based on something he had gleaned while surfing the Internet. Billick was such a techno-geek that the *New York Times* had done a story for its business section on the NFL coach who had become a computer whiz and how he used his knowledge in his job. One way he used it was to search for tidbits he could relate to the players that he thought sent some kind of message.

One day, on the field, he quoted something Redskins coach Joe Gibbs had said about training camp and the need for "every practice to matter to every single person on the field from the first snap to the last." Gibbs had gone on to talk about how mistakes could not be tolerated and had explained that some practices were so important that they had to be absolutely secret and away from any and all prying eyes.

When Billick was finished quoting Gibbs, he looked around at his players, standing or kneeling in a circle around him. "Let me tell you something about Joe Gibbs. He is and always will be a better coach than I am. He's won three Super Bowls. Now, we'll be okay when we play them because we've got better players and better assistant coaches. But I want to tell you one other difference between Joe Gibbs and me: I've won a game in this century."

The players thought about that one for a second, then cracked up. Gibbs had retired from the Redskins following the 1992 season and had been lured out of retirement by Redskins owner Dan Snyder in return for a five-year, $25 million contract. Since he hadn't coached a game since 1992, he hadn't won (or lost) in the twenty-first century. Billick *did* respect Gibbs, but he couldn't resist the joke.

Now, on a sultry Monday afternoon, Billick didn't want to talk about any other teams or coaches or anything he had learned on the Internet. He wanted to talk about mistakes. There were five things he had seen, three in the game and two in practice that morning, that he believed a team with

Super Bowl aspirations couldn't allow. The first three he had talked about briefly after the game: the Brightful fumble, the Stewart sack, and the Wilcox spike. "You can't get a team three-and-out on the first series of the game and then give them the ball back," he said, referring to the fumble. "Just can't do it." On Stewart, who had already admitted he had gotten carried away trying to make a play and should have known better, he said, "You have to think logically in that situation even though football's an emotional game. We don't need a touchdown there. If we get a field goal and it is 17–0, game's over. Psychologically, the other team knows that unless we start committing turnovers, they're not scoring three times on our defense." Wilcox's gaffe was the most understandable: a young player overexcited about making a play. "I didn't even think what you did was that big a deal, Dan," he said. "But we simply cannot give the officials the opportunity to blow their whistle. Don't put the game in their hands in any way."

He was also disturbed that the offense had not been able to get the ball in the end zone from the 2-yard line in practice that morning and that Josh Harris had fumbled the snap on the last play of the morning. "Remember what kind of team we think we can be," he said. "Jamal does not have to rush the ball for three thousand yards for us to win. Ray does not have to make seven thousand tackles for us to get to the Super Bowl. But you have to play intelligently. I need fifty-three guys who will not make silly mistakes when the lights come on. I've told you I know fifty guys who are going to be here. You have to help me pick the other three. I know you're all starting to feel a little pressure now. The games are started. I know a lot of people are going to make a big deal out of this game [in Philadelphia] Friday night. I understand. But those mistakes can't keep happening, not if you want to go to the Super Bowl and win the Super Bowl. If all you guys want to do is be a playoff team, maybe play a game or two, that's okay. But tell me now and I'll go spend the next month on my boat and meet you in Cleveland for the opener. I wouldn't get on you about this if it was stuff you couldn't do. But these are basics. Repeat mistakes like these and we won't come close to getting what we want out of this season."

Billick wasn't concerned — yet — about the mental errors. He just wanted to reinforce sooner rather than later the need not to make them. His reference to feeling pressure, the last thing he wanted anyone feeling in mid-August, came on two fronts: T.O. and Deion. Both were unavoidable. The day in March when the special master had allowed Terrell Owens to go to Philadelphia, the Ravens had known they would face Owens and the Eagles twice, both times in Philadelphia: once in the exhibition season and again on Halloween. Billick didn't really care about the outcome of the exhibition game. He would stick to his plan regardless of the score. But he knew there would be questions about Owens and about the anger Ray Lewis had expressed after Owens had ditched the Ravens in favor of the Eagles. He wanted it downplayed as much as possible.

Deionmania had now taken on a life of its own. Within the team, it was now a given that Sanders was coming. Billick was still pushing to get him into camp soon. Training camp would actually break before the third exhibition game, so this was the last week that Sanders could be in a camp atmosphere to try and get into football-playing shape. Newsome was still negotiating a contract with Sanders's agent, Eugene Parker. He had laughed when Parker, an old friend, had thrown out the notion that Sanders's return had nothing to do with money.

"Eugene," Newsome had said. "You know and I know, it's *always* about the money."

Newsome had, in fact, offered a $1 million contract laced with incentives based on playing time and performance. Even though it wasn't about the money, Parker had told Newsome straight-up that it wasn't acceptable. Newsome wasn't surprised. Business was business.

Sanders had stayed in touch with Lewis and Fuller, updating them on his workouts and his progress. His plan was to be in camp before the last exhibition game on September 2 in the Meadowlands against the Giants. Ideally, he wanted to play in one game before the season began but wasn't certain if that would happen. He had surprised Newsome by tracking him down on the golf course one afternoon when Newsome and the scouts were holding their annual golf tournament. "I need some tapes," Sanders had said. "Tapes of your defense and of the first three [regular-season] opponents. I want to do some studying."

Newsome was happy to hear Sanders say that. Clearly, he was planning to show up as prepared as he could be. Publicly, the team was saying nothing about Deion. Whenever Newsome or Billick was asked about him, their answer was direct and honest if not complete: "The man's retired."

*   *   *

The Ravens prepared for each exhibition game the same way they prepared for a regular-season game, with the exception that everyone in uniform would play, regardless of the score. The offensive and defensive coaches put together a game plan and a complete scouting report.

The details in an NFL scouting report nowadays are almost mind-boggling. Thanks to computers, there isn't a tendency or a fact or a statistic that is unavailable to a coaching staff. Each week Jedd Fisch put together the offensive breakdown, and Mike Pettine put together the defensive breakdown. The report included things such as how many times a team threw on third and less than four vs. how many times it ran; how often it ran left or ran right; how many times the quarterback attempted passes of more than 10, 20, 30 yards; and how many times a team lined up in a double-tight-end set vs. its regular set vs. a three-wides, four-wides, or a five-wides look. The same things were charted on defense: blitz tendencies, when a team went to a nickel or dime package (extra defensive backs), when it went to a heavy (extra lineman) set, and on and on and on. One could completely drown studying everything the computer spit out. The coaches went through most, if not all, of the computer information among themselves, then passed on the highlights to the players.

Fisch and Pettine were part of a new breed of coaches in the NFL. Expertise on the computer was part of their job. Neither coached a specific position — though both aspired to do so — but worked instead as an assistant to the coordinator on his side of the ball. That didn't mean they didn't have on-field responsibilities during practice, but they weren't as specific as for coaches working with one group of players. Pettine was thirty-nine and had grown up in Doylestown, Pennsylvania, where his father was a successful high school coach. He had played at Virginia under George Welsh, then had worked for his dad before becoming a high school head coach himself. He had been very successful his last five years — winning forty-five games — and had received some national fame when his team was featured in the first edition of ESPN's *The Season*, the once original (though now completely hackneyed) idea of following a given team from up close for all or part of a season. He had come to the Ravens in 2002 and was now considered more than ready to move up to being a position coach if, as expected, members of the staff moved on to other jobs at the end of the '04 season.

Fisch was already in his fourth season in the NFL at the age of twenty-eight. He was Jim Fassel's officemate, sharing an office that probably wasn't a quarter as big as the one Fassel had occupied a year earlier as the Giants' head coach. Fisch and Fassel were an interesting pair: Fisch soaking up Fassel's coaching experience, Fassel learning about computers from the younger man. Fisch had decided as a high school senior in Livingston, New Jersey, that rather than pursuing a tennis scholarship to college, he wanted to go to the University of Florida and learn coaching from Steve Spurrier. He had watched Spurrier's teams play, knew coaching was what he wanted to do, and figured Spurrier was the best teacher he could possibly have.

Of course, he had absolutely no connections at Florida and, even though he could have played tennis at a number of Division 1 schools, Florida — consistently ranked in the top ten nationally — wasn't one of them. So he applied early-decision to Florida. And no place else. He didn't get in. Undeterred, Fisch picked up the phone and put in a call to the admissions director. He introduced himself and explained that he had applied early-decision to Florida and failed to get admitted.

"Which means you and I have both got a problem," he said. "I have a problem because I haven't applied to school anyplace else and if I'm not in school next fall, my parents will kill me. You have a problem because fifteen years from now when I'm an NFL head coach and I'm looking to give my alma mater a million dollars a year, that school isn't going to be Florida."

Whether that little bit of cockiness swayed the admissions director is hard to say, but Fisch was eventually admitted. He then talked his way into the football office as an undergraduate assistant and had on-field duties by the time he was a senior. He also worked, while still in college, as an assistant coach at a nearby high school. After Fisch coached one year of semi-pro ball, Spurrier brought him back to Florida. In 2000 he recommended him to Dom Capers, who was looking for a young coach to help him start putting together the expansion Houston Texans. The only setback to his coaching career had been a major health problem. In April of 2003 he had returned from a run and found himself unable to breathe. He ended up in the hospital and had to undergo emergency surgery for an aortic tear in his heart. He was completely recovered, although he still had a long scar running down his chest as a reminder of what he had been through.

Fisch and Pettine were responsible for getting the computer breakdowns to the coaches early each week so they could begin studying them to formulate a game plan. The coaches also received a scouting report on the upcoming opponent from George Kokinis or Vince Newsome, who usually took turns watching the next opponent play in person the week before it played the Ravens. With the Eagles there weren't a lot of secrets: everything they did on offense started with quarterback Donovan McNabb. They would throw deep often and would try to find Owens deep early. Their secret weapon was diminutive running back Brian Westbrook. On defense it was even simpler: the Eagles would blitz, blitz, and then, for variety, blitz some more. The question was knowing where the blitz would come from, not whether it was coming.

The preparation was really practice at this point in the summer. The coaches wanted the players to study their scouting reports and the tape they showed them so they would be in the habit of doing those things and know what to look for when they received their first real scouting report of the season prior to the opener in Cleveland. Everything now was geared to being ready to play at 100 percent on opening day. This is more true in football than for any other sport because the season is so short. No one wants to stumble out of the starting blocks in September. History has shown that an 0-1 start isn't a disaster, 0-2 is courting disaster, and 0-3 means you are finished. In other sports an 0-3 start is meaningless. In football, it simply can't happen if you consider yourself a playoff contender.

Billick wanted the focus for the week to be on viewing the game simply as another step toward the goal of being ready to play on September 12. He didn't want anyone — especially Ray Lewis — engaging in any kind of war of words before the game with T.O. "Someone asks you about it, the answer is simple," he told his players. "He didn't want to be a Raven. That's fine with us. It isn't worth further discussion."

Even as he said those words in the meeting room, there was still just a hint of anger. Owens had dissed his team, his organization. But Billick wasn't going to allow it to become a focal point. Certainly not in August. Since the Olympics had just ended, Billick threw up a photo of Michael Phelps, the brilliant swimmer from Baltimore who had won eight medals —

six of them gold. "The kid lost two races, one of them a relay, and people say he didn't meet his expectations," Billick said. "But he didn't stop because of that. He went on and won the rest of his races. We got a shutout last week. No reason not to get another one this week, but if they score, we don't let down. We try to shut them out the rest of the game."

The team traveled to Philadelphia on a chartered train, something it had been doing on East Coast road trips — Philadelphia and the Meadowlands — for several years. The train was big enough that everyone had room to spread out, and it took little more than an hour to get from Baltimore to Thirtieth Street Station in Philadelphia. From there, they bused straight to the stadium. For an exhibition game, there was no point in staying overnight. Because the game was on CBS and would start at eight o'clock, it would be after two o'clock in the morning before they got home.

An NFL exhibition game is a real game in the sense that the public has to pay full price for the tickets, the games are on TV and radio, and all sorts of judgments will be passed by media and fans based on what they see in the game. It is also real in the sense that major injuries occur because football is always a physically dangerous game, whether the game being played counts in the standings or not.

But the atmosphere in the locker room is different than for a real game. For one thing, especially on the road, everyone is packed in tight because there are more than eighty players dressing in a locker room built for about fifty. The coaches are far more relaxed. Billick and Fassel sat in Billick's office prior to kickoff, trading stories about their days as college coaches. The assistant coaches, all dressed in NFL-required Ravens gear, all had their shirts pulled out so as to be more comfortable on a warm, humid night. Except for Mike Nolan, the staff's fashion plate. His shirt was neatly tucked in. "No Andy Reid/Mike Holmgren look for our man Coach Nolan," Rex Ryan kidded, referring to two of the heftier NFL head coaches, one of whom would be on the opposite sideline for this game.

Fassel asked Billick what the latest was on the Deion watch. "I'm hoping next Thursday," Billick said. "But it may be after the Detroit game." Detroit was the next week's exhibition opponent. There would be only one more preseason game left after that.

Because NFL teams play only ten home games a year and charge fans a lot of money for all of them, every game is an event. In most stadiums these days, a number of fans pay extra money for the privilege of standing on the field behind a rope and watching the players warm up. Player introductions — for the home team — are long and loud. In Philadelphia, the introduction of the Eagles was sponsored by Levitra, the male sexual-enhancement drug, which was one of the league's corporate sponsors. NFL commissioner Paul Tagliabue had no trouble taking sponsorship money from Levitra or putting out calendars of the various team cheerleaders dressed in very little, but he had been shocked by the infamous Janet Jackson/Justin Timberlake wardrobe malfunction at the Super Bowl. Imagine what might have happened if Timberlake had been using Levitra.

The loudest cheer of the pregame introductions was for Owens. The screeching player intros, complete with fireworks, a fight song, and the players running out of a giant Eagles helmet through a cordon of pom-pom-shaking cheerleaders, climaxed with a video tribute to Philadelphia's most famous fictional athlete: Rocky, complete with the music. Then, finally, it was time to play.

It didn't take long for the defense to lose its shutout. After the offense had failed to move the ball, Dave Zastudil punted and the Eagles took over on their own 19. On the opening play, McNabb play-faked, freezing Gary Baxter for an instant. Owens raced behind Baxter, caught the perfectly thrown ball in stride, and was gone. Touchdown. The Eagles' new stadium, Lincoln Financial Field, isn't nearly as loud as Veterans Stadium, the old concrete bowl the team played in for more than thirty years, because, unlike the Vet, it is open at both ends and the noise escapes. But as Owens raced into the end zone, the roar was deafening.

Of course, there really is no such thing as a big play in an exhibition game. The most significant moment of the night would come on the next series, when Eagles running back Correll Buckhalter would suffer a season-ending knee injury. But the way the Owens touchdown occurred, so swiftly, so decisively, sent a shiver through the Ravens sideline. The CBS cameras would show Lewis comforting Baxter after the play, and Nolan would later blame himself for not having help on the left side of the defense for Baxter, but there was an unmistakable feel — if only for an instant — that perhaps the defense wasn't as infallible as it had appeared a week earlier.

"It's just football, G.B., that's all it is," Lewis said, repeating one of his mantras. "Sometimes you get beat. It's part of the game. Nothing more. Next play. Move on to the next play."

The Ravens would do that. With the team down, 10–3, Ed Reed intercepted a McNabb pass and lateraled to Will Demps, who took the ball into the end zone. The defense gathered around Demps to celebrate. That's an NFL no-no. Excessive celebration. The flag flew and Billick's headset flew off about a millisecond later. "Dammit, Ray," he said, directing his anger at the leader of the defense. "You guys simply cannot do that. You can't get us penalized like that. What did I tell you guys about not giving them the chance to throw a flag?"

Billick might not have stayed angry for long if Wade Richey's kickoff, pushed back to the 15-yard line by the penalty, hadn't been fielded by Eagles rookie J. R. Reid at the 20 and run back for a touchdown. "I told you we'd pay!" Billick roared. "When are you guys gonna learn you can't make mistakes like that!"

The final score was 26–17, Eagles, the second half dominated by rookies and free agents trying to make an impression while the game dragged on toward midnight. By the time it mercifully ended, even the eager Eagles fans were on their way home, if only to get out of the stifling heat.

The good news was there had been no major injuries.

Except perhaps to the team's psyche. Owens didn't catch another ball the rest of the night. He didn't have to.

10

Getting Serious

WHEN THE TEAM RETURNED to Westminster following the Eagles game, the mood was different. Two preseason games were in the books. Training camp was almost over. Billick had planned to break camp after practice on Tuesday morning, August 24, but decided to send everyone home after the annual rookie show on Monday night. Almost always when the choice is between slightly overworking or slightly underworking, Billick leans toward the latter, especially in preseason. The one and only exhibition game in which the starters would play extensively was the following Saturday. The first cuts would take place the following Monday. Most of those decisions had already been made, and a number of players were keenly aware that they were in the final days in which they were guaranteed to be paid for playing football.

The best thing about camp had been the lack of injuries to starters and key players. B. J. Sams was close to returning from his hand injury. No one had expected Peter Boulware or Anthony Wright, both still mending from surgery, to be involved in camp at all. Defensive tackle Marques Douglas had injured an elbow, and at first it had been feared he might be out six weeks. Now it appeared likely he would be back for the final exhibition game. Anthony Weaver had an ankle injury that did not appear to be serious. Todd Heap had been out for a couple of weeks with a broken nose and rotator cuff problem in his shoulder, but neither injury threatened to keep him from being ready to start the season. The three players currently slated for injured reserve had never played a down in an NFL regular-season game: Trent Smith, Derek Abney, and Matt Zielinski.

The one serious problem that had cropped up was the health of Orlando Brown's mother. She had been hospitalized just prior to the first exhibition game, and Brown had been excused from camp and from the games to spend time with her. She was a diabetic with blood pressure problems, and her condition was extremely serious.

Everyone associated with the Ravens knew how close Brown was to his mother and how emotional he was in normal situations, much less one as dire as this. Brown was one of the more remarkable and unlikely stories in NFL history. Brown's nickname was Zeus, which made sense since he was just about the biggest man anyone had ever met. Even among the behemoths of the offensive line, Brown stood out. He was six foot seven, 360 pounds, and, if it were possible, looked bigger than that. The irony was that his mother gave him his nickname when she was pregnant with him, and when "Zeus," was born — several weeks premature — he weighed three pounds and five ounces.

"My mother never thought she would be able to get pregnant," he said. "When she did, she was forty-two years old. She decided that the baby was some kind of a gift from the gods and told her students [she was a junior high school teacher and taught a class in mythology] that she had already nicknamed the baby Zeus." It didn't take long for the preemie to grow into his nickname. By the time Brown was a teenager, growing up in Northeast Washington, D.C., he weighed more than 300 pounds and was playing on both the offensive and defensive lines at H. D. Woodson High School. To make extra money, he worked as a bouncer at a strip club not far from the school. "They never guessed that I wasn't eighteen," he said. "I looked a lot older."

Brown did just enough work in school to graduate but never worried about the SATs. He had decided to be a football player, and school wasn't a priority. He landed at Central State, an NAIA school in Ohio that had no SAT requirement for admission or, more important, to play football. After a year at Central State he transferred to South Carolina State (still without having taken an SAT) and was eventually shifted from defense to offense as a senior. His size drew the attention of some pro scouts but he really had never been taught the nuances of playing the offensive line, so there was almost no chance he would be drafted.

The Cleveland Browns had sent Scott Pioli to South Carolina State to work out one of Brown's teammates. Pioli couldn't help but notice Brown, who had lingered near the practice field when he heard an NFL scout was in town, and asked him if he wanted to work out for him. Brown did. Pioli was impressed, especially when Brown decided to show him how aggressive he could be by charging at him while he was trying to get video of him to take back to Coach Bill Belichick.

"I said, 'You want aggressive?'" Brown remembered. "I'll show you aggressive."

The Browns decided to offer Brown a free-agent contract. When he got into minicamp it was apparent he had great potential but very little idea of how to play. There were no practice squads in those days, so the only way to keep a player under contract who wasn't going to be on the active roster was to hide him on injured reserve. It was common for teams to create injuries for players they thought had potential in order to get them onto IR. When the Cleveland coaches told Brown they wanted him to get "injured" in the team's final preseason game, Brown objected. "I'm not faking an injury," he said. Even though the coaches tried to convince him that the injury was for his own good and that it was not unusual, Brown was still skeptical.

"Then the game starts and I get knocked down on one of the first plays, I don't even know by who," Brown said, laughing. "Next thing I know, before I can even start to get up, all the trainers are out there, saying, 'Stay down, Zeus, we'll take care of you.'"

He was placed on injured reserve the next day with a shoulder injury. Brown has nothing but good things to say about Belichick, who attended his wedding. But his memories of his early days in Cleveland are of Belichick screaming at him almost nonstop. "I think he thought my first name was 'Stupid,'" Brown said. "Every time I did something it was 'You stupid ——, I told you not to do that.' He never let up on me. He taught me how to be a football player. When I started to make money, first thing I did was buy my mother a car. If Belichick didn't have plenty of money, I'd have bought him a car, too."

Midway through the 1994 season, Brown became a starter at right tackle. He remained there for the Browns and then for the Ravens through the 1998 season. When the expansion Browns came into existence in 1999, one of their first free-agent signees was Brown. He was twenty-eight years old, back in the city where he had started, making big money. He could not have been happier. He had started sixty-nine straight games for the Browns/Ravens before missing the last three games of the '98 season with an ankle injury. With the new Browns he was a starter and a key player on the team for the first fourteen weeks of the season. Then, in week fifteen, in a game against Jacksonville, one of the all-time fluke injuries in the history of football changed the course of his career and his life.

It was midway through the second quarter and the Browns were driving. Referee Jeff Triplette called a false start on Browns center Jim Bundren and tossed a penalty flag in his direction. Back then, referees were instructed to throw penalty flags in the direction of the offender. Penalty flags are weighted at one end by a tiny beanbag so they don't float in the wind but rather stay put once they land on the field. Somehow, Triplette threw the flag right at Brown. Instead of landing near Bundren, it went through Brown's face mask and smacked him in the right eye. Brown screamed in pain because the weighted part of the flag had scratched his cornea. Enraged, he charged at Triplette and knocked him over before he was pulled away. He was ejected from the game, which was a moot point since he couldn't see out of his right eye anyway. To add insult to injury, the league suspended him for the final game of the season, meaning he lost a week's pay while wondering if he would be able to play again.

The injury proved to be serious. Brown had to have surgery on the eye and was out of football for the next three seasons. During that time he sued the NFL for loss of income and was awarded a settlement reported to be about $10 million, even though both sides agreed as part of the deal not to talk about how much money the league paid Brown. At the end of the 2002 season, Brown was cleared by doctors to play football again. The Ravens, who needed a tackle to bookend with Jonathan Ogden, decided to take a chance that Brown could still play and that he could stay healthy. He had done both in 2003, and the team was counting on him to anchor the right side of the line again in 2004.

His mother's illness concerned everyone in camp. The entire team was aware of how close Brown was to his mother and everyone knew he had been through a difficult off-season because of a nasty custody battle with his ex-wife over their three children. Brown had always been high-strung, even putting aside his understandable (though not excusable) bull rush on Triplette. Players on other teams often tried to bait him into committing penalties, either through trash talking or unseen grabbing and pushing in the pile. His temper had cost the team in the Tennessee playoff game when Jevon Kearse had taunted him into committing a personal foul just prior to the Ravens' final punt of the game. That 15 yards had allowed the Titans to get just close enough for Gary Anderson to sneak his game-winning 46-yard field goal over the crossbar. The referee who had called the personal foul on Brown? Jeff Triplette.

Brown was one of those people who was a delight to be around 99 percent of the time. He was outgoing and friendly, probably as well liked as anyone on the team. If you asked staff members which player they enjoyed the most, many would say Brown. But when he lost his temper, it could get scary in a hurry. At halftime of a game the previous season, Brown had become so frustrated with offensive line coach Jim Colletto that he had started screaming at him to leave him alone and just let him play the game. Billick had stepped in and calmed things down before they got worse.

There was no doubting that Catherine Brown's illness was devastating to her son. He had called Billick before the Eagles game to say he felt guilty about being away from the team but was afraid if he left his mother's side, she might die while he was away. "You stay there as long as you need to and do what you have to do," Billick told him. "That's your first priority."

The final day of camp — Monday, August 23 — got off to a good start when Orlando Brown walked into the locker room and pronounced himself back with the team. Everyone was glad to see him. The rookie show was scheduled for that night, the final rite of passage for the rookies. The days of serious rookie hazing are long past in the NFL, in part because training camp isn't nearly as intense as it once was. Rookies are still expected to round up food for the veterans on the road and still have to sing at dinner. The only true hazing in the Ravens' camp came after one morning practice when the top two draft picks — Dwan Edwards and Devard Darling — were tied to a goalpost while a group led by Ray Lewis, Gary Baxter, and Adalius Thomas showered them with shaving cream, Gatorade, and ice-cold water. When the bucket of water was empty, it was placed on Darling's head. The two of them stood quietly while they were serenaded, for reasons no one could explain, with an off-key version of "Down by the Riverside." They were freed after a few moments. Lewis checked to make sure they were okay, adhering to Billick's rule that no one get hurt during hazing.

The way rookies react to being hazed can give coaches some insight into their character. Edwards and Darling simply accepted their fate without complaining or arguing or even asking for mercy. They understood that it was part of the drill. Jim Fassel remembered three years earlier, when tight end Jeremy Shockey, his first-round draft pick, had arrived at camp without any sleep because of a screwup in his travel plans. He had practiced, gone to dinner, and had immediately found himself being ordered to sing by veteran linebacker Brandon Short.

"He said, 'Just let me finish eating first,'" Fassel remembered. "That wasn't good enough. Short walked over and said, 'We tell you to sing, you sing *now.*' Well, next thing I know, he and Shockey are going at it. I jumped in and screamed at 'em both but I remember thinking, 'I got my guy. This is a real player.' Shockey went on to have a monster rookie year and helped the Giants reach the playoffs before the fame and fortune of New York caused him to implode on and off the field. Edwards and Darling weren't likely to become luminous stars, but they weren't likely to self-destruct, either.

The good mood of the morning was broken by two incidents: one minor, one not-so-minor. The first was a fight between Ron Johnson and Gerome Sapp, two players struggling to retain their spots on the team. Sapp was a defensive back and special teams player who had made the team a year earlier as a sixth-round pick out of Notre Dame. He was one of the most highly regarded people in the organization, one of the players asked to come in and talk to the rookies during orientation sessions about dealing with the pressures of being in the NFL. Everyone knew that the first cut day was a week away, and tensions were high. Billick doesn't like fights in practice, and his teams don't have them very often. He threatened everyone with gassers — repeated wind sprints — if it happened again, but he understood why the players were on edge.

Near the end of practice, the first significant injury of the preseason took place. During a pileup, someone rolled onto center Mike Flynn's shoulder when he was twisted in such a way that he heard something crack. "I knew right away it wasn't good," he said. "The sound was all I needed."

He was right. He had fractured his right clavicle. Leigh Ann Curl, the team's surgeon, made the drive from Baltimore to examine him and by lunchtime word had come back that Flynn would be gone for eight weeks. Flynn had missed one game in four years and had just signed his first big contract during the off-season, a four-year extension that was worth almost $4 million. That contract had marked a moment of arrival that Flynn had doubted would ever come in his football career. He hadn't been offered any Division 1-A scholarships coming out of high school in Springfield, Massachusetts, and had ended up at Maine, a Division 1-AA school. "Almost everyone who played football at Maine was like me," he said. "We were the 1-A rejects, guys who weren't quite good enough to get a 1-A scholarship. A lot of us had a chip on our shoulder because of that. We all had stories about the 1-A program that said it wanted us but didn't offer [a scholarship] in the end. In some ways, I think it made us better players because we all felt as if we had something to prove."

Flynn never thought seriously about the NFL until very late in his college career. He had torn up his knee midway through his sophomore season and thought perhaps he might not play again. But he came back and was first team all–Yankee Conference as a senior, playing at tackle. Even so, at six-three and 270 pounds, he was undersize for an NFL lineman. He signed with the Ravens as a free agent, thought he was doing well in training camp, and then was cut after the third preseason game. "Awful feeling," he said. "I remember driving home, thinking, 'What am I going to do now?'" He didn't want to give up football; he had felt competitive enough in camp to think he might have a chance to play in the NFL. He had a burst of hope when the Tampa Bay Buccaneers signed him to their developmental squad, but learned how cruel the NFL can be when he was released six days after signing because the Bucs had found another player they believed had more potential. He went home — again — stayed in shape, and hoped the phone would ring. It did — in November — when the Jacksonville Jaguars called to offer him a spot on their developmental squad.

Flynn accepted and walked into a locker room where he knew no one and no one knew him. "It was a lot different than going to a team in the spring where there are a bunch of you who are rookies and in the same boat," he said. "I didn't know anyone. I think I had dinner just about every night I was there by myself. The people at the Cracker Barrel near my apartment all knew me by name. They were probably my best friends down there."

Flynn lived the lonely practice squad existence in Jacksonville for a month, until he got a call from the Ravens. He had, in fact, made an impression on the coaches in training camp, and when the team found itself low on offensive linemen because of injuries, Flynn was offered the chance to sign on to the active roster for the last three weeks of the season. He never made it into a game but felt as if he had his foot in the door. He sweated out training camp the next summer, wondering if he was going to get cut again.

"On one of the cutdown days George Kokinis came and knocked on the door," Flynn said. "When I saw him, my heart sank. I remember thinking, 'Not again.' Turned out he was looking for my roommate. I remember turning around and saying to the guy, 'Hey, guess what, George is here looking for *you.*' Then I felt bad." He smiled. "But not that bad."

He was inactive most weeks that season but played the last three weeks — his first action in the NFL after almost two years of waiting to play. The following year he played regularly on special teams. He became the starting center a year later and was now one of the key players on the offensive line. It is the center who makes all the calls for the linemen, which makes him the quarterback of the group. Flynn's injury would hurt the team psychologically as much as anything else. His replacement, Casey Rabach, was the team's best backup offensive lineman, a good enough player that there had been talk of moving him to right guard to compete with starter Bennie Anderson. Now there was no choice but for him to play center. Rabach was a good player, but without Flynn, the character of the line changed. Flynn was New England fiery; Rabach Midwest (Wisconsin) laid-back. What's more, with Rabach starting, there was very little depth on the line.

"I'll be back after the bye week," which came after the fifth game, Flynn vowed. "I hate the idea of not playing. Playing is what I do."

Billick addressed Flynn's injury with the team after the final practice of camp that afternoon. "Losing Mike is a blow," he said. "But I know Casey will do well. [Damian] Cook and [Lenny] Vandermade, this is your chance. Remember what I told all of you guys about how things always change in football. The one thing I can tell you for sure is that this is not the last adversity or the worst adversity we'll face before the end of the season."

He paused to let that sink in. "Now, you rookies better have a good show tonight because I'm giving you guys tomorrow off. So don't let me down."

The rookies came through. The show was hosted by Brian Rimpf, the offensive lineman from East Carolina who had been the team's final draft pick, and Brendan Darby, a free-agent tackle out of San Diego State who was the longest of long shots to make the team. The evening was a typical send-up of the veterans and coaches. There was a skit on the "Billick modeling agency," complete with a shirtless "Billick" talking about his clientele. There was a re-creation of a linebacker drill with linebacker coach Mike Singletary criticizing everyone, interrupting his diatribe only to say, "Perfect, Ray, that's perfect. Exactly right, Ray." Kyle Boller, who had been part of the rookie show a year ago, got nailed for constantly having two or three coaches hanging on his every move.

It was all good fun and everyone laughed heartily. For many of the rookies, the show was a farewell. Training camp was over. They would get to play one more time, on Saturday night against the Detroit Lions, and then they would hold their breath, hoping they wouldn't be called up to the second floor the following Monday. The locker rooms and player meeting rooms are all downstairs. The coaches' offices are upstairs. Players generally understand that a call to the second floor is never good news. Especially on cutdown day.

Most of the players and coaches headed back to Baltimore after the rookie show. A number of staffers stayed behind to finish up the business of camp the next day. By noon, the sign outside the Best Western had been changed. ROOMS AVAILABLE, it said.

*   *   *

The third exhibition game is by far the most important one of the summer. For the veterans, it is the one game in which they are expected to play extensively enough to get a real feel for where they are, with the start of the season only two weeks away. For those trying to make the team, it is their last chance to make a case to the coaches to keep them around for at least one more week. Some know their time is short.

Clint Greathouse, the rookie punter, had flown several members of his family in to Baltimore for the game. "Maybe I'll get another chance somewhere down the road," he said. "I hope so. But if I don't, I got to be in camp and run through the tunnel with an NFL team for three games. I want my family to see me do that."

Others were still hoping. At least fourteen players would have to be cut on Monday. (Players on the injured list did not count against the limit of sixty-five.) Most would be rookies, but a few would be veterans. An extra spot on the roster would have to be created for Deion Sanders, who was now expected to show up on Tuesday to take his physical and sign his contract. Deionmania had ebbed slightly since the initial story that he was considering a comeback, but everyone knew it would peak again the minute he showed up. Ozzie Newsome and Eugene Parker had agreed in principle to a contract that would pay Sanders about $1.5 million plus incentives based on how much he played and how well he performed. In NFL terms, that was cheap for a player who was going to the Hall of Fame — cheap, that is, if he could stay healthy, which he had struggled to do during 2000, his last season as an active player.

Billick was concerned with the number of nagging injuries that had suddenly cropped up. In NFL jargon, injured players are referred to as "down," healthy ones are referred to as "up." For the Lions game, the Ravens had a lot of guys down: Flynn, who was going to be gone for a while; Todd Heap, still nursing his shoulder injury; Marques Douglas and Anthony Weaver; Devard Darling, the rookie wide receiver, who had a foot injury; Corey Fuller, who had suffered a calf injury early in the Eagles game; and Travis Taylor, who had a groin pull — a major concern because it was the sort of injury that could linger. The last thing the Ravens needed with their already-thin receiving corps was to have Taylor, who was the most dangerous in the group, hobbling. Still, the team was taking the optimistic approach: let's have our nagging injuries now rather than later.

The flip side was that B. J. Sams had been cleared to play. With the first cuts coming the following week, the coaches wanted to get a look at him to decide whether to keep Lamont Brightful around for the final exhibition game. Brightful and Kareem Kelly, who had been given the chance to return a couple of kicks in Philadelphia, had done nothing to convince anyone that they were the answer. The coaches were hoping the answer was Sams.

The Detroit game would be the closest the Ravens would come to creating a regular-season atmosphere before the season actually began. Billick didn't make them spend the night at the downtown Hyatt, as they would the night before a regular-season game, but he did have them report to the hotel for the pregame meal — which began four hours before kickoff — to get into the habit of establishing their pregame ritual for home games. Unlike on the road, where they bus from the hotel to the stadium, the players are on their own to get there at home. Many are dropped off at the hotel by their wives and then share a ride to the stadium, which is about a five-minute drive from the hotel.

Billick walks to the stadium. He began walking from the team hotel to the stadium for home games while he was in Minnesota. Kim would drop him off on Saturday night, then she and the girls would drive to the game so the family could all ride home together after it was over. Billick would walk about a mile from the Vikings' hotel to the Metrodome before the game. Occasionally this could be risky. "One day it was so cold, I think I was on my way to getting frostbite. I was shivering, having trouble walking. I was crazy to be out there. Fortunately, one of our security guys came by and made me get in his car. Actually, I didn't really argue with him. I was too cold to talk anyway."

It never got that cold in Baltimore. When Billick first arrived, he had asked Vernon Holley to help him map out a walking route from the hotel to the stadium. Like a lot of NFL security people, Holley is a retired cop, having worked as a homicide detective for the Baltimore City Police Department for most of his twenty-three years on the force. He and Billick found a route that took them through a restored city neighborhood to the foot of the Hamburg Street bridge. From there they walked across the bridge, arriving on the concourse outside the stadium. Once Billick had the route down, he thanked Holley.

"What time do we leave?" Holley had asked him.

"We?" Billick said.

"You're a head coach now," Holley told him. "You aren't walking through throngs of fans without security."

"It's okay, Vernon," Billick said. "We aren't on a losing streak yet. I'll be fine."

"I'm sure you will be," Holley answered. "But you'll be fine with me walking next to you. This is *not* your decision."

At six foot five, Billick is a lot bigger than Holley. He's also a few years younger. "Vernon is one of those guys who is as nice as anyone you'll ever meet," Billick said. "But there are moments when you can see why he was a homicide cop. I just said, 'We'll leave two hours and twenty minutes before kickoff.'"

Which they have done before every home game for six years. Billick tried walking to the stadium on the road a couple of times early on but found that the notoriety he had acquired as a head coach (and an outspoken and controversial one) made it difficult for him to make the walk without encountering a few fans who weren't that thrilled to see him. "Actually, most of them were nice or funny," he said. "But there were always a couple who went a little too far."

The last road walk had been on a trip to Nashville for a game against the Tennessee Titans. As Billick and Holley neared the stadium, a car passed them with two men in it who appeared to be already drunk. Their message to Billick for the day did not include the words "Good luck, Coach." The car went past. A few minutes later Holley saw that it had circled back and was coming near them again.

"Coach, walk on the inside, away from the curb," Holley said.

"Vernon, it's okay. . . ."

"Coach, do what I'm telling you to do, please."

Billick complied.

The drunks came past, repeated their profanities, and moved on.

That sort of thing is never a problem in Baltimore. After six years, the fans now know exactly when Billick and Holley will cross the Hamburg Street bridge. Many are tailgating in the parking lots that fan out on either side of the bridge, and they cheer Billick heartily as he passes. Most fans on the bridge wish him luck or shake hands. There are regulars. One woman stands about a third of the way up the bridge and insists that Billick give her a pinky shake for good luck. Another waits at the bottom of the bridge to take a good-luck picture, occasionally with friends. Billick always complies. For the past two years, the same guy had passed Billick on the bridge in almost the same spot and said, "Fire Cavanaugh," and kept on walking. Billick's response was usually a laugh or "Matt sends his best to you, too," also without breaking stride.

One week a national TV crew wanted to get Billick on tape walking across the bridge, but someone fell asleep at the switch and the camera wasn't on as Billick and Holley reached the top of the bridge. The producer ran up to Billick and explained what had happened. "Really sorry to hear it," Billick said.

"Any way you can go back to the bottom of the bridge and walk back up again?" the TV guy asked. Billick looked at him for the smile that would indicate he was kidding. There was none. He laughed anyway and said, "You're joking, right?" and kept on walking.

In addition to the picture lady, Billick is also greeted at the bottom of the bridge by a woman named Downtown Diane who works for WQSR, the flagship station on the Ravens' radio network. Diane conducts a brief interview with Billick as he walks briskly (she has to run to keep up since she is about five foot two) toward the entrance to the stadium. The interview usually goes something like this:

"Coach, big game today. Do you think the team is ready?"

"Well, I certainly hope we're ready. The [fill in team name] are a very good team and we're going to have to play a great game to beat them."

"Coach, what does the team need from the fans today?"

"We need everybody loud, really loud. They have a [young and inexperienced/old and experienced] quarterback, and anything we can do to rattle him is going to help our defense."

"Anything we should know about injuries or lineup changes?"

"No, can't think of a thing." (If Jamal and Ray Lewis had woke up too sore to play, that would still be Billick's answer. Like every NFL coach, he doesn't give away anything about any kind of lineup change until the last possible moment.)

"Coach, good luck today. We're all behind you."

"Thanks. We need all the help we can get."

It may not be the most scintillating radio in history. Still, Billick is the only NFL coach who submits to a weekly chat while walking into the stadium. It makes the fans feel closer to him, because in a sense, he's no different than they are. He walks across the bridge that many of them walk across, chats about the game, and enters the stadium. The only difference is he doesn't have to go through a patdown or have his bag checked by security.

Saturday, August 28, was hot and humid in Baltimore, one of the first truly unpleasant days of the late summer. The atmosphere in the pregame locker room was a lot more tense than it had been before the previous two games. The starters were treating this like a real game; the younger players like a final exam. If there was any doubt that the game was to be treated like the real thing, it was erased almost as soon as Ray Lewis walked into the locker room. There may be no one in football who has a game face like Lewis's. Like his idol, now coach, Mike Singletary, Lewis's eyes radiate intensity from the minute he enters the locker room until the game is over. He almost always keeps up a running commentary that is alternately funny and insightful, if not always logical. Lewis keeps up such an endless monologue that some players keep their headphones on before the game just to shut him out. Others enjoy hearing him. Still others find that listening to him either inspires or relaxes them.

"We need to show [Lions running back] Kevin Jones what the NFL is about!" Lewis shouted as the linebackers prepared to take the field for pregame warm-ups. "I hope he doesn't think this is a preseason game, because it's not. This is personal. It's football; that means it's personal!" Turning to outside linebackers coach Jeff FitzGerald, he said, "Come on, Jeff, don't keep us in here too long. We're ready to get out there. We need to get out and hit somebody!"

The time when the linebackers would leave the locker room was written on the greaseboard just inside the locker-room door. It wasn't up to FitzGerald to change the time, and Lewis knew it. He was just letting off steam.

"Ray may be the only guy I know who can get intense talking about cereal," Todd Heap joked.

Like every football team, the Ravens' pregame routine is identical before every game. The players take the field in stages, by position. The kickers and their holders and snappers go out first, and the others follow one group at a time. Most players greet a few players on the opposing team whom they know. When the Ravens are at home, Billick always seeks out the opposing head coach at some point. It may be when he first arrives at the stadium and walks the entire field from one end to the other, one corner to the other, or it may be later, during warm-ups.

"I always think when you are the home team, it is up to you to seek the other guy out, almost as if you are the host," he said. "I know I appreciate it when other guys do it for me on the road, and I'm disappointed when they don't. So, I always do it, whether it's a friend, someone I hardly know, or even when it's someone I might not like."

The players return to the locker room about twenty-five minutes before kickoff. The coaches leave them alone to relax for a few minutes. In the Ravens' locker room, the players gather in a circle, holding hands to say a prayer as soon as they come back in from warm-ups. This was something the team leaders — notably, Lewis — had decided to do for the 2004 season. Billick had always had everyone kneel to say the Lord's Prayer as the last thing they did before taking the field, but Lewis and others had decided praying as a team with no coaches in the room was something they needed to do to feel closer.

Most of the players were fine with that idea. A few felt uncomfortable with it because they felt there was peer pressure to take part. "I can't not do it," said one player, "because I'm afraid some of the guys will be offended. But I'm not comfortable with asking God for help in winning a football game."

A couple of players — backup running back Chester Taylor and long snapper Joe Maese — always went to the bathroom during the prayer, preferring not to take part. Everyone else joined in. Different players led the prayer from week to week. Often it was Lewis. Sometimes it was Marques Douglas, one of the leaders of the team's Bible study. Other times it was Corey Fuller or Matt Stover. Usually Rod Hairston, the team chaplain, would ask one player to lead the prayer.

Just before it is time to leave the locker room, Billick walks to the center of the room and says the same five words: "Okay, let's get it up."

That is the signal for the team to form a circle around him for a pregame speech. Except that Billick rarely gives speeches. He reminds the players about the keys to the game that have been talked about all week and talks about the effort needed to win. When he is finished, everyone who is playing in the game leaves the locker room by a back door that takes the players through the bowels of the stadium to the tunnel where they will be introduced. Everyone not in uniform — injured players, assistant coaches, doctors, trainers — leaves through the front door and enters the field from two stairways that spill out onto the sidelines directly behind the team bench.

"Nothing worse than going out this door," Mike Flynn said on the night of the Lions game as he walked to the front door dressed in street clothes, his arm in a sling. "You walk out this door, you're just some guy. You come out of that tunnel, you feel like you're a god."

Like every other team in the NFL, the Ravens hype their introductions to try to get the crowd jazzed for kickoff. They do not have a goofy foam helmet they run out of, but they do have cheerleaders who form a cordon, first for the players not being introduced and then for the players being introduced individually. (The cheerleaders are paid $50 a game plus two tickets, making them, arguably, the most underpaid performers in football.) Before each game, coaches decide whether to introduce their offense or their defense. When the defense is introduced in Baltimore, the player introductions officially become an event because the last player introduced is Ray Lewis.

It is during introductions that the entertainer in Ray Lewis is clearly on display. Even before the PA announcer gets to his name, Lewis goes into his act. He pounds his chest. He screams to the fans and waves his arms and then when the music starts — a song by the rapper Nelly — he does the Dance. By the time he is finished and runs into the arms of his teammates, the dead in Baltimore may very well have been awakened.

The Lions game answered one question very quickly. After the Lions had stalled on their own 42 on the opening drive of the game, punter Nick Harris lofted a 47-yard punt that Sams caught on the 11-yard line. He cut one way, then the other, found a seam, burst by several would-be tacklers, and was gone, 89 yards for a touchdown. It was an electrifying play, the very first time Sams had caught a punt in any kind of NFL game. That the play was nullified because Musa Smith was called for running into the kicker didn't change what Sams had done.

He was greeted like a returning astronaut when he came to the sideline even while the Detroit offense was trotting onto the field to continue its drive.

"Congratulations, kid, you just made the team," Matt Stover said to Sams, offering him a handshake.

"I hope you're right."

"Oh, I'm right," Stover said. "You're on the team."

On the Lions' next punt, Sams had another good return, this one for 15 yards. This time Chester Taylor was called for an illegal block, bringing the ball back. "How many times have we talked in meetings about where to put your hands when blocking?" Billick asked everyone and no one, clearly frustrated.

Preseason games are often filled with penalties. There are a lot of backup players in the games, and the officials are trying out their flags to make sure they work. In this game, everyone seemed to get involved in the foulfest. Even the normally perfect Jonathan Ogden was called for lining up in the neutral zone. Of course, Ogden was convinced he had not lined up wrong and spent several plays demonstrating to the officials what he had done so they would understand what a terrible mistake they had made.

"I try not to let the crazy man come out in the exhibition season," he said. "But sometimes I can't help myself."

The game was not filled with artistic moments. With the Lions leading, 6–3, at the half, Matt Cavanaugh decided to leave the first-team offense (minus Jamal Lewis, who didn't need any more banging) in for the first series of the second half. The decision had nothing to do with the score. Cavanaugh thought that Boller and his receivers needed some extra work and that Chester Taylor and Musa Smith should get some snaps with the first team. The strategy worked well. Taylor went 84 yards for a touchdown (no penalties) on the first play from scrimmage, to give the Ravens a 10–6 lead, and then Smith played the next series before Boller and the rest of the starters retired for the night.

There were good moments and bad moments the rest of the way. The second-team defense stymied Detroit's offense completely. Gerome Sapp, fighting for his roster spot, had an interception and a fumble recovery. Clint Greathouse got two chances to punt — adding to his tape collection with his family watching. On the other hand, the offense struggled in the so-called red zone. *Red zone* is a relatively new football term, one that describes the area inside the 20-yard line. How offenses perform in the red zone is often seen as a key to their success or failure. *Red zone* is another of those terms — like *crunch time, stepping up,* and the always popular *escapability* — that has been overused to the point where it is now part of the jock-cliché culture. The perfect TV sound bite from an NFL player or coach describing his team's success might sound something like this: "We really stepped it up at crunch time, especially in the red zone where [fill in quarterback's name] escapability really helps us give 110 percent effort on every play." There is even a ketchup that sponsors plays in the red zone, turning it into the [ketchup's name] red zone.

With or without ketchup, the Ravens didn't step up in the red zone in the second half. On one play from the 9-yard line, Ron Johnson was caught in motion — causing Billick to tear off his headset in anger. Then Kordell Stewart threw an interception. One series later, having moved the ball 79 yards to the 1-yard line, the Ravens failed to score on three plays. Musa Smith fumbled but was rescued by a Detroit penalty. Chester Taylor was stopped for no gain, and then Stewart fumbled the next snap and was not saved by a Detroit penalty. Everyone felt a little better when the Ravens went 75 yards to score the clinching touchdown on the next series. But with the season now two weeks away, there was clearly work still to be done.

11

The Turk

BRIAN BILLICK ALWAYS TELLS his players to enjoy every victory, regardless of when or how it comes. But he didn't spend a lot of time enjoying the win over the Lions. He was concerned about the continuing mental errors he was seeing and told the players they were going to have to deal with that issue before the regular season began, when they would pay a serious price for such mistakes as blocking in the back on a punt return, running into the kicker, or being penalized and turning the ball over in the red zone. Those were matters that would be dealt with over the course of the next two weeks. The more pressing issue was the cuts that were to come on Monday morning. "This is the part of the business I dislike the most," Billick said. "But as you all know, this *is* a business and we've got to make some tough decisions here in the next day or so. Whatever happens, I want to thank every one of you for the effort you've given us."

The coaches would meet Sunday to finalize the cut list. The rookies and second-year players who were staying at the Hilton Garden Inn were told that a bus would pick them up at 6:30 on Monday morning to bring them over to the complex. Everyone else had to be in the building before nine o'clock for a team meeting. Those who were leaving would be gone by the time the meeting began.

There wasn't going to be a lot of argument among the coaches about this list. The first cut would not be that difficult. Many of the players leaving would be "slappies," kids who were good college players but a clear step or two away from being good enough to play in the NFL. The question for

Billick was exactly what to say to those players in their exit interview. He didn't like the idea of killing dreams by saying something like "Listen, son, you can't play at this level — you need to go get a job." But he wanted to at least put that thought in the minds of those he didn't feel could make a living playing football. "It's not my place to tell them to stop," he said. "But for some of them, the time has to come to start thinking about the next thing."

It helped Billick that he had been in the shoes of the players he was cutting, having been cut twice in training camp before coming to the realization that he needed to move on with his life. "I can honestly say to them, 'I've sat in that chair, I know how you're feeling,'" he said. "That may make them feel better about me, that I really do empathize, but it doesn't make them feel better about what has just happened."

The Sunday meeting was relatively brief. The only serious debate was about a rookie linebacker from Baylor named John Garrett. The coaches liked his attitude and aggressiveness, but he was caught in a numbers game. There just weren't any openings in the linebacker corps for a rookie and, at least at the moment, the coaches liked another rookie linebacker named Brandon Barnes a little bit better as a developmental squad player. Teams frequently do not get all eight players they want for the developmental squad because everyone has to pass through waivers first, and often another team grabs someone for their active roster off the waiver wire.

There was some talk about the second round of cuts since they would be made in only five days, after the final exhibition game against the New York Giants on Thursday in the Meadowlands. At least two veterans would be cut that day: Ron Johnson and Lamont Brightful. Both were being kept around essentially because they were needed to play in the second half of the Giants game. Johnson's fight with Gerome Sapp and his thoughtless penalty on Saturday had been the final straws for him, and B. J. Sams's performance against the Lions had sealed Brightful's fate.

The one surprise on the possible cut list was Sapp, who had been the defensive player of the game on Saturday. Mike Nolan was disappointed in the way Sapp had developed, feeling that, as bright as he was off the field, he had struggled to pick up concepts on the field. Gary Zauner spoke up in Sapp's defense, saying he was one of the team's better special teams players.

"Will he ever pick up the concepts you're talking about?" Billick asked Nolan.

"I'd love to say yes," Nolan said. "Because he's a great kid. But I think the honest answer is no."

Billick turned from Nolan to Zauner. "How good is he? Is he just good, or is he *really* good?"

"In my opinion, really good," Zauner said. "Special teams is attitude, and he's got as good an attitude as anyone we've got."

They decided to let the question simmer until Friday.

It rained the next morning, appropriate weather for what is always a grim day around a football complex. Relatively speaking, Billick and Ozzie Newsome had the easy jobs. Billick would conduct what amounted to an exit interview, and Newsome would then go through administrative details. The dirty work would be done by the team's three youngest scouts, Daniel Jeremiah, Jeremiah Washburn, and Chisom Opara. All three had been good college football players: Jeremiah at Appalachian State, Washburn at Arkansas, and Opara at Princeton. A year ago Opara had been a free agent in the Ravens' camp and Jeremiah had "turked" him.

The Turk is one of football's oldest phrases. Whoever it is who gives a player the news that he's cut, or sends the message with the unmistakable request "Coach needs to see you and bring your playbook," is called the Turk. That is, unless you are Orlando Brown. He called the young scouts "reaper," and always turned his nametag away from them whenever they came near his locker, as if that might prevent them from knowing who he was. Brown had never been turked, but like most older players, he always wondered when that day might come for him.

Jeremiah, Washburn, and Opara spread out in the locker room as the players began filtering in soon after 6:30 on Monday morning. Technically, everyone was supposed to report to his position coach. When one of the Turks walked into the meeting room — or the locker room before reaching the meeting room — and told a player he was needed upstairs, that player knew what was coming. The mood on cut morning is always somber. Those not getting cut feel for those who are. Some are losing friends or seeing players they like and respect lose their jobs. All of them understand that someday they may be the ones being asked for their playbooks.

"Not a lot of laughter on cut mornings," kicker Matt Stover said. "You sort of try to tiptoe around because you know it's a painful day for a lot of people."

Stover had memories of one awkward experience from the year before. Jeremiah and Washburn had been the Turks that day, and both had showed up for work wearing, appropriately enough, black shirts. Quietly, they made their way around the locker room, finding players and asking them to go upstairs. Finally, every player being cut had been rounded up, except for one, wide receiver Milton Wynn. Stover was sitting by his locker when Wynn walked in. Thinking that all the cuts had already occurred, Stover clapped Wynn on the back and said, "Must be a relief for you not having any of those guys in the black shirts looking for you, huh, Milton?"

Jeremiah had just walked back into the locker room in search of Wynn and he heard what Stover was saying, too late to get his attention and call him off. "I felt awful," Jeremiah said. "I had to walk over right after that, in my black shirt, and say, 'Milton, I need to take you upstairs to see Coach.'"

The only person who felt worse was Stover. "I was sick, almost literally sick," he said. "I just didn't think. I told Milton before he left how terrible I felt. He was good about it. He just said, 'Matt, I wouldn't be any less cut if you hadn't said anything.'"

Occasionally the scouts make a mistake. Jeremiah had been sent down to get an offensive lineman named Jason Thomas the previous year. He had walked into the offensive line meeting room, put his hand on Thomas's shoulder, and quietly told him he needed to come upstairs. Jeremiah was halfway up the stairs before he realized that the player walking in front of him was Damion Cook, not Jason Thomas.

"Damion, I'm sorry, I got the wrong guy," he said, watching Cook's knees sag in relief. Jeremiah returned to the meeting room to get Thomas. Seeing him come back for a second player, Jonathan Ogden said, "What's going on here today, are you guys trying to cut the whole team?"

Perhaps the ultimate case of mistaken identity had happened to Jim Fassel when he was coaching the Giants. "We were making some cuts on an off day, so the players didn't have to come in," he said. "I was calling guys at the hotel and asking them to come in. Course, they knew what it was about, but there's just no easy way to do it. There was a guy named Ryan

Smith we had to cut. I called the hotel and asked for Ryan Smith. The operator put me through. He answers the phone. I said, 'Ryan, it's Coach Fassel.' He says, 'Oh my God, you're cutting me.' I told him how sorry I was, gave him my usual speech, thanked him, and all that. He asked me what he'd done wrong and I told him he just wasn't quite good enough to play for us, but I thought he had potential as a long snapper.

"He says, 'Long snapper? Coach, I'm not a long snapper.' Now I think the kid's crazy, or I'm crazy. I said, 'Ryan, is that you?' He said, 'Yes, Coach, it's me.' I said, 'Ryan Smith?' There's a long pause and he says, 'Oh God, Coach, Ryan Smith's my roommate, this is Ryan Phillips!' I made his day right there. He said Ryan Smith was out. I told him to have him call me when he got back."

Billick normally keeps some kind of background music playing in his office throughout the day — jazz early, classical later. On cutdown day, there's no music. Once the players started filtering in, one of the young scouts was assigned to stand in the doorway to identify each player as he came in. As in, "Coach, Don Muhlbach is here."

Billick knew just about all the players in camp on sight. But he wanted to be sure not to make the same mistake he had made three years earlier when Terry Jones came into his office on cut day. Neither Billick nor Jones is exactly sure how Jones found himself in there: Billick thinks Jones wandered in to ask a question about scheduling; Jones remembers Billick having said he wanted to speak to all the rookies that day one way or the other. Jones was a fifth-round pick out of Alabama who thought he was going to make the team as a backup tight end.

When he sat down, the look on Billick's face told him differently. "You've worked really hard for us, and that makes this really tough." Jones felt his stomach drop to his shoes. The coaches had told him he was doing well. He had been almost certain he would make the team. "I don't think this is the end for you," Billick continued. "You're the only one who can decide how long you want to chase the dream."

Jones, who thought he might cry, just nodded his head as Billick talked.

"Do you have your degree?"

"Yes, sir, I do."

"That's good, that's important. Where do you think you'll go right now?"

"I hadn't really thought about it, but I guess I'll go back to Birmingham."

Billick stopped. Birmingham? The next player on his list of cuts was from California. He looked at Jones closely.

"Oh my God," he said. "I've got the wrong guy. I'm not cutting you. You're on the team."

Jones thought he might pass out. He was taking deep breaths to keep his composure. "I'm not cut?" he asked. "I'm on the team?"

"Yes, you're on the team," Billick said. "Terry, I'm so sorry, I made a terrible mistake."

"Oh thank God," Jones said.

Billick didn't want that scene repeated, although he had once intentionally told a player he knew had made the team that he was being cut. That player was John Jones, a talented tight end with a questionable work ethic. Billick wanted to get his attention, so he called him in and told him he had been cut. Jones was, predictably, shocked and devastated. After letting the news sink in, Billick walked around his desk and said, "You aren't cut, John." Jones leaped to his feet and threw his arms around Billick, going from low to high in seconds. "I wanted you to know what it felt like to be cut for a few seconds," Billick said. "Because I want you to work to make sure that day never comes."

Most of the time, the meetings in Billick's office were brief. Billick would give his speech about deciding when to give up the dream, offer up the possibility that NFL Europe could be a good training ground if a player wanted to continue his career. Very few — if any — ever told Billick they were done, because very few, if any, thought of themselves as done. Twice during his player meetings Billick opened the conversation by saying, "How's it going this morning?" Then he caught himself: "Now there's a stupid question."

Not everyone got the same speech. Billick told Muhlbach he believed he could snap in the NFL. "I believe it because Gary Zauner believes it," he said, "and Gary is almost never wrong about these things." He pointed out to offensive linemen such as Eric Dumas and Brendan Darby that it often took longer for offensive linemen to develop than players at other positions. "Mike Flynn got cut a couple times before he stuck," he said. "Bennie Anderson came in here as a camp guy, a body to get us through July and August, and now he's a starter." He was honest with Brian Gaither, the free-agent quarterback. "What I saw of you on tape excited me," he said. "For some reason, maybe it was lack of snaps, I don't know, I never saw that in camp."

The two toughest meetings were with John Garrett and Kareem Kelly. "I want you to know it took us fifteen to twenty minutes before we decided to make this move with you," he told Garrett. "There's certainly a chance we'll bring you back for developmental. You're a good football player."

Kelly was different. He had bounced around — cut by the New Orleans Saints, signed to the Ravens developmental team, kept around with the idea he might make the team at wide receiver. "I know you've been through this before," Billick began. "So have I. The problem has been consistency. We just haven't seen it. At some point you need to figure out if you're done chasing this dream. Have you given any thought to what you'd do? Do you have your degree from USC?"

"No, Coach, I don't. But I'm not done chasing."

There was no small talk as Kelly left the office. "He thinks we screwed up," Billick said after Kelly had walked down the hall to do his turn with Newsome. "He'll leave here believing we didn't give him a chance."

Kelly had a minor injury, which meant he would have to negotiate an injury buyout with Newsome. Billick was standing in the doorway, watching Kelly walk down the hall, when he saw a familiar face approaching.

"I'm back," Chris McAlister said, shaking hands with Billick.

"Good to have you back," Billick said to his All-Pro cornerback who hadn't been in training camp for a single day because of his ongoing contract dispute with the team. "When you get done with your physical, let's talk."

"Absolutely," McAlister said. "I'm ready to go."

The Ravens' prodigal-son cornerback had come home. The Hall of Fame cornerback was due to arrive any minute. Fourteen lockers were being cleaned out. Fourteen men would be making the drive of shame along with dozens of others who hoped to make their living playing pro football. Their names would appear in small agate type the next day in newspapers around the country under the heading "Waived." Perhaps the words "Dream Shattered" would be more appropriate.

*   *   *

The Ravens had one final preseason game to play. Chris McAlister would play in that game. That made everyone in the organization happy since he was a key part of the defense. What's more, everyone understood why he had waited so long to show up. Each year, NFL teams have the right to "franchise" one player who is eligible for free agency, meaning that if he signs somewhere else, the team has the right to match the offer or be compensated with two first-round draft picks if the player ends up leaving. In return, a franchise player must be paid whatever the average salary is for the top five players at his position. McAlister was in his sixth NFL season and had been franchised twice by the Ravens. In 2004 he would be paid $7.1 million.

The Ravens had talked with McAlister about a long-term contract, but they had been reluctant to agree to the kind of money — notably, the kind of signing bonus — they knew it would take to secure a player of his caliber and reputation. The reason was simple: they just weren't sure what they would be getting if they made that kind of commitment. There was no questioning his ability to play the game. He was the prototypical lockdown cornerback, gifted with speed and size (six-one, 206), a nose for the football, and a penchant, like safety Ed Reed, for making big plays.

But McAlister wasn't like Reed, who hung out with Ray Lewis, looked up to Ray Lewis, and seemed mature beyond his years. McAlister wasn't like anyone on the Ravens. He hung out with no one and had no role models. He was a loner — at least, in the locker room — a high-strung personality who frequently clashed with the coaching staff. In 2003, when the Ravens had spent the week in San Diego prior to playing there because a hurricane was sweeping through the East Coast, McAlister had been the one player on the team who had ignored Billick's request that the players remain on an East Coast clock, meaning he wanted them in their rooms at seven o'clock, lights-out at eight, and awake for breakfast at five. McAlister made a point of missing the curfew, made sure everyone knew about it, and then walked into the morning meeting the next day late.

Billick isn't exactly Tom Coughlin when it comes to rules, but he does expect players to be on time and he does not expect them to make a point of ignoring what he tells them to do. He called McAlister in after the morning meeting and told him he was sending him home. "You aren't playing Sunday," he said. "You've let your teammates down. I let you play, I'm letting them down, too."

McAlister was stunned. He had expected to be yelled at and to be disciplined, but he hadn't expected Billick to simply tell him to go home. He was angry. Only later did he understand why Billick did what he did. "I was an asshole," he said. "I was trying to prove something, although I'm not exactly sure what. The only thing that saved me is that the team went out and won without me. Thank God. Because if they had lost, I think it would have been very difficult for me to walk back into that locker room. It wasn't easy as it was. I had to go around and apologize to everyone, but at least I could look them in the eye, tell them I was sorry, and there were no lingering hard feelings because I didn't cost us a game."

No lingering hard feelings, but lingering doubts. McAlister had always been the gifted kid who tended to make things harder for himself than they should have been. He was the son of a great football player, James McAlister, a star running back at UCLA who later played for the Philadelphia Eagles and the New England Patriots. He still remembered when he was little his dad showing him film of his playing days. "He would get out this reel-to-reel stuff and show it to us on the wall," McAlister remembered. "It was snowy and hard to see, but you could tell he was great."

The son was a natural athlete just like the father. Chris played everything as a kid, but he always wanted to be a football player, to be just like his father. He was heavily recruited as a high school senior after being named California player of the year while playing quarterback at Pasadena High School. He rushed for more than 1,000 yards and threw for more than 1,000 yards as a senior. A lot of colleges thought his future was as a running back. His father put an end to that talk. "He said to me, 'You don't want that, it beats your body up,'" McAlister remembered. "I knew he knew firsthand. I was already six-one as a senior in high school. He pointed out that there were very few defensive backs in the NFL over six feet. He thought that might be the best route for me even back then."

More than anything, McAlister wanted to follow in his father's footsteps to UCLA. The problem was his SAT score. "I never even thought about SATs until I was a senior," he said. "Then I realized I had to take them. First time, I bombed. Second time, I got better. Third time I was

760, which under the old rules would have made it. But that was the year they changed the rule, so instead of 700 being good enough, I had to make 810. My parents got me a tutor. I studied, I learned how it was better not to answer questions if you weren't sure, the whole thing. Took it one last time. Made 1010. Hallelujah! I'm going to UCLA! Sent them the score and waited for the call saying welcome to UCLA. Instead, I get a call saying, 'Admissions is concerned about the jump in your score. They're sending it to the NCAA to be investigated.' I couldn't believe it. I was crushed."

UCLA's decision to submit McAlister's SAT for investigation "froze" his score, meaning he could not use it to gain admission to any college. His father was so upset that he divorced himself, for all intents and purposes, from his alma mater. McAlister went into a funk. "They had taken my dream from me," he said. "I didn't want to go anywhere, do anything. I spent the whole summer around the house, just sulking."

It was mid-August when his mother came into his room one day with neither tea nor sympathy. "You've got a choice," she said. "You can go enroll in a junior college and get yourself eligible to play college football or you can go get a job. But you aren't going to sit in this house and do nothing."

"Surprisingly enough," McAlister said, smiling, "I opted for the chance to play football again."

He enrolled at Mt. San Antonio College, not that far from his home. He played that fall but didn't really bother with school. He was still seething about the SAT, so, in protest, he didn't bother going to any classes. At the end of his first semester, word came down from the NCAA: his test score had been verified. He was free to go to any college in the country. There was only one place he knew he *wasn't* going: UCLA. He opted for Arizona in the second recruiting go-around, in part because it was warm and not far from home, in part because the Wildcats had recruited him from day one as a defensive back.

Before he could get there, though, a moment of immaturity —"actually, stupidity," he said — landed him in trouble that would linger through his college years. Walking out of a department store one day, McAlister spotted a jacket he liked. Money was never an issue in his life, so the thought of getting something for free wasn't what caused him to try to walk out of the store with the jacket. "I looked around and thought, 'I wonder if I can get away with this,'" he said years later. "Don't even ask me why I thought that, because I don't know. I just did it."

And got caught. "Probably lucky," he said. "If I'd gotten away with it once, I might have been tempted to see if I could do it again. They stopped me in my tracks right there." He was charged with petty theft and sentenced to fifteen hours of community service. Except he didn't bother going back to serve those fifteen hours. In the fall of 1998 the judge decided that if McAlister didn't want to bother with his community service time, he could serve ten days in jail instead. By then, McAlister was an All-American cornerback for the Wildcats and a surefire first-round draft pick.

The petty-theft charge was not a major concern to most NFL teams. The rest of McAlister's record was clean, and his talent was unquestionable. The Ravens liked the way he played — very hard, very intense; he was clearly someone who loved to play. "That has always been Chris's strength," Ozzie Newsome said. "He's made some mistakes, but we've always known when it was time to work, time to play football he was going to be there."

McAlister made the usual rounds for interviews with teams that might draft him. He expected the shoplifting issue to come up. He didn't expect to walk into the office of newly minted Redskins owner Dan Snyder and have the conversation begin with "So, I understand you've got some jail time coming up, huh?"

"I remember thinking to myself, 'Boy, do I hope this guy doesn't draft me,'" McAlister said. "Even though they were picking number seven and it would have been a big deal to go that high, I just instantly disliked the man. I mean, look, I was embarrassed by what I'd done and I told everyone who brought it up how dumb it was. No debating it. No excuses. But that's not the way you expect someone you've just met to greet you. If he thought I was such a bad guy, why fly me in for the interview in the first place? It was as if he wanted to make me feel small right away. I didn't like that."

McAlister was relieved when the Redskins used their pick to take Champ Bailey and was delighted when the Ravens, picking tenth, took him. McAlister didn't start the opener, but in his role as the nickel back, he had an interception that he almost returned for a touchdown. "Rod Woodson, peeling back to block, tripped me up on the two-yard line," he said. "I told him he was just trying to keep me from doing something he hadn't done." He was in the starting lineup by the fifth game and finished the season with five interceptions. He soon became established as one of the better cornerbacks in the NFL, someone who could come up and stop the run but was also difficult to throw against. In his second season, the Ravens won the Super Bowl. McAlister was established as a star, and he behaved like one.

"I was absolutely living the good life," he said. "I traveled all the time and I spent a lot of money wherever I was. I had the money, so why not spend it? When my first contract was up, if my football career had ended at that moment, I wouldn't have had any money at all. I spent everything I had."

It was that lifestyle along with his loner style in the locker room that concerned the Ravens. No one in the organization thought he was a bad person; in fact, almost everyone liked him. But his moodiness was a concern, as was the incident in San Diego, which to many was a microcosm of who McAlister was. It didn't alienate McAlister from his teammates, but it did distance him even more.

That *didn't* mean the Ravens didn't want to sign him. They just weren't ready to make the kind of commitment to him that they normally would make automatically to a player of his caliber, the kind of commitment they had already made to players like Ray Lewis and Jonathan Ogden and would almost certainly make in a few more years to Ed Reed and Todd Heap.

McAlister hadn't helped the situation in June when he had been quoted as wondering why the Ravens wouldn't give him a long-term deal when he wasn't one of the players on the team who had been arrested or been in trouble during his pro career. Those comments were upsetting on two levels: they were a swipe at his teammates, and McAlister had the shoplifting incident in college, had been suspended by his team, and had once tested positive for marijuana and had been charged with DUI — although the charge was later dropped. None of the incidents by themselves were that serious, but they hardly made McAlister a poster boy for good behavior.

No one on the team was upset with him for staying out of camp. That was what franchise players did. Since they didn't have a contract, they didn't receive a signing bonus — the key to all NFL contracts these days. NFL players receive their entire salaries during the seventeen weeks of the regular season. That means a franchise player would be putting his body at risk for the roughly $1,000 a week players receive during the exhibition season. That makes no sense, so they stay out of camp until the last possible moment. Coming in before the last exhibition game was an indication to his teammates that McAlister wanted to be ready for the season opener on September 12 in Cleveland.

"I don't have any problem with you staying out of camp," Billick told him on that first day back. "Business is business. You and I don't have to be friends, but we do need to work together as business partners because that's what we are. I don't want to hear that the media has been able to get you to rip your teammates. You need to not do that again."

McAlister said he understood. He was there to work and help the team. "I really was glad to be back," he said later. "It felt weird being out on the West Coast, sitting around knowing my teammates were going through two-a-days. Then, watching the exhibitions on TV, I was saying to myself, 'Hey, I'm on that team, what am I doing here?' I really wanted to get back to playing football. I missed it."

McAlister was warmly greeted when he walked into the locker room. All the Ravens knew one thing: prodigal son or not, McAlister made them a better team. Which, in the NFL, is what matters.

"It's just football," Ray Lewis always said.

With McAlister in uniform, Lewis's football team was now capable of playing better football.

The last exhibition game was a headache for almost everyone. The players and coaches really didn't want to bother with another game. They wanted to start getting ready to play real games. Everyone worried about someone getting hurt while playing a meaningless game. The coaches were concerned about getting through the game without injuries and with minimal playing time for the players who mattered most. Many of the players who would play in the second half would be cut the following day. Some had been kept on the roster for the final week for the specific purpose of using up minutes so that starters and key backups could stay out of harm's way.

Traditionally, the Ravens have played their last exhibition game against the New York Giants. It is a logistically easy trip for whichever team travels, and since Billick and Jim Fassel were friends, they made sure to get through the game as quickly and painlessly as possible. "I'm not sure either one of us ever used a time-out," Fassel said.

This trip would be a little bit different. For one thing, Tom Coughlin was now the Giants' coach and he took pregame *meals* seriously, not to mention something resembling a football game. Coughlin was already getting hammered in the New York media for his inflexible ways, personified by his decision to fine a player for being five minutes early to a meeting because, in his mind, five minutes early wasn't early enough. The game would also be a homecoming for Fassel, returning to the stadium where he had been the head coach for seven years.

There was also one more problem: the Republican National Convention was winding up across the river in New York City that night and, with President George W. Bush scheduled to speak, security everywhere within a hundred miles of New York was airtight. The Ravens had already been told the only way they could leave Giants Stadium after the game was by bus. No planes or even trains were being allowed into or out of the area until one hour after Bush finished his speech. Football teams are not accustomed to traveling by bus except to and from an airport or hotel or stadium. Normally the Ravens would charter a train into and out of Newark for a game at Giants Stadium. That option would not be available for the return trip.

The most important thing was getting through the game.

And the arrival of Deion.

Newsome and Eugene Parker had finally agreed on a contract the previous weekend, with Sanders getting $1.5 million guaranteed, plus incentives. He was planning to report Tuesday, take his physical, deal with the media onslaught, and then travel with the team to the game on Thursday. Once he signed, the Ravens would have to cut an additional player, someone who was going to be cut anyway but would have been available for the Giants game if Sanders weren't on the roster. There had been a lengthy conversation on Sunday before the initial round of cuts about holding off on signing Sanders until Friday. That idea was eventually abandoned. Parker and Newsome had agreed that Sanders would report Tuesday. It was too late to change the plan.

Sanders ended up traveling to the game on his own because Billick and the coaches wanted him to get in an extra workout after the team left for New Jersey. He arrived at Giants Stadium a couple of hours before kickoff, looking every inch of Prime Time, hugging the players he already knew, shaking hands with the ones he was meeting for the first time. He walked onto the field for pregame warm-ups dressed in a black shirt, with a gold crucifix around his neck, shorts, and a brand-new Ravens cap. "There's a part of me that wants to ask him for an autograph or something," cornerback Gary Baxter said. "I mean, that's Deion Sanders we're talking about, not just some nickel back we just signed."

The new nickel back appeared to be very happy to be with his new team and he was clearly pleased when Lewis asked him to lead the team's pregame prayer. He did so in a loud, enthusiastic voice, giving thanks for "our ability to play and love this childish game." His "amen" was echoed loudly around the room. When he walked to the sideline after the team had been introduced, head linesman Jerry Bergman called out to Billick, "Hey, who's the new guy?" Sanders walked over and hugged Bergman. He was clearly delighted to be back.

"Always be nice to the officials," he counseled. "You never know when you're going to need them." Everyone laughed. "No, I'm serious," he said. "I used to say to guys, 'Hey, if I'm using my hands too much, tell me, if I'm doing something wrong, let me know.' You do that, they'll warn you, give you a heads-up. It's a lot better than finding out when that flag lands at your feet."

Sanders' feel for football was obvious throughout the game. He seemed able to call almost any play before it happened. On one third-and-3 for the Giants, he began screaming, 'Run, run,' an instant after the offense had lined up. How did he know that with such certainty? "You look at the linemen's knuckles," he said. "If they're flat on the ground, it's a run because they're going to push forward on them. If they're up in the air, it's a pass, they're getting ready to backpedal." When someone said that Sanders had wasted his time working in a studio and should have been in a booth as a color commentator, he shook his head emphatically.

"No way, man," he said. "Not enough face time in the booth. I'm not going to put on one of my suits to be on camera for forty-five seconds all day long."

The only person with more people to greet than Sanders was Jim Fassel, who was greeted by most in the stadium as a returning hero. He hugged co-owner John Mara and was bearhugged by Giants star Michael Strahan, who made it clear he wished Fassel were still coaching on his sideline. Fassel did a double-take when he saw Sanders in the locker room. When he had left the Sunday meeting, the plan had been to sign Sanders on Friday. "I told everyone he wouldn't be here tonight," he said. "I'm going to look real plugged-in with my new team, huh?"

The game itself was just about everything the Ravens did not want it to be. On the Giants' first series, quarterback Kurt Warner found receiver Tim Carter behind McAlister for a 50-yard gain. Welcome back to the NFL, C-Mac. That wasn't all bad, because as McAlister said afterward, "Better to get blooded now rather than later."

If that had been the worst moment of the first quarter, no one would have complained. But it wasn't. With 2:57 left, on what was almost undoubtedly the first-team offense's last series, the Ravens had a first-and-goal on the Giants' 7-yard line. The call was a routine sweep left, with Chester Taylor, already in the game for Jamal Lewis, following Ogden and Edwin Mulitalo. Taylor bolted to the 3-yard line before he was piled up. As the players unpiled, though, one person didn't get up: Ogden. He was on the ground, reaching for his right leg, clearly in a lot of pain.

The Ravens' sideline went silent while trainers Bill Tessendorf and Mark Smith raced to Ogden, followed by Andy Tucker and Leigh Ann Curl, the team's head physician and surgeon, respectively. Watching the medical people work on Ogden, Billick, hands on hips, face a blank mask, kept saying repeatedly: "Get up, get up. Come on, get up. Please get up."

Ogden was finally helped to his feet and went to the sideline, walking very slowly, supported by Tessendorf and Smith. As he went by Billick, headed for the bench to be examined, Billick patted him on the head. Tucker walked by Billick and in the softest voice possible said simply, "Knee."

Billick was pale. So was everyone else. On the next play, Boller hit Kevin Johnson in the end zone for a touchdown. It was the offense's best drive of the preseason. No one on the Baltimore sideline so much as cracked a smile. If Ogden was seriously hurt, all the hopes that had been discussed since minicamp were seriously jeopardized. Ethan Brooks, who went in to the game in his place, was a competent NFL offensive lineman, a good backup to have on your team. But he couldn't possibly be anything close to Ogden for the simple reason that there wasn't a left tackle in the game as good as Ogden. He was the heart and soul of the offensive line, the person Jamal Lewis liked to run behind, the key protector for the young quarterback.

While Tucker and Curl examined Ogden, McAlister intercepted a Warner pass on the sideline and returned it 23 yards for a touchdown, giving the Ravens a 14–3 lead. As he came off the field with a big smile on his face, Billick grabbed him. "Don't think that means you can miss training camp every year," he said. He was smiling when he said it, but McAlister knew he meant it.

In the meantime, everyone was still more focused on what Tucker and Curl were doing than on what was going on on the field. Finally, they reported to Billick: It was, they were almost certain, a sprained MCL. They couldn't feel a tear in the ligament, although an MRI would have to confirm that. They were confident it wasn't a major injury.

"Will he be ready for Cleveland?" Billick asked.

"Maybe," Tucker said. "We've got ten days. He'll need every single minute."

Ogden had his leg stretched out with ice on it, but he was smiling again. "I scared the hell out of myself for a minute there," he said. "I had a sprain on the other leg once, and that's what this felt like when I came off. It's a relief, knowing it isn't serious."

Everyone was breathing again. Even if Ogden didn't play in Cleveland, it would be just one game. That was a big deal — every game in the NFL is important — but it wasn't a disaster.

The rest of the game was comic relief. Midway through the second quarter, with most of the starters out of the game, word came down from the press box to Jeff Friday that nine Ravens had been spotted with uniform violations. Friday was the Ravens' strength coach. But on game day, he had a number of duties that had nothing to do with strength. He was the "get-back coach," which literally meant he was in charge of making certain players and coaches did not get too close to the field while the game was going on. In the heat of the game, people instinctively move closer to the action. It was Friday's job to move them back, either by asking, yelling, or occasionally pushing them backward. The job is considered so important that the officials always ask before a game who a team's "get back" coach is.

Friday was also in charge of charting time-outs so everyone knew from possession to possession whether a TV time-out was coming up or if play was continuing. There are five TV time-outs in each quarter of each NFL game (which means there is exactly one hour during each game when everyone simply stands around waiting for the signal to play), and Friday kept track of how many had been used and checked with the TV official stationed on the sideline to learn if a time-out was coming up after a change of possession, a score, or a kickoff. The answer, more often than not, was yes.

Friday's last assignment was his most difficult. The NFL has — to put it mildly — strict rules about players' uniforms. They must conform in every way possible. Anything that is even a little bit different is against the rules. Different-colored socks? Not allowed. Towel? Against the rules. Uniform shirt worn outside the pants? No way. Uniform cut differently? Verboten. And so on. The rules apply to everyone on the sidelines. Leigh Ann Curl had received a call from the press box a year earlier because she was wearing a shirt with an Under Armour logo underneath her Ravens-issued (Reebok) jacket during a game. "I had unzipped the jacket just a little and I guess a tiny bit of the Under Armour logo [Under Armour is a Ravens sponsor but not an NFL sponsor] was showing. They nailed me."

In every NFL stadium, a former player is paid to act as the league's "clothes Nazi." Before the game he walks among the players during warm-ups, noting any possible violations. He lists them all on a league-provided form and gives them to the "uniform coach"— Friday, in the case of the Ravens — before the game. It would then be Friday's job to make sure the players were aware of the violations and would correct them before game time. If a player is still in violation when the game starts, the CN (clothes Nazi) phones down to the sideline. If that warning is ignored, a report is sent to the league and the player is subject to a fine. Some players simply ignore the warnings and pay the fines because they want to make a fashion statement. Occasionally a player appeals the fine and wins because of a misunderstanding.

In Baltimore, the CN was Bruce Laird, a former defensive back for the Colts who was also a weekend talk-show host. Laird still looked as if he could jump in uniform and play, and the players respected him enough that they rarely gave him a hard time when he let them know about their violations. Typically, Laird would find between twenty and thirty violations during pregame and hand the list to Friday, who would go through the locker room to try and get everyone straight before kickoff. It was not in Laird's nature to play the role of hall monitor, but he — like all the other CNs — knew that Big Brother was watching in the NFL offices in New York.

"I've gotten memos because they'll look at the tape and see some kind of minor violation," he said. "I got one once because a player had written his number on the back of his shoes and I didn't catch it. It's amazing some of the things they worry about."

The CNs are paid $500 a game and get parking close to the stadium. "If it wasn't for the parking, I might give it up," Laird joked. "It's a lot of work and headaches for what they pay you."

In New York, the CN was Joe Morris, the former Giant running back who had been a key player on their Super Bowl–winning team in 1986. The New York CNs have to be especially vigilant because, more often than not, there are league officials in the press box for games played in Giants Stadium. That was why Morris had sent word to Friday right away instead of waiting until halftime. When Friday began telling players that they needed to — among other things — tuck in uniforms, roll down socks, and remove towels hooked to belts, there was a mini-revolt.

"We're not even still in the game," said Kyle Boller, nailed for untucking his jersey after coming out of the game.

"This is going too far, it really is," agreed Ray Lewis, guilty of the same crime. "Tell the guy we want to talk to him."

Friday sent word up to the press box that his players would like to talk to Morris. A few minutes later Morris emerged from the end zone tunnel. Those who had seen him play for the Giants did a double-take as he approached the sideline. Since his retirement, Morris had put at least fifty pounds on to a five-foot-nine frame. As a running back, he had been built solidly, stocky and low to the ground, tough to tackle. Now, dressed in shorts, a golf shirt, and sandals, he looked like the before picture in a health-club commercial. As soon as he walked behind the bench, the players pounced.

"You can't fine us, we're not even in the game anymore," Boller said as Lewis and Ed Reed walked up to join him.

"I don't want to fine anybody," Morris said. "I'm just trying to do my job."

"You fine us, you're going to have to fine everyone in the league," McAlister said, joining the group.

"You working on commission?" Reed added.

Morris laughed. He had been a player once and he knew how players thought. "Guys, do me a favor, tuck your uniforms in and pull your socks up at halftime. We'll let that be the end of it. I won't even write it up for your uniform coach."

Everyone looked at Lewis, always the leader. "Okay, man, we'll take care of it," he said. "But try to remember it's just a preseason game."

"I know," Morris said. "But that doesn't mean they aren't watching me. Okay?"

Everyone seemed to agree on that. "Who is that guy?" McAlister asked as Morris walked away. When someone told him it was Joe Morris, he was clearly surprised. "Joe Morris, the running back?" he said. "That guy was a great player. Maybe I shouldn't have yelled at him so much."

That pretty much ended the shouting for the evening. The Giants were booed by their fans at halftime, and it didn't get much better for them in the second half, even with both teams deep into their bench. The officials kept the flags to a minimum, and the second half went quickly — except when Coughlin insisted on using all his time-outs in the final three minutes, trying for a consolation touchdown in a meaningless game. "What's he thinking?" Fassel asked Billick. "All you do is risk someone getting hurt at this point."

The news that Ogden's injury appeared minor loosened things up on the bench. "Hey, Deion, I'm glad you're here," Matt Stover said, sidling up to Sanders. "Means I'm not the old dog around here anymore."

"How old are you?" Sanders asked.

"Thirty-six."

"Damn."

Sanders was thirty-seven. In fact, he was planning to wear number 37 (he had worn 21 in the past, and McAlister had offered to make him a deal for it, but he didn't want it) because his kids wanted people to know exactly how old their dad was every time he made a play. The final score was 27–17. Billick rarely presents game balls after games — he lets the coordinators decide who should get them — but in this case he made an exception.

"I think there's someone in here who deserves a little special recognition tonight, don't you, guys?" he said. Then with a big smile on his face, he flipped a ball to Fassel, whose smile was even wider. "I'll find a place for this one," he said. "I promise you, it will go in a prominent place."

There was laughter all around the room. Everyone was having a good time. They were convinced that the fun had only just begun.

12

Crossing the Street

THE SECOND ROUND OF CUTS would be tougher than the first because many of the players being let go were good enough to play in the NFL. What's more, decisions had to be made on which players were likely to make it through waivers so they could be re-signed for the developmental squad. Some of the cuts were veterans: Ron Johnson had pointed out to Billick coming off the field in New York that he had played the entire second half without picking up a penalty. Billick felt a twinge of sadness because he knew that that half had been Johnson's last as a Raven. The same was true of Lamont Brightful, whom everyone on the team liked. He had simply been beaten out of a job by B. J. Sams. Javin Hunter had willingly switched from wide receiver to cornerback and had shown flashes of potential. But not enough to make the team.

There was considerable debate about Lance Frazier, a tough little rookie cornerback from West Virginia. The coaches loved his attitude, felt he had the potential to become an NFL cornerback, and thought he would be an asset on special teams. But Frazier wasn't as good as Chad Williams or Ray Walls, the team's two young backup defensive backs, and Corey Fuller was going to make the team because of his experience and the strength of his personality in the locker room. Frazier might have made the roster as a special teams player, but the Ravens already had several players who were strictly special teamers, notably Harold Morrow and Ovie Mughelli, technically running backs but on the roster strictly because of their special teams ability.

In the end, it was Ozzie Newsome, who rarely spoke during cutdown meetings unless specifically asked his opinion, who stepped in to cut off debate. "Fellas, I understand why you love him," he said, addressing the defensive coaches. "He's a great kid, he's a worker, but what would happen to us if someone got injured and he had to play corner? He's just not good enough to do that. He's not big enough or experienced enough. I'd love to keep the kid, but in the end, we really can't."

That pretty much finished the discussion on Frazier.

There was another issue that had to be dealt with: Ogden's likely absence the first week. Ethan Brooks would step in as the starting left tackle, but another lineman who normally either would have been cut or kept on the developmental squad would have to be activated. Deciding to move Tony Pashos, a second-year tackle who had spent his rookie year on injured reserve, from the developmental squad to the active squad wasn't that difficult. Deciding whom to cut wasn't nearly as easy. The scouts, led by Phil Savage, wanted to cut Morrow on the grounds that he was a specialist on a team filled with them. The Ravens carried two placekickers — Matt Stover for field goals and extra points and Wade Richey to kick off — in addition to Morrow and Mughelli, who weren't likely to play a down from scrimmage all season.

Each NFL team is allowed to suit up forty-five of its fifty-three players each week, a rule that makes coaches crazy. "If you're paying fifty-three guys, why not play fifty-three guys?" Billick always says. Among the Ravens' forty-five each week were the two placekickers, the two special teams players, long snapper Joe Maese, and punter Dave Zastudil. That left only thirty-nine spots for everyone else. Nevertheless, the suggestion that Morrow be dropped from the opening-day roster brought a scream of pain from Gary Zauner, who had coached him both in Minnesota and in Baltimore.

"You kill me if you take Morrow away," he said. "The guy is the best wedge buster we have and he's the emotional leader of our kick teams. Plus, he's one of our best guys in the locker room."

No one doubted what Zauner was saying. But cutting him for the week still made the most sense. If a younger player like Gerome Sapp or Mughelli were cut, he would have to clear waivers and would probably get picked up by someone. Because he was in his ninth year in the league,

Morrow would not have to clear waivers. Players with four years in the league are not subject to waivers when cut from a team until after the trading deadline, which comes at the end of the sixth week of the regular season. Morrow would become an instant free agent. "We would need to love him up," Billick said. "Tell him it's just a one-week thing and we want him to be part of this team so he doesn't sign with anyone else. I think if he's certain we're going to bring him back right away, he won't go anyplace else if he has the chance."

Newsome was shaking his head. "It's not that simple," he said. "He's on the roster the first week, his salary is guaranteed the entire season. If he's not on the opening-day roster, it isn't guaranteed."

Billick nodded. "I think if I tell him man-to-man that we're absolutely planning on him being here all season, he'll be okay. I think he knows I wouldn't lie to him."

"What if something happened," Savage asked, "and we had to cut him?"

Billick was silent for a second. "Cross that bridge if we get to it," he said. "Let's hope we don't."

There was one other issue. The plan all along had been to put Clarence Moore, the six-foot-six wide receiver the Ravens almost hadn't drafted in the sixth round because they had a wrong phone number, on the developmental squad. He had shown flashes during preseason of being ready to contribute right away, but the feeling was that he should start the season on developmental.

"You can't do that," David Shaw, the wide receivers coach, said, seeing Moore's name on the developmental list. "Every game we've played, the first question the receivers coach on the other team has asked me is about Moore. There's absolutely no way in the world he'll make it through waivers. We'll lose him."

No one argued with Shaw's analysis. They could all see Moore's potential. Someone was bound to take a chance on him. The Ravens didn't want to lose him.

Billick clicked a few buttons on his computer and, magically, Moore's name was removed from developmental and moved to the fifty-three-man roster. That decision meant that Josh Harris, the team's other sixth-round draft pick, would end up on the developmental squad instead of being kept

on the roster as the number three quarterback. "Who's our third quarterback if Kyle and Kordell both get hurt?" Billick asked Matt Cavanaugh.

"Randy Hymes," said Cavanaugh, referring to the wide receiver who
had been a quarterback in college.

Everyone hoped Hymes would spend the following Sunday catching
footballs, not throwing them.

Saturday morning got off to a bad start. There had been discussion the previous day about what to do with Brandon Barnes, a rookie linebacker the
coaches wanted to keep around on the developmental squad. It was the
wide receiver position that created the dilemma. Several of them were
nicked: Travis Taylor had a pulled groin and was questionable for Cleveland, and Devard Darling, the rookie, was also a question mark with a leg
injury. That meant a wide receiver — in this case, Todd Devoe — who
would have been cut had to be kept around at least for an extra week.

Somehow during the course of the debate, there was a communications
mix-up: the defensive coaches thought Barnes was being kept around.
When he arrived the following morning, he was sent to the weight room
for his normal morning lift. When George Kokinis saw the cut list without
Barnes's name, he realized something had gone wrong. It was Mike Singletary who had to go into the weight room and tell Barnes he needed to take
him upstairs to see Billick. As fierce a football player as he once was,
Singletary is a soft-spoken, deeply religious man with a gentle streak never
evident on the football field. He looked almost as stricken as Barnes when
he brought him into Billick's office.

Even Billick was a little bit pale. Cutting a player was one thing. Cutting
him less than thirty minutes after he thought he had survived the cut was
another. "I am really sorry about this," he said. "There was miscommunication. We're waiving you today. There's still a chance we'll bring you back for
developmental, but you're free and clear to sign with anyone else." Technically, that's true of every player put through waivers. The ones the Ravens
wanted for developmental were told to "sit tight," unless someone picked
them up for their active roster. "You have to hang loose the next couple
days and see what happens."

Barnes was in pain. "Oh man, Coach," he said, almost pleading for a reprieve.

"I know," Billick said. "I'm sorry. There's no good way to do this, and we're doing it in a very bad way."

The rest of the morning wasn't a lot easier. Billick tried to explain to Lamont Brightful that he believed he had lost his confidence somewhere and needed to get it back. He told Javin Hunter he honestly believed he could be an NFL cornerback. "You showed me you can do this," he said. "We have injuries, we might very well call you back."

"Coach, I think I can play the position in the NFL," Hunter said.

"So do I," Billick said.

He wasn't as encouraging when Dave Revill, a safety from Utah, asked if there was any chance he might be brought back to the developmental team. "Dave, we're stacked at cornerback," Billick said, not mentioning there had been no discussion about keeping him for developmental.

The last player Billick had to cut was Ron Johnson, who showed up in the locker room just a few minutes before the team's scheduled nine o'clock meeting. He was walking into the locker room when Chisom Opara, again playing Turk along with Jeremiah and Washburn, spotted him. "Ron," Opara said, waving an arm to indicate he needed to talk to him.

As soon as Johnson saw Opara, he went pale. "Oh shit," he said.

Opara explained that Billick needed to see him upstairs.

Stunned, Johnson made the long walk up the back steps. Jeremiah was standing outside the office when he got there. Johnson didn't even look at him as he went by. When he sat down, Billick thought, for the first time since he had met him, he saw fear in his eyes. "The thought suddenly occurred to him that this might be the end for him," he said.

He was honest with Johnson. "You have the ability to play in this league, Ron," he said. "You need to think about why you're sitting here right now. You've never embraced the idea of special teams. Look at someone like Harold Morrow. You have more ability than he does, but he's in the league because he's embraced the idea of being a special teams player. You need to do that with your mind, your body, and your soul. You do that, you can still play in this league."

As Johnson left, Jeremiah asked him about his playbook.

"It's at my house," Johnson said. "I'll get it to you."

"How about if I follow you back there when you're done here and save you the trouble," Jeremiah said, trying to be diplomatic. In the NFL, there are no ifs, ands, or buts about turning in playbooks once you are no longer with a team. In fact, during the season, players are required to turn in their game plans from the previous week before they get a new one just in case the old one somehow falls into the wrong hands down the road sometime.

Johnson gave Jeremiah a look that told him he hadn't bought his attempt at diplomacy.

"What, you don't trust me?" he said.

"Ron, you know it has nothing to do with trust," Jeremiah said.

Billick watched Johnson and Jeremiah walk down the hall and sighed. It was a couple of minutes before 9 A.M. and it had already been a long morning.

"Whenever I have to make these cuts, I always think about what Clint Eastwood said in *Unforgiven:* 'When you kill a man, you not only are ending his life, you're taking away everything he ever had or is going to have.' Every one of these guys has to emotionally sell himself on the dream to even have a chance to play. Then, one day, I sit in front of them and say, 'You're fired.' Maybe the dream isn't dead for all of them, but it is for some of them."

The roster was now set. They would have to sweat a little bit when the eight players ticketed for developmental went through waivers. Newsome had heard through the grapevine that a couple of teams, notably Tennessee, might try to sign Josh Harris. The only light moment in the entire cutdown process had come when Newsome had finished his exit interview with Rashad Holman, a free-agent cornerback.

"Mr. Newsome, before I go can I ask you a favor?" Holman had said.

"Sure," Newsome said. "I'll do it for you if I can."

"Would you sign an autograph for me?"

Newsome laughed. That he could do.

The meeting room had empty chairs for the first time that morning. "This is our sixty-one," Billick said. "We're all in business together for the next seventeen weeks and we know what kind of potential we have. Every single person in this room will impact the kind of season we're going to have." He paused and smiled. "You guys might as well get comfortable because this is going to be one of my long speeches."

Billick picks his spots when it comes to long speeches. He knows most football players get antsy if they're squeezed into chairs for too long, and he would rather have them looking at tape while doing that than listening to rah-rah, win-one-for-the-Gipper talks. A few times a year he makes exceptions to that rule: at the start of the first minicamp, the first evening of training camp, and the first week of the season. After that, if he talks for more than five minutes in a meeting, it is only because there is some kind of crisis to be dealt with.

His theme for 2004 from the beginning had been based on a self-help business book called *Good to Great.* That was an appropriate slogan for this team. It had been 10-7 a year earlier, a division champion and a playoff team. That was good. Now was the time to move up to great. Any lengthy Billick talk is peppered with computerized graphics and photos and words of wisdom. He went through the basics of the book, things such as "Simplicity of Purpose — when you are working, work, when you're off, be off." The point being, come to practice focused and not show up tired because you are partying at night. Another point: "Confront the Brutal Facts." Injuries were going to happen. The Jamal Lewis situation remained unresolved. There would be personal crises. Mike Singletary's mother had died suddenly the first day of minicamp. Orlando Brown's mother was near death as they spoke. Mistakes would be made. All these things had to be confronted.

There was more. "Culture of Discipline." (Billick showed a photo of his father in his test pilot's uniform as an example of someone with a job in which the smallest mistake could be fatal.) "Momentum as a Force" was another building block.

Then came the potential pitfalls: "Separate Agendas, Selfishness, Pulling a [Building] Block Out," and the always critical "Listening and Reacting to Those Who Don't Know or Care." That led to a film clip from *The Natural,* in which Robert Duvall explains the power of the press to Robert Redford.

Billick gets along well with the local media in Baltimore most of the time and with many in the national media because he's accessible and quotable and, encouraged by Kevin Byrne, makes his team more open than almost any in the NFL. But like most coaches, he will use the media as a blocking dummy when it suits him. Frequently, he will stand in the circle at the end of practice and nod in the direction of the media, standing well out of earshot, waiting for practice to end, and say something like *"They* don't understand what this is about. . . . *They* are going to ask you questions there is no reason to answer."

This time, Billick talked about the media's agenda, which has to be different than a team's. "They want to control what you say, and you can't let them do that," Billick said.

From there, he launched into a lengthy analysis of what the team had accomplished in the past: the number of Pro Bowl appearances, the lock Hall of Famers in the room (Ray Lewis, Jonathan Ogden, Deion Sanders), the statistics from prior seasons. The realistic goal, according to Billick, was to go 12-4. That should be good enough to win the division and perhaps home-field advantage throughout the playoffs. The way to do that was to go 8-0 at home and no worse than 4-4 on the road. He even broke the season down into blocks and what a realistic record for each block would be: 4-1 before the bye week was not an unreasonable goal. There wasn't a team on the schedule the first five weeks they couldn't beat: at Cleveland, Pittsburgh at home, at Cincinnati, Kansas City at home, at Washington. Only one of those teams (Kansas City) had finished above .500 the previous season. The first three were division games, meaning they had a chance to take control of the division early.

The last graphic was right to the point: It showed a calendar with "September 12th at Cleveland" highlighted. Underneath were two words: "It Begins."

As soon as that graphic disappeared from the screen, another film clip came up. This was entirely different from the one from *The Natural*. It was from the crime family movie *GoodFellas*. In the scene, Ray Liotta's future wife has complained about being hit on by her neighbor across the street. Liotta doesn't say a word, he simply walks across the street and pummels the neighbor brutally, leaving him screaming for mercy. It is a visceral, bloody moment.

The players loved it. As soon as the clip ended, the lights came up. "Doesn't matter what they say this week," he said. "There's no need to respond at all. Just make sure we walk across that street on Sunday."

*　　*　　*

Standing on the sideline during the final moments of the Giants game, left guard Edwin Mulitalo took a deep breath as he watched the rest of the offensive linemen enjoy the victory. "It's all different from here on in," he said. "I remember my rookie year, being shocked at the difference in intensity between the exhibitions and the regular season. It was like two different sports."

That was evident the minute the Ravens began preparing for the Browns. There was less joking around on the sideline. Each series, each play seemed to have more purpose. Mistakes were corrected quickly and sharply. There was a crispness to what was being done that hadn't been there in August. There was also considerable concern that the schedule sent them to Cleveland to open the season.

The new Browns were beginning their sixth season, and the days when a Ravens trip to Cleveland was a media circus were, for the most part, gone. The fans in Cleveland were far more focused on the question of whether Coach Butch Davis could right a sinking ship than on their anger over the departure of the Art Modell Browns. But that didn't mean this would be an easy game. The Ravens had embarrassed the Browns twice in 2003, beating them 33–13 in Baltimore and 35–0 in Cleveland. What's more, Jamal Lewis had run roughshod over the Cleveland defense, setting an NFL single-game record with 295 yards in the first game, then settling for 205 yards in the second. The Browns had a new quarterback, free-agent signee Jeff Garcia, and a lot to prove to themselves and their fans. The setting would be emotional, and the Ravens had to be prepared to deal with it. That was why Billick had tried to set a tone early with the *GoodFellas* clip.

There were also more practical concerns. The offensive line, which had dominated the two Browns games the previous season, was hurting. Ogden was not going to play. Mike Flynn was also out. And Orlando Brown was commuting back and forth to the hospital during the week. The doctors had told him his mother had only days to live. There was no telling what his mental state would be on Sunday.

The Ravens had a lot of confidence in Casey Rabach, Flynn's replacement at center. Rabach was in his fourth NFL season, and the sense on the coaching staff had been that he was ready to be a starter. The plan had been to give him a chance to beat Bennie Anderson out for the right guard spot, but that had changed with Flynn's injury. Rabach was better suited to playing center anyway because of his relatively "small" size for an offensive lineman: six foot four, 300 pounds.

Replacing Ogden was an entirely different situation. No one was going to be Ogden, everyone knew that. Ethan Brooks was one of the most well liked players on the team, and his presence on an NFL team was testimony to his determination. In fact, in a league filled with unlikely stories, his was one of the most unlikely. He had grown up in Simsbury, Connecticut, where his father was a teacher and later the developmental director at a small prep school. His mother had grown up in France and knew very little about football. Ethan was the second son, big like his dad, quiet like his mom. Painfully quiet.

"I actually had a pretty bad lisp when I was young," he said. "I can remember when I was little, whenever I would say something my grandmother would make a comment about my lisp. After a while I just said, 'Heck with it, I'm not going to say anything.'" The lisp was corrected when he was eight after a painful procedure that involved maneuvering his tongue into a different position so that he could move it in a certain way so as not to lisp. "By then, I was in the habit of not talking much, so I just stayed quiet," he said. "I think it was my nature to begin with; that exacerbated it."

He was a good high school football player, but not so good that Division 1 schools were lining up to offer him scholarships. "I went to a small prep school and we had awful teams," he said, laughing. "My sophomore year we were 4-4, and that was the best record the school had ever had. I'm not sure I ever came on the radar screen for any of the big schools." There were several 1-AA opportunities, including Lehigh and Bucknell, both good academic schools that played good 1-AA football — especially Lehigh. Ralph Brooks had gone to Wesleyan, which was part of the famed "Little Three" (Wesleyan, Williams, and Amherst) and had been a good enough player to get invited to the Baltimore Colts' training camp in 1959. But back problems had ended his career. Wesleyan wasn't very good in football when Ethan graduated from high school, but Williams was a Division 3 power. Ralph Brooks pushed his son to go there: great education, very good small-time football.

Ethan didn't want to go. "Believe it or not, I had NFL aspirations even in high school," he said. "I can't tell you why. Ego, I guess. I thought I could do it. I didn't think Williams was the best route to the NFL. But I didn't think it would be a problem because I never thought I'd get in."

He didn't think he'd get in because even though he had very good grades, his SAT score was 1,170 — sky-high for a football player at most schools but low at Williams. Then, much to his surprise and dismay, he got in. "I was all set to go to Bucknell," he said. "I liked it when I visited and the football was at a higher level in terms of competition. When I was at Williams for my visit, I noticed that I was already bigger than almost anybody there. I just didn't think it was the best road for me."

His father thought different. On the day he had to make his college decision, he told his father he had decided to go to Bucknell. "Before you make a commitment," his father said, "Give it some more thought. Take your time."

Ethan got the message. He called several of his friends to tell them his father wanted him to choose Williams. They all agreed with his father. He chose Williams.

He started out in premed, thinking being a doctor was a good backup plan if he didn't make the NFL. A couple of Cs in biology convinced him that psychology would be a fine major. He became a good player at Williams, in part because he was much bigger than most Division 3 players at six foot six and 270 pounds. He played on the defensive line on very good teams — the Ephs were 15-0-1 his last two years, the tie coming in Brooks's last college game against Amherst. The game was played in a driving rainstorm and ended 0–0. "To this day I think of that as my worst loss," Brooks said. "It was a tie, but it felt like a loss, especially against Amherst." By the time he played that last game, he was getting attention from some NFL scouts. It is not unheard-of for D-3 players to make it in the NFL, although it is certainly unusual. He was drafted in the seventh and final round by the Atlanta Falcons (the 229th overall pick) and was thrilled just to have a shot to make it in the NFL. He had been told by all the scouts who came to work him out that his future was as an offensive lineman because of his size. But halfway through training camp the Falcons moved him back to defense because of injuries. "It was okay with me because it meant I was going to be on the team," Brooks said. "I had gone into camp hoping to make the practice squad."

He ended up on the active roster on defense. "When I realized I had a chance to get drafted, I got all these NFL game tapes and began watching them all the time," he said. "I was just amazed by the size and the speed of all the players." He laughed. "It was a long way from the NESCAC [the league Williams plays in]. "To find myself competing with guys like that so quickly was almost a shock."

During that first year in Atlanta, one of his teammates, Chuck Smith, asked him if he would go with him to dinner one night. Smith had a date who wanted to bring a friend with her, and Smith wanted Brooks to ride shotgun to engage the other woman. Reluctantly, Brooks agreed. Because of his size and shyness he hadn't dated a lot in college and he was way too busy trying to keep his head above water as a rookie pro to worry about a social life. As soon as the two women walked into the restaurant, Brooks was happy he had said yes. Jacqueline Smith was petite (five foot two, 115 pounds), pretty, smart, and funny. She had grown up a tomboy in a tiny Georgia town, had come to Atlanta to go to college at Morris Brown, and loved to talk about sports. Brooks felt comfortable with her right away. A romance bloomed quickly.

"It was one of those things where, when you haven't ever been serious with someone, you kind of know right away that this is it," he said. "She worked [as a paralegal] right near where I lived, so most nights we would get together."

By the spring of 1997 they were engaged, and that summer they were married. The NFL is not a sentimental place. Dan Reeves had replaced June Jones as coach of the Falcons, and one week into the season he cut Brooks, replacing him with someone who had played for him in Denver. Six weeks into his marriage, Brooks was unemployed. The St. Louis Rams picked him up with five weeks left in the season and, although he didn't get into any games, signed him for 1998. He played that season in St. Louis as a backup offensive tackle and on special teams.

It was during that fall when Jackie first began experiencing back pain. There was a knot in her back that she and Ethan both assumed was caused by some kind of muscle pull she had suffered while exercising. Except that it kept getting worse. One doctor told her to stop exercising for a while and the pain should abate. It didn't. Finally, she went to have tests done. Ethan was in Connecticut visiting his family for a few days when the results came back. "They think it might be cancer," Jackie told him on the phone.

"At first, I didn't really panic," he said. "We went to see a specialist and he told us it was non-Hodgkin's lymphoma, which is one of the more curable forms of cancer. They didn't want to operate, but she had to start chemo."

As luck would have it, the Rams released Brooks soon after he learned his wife had cancer. Both the Cardinals and the Cowboys called, offering him contracts to come to training camp. He turned them down. "I just thought I was supposed to be with her at that point," he said. "Certainly I didn't want to be away from her."

After Jackie endured four months of painful chemo, the doctors told Ethan and Jackie that they thought they had it, that the cancer was gone. For a while they were encouraged and were ready to get on with their lives, the scare behind them. Ethan accepted a free-agent contract to play for Arizona in 2000. He and Jackie agreed that he would go to training camp alone so she could stay in Atlanta near her doctors and her job until they saw whether he made the team. On the phone, she told him all was well, but something didn't sound right to Brooks. He made the team, and Jackie came out to join him in Phoenix.

When he saw his wife again, Brooks knew she wasn't healthy. She was weak and depressed. Soon after she arrived in Phoenix, she woke up in the middle of the night in so much pain that Ethan had to take her to the emergency room. That was when he found out that the cancer had come back. It was in her lungs and now, according to the doctors, in her kidneys. She had kept it from him while he was in training camp.

"From that point on, it was a fast slide downhill," he said. "It was a nightmare for me, but much, much worse for her."

Jackie needed dialysis two days a week. There were more trips to the emergency room. Brooks told only a small handful of people on the team that his wife was sick, never letting on how dire the situation had become. Soon after the end of the season, a doctor quietly told Ethan and Jackie that there really wasn't much more that could be done other than trying to make her as comfortable as possible.

"I'll never forget the look on her face when he said that," Brooks said. "I didn't realize it, but she had been in denial about how sick she was. She said to the doctor, 'Are you telling me I'm going to die?' It was heartbreaking."

A couple of weeks later the Cardinals told Brooks they were going to release him. He hardly noticed. On March 3, 2001, Jackie died.

Everyone told Ethan he needed to keep as busy as possible once the funeral was over. He agreed to sign with the Denver Broncos, which turned out to be a major mistake. "My agent and I didn't understand that they basically just wanted me as a camp body," he said. "They drafted some linemen that they liked and I never really got a chance to even compete for a job. I got into one series of the first exhibition game and that was it."

A camp body, in NFL vernacular, is just that: someone brought into camp to fill a uniform during early practices and exhibition games and to be around in case a slew of injuries hits a team. Brooks was cut after the third exhibition game, a relief, because he was miserable and just wanted to get out of Denver.

He went back to Atlanta, to the town house he had bought soon after Jackie died. "It was right across from the apartment where we had lived," he said. "We had talked about buying a house there and, on the spur of the moment, I bought it. Somehow, I thought it might make me feel better, to live where we had talked about living. I was wrong."

He began drinking heavily, hanging out in Buckhead, the same section of town that had brought Ray Lewis so much grief. "I can remember a few times just walking down the middle of the street, shouting at people, hoping someone would start a fight," he said. "Some nights I think I was just hoping someone would run me over. I was lucky. I never got in a fight, never got arrested. One night I drove home absolutely drunk. That's when I realized I had to get out of there."

He went home to Connecticut and began to piece his life back together. He worked out with his brother, a strength and conditioning coach, and found solace in his boyhood home. He thought he wanted one more chance to play again but wasn't sure. No one from the NFL called when the season ended. In March he went to Boston with his brother for a clinic being conducted by a trainer. Afterward, he talked to the trainer about needing a regimen like the one he was talking about. "If you want to work with me, come to Arizona," the trainer said. "But be there by Wednesday."

That was in four days. Brooks thought about it. He wanted to go. "That told me I still wanted to play," he said. "The fact that I was willing to make that kind of commitment to work on the spur of the moment."

It was June before anyone called. The Ravens had gone through their salary-cap purge and were searching for experienced players, especially experienced players who wouldn't cost a lot of money. He worked out for Jim Colletto and signed a contract at the start of training camp. He went to camp hoping to make the team as a backup and ended up starting thirteen games because of injuries on the offensive line. That was a mixed blessing. Being back in the league was great, getting to play certainly an opportunity. But there were times when he felt overmatched by getting extensive playing time. Even so, the Ravens gave him a $250,000 signing bonus and a two-year contract for $1.25 million before the start of 2003. Not exactly Jonathan Ogden money, but more than Brooks ever dreamed of making as a football player when he was at Williams. He played less in 2003 — starting three times — but felt more confident when he did play.

Most important, perhaps, he felt very comfortable in the Ravens' locker room. The other players enjoyed his dry sense of humor, and on an offensive line full of talkers, his quiet demeanor fit in well. The other O linemen had nicknamed him Big Swede, after a huge, silent character in an Eastwood movie (Eastwood was very big among the Ravens players and coaches), and he took to the nickname. He even asked Kevin Byrne if it might be possible sometime when he was introduced as a starter to be introduced as Big Swede. Byrne told him that was unlikely. He had finally reached the point where he was dating again, seeing a woman from Atlanta who worked as a flight attendant.

"I don't like to talk about things like finding perspective," he said. "But I wake up every morning and realize how lucky I am to be alive and to be completely healthy. When I hear people talk about tragic losses, I just kind of laugh to myself. A lot of people in this sport have no idea what a tragic loss is."

Like it or not, Ogden's injury meant Brooks would spend the week back in the spotlight, something he had never been comfortable with. The Browns had an outstanding right defensive end in Courtney Brown, and Brooks knew he would be under pressure all day. The coaches, he knew, would adapt the game plan to the fact that he was playing instead of Ogden: they would run right more often than usual, and Boller would frequently be limited to three-step drops when passing in order to get the ball off more quickly.

"Swede will be fine," Ogden said after going through some light agility drills apart from the team on Wednesday. "My question is, how will I do having to stand there and watch? I just hate that."

The first week of the season is always fraught with issues, some major (Ogden's absence), most minor. As Billick had expected, the Browns were talking — which was exactly what he wanted. One of their linebackers had predicted that Jamal Lewis wouldn't come close to gaining 100 yards in the game. One of their offensive players had called Ray Lewis overrated. Those two comments appeared under the dictionary definition of *bulletin board material* — great to post on the locker-room bulletin board to get the players riled up.

There were also logistics to be dealt with. Each week on Wednesday, every team is required to file an injury report with the league and with its opponent. Any player who has any kind of injury is supposed to be listed. Those who are nicked and virtually certain to play are officially listed as "probable." A player who is missing practice time but may play is listed as "questionable." If a player is too hurt to practice but might somehow play on Sunday (usually meaning he will take some kind of painkiller to get on the field), he is listed as "doubtful." Those on the injured list or who are definitely out of a game are listed as "out."

NFL teams constantly play mind games with injury lists. If there is any doubt in an opponent's mind about the status of a key player, coaches never list him as out or even doubtful, because they want the opponent to have to prepare as if it might have to face him. Ogden would be listed as questionable even though he was almost certainly out. The Browns would not know for sure until 11:30 A.M. Sunday — ninety minutes before kickoff — when each team has to submit its list of eight inactive players. As with all things, the NFL attempts to be vigilant about the use — or abuse — of the injured list. If a team lists a player as out or doubtful and he plays, the league may request practice tape from the team. If the injured player shows up practicing on tape, then the team may be subject to a fine for listing a player who was healthy enough to practice as doubtful or out. The flip side occurs if a player not listed on the injured list doesn't play. If the practice tape shows that he didn't practice and the team didn't list him, a fine is also likely.

There's no doubt that the league monitors the injured list closely in the interest of fairness, so teams can't simply lie or even hedge too much about injuries. Of course, the injury list is also important to gamblers since knowing who will and won't play affects betting lines and who bets on whom. The league would love people to believe that its popularity is based solely on the wonders of the game, the competition, and the remarkable athletic ability of the players. The fact is that a large chunk of the league's popularity is driven by the fascination people have with betting on the games, both legally and illegally.

On Wednesday afternoon the Ravens and Browns were playing injury-list chicken with each other. The Browns said that their list wasn't quite ready and that they would fax it to the Ravens at any minute. The Ravens responded by saying theirs would be ready just as soon as the Browns' was. "We won't show you our list until you show us yours," Kevin Byrne said, mimicking a taunting first-grader. "It all gets a bit silly at times."

The lists were finally exchanged, the fax buttons pushed at almost the same instant. The only real question mark among the Ravens was who would start at running back for the Browns. Lee Suggs, normally the starter, was listed as questionable. If he didn't play, William Green, who had been a starter before off-field problems had benched him, would play in his place.

The other issue was the production meeting. Every week NFL teams are required to produce coaches and players as requested for a meeting with a crew from the network televising that week's game. Every NFL game is on network television, either CBS or Fox for Sunday afternoon games; ESPN on Sunday night, or ABC on Monday night. One of the things the networks demand in return for the billions of dollars they pay the NFL — hundreds of millions per network — is the right to sit down alone with players and coaches on either Friday or Saturday prior to a game.

The networks hope to get a number of things from the meetings. First, perhaps foremost, is the opportunity for the announcers to say, "You know, when we talked to Ray Lewis yesterday, he told us . . ." They're also seeking information: confirmation on injuries, who is out and who is not, who may be playing a little bit gimpy. Game plans: are any surprises planned, is there someone who may be more involved than the other team might think? There are technical questions about offensive and defensive schemes, almost always asked by the color commentator so he can reference those things during a broadcast. Frequently you will hear color commentators say things like "The Ravens are a team that doesn't like to play cover-two very much," without ever explaining what cover-two is. (Cover-two, for the record, is when the safeties play a deep zone, designed to cut off any long passes.)

Frequently, the network production teams arrive on Friday in the city where a game is being played and hold their production meeting with the home team's coach and players on Friday afternoon. Occasionally they do it on Saturday morning. The visiting production meeting is almost always held in the team hotel as soon as the team arrives on Saturday afternoon. The network generally sends four or five people to the meeting: the game producer, director, and the "talent"— play-by-play man, color commentator, and, if there is one, the sideline reporter.

CBS did not consider Ravens vs. Browns a marquee matchup, so the network's number three crew would work the game. The announcing team would be Kevin Harlan and Randy Cross, the ex-49er. The producer was Ross Schneiderman and the director was Suzanne Smith. On Wednesday, as was standard procedure, Schneiderman called Kevin Byrne with his request list for the production meeting: Billick, Ray and Jamal Lewis, Deion Sanders, Kyle Boller, Todd Heap, Terrell Suggs, and Ed Reed. The standard was to request between four and six people.

"That's a lot of people," Byrne said.

"It's the first week," said Schneiderman. "We have a lot more questions now than we'd have later in the season."

Byrne didn't think that was unreasonable. He had two concerns: one was Sanders, whose parting with CBS over the issue of how much the network was willing — or not willing — to pay him had been quite public. The other was Suggs. Three times during his rookie season, Suggs had been requested for production meetings; twice he had been a no-show. Since the team had been in Baltimore, Byrne had had only one player miss a production meeting once. In one season, Suggs had tripled that number.

Byrne knew that Suggs wasn't being a bad guy. He was just a kid, still adapting to the responsibilities of being a professional football player. Even now, in his second year, he would not turn twenty-two until almost halfway through the season. Suggs could say things in the locker room that might have started fights if he were older. Instead, everyone just laughed and said something like "T-Sizzle [his preferred nickname], when are you going to grow up?"

Byrne had decided it was time for Sizzle to start growing up when it came to media responsibilities. He told him that CBS had asked for him for the production meeting in Cleveland and that he had better be there. "You already hold the record for no-shows," he told him. "Don't extend it."

Sanders proved to be easy. He said he would gladly do the production meeting. "I have no hard feelings toward CBS," he said. "Almost all of the people I worked with there were good to me. I consider them friends. No problem."

As soon as the team arrived at the Ritz-Carlton in Cleveland, Byrne sent Chad Steele to start rounding up players while he went to scout out the room CBS had reserved for the meeting. The CBS people were waiting — Cross and Smith sitting on one side of a conference table, Harlan and Schneiderman on the other. They had flip cards and notebooks in front of them. A seat at the head of the table was left empty for whoever was being interviewed. Byrne sat at the far end of the table. In an upset, Jamal Lewis arrived first. Production meetings are done by pecking order in terms of the players. Biggest star first, second-biggest second. The reason for that is simple: the sooner you finish, the sooner you can go to dinner. Apparently the Lewises had switched because Ray was going to dinner with Sanders and had to wait for him to finish anyway. Sanders would follow Ray Lewis.

Each network has a slightly different approach to the production meetings. In a CBS meeting, the analyst takes the lead, asking mostly technical questions. Naturally, Cross asked Jamal Lewis about Ogden's absence. "Ethan will be just fine," Lewis said, then paused. "Of course I've never played without J.O. It will be different."

Schneiderman had promised Byrne that each player would be kept no more than ten minutes in return for his agreeing to bring six of them. (CBS had agreed to drop Ed Reed.) When the discussion with Jamal inched toward fifteen minutes, with Ray standing outside with Steele, Byrne gave a quick wrap signal to Schneiderman. The last thing anyone in the room wanted was Ray getting impatient and walking off.

Of course, when he walked into the room, one might have thought that being in the production meeting was a true-life highlight for Lewis. He hugged Cross, player to player, then shook hands warmly with everyone else. The Ravens require that players dress neatly when they travel, so Lewis was still wearing the blue and white pinstripe suit, yellow shirt, and matching tie he had worn on the plane. He was both funny and charming as he talked, discussing Boller's newfound presence in the huddle. "It's tone of voice," he said. "He has more presence." When they asked him about the Browns, Lewis laughed and said, "I don't expect any surprises. I've been playing these guys for nine years."

Everyone nodded. Lewis was starting his ninth year in the league. Of course, the Browns had only been in existence for six years.

Midway through Lewis's interview, Sanders burst into the room. He was dressed as Prime Time — white suit, wide-brimmed Panama hat, giant gold crucifix around his neck. There were more hugs, more funny stories, and more talk about how thrilled Sanders was to be back. "Right now, I just want to be a nickel back," he said. "But that might change with time."

That got everyone's attention. When Billick came in, Cross and Harlan immediately asked if Sanders might be returning punts or playing on offense. "Not yet," Billick said. "Right now I see him getting fifteen to twenty snaps, and those will be on defense. Down the road, when he's ready for more snaps, yeah, we might use him to return kicks. He's been going to special teams meetings."

That made CBS's day. They would be able to tell their viewers in detail about Billick and Sanders's plans down the road. Clearly, Deion's return would be a big part of the CBS story the next day. And Cross could say, "Brian Billick told us last night that Deion is already sitting in on special teams meetings."

Everyone left the room happy. Especially Kevin Byrne. Terrell Suggs had shown up on time.

13

Sucker Punch

SUNDAY DAWNED CLEAR AND COOL, a perfect end-of-summer day for the start of a football season. The new Browns Stadium that Art Modell had once dreamed of sparkled in the morning sun as tailgaters began arriving on the shores of Lake Erie, most of them abuzz with anticipation at the new beginning that an 0-0 record means for all thirty-two NFL teams each September.

If one had any doubts about the NFL's grip on American culture, picking up that morning's *Cleveland Plain Dealer* would wipe them away quickly. In addition to the regular Sunday sports section with the usual advance stories about the Browns-Ravens opener, there were two special sections devoted to the Browns. One looked back at the fortieth anniversary of the Browns' last championship, the 1964 team led by the great Jim Brown, quarterback Frank Ryan, and Hall of Fame receiver Paul Warfield. There was no escaping the irony of the fact that the Browns' victim in that championship game had been the Baltimore Colts and that the owner of the team that year had been a young businessman named Modell. The second special section looked ahead to the new season, one filled with question marks with the arrival of a new quarterback — Jeff Garcia — and speculation about the future of fourth-year coach Butch Davis. When Davis trotted onto the field for warm-ups he looked considerably heavier and older than the confident young coach who had arrived on a white horse from the University of Miami in 2001 and led the team to the playoffs in his second season at the helm.

The Ravens weren't the least bit concerned by any of that. The buildup to the game was proof that time does heal most wounds. Almost none of the pregame talk had been about the ex-Browns taking on the current Browns or about Modell and his departure from the city. It hadn't come up even once in the CBS production meeting, and other than a lone sign in the lower corner of the stadium urging Hall of Fame voters to continue to overlook Modell, it was apparent that most people in Cleveland were far more concerned about Garcia's throwing arm than they were about their former team.

Billick had shown the team the Ray Liotta "across the street" tape again the night before in their Saturday night meeting. After reminding the players that "we're already across that street," he turned the meeting over to Ray Lewis.

This wasn't unusual. The coaches treated Lewis almost as a player/coach. Each week, Lewis would give Mike Nolan a list suggesting possible calls for the defensive script. Most teams script their first fifteen plays on offense, based on down and distance. The Ravens do the same thing on defense. When he first became defensive coordinator in 2002, Nolan encouraged Lewis to make suggestions about the defensive game plan. Eventually, those suggestions had been formalized into a list of specific calls Lewis thought would be effective at the beginning of the game.

Lewis would also go to Billick several times a year and ask if he could speak to the team. There was no pattern to it: he was as likely to do it on the field after practice as in a scheduled team meeting. Billick always told Lewis that it was fine with him, in part because he thought hearing a different voice was healthy for a team, in part because, like Nolan, he trusted Lewis's instincts. "I always scale back what I'm going to say when Ray asks to talk," he said. "I'm pretty certain that his message is going to be one that I'm in agreement with."

On the first Saturday night of a new season, Lewis's message was about football and the potential for the team to do big things but also about the experience they were all about to go through together. "We're living our lives together," he said, his voice, as always, full of passion. "We will never again be together as a group this way when this season is over. Never. We all know how things change. We should remember that on every single play. All we need to do is make every play in every game important. Play it as if you'll never play the game again. We do that and then, whatever happens, we can walk away when it's all over and feel good about ourselves and about each other. Every single play. That's what football is. I pledge to give you everything I have on every single play. I want all of you to pledge that to yourselves and to each other."

Now they went through their pregame rituals, familiar ones to the veterans, new ones to the rookies. For those who had gone through them before preseason games, the change in the way they felt was almost unnerving. There was very little of the locker-room chatter that went on before preseason games. No one joked about how many series the starters would or wouldn't play. Three hours before kickoff, Jim Colletto sat on a bench in the empty stadium and looked around while Matt Stover, Wade Richey, and Dave Zastudil stood at midfield checking wind currents and angles.

"This will be a very tough football game," Colletto said with a sigh. "They've got a huge offensive line, plus openers are always emotional, especially for the home team. Their feeling has got to be that this is a must-win game if they're going to have any kind of season." He worried about Ethan Brooks. "Ethan's good enough. We just have to keep him from getting tight and down on himself the way he can." He smiled. "I told him not to drink any coffee this morning. The last thing we want is for him to be hyper."

Billick arrived, as he always did, on the second set of buses. The first buses always leave the hotel three and a half hours before kickoff. Many players and coaches like to be in the stadium very early just to relax, stretch out, perhaps walk the field. The kickers are always the first ones out. There isn't a wind current on the planet Earth that Stover hasn't studied or dissected during his fifteen years in the NFL. Almost always, the other team's kickers will be on the field doing the same thing, and a conversation, in a language spoken only by kickers, nearly always ensues.

The second wave of buses leaves two and a half hours before kickoff. The Ravens rarely stay at a hotel more than five or ten minutes from the stadium, and since NFL buses always receive a police escort, it takes almost no time to arrive inside the bowels of the stadium. Billick is as superstitious — or, in his terms, "ritual oriented"— as anyone. He drops his bag in the locker room, walks out to the field, and circles the perimeter. He then spends a few minutes chatting with the opposing head coach (if he encounters him at that point) before heading back to the locker room.

Ninety minutes before kickoff, each team makes its list of eight inactive players known. That was the moment when the Browns knew for certain that Ogden was out. That was also the time when two of the game officials met with each coach. Billick is not a believer in making small talk with the officials. After handshakes, he looks at his watch and says, "I've got 11:31:20 right now." This is so the schedule the team is following leading up to kickoff is identical to the one the officials are following. When the NFL says kickoff is at 1:08, it does not mean 1:05 or 1:07, it means 1:08. Billick then told the officials that Jeff Friday was both his get-back and uniform coach. (The officials don't worry about sock levels, but they do randomly check one lineman coming out of the locker room before each half to make sure no foreign substances — like Vaseline — are on his uniform. Friday is charged with delivering the requested lineman.) Billick went on to say that Matt Simon would be on the headphones with the coaches in the press box in case of a possible challenge on a call but that he (Billick) would be carrying the red flag that is thrown if there is a challenge.

"Trick plays?" the officials ask.

Most of the time the answer is no, but Billick always reminds them that his punter is left-footed (which affects where the referee stands on punts) and finally tells them who his captains are for that day. The meeting rarely lasts more than five minutes.

Normally, for the opener, Billick's captains would be the most established player he had on each unit: Ogden on offense, Lewis on defense, and Stover on special teams. With Ogden out, Billick had decided to make Orlando Brown the offensive captain. This would be an emotional day for Brown. His mother had died the day before, and he had made the decision to play, knowing, as athletes often do, that his mother would want him to. The players were all aware of what had happened, and Lewis made mention of it in the pregame prayer.

Billick's pregame speech was brief. There really wasn't much need to say anything. They all knew what needed to be done and what the game was going to be like. Billick did tell a white lie, hoping for a small edge. "They've decided to introduce our offense," he said. "I don't know why they would want to introduce Jamal Lewis in this stadium, given what he did to them last year, but that's their choice."

Everyone hooted about that one and how sorry they would soon be. Of course, it wasn't the Browns' choice to introduce the offense. It was the Ravens' choice. Each team decides each week which unit it will introduce.

The only change Billick made was what he thought was a minor one: eliminating the Lord's Prayer from the pregame. In the past, the last thing the team had done before taking the field was say the Lord's Prayer together. Billick thought one prayer was enough. "I told you in camp this was your team," he said. "You guys have taken it upon yourselves to say a pregame prayer of your own, and that's exactly how it should be."

They came out of the tunnel, hearing the usual catcalls and challenges and profanities that visitors almost always hear in visiting stadiums in the NFL. Players learn to turn a deaf ear because doing anything but that can only lead to trouble. For the toss of the coin, Lewis, Stover, and Brown had to walk around a massive platform that had been set up at midfield for G. E. Smith, the former *Saturday Night Live* bandleader, and his band, who were going to play the National Anthem. Smith stood on the platform, peering down at the players and officials as they gathered at midfield.

The toss of the coin did not go especially well. Billick knew that Brown was in an emotional state. He had spent time with him on Saturday after hearing the news about his mother's death to make certain he was okay to play. Brown assured him that he was. But as the Ravens' captains and the Browns' captains shook hands, Brown was starting to lose control. He slapped hands hard with the Browns' captains, then informed them in no uncertain terms what was about to happen to them. Matt Stover wasn't certain exactly how many times the word *motherfuckers* was used, but he estimated it was more than one time and probably less than a hundred. Andra Davis, one of the Browns' captains, finally decided he had heard enough.

"What the hell is wrong with you, man?" he shouted. "Just shut the fuck up and let's play football!"

The officials got in between Davis and Brown before anything more than shouting could take place. The season hadn't yet started and the first fight of the year had almost broken out.

"Don't ever send him out there again," Stover said to Billick when the three Ravens returned to the sideline.

Billick grabbed Brown. "You need to get ahold of yourself," he said. "Don't let these guys get to you. That's *not* the way to deal with this."

Brown was near tears — for obvious reasons. "Zeus, are you okay?" Billick asked. "Look me in the eye and tell me you're okay."

"I'm okay!" Brown screamed.

Billick hoped he was telling the truth.

Standing a few feet away, Kordell Stewart, who had played all but one year in his NFL career in a division that included the Ravens, Steelers, Browns, and Bengals, shook his head. "This division is different than the others," he said. "Everything is personal. It's never just about football."

At precisely 1:08 the season began with Wade Richey kicking the ball off to the Cleveland 3, where Dee Brown fielded it and returned it to the 33. Chad Williams made the first official tackle of the season. The defense proceeded to move the Browns' offense 4 yards backward in three plays. A near-perfect beginning. Unfortunately, the offense couldn't match the defense — coming up a yard short of a first down on a Kyle Boller pass to Todd Heap. Late in the first quarter, the offense had its first real chance to score. Starting at their own 12, aided by a Browns penalty, the Ravens moved to a third-and-1 at the Browns' 49.

Matt Cavanaugh knew that the Browns expected the Ravens to do what they did best in that situation: pound Jamal Lewis into the line to pick up the yard and hope he might get into the secondary for a long run. He called, instead a play-action pass deep, Boller pulling the ball out of Lewis's stomach, drifting back, and lofting a perfect pass down the middle to Travis Taylor. As Taylor accelerated to run under the ball, he felt his groin muscle pull. He missed the pass and went down in pain. David Shaw had asked Taylor before the game if he was absolutely certain he was healthy enough to play. Billick had kept the rookie Devard Darling active just in case Taylor couldn't go. Taylor had told Shaw he was fine, ready to go.

"I like the toughness," Shaw said later. "Now I have to question the judgment."

NFL players frequently play with injuries. They learn to deal with pain almost as a constant during the season. Some take painkilling shots in order to get on the field, knowing that when the painkiller wears off, they will be in agony. There are only sixteen games a year. To miss one is a big deal. Taylor didn't want to let his teammates down. He was also in the final year of his contract and wanted every possible chance to show the Ravens they needed to re-sign him for big money in 2005. Now his body had let him down. As a result, instead of lining up for an extra point, the Ravens lined up to punt.

The rest of the first half was no less frustrating. The offense couldn't get anything going. Without Ogden, the running game sputtered. The Browns, helped by a short Zastudil punt that put them in business at the Baltimore 45, managed to move to the Ravens' 20 to set up a 37-yard Phil Dawson field goal. That was all the scoring in the half.

There may be nothing faster in sports than an NFL halftime. It is only twelve minutes long — as compared with college football, which is twenty minutes — and everything happens in a blur. Billick rarely says anything to the team; he leaves most of the talking for the coordinators. Only if he is extremely upset about something does Billick address the team. The players and coaches split up, the offense going to one side of the locker room, the defense the other. The offensive coaches meet in Billick's office, while the defensive staff huddles in any corner they can find. They go over which plays and calls worked in the first half and which did not. Suggestions on changes are tossed around. Matt Cavanaugh always writes down a list of calls he wants to make in the second half and then puts the plays on a screen so he can go over them with the players. Mike Nolan uses the old-fashioned greaseboard for anything he wants the players to see.

"There's not that much you can do at halftime," Nolan said. "You try to make some corrections if you see some things that are being done wrong or if the other team has surprised you with something. That doesn't happen too often in the NFL, though, they usually know what you're doing and you know what they're doing."

For the players, halftime is, for the most part, about relaxing. Some head straight for the training room for treatment for an injury that wasn't serious enough to cause them to leave the game but hurts nonetheless. The doctors and trainers probably work the hardest during the break because there are always players who need something taped or looked at or sometimes given a painkiller for. On occasion, Bill Tessendorf, who has been with the Browns/Ravens for thirty-two years and is trusted implicitly by every person in the organization, will walk out of the trainers' room, find Billick, and quietly tell him that someone is "down for the day"— out for the rest of the game.

No one felt any need to change anything on defense. For the most part, they had shut the Browns down. Gary Baxter had cut his thumb on someone's helmet during a punt return but had come back to play. Deion Sanders had walked onto the field in nickel situations, with Corey Fuller screaming the play calls at him from the sideline. The Browns had made no attempt to throw at him.

The problem — again — was the offense. There just weren't very many holes for Jamal Lewis, whether he ran left or right. Brooks was holding up okay, but he simply wasn't Ogden. They had known that going in. Boller had been under pressure often when he had tried to throw and had spent a good deal of time sprinting out of the pocket and throwing the ball away. Todd Heap had made a couple of catches to pick up first downs, but that had been just about all the passing offense they had been able to muster. All the preseason talk about how different the passing game was going to look had not been borne out so far.

Six minutes into the third quarter, the Ravens finally got on the board. Heap made a spectacular one-handed catch that was good for 24 yards and a first down on the Browns' 28. Three running plays picked up only 4 yards and they had to settle for a Matt Stover 42-yard field goal. Still virtually automatic at the age of thirty-six, Stover drilled the kick for the team's first points of the season and the game was tied, 3–3. The sense on the sideline was that the Browns were about to go away. The defense wasn't going to give them anything and the offense was slowly getting its act together.

Then right guard Bennie Anderson was called for holding, shutting down a Ravens drive and, after a Zastudil punt, the Browns started from their own 42. There was no reason to believe at that moment that there was any chance they were going to move the ball. Their offense had produced less than 100 yards in just under three quarters. Jeff Garcia, the Browns' new quarterback, threw two incomplete passes and the punt teams on both sidelines gathered, expecting yet another punt. It never came. Garcia found Kellen Winslow down the sideline for 21 yards. Winslow, the rookie tight end from Miami, had been called for an illegal block in the back on the previous punt but made amends by leaping high over Ed Reed to pull the ball in at the Ravens' 47. It was the Browns' fifth first down of the game, and they were still a long way from scoring territory.

Two plays later, they weren't. Garcia made a play-action fake to William Green on second-and-9 and, for some reason, the entire secondary froze. Quincy Morgan raced behind Baxter and Reed, caught the ball in stride, and scored, untouched. With twenty-four seconds left in the third quarter, the Browns led, 10–3.

The Baltimore bench was in shock. If Billick and Nolan had a concern during the preseason, it had been a disturbing tendency to give up what Billick called "explosion" plays — a big play in which the defense gets blown up. There hadn't been many of them, but there had been enough that Billick had mentioned it to the team during the week. "Eliminate those plays and we're virtually unscored on in preseason," he had said. "We can't let them happen now, because now it's real."

Now it was very real. The 10–3 deficit at the end of the third quarter looked a little bit like a mountain, given the struggles of the offense. Boller tried. He found Dan Wilcox open for what would have been a 20-yard gain — except that Wilcox fumbled the ball and, even though Kevin Johnson managed to recover it, the gain ended up being 13 yards to the Ravens' 49 instead of 20 to the Cleveland 44. Two plays later, Boller tried to go deep again on a first down from the Browns' 40. Browns cornerback Anthony Henry ran stride for stride with Johnson and intercepted the ball at the 7. That wasn't a complete disaster because of the field position. If the defense could get a three-and-out, the Ravens would probably get the ball back around midfield. Soon enough, the Browns faced third-and-10 from the 7.

Then, once again, the defense got blown up. This time Garcia found Andre' Davis behind Will Demps for a 51-yard pickup to the Baltimore 42. Seven plays later, Dawson kicked a 25-yard field goal, and the margin was 13–3. The Ravens now needed two scores. What's more, the Browns had taken more than six minutes off the clock. Time was short, the situation desperate. It got no better. Knowing the Ravens had to pass, the Browns ignored the run completely and began teeing off with their pass rush. Kenard Lang, who had been held in check fairly well all day by Brooks, blew by him and sacked Boller on the 14-yard line. The next play was like an instant replay: Lang going around Brooks, Boller going down.

The difference was that Boller fumbled this time and Michael Myers recovered on the 6. Billick futilely challenged the play, hoping that the replay might show that Boller was in the motion of throwing when he was hit. He wasn't. It took three plays for the Browns to score, Garcia sprinting untouched around the right side on third down. He ran right through the end zone and made a leap into Cleveland's infamous Dog Pound to celebrate what was now clearly an opening-day victory with the jubilant fans.

The final was 20–3. The stadium was shaking with joy by the time Heap caught Boller's last pass of the day and was tackled at midfield as time ran out. There was little postgame lingering on the field. This was not what they had in mind to start the season. Gary Zauner walked around the locker room, reminding people it was just one game, but it felt worse than that.

Steve Bisciotti, 0-1 as an owner, stood in the back of the room as Billick talked, twisting the cap of a bottle of water on and off, his stomach tied in a knot. "I almost never make predictions," Bisciotti said. "But when we went on our family vacation in June, I told everyone I thought we'd be 5-0 at the bye. I really thought we'd do that. Now, we're 0-1 and the offense doesn't look even a little bit better than it had been the year before. I felt awful."

His sentiment was shared by almost everyone in the room. They hadn't come close to crossing the street.

14

Must Win

THERE ARE FEW PLACES on Earth more tense than the headquarters of an NFL team on the morning after a loss. The misery ratchets up about 100 percent when the loss is in the opening game against a team that you expected to beat. Walking the halls on the morning after the Ravens' loss in Cleveland brought the Simon and Garfunkel song "The Sounds of Silence" immediately to mind.

The Monday routine in Baltimore is the same during the first half of the season, win or lose. The coaches and personnel staff meet at noon, first to go over any roster changes that need to be made and discuss the status of injured players, then to go through what they saw of each player on tape that morning. The mood on the morning of September 13 in the Ravens' draft room was grim. Not only had the team lost the game badly, but the trainers and doctors now agreed there could be no further delay for the knee surgery needed for Kelly Gregg, the defensive tackle who was considered the mainstay of the defensive line. Gregg was one of those free-agent stories the Ravens reveled in. He had spent a year on the Cincinnati Bengals' practice squad and then been signed and released by the Eagles before Rex Ryan recommended that the Ravens sign him as a free agent in the spring of 2000.

When Gregg walked onto the practice field, Billick took one look at his squat physique — 6 foot, 300 pounds — and said to Ryan, "What's the deal on this guy, Rex, did you owe someone a favor?"

He changed his tune quickly when he saw Gregg play. He was quicker than he looked and a fierce competitor on every single play. Now losing him to an injury made the loss in Cleveland feel even worse. Gregg had hoped the knee would hold up until the bye week so he could perhaps miss no more than one game, since the surgery was expected to keep him out three weeks. He had stood on the sideline through most of the second half in Cleveland, hoping the knee would stretch out enough for him to play, but it had been to no avail.

There was also the issue of bringing back Harold Morrow. The plan all along had been to re-sign him after the Cleveland game, and the play of the special teams — at one point there had been penalties on three straight kicks — had made his return even more of a necessity. That meant the first order of business at the Monday meeting was deciding whom to cut to make space for Morrow. This wasn't at all like a training-camp cut, because it involved someone who had proven himself good enough to play in the NFL — probably a veteran since there were so few rookies on the team.

"I need a name," Billick said quietly.

There wasn't a sound in the room. Billick repeated himself, acting as if perhaps no one had heard him the first time. "I need a name."

It was Phil Savage who finally spoke up. "What kind of production," he asked in his quiet way, "are we getting out of Cornell Brown?"

The question was directed at two people: Mike Nolan and Gary Zauner. Brown was an eighth-year player who had been drafted by the Ravens and had spent his entire career, except for a one-year sojourn in Oakland, with the Ravens. He was one of the best-liked players on the team, a special teams leader who had always been considered a solid backup at linebacker.

"If you want the truth, he's not getting many snaps for me," Nolan said. "But his value is having someone experienced to take some of the weight off of AD." Adalius Thomas had emerged as a starter at outside linebacker in Peter Boulware's absence but was also a critical special teams player.

Zauner, arms folded, understanding that one of his guys was in jeopardy, nodded. "He's not what he used to be for me," he said. "But he's still one of my leaders."

They tossed Brown's name around for a while. Clearly they would be cutting a fading player if Brown was let go. There was also a chance he might not be signed by another team and would be available to come back later in the season if something opened up.

Finally, George Kokinis, the pro personnel director, in a voice that might have been even softer than Savage's, said simply: "Are there issues here that make it impossible for us to consider Corey Fuller?"

Billick had been waiting for someone to bring up Fuller's name. He knew that, for a lot of reasons, cutting Fuller was the clear-cut move to make. Fuller was thirty-three years old, in his tenth season, and near the end of his career. He was at the bottom of the depth chart for the defensive backs and had been inactive for the Browns game — the first time in his career he had been inactive when healthy for a game. He had missed most of the last three exhibition games after hurting his leg in the Eagles game.

Everyone knew the issues Kokinis was talking about. Fuller was best friends with Ray Lewis and Deion Sanders. While both men would intellectually understand Fuller's release, they would be hurt by it, especially Sanders, who had first been tempted to come back by Fuller's phone call in July.

"There are good reasons why it should be Corey Fuller," Billick said, surprising most of the people in the room. He and Fuller had become close when Fuller was playing in Minnesota and Billick was coaching there, and Billick had played a major role in bringing him to the Ravens in 2003. "But I think we're going to need him before this is over. I've never coached a year in my career where the team didn't get into November and need a veteran presence in the defensive backfield. We may not need him right now, but down the road we're going to need him."

That eliminated Fuller. Or so it seemed.

Savage, who believed that there was no doubt Fuller should be the cut, threw out another name. "We did talk about Gerome Sapp during preseason, didn't we?"

Zauner was shaking his head immediately. "You're gonna give me back Morrow and take away Sapp? He's my second- or third-best guy."

"Gary, we can only have so many specialists on this team," Savage said. His tone was even, but there wasn't any doubt about the tension that existed between him — and the other scouts — and Zauner. They all thought Zauner had undue influence over Billick, something Billick readily admitted.

"Gary makes them crazy," he said. "Because when it comes to special teams, he's almost never wrong. Look at Will Demps. He found him on the street. Look at B. J. Sams."

In fact, as if Sunday hadn't been bad enough, Ozzie Newsome had been forced to pay Zauner the $2,000 he had promised back in April when Zauner had pestered him to get Sams into minicamp. That was Life with Zauner: he might make you nuts sometimes, but his judgments were almost always sound.

"George, how do you rate Sapp as a special teams player?" Zauner asked, knowing that Kokinis spent hours and hours looking at tapes of players around the league.

"He's very good," Kokinis said. "Probably number two on our team. Would help just about anyone in the league."

Billick jumped in. "Mike, how do you feel about his progress as a DB?"

Nolan hesitated. "To be honest, Brian, not great," he said. "Don't get me wrong, I love the kid. He's great in the classroom, he's got a great attitude. But on the field, there's something missing. He doesn't have great football instincts."

Football instincts are something that can't be taught. You either have them or you don't. Sapp, one of the brighter people on the team, simply wasn't gifted with the ability to make the right decision on the field without having to think about it.

Billick turned to Newsome. Because Fuller and Brown had been in the league for more than four years and because the season was less than six games old, they could be terminated without clearing waivers — meaning the chances of getting them back, either in a week or in a month if needed, were better than with Sapp, because as a second-year player, he would have to clear waivers. "Ozzie, if we waived him, what are the chances he gets picked up?" Billick asked.

"I would say very good," Newsome said. "In fact, I'm almost certain Indy would pick him up. They need a guy just like him for special teams and as a backup safety."

Billick sighed. They had been going at it for close to an hour. A decision had to be made. "I hate doing this," he said finally. "But I think it has to be Cornell. If we love him up like we did with Harold, maybe he won't jump right to another team."

"Or there might not be another team," Savage put in.

The decision was made. Cornell Brown, a man they all liked and respected, would be cut.

* * *

That decision lasted less than twenty-four hours.

The next morning, while the coaches were beginning to prepare their game plan for Pittsburgh, Nolan went to see Billick. The rest of Monday hadn't been much better than the personnel meeting. The film sessions (film hasn't been used in the NFL for years, but everyone still calls looking at game tape a film session) had been full of tension. David Shaw, the normally mild-mannered wide receivers/quarterbacks coach, had gotten on the wideouts about their lax run blocking. He had shown them no fewer than half a dozen plays where the lack of a block by a wide receiver had been the difference between a short pickup for Jamal Lewis and the kind of breakout run that might have changed the game. He had met one-on-one with Travis Taylor, who was going on the injured list for four weeks, to tell him in no uncertain terms that there was a difference between being tough and being foolish — and playing with a groin injury that didn't allow him to run at full speed was foolish.

Nolan had tossed and turned on Monday night for several reasons. He was still unhappy with the performance of the defense and was very nervous about cutting Brown. Part of it was personal: he liked Brown. More of it was the notion of leaving his defense without any experience behind the two starting outside linebackers, Adalius Thomas and Terrell Suggs. "I think we're making a mistake if we cut Cornell," he told Billick. "We're leaving ourselves too thin at linebacker. Corey Fuller probably ought to go, but under the circumstances, I think it has to be Sapp."

Billick listened. He and Nolan had worked together for four years. Their personalities could not have been more different: Billick was loud and direct; Nolan more subtle, with a dry sense of humor. Billick didn't keep much inside; Nolan internalized constantly. Billick knew this was an important year in Nolan's life. He had reached that level as a coordinator where his name was being mentioned for head coaching jobs. He had worked his entire adult life to get to this point, and the consensus was that a good year for the Ravens' defense would probably make Nolan a hot name when the season was over. Nolan had thought he was going to get interviewed after the '03 season for the Bears job, but it hadn't worked out. He was prepared — he had his résumé in his computer and a folder

Brian Billick: Always searching for an edge.
© Phil Hoffmann

Ozzie Newsome:
The quiet groundbreaker.
© Phil Hoffmann

Steve Bisciotti: The owner with no desire to be famous accepts his first victory game ball.
© Phil Hoffmann

Ray Lewis: Always the leader.
© Phil Hoffmann

Jonathan Ogden: The prototype of a left tackle.
© Phil Hoffmann

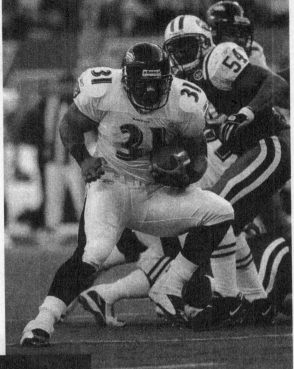

Jamal Lewis:
A long, hard year.
© Phil Hoffmann

Kyle Boller: A lot tougher
than he looks.
© Phil Hoffmann

Ed Reed: An
emerging superstar.
© Phil Hoffmann

Deion Sanders:
Still great . . . when healthy.
© Phil Hoffmann

B. J. Sams:
Gary Zauner's latest
discovery.
© Phil Hoffmann

Gary Zauner and Matt Stover: Discussing wind currents and other matters.
© Phil Hoffmann

Mike Nolan, with Ray Lewis: Following in his father's footsteps.
© Phil Hoffmann

Chris McAlister: New contract in '04, new Chris in '05?
© Phil Hoffmann

Ray Lewis does his pregame dance.
© Phil Hoffmann

Todd Heap: Ten games missed, and he was missed in all.
© Phil Hoffmann

Mike Flynn: A burning desire to play.
© Phil Hoffmann

Jim Fassel, with Boller: The teacher and his star — and only — pupil.
© Phil Hoffmann

Matt Cavanaugh: The one man in Baltimore who couldn't win in '04.
© Phil Hoffmann

Ethan Brooks: An unlikely NFL player.
© Phil Hoffmann

Brian Billick: A fairly calm sideline moment.
© Phil Hoffmann

marked "Head Coaching Material," which included a list of the things he would say if interviewed and coaches he would try to hire for his staff. Even so, Billick had no doubts about Nolan's focus. He knew Nolan had only one speed when it came to his job: all-out.

Nolan is a coach's son. His father, Dick Nolan, had been the head coach of the San Francisco 49ers for eight years and the New Orleans Saints for three. As a result, Nolan and his five siblings had grown up around the game. He and two of his brothers had spent years working as ballboys for the 49ers. The game had stuck to Nolan, not his brothers.

"You see it in your own children when you grow up and realize everyone has a different personality," he said. "I just loved it right from the beginning. Most of my boyhood memories center around football and football players. Back then, my brothers and I were *it*, we were the team's ballboys. Now you've got so many kids running around a team, you don't know where half of them came from. I was the one in the family who got upset when people said bad things about my dad. I was the one who wanted to start fights. And when he got fired, I was the one who said, 'I'm gonna do this, too, and it won' t happen to me.' Of course, I did it and it has happened to me."

Nolan played like a typical coach's son: he understood the game inside and out and made plays because he was usually a step ahead mentally. He wasn't nearly as good a player as his father, who had been a star cornerback for the New York Giants in the 1950s. "I don't think I understood it until I was older, but I grew up a celebrity's son," Nolan said. "My dad was so popular when he played in New York that they used him one year as the Marlboro Man in that giant ad in Times Square. But he was so devoted to my mom and to all of us that it never really felt like that. When he became a coach, it was perfect for me. It's funny, though, even when I was little, I always liked being around the defensive players more. Can't tell you why, I just liked the defensive mind-set more. Those were the guys I hung out with when I was little. And, except for one year when I coached offense [for the Ravens in 2001 before becoming defensive coordinator the next season], I've hung out with defensive guys as an adult."

Nolan was a cornerback himself, a solid high school player who might have been recruited by some Division 1 schools if he hadn't suffered a serious eye injury just prior to the start of his senior season. An accidental poke through the helmet by a wide receiver landed him in the hospital for a week with a patch on his eye and some question about whether he'd see out of it again. This was in the fall of 1976, a year after his father had been fired by the 49ers. Even though his dad was no longer the coach, a number of 49ers came to the hospital to see him, something Nolan never forgot. "Remember, professionally, my dad didn't matter to them anymore," he said. "But they somehow got word and they came. It meant a lot.

"It had been crushing to me when Dad got fired. We all knew it was possible and when he got called into a meeting the day after Christmas, he said to us, 'Guys, I doubt this is good news. You give people good news before Christmas, not after.' Seeing him after that happened was tough. He'd never known anything but success. It was not an easy time."

Neither was the period right after Nolan's injury. His sight came back and he was able to play a little by the end of the season. Still, any chance that he might get recruited had gone by the boards. Which is where his father's football contacts came into play — not for the last time. Rich Brooks, who had been on Nolan's staff, had just gotten the job as head coach at the University of Oregon. Dick Nolan called him and asked if he would give his son a chance to make his team as a walk-on. Brooks was more than willing to do that. When Mike arrived in Eugene, Brooks told him: "If you're ever a starter, I'll put you on scholarship."

Mike thought that was a reasonable deal, though it seemed unlikely ever to occur. He got into one game, the last one of the season on kickoff coverage, as a freshman. At the start of spring practice, he was fourth on the depth chart at cornerback. Then, in forty-eight hours, it all changed. "Our number two cornerback was also our number three quarterback," he said. "One day in practice, our number one cornerback collides with the number two quarterback. They both get hurt. Now the number two corner has to move to offense because we're a quarterback short. All of a sudden, we've lost two corners in one day — one to injury, the other to a position switch. Then, the day after that, the number three corner is declared academically ineligible. In two days, I went from number four to taking every snap because there was absolutely no one behind me."

By summer practice, Brooks had brought in a couple of freshmen and a junior college corner, but none of them beat Nolan out of the job that was now his. He proudly called his father to tell him he didn't need to pay tuition for him anymore, then went on to start for the next three years. He even made it to training camp with the Denver Broncos as a free agent before being let go on the second-to-last cut. In those days — 1981 — that meant he had outlasted a lot of players. "I wasn't big enough or fast enough, it was that simple," he said. "Dan Reeves brought me to camp as a favor to my dad, but I think I did better than they expected me to. I knew where the ball was going most of the time."

After he was cut, Reeves asked Nolan what he planned to do. "Coach," he answered. Reeves shook his head. "I was hoping," he said, "that you were going to be smarter than that."

Nolan knew firsthand what Reeves was talking about, but there was no question in his mind that coaching was what he wanted to do. He started as a graduate assistant at Oregon, then began making the rounds: Stanford, Rice, and LSU, where he coached linebackers. In January of 1987 he was updating his résumé and left a message for Reeves in his office, asking him if it would be okay to add his name, since he was thinking that perhaps his next move might be to the NFL. Reeves called him back the next night.

"Listen, I'm in Cleveland right now, getting ready for the conference championship game, but before you do anything, I want to talk to you," he said. "I'm going to make some changes on my staff after the season, so sit tight until we're done."

Nolan was stunned by the call. He had completely forgotten that the Broncos were about to play in Cleveland, with a trip to the Super Bowl at stake, when he had called Reeves. The next day produced "the Drive," John Elway's 98-yard masterpiece that Ozzie Newsome and the city of Cleveland have yet to get over. The Broncos went on to lose the Super Bowl to the New York Giants, and Reeves asked Nolan to come to Denver to talk to him.

"You know anything about coaching special teams?" he asked Nolan.

"Not a thing," Nolan answered.

"Good, you're hired."

Nolan spent the next ten seasons with Reeves, six in Denver and four in New York with the Giants. Reeves made him linebackers coach after two seasons in Denver and took him to New York as his defensive coordinator. Nolan was thirty-three, one of the youngest coordinators in the league his first year, when the Giants' defense gave up fewer points than any team in the NFL. Reeves got fired after the 1996 season and Nolan landed in Washington, working for Norv Turner. That worked fine for two years, until the Redskins were bought by one Daniel M. Snyder, a thirty-four-year-old whiz kid entrepreneur who seemed to think that being successful in business and being a football fan made you a football expert.

"I still remember my first meeting with him," Nolan said, shaking his head. "He was sitting at his desk, smoking a big cigar. First, he did about fifteen minutes on how he got to be rich. Then he said to me, 'If I guaranteed you a fifty-thousand-dollar bonus for getting our defense to be in the top three in the league, would that be an incentive to get you to work harder?'

"I told him no, it wouldn't, because with or without a bonus, I was going to give heart and soul to the job. He looked at me and said, 'You're probably another one of those guys who lets his wife tell him what to do, aren't you?'

"Now, that made me laugh. I tell young coaches that they better be sure when they take a new job that their wife can be happy. See, the coaches have it easy. We get someplace and we're spending all our time doing what we love: coaching. We're in meetings, we're planning, we're working with the guys. We're not the ones who have to find new schools and new doctors and a new place to shop and send out change-of-address stuff and get phones hooked up. Your wife is doing all the work, so you better be sure she's comfortable with wherever you're going, because if she's not, everyone is going to be miserable.

"I didn't say anything like that to Snyder, because I knew it was pointless. He was so busy spewing profanities all around, I just wanted to get out of there."

For a football coach to notice someone else's profanities is remarkable, since profanity is the official language of the NFL and most professional sports leagues. That meeting with Snyder proved to be the beginning of a less-than-beautiful friendship. Early that season, after a Redskins loss, Snyder told Nolan that his defensive calls were "too vanilla." Like the other coaches, Nolan had figured out by then that trying to explain football to Snyder was pointless, since he already had the game figured out. A few days later a gallon of 31 Flavors ice cream showed up on Nolan's desk with a note that said, "This is what I like. Not vanilla."

Nolan laughed and sent Snyder a note: "Thanks for the ice cream. My kids enjoyed it."

"The first time it was actually kind of funny," Nolan said. "I didn't mind it at all."

The next time wasn't as funny. The Redskins lost on the road to Dallas, and Nolan went into his office late Sunday night to start looking at game tape. When he arrived, there were three giant canisters of melting 31 Flavors ice cream on his desk with another note: "I wasn't joking. I do *not* like vanilla."

This time Nolan was less than amused.

As it turned out, the Redskins defense, after an awful start, righted itself the second half of the season and the team made the playoffs and even won a first-round game before losing in the divisional round to Tampa Bay. That was the off-season when Snyder went crazy spending money, signing (among others) aging free agents Bruce Smith, Jeff George, and Deion Sanders — completely undermining the work Turner and fired general manager Charlie Casserly had done to rebuild the team. Nolan left to become defensive coordinator with the Jets. Even though the Jets' defense improved from twenty-first to tenth statistically during the 2000 season, Nolan was looking for work again when the season ended after Coach Al Groh bolted the Jets to become the coach at the University of Virginia. Billick then hired him as tight ends coach, and a year later, when Marvin Lewis was lured to Washington by Snyder — becoming the first million-dollar-a-year coordinator — Nolan became the Ravens' coordinator. After the Ravens' still-young defense finished the 2003 season ranked fourth in the league (with Ray Lewis voted Player of the Year), Nolan was named to *USA Today*'s "All Joe" team. The "All Joe" consists of players and coaches who are "hard-working, successful, but overlooked."

This season was Nolan's chance to no longer be overlooked. He knew it, Billick knew it, everyone in the organization knew it. Nolan had some concerns about his defense: Chris McAlister had missed most of camp, and so had Sanders. The defensive line was full of great people who were eager but undersize. And there had been the early penchant for giving up big plays. Now Nolan was concerned that cutting Cornell Brown was going to leave him essentially one deep at the linebacker spot. It would mean that backup defensive end Jarret Johnson would have to take snaps in practice at linebacker in case of an injury. Sapp was more expendable to the defense, if not to special teams.

Billick told Nolan he would give it some thought. Then he went and talked to Newsome. This was their way: hash things out, reach a consensus between the two of them of some kind. In the end, this was Billick's decision, but he always sought Newsome's input. The two of them decided Nolan was right about Brown. They also decided it was time for Billick to talk to Corey Fuller. The players were off on Tuesday. Billick would talk to Fuller on Wednesday after practice.

The next day could not have been more miserable. To begin with, it rained. Although the team's new facility would not be ready to move into until mid-October, the indoor practice facility was ready and had already been used on several occasions in poor weather. Billick wanted to move practice indoors, but Dick Cass told him there was a problem: the carpenters union was embroiled in a dispute with the construction firm over the number of union carpenters being used on the job. As a result, the carpenters were picketing in the driveway leading into the facility. The Ravens didn't want to get into the middle of a political battle, so driving team buses across the picket line — a TV photo-op if there had ever been one — was out of the question. They would have to practice in the rain.

Billick was already dreading making a decision on Fuller or Sapp. Then, practice was predictably wet and sloppy, players slipping and falling, no one completely focused. "Completely understandable under the circumstances," Billick said. "Wednesday is usually a bit sloppy anyway. It's the first day back; you're starting to put in the game plan. Thursday is the day you expect and need to see guys get after it. But with everything else going on, I snapped a little bit."

He got angry with the players, questioning their effort and concentration, wondering if they had what it took to be the team they had been planning on being. "If this is the best you've got come Sunday, let me know," he said. "I won't even waste my time showing up. I'll go spend the day on my boat." He then told the receivers he wanted them to each catch fifty balls from the ball-throwing machine before they went inside. He said please, but he wasn't making a request.

Then he asked Fuller to stay behind and talk to him. They walked over by the rolled-up tarpaulin on the side of the practice field. Billick explained to Fuller what was going on. If they cut him now, he would still receive full pay for 2004 regardless of whether he came back, because he had been on the opening-day roster. What's more, because of his veteran status, he wouldn't have to clear waivers. He could be back as early as next week. Fuller and Billick had known each other a long time. They liked and respected each other. As soon as he mentioned the word *cut* to Fuller, Billick knew what his response was going to be.

"The thing you occasionally forget as a coach is that a personal relationship with a player doesn't exempt you from hurting his feelings," Billick said. "The game is full of hurt feelings, I know that's part of it. But I could see this was one Corey couldn't handle."

Fuller is a proud, sensitive man. He had grown up in Tallahassee, Florida, and, like a lot of inner-city kids, had figured out early in life that playing ball was his route out. He had never been a partyer. "I never smoked, never drank, never did weed, nothing," he said. "For me it was all about getting a scholarship to college."

He was good enough to be widely recruited as a senior, but when Florida State showed interest, there was no doubt where he was going to end up. "To begin with, Deion Sanders was my hero," he said. "I wanted to play corner at Florida State just like he had. Plus, when Coach [Bobby] Bowden came to my house to visit, the entire neighborhood lined up outside to watch him walk in and walk out. It was like Elvis had come to town or something."

Fuller went through ups and downs at FSU: injuries, not playing as much as he wanted early. But the real trauma came during his sophomore year when his little brother, Fred Bates (his mother's maiden name was Fuller, which Corey took after she and his father split), was shot and killed during a dispute on the street. Corey was on a road trip in St. Petersburg with some teammates when his mother called with the news.

"Fred was a better athlete than I was," Fuller said softly. "But he hurt his back before his senior year and couldn't play. He had always leaned toward trouble at times and he went back to it. He got into some kind of a fight with this guy, went home, and then came back. They both had guns. The guy shot him in the back."

His brother's death caused Fuller to change his major to youth counseling, an area he has been active in throughout his football career. He was drafted in the second round by the Minnesota Vikings, which was where he met and befriended Billick, even though Billick coached the offense. "He was a players' coach, even then," he said. "He and Cris Carter fought like cats when he first got there, but they ended up being close friends. He was someone everyone on the team liked being around."

Fuller left Minnesota to sign with Cleveland in 1999, the same year Billick left for Baltimore. He was cut in 2003 as part of a Butch Davis purge of just about anyone over thirty and signed with the Ravens. He had gone through a strange and troubling off-season in 2004: first the incident in which he had been attacked by armed gunmen outside his house and then his arrest for allegedly running a gambling ring inside his house.

"They kicked the door down and came in with dogs," he said. "What's that tell you? They thought they were going to find drugs. They had a warrant to search anywhere for anything. They didn't find anything. My lawyer tells me they've got no case at all, that we're up 21–0 in the fourth quarter and we've got the Ravens defense on the field. [That analysis would prove accurate; the charges were dropped after the season.] But it still hurts me to see my name in the paper as if I'm some kind of criminal. I'm not. Ask the police what they found in the house: nothing. I wouldn't even let other people drink or smoke in my house. That's the way I've always been."

Fuller had been thrilled to be back playing for Billick. "Veteran players in the league know he's a good guy to play for because he treats you like an adult and he's completely honest," Fuller said. "If Brian Billick asked me to run through a wall, I'd do it."

But allowing Billick to cut him was another story. Fuller told Billick that he thought he belonged on the active roster, that he still had plenty to contribute to the team. He was healthy, he was ready, he wanted back on the field. Billick knew that if he cut Fuller, he would not only lose him, but it could damage morale in the locker room because Fuller's pain would no doubt be passed in some form to Lewis and Sanders. When they were finished talking, he went back upstairs and told Newsome there was no choice: Sapp would have to be cut. Then he stalked back down the hall and did something he almost never does when he is alone in his office: he shut the door.

"I felt a little bit like I was in the scene in *Young Frankenstein* where Marty Feldman and Gene Wilder are digging the grave," he said. "It's awful, dirty work, gross and disgusting. They're exhausted and filthy. Feld-man finally looks at Wilder and says, 'Well, it could be worse. It could be raining.' As soon as he says it, the sky opens up. That's the way I felt at that moment.

"I certainly didn't want to cut Corey and we couldn't cut Cornell. But we had to have Harold back. We were cutting a good kid and a good football player because of a circumstance that might very well be resolved by Mon-day. Only we couldn't wait until Monday."

Newsome volunteered to deliver the news to Sapp. He had drafted him a year earlier and he always felt responsible if a draft pick failed — regard-less of the reasons for that failure. The sun had come back out on Thursday, and the team had gone through its regular Thursday morning walk-through. A walk-through is just that: once the game plan has been given to the players on Wednesday morning, they begin looking at tape of the op-position. Then, before lunch, they go out onto the artificial-turf practice field (the only one in the old facility where no one can look out a window and peek at what's going on) and mimic the plays they are going to run and expect the opponent to run, in what amounts to slow motion. There' s no hitting involved, just gaining familiarity with the plays that they will run at full speed in practice that afternoon.

Sapp was jogging off the field with the other defensive backs when Newsome, leaning against the same tarp where Billick and Fuller had talked the day before, called his name. Smiling, Sapp turned back to trot over to Newsome. "What's up, boss?" he asked.

When he saw the look on his boss's face, he knew exactly what was up. Newsome explained to him he had done nothing wrong and, if he cleared waivers, the team would do everything it could do to bring him back. Bil-lick walked over to reinforce to Sapp how much the team thought of him. Of course, if they had told him they planned to nominate him for the Nobel Peace Prize, it wouldn't have mitigated the shock Sapp was feeling at that moment. "You see that stunned look and you just feel awful," Billick said.

Sapp shook hands with both men, thanked them for giving him a chance, and walked slowly into the locker room. The first person he en-countered was Trent Smith, like him a 2003 draft pick. Smith could see in his friend's eyes that something was wrong.

"You okay?" he asked.

Sapp shook his head. "They cut me," he said.

Smith felt his stomach tighten. There was nothing he could say and he knew it. Sapp didn't stick around for lunch. To the surprise of most, he cleared waivers. But the following Monday — as Newsome had predicted — he was signed by the Colts.

There was one small bit of comic relief. On Wednesday, Kevin Byrne had received an e-mail forwarded to him by the Cleveland public relations office, from Andra Davis. When he had learned after the game that Orlando Brown had lost his mother on Saturday, Davis felt guilty about their confrontation during the coin toss. He sent Byrne a heartfelt apology and asked him to pass it on to Brown: "Please tell Orlando how sorry I am about what happened," he wrote. "I am amazed by the courage he showed playing in the game on Sunday. I doubt if I could have done what he did. Please tell him how sorry I am for his loss and wish him my very best."

"I guess the guy must have been way out of line," Byrne said, reading the note. He had been unaware of what had happened on the field, since he had been up in the press box. On Thursday morning he took the note to Brown, who read it and laughed. "Kevin, this guy's got nothing to apologize for," he said. "I was the one who was motherfucking him. He didn't do anything wrong. It was all me."

Byrne laughed. "It's a nice gesture, though, isn't it, Zeus?"

"Oh yeah," Brown said. "But the motherfucker's got nothing to be sorry for." Like a lot of players and coaches in the NFL, Brown uses profanity both to show anger and as a term of endearment.

That wasn't the only apology issued that day. After practice, Billick apologized to his players for being snappish on Wednesday. "It was a bad day all the way around," he said. "Between the weather and the union situation, the slipping and sliding plus the decision we had to make on Gerome, I wasn't feeling real good about things. I want you guys to understand one thing: there's nothing in the world I enjoy more than being out here with you. That's what makes all the other stuff worth putting up with. So, if I went a little overboard, I'm sorry."

With that behind them, all the Ravens had to do was worry about the Steelers. The two franchises had been rivals forever, first when the team was in Cleveland and just as much since the move to Baltimore. The Ravens were 5-11 against the Steelers since the move and had lost to them the first five times they had played them in M&T Bank Stadium (including the game that opened the stadium), finally ending that string in the '03 season finale with a 13–10 overtime victory. Even that win had been controversial since the Ravens had clinched the division title earlier in the day when the Cincinnati Bengals had lost their game and some people thought Billick should have rested his starters that night. In fact, earlier in the week Steelers linebacker Joey Porter had called Billick "stupid" for not playing subs in that game once Jamal Lewis had gone over 2,000 yards rushing for the season, which he did on the Ravens' first drive.

This was not even close to the first time that Porter had been involved in trash talking with the Ravens. He had missed the start of the previous season because he had been involved in an accidental shooting outside a bar in Denver. Walking out of the stadium after the season opener in which the Steelers had beaten the Ravens, Ray Lewis had passed Porter and said, "Hey, Joey, we hope you're better soon. You're in our prayers."

Whether Porter misunderstood what Lewis said or his intent in saying it, his response was to start screaming profanities at Lewis. He had briefly followed Lewis to the Ravens' bus before thinking better of it and heading the other way, still screaming at the top of his lungs.

Billick didn't mind playing the Steelers coming off the embarrassing loss in Cleveland. "These guys are exactly who we need to be playing right now," he said. "We need a game that makes it easy for us to get back to where we need to be emotionally, and there's no one better to do that than these guys."

If there was any doubt that the team was getting where it needed to be, it was erased by Friday's practice. Friday is normally a day when practice is dialed back a little. Many of the Ravens wear different numbers than normal — Sanders, for example, wore 2, his old high school number — and if anyone is the least bit sore or tired, he will sit out. Pads are never worn and most of the practice takes place at about three-quarter speed. On this Friday, Orlando Brown and T. J. Slaughter got into a fight. It wasn't anything serious, just the usual wrestling match with the normal profanities shouted before it was broken up. Billick, who normally doesn't like fighting in practice, didn't mind it this time.

"It was actually a teaching opportunity," he said. "I liked the emotion, but I told them they had to be disciplined in this game, that there were going to be times when someone wanted to draw them into something and they couldn't afford to let it happen."

Things were looking up. Jonathan Ogden was ready to play. The weather report for Sunday was good. The Ravens gathered, as they always did before a home game, at nine o'clock on Saturday night at the downtown Hyatt in Baltimore's Inner Harbor to go through their pregame routines. There were four meetings each Saturday: special teams, offense, defense, and then the entire team together. All four usually took less than an hour in total. They were final reminders of what to look for. Most of the time, Matt Cavanaugh and Mike Nolan would ask the video people to put together some kind of inspirational tape for the end of their meeting. For music, the video guys had selected the hip-hop song "Let's Get It Started," which was becoming a pregame anthem in most NFL stadiums. The implication was clear: last week had not been a start. This week needed to be.

Billick rarely backed up his talk with any tape. In this case he made an exception, showing tape of the regular-season finale from 2003, the 13–10 overtime win. "The blueprint is there," he said after showing them a series of successful plays. "You lived it. Now let's go out and play it."

The next day they did just that. During pregame warm-ups, Joey Porter approached Billick, hand outstretched. "Coach, I'm sorry," he said. "I didn't really call you stupid."

"No problem, Joey," Billick said, accepting the handshake. "I probably am stupid."

The feeling in the locker room before the game was clearly different than in Cleveland. There, they had quietly hoped they would handle the circumstances: hostile stadium, no Ogden, questions to be answered about the offense. The questions were still there. But Ogden was back and the crowd would be very much in their corner as soon as they walked onto the field. Knowing what was at stake, the players were almost manic as they waited. Ray Lewis was screaming at the top of his lungs over and over: "This opportunity only comes around once in a lifetime, fellas! Once in a lifetime! I will tell you one thing for sure: We are *not* skipping that prayer!" Lewis and Billick had talked during the week about skipping the Lord's Prayer in Cleveland. Billick had told him the minute they walked out the door without saying it, he felt as if something was wrong. So, it was back.

As Lewis screamed, Ed Hartwell, his partner at outside linebacker, kept doing push-ups, clearly seeking some kind of relief for the tension. Chris McAlister and Ed Reed, facing into their lockers, wore headphones and yelled lyrics out at the top of their lungs. Matt Stover lay flat on his back, feet on a stool, eyes closed, as if seeking some sort of Zen place where he could clear his mind. When Lewis wasn't shouting, Corey Fuller and Harold Morrow were. "Fellas, you've got to realize we are God's Chosen Few!" Morrow said. "Only a few get the chance to do this. It killed me to watch you guys on TV last week. We need to bring *passion* to every play today!"

One of the quietest people in the locker room, especially on the defensive side of the room — the defense dresses at one end of the room, the offense the other — was Deion Sanders. He sat quietly in front of his locker, watching and listening the way a teacher might observe his or her students at recess. Sanders had been involved in fifteen plays in Cleveland, and the ball had never been thrown his way. He didn't think that would be the case in this game. He had lobbied Billick heavily during the week to put in a few plays for him at wide receiver. Billick was tempted — especially after the way the wideouts had played in Cleveland — but still thought it too soon. "He's got qualities as a receiver our other guys don't have," he said. "But I'm afraid if I push too hard too soon, he'll break down. I don't want that to happen."

During the pregame meal, Sanders sat down with David Shaw to again ask why Billick didn't want to give him some plays on offense. "It isn't that," Shaw told him. "He just doesn't want to go too fast. Be patient. It's going to happen."

"I'm thirty-seven," Sanders said, smiling. "I'm too old to be patient."

He did understand Billick's reluctance to push him, but he also wanted more plays. He wasn't used to watching. Ninety minutes before kickoff, Sanders had been approached by Kevin Byrne. For home games, the Ravens traditionally introduced twelve players — eleven from the offense or defense and a twelfth man, usually someone from special teams who they think will help fire up the crowd. Billick wanted Sanders to be the twelfth man introduced. When Byrne explained what Billick wanted, Sanders shook his head.

"Kevin, I haven't done anything yet," he said. "I don't deserve to be introduced. Someone else should do it."

Byrne said he understood, but Billick wanted to fire up the crowd. "Ray will fire up the crowd, you know that," Sanders said. "Let me do something before I run out there and get cheered."

Byrne told Sanders this wasn't really a request. Reluctantly, Sanders agreed.

When the Ravens were introduced, Sanders burst out of the tunnel at the sound of his name, waving his arms at the crowd, circling to face all sides of the stadium, then leaping into the arms of his waiting teammates. It was as if he had stepped into a phone booth en route from the locker room to the field, taken off the clothes worn by the mild-mannered Deion, and emerged from the tunnel as Prime Time.

"That's exactly right," he said later, laughing. "The real me never wants to go out of the house. I like being at home with my wife and my kids. I spend all my time in sweats and have no need to go out and see people. But I understand business and there is a business aspect to all this. If I'm going out, I like to dress up. My daddy was like that, I guess I picked that up from him. And I know what people expect of me when it's time to perform. I'd have preferred not to be introduced. But if they're paying me and they ask me to do it, I'll give them everything they want and expect from Prime Time."

The team proceeded to do the same thing. On the opening series of the game, the offense did what it hadn't done in sixty minutes in Cleveland: put together a sustained drive that ended in a touchdown. The defense gave the Steelers almost nothing. The only real setback of the first twenty-eight minutes of the game was almost comical: offensive line coach Jim Colletto got so excited during a long run by Chester Taylor that he got too close to the sideline and accidentally clipped the side judge running past him with the pen he was carrying. Colletto was whistled for a 15-yard penalty for interfering with the official — intent was irrelevant — and Jeff Friday felt miserable that he had failed in his job as get-back coach.

The last two minutes of the half didn't go nearly as well.

With the Steelers trailing, 10–0, and needing a jolt, quarterback Tommy Maddox decided it was time to test Sanders. On third-and-long, with Sanders in single coverage against the speedy Plaxico Burress, Maddox tried to find him deep. Forced to run all-out in a game situation for the first time, Sanders sprinted back and just got into position at the last second to knock the ball away. But he came up limping badly. He came out of the game and went directly to the locker room, with Leigh Ann Curl right behind him. "I tore my hamstrings," he told her. As soon as Sanders got his uniform pants off, Curl could see that Sanders's self-diagnosis had been accurate. Both hamstrings were already discolored badly. Sanders was done for the day, probably a good deal longer than that.

The lead was still 10–0 when the offense again pushed deep into Pittsburgh territory in the final minute. Trying to get into position for a field goal, Lewis went off left tackle. Somehow, in the pileup, Todd Heap's ankle got rolled and stepped on. No one really knows exactly what happens in pileups, but the chances were almost 100 percent that it was an accident. What happened next was not. Heap limped to his feet and, with the Ravens out of time-outs, tried to line up so Kyle Boller could spike the ball to stop the clock for a Stover field goal attempt. He was clearly hurt; everyone in the stadium could see that. As soon as the ball was snapped, Boller spiked it. At the same moment, Joey Porter slammed into Heap, knocking him backward and off his feet.

The Ravens' sideline went crazy. Porter hadn't done any further damage to Heap, but everyone saw it as a cheap shot. Billick and Porter's newfound friendship was clearly over. While Heap was being helped off, Billick took turns screaming at the officials to throw Porter out of the game for unsportsmanlike conduct and at Porter. Stover came in and made the field goal for a 13–0 lead as time expired and the fans let Porter know their thoughts on his conduct as he left the field. Billick was still steaming in the locker room.

"We are going to go out there and show these guys what we think of them!" he yelled. "All my years in football, that's the cheapest, dirtiest, most bullshit play I've ever seen. I don't want any retaliation, we can't let them get to us that way, but let's let them know how we feel about what happened."

The Steelers never really challenged in the second half. Late in the third quarter Terrell Suggs sacked Tommy Maddox, who came up hurt, forcing the Steelers to bring in Ben Roethlisberger, their rookie quarterback. Roethlisberger had been the eleventh pick in the draft, taken after Eli Manning and after Philip Rivers. The Steelers saw him as their future, not necessarily the present. He was shaky when he came in but got lucky when a pass that Ed Reed would have returned for a touchdown slipped through Reed's hands and was caught by Burress, who took it to the 1-yard line. The Steelers scored from there, which didn't make anyone happy. What made Billick even more unhappy was Reed getting whistled for an unsportsmanlike penalty for taking his helmet off in frustration after the Pittsburgh touchdown. It was the second penalty on a Raven for taking a helmet off in the game: Sanders had returned a punt in the first half and, after taking the ball to the Steelers 31, had taken *his* helmet off — an automatic penalty in the NFL because the rule-makers consider that showing off and attempting to show up the other team.

Another touchdown brought the Steelers to within 23–13, but a Chris McAlister interception returned for a touchdown sealed the deal late in the fourth quarter, allowing everyone to breathe a sigh of relief. They had made too many mental errors to count, and two key players — Heap and Sanders — had left the game injured. But they had the victory they absolutely had to have against a bitter rival.

"I swear to God, I'm going to have your helmets glued to your heads if I have to," Billick said, able to smile in the locker room when it was over. "I told you that was the team we needed to play, and you guys went out and showed what kind of team we really have here."

Billick was holding a football as he spoke, standing as always in the middle of the locker room, with most of the players and team personnel kneeling around him. Normally, game balls are decided on by the coordinators and handed out later in the week during meetings. Billick had already presented one game ball — to Fassel in the Meadowlands. Now he wanted to present another one. "I think our new owner deserves this ball, don't you guys?" he said, flipping the ball to Steve Bisciotti, who was standing outside the circle. "He's building us a great new facility and we all know how hard he's worked to give us the best possible chance to compete."

Bisciotti had thought at various times about getting a game ball whenever his first victory as an owner came, but he had been so involved in the ups and downs of the game that any such thoughts had vanished by the time he walked into the locker room. He had a big grin on his face as he caught the ball. At that moment everyone in the locker room was smiling. It had been a long seven days since the loss to Cleveland. The next seven wouldn't seem nearly as long.

15

God and the NFL

ON THE NIGHT BEFORE the Steelers game, twenty members of the Ravens gathered in one of the downtown Hyatt's third-floor meeting rooms. It was 8:30 in the evening, half an hour before the start of the special teams meeting. On the Ravens' itinerary for the weekend, Saturday night always begins with Fellowship. This is not a formal chapel service, but it is certainly a religious gathering, led by Rod Hairston, the team chaplain.

The group that attended the Fellowship meeting each Saturday was almost always the same. Brian Billick sat in the back of the room in a chair pulled back and away from the rows of chairs that were lined up in front of Hairston. Several assistant coaches were scattered around the room: Mike Nolan, Johnnie Lynn, Mike Singletary, David Shaw, Wade Harman, Matt Simon, and Phil Zacharias attended weekly. Ray Lewis always sat near the back of the room, flanked by Corey Fuller and Deion Sanders. Almost all the players in attendance were African American. The only white players who came every week were placekicker Matt Stover and backup offensive lineman Tony Pashos. In one sense, that wasn't a surprise. For the most part, the African American players, many of them from the South, had grown up with very strong roots in their church.

"It was just an automatic in your life right from the start," said Ray Lewis. "My certainties in life were simple: family and God. Everything else came after that."

Hairston, who has at times been a controversial figure within the team, was conscious of the racial makeup of his Saturday night flock and candidly admitted that it was something that concerned him. "I would like to think that it has nothing to do with race, mine or theirs," he said. "But there are times when I wonder."

Religion plays an important role on every football team — more so, it seems, than in any other sport. At times it can bond a team or at least certain players on a team. It can also be divisive, especially if there are those in the locker room who feel that everyone else should believe the way *they* do. Why religion is so important in football is the subject of considerable debate. Some believe it is because of the sport's violent nature, that the potential for serious injury causes players to look for comfort and to want to believe that some kind of higher power is protecting them, even in those moments when a serious injury occurs. There is also the southern influence. A lot of pro football players are from the South, and as Ray Lewis pointed out, many come from deeply religious backgrounds. Most football teams take their cue on all subjects from their leader, and there is no question that Ray Lewis leads the Ravens. When he stands in the middle of the locker room and shouts for everyone to form a circle and hold hands for the pregame prayer, no one is likely to argue with him.

Brian Billick is keenly aware of the importance of religion to his football team. He is not one of those football coaches who invokes God when discussing his team's successes and failures. He is quietly religious, someone who makes a point of making it to Fellowship each Saturday but almost never discusses religion publicly. He rarely pushes any of his players when it comes to religion, although he will occasionally bring up to the team a message Hairston — called Rev within the team — was trying to get across in Fellowship. Billick and Hairston consult each week about the topic of Hairston's Saturday night sermon. Hairston sends Billick an e-mail each week telling him what he plans to talk about. Sometimes Billick will make a specific suggestion about relating the sermon to whatever the team's circumstance is that week. "I try to be sensitive to where we are as a team," Hairston said. "My message can have something to do with sticking together or not giving up or taking responsibility for one's life."

Hairston's athletic career was ended prematurely by an eye injury he suffered as a teenager in Norfolk, Virginia. He went to Virginia Tech, where he became friendly with a number of the athletes on campus through a

Bible study group called Campus Crusade for Christ. That was when he first began to think of the ministry as a career and was first involved in talking to athletes about their relationship with God. He graduated with a degree in finance and spent two not-so-happy years working as a commercial banker. "I knew that wasn't what I was meant to do," he said. "I had believed it in college, but it took me two years to figure it out for sure."

He joined Athletes in Action, the ministry group that puts together barnstorming basketball teams made up of players who give their religious testimony at game sites around the country. He was initially a fund-raiser, but one night when the team was in Roanoke, the minister traveling with the team turned to Hairston and said, "Boy, do you preach?" Hairston said, "I can, sir," and he did. After that he was hooked on the idea of becoming a preacher. "It was infectious," he said. "I took speech classes to help me get better at delivering my message."

His first assignment as a minister was at Howard University (where he met his wife). From there he went to UCLA for six years before joining a church group in Carey, North Carolina, in 1998. When the ministry closed the next year, a friend of his named Mike Bunkley, who had worked as a chaplain with the Carolina Panthers, told him that he had heard the Ravens were looking for a chaplain. Joe Ehrmann, who had been the team chaplain, was leaving and looking for a successor. Hairston met with Ehrmann and then with Brian Billick, who told him he saw the chaplain as another resource who could help the team.

In hiring Hairston, the team brought in someone who was vocal and charismatic, in many ways an old-time southern preacher who, while he might not bring outright fire and brimstone to his sermons, certainly brought passion and deep belief. Many of the players, especially those raised in the South, were drawn quickly to him and greeted his presence with great enthusiasm. Others weren't as comfortable, thinking that Hairston wanted more control over the religious direction of the team than a chaplain should ask for or be granted.

By 2002 there was a clear division within the locker room. Matt Stover and Peter Boulware, best friends and two of the more devout members of the team, wanted to start a separate Bible study group. Hairston generally met with players for Bible study on Thursday nights. Stover and Boulware wanted to form their own group that would meet on Wednesday night, a group led by a friend of Boulware's named Darryl Flowers who worked with Champions for Christ, a group that was in essence a competitor of Campus Crusade for Christ, the group that Hairston had worked with since his college days. Hairston objected to the presence of the people from Champions for Christ inside the team. Stover and Boulware objected to his objections, and angry words were exchanged.

"I had experience with Champions for Christ when I was at UCLA," Hairston said. "They were very aggressive in the way they approached players and dealt with players. I saw players hurt by them, by the fact that they wanted to be extremely controlling. There was one kid they told not to date a woman because she couldn't speak in tongues. They have a belief that true believers can speak in an unknown language to God. I have great respect for Peter and Matt, but I was uncomfortable with Champions for Christ and I told them that. Peter, I know, was very angry with me about it. I told Peter that if Darryl wanted a separate ministry and they wanted to be a part of that, it wasn't any of my business. But within the team, Brian and the Modells had asked me to provide religious leadership and I intended to do that."

A meeting to try to mediate the dispute was set up in the home of tackle Harry Swain. More angry words. Boulware and Stover accused Hairston of being controlling and territorial. He responded by saying he wasn't comfortable with people he didn't know coming in to form a ministry in a place where he had been hired to be the minister.

The dispute finally landed in Billick's office, about the last thing he wanted to deal with during the season. He sided with Hairston. "Rod is the team chaplain," he said. "He works with me during the season, and I'm comfortable with the messages he's trying to send to the players. I certainly can't control what players do away from the facility. I don't want to control what they do. But anything that was happening in our locker room, in our facility, was going to go through Rod. But I told them if they couldn't all work together, I'd just abandon the whole thing completely. Religion should unite people, not divide them."

A lovely thought, even though history has proven that religion divides at least as often as it unites. Stover and Boulware eventually agreed to follow Hairston's lead and not form any kind of separate Bible study group. Both men now say they regret what happened. Stover always attended the

Fellowship service on Saturday night and Boulware was planning to attend again when he was healthy.

Even in 2004, two years removed from Hairston vs. Stover/Boulware, there was still some tension. Later in the season, when the Ravens went to Philadelphia, Deion Sanders told Hairston he wanted to bring Irving Fryar, the former wide receiver who now has a ministry, to speak on Saturday night. Hairston doesn't often bring speakers in. Clark Kellogg, the former NBA player turned TV commentator, would speak to the team in October, and Chris Zacharias, younger brother of assistant coach Phil Zacharias, would speak to the team on Christmas night in Pittsburgh. That was it. Hairston told Sanders he would prefer he not invite Fryar.

"Why not?" Sanders asked.

"Because I don't know him," Hairston said. "I like to know people who come in and speak to the team."

"But you know me," Sanders said, not happy.

The dispute landed — again — on Billick's desk. Again he backed Hairston. "Nothing against Irving Fryar," he told Sanders. "I just don't think this is the right time."

Hairston often likes to finish his sentences when he's preaching by saying, "Can I get an amen on that?"

He always gets his amen. Some just say it louder than others.

The victory over the Steelers was a morale boost for everyone. One of the things that makes football different from other sports is that every game really does matter. Winning hides concerns; losing magnifies them.

Even so, there was genuine concern about the two key injuries that had occurred on Sunday: Todd Heap's ankle and Deion Sanders's hamstrings. The good news was that Heap's ankle wasn't broken. The bad news was he had a very serious ankle sprain; in some ways a clean break would have been better. The estimate was that Heap would be out at least two weeks, perhaps as long as six. The hope was that he would be back after the bye week — meaning he would miss the games against Cincinnati, Kansas City, and Washington.

There were few people on the team more important than Heap. What the Ravens lacked in wide receivers, they made up for — to some degree —

in talented tight ends. Heap was the key to that strength, a soft-handed receiver who was a tough matchup for defenses and could get deep into the secondary. He was one of the Ravens' poster boys, a six-foot-five, 250-pound, blond-haired, blue-eyed Mormon with an easy smile and a friendly demeanor. He loved to talk at length about his two-year-old daughter's latest achievement and was always on the list of players asked to take part in community relations projects. Heap was so aw-shucks in his approach to people that Steve Bisciotti affectionately referred to him as Howdy Doody.

The joking stopped when he stepped on a football field. Heap had been the Ravens' number one pick in the draft right after their Super Bowl victory, an example of their philosophy of drafting the best player on the board regardless of position. The team already had Shannon Sharpe, a future Hall of Famer, starting at tight end, but they thought Heap was too good to pass on. As it turned out, Sharpe left a year later and Heap became a Pro Bowler in his second season in the league.

"I never thought in terms of those things," he said. "I remember when I first got to college [at Arizona State] I would sit around with the other freshmen and everyone was talking about *when* they turned pro, *when* they were going to be in the NFL, *where* they thought they might go in the draft. I remember thinking to myself, 'What are these guys talking about? None of us have even proved we can play in college yet.' I always took the approach that if I worked hard and reached my potential, good things would happen to me as a player."

That was exactly what had happened. Only now, Heap was out and no one knew when he would be back. The good news was that tight end was the Ravens' deepest position. Terry Jones was a proven player and Daniel Wilcox had been the most pleasant surprise of training camp. But neither of them was Heap, who not only made plays but also helped open the field up for other receivers because he required so much of the defense's attention. His absence would force the offense to make adjustments.

Sanders's absence wasn't as big a deal but was still significant. In his absence, Chad Williams, a third-year player from Southern Mississippi became the primary nickel back and Corey Fuller again became a factor — as Billick had predicted he would — in the defensive backfield. Sanders had been brought in because the Ravens felt his presence would make life very difficult for quarterbacks in long-yardage situations. Now the team was back where it had been before it signed either Dale Carter or Sanders. What's more, Sanders's presence affected the other team psychologically. They had to prepare for him not only in nickel situations but quite possibly on kick returns and even on offense. That threat was now gone, and no one was sure for how long.

"I'd like to be back on Monday night," Sanders said, referring to the game in two weeks at home against the Kansas City Chiefs. He smiled. "After all, that *is* prime time."

Going back to Cincinnati — injured — made the week bittersweet for Sanders. As the team bus made the trip from the Cincinnati Airport in Covington, Kentucky, to the team hotel in downtown Cincinnati, Sanders recognized the spot on I-71 where he had tried to kill himself seven years earlier while he was playing baseball for the Cincinnati Reds. His seemingly perfect life — rich, two-sport superstar with all the endorsements one could possibly hope for — had gone off the tracks. His wife was divorcing him and he was separated from his children. He was lonely and unhappy and lost.

"In a way, I should have seen it coming," he said. "The year before, my wife had taken me to a counseling session, which turned out to be an important point in my life because it was with the man who's now my pastor and mentor, T. D. Jakes. Even though I knew during that session that my marriage was over, that it couldn't be fixed, he said a lot of things to me and about me that made sense. At one point he looked me in the eye and said, 'Deion, you need help. I'm afraid you might be suicidal.' I didn't believe him. Of course, he was right."

Sanders knew he was searching for something — but he wasn't sure what it was. He had left the San Francisco 49ers after the team won the Super Bowl because he wanted another challenge. Then he won a second Super Bowl, this time in Dallas. Not good enough. He decided to try baseball again. "I kept looking for something that was going to make me happy," he said. "Of course, I was looking in all the wrong places. Then, in a year, my dad died, my stepdad died, and I got divorced and couldn't see my children. I felt miserable and alone."

It was a May night in Cincinnati and Sanders was alone in his car and, he thought, in life. He decided to escape and drove his car off the side of the road at a spot where he knew there was a sharp decline, figuring the car would roll over once it landed and that would be that. "Landed perfectly, straight up, like a cat landing on its feet," he said, laughing at the memory. "There wasn't a scratch on the car and not a scratch on me. I sat there, thinking to myself, 'You are so messed up, you can't even get killing yourself right.' I actually started to laugh. The police came and helped me get the car out, and I just went home as if nothing had happened."

Something important *had* happened. Sanders knew he had hit rock bottom and needed to change his life. He turned to God. "I knew I needed to put myself in the hands of someone, and He made the most sense," he said. "It wasn't as if I hadn't had religion in my life before that, I did. But not this way. When I was a kid we went to church on Sundays, but I was *at* church, not *in* church. There's a difference. I certainly hadn't been saved. As soon as I turned my life over to God, things got better. I saw things more clearly and began to have a better understanding of how lucky I am, even if I have had some setbacks. Everyone has them. The question is, how you deal with them."

Sanders began dating Pilar Biggers, a woman he had met while playing on the West Coast. They married and he started a second family. He had decided to quit football after one season with the Washington Redskins because he didn't feel his heart was in the game anymore and because he was convinced that playing for the newly hired (and soon to be fired) coach, Marty Schottenheimer, wouldn't work for him. "One of Marty's sons was in a bar or a restaurant someplace and he was telling people that his dad was going to make life so miserable for me in training camp that I'd just quit and walk away from the money they owed me," Sanders said. "Only trouble for him was, a close friend of my agent was in there and overheard him. When I heard that I said, 'Man, I certainly don't need this.' I called Dan Snyder and told him what was going on. He flew up right away, we talked, and we made a deal. He was good about it. He understood. He only asked one thing of me: if I ever came back, not to come back to a team inside the division. I gave him my word and we parted friends."

Sanders had gone on to work for CBS, a job he enjoyed — in spite of his tempestuous relationship with Boomer Esiason on and off the set. Even after he made the decision to come back and play, he still believed there was a chance he would end up working for CBS again. "I liked the people there," he said. "I had a very good relationship, still do with [CBS Sports president] Sean McManus and with [executive producer] Tony Petitti. If I don't play again next year, I could easily see myself back working for them again. We all made a business decision. I have no hard feelings and I don't think they do, either."

The decision to return to football had more to do with unfinished business than anything else. Sanders consulted three people before making up his mind: Michael Jordan; Nancy Lieberman, the Hall of Fame basketball player; and his pastor, T. D. Jakes. Jordan told him the only thing he had to be prepared for if he came back were those who criticized him for not moving on with his life or for coming back for the money. "Neither of those things bothered me," Sanders said. Lieberman, who Sanders had coached with in a women's basketball league in Dallas, told him she was convinced that he had left the game before he really wanted to, that he needed to go back if only to have closure, that her sense was that he had never been at peace with his decision to quit.

Jakes expressed no opinion when Sanders approached him one Sunday morning after services. Instead, he asked a question: "If you walk away and don't play, will you have any regrets?"

Sanders thought about that for a moment. "I would wonder if I missed out not trying it again," he said.

"Then you should play," Jakes told him. "But only do it if you believe you can be passionate about it again. If you aren't passionate, there's no reason to bother with it."

Sanders soon found that the passion was there. "I was getting angry during my workouts at home when one of the receivers I was working with would beat me deep," he said. "Really angry. I said, 'Okay, you feel this way about it, let's go play.'"

Sanders was genuinely happy being back playing football again. That was clear from watching him in practice, in the locker room, in meetings. He made a point of sitting near Chris McAlister during defensive meetings because he thought he could make points that would help McAlister, not just technically but in terms of attitude and approach. "The kid has so much potential," he said. "I see some of myself when I was young in him. I think I can help him."

Now, though, Sanders would be reduced to helping as a cheerleader and unofficial assistant coach. It didn't make him happy at all. But as the bus rolled past the spot where he had failed in his suicide attempt, he smiled to himself in the darkness of the bus and thought, "I've come a long way since that night."

The weather in Cincinnati was close to perfect. The morning was cool and breezy, with the temperature climbing toward eighty degrees by game time. Brian Billick's main pregame concern was his team's frame of mind. Getting the players in the right mood before Cleveland and Pittsburgh had not been difficult. There was bad blood between the franchises and the players.

With the Bengals it wasn't that easy. Perhaps it was because they had been mediocre — or worse — for a long time. The team had reached two Super Bowls — after the 1981 season and after the 1988 season — and had lost in each case to the San Francisco 49ers, the second time when Joe Montana had produced one of his classic late-game drives to pull out the victory in the final seconds. But there had been very little to cheer about and plenty to either laugh or cry about in Cincinnati since then. Under Mike Brown, who had succeeded his father, the legendary Paul Brown, as the team's owner, the Bengals had become known as one of the NFL's cheapest and worst-run franchises. The team had even tried to impose a gag order on players several years earlier in order to keep them from criticizing management.

But there had been hints of improvement the past two years, most of them attributable to the hiring of Marvin Lewis, the former Ravens defensive coordinator, as the head coach. Lewis had been praised universally for turning around the attitude of the franchise before he had coached a single game in Cincinnati. The team's newfound confidence had produced an 8-8 record in 2003, including a win against the Ravens in Cincinnati. Normally, that loss would have provided Billick with a place to begin the job of getting an angry game face on his team. But it wasn't that simple. Many of the players, especially on the defense, had fond memories of Lewis. They all wanted to see him do well. There was no way that the *GoodFellas* "crossing the street" tape was going to be played for this game.

"The people in this town are too damn nice," Billick said, standing on the field in the empty stadium two hours before kickoff on Sunday morning. "They don't even really boo you or get on you coming out of the tunnel. I remember the first time we played in Cleveland, we come out of the tunnel and we just get pelted with stuff. I turned to the security guard walking with us and said, 'You need to do something about that before halftime.' He looked at me and said, 'Fuck you!' I can deal with that. It helps get everyone ready to play. But here, they're almost polite. I prefer coming into a place where they really hate our guts and want to get in our faces."

Because he knew he couldn't make the game personal, Billick tried making it professional: "This is the team we're going to have to beat to win the division, guys," he said, not sure if that was true but willing to take a swipe at convincing his players it was. "They beat us here last year; there is no reason for them to believe they can't beat us here again. We need to go out and show them why they're wrong."

This was not the same Bengals team that had beaten the Ravens a year earlier for one key reason: Lewis had made the decision in the off-season to make Carson Palmer his starting quarterback even though veteran Jon Kitna had produced the best season of his eight-year career in 2003. Palmer had won the Heisman Trophy at USC in 2002 and had been the first player taken in the 2003 draft, the same draft in which the Ravens had taken Kyle Boller with the nineteenth pick. He had held a clipboard throughout his rookie season, watching Kitna run the team. Lewis had decided during the off-season that Palmer was the future of the franchise and was going to take his lumps learning to play at some point, so why not do it now? The Bengals were 1-1, having lost to the Jets in New York before coming home to beat the already woeful Dolphins. The Ravens were convinced they could force Palmer to make the kind of mistakes one could expect from a quarterback making his third NFL start.

Like many NFL teams, the Bengals were playing in a new stadium. Paul Brown Stadium was one of two stadiums the city of Cincinnati had built to replace Riverfront Stadium, one of the multipurpose stadiums built in the early 1970s that managed to be bad places to watch both baseball and football. The new trend was to build baseball-only and football-only stadiums. The new baseball stadium, Great American Ball Park, sat directly across the parking lot from the football stadium. Walking onto the field for his pregame walkabout, Billick looked at the stands and said, "Mike Brown must have gotten a great deal on green seats." Every seat in the stadium was green. The Bengals' colors are brown and orange.

As he crossed the field, Billick encountered Lewis, still dressed in sweats. They hugged and spent some time chatting about the quality of the turf in the stadium, the prospect of the Bengals' moving their training camp to downtown Cincinnati, and Lewis's son, Marcus, who was a high school freshman. "It's scary, Brian," Lewis said. "He reminds me of [Bill] Belichick. His whole life is wrapped up in football already." That led to a conversation about the mellowing of Belichick in recent years. Lewis went so far as to report that he had played in an off-season golf tournament with Belichick and found him to be "absolutely loose and having fun."

Billick, who had heard innumerable stories about the Cleveland version of Belichick from Newsome and others on the Baltimore staff, found this information slightly short of astounding. What may have been more astounding was the sight of Buddy Ryan, the former Eagles and Cardinals coach, standing on the sideline before the game, taking pictures like a tourist. Ryan had flown in to see his son Rex and watch the game. Once, Ryan had defined toughness and meanness as a coach; his 1985 Chicago Bears' defense was one of the most feared and famous in NFL history. Now, at seventy-five, he stood with Rex, smiling proudly as the other coaches came up to shake hands and say hello.

"Dad, I've got a greaseboard set up in the locker room for you if you want to come in and help us make some adjustments," Rex Ryan said.

"How fast can your guys learn the four-six defense?" his father replied, referring to the defense he had made famous in Chicago.

Most of the Ravens were convinced the Bengals couldn't muster enough offense to seriously threaten them, even though there were five starters — if you included Sanders as a starter — on the inactive list: Mike Flynn was still several weeks away from returning; Kelly Gregg was missing his second game after knee surgery; Travis Taylor's groin still wasn't 100 percent; and Heap was out for several more weeks. Additionally, Ethan Brooks was also out with a leg injury, meaning the offensive line was very thin if anyone went down. "The only good thing about being inactive," Brooks had said at breakfast, "is I can eat all I want and not worry about it."

Early on, it appeared the Ravens would have a relatively worry-free day.

After the Bengals failed to move on their opening drive, the Baltimore offense took the ball and moved quickly down the field. Billick's jitters about the game were apparent early. After Jamal Lewis broke an 18-yard run to put the ball on the Bengals' 4-yard line, Billick's only comment when Lewis came out for a breather was "How about putting that ball in the end zone?" Two plays later, when Boller was forced to throw the ball away on third-and-2, he was barking as the offense came off the field: "Run the plays the way we practice them!" They all understood. He didn't want field goals, he wanted touchdowns. They settled for a Stover field goal to make it 3–0. It was 10–0 soon after that: ducking and weaving between tacklers, B. J. Sams returned a punt 63 yards, setting them up at the Bengals 8 late in the first quarter. Boller scrambled into the end zone on third-and-7 and spiked the ball so hard that it bounced through the end zone and into the tunnel leading to the locker room.

Midway through the second quarter, Boller fumbled going into the end zone on a scramble that would have made the score 17–0. The defense quickly made up for that mistake when Ed Reed intercepted Palmer at midfield. Four plays later, Boller threw his first touchdown pass of the season, finding Randy Hymes on a crossing pattern. Hymes sprinted to the left sideline and scored from 38 yards out. It was 17–0 and there was complete jubilation on the sideline. They were dominating a good team. The fumble aside, Boller was looking precise and confident. Hymes had been a quarterback in college, playing at Grambling, and was developing into a solid receiver who had a knack for getting open. Because Grambling was in the Southwestern Athletic Conference (aka the SWAC) his nickname was — surprise — SWAC. The entire team was screaming his nickname as he came to the sideline, beaming after his catch and run.

Still, the Bengals drove late and kicked a field goal as time expired to make it 17–3 at halftime. The Ravens' offense stalled in the third quarter and the Bengals crept to within 17–6. Then another Boller fumble early in the fourth quarter brought the Bengals closer. As the defense dug in on third-and-goal to try to keep the Bengals out of the end zone, Boller sat on the bench, muttering, "Come on, defense, bail my ass out."

They did, forcing the third Shayne Graham field goal of the day with 9:03 left, making the score 17–9. Then, on the Ravens' first play after the kickoff, Jamal Lewis and the offensive line bailed everyone out when

Lewis broke through the left side and sprinted 75 yards for a clinching touchdown. The score made it 23–9 and even provided a few laughs at Billick's expense. Wound up and excited after the touchdown, Billick failed basic arithmetic, somehow thinking that a two-point conversion would put his team up 17 — meaning Cincinnati would have to score three times to catch up — when in fact it would have put them up only 16 — meaning two touchdowns and a pair of two-point conversions could still tie. He went for two, the conversion failed, and the lead was 14. When he was asked in his postgame press conference what had happened, Billick just shrugged and said, "I flunked math in school."

The Bengals' last gasp ended with 5:08 to go when Marques Douglas sacked Palmer on a fourth-down play from the Ravens' 25. As most in the crowd of 65,575 left their green seats to head for the parking lot, Deion Sanders turned around, a big smile on his face, and said, "Where's everybody going? This is just starting to be fun."

It was fun, although there were some warning signs that everyone chose not to be too concerned about. Palmer had thrown three interceptions and had lost a fumble, but he had also passed for 316 yards, more than 200 yards of that total to wide receivers Chad Johnson and T. J. Houshmandzadeh, who had combined to catch 15 balls. The defense had given up more than 400 yards in total offense but had been able to make plays when the Bengals got close.

The victory left everyone in a buoyant mood. "Winning on the road in this league is one of the hardest things to do in sports," Billick told them as they knelt around him in their postgame circle. "We made some mistakes that we'll talk about, but the important thing is we made plays. There isn't any doubt in their minds or in anyone's minds about who the best team is in the division. We're 2-1 and the goal now is to be 4-1 when we get to the bye week. Enjoy this one. You earned it."

16

Warning Signals

THE SENSE NOW was that the debacle in Cleveland had been an aberration. The Ravens were tied with Pittsburgh for first place in the division at 2-1 but felt they had already proven their superiority to the Steelers in week two. Playing the Kansas City Chiefs on Monday night, they all knew, was a potential trap game. The Chiefs had been 13-3 a year ago after starting 9-0. They had started the new season 0-3, losing to Denver, to Carolina, and, shockingly, at home to the Houston Texans. Everyone knew they were better than they had shown. They still had a huge offensive line, a solid quarterback in Trent Green, an excellent running back in former Raven Priest Holmes, and a superb tight end in Tony Gonzales. The defense was suspect, but any team with an offense as good as Kansas City's had to be considered dangerous.

"I don't see any way we look past them," Steve Bisciotti said as he watched practice on Thursday afternoon. "To begin with, we know they aren't really an 0-3 team, they're better than that. What's more, even if we think that a little bit, we're playing on Monday night. I don't see us having a letdown playing on Monday night."

Monday Night Football isn't even close to being the phenomenon it was once upon a time when Howard Cosell, Don Meredith, and Frank Gifford became icons in American culture during the 1970s. Even the production staff, men such as Don Ohlmeyer and Chuck Howard and Chet Forte, the latter two having passed away several years ago, became stars. ABC Sports had no budgets; people just spent whatever money they wanted to spend.

The arrival of the *Monday Night Football* crew in a town was greeted with only slightly less enthusiasm than the Beatles' arrival in New York in 1964.

Now, *MNF* is like an aging beauty queen. Everyone knows there was once something great there and the queen has to be treated with a certain amount of reverence. But it isn't the same. *MNF* is the longest-running prime-time show in the history of network TV — 2004 was its thirty-fifth year — but the ratings aren't close to what they once were (11.0, the lowest in history, in 2004), about half of what they once were, and the arrival of the *MNF* crew in town is greeted with more of a whimper than a bang. The network's decision to abandon *MNF* after the 2005 season hardly came as a surprise to anyone. The magic had disappeared long ago.

ABC had hired John Madden three years earlier to boost ratings after its disastrous experiment with alleged comedian Dennis Miller. Miller had two weaknesses as a color commentator: he knew nothing about football and he wasn't funny. Other than that, he was an excellent choice. Madden hadn't boosted ratings, in large part because announcers rarely affect ratings. Good games boost them; bad games hurt them. Simple as that. Beyond that, he has become at times almost a parody of himself at this stage of his career, almost as much a video game — *Boom! Hey! Look at the fat guys up front!* — as an analyst. His partner, Al Michaels, remains one of the smoothest play-by-play men going, but his massive ego frequently tramples on Madden and the broadcast. Michaels didn't even show up for ABC's pregame production meeting. Generally speaking, the networks treat the weekly production meetings as if they are negotiations for nuclear arms reductions. There is some justification for this. After all, the networks pay the league billions for their TV rights, and the production meetings are considered an important perk. Because nothing said in the production meetings will be used before the game begins, players and coaches tend to be a little more candid than they are when speaking to the media during the week. Madden considered the production meetings sacred ground, somewhere between attorney-client privilege and the Catholic confessional. Michaels apparently didn't feel quite as strongly. When Billick and the requested players met with the ABC crew, Michaels was present only on the other end of a speakerphone.

Still, *MNF* coming to town was at least a semi-big deal in Baltimore. The Ravens hadn't played on Monday night terribly often in their nine-year history. During their first four seasons in Baltimore they had played once on a Thursday night but never on Monday night. In 2000, the year they won the Super Bowl, they made zero Monday night appearances. The next year, as Super Bowl champions, they were on twice. In 2002, the "salary cap" year, they were on once, and in 2003 they weren't on at all. That made a total of three Monday night appearances in eight years. "I guess you are whatever it is the networks perceive you to be," Billick said. "Except in '01, we were not perceived to be an important enough team to play on Monday night. I was actually surprised when they gave us the Denver game in '02. I think they did it because they thought we'd get killed and some people would enjoy seeing that."

The players liked playing on Monday night because it was a chance to be seen by all their peers. The same wasn't quite true of the ESPN Sunday night games because a lot of teams were still en route home from the road when those games were played and a lot of players didn't want to watch another football game a few hours after playing one of their own. On Monday night, most of the league watched. Billick had made that point to the team during the week: "This week and next [the Redskins game was a Sunday night ESPN game] are a chance for you guys to show the whole country what kind of team you are." One might wonder if professionals really care about showing off for the country. In truth, they do.

Billick has been accused on occasion of having a chip on his shoulder when it comes to the networks and the league office. In 2003 he had publicly suggested that the Ravens wild-card game against the Tennessee Titans had been scheduled as the weekend's kickoff game at 4:30 on Saturday afternoon because the league didn't think either team was a TV draw. "I don't think anyone sits up there in New York and says, 'Let's screw the Ravens,'" he said. "In fact, I'm inclined to think the opposite: I don't think anyone up there in New York gives us much thought at all. We're in a mid-size market and we've been a defensive-oriented team most of the time I've been here. They just don't really care about us one way or the other."

Now, with *MNF* coming to town, the phones around the facility began to jump. The league always sends extra people to Monday night games, especially if the game is close to New York. Paul Tagliabue would be at the game. Bruce Laird, the Ravens uniform Nazi, would have to deal with having an extra "observer" sent by the league at his side. If Laird missed a hanging shirttail or socks pulled up too high, there would be hell to pay.

There was also the Michael Powell issue. Powell was the head of the Federal Communications Commission, a job he had clearly been given on pure merit, having nothing to do with the fact that his father was secretary of state. He had worked very had to turn the FCC into an Orwellian type of organization, making sure the networks knew that Big Brother was watching for any sign that they might be straying from Powell's definition of pure American virtue. CBS was about to pay a heavy price (a $550,000 fine to twenty-one affiliates) for the infamous Janet Jackson "wardrobe malfunction" at the Super Bowl. ABC, in full suck-up mode, had invited Powell to the game, not only to watch it but as a halftime guest. No doubt America was on the edge of its seat waiting to hear that interview.

Powell's presence would prove to be a headache throughout the week. On Monday, ABC's *MNF* producer, someone named Fred Gaudelli, had called Kevin Byrne to ask if the Ravens could supply Powell and his people with a luxury box to watch the game from. All of the Ravens' luxury boxes were sold out. Byrne said the Ravens couldn't supply a box but would certainly have tickets for Powell and company. Not satisfied with that answer, Gaudelli called Dick Cass, apparently believing the team president has the power to create a box out of thin air. Cass gave him the same answer. Powell did not want to sit among the great unwashed in the stands. Byrne made a suggestion: the team would provide Powell with two press passes so he and a second person could sit in the press box. No, that wasn't good enough because Powell had Secret Service protection and at least one agent had to be with him. Finally, Byrne and Cass came up with an idea: Art Modell had a double box that was rarely full. They asked Modell if he would mind entertaining Powell and posse, and Modell said he would do it.

Hallelujah. The Ravens would not be subjected to an FCC fine for failing to make Michael Powell feel like royalty.

That left the issue of actually playing the football game. Because of the extra day to prepare, Billick gave the players Tuesday and Wednesday off, not wanting them to wear themselves out before game time finally rolled around thirty-two hours later than it would for a normal 1 P.M. kickoff on Sunday. The coaches used their extra day to do a walk-through at the new facility. The team would be moving in right after the Redskins game, which would be played six days after the Chiefs game. Workmen were everywhere in the building. It was hard to believe it was going to be up and running in less than two weeks. "Every time I look at it, I think there's no way we can get in there when we're supposed to," Dick Cass said. "But whenever I ask, they tell me we'll absolutely be in there, no question about it."

Everyone in the organization was a little bit on edge about literally moving the entire franchise into a new building in midseason. The decision to move in October had been made months earlier, when it became clear there was no way to finish the project before the season began. Bisciotti didn't want to wait until the season was over, so the compromise of moving during the bye week had been struck. It was still risky. If anything went wrong during the move, the team could find itself without a home — or at least, a finished home — while trying to prepare for the post-bye-week game against the Buffalo Bills.

The calm in the moving storm was Cass, whose presence represented the only major change Bisciotti had made in the organization once he officially became the team owner. As part of Bisciotti's deal with Art Modell, David Modell was being paid $1 million for the season to be a "consultant." Both Modells were still an occasional presence at the facility — Art Modell still came to practice once or twice a week and sat, as always, in his golf cart, watching the proceedings. He had a big office in the new facility, and Bisciotti was planning to unveil a painting of him that would hang in the reception area of the new building.

It was evident, though, to those who knew them, that both men were going through withdrawal. The Ravens — and before them, the Browns — had been the centerpiece of their lives, and now, while they were welcome visitors, that's what they were: visitors. Nothing Bisciotti or Cass or Newsome or Billick did would change that. Many in the organization worried about Art Modell's health. "He's seventy-nine," Kevin Byrne, who may have been closer to Modell than anyone other than Newsome, said one day. "A lot of men his age struggle when they lose their wives. Art hasn't lost this wife, but he's lost his mistress — the football team."

Bisciotti and Cass did all that they could to make Modell feel comfortable. Neither had an office in the old facility, and neither asked for one. They used Modell's office to conduct meetings but never sat at his desk.

Instead, they used a round table that sat behind the desk as a gesture of respect to the former owner.

Cass was fifty-eight, a lawyer who had spent thirty-two very successful years with one law firm, Wilmer Cutler Pickering, a prestigious Washington firm that he joined soon after graduating from Yale Law School. A glance at Cass's résumé would tell you that he had always been an achiever: the son of a career Coast Guard officer, he had lived on both coasts as a kid, moving about every two years, but had spent a lot of his time in the Washington area, growing up a fan of the Senators and the Redskins. He had gone to Mercersburg Academy because his parents wanted some stability for him and his brother, Bill, who was four years older. From there it had been Princeton and then Yale Law — Yale because Harvard, where he was also accepted, didn't offer him as much financial aid. He met Heather, his wife, while he was in law school and became an acquaintance of a very smart female student who was a year behind him.

Years later, when Bill Clinton ran for president, the Casses were stunned when they saw his wife. She didn't look anything like the Hillary Rodham they had known at Yale. "She was thinner and blonder and the thick glasses she had worn were long gone," Cass said, laughing. "We had trouble believing it was the same person."

Bill Clinton was two years behind Cass at Yale, but Cass can't remember seeing very much of him. "Part of it was I was third-year and he was first," he said. "The other part was that he was always out politicking — even then."

As good a student as he was, Cass's true passion was sports. He played everything in high school and went to Princeton hoping to play football and baseball. A knee injury his freshman year ended that dream — he spent most of the second semester on crutches — but Cass never stopped loving sports. When Wilmer Cutler was approached in the late 1980s by someone named Jerry Jones who was looking to buy the Dallas Cowboys, Cass was thrilled to get involved. He helped Jones buy the Cowboys and remained an adviser and confidant to him while he rebuilt the franchise. That experience led to the NFL's recommending him to the Jack Kent Cooke estate when the Redskins were being sold and eventually to the league's recommending him to Steve Bisciotti. The two men became friends while working together on Bisciotti's purchase of the Ravens, and

Bisciotti asked Cass during the 2002 season if he would be interested in becoming team president once he became the majority owner.

"I jumped at it," Cass said. "I had a very successful practice, but the chance to be involved in running an NFL team? I wasn't going to pass that up. This isn't just work, it's fun."

Cass quickly became popular with the team's hierarchy. He is one of those very smart people who never talks down to anyone. His only request came early, when he heard Billick and the coaches referring to less-than-stellar players as "slapdicks."

"Is there any way," he asked, "I can convince you guys to call them, 'slaptoms?'"

When he wasn't fending off ABC's demands for luxury boxes, Cass was having a hectic week. The Jamal Lewis drug case was reaching a climax. A trial date had been set for November 1, but Lewis's attorneys had entered into a plea-bargain negotiation with the prosecutors in Atlanta.

Almost from the beginning, Cass had been the team's point man on the Lewis case, which made sense since he was the resident lawyer. Early on, Ed Garland had told Jamal Lewis and the team that chances of a conviction in the case were "90–10 in our favor." Like everyone else in the organization, Cass believed that Jamal had been set up and that the prosecutors had chosen to indict him far more because of his name than because of what he had done. But the lawyer in him saw danger in going to trial. One day during training camp as everyone watched afternoon practice, the subject of a potential trial came up. Bisciotti began talking in his animated way about how unfair the whole thing was and concluded by saying, "There's absolutely no way they'll ever get a conviction. They've got no case at all."

Very quietly, Cass said, "Steve, they've got a case."

Cass's concern was simple: technically speaking, Lewis had broken the law by using his cell phone to set up the meeting that eventually led to a drug deal. While it was certainly possible, perhaps even probable, that a jury would understand that Lewis had played a minor role in the drug transaction (he hadn't even been present when the meeting took place) and was hardly the felon they would have to think him to be in order to convict, there were no guarantees. Depending on the makeup of the jury, they might see him as someone who had made a mistake at the age of twenty or they might see him as a star athlete trying to beat the system, claiming innocence when everyone knew that star athletes were never really innocent.

By September, Garland had revised his 90–10 estimate to 70–30. Basically, that meant he saw the odds as two to one in Lewis's favor. Not exactly overwhelming, especially considering that if found guilty, Lewis faced a minimum sentence of ten years in prison. Even with parole, that would, for all intents and purposes, be the end of his football career. The consensus became that a trial might be too risky. The prosecutor had discussed a possible plea bargain. Lewis, backed by the team, instructed Garland to see what the prosecution was offering.

When word came back initially that there had to be jail time, Lewis was angry and inclined to say no. "I'm not a criminal," he said later. "I don't like the idea of going to jail and I don't like the idea that people are going to look at me and think of me as some kind of druggie or drug dealer. I'm not either one of those things."

The prosecutor wasn't really concerned with any of that. He wasn't going to let Lewis off without jail time if there was going to be a deal. What's more, Lewis would have to admit in court that he had made the phone call that had led to the meeting. Lewis didn't have a problem with that. He had made the call and he knew he had made a mistake in doing so. The bargaining went back and forth. A deal began to take shape: Lewis would go to jail for four months, but his sentence would not start until the off-season. He would then spend two months under house arrest but would probably be able to participate in any preseason workouts that were going on at that point. The advantages for Lewis were obvious: he would not miss any games and he would not have to run the risk of putting himself at the mercy of the jury. The disadvantages were just as obvious: he would go to jail, and some people would just assume he was all the things he did not want to be thought of as: a criminal, a druggie, a drug dealer. Lewis was fully aware that there were many people who still thought of Ray Lewis as a murderer and he *hadn't* plea-bargained.

Still, this took serious risk out of the equation. The other issue was the NFL. Once Lewis pleaded guilty, the league would have to decide on a penalty for the conviction, and the likelihood was that he would be suspended almost immediately. Four games was possible under the league's rules. Cass flew to New York to get a sense from Paul Tagliabue of how the league would likely react if Lewis accepted the deal that was now on the table. Tagliabue wasn't going to make any official pronouncements, but the message Cass got was clear: Lewis had not technically been a Raven yet when the incident had occurred. He had been drafted by the team in April but had not yet signed a contract when the incident took place in July. The players union might be able to make the case that the league didn't have jurisdiction to penalize him. Tagliabue didn't want them making that case. If the union and Lewis didn't appeal, he was inclined to limit Lewis's suspension to two games.

That put all the pieces of the puzzle in place. Once Cass had the unofficial word that the suspension would be two games, Garland was instructed to make the deal. Lewis would have to fly to Atlanta the following week to appear before a judge and submit his plea. The league would announce the suspension immediately, but it would not go into effect until after the game in Washington, meaning he would miss the first two games after the bye week, against Buffalo and Philadelphia.

"If it had gone to trial, he probably would have missed two games while the trial was going on and he would have been at risk," Cass said. "This way he misses two games, he deals with the jail time in the off-season, and we go into next season knowing it is behind him and behind us."

Except, of course, for the fact that, as Lewis well knew, some people would put the druggie label on him for the rest of his career. "If I told you that doesn't bother me," he said, "I would be lying to you. I did smoke some marijuana when I was younger. But I've been clean for a while now and I've never done hard drugs and never once sold drugs. But I know there will always be people who will think I did all those things."

He sighed. "I made a mistake. No one can say I'm not paying the price for it."

Billick's concern about playing an 0-3 team that should not be 0-3 was apparent when the team met on Sunday night. He talked about watching three games that day, all of them involving winless teams: Tampa Bay, Miami, and Buffalo. "They were all close games," he said. "All of them played very, very hard, almost desperately. You could see the burden they were carrying around, but in the end that burden got to them. You have to expect this team to come in here and do the same thing. Be prepared to play a desperate team, because that's what they are."

He talked about the "noise" around the game. The sideline would be packed pregame. ABC was sending 175 people. With the kickoff so late — nine o'clock — there would be a lot of pent-up emotion on both sides when the game started. "Don't put us at risk by losing control of your emotions," Billick said. "Don't turn the control card over to the officials."

Billick knew Jamal Lewis was upset about the plea bargain, which had been announced on Friday. He spent some time with him on Monday, telling him not to worry about how it might affect the team. Billick was still angry at the prosecutor for insisting on jail time. "You're telling me he needs to go to jail at taxpayer expense? Why, so he can be rehabilitated? Come on."

Rehabilitation had nothing to do with the deal that had been cut. The jail time was there so the prosecution could say that it had a legitimate case when it indicted Lewis. That notion didn't make Billick any happier.

The weather that night was close to perfect. Billick and Vernon Holley walked across the Hamburg Street bridge shortly before seven o'clock, with the sun beginning to set while the fans in the parking lots screamed Billick's name. He smiled and waved like a political candidate working a room. This was a very big room.

Inside the stadium, even with kickoff two hours away, the atmosphere was amped up. One of the first players on the field was Deion Sanders. He had practiced twice during the week but still felt a little bit sore. Part of him wanted to play in the game, especially in the spotlight of Monday night. But he knew it would probably be a mistake. He had talked to Billick on Saturday, and Billick had urged him to be cautious, saying that missing one more game was better than running the risk of missing eight.

"They use two tight ends a lot," Sanders said, standing in the locker room while the other players put their uniforms on. "I probably wouldn't be needed for that many snaps anyway. I think Coach Billick's right. I have to look at this long-term."

The pregame locker room was the loudest it had been all year. Ray Lewis was in full voice, screaming repeatedly, "This only comes around once! Everybody understand? This only comes around once!"

Terrell Suggs walked over and said to Lewis, shouting because no one speaks in a normal tone of voice pre-game, "Ray, what does pressure do?" The question was a setup. "All I know is that it breaks a pipe," Lewis answered. "So imagine what it does to a human being!"

Both teams were overheated at the start. After B. J. Sams returned the opening kickoff to the Ravens' 32, several players came up pushing and shoving. Billick wasn't the least bit happy when he saw that. He had warned the players again in the locker room about controlling their temper, especially since the referee in the game was Jeff Triplette — Orlando Brown's nemesis from both the beanbag-in-the-eye incident and the late personal foul in the playoff game. Triplette and crew kept their flags in their pockets on the kickoff, and the offense quickly pieced together a drive. Jamal Lewis picked up 18 yards on the first play, and Boller converted a third-and-8 with an 11-yard pass to Randy Hymes. They stalled just outside the Kansas City 32, and Billick looked at Gary Zauner.

Prior to each game, Matt Stover walks the field, checking the wind and the condition of the turf. Once he gets a sense of both, he tells Billick and Zauner what yard line the offense needs to reach at both ends of the field for him to attempt a field goal. Stover had started giving Billick a yard line early in Billick's first season as coach after Billick had sent him in to attempt a 53-yard field goal and he had missed it. "He jumped me in front of the whole team for missing," Stover said. "I know now that's just the way he is during a game and it's no big deal. But at the time, it upset me because he had asked me to make a kick I couldn't make under the conditions and then jumped me for not making it."

Stover was in his tenth NFL season at the time, his ninth as the regular placekicker for the Browns/Ravens. The next day he walked into Billick's office and told him he didn't appreciate being called out in front of the entire team for a kick he probably should not have been asked to attempt. "I said to him, 'Look, you need to trust me, I've been doing this a long time. I'll give you a yard line before the game and if you ask me to make a kick from there or inside, I'll make it. If I can't kick far enough for you or if I start missing from the yard lines I give you, cut me. But this isn't going to work unless you trust me.'"

Billick agreed to trust Stover, and their relationship has been rock-solid ever since. Stover's only moment of insecurity came when Billick hired

Zauner, whom he had worked with in Minnesota, prior to the 2002 season. One day in training camp, Zauner ordered six straight time-running-out field goal drills from different distances. Racing on and off the field in the heat, Stover missed a couple of kicks. Later he confronted Zauner, telling him he thought the drill had been unfair to him. Zauner said he was just trying to see how the entire field goal unit performed under adverse conditions.

"And the scouts aren't standing over there, noticing every kick I miss?" Stover answered. "You know how this game works, Gary: a kicker's only as good as his last kick. You're trying to make me look bad."

Zauner insisted that wasn't the case, and the two of them ended up in Billick's office hashing the whole thing out. "Which is exactly what we did," Stover said. "I wanted to make it clear to Gary that he was the boss and I'd do whatever he told me to do. But I also wanted us to have the same kind of understanding I have with Brian about reasonable expectations."

At thirty-six, Stover was the last of the old Cleveland Browns still in a Baltimore uniform — not counting Orlando Brown, who had left the team and come back. If you were to bump into him on the street, with his neatly cropped black hair and glasses, your first guess would be that Stover was either a schoolteacher or an aspiring Republican politician. But he is one of the most respected players on the team because of his work ethic — he works out year-round, believing that the key to keeping up his leg strength is to keep his body in perfect condition — and because he almost never misses a kick. "It takes six years in this league for a kicker to be thought of by the other guys as a football player," he said. "Even then, you better keep making kicks." He laughed. "I like to remind guys that I've made twenty-two tackles in the NFL."

Stover knows how many tackles he's made, how many kicks he's made, and where he made them from. He has an encyclopedic memory of both his successes and failures and can usually tell you not only where he missed a kick from but why.

He grew up in Dallas and dreamed of being an NFL placekicker when he was in high school. A friend of his had pointed out to him that there weren't very many NFL kickers who weighed 155 pounds, so he began weight training and built himself up to 170 pounds by the time he went to college at Louisiana Tech. He was selected in the twelfth round of the 1990 draft by the New York Giants, coached at the time by Bill Parcells.

"I think I was one of two kickers drafted that year," he said. "First day I was in camp, Parcells said to me, 'Don't make me look bad, kid.' Welcome to the big leagues."

His first season in the big leagues was spent on injured reserve after he injured a quadriceps muscle late in training camp. If he had stayed healthy, he might have ended up kicking on a Super Bowl team because Raul Allegre, the regular placekicker, got hurt early in the season. The Giants ended up signing Matt Bahr, who kicked five field goals in the NFC Championship Game, including the game winner as time expired, to beat the San Francisco 49ers, 15–13. "It was probably a good break for everyone that they ended up signing Matt," Stover said. "I'm not sure Parcells wanted a rookie kicker in that situation. I'm not sure I wanted a rookie kicker in that situation, either."

Stover was on the sidelines during Super Bowl XXV against the Buffalo Bills, which ended with Scott Norwood's infamous miss from 48 yards out that gave the Giants a 20–19 victory. To this day, Stover admits he had mixed emotions as Norwood lined up the kick. "There is a part of me that can never root against another kicker," he said. "I can identify with anyone who is put in that situation. I have never, to this day, talked to Scott Norwood about that kick, but I think I have an idea how he feels. It was not an easy kick. People act now as if he missed a chip shot. It was forty-eight yards on a grass field with a swirling wind. He just jumped on it a little too much, and that carried it wide. I was thrilled we won the game, but I felt for Norwood. I still feel for Norwood."

Stover signed with the Browns after his rookie season and has been with the franchise as the primary kicker ever since. He had just signed a new five-year contract with the Ravens after flirting with the Jacksonville Jaguars during the off-season. In the end, the Ravens gave him the money he wanted — a $1 million bonus and an annual salary averaging about $1 million — even though they knew he wasn't likely to change teams at this stage of his career. The Ravens had brought Wade Richey in to handle kickoffs two years earlier, and while Stover was close to Richey and readily conceded that Richey had a stronger leg, there was a part of him that still wanted to kick off.

"Intellectually, I know why they did it," he said. "Can I kick off as deep as Wade consistently? No. Does it help me save my leg to not kick off? Yes. Do I still want to kick off? You bet. And I train to be ready to do it."

There are two very clearly defined sides to Stover's personality. One is the almost manic competitor who lies flat on his back on the locker-room floor before games, legs on a stool, eyes closed, shutting out the world until it is time to brush his teeth (yes, brush his teeth) and go out on the field. The other is the deeply religious, born-again Christian who can recite lengthy verses from the Bible and can work scripture or biblical sayings into almost any conversation. The two sides of Stover often come together on the field, according to Dave Zastudil, who is the team's punter and Stover's holder.

"There are times when we're lining up for a kick and I have to keep from laughing at some of the things coming out of Matt's mouth," Zastudil said. "He'll be screaming to himself, 'You *have* to make this, Matt, you have to concentrate. Oh, Lord Jesus, please let me make this kick, give me strength right now. Come on, Matt, right through those goalposts. Lord stay with me now!'"

And that might just be on an extra point.

Stover points to the sky in thanks after every kick — make or miss — although teammates occasionally note that he tends to point with a bit more enthusiasm after a make. "That's just because I'm pumped," he said, laughing.

Now, with the ball just outside the yard line that Stover had designated before the game, Billick looked toward Zauner, who turned to Stover, standing, as always, a couple of feet away in a potential field goal situation. "Let's go," Stover said, indicating he wanted to try the kick.

Stover, Zastudil, and long snapper Joe Maese trotted into the huddle and Zastudil knelt on the 40-yard line, meaning the kick would be a 50-yarder. Stover hadn't attempted a kick that long since 2002, but with plenty of adrenaline pumping, he nailed the kick perfectly and it cleared the uprights with a couple of yards to spare. Billick shook a fist and the Ravens led, 3–0, with less than four minutes gone in the game.

The lead didn't last very long. Richey's kickoff went out of bounds, setting the Chiefs up at their own 40. They quickly sliced through the defense, needing ten plays to get into the end zone on a 3-yard Trent

Green–to–Jason Dunn pass. It was 7–3. The Ravens went three-and-out and the Chiefs promptly drove into field goal range to make it 10–3. Early in the second quarter, the Ravens answered with a play they had been practicing since camp, a trick play that had worked in the Pittsburgh game only to be called back by a penalty. Boller handed off to Lewis, who flipped it back to Boller, who then found Randy Hymes open for 57 yards and a touchdown. Matt Cavanaugh liked to call it a "Jamal-flicker" rather than a flea-flicker. By any name, it worked and the game was tied at 10. To the amazement of everyone in the building, the Chiefs' offense continued to dominate the Ravens' defense, going on another lengthy drive — 79 yards — to take back the lead, 17–10. This time the Ravens replied with a punt return: B. J. Sams, who was rapidly becoming a star, fielded a punt at his own 42, cut back against the swarming Chiefs, and was gone — 58 yards for a touchdown. It was his second huge return in two weeks. This one tied the game, 17–17, at halftime.

Even though the game was tied, Billick sensed trouble. It had taken a trick play and a punt return for the Ravens to stay even. The Chiefs already had 212 yards in offense, including 105 yards rushing. The Ravens rarely gave up 100 yards rushing in an entire game, much less a half. Though Billick doesn't usually speak to the team as a unit at halftime, he made an exception in this case.

While Mike Nolan was still huddling with his coaches, Billick walked into the defensive meeting room. "Hey, fellas, we have to get off the field on third down," he said, noting that the Chiefs had converted five of their nine third downs. "We told you this was a big, physical football team. Now you can see that. But that's not what's hurting us. Mental errors are hurting us. That's not us." He left Nolan to talk about the technical changes that needed to be made and walked out to listen to Cavanaugh talk to the offense. When Cavanaugh was finished, he decided to talk to the team as a whole.

"Everybody up here," he said as the defense made its way out of its meeting room toward the front of the locker room, where the offense was grouped. When some of the defensive players, perhaps not hearing him because they weren't accustomed to being called together at halftime, lingered a bit, Billick barked at them: "Everybody get up here *now!*"

They picked up their pace. When they were gathered in front of him, he said, "We all know we're better than we showed that half. The good news is we got out of it tied. Defense is up now, so let's set the tone right away and let these guys know who the better football team is. They'll wear out mentally as long as we don't keep giving them opportunities."

The Chiefs' opening possession of the third quarter was a microcosm of the game. Facing third-and-10, Trent Green dropped to pass and was under pressure from Maake Kemoeatu, the huge third-year defensive lineman who was getting extra snaps in the absence of Kelly Gregg. No one on the team ever even attempted to call Kemoeatu by his first name. He was "Kemo" to everyone. Like starting right guard Edwin Mulitalo, he was Polynesian —"Polynesian men tend to be very big," Mulitalo, six foot three and 345 pounds, explained. Kemo was six-five and 340. He and Mulitalo were one of the highlights annually of the rookie show. Once the rookies were finished, the two of them would get up and perform a Polynesian war dance (in 2004 they had been backed by two rookies of Polynesian descent), which left the whole room whooping and hollering. "Legend has it that when our men would go down to the beaches and perform the dance, the invaders would look at them and see how big they were and turn around and leave," Mulitalo said. He had performed the dance as his part of the rookie show in 1999, and Billick had liked it so much that he asked Mulitalo to reprise it each summer.

Now, Kemo danced past the Chiefs' offensive line and seemed to have Green in his grasp for a critical sack. Green pulled free and scrambled to his right. Kemo stayed with it, coming up from behind to grab him again. Somehow, Green wriggled free a second time and found one of his receivers, Chris Horn, in an open seam 16 yards downfield. Instead of forcing the Chiefs to punt from inside their own 15 with the crowd roaring, the defense stayed on the field while the Kansas City offense started a new set of downs from the 36. Seven plays later, the defense finally got a third-down stop when Chris McAlister nailed Gonzalez for no gain on a third-and-3. By then, though, the Chiefs were at the Ravens' 20 and kicker Larry Tynes drilled a 38-yard field goal for a 20–17 lead. The defense had been on the field for more than six minutes.

After the offense picked up one first down and stalled, the defense surrendered another touchdown on a thirteen-play, 80-yard drive that took the game into the fourth quarter. Priest Holmes, the ex-Raven, scored the touchdown from the 1-yard line to make it 27–17. The once-festive crowd had become almost silent. The offense did manage to put together a touchdown drive to close the gap to 27–24 but failed to threaten again, getting the ball twice more before game's end without ever crossing midfield. The stands were rapidly emptying when Trent Green took a knee at nine minutes after midnight to run the final seconds off the clock.

The trap game that they hadn't believed could trap them had done just that. "I can't believe it," Sanders said as they trudged up the tunnel. "This is crazy."

Disbelief was the feeling in the locker room. It was one thing for the defense to give up yardage the way it had in Cincinnati. In that game, they had been able to dig in and stop the Bengals whenever they got near the goal line. That had not been the case this time. The Chiefs had rushed for an astonishing 178 yards — 125 of them by Holmes — and Green had passed for another 223. They had been burned consistently on third down. Beyond that, the Chiefs had done something no one in Baltimore believed possible: they had made Ray Lewis a non-factor. Lewis had been miked by ABC during the game (networks loved to mike Lewis because he was always talking) and at one point the mike had picked up a conversation between Lewis and Mike Nolan in which Lewis told Nolan that he had to find a way to keep him from being double-teamed on every play.

"He's *not* being double-teamed," John Madden screamed. "He's just being kept away from the football."

Billick and Nolan knew that the Chiefs had one of the best offensive lines in the league. Very few teams would be able to get someone as big and as fast on Lewis as consistently as the Chiefs had. They decided it was just one game. What they had to be concerned about was a defense that had given up close to 400 yards for a second straight week. What's more, they now had a short week to prepare to make the trip down I-95 to play the Redskins. At least that would not be a trap game. After what had just happened, no one was concerned about overconfidence.

17

Make Mine Vanilla

EVEN BEFORE THE SEASON BEGAN, the fifth week had been circled on everyone's calendar as one filled with potential pitfalls.

To begin with, it was the week before the Move. Everyone was under orders to have everything packed in boxes so the movers could transport the entire franchise five miles down the road to 1 Winning Drive on the morning after the Redskins game. As a result, the building was chaotic with boxes everywhere, tables sitting in hallways, some computers still working, others not.

There was also the issue of the opponent. Because the Redskins were in the NFC and the Ravens were in the AFC, they played each other only once every four years. That meant there wasn't the kind of ongoing rivalry or bitterness that there might have been had they been in the same division. Even so, there was no love lost between the two franchises. The last time the Ravens had played in Washington had been during their Super Bowl season. It had come in the midst of their five-week no-touchdown drought, and the result had been a frustrating 10–3 loss. That wasn't all. There had been problems getting the Ravens' buses into the parking lot and there had also been the charming specter of the public address announcer urging the fans to chant, "The Ravens suck!" during pregame warmups. That little bit of class was courtesy of Dan Snyder, then in his second year as the team's owner. Snyder had ridden into town and started firing people almost the day he arrived, including a public relations secretary who had been with the team for twenty-six years. One of those caught in the purge was longtime public address announcer Phil Hochberg. Apparently the problem with Hochberg was that he was far too professional. He was an old-time PA guy who didn't believe in screaming hysterically when the home team picked up a first down or in whispering so he could barely be heard if the visiting team happened to do something good. He certainly would not have been willing to scream, "The Ravens suck!" So he was gone, replaced by a rock 'n' roll deejay who was willing to say or do anything that Mr. Snyder ordered.

The Snyder regime may have been best explained by something that had happened to Phil Hoffmann, the Ravens' team photographer. Getting on the elevator after the game in 2000, Hoffmann found the woman who operated it in tears. When he asked her what was wrong, she told him that she had made the mistake of letting someone get on the elevator with Mr. Snyder. "I'm sure I'm fired," she said. "Mr. Snyder doesn't let *anyone* ride the elevator with him."

With stadiums that are only thirty-five miles apart and fan bases that don't especially like each other, it is natural the teams would not be especially close. But it went beyond that. Steve Bisciotti was already being called the anti-Snyder in NFL circles. Nothing happened in Redskinland without Snyder being in the middle of it. Every player signing featured Snyder and the player posing for photos. On draft day Snyder loved making a spectacle of flying the Redskins' first-round pick to the team's headquarters on his helicopter. Bisciotti could afford a helicopter, too. He didn't have one. On draft day he sat upstairs in the draft room while Ozzie Newsome, Brian Billick, Phil Savage, and Eric DeCosta talked to the media. Bisciotti has said he wants to be the least-known owner in the NFL. Snyder may be the best known — and the least liked. When he does interviews, Bisciotti is honest and open. Snyder prefers whispering "off-the-record" leaks to his chosen few media sources.

There were a number of key Ravens who had a history with the Redskins. The most notable was Deion Sanders, who was ready to play and knew he would be resoundingly booed when he stepped onto the playing surface at FedEx Field. (The stadium had initially been named for Jack Kent Cooke, the late Redskins owner. Snyder's first act as owner had been to take his name off the stadium. He called it Redskins Stadium until he could make his corporate deal.) Unlike a lot of people who had dealt with him, Sanders had no problems with Snyder. The same was true of Jim Fassel, who had interviewed for the Redskins job the previous January, only to lose out when Snyder was able to lure Washington icon Joe Gibbs out of retirement. "No hard feelings at all," he said. "If I were Dan Snyder, I'd have hired Joe Gibbs, too."

Mike Nolan's memories of Snyder weren't nearly as warm. The vanilla ice cream incident in 1999 had been symbolic of their relationship, or non-relationship. Later in the season, when Nolan told the ice cream story to Leonard Shapiro of the *Washington Post* for a piece Shapiro was writing on the ups and downs of life as an NFL coordinator, Snyder's spokesman Karl Swanson called both Shapiro and Shapiro's boss to hotly deny the story and demand a correction. In the interest of fairness, Emilio Garcia-Ruiz, the *Post*'s sports editor, asked Mark Maske, who had covered the Redskins while Norv Turner had been the team's head coach at the time of the incident, to call Turner, now the head coach in Oakland.

"Is there any way we should print a correction or an apology to Dan Snyder for this story?" he asked Turner.

"Absolutely not," Turner answered. "Not only did he do it to Mike, he said to me the next year, 'Do I have to send you ice cream, too?'"

Jeff FitzGerald, now the Ravens' inside linebackers coach, was with the Redskins when the incident occurred. "I saw them wheeling the three canisters into Mike's office," he said after hearing about the denial.

When Swanson was contacted after the season for a comment on the ice cream incident, FitzGerald's eyewitness account and Turner's comment were included in the e-mail. A swift response came back: a statement from Redskins personnel director Vinny Cerrato saying *he* had been the one who had sent the ice cream. Cerrato went on to take a couple of swipes at Nolan, claiming the improvement in the Redskins' defense during the 1999 season was the result of hiring Bill Arnsparger as a consultant.

At least now people in the NFL may have some understanding of why Cerrato remains on the Redskins' payroll. He is both Snyder's fall guy and hatchet man.

Nolan laughed when he heard that Cerrato was taking the fall for the ice cream. He long ago reached the point where he laughs when the story comes up. His concerns the first week in October had a lot more to do with Redskins running back Clinton Portis, Gibbs's offense, and the 800 total yards his defense had given up the previous two weeks.

Billick believed his job — besides packing his desk — during the week was to restore the team's confidence. The loss had been the kind that can make a good team question itself. Even though the final margin had been only 27–24, that score was deceiving. The Chiefs had clearly outplayed the Ravens on both lines, and their offense had been the dominant factor in the game. "We had a bad game, guys, and we still only lost by three points," Billick told the players on Wednesday, choosing to leave out *how* the team had stayed close (punt return, trick play). "I've said before, I'll say it again, we all *know* we have everything it takes to be a very good football team right here. Were we a good team last year? Well, last year we were 2-2 at this point and we'd given up eighty-four points. This year, we've given up eighty points. Everything we want is still out there. We can't be 4-1 at the break like we hoped. But we can be 3-2."

Billick had mixed emotions about matching up with Joe Gibbs. His training-camp joke about Gibbs not having won a game in the twenty-first century was no longer true since the Redskins had won their opener against Tampa Bay. Most of Washington had started making Super Bowl plans after that game, but the town quickly came back to Earth when the Redskins proceeded to lose their next three games, to the Giants, Cowboys, and Browns. A little bit of the bloom was off the rose, but Billick knew playing at home on a Sunday night against the Ravens, trying to avoid a 1-4 start, the Redskins would be a dangerous team.

"They're doing a lot of the same things he [Gibbs] did the first time around," Billick said. "I think our defense will handle their offense. Their defense is really good, though, really good."

Translation: he was still worried about his offense.

Kyle Boller had not played poorly in the season's first four games and had in fact had some excellent moments. He was still being pilloried locally, though, especially after the offense had failed to move the ball at all in its last two possessions against Kansas City. Baltimore appeared to be equally divided: 50 percent of the fans thought Boller was a bust (after thirteen career starts); the other 50 percent thought (still) that Matt Cavanaugh should be fired. What no one ever brought up was how different life would be for both men if the team had a wide receiver who was a legitimate deep threat (as in Terrell Owens) or if Todd Heap were healthy. Owens was in Philadelphia wowing people, and Heap was still a few weeks away from even thinking about playing again.

As if the uncertainty following the Kansas City loss, the distractions of the move, and knowing just how much the Redskins were going to want to win the game weren't enough, there was also Jamal Lewis's absence from practice on Thursday. Missing one practice was hardly a big deal for Lewis. The reason he missed practice was what was disturbing: he had to fly to Atlanta to enter his guilty plea in court to complete the plea bargain that had been agreed to the previous week. Kevin Byrne went to Atlanta with Lewis, and Lewis spoke to the media after he finished in the courtroom.

"I made a mistake," he said. "I hope young people understand that. I know I'm a role model for a lot of young people and I have to pay for the mistake I made."

If his lines sounded scripted, it was only because he had been briefed the day before by his lawyers on how to handle his post-court comments. Any complaining about the prosecutor's actions or what had gone on could anger the judge enough that he might not go along with the prosecution's sentencing recommendations. That wasn't likely, but there was no sense in taking any chances. What's more, Lewis honestly believed he had made a mistake. He didn't believe he should serve time in jail, but he understood why he was going to have to.

Byrne was with Lewis when he spoke to the media. His mother and other members of his family were not there. He had told them not to come. This was one moment in his life he didn't want them to have to take part in.

Saturday was the team's last practice at the old facility. It was a gorgeous morning and everyone was in a good mood. Four days of separation from Monday night certainly helped. So did the knowledge that they were about to get a break in the routine. The team had reported to camp on July 29 — ten weeks earlier. There had been virtually no letup since then. The week off would do everyone good.

When practice ended, Billick briefed the players on the schedule for the next night, then turned to leave. "Hey, Coach, did you forget?" several players, led by Adalius Thomas, yelled. Billick turned back, puzzled. "This is our last practice here."

Billick laughed. "I *did* forget," he said. "We should commemorate the moment. Listen, this field has served us well. Let's go out there and put on a performance tomorrow worthy of that. And by the way, let's also remember to thank the new guy [Bisciotti] for spending thirty-five million dollars [actually $31 million] on the new place."

They came together one more time as a group before leaving the field. No one looked back. The city of Baltimore had sold the facility to nearby Villa Julie College. A lot of great football players had practiced on the field they were leaving behind. The athletes who would use it in the future would not be nearly as talented, nearly as famous, or nearly as well paid.

Joe Theismann was at practice. It was difficult to believe that it had been nineteen years since Theismann's career had suddenly and horribly ended when Lawrence Taylor had snapped his leg while sacking him during a Monday night game. Theismann was now fifty-five, a grandfather. He still looked youthful enough to take a few snaps if need be. Theismann was part of ESPN's Sunday night crew, sharing the booth with Paul Maguire and Mike Patrick. It could be argued that of all the networks' on-air crews, the one on ESPN took itself the least seriously. Perhaps it was because the three men in the booth had been together long enough that they were completely comfortable, or because their producer, Jay Rothman, went against the ESPN/ABC prototype and looked at what he was doing as several notches below life-and-death.

No one understood that better than Mike Patrick. This would be his first game back since undergoing open-heart surgery during the summer. A longtime smoker, Patrick had finally paid the price. There are few people in the business better liked than Patrick. Each of the Ravens invited into the production meeting that day made a point of giving him a hug and welcoming him back.

An ESPN production meeting is unlike those of the other networks. It is far less formal. There is no particular order to it. In fact, when Rothman, Maguire, Patrick, and sideline reporter Suzy Kolber were a couple of minutes late, Theismann began talking to Jamal Lewis, the first Raven in the room, by himself. He started with straight football questions and waited until everyone else arrived before getting into questions about his day in court. It was Rothman who asked if he thought the two-game suspension — which had been announced the day before — was unfair.

"Unfair?" Lewis said. "Hell no, it wasn't unfair."

Would he appeal?

"No. I'll serve my two games and that will be the end of it."

That was the way he wanted it. It was also the unofficial deal Cass had made with the league.

The last player ESPN had requested was Chris McAlister. Theismann asked him if not having a contract bothered him at all. "I'd be lying if I told you it didn't bother me," McAlister said. "I'd like to feel certain I'm going to be here for a long time. There's a definite feeling of insecurity because of the situation."

While McAlister was speaking, Newsome was upstairs finalizing a deal with McAlister's agent. Two hours later the deal was sealed. The following morning it was announced: it would be for seven years, $60 million, with a $12 million signing bonus. The Ravens — Bisciotti, Cass, Newsome, and Billick — had decided that McAlister's willingness to commit to a longer-term deal than a year ago, along with the maturity he had shown since returning to the team, made signing him a worthwhile gamble, even if it was an expensive one. McAlister had been counseled by Deion Sanders to stay with the Ravens rather than wait them out and go the free-agent route.

"I told him he didn't want to go someplace where he would have to go in and be the Man because he was the highest-paid player on the team," Sanders said. "Sure, maybe Champ Bailey was getting paid a little more [in Denver] because he's expected to come in there and be the star of their defense. I've been in that position, I know what it's like, and it isn't easy. I told him here everyone knows him. They know his strengths and his weaknesses, and that's good. He wouldn't have to prove himself to a whole new group of people. Plus, here he's got Ray, he's got Ed Reed, he's got a great defense. It isn't all on him."

McAlister listened to Sanders, although the Ravens' willingness to pay him top cornerback money undoubtedly had more to do with his decision to commit to the team long-term than anything else. Saturday was a hectic day for him. After practice — and before his meeting with ESPN — the defensive backs decided to hold a rare players-only meeting among themselves after their normal post-practice meeting with their coaches, Johnnie Lynn and Dennis Thurman.

They all knew that Sanders's absence in the last two games had been a factor in their inability to come up with enough plays, but they also knew they had to play better. Ed Reed had produced two interceptions in the Cincinnati game, but McAlister and Gary Baxter had been burned on the inside frequently by the Cincinnati receivers. Against Kansas City, the malaise had stricken all of them. They had given up key receptions all over the field and hadn't done enough to help stop the running game. A lot of attention had been focused during the week on Madden's shot at Ray Lewis. The DBs, notably Reed, who was closer to Lewis than anyone on the team, thought it unfair that so much of the heat had been focused on Lewis. The meeting wasn't long, but the consensus was clear: "We've got too much talent to be giving up so many plays," Reed said. "It needs to change. Now."

That meeting ended at 12:30, and McAlister's ten minutes with ESPN ended at 1:30. Shortly after three o'clock he had a new contract that made him a very wealthy young man. "You won't regret this," he said to Ozzie Newsome.

Newsome hoped those words would prove to be true.

There may not be a less-appealing stadium in football than FedEx Field.

"Reminds me of a hot dog stand stuck in the middle of nowhere" was Ravens assistant coach Mike Pettine's apt description.

It was a bad idea to begin with — built, as Pettine said — in the middle of nowhere, with too few access roads leading to and from the Washington Beltway, a highway choked by traffic under normal conditions, a complete disaster with 90,000 people trying to get into or out of a stadium located a couple of miles away. If Dan Snyder wasn't especially gifted when it came to human relations, he did know how to squeeze every last dollar out of a business deal. Since buying the team, he had expanded the capacity of the stadium to include obstructed-view seats (and then became furious when the *Washington Post* wrote about fans who weren't happy with them) and seating behind the end zones that came dangerously close to the playing field. Snyder had even tried to prevent fans from parking on the other side of the Beltway (without paying his $25 parking fee) by claiming it was too dangerous for them to walk to the stadium from there. Only a court ruling — after several fans brought a lawsuit — had stopped him from continuing that charade. Fans were urged to "be in their seats early" for the simple reason that if you weren't, you might spend the first half trying to get into the parking lot.

Nonetheless, people still came to see the Redskins play. Because Washington had been without a baseball team since 1971 and the hockey and basketball teams had had little success, the Redskins were an even bigger deal in Washington than the NFL team is in most cities. When Joe Gibbs returned — most Redskins fans believed he had descended from eleven years in heaven, where God had been sitting at his right hand — the local TV stations broke into programming to cover his press conference live. On the first day of minicamp the *Washington Post* put the story on the front page. Not the front page of the sports section, the front page of the newspaper. One giddy *Post* columnist all but handed the team the Super Bowl trophy that day.

Reality was now beginning to set in. There was even some soft grumbling about Gibbs's key off-season acquisition, veteran quarterback Mark Brunell. The Ravens knew a lot about Brunell, having played against him frequently when they were in the same division as Jacksonville. They had great respect for his toughness and smarts, but the Brunell they had seen on tape in a Redskins uniform didn't resemble the young Brunell they had faced in Jacksonville. "He still worries me," Mike Nolan said. "It's only four games. Give him time and he can still cause a team a lot of problems."

The key was not to give him time. The best way to do that was to force the Washington offense into passing situations, and that meant bottling up Gibbs's other important off-season acquisition, running back Clinton Portis. Like the rest of the team, Portis had looked great on opening day, mediocre since. "He's very shifty and he can make you miss," Nolan told the defense. "But if you hit him, he'll go down. He's not going to break a lot of tackles. Tackle smart and we'll get him on the ground."

The pregame atmosphere on the field was almost as festive as Monday night in Baltimore. Steve Bisciotti was on the field prior to the game, feeling a little bit like a football player in that he was about to undergo neck surgery that he had put off until the bye week. "The doctor says I have to do it," he said. "I'll probably be in rough shape for a few days, so this way I won't miss a game next weekend. I should be able to make it to the Buffalo game in two weeks if all goes well."

The first person Bisciotti saw when he walked onto the field was Mc-Alister, who came over to him, threw his arms around him in a hug, and said, "Thank you."

Gary Baxter was a step behind McAlister and said to Bisciotti, "Me next."

"You mean you want a hug, too?" Bisciotti asked.

Baxter laughed. He wasn't talking about a hug, he was talking about a contract. His was up at the end of the season, and unlike several players whom the team planned to let walk, Baxter's Ravens future was still being debated. Everyone in the organization liked him personally. He had a great attitude and loved playing on a winning team, having played on horrible teams during his college career at Baylor. The question was whether he was worth big-time cornerback money when the team had just committed huge money to McAlister and would undoubtedly be paying Ed Reed a lot in the near future when he reached free agency. There was one other unwanted issue: Ray Lewis's contract had been redone two years earlier, seemingly locking him up for seven years. He now had a new agent who was telling the team that Lewis needed a new contract in the wake of his being chosen the NFL's Defensive Player of the Year in 2003. The team felt it had given Lewis an $18 million signing bonus and an annual salary of close to $10 million a year because they felt he was the best defensive player in football and there was no need to pay him again. What's more, giving him a raise would throw their salary cap structure into chaos. And yet, because it was so important to keep Lewis happy, they couldn't just tell the agent to take a hike.

Even with his new contract, McAlister had money on his mind before the game. "I bet JO [Jonathan Ogden] a hundred bucks on UCLA-Arizona, and you can be sure he's going to want to collect," he said, laughing. Most of the time when two players' alma maters played each other, the Ravens involved would bet $100 on the game. The one sure thing about making a bet with Ogden was that if you lost, he would collect; if you won, he would pay off.

There was one other pregame problem. As the sun was setting, the temperature was dropping rapidly. Sanders came onto the field for warm-ups wearing a bandana around his neck to keep it warm. The uniform Nazis were swarming. The bandana would have to go when the game started, regardless of temperature.

Sanders had one other problem: a cap on one of his teeth had fallen out and he needed a temporary cap. Leigh Ann Curl sent someone to ask the Redskins team doctors if they had a dentist on the sidelines or could find one who could give her a temporary cap for Sanders's tooth. They did. If there is one group in the NFL that is truly collegial, it is the team doctors. Most teams have at least three or four doctors on the sidelines. It is part of the pregame ritual for the home-team doctors to cross the field to welcome the visiting-team doctors. They exchange stories about different injuries they are dealing with, even on occasion trade advice on specific cases. At game's end, the doctors always find one another much the same way the kickers find one another, the long snappers find one another, and the linebackers find one another. Curl told Sanders that a temporary cap was on the way.

"That's good," he said. "But what I really need is a dentist."

For the Ravens, the first half supplied what seemed like a trip to the dentist. Watching the offense was especially painful. The first quarter produced three series of three-and-out and one series in which Kyle Boller completed a first-down pass to Kevin Johnson. Even so, the Ravens never ran a play on Washington's side of the field. The only good news was that the Redskins' offense wasn't doing much better against the Ravens' defense, producing a total of two first downs, also without threatening to cross midfield. The clicking sound people heard as the teams changed ends of the field after fifteen minutes was the sound of TV sets across America being turned off.

Amazingly, the Ravens' offense was worse in the second quarter. Instead of giving the Redskins the ball courtesy of Dave Zastudil punts, the Ravens started giving them the ball courtesy of Kyle Boller passes. First Fred Smoot grabbed an errant throw aimed for Dan Wilcox and returned it 17 yards to the Ravens' 28. With 8:40 left in the half, the Redskins' first play of the ensuing series was the first time in the game either team had been in the other's territory. The Redskins managed to pick up one first down before being stopped at the 8-yard line. Kicker John Hall made a 26-yard field goal with 5:42 left in the half, and the Redskins had a 3–0 lead.

The Ravens managed to pick up a first down on their next series, but then a Boller pass intended for Randy Hymes was deflected to Shawn Springs. A tripping penalty on Hymes moved the ball to the Ravens' 43, but the defense dug in and Terrell Suggs sacked Brunell on third-and-10, forcing a punt. The Ravens took over on their own 14, looking to at least run the clock out and get to the locker room down 3–0. After two Lewis runs, Boller hit Clarence Moore with a short pass that gave the Ravens a first down with under two minutes to play. But three plays later, trying to pick up another first down, Boller's pass for Kevin Johnson was again tipped and ended up in the hands of backup safety Todd Franz. He took the ball back to the 8-yard line. Even the Redskins' offense couldn't squander this chance: Brunell found Chris Cooley in the end zone with 26 seconds left, and the halftime lead was 10–0.

The way the Ravens' offense was going, that lead looked almost insurmountable. Although two of Boller's interceptions had been deflections, they were as much the result of poor reads as poor throws. He wasn't the only one struggling. Lewis had a total of 19 yards on ten carries, which meant neither he nor the offensive line was getting anything done. The defense had been solid, but it needed some help. Billick opted for the "we're okay" route with the players at halftime. "We have to stick together right now," he said, not wanting to see any finger-pointing. "We go back out there and play our game and we'll be fine. We've made some mistakes, it's okay, we're only down ten. We'll make a play and turn this thing around."

Calm as Billick was, there was clear tension in the locker room. They simply could not afford another loss to a sub-.500 team. The last thing they wanted was to spend two weeks listening to people talk about how they were 2-3 and had just lost to the *Redskins.* Billick, Matt Cavanaugh, and Jim Fassel were all baffled by Boller's performance but knew that jumping on him at that moment was the worst thing they could possibly do. Matt Simon, the running backs coach, pulled Jamal Lewis aside as they started to leave the locker room. "Thirty minutes," he said to him. "Make the most of it."

Lewis knew what Simon was saying. It would be three weeks before he would play football again once the game was over.

The second half didn't start any better than the first. On the second play, Ray Lewis came off the field holding his shoulder, clearly in pain, his knees almost buckling as he reached the trainers. Brunell promptly completed a pass to Laveranues Coles for a first down at the Washington 32. It turned out that Lewis just had a stinger in his shoulder. Stingers can be very painful because they are just that — a stinging sensation caused by a hard hit — but they don't involve any broken bones. Lewis came back two plays after coming out, and the defense forced a punt. The offense was no better: three-and-out again. It was beginning to look as if the defense was going to have to score for the Ravens to have any chance to come back and win.

Mike Nolan wasn't necessarily thinking that, but he was thinking the defense needed to make something happen. They had been resolute in the first half but hadn't created any turnovers. That made six straight quarters without a turnover. With the Redskins facing third-and-6 on their own 37, Nolan decided to take a chance. He called "3-2 jacks," a safety blitz that had Ed Reed blitz from the left side. Since Brunell was left-handed, that would mean if Reed could get to him, he would be coming at him from his blind side. Billick heard the call in his headset and liked it: they had to try something even if it was a little bit dangerous.

Reed smartly delayed for a split second on the snap, which appeared to lull Redskins' running back Ladell Betts, the player assigned to pick up a blitzer, into a false sense of security. As Brunell started to roll left a step, Reed exploded past Betts and was on Brunell in an instant. Even before Reed got his hands on Brunell, Billick could sense a big play about to happen: "Get him!" he screamed. "Get him!"

Reed had him. Brunell's arm was up to pass and Reed knocked the ball cleanly from his grasp. He stumbled for a step, then took off after the ball, which was now rolling on the ground. "Go, Ed Reed! Go, Ed Reed!" Billick was screaming, running down the sideline in the direction of the rolling ball as if to make sure Reed could see it. Reed saw it. He picked it up in full stride at the 22-yard line and was gone down the sideline for a touchdown. The Ravens' bench exploded, pent-up anxiety coming out of everyone at once.

Gibbs, who had already been criticized in the local media several times for wasting time-outs by challenging plays that had no chance to be overruled, challenged again. Instant-replay challenges hadn't existed during Gibbs's first stint as a coach, and he had actually hired someone to sit in the coaches' box strictly for the purpose of advising him when to challenge and when not to. Clearly, the man wasn't earning his money. There was no way the play was going to be overturned, Brunell's arm hadn't even been close to going forward. The play stood, and Matt Stover's extra point made the score 10–7.

In an instant, one play, one call — 3-2 jacks — the entire game had turned around. The Ravens' bench was alive again. The stadium, which had been enveloped in noise most of the night, was almost quiet. The Ravens kicked off and the Redskins, having had no success throwing the ball, decided to try to move the ball on the ground. Portis picked up 9 yards on two carries. On third-and-1, Brunell again gave the ball to Portis. But Reed knifed in seemingly untouched and got to Portis before he could get close to the line of scrimmage and nailed him for a 2-yard loss. It wasn't a turnover, but it was another huge play. The Redskins had to punt again.

Billick and Gary Zauner decided it was time to try to make something happen on special teams. They sent Sanders out with B. J. Sams to return the punt. As soon as Sams fielded Tom Tupa's spiraling kick, Sanders cut behind him, apparently to take a handoff. He was running left, Sams right. When the Redskins' cover team saw Sanders circle behind Sams, they bought the fake — if only for an instant. Sanders took off to the left without the football. Sams, with an open lane, raced to his right and went down the sideline 78 yards for a touchdown. Without running a single offensive play, the Ravens had gone from a 10–0 deficit to a 14–10 lead in a little more than two minutes. Nolan's 3-2 jacks call had started the turnaround. Reed had made two brilliant plays. And Sams, with a little help from Sanders and his blockers, had finished off the sudden turnaround.

The Redskins were staggered. Their offense picked up a couple of first downs on the next series, but then Brunell tried to throw deep on a third-and-9 from his own 48 and Sanders stepped in front of Coles in the end zone and intercepted. There was still a quarter to go, but the game was over. Lewis and the offensive line took complete control the rest of the way, killing more than five minutes with a drive that culminated in a Stover field goal, then running the clock out in the final 4:42, the game ending with Boller kneeling on the Redskins' 11-yard line. The offense had held the ball for an astounding 12:33 in the last quarter. Lewis carried 16 times during the Ravens' last three drives for 90 yards. The defense gave up an astonishing total of 107 yards for the game — only 43 of them in the second half.

By the time Boller knelt on the final play, about the only fans left in the stadium were those in purple and white who had managed to get tickets. They had been hardly noticeable during the first half, drowned out by the Washington fans. Now they appeared to be everywhere.

For the first time all season, there were heartfelt hugs of congratulations in the locker room. Pittsburgh had been a big win because it was the Steelers and they had been 0-1, but they had been in control almost the entire game. This had been an escape. The defense had started it, the special teams had continued it, and then the offense had finished it with complete ball control in the fourth quarter.

"We're going to give a special game ball tonight," Billick said. "We're going to give it to Jamal Lewis [cheers all around] not only because of the way he ran in the second half but because we want him to know two things: when he comes back, we'll be here waiting for him and we'll be waiting for him with a 5-2 record."

More cheers and more hugs. Everyone seemed to be smiling.

As the defensive coaches made their way to their lockers, Mike Pettine's voice could be heard clearly above all the shouting: "Someone send Dan Snyder some ice cream," he said. "And make sure it's vanilla."

Mike Nolan said nothing. He didn't have to. Three-two jacks had done all the talking that needed to be done.

18

Making a Move

WHILE THE RAVENS WENT ABOUT MOVING from their old facility to the new one during their bye week, two players were the subject of most of the buzz in Baltimore: Ed Reed, who had announced himself as a big-time defensive star in the Redskins game, and Kyle Boller, who had probably played his poorest game since his rookie debut in Pittsburgh.

Before the players took off for a few days — Billick had them come in briefly on Monday and then gave them off until Saturday — Boller met with Matt Cavanaugh to discuss what had happened in the Washington game. The care and feeding of Boller was a sensitive subject for everyone associated with the Ravens. Every time he made a mistake or looked the least bit vulnerable, the wolves were ready to pounce. They pounced on Boller for not being as advanced as rookie classmates Carson Palmer and Byron Leftwich. Now they were beginning to point out that Ben Roethlisberger, the Pittsburgh rookie, was unbeaten since Tommy Maddox's injury in the Ravens game. They also pounced on Ozzie Newsome for trading a first-round pick to get Boller in the 2003 draft and on Billick for never having developed a quarterback as good as the ones he had coached as the coordinator in Minnesota.

And they jumped on Cavanaugh, again. Which was fine with him. He was fully aware that if the offense didn't improve, he wasn't going to be back in 2005. He had enough self-confidence to believe there was another job out there for him if that occurred. "I've been cut, I've been fired, and

I've been ripped from stem to stern," he said. "I can handle it. My concern right now is Kyle."

Boller never appeared rattled by the criticism that seemed to be growing with each passing week. He addressed it with a smile on his face when he spoke to the media. After the Redskins game, he had cheerily greeted his parents (who flew in from California for most games) and talked about how pleased he was that the defense and special teams had been able to rally the Ravens while the offense sputtered. But Cavanaugh and Fassel both knew that, tough-minded as he was, Boller was twenty-three and that the criticism had to hurt. Cavanaugh talked to him quietly that Monday about getting away and relaxing for the next few days and coming back to start fresh when preparing for Buffalo. That was what the bye week was all about, anyway. Fassel suggested that the two of them get together someplace away from the facility the following week.

No one had to worry about Ed Reed's mental state. At twenty-six, he was clearly emerging as a full-fledged star. It wasn't as if his first two years in the league had been unimpressive. As a rookie he had intercepted five passes and blocked two punts, returning one for a touchdown. In 2003 he had seven interceptions — one for a touchdown — and blocked two more punts, returning *both* for touchdowns. That meant the touchdown he had scored against the Redskins was the fifth of his career. There were offensive players who had been in the league just as long who had not scored that often.

Reed's nickname on the team was "Little Ray." Like Lewis, he wore a black scullcap under his helmet. Like Lewis, he enjoyed celebrating after making big plays. Like Lewis, he was deeply religious. When the defense was introduced before a game, Reed and Lewis were always the last two players to come out of the tunnel. While the rest of the team gathered near the field, they would stand back and apart, each crossing himself repeatedly before moving into the tunnel. Reed was a regular at Lewis's Thursday night get-togethers at his house. Like Lewis, he had gone to Miami. Unlike most of Miami's star players, he had stayed five years, had gotten his degree in four, and had never been accused of an attitude problem. That, he said, dated to his upbringing in St. Rose, Louisiana.

"Where I grew up, there were two paths you could take," he said. "One led to trouble, the other led out. My way out was always going to sports, football especially. For as long as I can remember, I played football, from peewee on up. And for as long as I can remember, I loved football. I didn't just love to play, I loved the way it felt. There's a feel to being part of the game, the way it feels before the game, the way it feels in the locker room and on the field, the way it feels after the game — whether you win or lose, there's a feel to it I'm not sure I can describe, I just know I've always loved it."

Reed grew up in a big family — the second of five boys. His dad, Ed Sr., was (and still is) a welder; his mother, a dietician. His elder brother was an excellent baseball player, but Ed was always into football first and foremost. Because his parents were always working, they would sometimes let him stay over at a friend's house if he had an early game because it was tough for them to get him to the game and then make it to work. "They came to a lot of my games, though," he said. "They were always there for me."

Like a lot of kids growing up in tough neighborhoods, Reed benefited because he was identified early as a gifted athlete. "When people see that you have a chance to get out, they want to help you," he said. "There were times when I would start in the wrong direction and one of my cousins or friends would grab me and say, 'Oh no, not you, you stay away from this.'"

Reed stayed out of trouble, but he also stayed out of school more than he should have. "I was like a lot of kids," he said. "I showed up when I needed to — for a game."

By the time he got to high school, he was behind academically. He took only two ninth-grade classes — the rest were eighth-grade — as a freshman because he wasn't ready to be a full-fledged freshman, except in sports. Early in his sophomore year, Jeanne Hall, the school secretary, made a proposal to him: Come stay at my house. Your parents have enough going on with four other kids. I'll make *sure* you get to school every day. Reed and his parents agreed. "It might have been the most important decision of my life," he said. "I'm not sure I'd be here today if not for Miss Hall."

Jeanne Hall got him to school every day, and a man named Ned Paquet, who frequented the local schoolyards, kept pushing him to work harder in school. "He was just a local guy who liked to mentor kids he thought had potential," Reed said. "He picked me out early. He would show up after I got done playing and give me a little shove and say, 'You been getting your schoolwork done? You want a scholarship, you need to get your work done.'"

By his junior year Reed was thinking about a scholarship. He had been contacted by Miami, where the receivers coach, Curtis Johnson Jr., was from St. Rose. His father, who still lived in St. Rose, had told him about Reed and he went to see Reed while back home, visiting. "His message was pretty direct," Reed remembered. "He said, 'You've got the talent, you haven't got the grades or the ACTs. If you want to come to Miami, that's what you have to work on.' So I did."

He pushed his grade point average to 2.7 and got a 17 on the ACT — two points higher than the 15 that he needed. By his senior year, other schools, seeing his talent — and now, his grades and ACTs — were onto him, but he was committed in his mind to Miami. He went there and immediately got hurt, breaking an ankle early in his freshman season. "I was upset at the time," he said. "I wanted to play — I mean, play right away — and now I couldn't. But it was probably the best thing that happened to me. It gave me a chance to get used to college, to learn how to fit in, to watch the older players and learn from them. By the time I started to play my [redshirt] freshman year, I was ready."

His career was a steady progression. By his junior season he was the Big East co-player of the year and was being told by scouts that he might be a first-round pick. But he was concerned that if he went to all the predraft camps and the combine and did all the workouts for teams, he wouldn't graduate in the spring. Plus, he thought Miami had a chance to be very good the next year even though Coach Butch Davis was leaving to coach the Cleveland Browns. He stayed, and the decision turned out to be exactly right. He graduated in the spring. The Hurricanes went undefeated and won the national championship in the fall. And the following April, after some nervous moments, he got the call from Ozzie Newsome telling him the Ravens were taking him with the twenty-fourth pick in the draft.

"To be honest, I didn't care where I went," he said. "I just wanted the chance to test myself at the next level."

He was tested right away, starting all sixteen games. He and Ray Lewis — both Miami guys — became best friends. A year later he made the Pro Bowl. Now, in his third season, people were starting to say he might be the best defensive player in the league. That was fine with Reed.

He was confident that Lewis could handle hearing that kind of talk without his ego being bruised.

"I'm no different now at twenty-six than I was when I was six playing peewee," he said. "I just want to play football and keep getting better."

When the players came back from their four-day break, they reported to the new facility and were given a tour of the posh new locker rooms, meeting rooms, and, perhaps most important to them, the new weight room. Everything in the new building — which was, in all, 200,000 square feet, complete with stone and brick fronting and a castle turret — was at least twice as large as in the old one. For the first time in team history, there was an indoor field to practice on, certainly a luxury during the season for bad weather days, but a huge advantage in the off-season, when players would be able to work out no matter how cold or snowy the weather might be. The weight room was a huge improvement, too: for one thing, it was part of the main building, not a separate bubble the way it was in the old building.

"I'm not sure I'm worthy of working out in this place," punter Dave Zastudil said when he saw the new weight room.

"The best thing about it is we don't have to walk outside to go to the bathroom," strength coach Jeff Friday said, a key upgrade for everyone.

The locker room was big enough to comfortably fit the fifty-three roster players and the eight practice squad players with room to spare — room that would be used during minicamps, when the roster swelled. There would be no need, as there had been in the old locker room, to put temporary lockers in the middle of the room for the rookies and free agents. The coaches' offices were palatial. Every assistant now had his own office — as opposed to the old place, where many of them had to double up. Bisciotti and Cass went from no office space to having huge offices right next to each other. There were drawbacks. Unlike in the old building, where Newsome and Billick were at opposite ends of the hallway, now they were right next to each other, separated only by the space occupied by their assistants. In the old days, when something was going on, everyone knew it because the two men would take turns marching down the hallway to each other's offices. Now they could go back and forth unnoticed, a disappointment to all. Even the media, which had worked out of a trailer in the old place, had comfortable new quarters, complete with its own entrance and a freezer stocked with ice cream. The latter was a mixed blessing for most.

There were, predictably, some glitches. The washing machines and dryers that were needed to clean all the players' gear weren't working. Local firefighters work for the team to get the Ravens' laundry done in their spare time. Ed Carroll, the team's longtime equipment manager, had to send the firefighters to a Laundromat. "The hard part," he said, "was rounding up eight hundred quarters."

"It's amazing what you can buy these days with thirty-one million dollars, isn't it?" Billick joked.

Billick gave the players three days to get the hang of the new digs. On Wednesday morning, when the team gathered to begin a normal workweek in preparation for Buffalo, he announced that being late for a meeting because one got lost in the building was no longer a viable excuse. It was time to get serious and get back to work.

The Bills would come into Baltimore with a 1-4 record. Billick didn't want to sound like one of those coaches who makes every opponent sound like the 1967 Green Bay Packers, but he knew they were considerably better than their record. Two of their four losses had come on the final play; another had come in the last minute. They had a huge defense, which included Sam Adams, who had been a key part of the defensive line for the Ravens when they won the Super Bowl, and dangerous wide receivers who would make plays if quarterback Drew Bledsoe was given time.

The key to the game would be not giving Bledsoe time. He was a smart, veteran quarterback but lacked mobility. He was vulnerable to the sack and also was capable of throwing interceptions if forced to throw the ball quickly.

The week seemed to crawl by for everyone. They had been eager for the week off, but now they wanted to play again. For the first time all fall, the weather was truly lousy — cold and rainy, forcing three straight days of practice indoors. Billick began the week by ripping the league for not allowing a suspended player to train at the facility during his suspension. "Isn't it better for him to have some order in his life, to be working out, even if it's on his own, around people who know what they're doing?" he said. "What exactly do you accomplish by keeping him away?"

Nothing. As it turned out, the league agreed. The day after Billick's salvo, Ozzie Newsome got a note from the league office: the rules on suspended players had been changed. Lewis was welcome to work out at the facility, he just couldn't work out with the team. Whoops.

"I guess you could say this was one where we didn't get the memo," Billick said. "Literally."

Lewis was already home in Atlanta by the time the team got word. Plans were made for him to stay there through Sunday, then report back to Baltimore on Monday morning. With Lewis gone, the offensive game plan had to be adjusted somewhat because neither Chester Taylor nor Musa Smith was the pounding type of runner that Lewis was. The offense would try to run more to the outside and would include more short passes. The thought was that short passes would help Boller, too, because they were easier and less dangerous. Taylor would be the primary back; Smith would take Taylor's role, coming in on passing downs. Both men had known since the announcement of the trial date during training camp that this week was almost certainly going to come at this point in the season and both appeared prepared for it. The only hitch came early in the week when Kevin Byrne told Taylor there were several extra media requests for him. Taylor is one of the quieter players on the team, almost to the point of being a loner. When Byrne told him he would be expected to spend extra time with the media, he rolled his eyes. "So *now* they want to talk to me, when I'm the starter," he said.

"That exactly right, Chester," Byrne answered. "When you start, more people want to talk to you."

Byrne has been in public relations for almost thirty years and knows how to deal with players. He and his staff put out a booklet each year for the benefit of the players, telling them who the media are in Baltimore, what the players may be asked to do during the course of the season, and why it is important that they cooperate with the media. The players cooperate with him and with his assistants, Francine Lubera, Chad Steele, and Marisol Renner, in part because most of them do understand why they should but also because they know Byrne has the complete support of Billick, Newsome, and Bisciotti. If Byrne tells them he thinks something is important, they take him at his word. The players are expected to do the same. Chester Taylor did all the interviews Byrne asked him to.

Byrne had another issue to deal with during the week that had nothing to do with the Buffalo game. Each week NFL teams supply one key player for a conference call with writers from the opponent's city. This is usually routine: the Baltimore writers might ask for Drew Bledsoe and the Buffalo writers would ask for Ray Lewis or Kyle Boller. The only thing the PR people tried to do was make sure the same player wasn't asked to do the conference call every week. Ed Reed, coming off his huge game against Washington, was the Ravens' rep to the Buffalo writers for the week. Byrne was already in negotiations with Derek Boyko, his counterpart in Philadelphia, about the conference calls for the following week since the Ravens and Ray Lewis going to Philadelphia to play the Eagles and Terrell Owens was going to be a big story not only locally in the two cities but nationally.

The Baltimore writers wanted — surprise — Terrell Owens. The Eagles said no. "T.O. doesn't do conference calls" was Boyko's official excuse.

The Philadelphia writers wanted — another shock — Ray Lewis. As soon as the Eagles said no to T.O., the Ravens said no to Lewis. Byrne knew that Lewis wasn't going to want to get into any T.O. rehash, but once Boyko said no to T.O., he didn't even have to go back to Lewis to see if he would consider it.

Stalemate.

The issue was finally resolved the next Monday: Reed would talk to the Philly writers, and Donovan McNabb to the Baltimore writers. Peace was at hand. . . . Sort of.

Billick and the players weren't the least bit concerned about who was going to be on the next week's conference call. By the end of the week, everyone was a little bit tense. During practice on Friday, Terrell Suggs was teasing co–secondary coach Dennis Thurman in the way players and coaches often tease one another; silly macho stuff. Everyone on the team knew that Suggs was completely harmless, a constant talker who was best handled with laughter. Even though he was in his second season, he had just turned twenty-two and frequently acted younger than that. He was rapidly becoming one of the better pass-rushing linebackers in the league and had taken to punctuating his sacks with a dance that was so bad, no one wanted to tell him to stop because it was always good for a laugh. "He may be the only person I've ever seen who is a worse dancer than I am," Dick Cass had commented one day.

No one understood the give-and-take between players and coaches better than Thurman, who had played in the league for nine years (with thirty-six career interceptions) before becoming a coach. This time, though, he snapped at Suggs. "Sizzle, you need to learn when to just shut the hell up," he said, walking away from Suggs. There were other skirmishes, some on the field, some off. By Saturday night Rod Hairston felt compelled to begin his sermon by saying, "Fellas, I know this environment can wear you out." He went on to talk about opportunities that life presented one with; occasionally opportunities that appeared in the form of adversity.

Billick was fully aware of the tension in the locker room. Although he understood some of it was circumstantial — weather, time off, concerns about Jamal Lewis's absence — he was also beginning to think that "stacking," the psychological component he had heard about at the BCA convention, might be starting to infiltrate his team. "The Rev had a hell of a message tonight," he said. "It was about opportunities. This is an opportunity to prove we can overcome difficulties. We're without the league's best running back [Lewis], our best receiver [Todd Heap], and our starting center [Mike Flynn]. But I still think we have everything we need in this room to win this game. I told you before the season, we would face adversity. The way we deal with that adversity that we knew would come in some form will ultimately determine how successful we are."

"I wonder how we'll react to all of this," he said on Sunday morning while crossing the Hamburg Street bridge with Vernon Holley. The day was just about as miserable as the rest of the week had been. Billick's concern was apparently not shared by the team's fans. Rain or no rain, they were in a joyous mood on the bridge, delighted by the victory over the Redskins and convinced that the 1-4 Bills would be little more than a walkover. Billick didn't share their confidence.

He was even more concerned when he went on the field for pregame warm-ups. Something was missing. Because of the weather, there weren't as many people in their seats early as usual. It seemed to him that the players were flat as they went through their pregame routines and drills. There was very little of the usual chatter. Even Ray Lewis was relatively quiet. When Billick gathered the team around him before they went out to be introduced, he abandoned his normal pregame format. "I may be completely full of shit on this, I know I am on a lot of things and I'm not even sure if the way you warm up matters even a little bit," he said. "But what I saw out there just now was *not* a team ready to play an important football game. I'm gonna tell you guys something: *never* do you go out on this field if you aren't ready to play. You cannot go out there today and expect this crowd to pick you up. They're wet, they're cold, they're bundled up, and it's been three weeks since we last played here. You have got to provide the emotion. You can't count on anyone else to do it, not me, not the coaches, *you*. Now, if you aren't ready to go out there and play with emotion, don't go out there! Understand? Now, I'm going to go stand by that door and I want every one of you to look me in the eye and tell me you're ready to play. If you don't feel like you can do that, don't go out there!"

There was a lot of football rhetoric in the speech, but Billick's concern was genuine. His instincts had told him something wasn't right, and he thought he needed to get their attention before they dug themselves a hole the way they had in the Kansas City game. Billick always stands in the doorway and offers a word of encouragement to each player as he goes by. This time, he wanted the words to come at him, rather than from him.

They all said the right things going out the door, insisting they had gotten the message. But the game didn't start that way. After B. J. Sams returned the opening kickoff to the 30-yard line, Taylor tried to run left on first down and was nailed for a 2-yard loss. Boller dropped to pass on second down and was swarmed by defensive end Aaron Schobel and blitzing linebacker Jeff Posey, who blew by the left side of the Ravens' line. Boller fumbled, and Posey pounced on the ball at the 22. The game was forty-three seconds old and boos were wafting down from the stands. The fans might have been too cold to clap but they weren't too cold to boo. Bledsoe immediately found tight end Mark Campbell for a 16-yard pickup to the 6 and the bleak day looked even bleaker.

But the defense dug in and forced the Bills to settle for a field goal. Then the offense pieced together a twelve-play drive that stalled at the Buffalo 6 but still produced a Matt Stover field goal that tied the game. And then Deion Sanders took over. Facing third-and-9 from their own 45, the Bills lined up in shotgun formation. Bledsoe dropped back, was rushed hard, and tried to force a pass to running back Willis McGahee. Sanders stepped in front of McGahee and had nothing but 48 yards of Momentum turf between him and the end zone. With the stadium erupting, he waltzed into the end zone, then turned and put a hand up to stop his onrushing team-mates from mobbing him. It was time for Prime Time. He danced along the end line while everyone stood and watched. One could only hope that Suggs was watching; he could have learned a thing or two.

Once again the defense had completely changed the tenor of a game. The Bills went nowhere on their next possession and the Ravens opened the second quarter with what might have been their best sustained drive of the season — 83 yards in nine plays, with Sams, starting to get some snaps on offense, scoring on a sweep left from the 5-yard line. After the brutal start, they led, 17–3. That was the margin at halftime. By then the Ravens' defense had control of the game. The Bills managed a third-quarter field goal to cut the margin to 17–6, then marched to the Ravens' 5 with just under six minutes left in the game. But Chad Williams, in the game on third down, intercepted a Bledsoe pass on the 1-yard line and almost took it back all the way, finally running out of gas and being caught by wide receiver Eric Moulds at the Buffalo 6 after a 93-yard return.

Williams's not scoring hardly seemed significant at that point. What was likely the Bills' last gasp had been stopped. But on the first play after the interception, as Taylor swept left, Jonathan Ogden grabbed his left leg and went down in a heap. Just as in the Meadowlands when Ogden had gone down, the bench went from raucous — players were still teasing Williams about not scoring — to silent. Ogden was finally helped off the field, and as in the Meadowlands, Andy Tucker's initial diagnosis to Billick was one word: "hamstring." Billick groaned. He was certain, even without knowing the details, just judging by the way Ogden had looked coming off the field, he wouldn't play the next week in Philadelphia. No Lewis, no Ogden, no Heap going to play on the road against an undefeated team.

They settled for a field goal on that drive and the final was 20–6. Ogden's injury took a lot of joy out of the postgame locker room. Billick told them he was proud of the way they had gotten their act together after the poor start and told them to enjoy being 4-2. The defense had again been superb, intercepting Bledsoe four times, sacking him on four occasions, and keeping the Bills out of the end zone. The offense had been just good enough. Chester Taylor had produced 89 yards on 21 carries. Boller's numbers were hardly gaudy: 10-of-19 for 86 yards, but, after the fumble, he had taken care of the football. Sanders had finally gotten a shot on offense, but the reverse called for him had produced a 10-yard loss.

"We didn't run it right," he insisted when Fuller and Lewis gave him a hard time about producing negative yardage.

What was most important was the final score. A win was a win. But it had not come without cost. Playing the Eagles would be tough under any circumstances. Playing them without all three of the offense's Pro Bowl players would be even tougher.

If Billick liked opportunities created by adversity, he was going to love the next seven days.

19

The T.O. Dance

PART OF MIKE NOLAN'S POSTGAME ROUTINE every week was to circle the locker room to shake hands and have a quiet word with each of his players. The conversations were always brief, Nolan's comments ranging from "great job" to "hang in there," to "don't hang your head," depending on how the player and the defense had performed that day. Sometimes, he just said, "Thanks."

As he circled the room after the victory over the Bills, Nolan should have been flying high. For the second week in a row, the defense had been superb. It had not given up a touchdown, it had created four turnovers, and it had turned the game in the Ravens' favor with a big play.

Nolan felt none of that. More than anything, he felt slightly sick, his stomach twisted into a knot he couldn't untangle. "Deep down, I knew I'd been out of line," he said. "It was something that just happened in the heat of the moment. Almost as soon as I said it, I wished I could take it back."

The moment Nolan couldn't escape had occurred in the first half. Brian Billick leaves it up to his coordinators to call the game from the press box or the sideline. He and Matt Cavanaugh had decided before the season began that it would be better for Cavanaugh to move up to the press box. For one thing, it made him less of a target. For another, with Jim Fassel downstairs to eyeball Kyle Boller when necessary, Cavanaugh could get a better sense of the game from up above.

Nolan had always been a press-box coordinator, too. But, concerned about the big plays the defense had fallen prey to in the exhibition season and in Cleveland, he had decided to move downstairs for the Steelers game. "Normally I think you need to be upstairs, you see the game better from there," he said. "I like to joke that the only coordinators who work from the sidelines are the ones trying to get on TV to get head jobs. But I thought being down there, where I could communicate more directly with the guys, particularly Ray, since I talk to him so much during the game anyway, might not be a bad idea."

The new plan had worked well against the Steelers except for one miscommunication in the first half. Billick had challenged a catch made by the Steelers. When the challenge was upheld and the ball came back, Nolan wanted different players on the field. He asked Billick about calling time-out and thought Billick said okay. So he called time-out. The next thing he knew, Billick was screaming at him for calling time-out. By game's end, everyone was laughing about it — as is frequently the case when Billick explodes on the sideline. Most of the time he directs his anger at Gary Zauner, whom he has known the longest among his coaches and who tends to say things that might cause an explosion. Billick yells at Zauner so frequently that when Zauner's contract had come up for renegotiation a year earlier, Zauner put in a clause that allowed him to wear headphones to the press box that covered *both* ears at all times. Most coaches just cover one ear so they can hear what is going on around them. Zauner didn't want to hear what was going on — or what was being yelled in his direction.

The two games after Pittsburgh — Cincinnati and Kansas City — had gone so poorly for the defense that Nolan decided to end the sideline experiment and go back upstairs for the Redskins game. All had gone well that night, so he was back upstairs for the Buffalo game. The coaches' box is always a tight fit, regardless of the stadium. The Ravens' offensive coaches — Cavanaugh, Wade Harman, and Jedd Fisch — sat on the left side of the front row, with the defensive coaches — Nolan, Dennis Thurman, Mike Pettine, and Phil Zacharias — to their right. Bennie Thompson, the special teams assistant, sat behind them with his own phone and headset. Three seats separated Cavanaugh and Nolan, and since both men were almost always on headsets to the sideline, they rarely spoke while the game was going on.

With Jamal Lewis not in uniform, Cavanaugh — with Billick's approval — had tweaked the offensive game plan to throw the ball more often, even if a lot of the play calls were for short passes. Midway through the second quarter, after the defense had spent a good deal of time on the field (in part because of Sanders's interception return for a touchdown that put the defense right back on the field), Cavanaugh opened a series with two straight passes. One was caught for no gain, the other was incomplete. Chester Taylor then picked up a first down with a 12-yard run. On first down Boller again threw incomplete on another short route, this one to Musa Smith. That was it for Nolan.

"What the hell are you doing!" he screamed at Cavanaugh, who wasn't even certain at first that Nolan was yelling at him. Nolan went into a profane rant — out of character for him — screaming about giving the defense some rest and making calls that were best suited (in his mind) for the Ravens' offense. "Pass, pass, pass, what the f—— are you thinking?" he said. He continued in that vein for a couple more sentences before finally sitting down. By then, Cavanaugh knew that Nolan was talking to him and knew what he was saying.

"I was surprised," he said later. "And, yeah, sure, I was hurt. You don't expect that kind of thing from one of your own guys. I mean, we're all trying to win the game together. I didn't say anything, because I didn't think it would help anything if I did. But at that moment I was certainly a little bit steamed, to say the least."

The other coaches were stunned. Wade Harman, perhaps the gentlest soul among the coaches, was as white as a sheet, embarrassed and upset by what he had heard. The other defensive coaches didn't know what to say. They couldn't tell Cavanaugh, "Hey, just ignore him, you're doing fine," and, in effect, contradict their boss.

The person most upset with Nolan was Nolan. "I've been on the other side," he said. "I've been in Matt's shoes, been on the side of the ball that wasn't performing as well as everyone wanted it to perform. If anyone should have known better than to do something like that, it's me. But I didn't. I was frustrated and I let it out and took it out on Matt. I was out of line. Way out of line."

This was the stacking that Billick had been concerned about. There were several areas in which he thought he saw it: Boller was getting more and more heat each week, Jamal Lewis was dealing with the drug conviction, Chris McAlister had been dealing with his contract (Billick hoped that was now behind him), and the coaches — all of them — were thinking about their future. Which Billick could understand, because he had been an assistant coach once, too, and he had been a coordinator wondering when his chance to be a head coach was going to come.

"We went 15-1 the last year I was a coordinator," he said. "That made it a lot easier for me. I had two coordinators worried about next year — Matt's wondering if he's going to keep his job; Mike's hoping he can get another job. Rex Ryan's twin brother just became a coordinator [in Oakland], and he wants to know when he gets his chance. I had already told Phil [Zacharias] that he needed to look for another job at the end of the season and a couple of the other guys knew they were on the bubble and their future might depend on how we did. That can create a lot of tension."

Now the tension had exploded. When Billick heard what had happened, he decided to say nothing to Nolan — at least for the moment. "Mike's a bright guy and he's a guy who knows right from wrong," he said. "I was guessing — hoping — he'd do the right thing."

As soon as Nolan got home from the Bills game, Kathy, his wife, could tell something was wrong. His defense had dominated the game, and the look on his face was more what she would have expected after a 40–10 loss. He told her what had happened. She wondered if it had been as bad as he thought; perhaps Cavanaugh hadn't heard all or most of the rant. Nolan knew better. "He had to hear," he said. Then he went to bed and didn't sleep for most of the night.

The next morning he was in his office, getting ready to break down tape of the Buffalo game and start working on a game plan for the Eagles. Pettine and Thurman came in to ask about practice plans for the week. Nolan asked them to sit down for a minute.

"What happened yesterday in the box," he said. "Do you think I should apologize to Matt or just let it go?"

They both answered at once: "Apologize."

The way they answered erased any doubt Nolan might have had about what to do next. He walked down the hall to Cavanaugh's office. The lights were out and the offensive staff was in the room watching the Buffalo game tape. Nolan knew the entire offensive staff would know by now what had happened, so their presence didn't bother him.

"Matt, I wanted to apologize for yesterday," Nolan said. "I was out of line. I shouldn't have said what I said under any circumstances, but I certainly shouldn't have said it while you're trying to call a game. I'm really sorry."

Cavanaugh, sitting behind his desk, had stopped the tape when Nolan walked in. "I appreciate it, Mike," he said. "It's really good of you to come down here and say that. Thanks."

There were no hugs or even handshakes. Nolan was probably in Cavanaugh's office for less than a minute. He walked out feeling better. Cavanaugh felt better, too. The air had been cleared. But the tension wasn't likely to go away anytime soon.

It was bound to be a tense week under any circumstances. The game with the Eagles had been metaphorically circled since the day in March when the special master had urged the league to make the deal that landed Terrell Owens in Philadelphia, not Baltimore. The loss in the exhibition game, especially with Owens catching the 81-yard touchdown pass to start the game, had stung, but everyone knew that, ultimately, it was completely meaningless. This game would have plenty of meaning. The Eagles were 6-0, one of two undefeated teams remaining in the league. The other was the New England Patriots, who had extended their league-record winning streak to twenty-one games and were going into Pittsburgh to play the Steelers — who had not lost since their trip to Baltimore. If the Ravens and Patriots could win on the road, the Ravens would be tied for first place with the Steelers in the AFC North. If both home teams won, the Steelers would have a two-game lead over the Ravens. The consensus in the Ravens' locker room was that the Steelers were about to find out what it was like playing against one of the NFL's big boys.

Then again, the Ravens were also playing one of the NFL's big boys — and they were doing it without Jamal Lewis, without Todd Heap, and, as Billick had suspected the minute he went down, without Jonathan Ogden. The diagnosis was pretty close to what everyone had expected as soon as Ogden reached back and grabbed his left leg: a tear in his hamstring, meaning he would be out at least two weeks. As a result, Ethan Brooks would be playing in his place against a defense that probably blitzed more than any in the NFL.

Billick is a major movie buff who often likens real-life situations to movies he has seen. "This is like the scene in *Apollo 13*," he said, sitting in his office just before practice on Wednesday. "The guy starts throwing all sorts of stuff on his desk and he says to his people, 'Find something in here that will give them air up there.' We've got to throw everything we have on the desk and figure out a way to beat the Eagles."

One thing was certain: good play from only one side of the ball wasn't going to be enough. Donovan McNabb was having an MVP season at quarterback, unless — as many people believed — Owens was the MVP. They had become the most dangerous deep-passing combination in the league. With Jamal Lewis out, the offense was going to have to be able to move the ball through the air to keep the Philadelphia defense honest. Which meant that Kyle Boller had to play well — something he had not done for several weeks.

All of Boller's coaches — Billick, Matt Cavanaugh, and Jim Fassel — were searching for ways to jump-start his confidence. On Monday, Cavanaugh told Boller he would like him to take the lead in the Saturday night tape sessions. Normally on Saturdays, Cavanaugh would take the players through a dozen or so key plays on tape, calling out questions to players about blocking schemes or what coverage the defense was in or what a player's responsibility was on a given call. Cavanaugh wanted Boller to take over that role: in part to remind everyone that he was the team's offensive leader, in part to make him feel more involved in the game plan, and in part to let Boller know that no one was doubting his leadership of the team. Boller liked the idea.

To back that up, Billick called Boller in to tell him that regardless of what he heard or read, no one was giving any thought to changing quarterbacks. "If you're ever on the bubble as far as starting goes, you'll hear it from me, not from anyone else," Billick told him. "You aren't on the bubble, you aren't even close to being on the bubble. I know you can play better, and so do you. But there isn't any doubt in my mind that you're our quarterback and there shouldn't be any doubt in yours."

Boller told Billick there hadn't been any doubt in his mind, but he appreciated the reinforcement.

Last but not least came Fassel. Boller had already become close to Fassel because, unlike Billick and Cavanaugh, Fassel concerned himself only with

Boller. On Monday, Fassel suggested they go to dinner, get away from the facility and all the prying eyes, and just talk football and whatever else was on Boller's mind. Boller liked that idea. They went to a Ruth's Chris Steak House not far from Owings Mills and sat in a private room. Fassel ordered a bottle of red wine and they talked.

Alone with Fassel, Boller felt he could open up. He didn't think people were being fair to him, especially the now-growing list of people wondering why Ben Roethlisberger was racking up wins and putting up numbers as a rookie that were outshining Boller's as a second-year player. Roethlisberger was actually older than Boller by several months. More important, he was throwing to high-quality receivers with great speed: Hines Ward, Plaxico Burress, and Antwaan Randle El.

"I really thought coming into the season that TT [Travis Taylor] and I were going to have a big year together," Boller said. "And I knew that Todd would catch a lot of balls. Then they both get hurt. Don't people understand that?"

Many people didn't understand that. Boller was throwing to Kevin Johnson, who had great hands but had trouble getting open; backup tight end Terry Jones, who was a solid player and an excellent blocker but nowhere near the receiver Heap was; Randy Hymes, who had improved greatly but was still very inexperienced; and now the rookie Clarence Moore, who was becoming more important to the offense with each passing week.

"Not exactly anyone who resembles T.O. in that group, is there?" Fassel said.

"They're are all good guys and they're all working their butts off," Boller said. "But I can't remember the last time I had an easy throw, you know, one where the guy is so wide-open, there's no way I can mess it up."

"You have to be perfect almost all the time," Fassel said.

Boller laughed. "And, as anyone in town will tell you, I'm far from perfect."

They each drank a glass of red wine and looked forward to better things.

There was one piece of good news during the week: the Ravens and Jonathan Ogden had worked out what he expected to be his last contract. Ogden had turned thirty on the first weekend of training camp and had told the team he wanted one final long-term contract that would carry him to the end of his career. Even though he had now been injured twice during the season, the Ravens still figured Ogden was about as good a long-term risk as anyone in the game. He had been durable throughout most of his career, he kept himself in excellent shape, and he was one of those rare players they knew would never get into any kind of trouble. The deal was for seven years and $50 million. What was most significant to Ogden was the $20 million signing bonus because that money was up front and guaranteed.

Ogden has a way of carrying himself as if the weight of the world (like carrying 345 pounds isn't enough) is always on his shoulders. The most frequent answer he gives to people who ask how he's feeling is one word: *tired.* Whenever Ogden was asked to do something by the marketing or public relations people, he would roll his eyes, shrug his shoulders, and say, "Well, if you really need me . . ." And then he would do it. When word about his new deal spread, Ogden was universally congratulated. There wasn't anyone who didn't think he deserved the money and the extension.

Of course, Ogden found a dark cloud in his financial silver lining: "Now I *really* can't vote for John Kerry," he said, smiling.

The presidential election was a topic of conversation among some of the Ravens that week. Most of the players were either neutral, not interested, or Republican, like many Americans in the upper tax brackets. Ogden tended to lean more left than most of his teammates and was no fan of George W. Bush. "I can't possibly vote for him," he said. "I voted for Al Gore in 2000 even though I knew he'd raise my taxes, because he's an old St. Albans guy like me. I probably wasn't going to vote either way before this [the new contract]. Now I can't possibly vote for Kerry because he'll absolutely raise my taxes. I guess I'll have to sit this one out."

Most professional athletes aren't even registered to vote. Those who are almost always vote Republican. The most rabid Democrat on the Ravens was backup linebacker Bart Scott, who spent a lot of time in the locker room trying (to no avail) to convince some of his teammates that voting based strictly on who would tax you less was a mistake. He was shouted down most of the time, especially by those who somehow saw not supporting Bush as not supporting the troops overseas.

Billick supported Bush, partly because of taxes but also because of an interesting theory he had developed about the war in Iraq: "We need Bush in there to get us out of Iraq," he said. "He got us in, he's the best person to get us out."

Kevin Byrne liked to say that this was undoubtedly the kind of thinking that had caused Billick to vote for Jesse Ventura, the wrestling star, when he ran for governor of Minnesota. To his credit, Billick encouraged his players to vote — and did not try to tell them whom to vote for.

Most of the players weren't listening to any of the speeches given by either Bush or Kerry that week, but they were listening to speeches. Billick gave his on Wednesday morning.

"This is the kind of game where you can make an impression in a big-time way," he said. "You don't do it by beating Buffalo last week and, let's face it, you don't do it by beating Cleveland next week, even though it's important to win those games. This is the game you do it in.

"Gary Baxter, you want a big-time contract, this is the game to prove you deserve it; Mike Nolan, you want a head coaching job — this is the game people will notice; Gary Zauner, you want to walk in and demand to be paid like John Harbaugh [the Eagles special teams coach who made $350,000 a year], show me you deserve it in *this* game. You guys who think you're Pro Bowlers — this is the game to prove it."

Unlike a lot of coaches, Billick has no problem with the notion of singling certain games out as special. He has never taken the approach that "this game is our biggest of the season because it's the next one on the schedule." Beating the Eagles would be a bigger deal than beating the Bills or the Redskins or the Bengals. Beating Pittsburgh was turning out to be more important than they had realized — although any win over the Steelers was significant — but knocking off a 6-0 team on the road would reestablish the Ravens as one of the league's elite teams.

Ray Lewis felt some of that. He also felt as if the team wasn't as close-knit six games into the season as it should be. Even putting aside the Nolan blowup, he wanted to make certain there wasn't any finger-pointing from defense to offense or within the team at all. He talked to Ed Reed about some of his concerns on Thursday night and then went to Billick on Friday before practice to ask if he could speak to the team after practice. The question was really rhetorical: when Lewis wanted to talk to the team, he knew he pretty much had carte blanche to go ahead and talk. But he always asked Billick first, if for no other reason than to make sure he didn't catch him off-guard.

Practice on Friday was indoors — the weather was miserable again. When it was over, Lewis asked everyone to stay on the field for an extra minute. Whenever Lewis speaks to the team, his voice is considerably different than in the locker room when he is getting himself into game mode. The intensity is still there and so is the emotion, but his voice is soft, sometimes soft enough that those not standing or sitting close to him have to lean forward to hear him.

"We have a chance to do something special this week," he said. "This is our time to start making a real mark, to let people know how good we are. But if we are going to do that, we have to do it *together*. We cannot succeed as individuals, we can only succeed together. We need to be looking forward now, not back. What's happened up until now is over, it's gone. There's no reason to think about it or worry about it. There's nothing we can do about what was good or about what was bad. It's over. We're about today, tomorrow, and what comes after that. We can't be talking amongst ourselves about lacking offense or not making plays or not making calls. The defense needs the offense, the offense needs the defense, and we all need the special teams. This kind of chance doesn't come around very often. Let's take advantage of it. Let's do something special. Let's do it together."

They all listened intently when Lewis spoke. Perhaps it is all those Sunday mornings in church, but he sounds almost like a southern preacher when he talks to the team. There isn't usually any screaming or yelling or wringing of hands or calling for help from the heavens — that comes on Sundays in the locker room. But there is a sense that he is a true believer talking to other true believers. When it comes to Lewis's leadership, there is no doubt that the Ravens are true believers.

One of Lewis's flock was missing as he spoke. Outside, in the rain, Jamal Lewis worked out on his own. He would watch the game on TV on Sunday. He would be back with the team on Monday.

Halloween morning in Philadelphia was extremely warm and bright, the rain swept away. The square that surrounds City Hall was alive with people early, many of them already decked out in Eagles jerseys. The entire town appeared to be green and white. One couple stood in front of the plaque commemorating the fact that Mother's Day had been invented in

Philadelphia in 1908. He wore a number 5 jersey (McNabb); she wore 81 (T.O.). At the stadium, it would appear from the sidelines as if half the crowd of 67,715 was similarly dressed.

It felt more like September than the last day of October. The game-time temperature was 73 degrees, and it felt warmer in the sunshine on the field. In the locker room Ray Lewis was directing his pregame message at one person: Kyle Boller. "This is *your* day," he screamed at Boller. "These people are in for a major surprise. *Your day*. Remember that." He clapped Boller on the shoulder pads. Boller stared back at him blankly, not sure how to respond.

The toughest thing about playing in Philadelphia as the road team might be waiting for the endless pregame introductions. First there's the Eagles fight song. Then, of course, the theme from *Rocky* has to be played. Then come the fireworks (yes, in the daytime). And finally, the PA announcer stretches the name of each Eagle out for what feels like about a minute.

When the game finally kicked off, the Ravens got off to a brutal beginning. Trying to make something happen right away, the offense came out with Deion Sanders lined up as a receiver on the first play from scrimmage. Using Sanders as a decoy, Boller tried to throw deep to Travis Taylor, hoping to mimic the start the Eagles had gotten on the same field in August. It didn't work. Cornerback Lito Sheppard read the play all the way and broke it up. Two plays later Jevon Kearse beat Orlando Brown cleanly, sacked Boller, and caused a fumble. Fortunately, Brown was there to jump on the ball for a 7-yard loss.

Zastudil punted to the Eagles' 42, but Musa Smith was called for a personal foul on the play, setting the Eagles up on the Ravens' 43. On the Eagles' second play, McNabb tried to throw deep to Owens. Ed Reed rolled back in coverage to help Chris McAlister and intercepted the ball. But the official saw McAlister turn away from the ball, trying to fight Owens for it, and called him for interference. Instead of a turnover, the Eagles got the ball on the Ravens' 4-yard line. That made one sack, one fumble, and 54 yards in penalties with the game less than two minutes old. The defense stopped them there, though, and forced the Eagles to settle for a field goal, a major moral victory at that moment.

The Ravens pieced together an eleven-play drive midway through the quarter that ended with Stover kicking a 44-yard field goal that tied the game. The Eagles appeared ready to take the lead back when they drove to the Ravens' 5-yard line with a first-and-goal. But McNabb was hit hard by Ed Hartwell as he tried to cross the goal line and he fumbled. Will Demps jumped on the ball at the 1, averting the threat. The Eagles did take a 6–3 lead a few minutes later on a 41-yard field goal by David Akers but a three-point deficit at halftime didn't seem so bad. In most games, the Eagles had blown the opponent off the field in the first half. Mike Nolan had talked to the defense about withstanding their early attempts to make big plays and blow the game open. They had done that.

Boller had been efficient in the short passing game (14-of-17), and the defense had stopped McNabb on several key plays. Billick was animated at halftime. The game was being played the way it needed to be for his team to have a chance. "This is a big-time football game, guys," he said. "Let's keep it at our speed and our tempo." Nolan reminded the defense not to worry if the Eagles made a play. "We'll make the next one," he said. "Just don't catch yourself lingering after the play. Get back up and get ready for the next one."

The third quarter was a punting contest until the Eagles took over with 2:19 left at their own 16 and, as Nolan had known they would eventually, made a couple of plays. McNabb found Owens for 24 yards to the 40. Then he hit Chad Lewis for 10 yards and was helped out by another personal foul on the Ravens, this one on Maake Kemoeatu. McNabb then scrambled 13 yards for another first down, at the Ravens' 22. Again the defense — not lingering — dug in and forced an Akers field goal. It was 9–3 with a quarter to play.

The offense had been moving the ball all day but stalling when it got near scoring range. This time it moved quickly from the Baltimore 20 to a first down at the Eagles' 39 on a pretty Boller-to-Travis Taylor pass, good for 21 yards. But on first down, Chester Taylor, trying to push forward for an extra yard or two, fumbled. The Eagles recovered and the stadium, which had been nervous all day while the Ravens continued to hang around, got very loud.

It got louder. McNabb found Owens. Then he hit tight end L. J. Smith for 17 yards over the middle, a play Nolan had been concerned about all week because the defense had to pay so much attention to the outside receivers. It looked as if the Ravens would hold the Eagles to yet another field goal — which would still give them a two-score lead — when McNabb threw two incomplete passes from the 11. But on third down McNabb threw a short slant over the middle to Owens. He made the catch, dodged Baxter, twisted to the outside, and ducked past Reed into the end zone for a killing touchdown. The place went crazy. It went even crazier seconds later when Owens began to dance. End zone dances are a dime a dozen in the NFL, but this wasn't just *any* dance. This was an on-the-money, step-for-step imitation of the dance Ray Lewis does when he is introduced in Baltimore. Clearly Owens had studied tape of Lewis in preparation for this moment, and he carried it off perfectly.

Not everyone in the stadium knew what he was doing, but the Ravens did. Even without the music of Nelly, they knew exactly what they were seeing. They were not happy about it. They were also not happy to be down 15–3 (the Eagles went for two and failed) with 9:12 left in the game. Boller and the offense gamely came back and drove 72 yards, the key play coming on a leaping catch by Clarence Moore, good for 52 yards. Boller found Dan Wilcox for the touchdown from seven yards out, and with 5:52 still left, they were back in the game again, down 15–10. Perhaps Owens's dance had been a bit premature. The game clearly wasn't over.

The Ravens had two more chances. The defense held the Eagles to three-and-out, and the offense, starting from the 19, picked up one first down before stalling. Billick elected to punt with 2:01 left, hoping to use his time-outs — and the two-minute warning — to get the ball back in decent field position one last time. The strategy worked. The defense held, and the Ravens got the ball back at the 29 with 1:34 left. This was Boller's chance to be a hero back in Baltimore. This was the chance to do something special that they had talked about all week. On the sideline, Ray Lewis knelt on one knee, propping himself up with his helmet, and screamed at Boller: "Come on, cowboy, grow up right now! This is the time. Grow up, son! Be a star right now!"

Boller certainly tried. On first down he found Travis Taylor streaking across the middle for 23 yards into Eagles' territory at the 48. Quickly, he spiked the ball to stop the clock with 1:18 to go. A nervous rumble went through the stands. On second down Boller's pass to Chester Taylor was tipped. Third-and-10. He tried to force a pass into Kevin Johnson. It was broken up. Fourth down. Last chance. Boller dropped, scrambled to avoid pressure, and found Travis Taylor open inside the 30. The pass, thrown on the run, wasn't perfect, just a tad behind Taylor. But it was a catchable ball, the kind of pass a team's best wide receiver should make — has to make. Taylor had it, bobbled it, and dropped it as he was hit. If he had held on, they would have been on the Eagles' 25 with a minute still left. That certainly was a long way from the end zone, but the game would have appeared eminently winnable.

Now it was over. McNabb knelt twice to run out the clock. The camera crews made a beeline for Owens as soon as the clock hit zero. So did Corey Fuller. "You need to grow up, T.O.," he screamed. "Act like a man when you make a play. Your act is low-rent."

Actually his act was very high paying, and right now it was a huge success. The Eagles were 7-0. The Ravens were 4-3. Lewis wasn't going to be drawn into a verbal war with Owens. "If we didn't let him get in the end zone," he said, "he wouldn't have had the chance to do the dance."

Billick wasn't really concerned about T.O.'s dance. In fact, he was a lot more concerned about the two missed tackles on the play that had led to the touchdown. He was drained. Before speaking to the team, he made a point of shaking hands with Boller and telling him how proud he was of the way he had played. In the end, Boller hadn't pulled the game out, but in many ways he had grown up. He had completed 24 of 38 passes, many of them while running for his life. His only interception had come at the end of the first half on a Hail Mary into the end zone. He had put the ball where Taylor should have been able to catch it on the last drive.

"I feel like we just lost a playoff game," Billick told the team, his voice hoarse from yelling over the crowd most of the day. "If that's one of the best teams in the NFL — and I think it is — then we are, too. We came in here without some key people and we had a hell of a chance to win that game. Maybe we'll see them again. I hope that we do."

With good reason. The only way to see them again would be in Jacksonville on February 6. That was the day of the Super Bowl.

20

Second Chance

ALTHOUGH THERE WAS A LOT to feel good about as the Ravens boarded their chartered train for the trip home to Baltimore, it didn't change the fact that they were now 4-3. What's more, when they got home they learned that the Steelers had ended the Patriots' winning streak with a 34–20 victory. That meant the Steelers were 6-1 and had a two-game lead in the division race. The season would be halfway over in a week. The Browns were coming to Baltimore for a rematch of opening day. A loss to the Eagles was disappointing but understandable. A second loss to the Browns would be an unmitigated disaster.

Billick was concerned that there might be an emotional letdown during the week because they had put so much into the Eagles game. He had planned to remind the players after practice on Wednesday that the loss to Cleveland counted just as much in the standings as the loss to Philadelphia, but the team practiced so well that he decided he didn't need to say anything. "Historically, we've played well at home after playing poorly against a team on the road," he said. "I was afraid there might be some hangover after Philadelphia, but there wasn't."

For the third time in five games, the Ravens were playing at night. The game was an ESPN Sunday night game, a rare chance for a team like the Browns to play on national TV. The game would also mark Jamal Lewis's return to the lineup. Chester Taylor had played well in his absence, but with Lewis back, Billick and Matt Cavanaugh were hoping — even with Ogden still out — to pound the ball more and pass the ball less. No one was looking forward to that more than Lewis, who had been unhappy with the way the first Cleveland game had evolved and was, needless to say, eager to get back on the field and show people that his three-week break had not affected him.

"Watching on TV just about killed me," he said. "I knew I could have helped if I had been there."

Lewis had missed the start of the Buffalo game the week before because he had been in Atlanta and had failed to realize that a game between Baltimore and Buffalo wasn't likely to be televised there. "I never even thought about it," he said, laughing. "I turned on the TV at one o'clock and our game wasn't on. I never got the satellite package down there because I'm not there during the season, so why do I need it? I had to call a friend who had the satellite and go over to his house and watch."

He might have been better off not watching the Eagles game. Now he was back on the practice field and happy to be there. The news on the other two injured offensive stars — Jonathan Ogden and Todd Heap — wasn't as good. Heap had now missed five games and still wasn't close to being ready to play. The local radio shows were filled with callers who wanted to know why it was taking so long for a sprained ankle to heal. Heap was just as frustrated as the callers. "I can't believe it's taking this long," he said. "When it first happened and they said it wasn't broken, I was relieved. Now the doctors are telling me I might have been back faster if it had just been a clean break." Ogden had known the minute he got hurt that he would be out for at least two weeks. He had set the game in New York against the Jets on November 14 as his target date to return. Watching practice on Wednesday, he shook his head when the possibility of playing against the Jets came up. "I still can't touch my toes with my left hand," he said. "Every time I try to do it, the leg grabs up on me. I don't see it happening."

Ethan Brooks had played well against the Eagles, holding his own for most of the afternoon. There were other questions on the offensive line, though, especially on the right side. Orlando Brown, who had been riding an emotional roller coaster since July, had played that way: up and down. He had broken a finger early in the Buffalo game and had struggled all day, then had a predictably tough time in Philadelphia against the Eagles All-Pro Jevon Kearse. Bennie Anderson, who lined up next to him at right guard, was also having difficulty. Mike Flynn was finally ready to be activated, but with Casey Rabach playing so well at center and Anderson struggling, the plan was to get Flynn snaps at Anderson's spot.

This was an uncomfortable situation for all three men. Rabach and Flynn were best friends. They lockered next to each other and spent time with each other away from the field. Flynn was where Rabach wanted to be: locked into a four-year contract worth an average of more than $1 million a year — in addition to the $1 million signing bonus he had received. This was Rabach's year to prove that he was worthy of that kind of money, and he was in the process of doing just that. Deep down, he knew that he was probably going to have to go to another team to get paid the kind of money he was proving he was worth. The Ravens had already made a financial commitment to Flynn and didn't think Rabach was worth big money as a guard. Like Flynn, his best position was center. Rabach had been a third-round draft pick out of Wisconsin in 2001 and had patiently waited for his chance to be a starter. He had expected to compete with Anderson in training camp at the right guard spot, but that competition had come to a halt when Flynn got hurt.

Anderson was one of the most popular members of the team. He was one of the last survivors from the late, unlamented XFL, having played for the Chicago Enforcers in 2001. He had tried out briefly with the St. Louis Rams — his hometown team — after graduating from Tennessee State in 2000. "Didn't even make it to camp," he said. "They cut me in July before camp started. Needless to say, I didn't feel as if I really got a chance."

He spent the fall working out and coaching before signing with the XFL, where he was paid $40,000 for the season as a starter. That spring, looking for "camp bodies," Ravens offensive line coach Jim Colletto invited him in for a tryout. Every player who signs with a team as a "camp body" does so convinced that he will catch the eye of the coaches and make the team. Anderson proved to be one of those rare exceptions. He not only made the team, he became a starter and had become a mainstay. He had signed a two-year contract in 2003 and was hoping that 2004 would put him in a position to get a long-term deal with a big signing bonus. It had not gone that way so far. Whether his problems were being caused by Brown having a tough time playing next to him or because defensive linemen had figured him out was tough to say.

In any event, Flynn's return and Rabach's play at center meant that his playing time was likely to shrink over the next few weeks. Naturally, Anderson wasn't thrilled with that likelihood. Flynn was less than delighted with playing out of position and sharing time. Rabach simply felt uncomfortable because he knew his two friends were not happy.

"In a lot of ways this has been the toughest season I've ever had in football," Flynn said. "When I was young and still trying to prove myself, being on special teams or not starting was part of the deal and I understood it. I didn't want it to stay that way, but I understood it. Now I'm being paid all this money and it kills me that I can't go out and play the way they expect me to play. I know I've been injured and people understand that. Being in here the first seven weeks, seeing the guys getting ready to go play, and knowing I can't play has been brutal. My wife finally told me one night that I just had to calm down and not let it bother me so much."

Flynn was going through what many athletes experience when they are injured or when age has cut back on their playing time. He was *in* the locker room but didn't feel as if he was *of* the locker room. "It isn't as if the guys aren't friendly and encouraging, they are," Flynn said. "But the fact is, when you're hurt, you aren't part of the team. You aren't taking part in practices the way everyone else is. You aren't getting ready to play a game the way the other guys are. You feel almost invisible when you're in the locker room. I can't stand feeling that way."

One reason for Flynn's success is his intensity. In today's NFL he is a small offensive lineman at six-three, 305, although about average for a center. Before games, he would roam the locker room, headphones on, talking to himself, taking deep breaths to get himself ready to play. By nature Flynn was outgoing and friendly. On game days he was not someone to be trifled with. Moving to guard would make him one of the smaller players in the league at that position — by comparison, Anderson and Edwin Mulitalo each weighed 345 — and would put him at a position where he had little experience. He understood what the coaches were thinking, but it didn't make it any easier for him.

Everyone on the team had become concerned about the offensive line. In 2003 it had been one of the team's great strengths. Ogden had been his normal unbeatable self, Flynn had become one of the league's better centers, Mulitalo had become a player worthy of Pro Bowl consideration, and Anderson and Brown had been very solid. They had been healthy almost the entire season, and when one of them had been nicked, Rabach and Ethan Brooks had played well in backup roles.

This year the line had been in flux since the start of camp. Brown had been understandably distracted by his mother's death, Flynn had gotten hurt, Ogden had now been hurt twice, and neither Mulitalo nor Anderson had been the same player as a year earlier — perhaps because of what was going on around them. No one was exactly sure how Flynn's return would affect the play of the line. It should help — a good player returning to the lineup. But he was coming back to an unfamiliar position, and his presence could — almost surely would — create doubts in Anderson's mind, not only about the present but about the future. The Ravens needed to be able to run the football, especially in the second half of the season, when they would play the Jets, Patriots, Colts, and Steelers — arguably the four best teams in the AFC (they hoped other than themselves) — during the season's final eight weeks.

"I'm not exactly sure where any of them are mentally right now," Jim Colletto said of his players when the coaches met after the Eagles game. "We just have to keep mixing and matching until we find the best combination."

Not exactly the way you wanted to feel about your offensive line halfway through the season.

Playing at night is a mixed blessing for a football team. Players and coaches like the idea that they are playing in the only game going on at that moment; that, even on Sunday, a lot of the league and most of the country is watching them. There's a different feeling in the stadium at night. It isn't like a one o'clock game on Sunday, when fans roll out of bed to head downtown for their tailgates. They've had all day to get ready, they've probably had more to drink at their tailgates, and the fact that the game is on national television adds an extra bit of tingle.

The flip side is the waiting. Players like to wake up and get ready to play. Most are accustomed to early-afternoon kickoffs, which mean eating a pregame meal, getting to the stadium, getting in uniform, going through pregame drills, and then *playing*. There really isn't much time to accumulate pent-up energy or to think about the game. "You have to wake up ready to get right at it," Billick often says on the night before a one o'clock game. "You go from bed right to Jump Street."

That's not true with a night game. The day passes slowly. Some players watch other games on TV, others prefer not to. On the night of the Browns game, the Ravens already knew that the Steelers had beaten their second undefeated team in two weeks — this time it was the Eagles — by the time they began showing up at the Hyatt for the pregame meal. There is plenty of food available at the pregame meal: steaks, chicken, pasta, omelettes, lots of fruit, and, if someone asks, pancakes or waffles. Most players eat light, not so much because they are worried about having food in their stomachs at game time but because their nerves are too raw to eat very much. Many — if not most — football players have bad stomachs on game day.

The weather for Browns II was, again, close to perfect. "It's amazing how rarely we get bad weather here," Billick said as he crossed the Hamburg Street bridge, all the while giving his two walking companions grief about George W. Bush's victory over John Kerry the previous Tuesday. "Coming from Minnesota, it took me a while to get used to the notion that you could have a night like this in November."

Another Bush voter, Matt Stover ("I'm conservative economically, liberal socially," he liked to say) was, as always, one of the first Ravens on the field. "Now that Bush has been reelected, are you going to start collecting social security?" Browns punter Derrick Frost, a second-year player from Northern Iowa, asked Stover.

"Don't start with me, kid," Stover said, laughing. Frost was nine years old when Stover was an NFL rookie.

Kickers, punters, and long snappers are a cult in the NFL. They spend most of their time practicing apart from the rest of the team, and it is important that they get along because they spend so much time together. Because their jobs are so different from those of the rest of the team, they often have to look to one another for friendship and support and often become friendly with the kickers and long snappers on other teams since they all speak the same language. Stover could often be seen standing on the field three hours before kickoff, dispensing wisdom on subjects ranging from crosswinds to which flagpoles in the NFL could be trusted and which could not.

The pregame sidelines were alive with activity. Michael Phelps, the Olympic swimmer who had won six gold medals and eight medals in all in Athens, was on the field with his mother. He was scheduled to be introduced as the Ravens "twelfth man," an exciting prospect for him because he had grown up in Baltimore and was a Ravens fan. Phelps appeared completely at ease talking to players and coaches before the game. Two nights earlier he had been arrested and charged with driving under the influence. It was a mistake that far too many nineteen-year-olds make. The arrest would be big news and he would have to deal with being labeled some kind of drunk or miscreant even though he was a very good kid who had made a very bad mistake — one he readily admitted, without making any excuses. The police had agreed not to make the news public until Monday so Phelps could enjoy his moment running out of the tunnel with the Ravens.

As usual, the scouts congregated on the sidelines, talking about the college games they had seen that week. By now, Phil Savage and Eric DeCosta had each seen almost twenty college games apiece — picking up extra games by going to weeknight games and occasionally seeing a day-night doubleheader — in addition to numerous practice sessions. The draft was still more than six months away, but already the scouts were putting together a draft board, at least in their heads.

"I'll go out on a limb right now and say our first pick will be Dan Cody," DeCosta said. "Linebacker from Oklahoma. Our kind of kid."

Phil Savage wasn't even certain he would be in the Ravens' draft room in April. As he always did, he stood as close to the field as he could while the teams went through their pregame drills, watching the opposing team's players warm up. "You never know who will be available at some point in the future," he said. "You can always pick something up watching how a player gets ready for a game." He might have been watching the Browns a little more closely than he watched most teams. Since the euphoria of their opening-day win over the Ravens, the Browns had struggled. They were 3-4 and the whispers about Butch Davis's future had grown louder. Since Davis was one of those coaches who also controlled personnel decisions, his departure from Cleveland would probably mean the Browns would need a general manager. Savage would be at the top of anyone's list if a general manager's job opened up.

There was one pregame problem that had to be dealt with: Deion

Sanders's towel. Sanders was penciled into the offensive game plan and was also probably going to be back on a couple of kicks. He had a towel tucked into his belt so he could keep his hands dry throughout the game, something a lot of players do. Because a lot of players do it, the NFL (surprise) has a rule on how big the towel can be: six inches in length is the maximum. Knowing the NFL Big Brothers would be looking over his shoulder because of the game being on national TV, Bruce Laird had told Jeff Friday during pregame drills that Sanders's towel was two inches too long. Friday sighed and found Sanders in the locker room to tell him the towel was too long. Sanders sighed, got some scissors, and cut the towel by two inches. Crisis averted.

In the meantime, Corey Fuller was in full rant. Fuller's role with the team was one that seemed to shift from week to week. In many ways he was one of the team's respected elders because he had accomplished a good deal during his NFL career. But everyone — including Fuller — knew that the end of the season was going to bring a lot of change to Fuller's life. He was still with the Ravens in large part because of his close relationship with Billick and his friendship with Ray Lewis and Deion Sanders. The plan had been to move him to safety in preseason, but Dale Carter's illness and Sanders's on-again, off-again status had forced him to play cornerback. At thirty-three, he wasn't the player he had once been, which sometimes caused problems because he still thought of himself as someone who should be on the field more often than not. Mike Nolan saw him as more of a last resort.

There was no denying Fuller's passion for the game. Next to Lewis, he was the most verbal player in the locker room. Sometimes, when Lewis wasn't yelling at his teammates prior to a game, Fuller took up the baton. This was one of those nights. "Now, everyone in this room knows that we took these guys for granted the last time," he said, stalking around in a circle. "We better not do that tonight! We need to go out there and kick their butts on every single play! Every play! Everyone understand that?"

There was no response, so Fuller stalked over to Lewis, who was sitting in front of his locker, headphones on, listening to gospel music, as he often did before games. "Five-two, are you angry?" Fuller asked, addressing Lewis by his number (52) rather than name the way players often do. "I'm ready to hunt!" Lewis answered. "I'm ready to play football!"

"Y'all hear that!" Fuller barked. "Five-two is angry. We all might as well be angry!"

He was about to go on when Billick walked into the room. The Ravens were wearing black uniforms, a newly minted, third uniform that teams create nowadays as a marketing tool. "Our uniform color fits our mood," Billick said. "We owe these guys in a big-time way. Let's let them know that right away."

Any hope of that happening disappeared on the opening kickoff. Wade Richey's kick floated to Richard Alston at the 7. He started to his right, broke one tackle, then another, and then a third. While the message boards at either end of the stadium were still showing a picture of the Ravens' "Kickoff Kid of the Game," Alston was sprinting down the sideline for a 93-yard kickoff return. Fourteen seconds into the game, with many of the crowd still not in their seats, the Browns had a 7–0 lead. In a sense, Gary Zauner and his special teams players had seen this coming. On Saturday morning, sensing that a lot of people weren't paying serious attention during a tape session, Adalius Thomas and Bart Scott had called a players-only meeting for the special teamers. Apparently, there weren't a lot of people paying attention then, either. Alston's touchdown was more the result of poor tackling than anything brilliant either he or his blockers had done.

There was a good deal of anger on the bench after the touchdown. No one was any happier when the offense went three-and-out. The second series didn't start any better than the first. Boller tried to find Sanders on first down, but he was well covered and Boller had to throw the ball away with pressure coming. He took a hit, went down, and came up holding his shoulder. Behind the baby face, Boller is a physically tough player. He waved quickly to the bench to let trainers Bill Tessendorf and Mark Smith know he was okay. Kordell Stewart grabbed a ball and walked behind the bench to warm up, just in case. He had yet to take a snap all season. Two plays later, Boller completed a pass over the middle to Kevin Johnson and took a vicious hit from Kennard Lang after he released the ball. Lang was called for roughing the passer, and Boller popped back up to make sure everyone knew he was fine. The drive stalled soon after that, and Mr. Social Security came in and kicked a 44-yard field goal to make it 7–3.

In the meantime, Billick and Mike Nolan were conducting a lively dialogue on the headsets. Nolan and his coaches were using Sanders more and more each week. He had made a key interception against the Redskins and two more, including the one that turned the game around, against the Bills. He had played well against the Eagles. But with the passing game struggling and Sanders campaigning to play more on offense, Billick had given Cavanaugh the green light to use him. Each week there were a few more plays in the game plan for Sanders. "I just want to help," Sanders said. "I feel good. I'm only going to get a certain number of snaps on defense, why not let me help on offense?"

Nolan's answer to that was that he was too important to the defense to risk him on offense. Just as Gary Zauner was concerned with B. J. Sams breaking down because he was being given more chances on offense, Nolan worried that Sanders was more susceptible to injury being on the field more often, especially in a role he wasn't that familiar with. Seeing Sanders on the field with the offense, Nolan reminded Billick of his concerns about Sanders' being overused. "I heard you, Mike," Billick said. "We're keeping track of his snaps."

"I'm just worried that he's going to get hurt and we're going to be short on defense again," Nolan said.

"Mike, I'll tell you what I tell my wife in these situations," Billick said. "The first time you tell me something, I'm grateful for the reminder. The second time you bring it up, you're nagging me — and I don't like being nagged."

Nolan dropped the subject.

With or without Sanders, the offense struggled. Late in the first quarter, the Ravens started a series on their own 37 and on first down Boller dropped back to pass and got hit by Ebenezer Ekuban, who had beaten Orlando Brown with an outside rush. Boller fumbled and Ekuban recovered at the Ravens' 33. The defense stopped the Browns right there, but Phil Dawson came in and kicked a 50-yard field goal for a 10–3 lead. The boos — directed at the offense — were getting louder with each series.

The Ravens were able to get a field goal on their next drive, but not without a price. With a first down on the Browns' 28, Boller swung a quick pass in the flat to Sanders, who, seeing a little daylight, tried to take off before he secured the ball and dropped it. Sanders clapped his hands together in frustration, then reached down and grabbed his right foot in pain. He hobbled off the field and headed right to the bench, pulling his shoe off almost before Tessendorf or Andy Tucker and Leigh Ann Curl could get to him. He pulled off his sock and pointed at the second toe. A quick examination revealed a dislocation underneath the toe. Sanders asked the doctors if it was possible to tape it in such a way that it wouldn't slide and cause him pain when he tried to run or stop or cut. Neither doctor was terribly optimistic, but they agreed to try.

"He's going to see if he can run on it at halftime," Curl said. "But I think he's down for the night."

The only person who might have felt worse than Mike Nolan was Billick.

The rest of the half went better. The offense was able to move the ball, just not into the end zone. Stover kicked two more field goals, including a 36-yarder at the gun that gave the Ravens a 12–10 lead. The tension on the sideline was apparent in the last minute, when Zauner suggested that Billick call a time-out and Billick began screaming at him to let *him* worry about clock management. Zauner pulled his headset tighter and walked away.

Everyone was calm during the break. They had handed the Browns seven points to start the game but they were still ahead. The offense was moving the ball between the 20s, but not in the so-called red zone. The defense had been outstanding. The only piece of news during intermission wasn't good: Sanders tried to run on the sideline before the start of the second half, but as Curl had expected, the pain was too acute. He was through for the night.

The second half didn't start much better than the first. The Ravens picked up one first down before Zastudil had to punt from the Browns' 45. He lofted the ball toward the end zone and Ray Walls and Chad Williams sprinted after it, trying to down it inside the 5-yard line. Walls looked at Williams, Williams looked at Walls. Neither one of them seemed certain about who was supposed to make a dive for the ball. In the end, neither was able to get a hand on the ball and the Browns got the ball on the 20 after the touchback.

Zauner, who rarely screams during a game, was screaming as they came to the sideline: "Do you guys remember training camp?" he yelled. "Do you remember what we worked on? Do you remember talking about the need to communicate?"

No one scored in the third quarter, but the Browns, shut down all night, finally got a drive going that ate up more than eight minutes and culminated in Dawson kicking a 29-yard field goal forty-six seconds into the fourth quarter. Playing a game they had to win, against an opponent they believed they should dominate, the Ravens found themselves trailing, 13–12, with less than a quarter left to play.

Finally it was the struggling special teams that came through. After Dawson's field goal, the offense picked up two first downs before being stopped at the 48. Zastudil lofted another hanging punt in the direction of the goal line. This time Zauner inserted B. J. Sams, to take advantage of his speed. Sams ran the ball down on the 1-yard line and, leaping in the air so his feet wouldn't touch the goal line, batted the ball back toward the field of play. Chad Williams, a step behind him, downed it on the 1. Butch Davis challenged the play, claiming that Sams had his foot on the goal line when he knocked the ball backward. It took a while, but referee Walt Coleman finally ruled that the play stood, forcing the Browns to take over on their 1-yard line.

In Cleveland, in a similar situation — early fourth quarter, the game close, the Browns' offense backed up — the defense had surrendered a big play, giving the Browns control of the game. Now they dug in and gave up only one yard in three plays, bringing Frost into the game to punt from the very back of the end zone. Punters like to stand 14–15 yards behind the line of scrimmage to give themselves time to catch the ball, avoid the rush, and get the kick off smoothly. Frost had only 12 yards to the back of the end line, so he had to be careful. He had to move to his right to corral the snap, and with Ed Reed bearing down on him, he rushed the kick. It went right off the side of his foot, a clean shank, and flew out of bounds only 7 yards from the line of scrimmage. The offense was in business at the 9-yard line.

Cavanaugh wasn't going to try anything fancy at this stage, especially since a field goal would give the Ravens the lead. Jamal Lewis ran right for 4 yards. Then he ran left for 3 more. It was third-and-goal on the 2. This time Lewis went straight up the middle, diving into the end zone. With 7:07 left, the Ravens had the lead back, 18–13. This time, Billick had his math right, knowing that a one-point conversion would put them up by only six. If they could make a two-point conversion, a Browns touchdown and an extra point would only tie the score. He went for two, and succeeded — Boller finding Clarence Moore in the corner. In the midst of the celebration — one of relief as much as anything — everyone noticed a flag. Orlando Brown had allowed himself to get goaded into a personal foul. He was taking a painkiller for an arthritic knee and he had gotten hit in the eye — something he was obviously very sensitive to — and, even though he was wearing a protective face shield, felt pain and responded.

Billick had been lecturing the entire team on the subject of in-game discipline. They had been struggling with personal-foul calls all season. Now Brown's outburst would mean Wade Richey had to kick off from the 15-yard line after the 15-yard penalty. "For God's sake, Zeus, think out there!" Billick said as Brown came to the sideline. "When are you going to learn to keep your poise?!"

Angrily, Brown started to tell Billick what had happened. "I don't want to hear it now," Billick said. "You can't do that kind of stuff, you just can't."

"Fine, then," Brown snapped back. "I just won't play if you feel that way."

Billick followed Brown back to the bench "Listen to me, Zeus, you can't quit on us now. You can't let them play you for a chump. Get yourself calmed down."

The game was now in the hands of the defense.

Based on what had happened during the game's first fifty-three minutes, that should have been perfect for the Ravens. The Browns' offense had not been in the end zone yet and it needed a touchdown to tie. The penalty helped them, Alston returning Richey's kick to the 41. Jeff Garcia picked up a third-and-10 with a sideline pass to Frisman Jackson. Then he picked up a third-and-3, pulling the ball down and running up the middle to the Ravens' 35. Another quick-hitter to Antonio Bryant got the ball to the 21. Three plays later, on third-and-9, Garcia scrambled away from the rush and found Bryant again for a first-and-goal at the 5. The clock was down to 1:24. Running back Lee Suggs got nothing on first down. The clock ticked under a minute. Garcia dropped back again and looked over the middle for tight end Aaron Shea.

Anticipating a possible pass over the middle, Ray Lewis had dropped back to the goal line in coverage. He had told Ed Reed to cover the back of the end zone, that he would cover the tight end underneath. As Garcia tried to force the ball in to Shea, Lewis got his hand on the ball and deflected it into the air. Backing up the play, Reed saw the ball pop into the air and he reached down and scooped it off his shoetops 6 yards deep in the end zone. All he really needed to do was drop to a knee to down the ball and the Ravens would run out the clock. Instinct took over, though, and he took off, running past the stunned Browns before anyone could make a serious attempt to tackle him. He didn't stop until he crossed the goal line 106 yards later. The return was an NFL record.

Billick's immediate concern was that the replay official in the press box might look at the play to be sure that Reed hadn't trapped the ball. Replays would later show that Reed had caught the ball cleanly, but at the time Billick didn't know that and the last thing he wanted was an official's ruling the pass incomplete and giving the Browns two more shots from the 5-yard line. Once the ball was snapped for the extra point, the play could not be overruled. He was screaming at the kicking team to get the kick off as quickly as possible even while the defense was still mobbing Reed.

"Snap the ball!" Billick screamed as if the clock were ticking down and the kick was to win the game. "Snap the damn ball!"

The kicking team was apparently unaware of Billick's concern, because it went through its normal routine. By the time Maese snapped the ball, Zastudil put it down, and Stover kicked it through the uprights, Billick was screaming at Zauner. Even with the kick safely made and the chance of replay now gone, Billick still let Stover have it for not calling for the ball to be snapped more quickly. Stover, having played for Billick for six years, knew the best way to deal with him at that moment was to keep moving.

"There's no sense arguing with him at a time like that," he said later. "Because he isn't going to hear a word you say."

"He's right about that," Billick said, knowing that he can be a tad unreasonable at moments like that. "But I did want them to get the damn kick off. I didn't care if Matt kicked it backwards, it didn't matter. Just get the ball snapped."

The ball was snapped. There was no replay. The touchdown — correctly — stood. And after three hours in the dentist's chair, the game was finally over. It had taken more than fifty-nine minutes to put the Browns away, but they had finally done it. The final was 27–13. "That's one of the most deceptive scores you'll ever hear," Billick said.

Perhaps it was because it was close to midnight. Or perhaps it was because they realized they had been fortunate to win. Or maybe it was just exhaustion. In any event, the locker room hardly sounded like a winning NFL locker room. "Why's it so quiet?" Corey Fuller asked. "We won the game, fellas, we won the game."

They had won. They were 5-3 halfway through the season. Billick noticed the quiet, too, but said nothing about it. A win, as Billick always said, was a win. The easy half of the season was now over. Maybe that was why it was so quiet.

21

Stacking

THE MORNING AFTER THE WIN over the Browns, Brian Billick sat at his desk, brow furrowed, a yellow legal pad in front of him. When Billick is trying to think, he writes in longhand as opposed to using the computer. He had decided it was time to make a list of the issues he thought the team was facing and deal with them head-on. On his list, Billick wrote:

- Everyone knows Anthony [Wright] and Peter [Boulware] are going to be back soon. They'll need roster spots. Some guys feel the axe hanging over their heads.
- There's tension on the special teams. Is it the axe? Is it the fact that Musa Smith was down [inactive] on Sunday? Is Cornell Brown worried about his status with Boulware coming back?
- Kyle Boller is starting to feel pressure because of all the criticism.
- Gary Baxter's worried about his contract. So is Ed Hartwell.
- Kevin Johnson got only fifteen snaps on Sunday. He already told [receivers coach] David Shaw that he's unhappy about it.
- Mike Flynn got only four snaps last night. He's uptight. So is Bennie Anderson. Orlando Brown isn't happy, either.
- Todd [Heap] and Jamal [Lewis] aren't going to be Pro Bowlers this year. How does that affect their mind-set the last few weeks? Jamal telling the media he needs more carries after last night is probably an indication that he's uptight about things right now.

- Both coordinators are worried about their future. A lot of the coaches are wondering how their future might be affected by what happens with the coordinators.
- Gary Zauner's feelings are hurt because I yelled at him twice last night.

The easiest of those issues to deal with was Zauner. The two men had known each other a long time, and Zauner knew that Billick often said things on the sideline that he didn't really mean. Before the coaches and scouts had their weekly meeting on Monday, Billick called Zauner in to tell him he was sorry he had lost his temper the night before. Zauner understood. He also reminded Billick that there was a reason why he had insisted on wearing a headset that covered both his ears. "I know you're yelling," he said. "But a lot of the time I don't know *what* you're yelling."

They both agreed that was probably a good thing.

The noon meeting in the new boardroom would not be as simple. Like everything else in the building, the new boardroom was a far cry from what the team had worked with in the old building. To begin with there hadn't *been* a boardroom in the old place. The weekly meetings had been held in the draft room, with coaches often sitting on the floor because of a lack of space. That wasn't a problem here. There was a massive table in the middle of the room, a fireplace at one end, huge windows looking out toward the practice fields and the parking lot, and plenty of space around the table for those not seated at the table to spread out. The entire team could have met in the boardroom if necessary.

The poshness of the surroundings didn't cheer up anyone for this meeting. It hardly had the feeling of a morning-after-a-victory get-together.

Billick started with the medical report. Jonathan Ogden, as expected, was out for at least another week. Heap was still a couple of weeks away, and it was possible he might not play again for the rest of the season. That was the old bad news. The new bad news was Deion Sanders: the doctors thought he would miss at least two weeks. Given that he was thirty-seven, given that the injury was on his foot — different, though, from the injury that had plagued him while with the Redskins — two weeks might be optimistic.

They went through the coaches' analyses of the tape. Billick asked Zauner about Wade Richey's kickoffs, which had gotten shorter since the start of the season. "He may have a tired leg," Zauner said. "He's not been as good in the games as he is in practice."

Everyone knew why Billick had asked the question. Roster spots. Richey was clearly in jeopardy.

Once the coaches were finished, Billick pulled out his legal pad. "There's a simmering tension in this building," he said. "Some of it is normal mid-season stuff that's a part of every season. I understand that. But I think we need to address some of the issues that the players and all of us in this room are thinking about."

He went through his list while everyone listened. Then he asked for comments. There was a lengthy silence. Not surprisingly, it was Zauner who spoke first.

"I know there was concern among my guys about Musa being down," he said. "Bart [Scott] made the comment 'Which one of us peons is going to get cut.' I thought they played afraid on that opening kickoff. That's why we were messed up."

Billick understood the insecurity some of the special teamers were feeling because clearly changes were coming. "I'll go to special teams meetings this week," he said. "It's probably a good idea for me to remind them that we value them."

He then asked running backs coach Matt Simon if not being in the Pro Bowl was bothering Lewis. Perhaps that was why he had complained about his lack of carries (22 for 81 yards) after the game. "I don't think the Pro Bowl is bothering him," Simon said. "For one thing, he knows he couldn't go anyway, because he's going to be in jail."

They all laughed — uncomfortably — at that reminder.

"I just think the whole season has been difficult for him," Simon continued. "But I don't have any sense at all that he's pouting. He just wants to play better."

Billick turned to O. J. Brigance, whose title was director of player personnel. In reality, Brigance was the team's troubleshooter. When a player had a nonfootball problem, the person he was most likely to take it to was Brigance. His phone number was the one the players carried with them at all times in case they were involved in an accident or a fight or got into any kind of trouble. He was thirty-five and had been retired as a player for only two years, so he still remembered clearly what life as a player was like.

"Do you sense the tension?" Billick asked. "Or am I making this up?"

"No, you're not making it up," Brigance said in his quiet, deep baritone. "The tension is there for all the reasons you've brought up. I think getting it out in the open is a good idea. Let them know you're aware of it and you sympathize even if, in some cases, there's nothing that can be done about it."

"What about right here in this room?" Billick said. "There's tension here, too, isn't there?"

This time the silence stretched on. Billick wasn't going to break it.

Finally, Mike Singletary, probably the quietest member of the staff, spoke up.

No one in the room had a football résumé that compared with Singletary's. In the 1980s he had been the prototypical NFL middle linebacker, the heir to the Dick Butkus linebacking throne in Chicago. He had played twelve seasons for the Bears, had been the heart of their famous defense in 1985, and had been elected to the Pro Football Hall of Fame in 1998. He had decided to get into coaching in 2003 — eleven years after retiring as a player — and had joined the Ravens' staff.

Singletary was probably the most deeply religious member of the coaching staff, someone who always called both Billick and Nolan "Coach" out of respect for their positions of authority within the team. Nolan always asked him to speak to the defense about the upcoming game at least once a week because he knew that the players remembered how great a player he had been and that they had the utmost respect for anything he said about football. His weekly player reports were, generally speaking, the shortest of any, which worked well since those of Jeff FitzGerald, who worked with the outside linebackers, tended to be the longest.

Now Singletary cleared his throat and broke the silence. "Coach, I think you're right, there is a lack of cohesion within our staff right now," he said. "We aren't the team we need to be going forward. I don't think we know what we are or where exactly we're going from here. There are men in this room who feel this tension and aren't speaking up."

He paused to see if anyone wanted to speak up. No one did. He plowed on. "Coach, I'll be honest with you, I don't understand why we're using Deion on offense or on special teams. We *need* him on defense. Look at last night. When Deion was in the game, the Browns were one-for-six on third downs. After he got hurt, they were four-for-seven."

Billick knew that the Deion part of Singletary's speech came from Nolan. Or perhaps Nolan's comments the night before had come from Singletary. The two men were that close. He also knew that neither man was trying to nag, that they had genuine concerns. "I understand where you're coming from, Mike," he said. "Those are decisions I have to make."

Zauner brought up again the uncertainty his players felt. "Gary, that's the way the league is," Billick said. "We've got fifty-three on the roster; only forty-five can dress. I think it's a silly rule, but that's the rule."

Zauner, never one to back down, brought up Corey Fuller. What good, he wondered, was a backup cornerback who didn't play at all on special teams?

Mike Nolan had been squirming in his seat for a while. Clearly, he didn't want to say anything. But Zauner's special team complaints made it impossible for him not to. "Guys, I really don't want to say anything that's going to create divisions in here," he said, starting slowly. "I already spoke up once this season when I shouldn't have, and I know I was wrong for doing it. But here's a fact: we've got more guys on this team who are strictly special teams players than anyone in the league: We've got Stover, Richey, Maese, Zastudil, Morrow, and Sams. Only one of them [Sams] will ever take a snap on offense or defense. I think that makes it tougher on the offense and on the defense."

Cavanaugh jumped in behind Nolan: "I don't see what the big deal is about guys being up or not being up," he said. "When did players get so sensitive? Last week KJ [Kevin Johnson] came to me about playing time. We have to play the guys who give us the best chance to win. Geez, when I played, I was down all the time. Last I looked, guys still get paid, don't they? Brian, personally, I think you do a damn good job putting the best forty-five in uniform every week."

Billick knew it was time to break up the meeting. He didn't want it to degenerate into the offense and defense vs. the special teams, and that's where it was headed. Most Monday meetings lasted forty-five minutes. They were closing in on two hours. "I think you guys are right that I should address some of this with the team on Wednesday," he said. "I'll do that. We'll have to make some decisions on the roster next week. Jim [Colletto], I may need one of your guys to go. Gary, it might have to be Wade Richey."

They broke up. The tensions within the room and the team had certainly been addressed. Whether they had been resolved was another question entirely.

One person Billick had been right to be concerned about was Kyle Boller. He hadn't played poorly against the Browns (17-of-30 for 142 yards, no interceptions), but the lost fumble early and the offense's continuing struggle to score touchdowns — its only one had come after the poor punt put the ball on the Browns' 9-yard line — had given the fans more reason to boo Boller, who had become their favorite target.

On Monday night, before going to what had now become their weekly dinner, Boller and Jim Fassel appeared together on a local radio show. The host took some calls. Almost always when a player or coach appears on this kind of show, the calls range from complimentary to out-and-out fawning. Part of this is the intimidation factor and part of this is careful call screening. One caller apparently told the screener that he wanted to tell Fassel how lucky he thought the Ravens were to have him. He kept his word. Then, after he had finished complimenting Fassel, he said, "As for you, Kyle, I just don't understand why you're still here or why you still have a job. You were a loser when you quarterbacked Cal, and the only reason you aren't an out-and-out loser right now is because we have such a great defense. The sooner we get another quarterback, the better off we'll be."

Boller stayed cool. "Well, pal, all I can tell you is I'm doing the very best I can and I'm going to continue to do the best I can as long as I'm here," he said.

An hour later, sitting at Ruth's Chris, Boller shook his head. "There is no reason to let it bother me," he said. "Guys like that don't understand what's going on. I know that. But it really does get old. I hear the boos, I know what people are saying. I know that guy isn't alone. I know when a team does well, the quarterback gets too much credit. But there are times when he gets too much blame. I feel like I'm getting better, but a lot of times people don't understand why plays turn out the way they do."

"You are getting better," Fassel said. "A lot better. I know that, and you know that."

As he frequently did when talking to Boller, Fassel launched into stories about John Elway and Phil Simms. "When I first got to Denver [in 1993], John was nervous as could be," he said. "Dan Reeves had just been fired, and most people thought it was because of John. He said to me, 'If we don't do well, everyone in town is going to say, "They should have gotten rid of Elway, not Reeves."' Remember, this was after he'd already been in, I think, three Super Bowls. He'd had the Drive. But he was still nervous, still insecure. That's the nature of playing quarterback. Ten years from now, when you're a big star in this league, you'll still have nights when you feel insecure."

Boller nodded. These sessions were good for him because he felt he could tell Fassel things he didn't tell anyone else. He had gone that day for acupuncture treatment for his back and neck, both of which had been sore for several weeks. He had kept the injuries quiet because he knew he could play with the pain but also because he didn't want to sound as if he were making excuses. Fassel asked about the acupuncture.

"It was kind of weird," Boller said. "But it felt pretty good. I know it won't make me feel worse, and it might make me feel better."

Fassel took a sip of wine and said, okay, let me ask you a few questions. "What did you do well last night?"

Boller thought about it. "I didn't make any mistakes that hurt us after the fumble," he said.

"Fumble wasn't your fault, you never saw the guy," Fassel interjected.

Boller nodded. "I kept us on the field, we converted third downs well. But . . ."

"What?"

"I just wish Matt would call more of the plays I'm really good at," he said. "There are some routes we worked on all preseason, all through camp, that I feel confident throwing, and it seems like we've gone away from those."

"Tell him," Fassel said. "Go in there tomorrow *before* they put together the game plan and tell him. Don't wait until Wednesday when it's done; then, it's too late. You're right and I'll bet he'll agree you're right. Tell him the plays you want called. If I go in there and do it, that accomplishes nothing; then, I'm meddling. But if you go in and tell him this is what's best for you, he'll do it. I guarantee it. The job of a coordinator is to let his quarterback lead, and one of the ways you do that is to make calls he feels confident about."

Boller told Fassel about Cavanaugh's having him run the video meeting on Saturday nights. Fassel smiled. "That's smart coaching," he said. "That's good for you and good for the team."

He paused. "Now, tell me where you need to improve."

Boller thought a moment. "I'm still throwing the ball away sometimes too quickly," he said. "I don't want to force things, but maybe I've been a little gun-shy because I don't want turnovers, like in the Washington game. I need to know when to throw it away, when to try to make something happen."

"Which may be the hardest thing for any quarterback to learn," Fassel said. "Look at [Brett] Favre. He still forces things. Makes some of the worst throws you've ever seen."

"Yeah, but he's Brett Favre," Boller said. "He knows he'll make up for it."

"He didn't make up for it in Philadelphia last year," Fassel said, a reference to Favre's backbreaking interception in overtime of the Packers' playoff loss to the Eagles.

"Can you imagine the reaction," Boller said with a smile, "if I ever made a play like that?"

Fassel laughed. "Ten years from now, you'll make a play like that, and you know what? You'll come back the next year and be a better player. The best thing you've got going, Kyle, is your mind. You're going to keep getting better. Heck, you've got most things figured out now. You don't even need me."

Boller shook his head and didn't crack even a small grin when he answered: "Oh yes, I do."

The next morning Matt Cavanaugh was surprised when Boller walked in and asked if he had a minute. Players rarely venture onto the second floor except when someone tells them they're needed up there. Most agree there is almost never a good reason to venture upstairs. Now, on the players' day off, Boller was standing in Cavanaugh's doorway.

"Absolutely," Cavanaugh said, waving him in.

Boller told Cavanaugh that he thought there were some pass routes he felt good about throwing that hadn't been used enough in the offense. Cavanaugh asked him to tell him more. They talked for a solid thirty minutes. Boller even went to the board and drew up some of the plays he thought would work well in Sunday's game in the Meadowlands against the Jets. Cavanaugh was delighted. "The more input I get from Kyle, the better," he said. "Eventually, he needs to feel as if this is his offense. It doesn't matter how good J.O. is or Jamal or Todd. If he doesn't walk into the huddle feeling like it's his offense, it won't be and he won't be successful. That's one reason why I wanted him to be the guy doing the talking on Saturday nights. The guys don't need to hear my voice, they need to hear his. This was another step."

By the time he left Cavanaugh's office, Boller was excited about the game plan. "If we run the stuff we talked about, it'll be great," he said. "Matt told me we should talk that way every week."

On Wednesday, Billick followed through on his promise to the coaches to address the issue of uncertainty with the players. He told them not to take it personally if they were down for a week, that often those decisions were predicated on factors that had nothing to do with them but with injuries and with the opponent. "If we didn't like you and respect you as players, you wouldn't be here," he said. "Everyone can't play every week, that's an unfortunate fact of life in this league. But you all know that before the season's over every person on the fifty-three-man roster is going to play a role, so you have to stay ready because you don't know when that time will come."

Next to the Eagles, the Jets were the best team the Ravens had played since Pittsburgh, and when they had played the Steelers no one, including the Steelers, had known how good they or Ben Roethlisberger were going to be. The Jets were 6-2 but were coming off a frustrating loss at Buffalo. What's more, their starting quarterback, Chad Pennington, had gotten hurt in the Bills game, so Quincy Carter, the onetime Cowboys quarterback cut suddenly in preseason by Bill Parcells amid rumors of a positive drug test, would start.

For the first time all season, the weather on game day would be truly cold. The wind was whipping when the Ravens arrived at their hotel on

Saturday night, with the promise of a similar day on Sunday. Billick's emphasis in that night's meeting was on his belief that the Ravens would win almost all of the one-on-one matchups in the game. "They're about misdirection because, one-on-one, they can't stand in with us," he said. "We get them to stand in with us and they beat us, we'll just shake their hands. But I don't think that will happen."

Both the Ravens and Jets had agreed to allow NFL Films to mike key players and the coaches during the game. There would be no play-by-play and no narration. The story of the game would be told through the sounds picked up by the microphones. Since the tape would be edited into a one-hour film, no one had to worry about profanity or anything embarrassing making it onto the air. The fact that the two teams and the two coaching staffs respected each other and had no serious issues made it easier for Billick and Jets coach Herman Edwards to agree to the project — although it probably made it less sexy than if Billick and the Steelers' Bill Cowher had agreed to be miked for a game against each other.

The first thing the players noticed, even those who walked onto the field at 10 A.M. — three hours before kickoff — was the wind. There is no place in football like Giants Stadium during the second half of the season. Even on a relatively mild day, the wind swirls through the place, usually a cold wind. The game-time temperature was a relatively balmly forty-eight degrees, but on the Ravens' side of the field, where there was no sun at all, it felt considerably colder than that. Throughout the game, the temperature would drop and the wind would pick up.

The opening kickoff provided a scare — and a warning. B. J. Sams fielded the kick at the 6-yard line and returned to the 32. But he fumbled as he was hit, the ball flying loose. Fortunately, Bart Scott alertly jumped on it. Sams came to the sideline looking spooked. Since his touchdown returns against Kansas City and Washington, he had become a marked man for opponents' special teams and hadn't looked quite as confident.

The offense started the game with the kind of drive coaches dream about. Boller converted two third downs right away, including a third-and-16 on which he threw underneath to Musa Smith — back on the active roster, with Wade Richey down for the week — for a 25-yard pickup. By the time they reached the Jets' 8 with a first-and-goal after a crisp Boller-to-Moore completion, they had held on to the ball for almost nine minutes. Three plays later, they faced fourth-and-goal from the 1 after Boller had gained 4 yards from the 5 on a quarterback draw, a play Cavanaugh hadn't called for him all season. Billick decided to go for the touchdown for several reasons: to hold the ball for so long and only come away with three points would be deflating, he wanted to show confidence in Jamal Lewis and the offensive line, and he figured that even if the Jets held, his defense would force the Jets to punt a few plays later from inside the 10-yard line.

All very logical and reasoned. Football, of course, is not a game of logic or reason. Lewis tried to run left, not straight ahead but wide, a play call that never would have been made if Ogden had been playing left tackle instead of Ethan Brooks. John Abraham, the Jets' occasionally brilliant, oft-injured defensive end, knifed in and got him down at the 1 as the stadium exploded with the first real noise of the day. The Ravens had held the ball for fifteen plays and 9:44 and come away empty. Still, if the defense could hold and they got the ball back in good field position . . .

The defense didn't hold. On third-and-1 from the 10-yard line, Carter found his tight end, Chris Baker, across the middle for a key 19-yard pickup, to the 29. The Jets moved the ball almost to midfield before the defense finally forced a punt. Toby Gowin sailed the ball to Sams on the 12-yard line. Sams hadn't dropped a kick all year. He had fumbled a couple of times after being hit the way he had been hit on the opening kickoff, but he hadn't dropped a ball yet. Now, in the Giants Stadium winds, he called for a fair catch — and dropped the ball. The Jets' Kenyatta Wright fell on it. Four carries by star running back Curtis Martin later, the Jets were in the end zone and led, 7–0. To make matters worse, Chris McAlister wobbled off the field, clutching his shoulder. He had taken a hit to the shoulder in the Buffalo game — but not one serious enough to get him off the field. This *was* serious. It was a stinger, but it was a bad one, bad enough that he couldn't stand up straight. Corey Fuller had to take his place.

Later, when they watched the NFL Films' tape of the game, the Ravens' coaches would hear the Jets' coaches screaming at Quincy Carter and the offense to attack Fuller the minute they saw him in the game. Watching helplessly from the sideline and without having the benefit of hearing the tape, Deion Sanders knew they were going to do that. When the defense went onto the field with Fuller in McAlister's place, he called Ed Reed over. "You know you're going to have to shade to Corey's side," he said. "They're going to go right at him."

What could have been a great start had now become a terrible start. It got worse. After the teams traded punts, Boller was sacked twice on the offense's third series and Zastudil had to punt from the Ravens' 13. He floated a gorgeous punt that Santana Moss fielded at his own 28. Moss, a dangerous returner, got to the outside and slithered his way to the Ravens' 40. As it turned out, the ball came back because of a holding penalty. But Moss's run had forced Zastudil to try to get into position to make a tackle. As he ran down the field in the direction of the play, Zastudil got blindsided — he never saw the hit — and came off the field doubled over in pain, holding his left arm limply at his side. He went straight to the locker room, accompanied by Leigh Ann Curl. He had a severe shoulder separation. There was some talk among the players that perhaps Curl could give him a shot so he could play, but Curl quickly ruled that out. He was done for the day.

Which left the Ravens with quite a problem. Zauner, always prepared, had experimented a couple of times during camp with backup punters. The two candidates were Boller and Kordell Stewart, both of whom had punted in high school, as many quarterbacks do. Boller — perhaps because it had only been six years since he had punted, as opposed to sixteen for Stewart — had punted better when Zauner watched.

"Who's our backup punter?" Billick asked Zauner when he saw the pain on Zastudil's face.

"The best one is Boller," Zauner said.

"Who's the next-best one."

"Kordell."

"Tell him to get ready."

Billick wasn't about to risk his starting quarterback, knowing that the Jets were likely to put on an all-out rush when they saw a backup punter in the game. Zauner went to tell Stewart to warm up his leg.

"I don't think this is in my contract," Stewart said, trying to force a laugh.

While the Ravens were trying to figure out who would punt when they got the ball again, the Jets were methodically moving the ball downfield. Carter, doing as he was told, found Justin McCareins in front of Fuller for

16 yards. Then he threw a quick pass to backup running back LaMont Jordan, who took the ball 25 yards to the Ravens' 18. The building frustration was never more evident than on that play, when Ray Lewis was called for a late hit, moving the ball to the 9. Martin came back in on the next play and scored. The Jets led, 14–0, with 4:14 left in the half. The day was quickly becoming a disaster.

The offense went three-and-out. When Zauner called for the punt team, his punter was standing a few feet away from him, huddled in his Windbreaker. "Kordell!" Zauner screamed. "You're the punter!"

Stewart had forgotten. He tossed off the Windbreaker, raced onto the field, caught the perfect snap from Joe Maese, then dropped the ball quick-kick style, and managed to wobble a 31-yard punt to the Jets' 27. Moss returned it 8 yards.

"First time I've kicked in a game since high school," Stewart said to Sanders as he came off. "How'd I look?"

"Like you haven't kicked since high school," Sanders answered.

Stewart's kicking would have been funnier if the situation hadn't been so grim. On second down Carter went right back at Fuller, finding the fleet Moss breaking down the sideline. Reed came over and pushed him out of bounds on the 17-yard line after a 47-yard pickup. Any Jets score in the final two minutes, field goal or touchdown, would create a three-score deficit. The way the offense was going — one first down since the opening series — that would be almost impossible to overcome.

For some reason, Jets offensive coordinator Paul Hackett, frequently pilloried in New York for his notoriously conservative play calling, decided to get fancy at a moment when nothing but straight-ahead running between the tackles was needed. Looking, no doubt, to drive a stake into the Ravens' heart, he called an option pass on the next play, sending Jordan sprinting to his right, looking to throw the ball into the end zone.

"As soon as he took the pitch I knew he was going to pass the ball," Reed said later. "I could tell looking at his pads. He wasn't trying to get turned at all to run the ball, he was standing up straight. You don't do that if you're trying to run."

Running out of room as he ran toward the sideline, Jordan should have just run out of bounds. Reed and the rest of the Ravens had read pass all the way and the Jets receivers were covered. Jordan, inexperienced at making that kind of decision, panicked. He tried to fling the ball into the end zone, hoping someone in green would come down with it. If he had been watching the Ravens play all year, he would have known exactly who was going to come down with the ball. Fuller actually got a finger on it and deflected it right into the hands of Reed, who was four yards deep in the end zone. Seeing himself surrounded by Jets, Reed thought for a moment to kneel and let the offense start at the 20.

"But then I thought, 'I need to take a chance, try to make a play,'" he said. "Plus, when I make an interception, I always think to myself, 'These are offensive players out here. They don't know how to tackle.'"

Reed's instincts were on target. Bobbing and weaving, ducking tacklers, first in the end zone, then all over the field, he raced the length of the field again, and more, going 104 yards for a touchdown. The Ravens' bench, which had been completely silent a moment earlier, exploded. There was one problem: peeling back to try to get one last block for Reed, Will Demps had been caught blocking in the back at the Jets' 26. Instead of a touchdown, the Ravens got the ball on the Jets' 36 with 1:33 left in the half.

"I can't believe it," Demps said, coming off.

"Don't sweat it," Reed said. "The O will come through."

Optimistic words at that moment. They appeared to be more fantasy than optimism a few moments later, when the offense picked up 2 yards on three plays and faced fourth-and-8 from the 34. Billick called time-out and decided not to try a field goal. For one thing, it wouldn't mean that much. For another, it would be a 51-yarder, and even kicking with the wind, Stover would be working with a new holder (Boller) since Zastudil was in the locker room. He and Cavanaugh agreed on a pass underneath to Chester Taylor, in the game for Lewis because it was third-and-long. Taylor broke two tackles and took the ball all the way to the 11-yard line. Two plays after that, Boller threw a lob to Clarence Moore in the end zone, and he used all of his six-foot-six inch frame to go up and catch it. Touchdown. Instead of trailing by two touchdowns — or more — at the half, the deficit was only 14–7.

The game had been turned around completely. You could feel it in the Ravens' locker room. Even with McAlister, Zastudil, and Edwin Mulitalo — whose foot had gotten stepped on in a pileup — in the training room, the place was full of life. Mike Flynn had gone in to play center, and Casey Rabach was playing at left guard for Mulitalo. Everything was patchwork. It didn't seem to matter. "If I have to go out there myself and make a play, I will," Mike Nolan told the defense. Billick kept saying over and over, "We've got what we need to win this game, we just have to go do it."

Fassel checked in with Boller. "How you feeling, Seven," he said, calling him by his number.

"Never better," Boller said.

They quickly cut the lead to 14–10 on a Stover field goal midway through the third quarter. Stewart kept getting off punts that didn't go all that far but went far enough. The punt team, knowing it had to make plays, was making them. The defense had its second wind, and the Jets offense was going nowhere. It became a punting battle until the Ravens finally pieced together a drive in the fourth quarter. Boller, who had spent so much time in the off-season throwing balls to Travis Taylor, finally found him twice when it mattered: first for 23 yards, then for another 6. On a third-and-11 at the Jets' 16, he lofted another perfect pass to Clarence Moore, who — again — came down with it. Moore had come a long way from being a candidate for the practice squad in August.

The touchdown put the Ravens in the lead for the first time all day at 17–14 with 4:13 left in the game. The defense needed one stop and they could go home with a remarkable come-from-behind victory. But the NFL rarely works that way. LaMont Jordan, trying to make up for his critical second-quarter mistake, returned Stover's kickoff to the 45-yard line. On third-and-7 Carter picked on Fuller again, finding McCareins at the Ravens' 38 for a first down. Curtis Martin then took over, picking up 26 yards on two plays to put the ball on the 12. The clock was running down. Martin was stopped for a loss of 1 with fifty-five seconds left, setting up third-and-6. Herman Edwards used his first time-out. Carter picked up 9 yards — and a first down at the 4 — on a scramble on the next play, but for some reason, Edwards didn't take time-out and the clock ran all the way to eighteen seconds before the Jets ran another play.

Hoping to surprise the Ravens with a run, the Jets ran LaMont Jordan right, but Lewis and Ed Hartwell stopped him for a 1-yard gain. Fourteen seconds left. Time-out, Jets. Carter threw incomplete into the end zone, throwing the ball away with Adalius Thomas bearing down on him. Third down and three yards to go for a winning touchdown. Eight seconds left. The Jets still had a time-out. They could run one more play — as long as it wasn't a slow-developing one — and still have time for a tieing field goal if they didn't win the game with a touchdown. But there was confusion on the Jets' sideline, a recurring problem in endgame situations. Edwards ended up using his last time-out then, instead of saving it in case he needed it after the third-down play. Not wanting to risk getting tackled in bounds with no time-outs left, he was forced to send in the field goal team. Doug Brien made the kick with five seconds left and in a scene that could probably take place only in New York (okay, maybe Philadelphia), the fans booed their team for tieing the game and forcing overtime. Their anger was understandable, though; the Jets should have been able to take at least one more crack at winning the game, but clock mismanagement had forced them to kick the field goal.

The Ravens were thrilled, under the circumstances, to be playing overtime. The defense quickly held the Jets to three-and-out. Overtime is about two things: possession and field position. The Ravens had both, taking over at their own 44 after the punt. The offense couldn't move. But Stewart, the rookie punter, came up with a huge kick — punting the ball 42 yards, where it was downed by Thomas at the Jets' 9. They didn't have possession, but they did have field position. Again the defense forced a three-and-out. Sams very carefully fielded the punt at the Ravens' 41 and returned it to the 44. They were five minutes into the fifteen-minute overtime and the tension in the stadium grew each second.

On third-and-5, Boller scrambled to his right and found Kevin Johnson, who had been the invisible man for several weeks, across the middle. Johnson, who had always been known for his sure hands, took a big hit and held on to the ball at the Jets' 30. With the wind behind them, they might have been in field goal range right there. Stover prefers to kick from eight yards behind the line of scrimmage (some kickers will go from seven), so the attempt at that moment would have been 48 yards. Billick didn't want to take a chance, especially with Boller doing the holding. He had done okay so far, but Stover's last extra point had hit the crossbar before dropping over, and whether it was the hold or the kick didn't matter. It made everyone a little bit jittery.

Hoping to grind the ball closer to the goalposts, Boller handed the ball to Lewis, who was dropped for a 4-yard loss before he could take a step. Now the field goal would be 52 yards, a bomb even with the wind. They needed a few more yards. Boller threw incomplete to Travis Taylor. Third down. From the shotgun, he went back to Taylor and this time they connected, Taylor being brought down at the 24. It was short of a first down, but that didn't matter. It was now well within Stover's range.

The Jets called time-out. Larry Rosen, the sideline reporter for the Ravens radio network, couldn't resist a crack: "First time in history someone has called time-out," he said, "to freeze the *holder*."

He might have been right. Normally from 42 yards, even in the Giants Stadium winds, Stover was a near lock to make the kick. Now Maese needed a perfect snap and Boller had to get the ball down for him. "By that point I was so wound up, I was fine," Boller said. "As long as Joe gave me a good snap."

Stover was trying not to think about what might happen if the snap or hold wasn't good. He was just going through his prekick routine, talking to himself the way he always did.

"Time to go home," Deion Sanders said. It was getting close to dark by now and the temperature had dropped a good deal since kickoff more than three hours — and a lifetime — earlier.

Time was back in. Maese's snap was perfect. Boller put the ball down, laces away from the kicker, just as they are supposed to be, and Stover hit the kick perfectly. Sanders was trotting in the direction of the tunnel with the ball still in the air. The kick would have been good from 52 yards. For the first time all season, the Ravens celebrated a victory on the field. The Jets, understandably, were devastated. The Ravens were still pounding one another gleefully when they hit the locker room.

"Kordell, I knew we brought you here for a reason," Billick said. "But I didn't know *this* was it."

The game ball was Stewart's. In fact, he would be voted the league's special teams player of the week. He had punted five times for an average of 35.4 yards, including the key 42-yarder in overtime.

He wasn't the only hero, though: Reed had again turned the game around with his interception and return. The receivers had made big catches. And

Kyle Boller, the quarterback almost no one in Baltimore thought could come up big in the fourth quarter, had come up big in the fourth quarter. And in overtime.

"The best thing about it is now the guys know Kyle can get it done at the end of a close game," Billick said, relaxing in the locker room, taking his time to savor what he had just seen. "All of us *thought* he could get it done. Now we know. That's an important difference." He paused and smiled. "Especially when you get to the playoffs."

The Ravens were now 6–3. A lot of the stacking issues Billick had been concerned about on Monday were still in play. But talking about the playoffs was now a reasonable thing to do.

22

Best Record Ever

AS EXHILARATING AS THE VICTORY over the Jets was, there was work to be done even before the Ravens boarded the train for their trip home.

"I assume you have a punter in your back pocket someplace," Brian Billick said to Gary Zauner as they left the locker room.

"I'm going to start calling guys from the train," Zauner answered.

Dave Zastudil was going to be out for at least two weeks, perhaps longer. Kordell Stewart had performed remarkably as a stopgap, but the team needed a real punter. There were other injuries: Edwin Mulitalo's foot appeared to be okay, but Chris McAlister's shoulder was sore enough that it appeared possible he might not be able to play the following Sunday against the Cowboys. Jonathan Ogden was confident he would be ready to play against Dallas, but Todd Heap and Deion Sanders were still at least a week — possibly longer — away from playing.

The first order of business was finding a punter. Zauner was intrigued by the notion of bringing in Lee Johnson, the former Cincinnati Bengals kicker. Johnson was well over forty and had been out of football for a while but had the advantage of being left-footed, like Zastudil, meaning no adjustments would be needed. "How old is he, fifty?" Billick asked. "There has to be someone else."

There were plenty of someone elses. The life of an NFL kicker — placekicker or punter — is often a nomadic one. Few kickers were like Stover, sticking with one team for fourteen years. Except for elite ones like

Stover, kickers and punters were on and off rosters like steaks on a hot grill. One kicker whose phone number Zauner had in his back pocket was Nick Murphy, like Zastudil three years out of college but someone who had never kicked in the NFL. Murphy had been in the Minnesota Vikings' training camp twice and had spent the preseason in 2004 with the Eagles. He had kicked in NFL Europe for two years and had done very well there, leading the league twice, but had never made an NFL roster. Zauner had seen him on tape and knew he had a strong leg. The only real knock on him was that he had never set foot on an NFL field in a game that meant anything. Zauner called Murphy from the train and asked if he could be in Baltimore on Tuesday for a tryout. Murphy was in Phoenix, where he had gone to college at Arizona State, selling insurance and working out to stay in shape just in case his phone rang. Now — finally — it had. "First time in three years I even got a call for a tryout in-season," he said. "I was excited, but not overly excited. I knew I wasn't going to be the only guy they brought in."

He was right. By Monday afternoon Zauner and George Kokinis, the pro scouting director, had a list of ten punters they wanted to bring to Baltimore. One of Kokinis's jobs was to keep tabs on available players at every position in case of an injury. He was expected to be ready with a list of names if a player went down at any position.

Tuesday tryouts are a regular part of NFL life. Tuesday is tryout day for the simple reason that teams' facilities are nearly empty since it is the players' day off. Teams bring players in when someone is injured and when they think someone can make their team better — if not right away, then down the line. The Ravens had already turned over more than half the players who had started the season on the practice squad. One player they had initially brought in to look at for the practice squad, Darnell Dinkins, had proven to be such a good player that he had been on the forty-five-man roster for the past three weeks, getting snaps at tight end and on special teams.

The Ravens worked out the punters in two groups of five. All of them were, understandably, nervous, none more so than Murphy. "I got engaged this past summer," he said. "I think when I did that I knew the time when I could hang around and hope to get a [football] job was ending. I was running out of time — and chances."

Murphy hadn't played football until his family moved from St. Louis to Phoenix when he was thirteen, because he was a soccer player — a goalie — and soccer and football season in St. Louis were both in the fall. In Phoenix soccer was in the spring, so he decided to try football. "To be honest, the main reason I did it was so when people asked me later in life if I ever played football, I could say that I did," he said. "Funny reason to take up a sport, but that was it."

He was a decent wide receiver, but when the chance to punt came up his junior year, he decided to try it. "The motions that you make to kick the ball as a soccer goalie aren't that different than in punting," he said. "I knew from soccer I had a pretty strong leg, so I decided to try it."

He received no scholarship offers as a senior, so he decided to go to junior college for a year, hoping he would improve enough to be offered one. He did and several schools expressed interest, including Arizona State — his hometown school. He decided to go there and was All–Pac 10 by his junior year. He punted well enough as a senior that he was one of six punters invited to the combine in Indianapolis. His roommate for the week: Dave Zastudil.

"The one thing we had in common was we were all miserable," he said. "It was freezing in the dome, we had to get up at five-thirty the day we kicked, and then we got ten kicks and that was it. I didn't do horribly, but I didn't do well enough to get anyone's attention, I guess."

Zastudil did — ending up as the Ravens' fourth-round pick in the draft. Murphy ended up in camp with the Vikings as a free agent. He was cut after the third exhibition game and spent the fall working in a Pizzeria Uno. "I did a little of everything," he said. "I bartended, I waited tables, I valet parked. I wanted flexible hours so I could keep working out."

He went to Europe the following winter and played in Barcelona, where he had trouble getting used to the lifestyle. "Dinner at ten? Go out at midnight, stay up all night? Wasn't me," he said, laughing.

He was back in the Vikings' camp that summer but knew he didn't have much chance of making the team when the team drafted a punter in the sixth round. "They gave him a hundred-thousand-dollar bonus; they'd given me four thousand. I didn't even count against their roster since I'd been in Europe [meaning the team had a roster exemption for him during training camp], so what were my chances?"

Zero. He was cut again. This time he decided to get his insurance license — his dad had gotten into insurance late in life and done well. He went back to Europe, playing in Scotland (which he loved) and again leading the league. This time the Philadelphia Eagles signed him. "John Harbaugh [the Eagles special teams coach] was great to work with," he said. "He was completely honest with me from the start. He said it was Dirk Johnson's job to lose. But he worked hard with me. He told me he thought I'd had three really good kicks in Europe. Three! Imagine if I hadn't led the league, what he might have thought. But I learned quite a bit from him. I kicked well, probably as well as Johnson. John was straight-up with me. He said, 'Nick, you kicked well enough to win the job. But Dirk didn't kick poorly enough to lose it.'"

Murphy went home thinking he might be finished, but he kept working out, hoping for a phone call. And then one came from Zauner. He felt he had kicked well and went into the cafeteria to eat lunch. All the kickers were in there, eyeing one another nervously. There's a camaraderie among kickers, especially those who have been in and out of work. But now they all knew only one of them was going to be happy. Murphy went back to the hotel where he had spent the night, hoping if he wasn't going to get the call, he would at least get the bad news in time to fly home that night. The phone rang. It was Zauner.

"Can you get back over here?" he asked. "We want to get a contract done for you by the end of the day."

Murphy said he thought he could do that.

Murphy was introduced to his new teammates on Wednesday morning. Billick had spent a lot of the season reminding the team how good he thought it was, rebuilding confidence. He didn't think that was going to be a problem this week. "I'm going to be watching you guys closely this week," he said. "I'm going to be looking for little things. Are you sloppy in practice? Are you late getting in and out of lunch? Are you late for meetings, even by a little bit? Is the locker room a mess when you leave at the end of the day?

"There's nothing more dangerous than a desperate team, and this is a desperate team," he said. "They're wounded and they're angry. We can't afford to walk out there with an attitude that we expect to win the game just by showing up. We do that, we'll get beat. Guaranteed."

The Cowboys *were* a desperate team. They had surprised the NFL by making the playoffs a year earlier during the first season in Bill Parcells's latest return to coaching. But this year they were 3-6, and most of Dallas was screaming for Parcells to bench forty-one-year-old quarterback Vinny Testaverde in favor of Drew Henson, the much-hyped quarterback of the future. Parcells was, if nothing else, stubborn. Testaverde would start against the Ravens. "The only danger," Billick said, "is if Vinny gets hot — which he can still do. He could go out there and throw five interceptions. He could also burn us."

Billick and Ozzie Newsome had thought this would be the week they had to make two major roster decisions because Peter Boulware and Anthony Wright were going to return to the active roster. But neither man was ready. Wright's shoulder still wasn't 100 percent, so even though he was restored to the fifty-three-man roster — meaning that third-year backup offensive lineman Damion Cook found himself looking for work — the plan was for him to be listed as the third quarterback on Sunday. That meant he wouldn't count against the forty-five-man roster and would play only if both Boller and Stewart were injured. The Ravens had gone the entire season without a third quarterback because Josh Harris, who would have been it, had been relegated to the practice squad. Randy Hymes, the college quarterback turned wide receiver, had been the third quarterback until now.

Boulware had returned to practice a week earlier, excited that his knee finally felt healthy. He had practiced Wednesday and felt no pain at all. He was convinced he would be back on the field for the Dallas game. The next day he tried to make a cut during a drill and felt a searing pain in his right foot. He had torn a ligament on the bottom of his foot — a painful version of turf toe. Twenty-four hours after his comeback had started, it was over. The doctors told Boulware it was back to rehab. He wouldn't play again for the rest of the season.

"I know things happen for a reason," said Boulware, one of the most religious players on the team. "But right now I'm having trouble figuring out what the reason for this might be."

Even though they were struggling, the presence of the Cowboys in town was still a big deal. They were still America's Team, the guys with the stars on their helmets, and they were coached by Parcells, who would already be in the Hall of Fame if he didn't keep coming back after vowing never to coach again. This was his third comeback from retirement. He had quit the New York Giants in 1991 after winning two Super Bowls. He had come back to coach in New England, then left the Patriots days after taking them to Super Bowl XXXI in January of 1997 to take over the New York Jets. He had stayed in New York for three seasons, taking a woebegone 1-15 team to the AFC Championship Game in two years, then quitting a year later. He had cowritten a book titled *The Final Season* describing his exit, once and for all, from coaching. A little more than two years after the book was published, he was introduced as the new coach of the Cowboys.

Because the Cowboys, an NFC team, were the opponent, the game would be televised on Fox. The only time the Ravens, an AFC team, appeared on Fox each year was when they hosted an NFC team. AFC games were on CBS, NFC games were on Fox, and interconference games were televised by the visiting team's network. When the Ravens played at Philadelphia, the game was on CBS. (The Redskins game had been an ESPN Sunday night game.) When the Cowboys and New York Giants came to Baltimore, the games were on Fox.

That meant the Ravens would be dealing with a very familiar announcing team, since Dick Stockton, Daryl Johnston, and Tony Siragusa had worked two of the Ravens' preseason games, not as part of their Fox deals but for the Ravens' TV network. This is common practice in the NFL, network announcers working for specific teams in preseason. Along with Sam Adams, Siragusa had been half of the Ravens' twin-powers defensive tackle tandem during the Super Bowl run. He had retired after the 2001 season, and he was a natural to get TV work because he was outgoing and loquacious. He could also be obnoxious at times. No one enjoyed torturing rookies more than Siragusa, to the point where other veterans sometimes thought he went too far. He wasn't malicious, just a gigantic kid (six-three, 340 pounds) who often crossed the line when it came to outrageous behavior. One year he had brought a paintball kit to training camp and had gotten great joy out of sneaking up on people and spraying them. When the hotel complained to the Ravens about it, Siragusa was told to cease and desist. Soon after, he was caught trying to spray-paint a hotel employee who was working right outside the hotel entrance. "One for the road" was his explanation.

Siragusa was still a hero in Baltimore because of his role on the Super Bowl team and because he always seemed to have time for the extra autograph. In typical Siragusa fashion, he walked into the Friday production meeting late — he had been in the locker room chatting with some of his ex-teammates — sat down at the conference table (next to his walk-around guy/driver), and started asking Rex Ryan (who Siragusa had suggested be asked to the production meeting instead of either coordinator because of Ryan's tendency to be blunt) about what techniques "our" D line would use against the Cowboys.

Siragusa had also suggested that instead of asking for Ray Lewis, Fox should ask for Adalius Thomas. Another smart move. Thomas's nickname in the defensive room was "the coordinator" because he understood every assignment for every player at every position on every play of the game. Thomas told the Fox people that he had actually taken some snaps at cornerback during the week because with McAlister and Sanders both down for this game, he was the next alternative if someone should get hurt.

The Fox production meeting was different from CBS, ESPN, and ABC. For one thing, Siragusa was a wild card, apt to ask anything or say anything at any moment. He offered a prediction — unsolicited — that the Ravens would shut down Cowboys running back Eddie George. "Except for the playoff game last year, he's never done anything against our defense," he said. Daryl Johnston asked the kind of questions most color analysts ask. Stockton, one of the true staples of network play-by-play (he's been doing it since the mid-'60s), stuck to nuts-and-bolts questions about who might be in the game in certain situations and what sorts of things they should be alert for. It was in response to a Stockton question that Kyle Boller told the group that there was an option pass in the offense for Sunday, a pitchback play where Randy Hymes threw the ball across the field back to Boller. Stockton knew his style was different than a lot of play-by-play men, but he was completely comfortable with his approach. And why not? It had worked well for many years.

"I don't want anecdotes," he said. "I worry that if I get wrapped up telling a story, I may lose track of what I'm supposed to be there for: keeping the viewer apprised of down, distance, subs, time, injuries — the basics of the game. Daryl's there to break the game down, and Goose can come up with color or analysis from the sideline. There's only so much time between plays, and I don't want to have the viewer confused — thinking about a story about the quarterback's high school days when it's third-and-ten at a key moment."

If the Fox people should have gleaned two things from their time with the Ravens, they were that Jamal Lewis believed he had a chance to finally break out and have a big game against the Dallas defense, and that Kyle Boller was a very different player from two weeks ago. The Jets game might very well have given his teammates new confidence in Boller, which made Billick happy. Beyond that, it had clearly given Boller new confidence in Boller. His body language had changed 180 degrees in one short week. On Monday night, just seven days after he had felt the need to remind Boller he was still going to be a good NFL quarterback someday, Jim Fassel found himself talking his pupil down: "Don't get too excited," he told him. "What you did yesterday was terrific, but you have to keep moving forward. There are always ways to improve on and off the field."

Fassel's off-field suggestion for the week was that Boller invite members of the offense to his house on Thursday (which tended to be the night players socialized together) the same way Ray Lewis had members of the defense come over to his house. Boller followed through, and a few of the linemen did come over. The receivers were all busy. "Walk before you run, I guess," Boller said.

While Boulware and Wright were still struggling with injuries, one injured "Raven" was back at practice looking and feeling much better: Steve Bisciotti. The neck surgery he had undergone on October 12 had been every bit as painful and difficult as the doctors had told him it was likely to be. He had made it to the Buffalo game, although he admitted it wasn't easy sitting absolutely still in his box, knowing that any sudden movement — even in a neck brace — would cause him great pain. He hadn't been able to go to Philadelphia or New York, but now he was out of the neck brace and off antibiotics. "I'm finally starting to feel like myself again," he said, sitting in what would always be considered Art Modell's golf cart, watching Friday's practice.

His first season as majority owner had not been an easy one, even putting aside the surgery. He had always been an involved fan — anyone watching him at a Maryland basketball game could tell you that — but now, with his name at the top of the team's masthead, the games had become more personal, tougher to watch, especially if the team wasn't playing well.

"You can see it when you sit in the box with him," said Gary Wiliams, the Maryland basketball coach, who is a close friend. "He's always been into the games, but now it's different. When things aren't going well, he gets very quiet. Steve is usually the last guy in the world you sit with and think, 'I better not talk to him right now,' but in some of those close games, it's pretty apparent that he's not in the mood for small talk."

Dick Cass had also noticed the difference. "I think it has something to do with the fact that when something happens to the team, good or bad, he was involved in the decision making that may have led to what was happening and, maybe more important, he's sitting there thinking, 'Okay, what do we need to do next?' Steve's brain is always working, and now it's spending a lot of time working on the Ravens."

Bisciotti made no bones about the fact that being the majority owner was a lot different for him than being the minority owner. He was very comfortable with the way Ozzie Newsome and Billick ran the team, but the weekly ups and downs were now more difficult for him to take. "I remember thinking the day we played in the Super Bowl, when I was still minority owner, that I would never be more nervous than I felt right then. The way I felt going into the Pittsburgh game, facing the possibility of 0-2, went way beyond that — way beyond it. I was almost sick to my stomach before kickoff. I thought I might throw up. Then when we drove the ball and scored right away, I felt much, much better."

Now Bisciotti was decidedly upbeat. His body felt better and his team was playing better. "Typical Billick team, if you think about it," he said. "It's November and we're starting to build toward December. I really think if we can get through this Dallas game without getting anybody hurt, maybe get a couple guys back next week, we can go into New England and win. They're very, very good but they don't dominate teams. They're beatable. I think we're building to that."

First there was the matter of getting through the Dallas game. On Saturday night Billick again warned the players about not getting sucked into any confrontations with the Cowboys. Like everyone else in the room, he had seen the endless replays of the horrific NBA brawl in Detroit the previous night involving the Indiana Pacers, the Detroit Pistons, and a number of fans. He had also watched complete mayhem break out that afternoon during the Clemson-South Carolina football game. "Fellas, you simply cannot retaliate, no matter what happens in this game," he said. "This is a wounded, frustrated team. Who knows what they will do or what they will try, especially if they get behind. You retaliate, you're the one who will be gone. The league is very hyper right now. They're very image-conscious and what happened last night [in Detroit] will make them even more hyper. They're going to be watching what the NBA does and they're going to be watching for any misbehavior at all during a game. You guys have got to be disciplined and you've got to behave, because if you don't, the league's going to come down on you and on us. I guarantee it."

Sunday morning got off to a less-than-auspicious start. Shortly after arriving at the stadium, David Shaw went looking for Clarence Moore to go over a couple of routes with him before the team went on the field to warm up. He couldn't find him at his locker, so he went into the training room to see if he was getting taped. He was in the training room. He was not getting taped.

"He was lying under a white sheet, shivering uncontrollably, looking as pale as death," Shaw said. "He looked so bad, I was tempted to see if he had a toe tag on him. He looked awful."

Moore had contracted some kind of stomach flu, and the trainers were trying to get fluids into him, hoping he would feel good enough to play in the game. He didn't go out for warm-ups, leaving Billick with a decision to make since he had to submit his list of inactive players by 11:30. Before he went out on the field for pregame, Billick got another piece of bad news: Terry Jones, the number one tight end in Heap's absence, had a bad shoulder. The doctors had hoped he would be able to play, but it felt weak when he tried to warm up early and they were recommending he sit out as a precaution. Billick added Jones to the inactive list and told Zauner to let Wade Richey know he would be dressing for the game. The doctors told him they thought Moore would be able to play, so he left him up.

"The injury list is starting to get critical," Billick said. "Injuries are part of the deal in football, but so is luck. Right now, we aren't having a lot of luck in terms of who we've got injured."

Kevin Byrne put it another way: "We've got a lot of very highly paid football players watching football right now rather than playing it."

When Billick walked onto the field, he sought out Bill Parcells, the way he always made a point of saying hello to any visiting coach. The two men shook hands and Billick tried to make small talk.

"You know I met my wife when she was working for the Cowboys after I was a free agent in Dallas," he said.

"Uh-huh," Parcells said, turning away, clearly uninterested in any further conversation.

Billick shrugged and walked away, baffled and a little bit more fired up to, as he put it, "kick the guy's ass." He had been equally baffled in Washington when Joe Gibbs had made no attempt to walk over and say hello during pregame warm-ups even though the two men were standing no more than twenty yards away from each other. "Maybe it's a Hall of Fame thing," he had joked at the time. Gibbs, he had decided, was just so caught up in pregame preparations that he had forgotten to walk over for a courtesy handshake and hello. Parcells was different. He was just rude.

"Some guys have success and don't take themselves that seriously," Billick said. "I remember last year after we beat Denver, Mike Shanahan shook hands with me and said, 'Don't you ever get tired of kicking my ass?' " I just laughed and said, 'Nope.' Last I looked, Shanahan's won as many Super Bowls as Parcells has."

It was overcast when the game started, and the first quarter didn't brighten anyone's spirits. As Billick had feared, the team came out with little fire and quickly played down to the level of the Cowboys. The only person seen smiling even a little bit in the first quarter was Nick Murphy, who made his NFL debut after the offense quickly went three-and-out the first time it touched the ball. Murphy wobbled a low 41-yard kick to the Dallas 20 that was returned 18 yards by Lance Frazier — one of the last cuts the Ravens had made in training camp. Along with tight end Brett Pierce, another late cut, he had caught on with the Cowboys and was now a starting cornerback.

Murphy was greeted coming off the field by Stover. "Hey," he said, "you caught the ball, you kicked it, and you didn't get it blocked. Congratulations."

Murphy managed a smile. "I'm just glad it's over with," he said. "Now maybe I can start breathing."

On the Ravens' third series, things really began to unravel. On first down, Jamal Lewis picked up 4 yards running left and came up limping. He hobbled to the sideline, cursing in frustration. "Not again," he moaned as he was helped to the bench. "Not again."

While the doctors were making their way over to Lewis, Boller completed a short pass to Travis Taylor, who was hit by Frazier and fumbled. Frazier recovered the ball at the Ravens' 15. The defense held, but Billy Cundiff came in to kick a 19-yard field goal and the Cowboys led, 3–0. The boobirds could be heard warming up in the stands.

The offense finally began to move the ball on the next series. On the first play, Boller went right back to Taylor, who hung on for a 13-yard gain to the 35. Three plays later, on third-and-1, Musa Smith broke through a hole on the right side and charged into Dallas territory, picking up 12 yards and a first down at the 44 before safety Roy Williams brought him down.

But as Williams, coming up from behind Smith, made the tackle, everyone on the Ravens' sideline let out a gasp of horror. With Smith going forward and Williams pulling him backward, Smith's leg literally snapped — his body going one way, his leg going the other. You could hear the sound from the bench. Several players, seeing Smith fall backward and hearing the sound, ran away from the scene, screaming, "Oh my God!" Ray Walls, the backup safety, standing only a few feet from the play, ran back to the bench, buried his head in his hands, and kept screaming, "Oh no, oh no, oh no."

It was one of those football injuries that brings the game and the entire stadium to a halt. Almost before Smith could roll over on his back, the doctors were on the field. Once the horrified reaction from the Ravens' bench had subsided, the stadium became eerily silent. The injury was reminiscent of what had happened to Joe Theismann nineteen years earlier, not that different from what had happened to Trent Smith in the exhibition game a little more than a year ago. Standing on the sideline, Trent Smith shook his head and said quietly, "I just hope he's in shock like I was and not feeling the pain yet."

The doctors immobilized the leg immediately and put it in a temporary cast. Smith was helped by several teammates and the trainers onto the back of a cart that would take him out of the stadium to a helicopter that would fly him to the hospital. Surgery would be performed within hours. The only reason for the wait was to allow the swelling to go down. Roy Williams and fellow cornerback Terence Newman stood by the cart as Smith was loaded onto it and offered their hands and a pat on the back. Ray Lewis was kneeling on the sideline, head down, praying.

Musa Smith would say later that he *was* in shock during those first few moments. "I knew right away that it was bad," he said. "I looked down and I could see the bone sticking out of my leg. No one had to tell me how bad it was. But the pain then wasn't too awful. I just remember guys coming over and wishing me luck when they got me up on the cart."

Smith may have been the quietest man on the team. He had a unique family background, one he didn't like to talk about. Several years earlier, his father had been arrested and charged with allowing terrorist groups to use his Pennsylvania farm as a training ground. Smith also had two brothers, both of them in the marines. One was home, having lost part of his leg the previous spring in Iraq. The other was still in Iraq. "If I hadn't been a football player, I would have gone into the marines, too," he said.

He was an excellent football player who had starred at Georgia even while fending off questions about his father, who was now back on the farm in Pennsylvania. The Ravens had drafted him two years earlier in the third round and he had become a more-than-competent backup running back and a very good special teams player. The summer had been difficult for him: his wife had suffered a miscarriage, but he had been looking forward to getting a chance to play more in the fall. Now his season had ended in an instant, one frightening moment that left him wondering about his future. "All I remember," he said later, "was being angry. It didn't really hurt then. Only later."

Later, in the hospital, he would think dark thoughts, thinking that his football career was over and that it was all too unfair. But he soon talked himself out of that, vowing to come back and play again. "It wasn't easy, though," he said. "I just couldn't figure out why it had to happen."

It happened because awful injuries happen in football. Billick knew there was nothing he could say or do to lessen the shock of what everyone had just witnessed. The potential for injuries like the one Smith had suffered is there on every play in every football game. Worse things can happen — and have. Every year there are stories about players being paralyzed playing football; there are also stories about football players dying, usually on the practice field. More often than not, it happens to high school or college athletes who aren't in the kind of shape professional athletes are. But every-one in the NFL remembered the training camp death in 2001 of Minnesota Vikings offensive tackle Kory Stringer. Mike Solwold, the long snapper who had been released during training camp, had been standing a few feet from Stringer when he collapsed. Gary Zauner had been the special teams coach. Both men still had vivid, frightening memories of that day.

This wasn't nearly at that level. But the unspoken fear on the sideline was that Smith's career might have just ended at the age of twenty-two. Theismann's career had ended on that night in Washington. Trent Smith still wasn't back on the field sixteen months after his injury. Leigh Ann Curl's initial report was somewhat promising: "It looks like a clean break," she said. "If it is, he could be back next season."

At that moment, all anyone could do was hope.

The rest of the first half was as dreary as the first few minutes had been. Billick and Matt Cavanaugh tried the Boller-to-Hymes-to-Boller throw-back play three plays after Smith's injury, perhaps hoping to get everyone back into the spirit of the game. Unfortunately, the Cowboys read the play and Hymes was lucky to have time to throw the ball away. A last-minute attempt to drive for a tieing field goal was cut short when Kevin Johnson fumbled on the Dallas 43. It was 3–0 at halftime.

Billick decided to go the calm route during the break. They had done nothing on offense, but neither had Dallas. When the offensive coaches gathered in his office, he listened as they threw ideas back and forth for a minute and then he said, "Listen, fellas, you've got a rookie cornerback out there [Lance Frazier] and you aren't working him at all. I think you're let-ting him off the hook."

He thought about saying something about Smith's injury but decided against it. "There was nothing to say," he said. "We all felt badly, we were all concerned. But it wasn't the time for a 'win one for the Gipper' speech. We just had to get our act together and play like a good football team."

Eventually, they did. With Jamal Lewis down for the day — he had in-jured his foot — and Musa Smith out, they were down to one running back, unless Harold Morrow, who had last carried the ball in a game in 2001, was pressed into duty. What's more, with Terry Jones inactive, there was no true backup fullback if something were to happen to starter Alan Ricard. All of that meant one thing: Kyle Boller had to throw the ball. On the second series of the second half the Ravens went 78 yards for a touchdown — 74 of those yards in the air. What was more remarkable was who was catching the ball: Dan Wilcox, the late-spring free-agent pickup who had been cut six times in his career, made a spectacular catch over the middle for a 20-yard gain. And Darnell Dinkins, who had been home watching football on TV when the season began, made three catches, including a 17-yarder for the touchdown that put the Ravens ahead, 7–3.

Dinkins had been a George Kokinis/Jim Fassel discovery. Fassel had coached Dinkins in New York, keeping him on the team as a special teams player because he was so impressed by his intensity and enthusiasm. He had originally been signed by the Giants as a fourth-string quarterback but played with such abandon on special teams that Fassel kept him around. Cut during camp by new coach Tom Coughlin because he was injured, he had been sitting at home in Pittsburgh when Kokinis called and asked him if he wanted to try out for the practice squad. He had been so impressive that he had been moved up to the active roster for the Eagles game and was now getting a lot of snaps at tight end.

He was truly grateful to get another chance to play pro football. After college, undrafted and uninvited to any camp as a free agent, he had worked as a juvenile counselor for kids in trouble in Pittsburgh. He had thought that was going to be his career path before the Giants offered him the chance to try out. They sent him to NFL Europe, where he made enough of an impression on special teams to get a serious look from Fassel and his coaches. His attitude toward the game had been best summed up by what he had said to Wade Harman before going out to warm up before his first home game, the game against the Browns. Harman always gathers his tight ends for a final word and a hug by the locker room door before they go out. When he went to Dinkins, his new tight end said to him, "Can you believe this, Coach? It's a beautiful night and I'm getting paid to play football on national TV in a stadium like this. How can anyone be more blessed?"

The Ravens felt pretty blessed to have found Dinkins.

His touchdown opened the floodgates. On the next Dallas series, Ed Reed intercepted Testaverde at the Ravens' 35. Six plays later, Boller found Kevin Johnson isolated on Lance Frazier and threw right over him for a

31-yard touchdown to make it 14–3. Stover added a 50-yard field goal early in the fourth quarter. Testaverde then threw a strike — to Chad Williams, who returned it 44 yards for a touchdown. That was enough for Parcells. He yanked Testaverde in favor of Drew Henson. On his first play, Henson was sacked by Marques Douglas and fumbled. Terrell Suggs fell on it on the 1-yard line. Chester Taylor scored from there and, even though Murphy bobbled the snap and Stover didn't get to try the extra point, it was 30–3. The Ravens had scored 30 points in twelve minutes and seven seconds after failing to score for thirty-eight minutes and seven seconds. They had turned an ugly afternoon into an easy victory. The Cowboys scored a consolation touchdown late, and the final was 30–10.

Billick resisted the urge to say anything to Parcells during their brief handshake. Walking off the field, he heard the PA announcer say something that surprised him: "The Ravens 7-3 record is their best record after ten games in franchise history." Granted, the franchise was only nine years old. Still, Billick hadn't known that. He pointed it out to the players — admitting he hadn't known it — and told them they were now in a position to do something really special, going to play the Super Bowl champions on the road the following week.

"Championships are won on the road," he said. "This will be a great way to start doing that."

Not all the postgame news was good. Clean break or no, Musa Smith was done for the year. Jamal Lewis appeared likely to be down for at least a week, perhaps two. Several other players had been nicked during the game. Orlando Brown's knee was sore. Travis Taylor had suffered a minor concussion on the play in the first quarter when he had fumbled, but he hadn't told anyone until late in the game.

There was also another issue: Corey Fuller. With Sanders and McAlister down, Fuller had apparently expected to play most of the game. Mike Nolan and the defensive backs coaches, Johnnie Lynn and Dennis Thurman, had opted to use Ray Walls more often in the second half. At one point, when Lynn told Fuller that Walls was going to be in during the next series, Fuller screamed that he had been told earlier *he* was going to be in on the next series and insisted he was going into the game.

It was Sanders who stepped in at that point. "You do what the coaches tell you," he said to Fuller.

"But, Deion, I'm supposed to be in. . . ."

"I don't care what's supposed to be, I only care what is. He says you aren't in, you aren't in. You know that."

Fuller knew that. But he didn't like it.

When the game ended, Fuller went after Nolan in the locker room, telling him that he had been unfair and that he had disrespected him by playing Walls ahead of him. Nolan told him the locker room wasn't the place and this wasn't the time for an argument, especially after a 20-point win. He then went in to tell Billick he could expect a visit from Fuller. Before he was finished, Fuller was knocking on the door.

Fuller was angry, frustrated, flailing. "If you don't respect me, just cut me," he said at one point.

"Corey, I want you to calm down," Billick said. "No one here disrespects you. That's not what this is about. It's about what is best for the team and clearly defining roles. I promise you by Wednesday your role will be clearly defined."

They went around in circles for twenty solid minutes. Billick felt bad for both men.

"Mike has to be the bad guy in this for Corey," he said. "Corey's emotionally committed to me, and Mike's his boss day-to-day. He badly wants to be a contributor, but it's hard for him now. I've never seen a player who knows when the time has come to move on. If Corey's not there, he's very close. He certainly can't be an every-down back, he can't really be a nickel corner. He can be a backup safety, and that's about it. But it's tough telling that to him. He's a proud man, a competitor.

"Mike has to feel like a whipped dog right now. He's trying so hard to hold the defense together. We go out, beat up in the secondary the way we were, and shut them down completely. So, what happens? I'm trying to get him in to talk to the media to get him some attention and we have to spend twenty minutes shouting about Corey Fuller."

Billick sighed. "We're 7-3. Best record in franchise history. So why do I feel so damn tired?"

23

Mud Bowl

THE BEGINNING OF A NEW WEEK did not mean the end of the Corey Fuller incident even if both Thanksgiving and a game against the Super Bowl champions were both on the upcoming calendar.

When Mike Nolan looked at the game tape, he counted thirty-four snaps for Ray Walls and thirty for Fuller. He had believed the numbers were more lopsided in Walls's favor and was even angrier about the outburst when he saw how much Fuller had played in the game. Exactly how to handle him would have to be discussed again during Monday's personnel meeting.

Player-coach confrontations occur in football all the time. Occasionally, they are brief shouting matches. When they occur on the sidelines, on camera, they become a big deal. The most memorable Ravens coach-player confrontation had occurred a year earlier, when Jim Colletto had been trying to make a point about blocking schemes to Orlando Brown at halftime of a game against the Miami Dolphins. Brown, six foot seven and 360 pounds, had started screaming at Colletto, who was almost a foot shorter, weighed about 180 pounds less, and was twenty-six years older.

Brown was so frustrated that he began tearing apart his locker, yelling, "Just let me play the game!" at Colletto over and over again. Figuring that anything he said at that moment would further inflame Brown, Colletto called Billick over. Billick ordered Brown to sit down and calm down. "Look at me," he said. "If you can't look at me and you can't calm down, you can't play. He's only trying to help you play better. You should know that."

Brown calmed down, and nothing further was said. This was different. For one thing, Brown was a starter the Ravens had invested a lot of money in, so a brief blowup wasn't about to get him into serious trouble with the coaching staff. What's more, they all understood he was high-strung. Billick had learned after the incident in the Cleveland game (when Brown had been hit with a personal foul call on the two-point conversion after Ed Reed's clinching touchdown) that Brown's eyes had been affected by medication he was taking for a sore knee, which was part of the reason he had exploded when hit there on the play.

Fuller was different. He was clinging to his spot on the roster for dear life. There was a lot of feeling within the coaching staff that he should have been cut early in the season. What had kept him around was Billick's respect for him and that he had always been a good locker-room guy, someone who said the right things and did the right things. Now that was no longer the case.

"What upset me," Nolan said when the subject came up at the Monday meeting, "was when I looked at the film, he only had four less plays than Ray. On Sunday I thought it was more skewed than that and maybe he had a legitimate gripe, given that we had told both guys we were going to alternate them. That's essentially what we did."

Both defensive backs coaches, Johnnie Lynn and Dennis Thurman, said they thought Walls was the better player right now. "I love Corey," said Thurman, who had played defensive back in the league for nine years and knew how much tougher it became as you got older. "But I just don't think, at thirty-three, he can do the job anymore."

Everyone in the room expected Billick to support Fuller, and ultimately, his vote would be the final one. No one really expected Fuller to be cut at this stage of the season, but the issue appeared to be hanging in the air when Vince Newsome spoke up. Newsome (no relation to Ozzie) was the team's assistant director of pro scouting. He had also been a defensive back in the league, playing for ten years before a spinal injury had ended his career. He was soft-spoken, someone who voiced an opinion only when he felt strongly. Now he felt the need to speak up. "I think there's still value in Corey," he said. "Before you throw him out the door, I think you should consider the fact that you may need him again before the season's over."

"I never said throw him out the door," Thurman said.

That changed the tone of the conversation. Billick told Nolan he should sit Fuller down on Wednesday and tell him exactly what his role would be going forward. If Fuller objected, Nolan should send him to Billick. Everyone in the room was fairly convinced that Fuller wouldn't object. To begin with, he would have two full days to calm down. During the second half of the season, Billick gives the team both Monday and Tuesday off after wins (and occasionally after a well-played loss), so few players would be in the building until Wednesday. Beyond that, Fuller was smart enough to know he was on thin ice. It was also quite likely that Deion Sanders and Ray Lewis would make it clear to him that fighting the coaching staff wasn't a good idea.

The Fuller situation was upsetting to Billick, because he genuinely liked him, but was really a minor issue, given the week to come. Like the Ravens, the Patriots were a banged-up team. Both their starting cornerbacks were out for the season and they had the usual assortment of injuries that afflict NFL teams in late November. The Ravens would again be without two key offensive components: Jamal Lewis's foot would keep him out for at least a week, and Todd Heap, although finally starting to make progress, was still at least a week away. So was Deion Sanders. Chris McAlister thought he would be able to play, but he wasn't certain.

Dave Zastudil had been in so much pain after the team arrived home from New York that he pulled into Mike Flynn's driveway and slept on his couch. "I just couldn't go any further," he said. "The pain was unbearable." He was feeling considerably better and talking about perhaps punting in another week against the Cincinnati Bengals. Nick Murphy wished him no ill will but was fervently hoping he would delay his return at least another week. "I play in three games, I get a vested year," he said.

A vested year was a big deal to a player like Murphy. It meant that if he made a team in 2005, he would be paid $305,000, as opposed to the rookie minimum of $235,000. It would also mean he was only three years away from being a fully vested four-year player. Murphy had kicked well enough on Sunday that any thoughts about holding another round of kicking tryouts — always a possibility when a new kicker is brought in — had vanished. "He did exactly what I told him to do," Zauner said. "He caught it, he kicked it, and he didn't have a real bad kick in the bunch. He did fine."

The bigger news was the emergence of Darnell Dinkins as a legitimate target for Boller. Considering that he had never lined up at tight end in the NFL until the Eagles game, Dinkins had been a revelation. He was a good blocker, played hard on special teams, and could catch the ball. Plus, even though he was very quiet and deeply religious off the field, he had a little bit of a mean streak — the kind coaches like — on the field. Rex Ryan had been impressed the very first day Dinkins had practiced with the team, when he got into a scuffle with Jarret Johnson, something of a tough guy himself. "There's no back down in that kid," Ryan said. Coming from Ryan, that was the ultimate compliment.

Playing the Patriots was important to the Ravens on a number of levels. The first — and most obvious — was that they had won two of the last three Super Bowls, including the most recent one. They were 9-1, tied with the Steelers for the best record in the AFC. There was also the Belichick factor. Most of the Ravens' key front office people had worked with (or for) Belichick in Cleveland. Ozzie Newsome often talked about how much he had learned from Belichick about coaching and personnel. Everyone had nothing but respect for his football knowledge. But most of those same people had all sorts of stories about what a difficult boss he had been. Almost to a man, those who had worked with him were stunned by the emergence of the "new Belichick" in New England. He had gone from being a football geek who seemed to have all the qualities needed in a coordinator but few of those needed in a head coach to an absolute slam-dunk Hall of Fame coach.

He still seemed to make a point of not filling up notebooks during press conferences, but he had developed a good relationship with a number of key media people around the league. Clearly, he was the leader of this remarkable Patriots team and his players all looked up to him — not just for his football knowledge but for his leadership. The general consensus in the NFL — and the results bore this out — was that Belichick and his right-hand man, Scott Pioli, ran the best franchise in football. The Ravens, who had a very healthy self-respect for their way of doing things, wanted to believe they were every bit as good. The only way to prove it was to beat the Patriots — now and, more important, in postseason. The Patriots were king. No one could inherit the throne without knocking them from it.

"What they do is they wait for you to break," Billick said. "They don't give you anything quick or easy. If you want to score, you probably have to go ten or twelve plays and they just bide their time and wait for you to make a mistake. They almost know you'll screw up eventually. Kyle has to be ready to throw the ball fifty times in this game. That isn't necessarily a bad thing. If we're going to beat these guys and Indianapolis and Pittsburgh, we're probably going to have to do it late, which means he's going to have to make plays."

Boller had ended up 23-of-34 for 232 yards, his best day of the season, on Sunday. He had been voted player of the game, and when he had appeared on the video boards at the end of the game, many of the fans who had booed him lustily in the Buffalo and Cleveland games had cheered. That was the way of the NFL world. When Billick had looked at the tape of the Dallas game, he had said it easily could have been a "rat-killer"— an embarrassing rout — if his team had been healthy. But at this time of year, few teams were healthy. "It isn't so much how many injuries you have this time of year, because everybody's got 'em," Billick said. "It's *who* you have injured. We lost two running backs in one series on Sunday."

Jamal Lewis was actually flying to North Carolina on Monday to have his foot examined by a specialist. He was hoping someone — anyone — would tell him that the diagnosis of the Ravens' doctors, who believed he would be out at least two weeks, was wrong. In the meantime, the Ravens needed a backup running back, so they signed Jamel White, who had been waived earlier in the year by Cleveland and more recently by Tampa Bay. He would spend most of the week trying to learn the offense. Chester Taylor would have to take almost all the snaps on Sunday.

For the first time all year, the weather was likely to be a major factor. On the last weekend in November in Massachusetts, no one could even begin to predict what it would be like. One thing was almost certain: it would be cold. Kickoff had been moved back from 1 P.M. to 4:15 because CBS wanted it as the back end of its doubleheader. That meant the sun would just about be down by the end of the first quarter. Cold they could handle. Snow or sleet or rain would be another story. The playing surface in the new (third-year) Gillette Stadium was real grass, one of the few NFL stadiums — especially in a cold-weather city — that had not installed some kind of turf. When the stadium opened, the idea had seemed like a good one: players generally prefer grass because it is easier on their legs. But any kind of precipitation turned the field into an absolute swamp. The Patriots loved it because they were used to it. Quarterback Tom Brady's first comment after the Patriots had clinched home field throughout the playoffs the previous year had been "What this means is that someone's got to come in here and figure out a way to beat us on this terrible field."

The Patriots loved their terrible field. The worse the weather, the more they loved it.

Billick always changed the practice schedule on Thanksgiving, moving practice up to the morning so players and coaches could get home to spend the afternoon and evening with their families. Practice was earlier in the day this time of year anyway because Billick wanted to be outside as much as possible, and by late afternoon the sun was starting to disappear. The team always had a Thanksgiving celebration on Saturday, which was just a walk-through day. Families came to the facility to spend some time before the team left to fly to Providence, where it would stay on Saturday night, as Gillette Stadium was exactly midway between Providence and Boston.

Billick was pleased with practice on Thanksgiving morning. "I really think yesterday and today are as good as we've been all season," he said. "They understand where we are right now and the opportunity that's there for them this week."

Terrell Suggs probably summed up what everyone was thinking, saying over and over again, "They've got something we want."

Indeed they did.

The weather report for Sunday wasn't very good: wind and rain, the rain increasing as the afternoon went on. If the game had kicked off at one o'clock as originally scheduled, there might have been a chance to avoid the rain. Now it seemed unlikely.

It is truly a shame that the Patriots play their games in Foxboro. The franchise was launched in Boston in 1960, part of the then-fledgling American Football League. There may not be a better sports town in the country than Boston. Everyone talks about the Red Sox and their legendary fans, but the Celtics and Bruins have also had a fanatic following for years. The case can be made that the city is home to three teams that are among the signature franchises in their sport. The Celtics were the dominant dynasty in the NBA and still own far more titles (sixteen) than any other NBA team. The Bruins haven't won nearly as many championships (five), but the two they won in 1970 and 1972 were won with the great Bobby Orr as their backbone and Phil Esposito shattering NHL scoring records. Until October of 2004, the Red Sox were as famous for not winning championships as other teams are for winning them.

The Patriots never quite fit into that lore. Maybe it was because they began as part of an upstart league and never really found a true home in Boston. Maybe it was because they didn't make a Super Bowl until 1986 and then got blown out, 46–10, by the Chicago Bears when they did. Or maybe it was because they left Boston and moved to Foxboro — which consists of about six fast-food stops and four gas stations — in the late 1970s and built a stadium that looked like it came out of a kid's construction set in a spot with exactly one road — Route 1 — leading in and out of the place.

Gillette Stadium is a typical, modern NFL stadium, complete with all the amenities required by today's owners. It has a mock lighthouse that sits at one end of the field that distinguishes it from other stadiums, but it still is in the middle of nowhere since it is built on the same spot as the old Foxboro Stadium. These days, though, that doesn't matter. Nor, apparently, do the lack of access roads. Foxboro has become the pro football capital of the world.

The turnaround began when Bill Parcells took the Patriots to their second Super Bowl in January of 1997. They lost again, to the Green Bay Packers, but by a far more respectable score, 35–21. That appearance was sullied by the internal battle going on between Parcells and team owner Robert Kraft. Parcells left right after the Super Bowl to coach the New York Jets, and Bill Belichick, who had become his defensive coordinator for a second time (they had first been together with the New York Giants) after being fired by the Modells en route from Cleveland to Baltimore, went with him. In fact, Belichick was technically the head coach for a brief period while the Jets and Patriots negotiated compensation to the Patriots for the loss of Parcells.

When Parcells retired (again) after three seasons, Belichick was again supposed to be head coach. But he did to the Jets what Parcells had done to the Patriots — negotiating with New England to have complete control of the team rather than coach in New York, where Parcells was still hanging around as general manager. Technically, Belichick was the Jets' coach twice and never coached a game or ran a practice.

In New England he had built the league's model franchise, helped by Scott Pioli, an old Cleveland ally. The Patriots went 5-11 in his first season as coach (2000), then went 11-5 the next season after Tom Brady, who had been the 199th pick (sixth round) in the 2000 NFL draft, replaced an injured Drew Bledsoe at quarterback. The Patriots stunned the heavily favored St. Louis Rams in the Super Bowl at the end of that season, then, after missing the playoffs during the 2002 season (with a 9-7 record), they came back to go 14-2 and win another Super Bowl after the 2003 season. They had finished that season with a fifteen-game winning streak, and their only loss in 2004 had been at Pittsburgh. That meant they were on a 24-1 streak when the Ravens came to town.

It started to rain at about two o'clock on Sunday afternoon, which was fine with Mike Nolan. "The windier and rainier, the better," he said. "They do so many things in their passing game. If the weather takes a few of them away, that helps us."

Once again Billick was scrambling to decide who was going to be on his inactive list. Orlando Brown's arthritic knee had been sore during the week, but not sore enough for him to miss any practice on Wednesday or Thursday. Billick had told him to rest for most of the day on Friday. But by the time Brown got off the team bus Sunday afternoon, the knee was bothering him. No one wanted to play in this game more than Brown. He was convinced that he would never have played in the NFL if not for Belichick and he wanted to show his old coach that, at thirty-three, he still had it as a player. Now, about two hours before kickoff, he and Andy Tucker went out to test the knee. Tucker stood and watched while Brown got in his stance and tried to push off the already slippery turf in the end zone near the Ravens' tunnel. Each time Brown tried to come out of his stance, Tucker could see him wince. He went back and told Billick that Brown couldn't play. Ethan Brooks would have to start at right tackle. Brown was devastated as he climbed back into his street clothes.

The other big question mark was Chris McAlister. He had practiced lightly during the week, protecting the shoulder he had reinjured during the Jets game. Shortly after the team arrived in the locker room, McAlister told Nolan he didn't think he could play. He was concerned that the first time he took a hit, the shoulder would go again. Nolan suggested that the two of them talk to Billick about it. Nolan knew that going into this game without McAlister was potentially disastrous, given the quality of the Patriots' quarterback and their deep receiving corps. He wasn't about to push an injured player to play, but he also knew that playing two weeks after a stinger, even a bad one, was not risky even though a good hit could be painful.

Billick had not started the day well, taking a wrong turn when he arrived at the stadium and had turned away from the locker room rather than toward it. He had walked in to find Tucker waiting for him with the news that Brown was down. Now Nolan and McAlister walked in and shut the door.

"Poor Mike," Billick said later. "One week he's got one cornerback screaming he's not playing enough, the next week he's got another one saying he can't play at all."

Billick asked McAlister if he was concerned about risking further injury. McAlister said the doctors had told him that wasn't likely, he was just worried about his ability to tackle if the shoulder was still weak. That was a legitimate concern. Billick suggested that if he played on only the left side of the defense, the shoulder would probably not take a hard hit since he would be using his right shoulder most of the time to tackle running backs coming out of the backfield. Reluctantly, McAlister agreed. Billick told him to let the doctors know if it got too tough, and they would get him out right away. McAlister had had his shoulder injected in 2003 after a stinger but had vowed never to do it again, because he was still in pain "months" after the season ended. He did take a weekly shot — like many players — of a painkiller, but not one that numbed a specific body part.

Billick took a deep breath and walked out of the locker room and down the tunnel to take his pregame walk around the field. He got one step out of the tunnel, felt the rain coming down in sheets, and turned back. "Ritual isn't really *that* important," he said.

Nolan walked out of the tunnel and shook his head in disappointment. It was windy, but not windy enough. "If this was golf, the wind would matter," he said. "But it's not. A football's a lot heavier. Brady will be able to do what he wants to do. This wind won't affect him."

The skies were black by the time the teams took the field for the kickoff.

"The lighthouse is very appropriate today," Dick Cass had said before taking refuge in the dry owner's box.

The first half went about as well as the Ravens might have hoped. Not surprisingly, both offenses struggled with the conditions and the fact that they were facing an excellent defense. Boller had never played in weather quite like this in his life. "I remember in high school I played one game in the rain," he said. "But it was nothing like this."

Boller began the game without a glove on his throwing hand but had so much trouble keeping his hand dry between snaps that he tried a glove in the second quarter. That felt awkward and the glove quickly got wet, so he went back to his bare hand. Brady, who was far more accustomed to this sort of weather, wasn't having much more luck. He did come up with a critical completion early, finding David Patten for a 37-yard gain when the Ravens had the Patriots backed up with a third-and-12 on their own 3 in the first quarter. The Patriots didn't get any points out of the drive, but they did reestablish field position thanks to that play. Fortunately for the Ravens, Nick Murphy was doing an excellent job of keeping them in good shape in the field-position battle. The conditions didn't seem to bother him at all. He kept booming one good kick after another. For most of the first half, he was the closest thing the Ravens had to an offense.

The Patriots scored first, Brady piecing together a drive that bogged down at the Ravens' 10 when Marques Douglas sacked Brady on third down. Adam Vinatieri, likely to someday be the second placekicker (Jan Stenerud is currently the only one) voted into the Hall of Fame, came on to kick a 28-yard field goal that made it 3–0. It looked like that would be the halftime score until Corey Dillon decided to help out the Ravens. With the Patriots trying to run the clock out in the final minute deep in their own territory, Dillon took a handoff from Brady with fifty-six seconds left and, for some reason, ran out of bounds — stopping the clock. The Ravens had already used two time-outs. If Dillon had stayed inbounds, the Ravens would have had to use their last time-out. One more running play would have taken the clock to forty-five seconds — or less — and by the time the officials set the ball and started the play clock, the half would have been just about over by the time the Patriots punted.

Dillon is a talented back who had always had a reputation for finding trouble when he played in Cincinnati. He had fit in well with the Patriots, clearly happy to be on a good team. His mistake surprised the Ravens, but didn't really shock them. "The man can run out of bounds with the best of them" was Deion Sanders's comment.

The Ravens ended up using their last time-out after Dillon — staying inbounds — picked up 2 yards on third down. That meant Josh Miller had to punt with fifty-one seconds still left. B. J. Sams fielded the punt at the Ravens' 42 and returned it to the Patriots' 46. Amazingly, the Patriots had committed two major penalties during the punt: a face mask on linebacker Matt Chatham and an unsportsmanlike conduct penalty on Tedy Bruschi, the All-Pro linebacker. Those gaffes moved the ball to the New England 16 with thirty-six seconds left. This was remarkably un-Patriot-like, and Belichick was clearly perturbed by the sudden turn of events. The Ravens managed to get the ball to the 4-yard line, and Boller spiked the ball to stop the clock with nine seconds left. With no time-outs left, the only option was to try to throw the ball into the end zone and Boller's pass for Randy Hymes was broken up. They settled for a Stover field goal that tied the game at intermission.

"We've got them playing our game," Billick said. "Stay patient, keep doing what we're doing, and we'll win the game."

The locker room was alive with anticipation. Thinking you could walk into the stadium of the defending champions and win was one thing. Actually doing it was another. Nolan was still nervous. "Guys, we have got to hit the quarterback in this half," he said. "If we don't, he'll put up the thirty points he didn't put up in the first half. He's that good."

If it was possible, it was raining harder when the second half started. The field was pure mud, especially in the middle portion, where most of the play took place. It was amazing that anyone could run forward in the stuff. It was clear from the start that Belichick had read his team the riot act during halftime. The Patriots took the kickoff and moved down the field, and Vinatieri, clearly a good mudder, kicked a 40-yard field goal to make it 6–3. The Ravens offense, still struggling to find something, went three-and-out. This time Brady got his team to the Baltimore 30, and Vinatieri was good from 48 yards. Still, it was only 9–3. If they could just find some way to get the offense moving . . .

They couldn't. Another three-and-out for the offense. Murphy boomed a 51-yard kick, but it was largely negated by a 14-yard return by Troy

Brown and a personal foul on Bart Scott. The Patriots started at the Ravens' 48. Dillon, not running out of bounds, picked up 12 yards on three straight carries. A pass interference call on Adalius Thomas was worth 12 more yards, then Brady found Deion Branch across the middle for a first down at the Ravens' 5. Dillon carried to the 1 as the quarter ended. At that stage of the game, even a field goal was probably going to be a death knell for the Ravens because it would give the Patriots a two-score lead. Dillon made sure a field goal wasn't necessary on the first play of the fourth quarter, pounding in from the left side. Belichick, wanting a two-touchdown lead, went for two and got it (Dillon again), and it was 17–3. One couldn't help but wonder if Belichick had said something to Dillon about the out-of-bounds play at halftime because he ran with renewed vigor and toughness in the second half.

A two-touchdown lead was probably going to be insurmountable, but just to make certain there was no doubt, Bruschi, blitzing from the right side, sacked Boller on the second play from scrimmage and he fumbled the wet ball. In the ensuing scramble, a number of players had a shot at the ball, but it was backup defensive end Jarvis Green, playing in place of All-Pro Richard Seymour, who ended up on top of it in the end zone. The score had gone from 9–3 to 24–3 in less than a minute. The rest of the game was nothing more than forty minutes of misery for everyone, especially the Ravens, who had seen their hopes of an upset blow up completely. The play that summed up the day came on the last drive of the day, with the Ravens in a no-huddle offense, trying to get a consolation touchdown. Scrambling desperately, Boller picked up 13 yards to the Patriots' 35 with 1:20 to play. Except that play came back because Jonathan Ogden — of all people — was called for holding. Ogden gets called for holding about as frequently as lunar eclipses occur. It was the perfect punctuation mark to what had turned out to be a lost day in the rain, the wind, and the mud.

They trudged down the tunnel in absolute silence, wet and cold and sore and angry.

"That's where we need to get to," Billick said quietly. "The road to the Super Bowl probably goes right through here. We may very well be back here in January."

There was a lot of work ahead of them if they wanted to get to that point. The Patriots were 10-1. So were the Steelers, who had beaten the

Redskins earlier in the day. The Ravens were 7-4. Any realistic hopes of defending the division title were now gone.

"We have to focus on the wild card now," Billick said quietly as he dressed. "Which is fine. We can still get where we want to go that way."

It was the road they had taken to the Super Bowl four years ago. Billick would remind his team of that fact repeatedly. Their first job was to make sure they had the chance to get back on that road again.

24

Roadblock

REGARDLESS OF WEATHER or field conditions, the loss to the Patriots was sobering. They had been dominated in the second half in a way they weren't used to. Furthermore, the Ravens all knew that if they wanted to make any noise in the playoffs, they would have to go to a place like New England or Pittsburgh in bad weather conditions and win. Unlike 2000, when a wild-card team could host a first-round game — which the Ravens did — wild-card teams now opened on the road because there were four division winners, and each played at least one playoff game at home. The two wild-card teams from each conference were seeded fifth and sixth, regardless of record. The only way a wild-card team could host a playoff game under the new setup would be if both reached the conference final: then the fifth seed would play at home. That was an extremely unlikely scenario.

Billick's thoughts early Monday morning were not on the playoffs. He was sitting at his desk, watching tape, when Ozzie Newsome walked in with an e-mail from the league office. Apparently, the Patriots had complained about the fact that Orlando Brown had not been on the Ravens' injured list during the week and then had not played in the game. The league had e-mailed the Ravens demanding an explanation. "Here's the explanation," Billick said, exasperated. "He was hurt."

That would not be good enough for the league. Because so many coaches play games with their injury lists — wanting to make it as difficult as possible for an opponent to know whom to prepare for — the league tries to stay vigilant if it suspects someone is trying to pull a fast one. That's one reason why teams are required to tape their practices. If a player listed as out or doubtful shows up on a practice tape, that means the team was trying to hide that he was going to play. Conversely, if someone not on an injury list or listed as probable doesn't show up on practice tapes, that means the team is trying to hide the fact that he is injured. The Patriots — and the league — were accusing the Ravens of hiding Brown's injury.

"Here's my response to that," Billick said. "Why don't they e-mail [Bill] Parcells and ask him why Julius Jones was listed as doubtful all week before they played us and then carried the ball thirty times in the game on Sunday?"

The team's official response would be a little less heated. They would send the league practice tapes from Wednesday and Thursday showing Brown taking most of the snaps at right tackle. That would put an end to Zeus-gate.

As the Ravens began preparing for their rematch at home with the Bengals, Billick was far more concerned with rebuilding his team's confidence. He knew there had to be some doubts after the way they had been dominated in the second half by the Patriots. He decided to pull out the schedule chart he had shown them in preseason that contained his formula for a 12-4 record, which he had thought prior to the start of the season would be good enough to win the AFC North. With the Steelers 10-1, that wasn't going to happen, but 12-4 was still possible and would get them into the playoffs as the first AFC wild card. According to Billick's chart, the team was one game behind where it should be: he had figured on 8-3 going into December: 4-1 before the bye week; 2-1 in the Bills, Eagles, Browns block; and 2-1 against the Jets, Cowboys, and Patriots. The last two blocks had gone exactly as figured; the losses had even been to the teams they were most likely to lose to: Philadelphia and New England, both on the road. The only glitch had come early, when they had lost to Cleveland and Kansas City. One of those games had figured, in Billick's projections, to be a win.

Billick had them going 4-1 in the season's final stretch, which would now produce an 11-5 record. That, too, would almost certainly be good enough to make the playoffs. But it wouldn't be easy. There were three home games left: Cincinnati, the New York Giants, and the Miami Dolphins. Those three games should produce wins. All three teams were under 500 — the Dolphins were fighting with the San Francisco 49ers for the league's worst record and the first draft pick and had already lost Coach Dave Wannstedt; the Giants had started well under Tom Coughlin but were fading rapidly; the Bengals were playing better than they had early on, but Billick didn't think they could beat his team in Baltimore. The two road games were another story: at Indianapolis and at Pittsburgh. The Colts had started slowly but were now rolling, Peyton Manning heading toward a record-smashing season, and the Steelers still had only one loss — the second week of the season in Baltimore before Ben Roethlisberger became the starter at quarterback. They hadn't lost a game since Terrell Suggs had sacked Tommy Maddox and forced Roethlisberger into the lineup. To win either road game would be difficult. If they held serve at home and lost the two road games, they would be 10-6. History said that would be good enough to make postseason, but in 2004 the AFC was deep in potential ten-win teams.

"I'd rather not take any chances," Billick said. "We need to take the approach that we're going to win all five, but we damn well better win at least four."

It was on Tuesday that Mike Nolan and Mike Singletary asked Billick if they could talk to him privately about the offense. Billick knew what was coming. But he respected both men and knew why they were concerned. So he sat down with them in Nolan's office to listen.

"Coach, we keep saying we're an old-school team, but we aren't playing like one," Singletary said. "Mike and I both understand that the offense has to make adjustments with Jamal out, but we threw the ball thirty-five times on Sunday [with only twenty runs] in a driving rain. Is that really us?"

"I think Matt thought, and I tend to agree, that was our best chance to move the ball against that defense on that day, given the players we had on the field," Billick said.

Nolan was shaking his head. "Even if that's true, sometimes you have to think about your defense, too, especially in a game like that, where it's 3–3 at halftime. I've been on the offensive side of the ball and I know there are some times you have to try to just give your defense a breather, take some time off the clock even if you aren't putting points on the board. Three incomplete passes doesn't do that. We haven't done that for weeks. I know the offense is hurt, but so's the defense. With injuries and all the special team guys who were up, we only dressed nineteen guys on Sunday. There's not a team in the league dressing so few players on defense."

Billick felt he knew exactly where Nolan and Singletary were coming from. In addition to losing the game, Nolan had seen what had started out as an excellent defensive effort — on national TV — blow up into a lopsided loss, even if the offense had given up the last touchdown.

"You guys are stacking," Billick said. "I understand why, but that's what you're doing."

He walked back to his office and sat down. "Some days," he said, "I wonder if *I'm* not stacking."

Billick's talk to the team on Wednesday covered a lot of territory. He had given them Monday off in spite of the loss because he thought rest was more important at this point than going through the game tape. There just wasn't that much to be learned from looking at the New England tape. They had been outplayed in the second half. Move on.

He began the Wednesday morning meeting by again showing them the schedule chart. They had seen this before and he knew it. He also knew that he had already given them a lot of pep talks. So, after he finished reminding them that everything they wanted from the season was still very much there for them, he called them out.

He went back to *Good to Great,* the motivational book he had told them about before the season. One of the sections in the book was called "Confront the Brutal Facts." Knowing all the whispers going on in the locker room — all of which he heard in one form or another — he confronted them. He knew the defense wasn't happy with the offense — specifically the play calling. He knew the offensive line wasn't happy, either. They were a great run-blocking line being asked to pass-block 60 percent of the time.

"Here are the brutal facts, fellas," he said. "Defense, you've got a team backed up inside the 5-yard line on the first series of a game, you have to stop them! Offensive line, you aren't happy with how much we're passing, well, that's on you. We averaged under four yards a carry on Sunday and we didn't have a single run over ten yards. You want to put that on the backs? Or is it on you? You want thirty-five to forty run calls in a game, fine, I'm all for it: *earn* it. It's easy to point fingers. That's what losing teams do.

Winning teams look within and figure out how to get better. We do that, we can still have the kind of season we all want. If we don't, we won't."

It was probably as sharply as he had spoken to them all season. It was December now and there was no longer time to find a comfort level. The doctor in North Carolina had told Jamal Lewis the same thing the Ravens' doctors had told him: two weeks. That meant he wouldn't play Sunday. Deion Sanders wanted to play, but the pain in his foot was going to make it impossible. He and Lewis were limping around the facility in what appeared to be matching boots, protecting their wounded feet. They sat together at lunch on Thursday and talked about the off-season.

"Maybe, when I go away, I'll start working on a book," Lewis said. "I think I've got a story to tell and I'll have the time."

"When you come out, I'm going to interview you about it," Sanders said.

"For who?"

"I don't know, *60 Minutes* maybe. Nothing second-rate, I guarantee you that."

Lewis told the media on Wednesday that the doctors had told him he was out at least another week. Billick groaned when he saw that. "In the future, before you declare yourself out of a game, do me a favor and check with me," he told Lewis. "You don't need to tell everyone on Wednesday. Let 'em wonder a little."

Orlando Brown would not appear on any practice tapes in the coming week, nor would he appear in the game. Billick wondered if he would play in a game again during the season.

"He told me he didn't trust our doctors to get him better," Billick said. "I said, 'Zeus, who do you trust?' He said, 'No one.' I think that's accurate."

Dave Zastudil needed another week before he could think about coming back, but that was okay. Nick Murphy's punting had been about the only bright spot in the game on Sunday. He would get his three weeks and his vested year. Perhaps more important, he had proven to people he could punt in the NFL. "All I ever wanted was a chance to prove I can kick in this league," he said. "These guys gave it to me. Now I think I've really got a chance to make it someplace next season."

The best news of the week was that Todd Heap was taking snaps in practice. He still felt some tenderness in the ankle but was convinced he was ready to play. He was, in fact, dying to play. He had missed nine games. "It feels more like nine hundred," he said. "Standing on the sidelines is hard, especially when we're struggling. There have been times when I wondered if I would ever get better."

Even though he was better, Billick wasn't certain about playing him on Sunday. He wanted to be absolutely certain that he was 100 percent for the game in Indianapolis in two weeks. To do that, he needed at least one game under his belt — next week against the Giants. He called Heap in after practice to ask him what he thought. Heap, naturally, wanted to play. The trainers told Billick there was no reason to hold him out, that he wouldn't be risking reinjuring the ankle by playing him. Billick told Heap they would try it and see how he felt. Heap felt as if he had been paroled from jail.

Even though the current season was still hanging in the balance, it was time for the team to begin thinking about next season. Once the season ended — whenever that was — things would move fast. Already one coach — Wannstedt — was gone. Rumors were rampant that Butch Davis wasn't going to make it to the end of the season in Cleveland. Dennis Erickson had a long-term contract in San Francisco, but the 49ers had one victory and there was talk that 49ers owner John York might clean house and start over again at the end of the season. Mike Tice, a close friend of Billick's, still appeared to be at risk in Minnesota. Jim Haslett was certainly under the gun — again — in New Orleans.

When a head coach gets fired, all or most of his staff gets fired with him. That puts coaches on the market. It also opens opportunities for other coaches. Jim Fassel would be extremely interested in any of the head coaching vacancies. So would Mike Nolan. If Nolan got a job, he would probably want to take some of his staff — certainly Mike Singletary — with him. The Ravens had to know where they wanted to look if they found themselves with staff openings. They would also have to deal with the issue of Matt Cavanaugh. Before Billick sat down on the Friday before the Bengals game to meet with Steve Bisciotti, Ozzie Newsome, and Dick Cass, he knew he was going to have a hard time making a case to keep Cavanaugh. This pained him for the simple reason that he liked Cavanaugh and, after six years of working together, considered him a friend. But the offense was still lagging even though Boller was clearly making progress.

"The only good news about the Patriots game was that we came home and people around here were making excuses for Kyle having a poor game," Billick said. "Three weeks ago they would have buried him — regardless of the conditions or the quality of the opponent."

What made the Cavanaugh situation easier for Billick was Cavanaugh himself. He wasn't sitting around, feeling sorry for himself or feeling that being fired was going to be unfair. "If we don't put it together these last few weeks, I know what's going to happen," he said. "I'm a big boy. I know how this game works."

There was some talk in the Friday futures meeting about players, but not much. Those decisions would be made at the end of the season after each coach had submitted his end-of-season report on each of his players. That was the way the process worked. But there were certain players whose future with the team had already been decided. There was no need to discuss them. Newsome had already made some decisions in his own mind, not about specific players but about what needed to be done in the upcoming off-season.

Dating back to the Monday night loss to Kansas City, he had started to wonder about how good the team really was. He and Billick had made a conscious decision during the off-season not to, as he put it, "upset the applecart." They had re-signed all their free agents with the exception of wide receiver Marcus Robinson. They had pursued only one big-name or even semi-big-name free agent, Terrell Owens, and, for reasons beyond their control, they hadn't gotten him. They had chosen, essentially, to stand pat with a team that had gone 10-6 and won a division title, but in doing so, they had probably not addressed some weaknesses. Already, Newsome was formulating an off-season plan for 2005 that would be far more aggressive.

Billick was still more focused on 2004, because he had more control over the next five weeks than Newsome and his staff did. A general manager and his staff do their most important work between January and April: deciding whom to keep and not keep, whom to pursue and not pursue, and, of course, whom to draft and whom to try to sign after the draft. From May to August the general manager and the coach work in tandem, piecing together the team. From September to the end of the year, the general manager and his scouts might be able to help with a free-agent signing here, a recommendation there. But for the most part, they have to sit back and watch the coaches and players and hope that they have given the coach the right players to work with. Newsome had started to wonder in October if the Ravens had the right group. By the first week in December he was losing sleep, thinking quite possibly they did not.

Billick loses sleep during the season only on Sundays after a loss. The rest of the time he sleeps fine. He slept well on the Saturday before the Bengals game because he felt confident that the team was coming into the time of year when it did its best work. In five seasons under Billick, the Ravens were 20-9 in December and January, including 5-2 in postseason. What's more, this team, through all the ups and downs and injuries, hadn't lost two games in a row all year.

Billick was in an upbeat mood crossing the Hamburg Street bridge on Sunday morning. The weather was remarkable for early December: temperature at kickoff would be fifty-six degrees, with a comfortable breeze. It would have been a nice day for October; for December it was borderline miraculous. Billick's walks had been fraught with adventure recently. On the night of the Cleveland game, one of the yellow-jacketed security guards had walked up to shake hands with him just as he walked into the stadium.

"Good luck tonight, Coach," he said.

"Thank you, young man," Billick said, his customary response.

"Now I need you to make a promise," the yellow jacket continued while Billick started down the ramp.

"Name it," Billick said, thinking he was going to be asked to promise a victory.

"Boller messes up, you promise you'll get him out of there, okay?"

"Wouldn't count on it," Billick said, not breaking stride.

Apparently one of the yellow jacket's supervisors overheard the conversation. The guard was fired on the spot.

Vernon Holley decided not to tell Billick about what had happened because he knew Billick would not have wanted the man fired, regardless of how out of line his comment might have been.

"He's not even supposed to shake hands with him [Billick] or say anything," Holley said. "He might have survived that, but when he brought up Kyle and his boss heard it, he was done. He was probably out of the building before we got to the locker room."

Before the Dallas game, another fan approached Billick on the bridge and wanted to take a picture. Billick complied. "Coach, can I ask you one question?" he said, falling into stride.

"Sure, why not?" Billick answered.

"Who exactly is responsible for the offense?" the man said.

Billick stopped. "I am," he said, glaring down at the man.

"But what about Cavanaugh?"

"Matt takes his cue from me. You have a problem with the offense, you can talk to me about it."

The man opted not to continue the discussion.

Soon after he arrived in his office, Billick called Heap in to make sure one last time that he was absolutely ready to play. Heap, who was already in uniform, insisted that he was. "When you get out there in warm-ups," Billick said. "Limp around a little bit. Let's play with Marvin's [Lewis] mind a little."

Heap nodded and left, a huge smile on his face.

Gary Zauner came in next. "Richey's down," Billick told him, anticipating a question about Wade Richey's status.

"Really?" Zauner said. "He's been kicking better, and it saves Stover's leg. . . ."

"Okay," Billick said. "It's Richey or Todd Heap. You think I should go with Richey?"

"No," Zauner said. Then, in his never-say-die way, he added, "But what about Richey for Randy Hymes?"

Billick shook his head. "Can't do it. I need Hymes in case someone gets hurt."

Zauner shrugged. "Okay," he said. "I lose."

When the linebackers walked onto the field to warm up, Peter Boulware followed them down the tunnel and up the steps leading to the playing surface. He was wearing a boot on his foot, similar to the ones that Lewis and Sanders were wearing. The difference was, they were hoping to play again in a week or two. Boulware knew the soonest he would play in a real football game was the following September.

As soon as the fans behind the tunnel spotted Boulware, they began calling his name, hoping to get an autograph. Boulware signed a few, shook hands with several people near the bench, and sat down, a smile on his face that was anything but real.

"This is killing me," he said. "When I had the knee surgery, it was frustrating, but I kept telling myself I'd be back by midseason and the whole thing would be behind me. Then I'm back on the field for one day and I hurt my foot. I've had one day in a year where I was a healthy football player. To go back and face rehab again is very, very tough."

Two weeks short of thirty, Boulware had been a star football player for about as long as he could remember. He had grown up in Columbia, South Carolina, the son of a doctor and a furniture-store owner who expected all four of their children to do well in school and be successful. Peter did just that, becoming one of the most highly recruited football players in the country by his senior year. Since Florida State was *the* program in the country at the time, having just won the national championship in 1993, Boulware chose to go there. He redshirted as a freshman, was a part-time starter as a redshirt freshman the next year, began to emerge as a star as a sophomore, and exploded in his junior year with nineteen quarterback sacks in twelve games. Since he was graduating in the spring anyway, Boulware declared for the 1997 NFL draft and the Ravens, with the fourth pick that spring, made him their number one choice. He was a starter from day one, recording 11.5 sacks as a rookie en route to being named the league's defensive rookie of the year. By the time he lined up in Cleveland for the penultimate game of the 2004 season, he was on his way to a fourth Pro Bowl and had become the team's all-time sack leader. That was the day he hurt his knee.

"I've always known there was going to come a day when I couldn't play football anymore and that it would be tough," he said. "What this has brought home to me is that it's going to be even harder than I imagined. There's such a high running out of that tunnel and hearing seventy thousand people screaming. There's nothing else you can do in life that's going to give you the feeling you have when you're playing a football game or when you're part of a football team.

"I'm in good shape financially. I've got a car dealership back home in Tallahassee and I'm learning the business. I know that will be there for me when I quit, but there's no way it can replace this. I mean, when I sell a car, are there going to be seventy thousand people screaming my name like there are when I get a sack? I don't think so.

"Being in the locker room every day and going off to do rehab rather than going to practice is really hard. I've got enough ego to think that I can help these guys, that in a close game I can make a play or two that might be worth a few points and make a difference. Right now, though, I can't do a thing to help them, and that kills me."

On the sidelines, Boulware was a full-throated cheerleader, screaming play calls to the defense, pulling Terrell Suggs and Adalius Thomas aside to offer advice, congratulating anyone who made a big play. "It's better than being in the stands," he said. "In a few years, I won't even be on the sidelines anymore. Right after the foot injury, I was down, really down. But my faith and my wife have gotten me through it. I'm convinced I'm going to play again and play well. I'm also convinced that things do happen for a reason, that there's a reason why I'm going through this. Some days it's hard to figure out what it is, but I keep believing it's out there. Maybe at this time next year, someone else will be going through this and I'll be able to help him." He smiled. "Maybe I'll come back a better player because I'm well rested."

Boulware admitted that the second injury had severely tested his faith. He still had mixed emotions about what happened two years earlier when he and Matt Stover clashed with Rod Hairston over the religious direction of the team. "Religion should help bring people together," he said. "I know if you look at history, that hasn't always been the case, and that's the kind of thing you don't want to have happen inside a team. One thing I hope I'll never be is someone who says, 'If you don't believe the way I believe, then you're wrong or there's something wrong with you.' I don't feel that way. I felt badly about what happened. The last thing any team needs is for people to be fighting on the inside about religious beliefs.

"Coach Billick did the right thing, stepping in when he did. Unfortunately, it needed to be done because all of us were not handling it very well." Boulware hadn't been attending Hairston's Saturday night fellowship meetings because he didn't participate in the team's Saturday night meetings. "Next year, when I'm back playing, I'll go," he said, sounding almost as if he was hoping that would be the case.

They were still screaming his name when he went back into the locker room with the team. The screams were because of what he had done in the past. Boulware wanted to believe there would be screams soon for what he was doing in the future. "The day is coming for all of us when we can't play," he said. "I see that now very clearly. I just don't want it to be yet."

Those who would play on this day gathered in a circle in the Ravens' locker room thirty minutes before kickoff. Corey Fuller had been chosen to lead the prayer. Before he prayed, Fuller preached. "We've got all we need in this room to win this game," he said. "Let's remember we are God's chosen people, chosen to play this game. Think about how lucky we are to get to do this. We only get so many chances to do this, so let's not let this one go by without giving every single thing we have out there."

Clearly, Fuller could see the end of football, too.

Since it was December, Billick was ready to name his captains for the rest of the season. He alternated captains the first eleven weeks, sending different players out for the coin toss. (Orlando Brown had not been sent out again after Cleveland, much to Matt Stover's relief.) The captains Billick named for the rest of the season were no surprise to anyone: Ray Lewis on defense, Jonathan Ogden on offense, and Adalius Thomas on special teams. Billick added a fourth captain: Ed Reed. Given his play during the season, it would be almost impossible not to name him.

As had now become tradition, the first half was a defensive struggle. Reed, the newly minted captain, set up the Ravens' first points of the game when he and Will Demps hit Bengals tight end Matt Schobel near midfield on the opening drive of the game and jarred the ball loose. Reed picked it up and returned it to the 25. Chester Taylor got 14 on first down to the 11. Then, on third-and-7, Boller found Heap at the 5, who, with the crowd screaming, "HEEEEEEP!" fought his way inside the 2. He appeared to be close to a first down. Billick was screaming at referee Walt Anderson to measure, but Anderson stood with his fist clenched over his head, the signal for fourth down. Billick yelled some more, got nowhere, and decided to take the sure three points, much to the disappointment of the crowd. Stover's 22-yarder made it 3–0.

The score stayed the same until late in the first half when Carson Palmer, who had moved his team most of the half without putting any points on the board, found Chad Johnson deep for a 51-yard catch over Chris McAlister. It was Johnson's fourth catch of the game against McAlister. All day, he had been trash-talking McAlister, telling him he couldn't possibly cover him. That surprised no one. What was surprising was that McAlister said nothing in response. Everyone knew his shoulder was still hurting, but he was quiet — too quiet — throughout the half.

The Ravens shut the Bengals down after Johnson's catch, and Shayne Graham kicked a 41-yard field goal to tie the game with 2:25 to go in the half. The offense responded with an almost-perfect two-minute-drill drive. In fourteen plays, mixing in time-outs along the way, Boller took his team from his own 18 to the Cincinnati 4. When he was sacked at the Cincinnati 38 to set up third-and-18, Boller found Travis Taylor over the middle at the 14 to pick up the first down. Boller scrambled up the middle two plays after that to pick up a first down at the 4. With the clock running out, he spiked the ball to stop it with ten seconds left. A jump pass to Clarence Moore didn't work, and they had to settle for Stover and a field goal and a 6–3 halftime lead.

There was tension in the locker room at halftime. As in Cincinnati, the Bengals were moving the ball but not scoring. They still didn't have a touchdown against the Ravens in six quarters. That was good. What wasn't good was the uneasy feeling everyone had that Palmer and his receivers were capable of exploding at any minute. Johnson and T. J. Houshmandzadeh already had four catches apiece and Palmer had completed 13 of 16 passes for 129 yards. He was clearly a more mature quarterback than he had been when he threw three interceptions back in September.

Even more disturbing, particularly to Mike Nolan and the DB coaches, was McAlister. Something was wrong and they couldn't figure out what it was. He insisted that his shoulder was okay, but he looked almost lifeless on the field. The coaches had changed the defensive plan from the first Cincinnati game to give McAlister more help on Johnson, taking their chances with Gary Baxter on Houshmandzadeh. But even with help, McAlister seemed unable to stop or even slow down Johnson. Instead of turning him toward the middle of the field, where Ed Reed was shading to give him help, McAlister was allowing him to run routes to the outside, where there was no help.

Before he went to talk to his coaches, Nolan grabbed McAlister and took him into the hallway just around the corner from the lounge where the defense gathers at halftime. McAlister was surprised — and upset — when Nolan asked him to step outside.

"Mac, what's wrong?" Nolan said. "Are you okay? If something's wrong, tell me."

"I'm fine, Coach."

"You're not fine, Mac, you're not yourself. You are a much better player than what I saw on that field the first half."

"Am I?"

Nolan felt himself getting angry. He had his hand on McAlister's arm. Now he shook it slightly. "Chris, when I'm talking to you, give me your eyes."

McAlister had his head down when Nolan said it. He picked his head up, took a small step forward to get closer to him, and got almost nose-to-nose with him, their eyes almost touching. They stood like that for a second, saying nothing.

"Get in the room with the other guys," Nolan said, turning to talk to his coaches.

"I knew right then I'd lost him," Nolan said.

"I was angry," McAlister said. "Chad had caught a couple of balls on me, I knew that, but it isn't like he's some fourth-rate receiver. He's an All-Pro. We had given up three points in the half, that was it. I didn't see any reason why he should call *me* out of the room that way. I did get in his face a little bit when he told me to give him my eyes. I was pissed-off at that moment."

If the Bengals had put up a couple of touchdowns, maybe Nolan would have made the radical move of benching his All-Pro cornerback. But they only had three points on the board. Maybe he could get through thirty more minutes without getting burned too badly. Nolan wasn't even concerned with McAlister's confrontation. He was far more concerned with how McAlister was going to react to Chad Johnson.

The offense picked up where it had left off at the end of the first half, marching 85 yards after the kickoff in what might have been its most impressive drive of the season. Boller was sharp, completing passes to five different receivers, and Chester Taylor had 5 carries, including a 1-yard dive for the touchdown. Jamel White, the little running back signed a week earlier, came off the bench to set up the score with a 16-yard run. They kept the ball for almost seven minutes. The lead was 13–3. It was 20–3 a few minutes later. First, Clarence Moore, who had become the team's most dangerous receiver, committed an unpardonable sin, short-arming (not reaching for) a Boller pass over the middle, which allowed Bengals safety Madieu Williams to make an interception that wasn't Boller's fault. The play set Cincinnati up at midfield. But Palmer finally made a mistake, floating a pass intended for Johnson a bit high. Ball-hawking as usual, Ed Reed swooped in to intercept it at the 15. Darting and dodging the way he always did, Reed was at the 39 when he got hit from behind. Carrying the ball loosely as was his wont, Reed lost control of it. But the ball took one hop and was picked up by McAlister, who was trailing the play. Before anyone on the Bengals realized that he — and not Reed — had the ball, McAlister was gone, down the left sideline for a touchdown.

Now they had control. Whatever had been going on with McAlister in the first half was forgotten as he and Reed were mobbed on the sideline. Reed was shaking his head, angry at himself for the fumble. But it didn't matter. The lead was 20–3 with 2:29 left in the third quarter. The Bengals were shaken. Their offense stalled again and Kyle Larson floated a punt to B. J. Sams near the sideline. At the last second, Sams decided to fair-catch the ball, waving his arm in the air. Perhaps he lost his focus for a split second, maybe his arm blocked his vision of the ball for just a moment. Later, Sams wasn't sure exactly what happened.

The ball slid through his hands and bounced on the ground, with everyone in pursuit. The Bengals' Marcus Wilkins ended up on top of it on the Baltimore 19. It took Palmer two plays — a pass to Houshmandzadeh for 6 yards to end the third quarter and a 13-yarder into the end zone to Johnson to begin the fourth — and the lead was 20–10. Instead of beginning the fourth quarter with a three-score lead, the Ravens were in a game. More important, the Bengals now believed *they* were in the game.

The Ravens' offense went three-and-out. Palmer was suddenly brimming with confidence. It took him five plays to go 76 yards, the touchdown again coming on a pass to Johnson. Nolan was beside himself in the press box. The entire defense was suddenly in disarray, and McAlister again looked lost. "It isn't as if he was the first DB in history to have trouble with Chad Johnson, the guy is a hell of a receiver," he said later. "But it looked to me as if he wasn't even really trying. No one could say anything to him to bring him back at that point."

In seven quarters, the Bengals' offense had failed to score a touchdown on the Ravens, putting up a total of twelve points. Now it had scored two touchdowns — in a little more than four minutes. The sideline, which had been so joyful a few minutes earlier after the McAlister touchdown, turned grim and quiet. Even Ray Lewis had nothing to say, sitting quietly on the bench while the offense went back onto the field. Everyone came back to life when Travis Taylor broke loose for 47 yards on the first play of the next series. But with a first down on the Cincinnati 26, they couldn't put the ball into the end zone. Stover came in and made a 38-yard field goal to make it 23–17, but the margin was still less than a touchdown and there was all sorts of time — 8:34 — left to play.

The Ravens appeared to have the Bengals stopped on the next series when Palmer was called for intentional grounding after a blitz forced him to throw the ball away. That set up second-and-20. Palmer found Houshmandzadeh wide-open at the Ravens' 20. Three plays later, Houshmandzadeh was in the end zone, celebrating with the ball, and the Bengals had the lead, 24–23, with 5:38 to go. There were no boos. Just silence. The crowd was as shocked as the Ravens.

Houshmandzadeh had given the Ravens a break with his celebration because he was whistled for it and the Bengals had to kick off from the 15. Sams, trying to make up for his fumble, returned the kick 29 yards to the Ravens' 46. On the bench everyone had the same thought: this might be the most crucial drive of the season. The way the Bengals' offense was suddenly dominating the defense, the Ravens might not see the ball again if they failed to score now.

"Come on, O," Terrell Suggs yelled as they trotted onto the field. "Bail us out."

It was full-fledged role reversal.

Patiently, Boller and the offense did what they had to do. On third-and-6 from midfield, Boller hit Kevin Johnson for 11 yards and a first down at the Bengals' 39. They were chipping away, not necessarily eager to score quickly because they didn't want to give the Cincinnati offense time when — if — they scored to take the lead. Two plays later, Chester Taylor fumbled and the Bengals' Brian Simmons recovered. But there was a flag downfield: far from the play, cornerback Tory James had been called for holding. The NFL's new rules on defensive holding, which had been the subject of lengthy debate when the officials had come to training camp for their annual briefing of the team on rules changes, had bailed out the Ravens.

Taylor picked up a yard, to the 32. Then Jamel White, giving Taylor a breather, sprinted left and picked up 12 yards to the 20. They were now well into Stover's range. The goal now was to kill as much time as possible. The Bengals knew that. White picked up 6 more yards to the 14. The two-minute warning stopped the clock. A touchdown would be far better than a field goal because it would mean the Bengals would have to go the length of the field and score a touchdown. But Taylor was stopped for a 3-yard loss and the Bengals used their second time-out. Third-and-7. Billick and Cavanaugh weren't going to risk a turnover. The ball went to Taylor again and he was buried behind the line for a 7-yard loss. Worse than that, Casey Rabach had made one of the few mistakes he would make all season, being caught holding. The Bengals, hoping to push Stover out of range, accepted the penalty and moved the ball to the 27.

The flags on top of the stadium were whipping. The wind was clearly going to be in Stover's face. As he always did, Stover had trotted onto the field at the end of the third quarter to check the wind. He had told Zauner his yard line was the 30. That was now forty minutes ago. There was no guarantee now that the 27 was close enough. Aware of that, Cavanaugh called a short pass to Travis Taylor, trying to pick up a few more yards for Stover. But the pass was broken up. Stover would have to try from 45 yards.

These were the kicks that Stover was paid the big bucks to make. He went through his routine: head down, right arm up. Murphy was the holder. Even though he had now been Stover's holder for three games, he had never had to get a snap down at a moment quite like this. Joe Maese's snap was perfect and Murphy got the ball down. The kick wobbled in the wind, seemed to hang in the air for several minutes, and floated down toward the goalpost. It was on line, but was it long enough?

Yes. It dropped just over the crossbar and the bench exploded with relief. The Ravens led, 26–24.

The game was far from over. The penalty and the incomplete pass had stopped the clock and allowed the Bengals to save their last time-out. Palmer had 1:42 to work with. That felt like an eternity.

The Bengals started from their own 34, meaning they probably needed to go about 35 to 40 yards to give their kicker, Shayne Graham, a reasonable shot at a game-winning field goal. On first down, the Ravens' defense made a huge play: Anthony Weaver and Suggs got to Palmer before he had a chance to even think about looking downfield. Palmer ducked Suggs for a moment, but Weaver ran him down for an 8-yard loss. It was second-and-18, the ball now on the 26 and the clock running.

Standing on the sideline, Billick felt a wave of relief. "We did it," he thought. "We scared the hell out of ourselves, but when we had to come up with a play, we did. We're going to get out of this."

Even as those thoughts were going through Billick's head, Palmer was lining up in shotgun formation. The clock was at 1:13 as he dropped back. Houshmandzadeh was wide-open, working single coverage on Baxter with the Ravens still focused on Johnson. Palmer put the ball on the numbers and Will Demps had to come up to make the tackle. The play was good for 32 yards. All the relief Billick had felt disappeared. The Bengals were now at the Baltimore 42. Palmer raced up and spiked the ball to stop the clock with fifty seconds left. The Bengals were no more than 10 yards from field goal range and they still had a time-out to get their field goal team on the field.

Palmer wasn't done. With the entire defense gearing to stop Johnson and Houshmandzadeh, he went over the middle to tight end Matt Schobel for 11 yards and a first down. Again he spiked the ball. Then, from the 31, he went back to Johnson, running the same out pattern that he had tortured McAlister with most of the day. Johnson caught the ball running out of bounds on the Ravens' 9 with thirty-three seconds left. Now, all the Bengals wanted to do was line the ball up in the middle of the field and run the clock down as far as they could. Rudy Johnson tried to run up the middle — he picked up nothing — but the Ravens were in such disarray that they had twelve men on the field; Chad Williams had run onto the field as an extra defensive back and no one had come off. The ball moved to the 4. Palmer willingly took a 2-yard loss to line the ball up in the middle of the field and called time-out with two seconds left.

Graham had little more than an extra point, lining up on the 14 for a 24-yard kick. It was a no-doubter, straight up the middle as time expired. Final score: Bengals 27, Ravens 26.

The loss could hardly have been more devastating. Not only were they now 7-5, but their confidence, especially on the defensive side, had been punctured. The Bengals had scored 24 points in the fourth quarter. Palmer had finished with 382 yards passing, 200 of them in the fourth. Johnson and Houshmandzadeh had 10 catches each, Houshmandzadeh for 171 yards and Johnson for 161 yards.

Billick was calm in the crushed locker room. He told them they would have to come in to look at the tape on Monday because there were corrections that clearly had to be made. "You're going to hear a lot of negative things the next week," he said. "You can't buy in. Our fate is still in our own hands. But we definitely took a hit today. There's no denying that."

25

Crisis

MONDAY'S WEATHER was exactly what it should have been: bleak, rain spitting down the entire day, a cold wind sweeping across the parking lot as coaches and players quietly parked their cars and ran, heads down, into the building.

The hallways inside were completely silent. People passing one another simply nodded hello rather than saying anything. The cafeteria, usually a noisy, cheerful place at lunchtime, was almost as quiet as the hallways. There was nothing anyone could say that was going to mitigate or change what had happened on Sunday. Instead of being alone in the second wild-card spot, just one game behind the Jets, the Ravens were now tied with Denver for the second spot, with Buffalo, Jacksonville, and Cincinnati just a game behind. The worst part was the schedule. They had blown one of the home games that was considered almost a sure win, meaning they would now have to win the remaining two home games *and* almost certainly win in either Indianapolis or Pittsburgh. Even that would get them only to 10-6, and at this point, that was far from a lock to make the playoffs.

There were, however, more immediate concerns. The noon meeting was as somber as might be expected. The coaches went through their analyses of what they had seen on tape. For the first time in anyone's memory, there were even questions raised about Ray Lewis. Mike Singletary defended him. "He's worked hard on improving against the run," Singletary said, a reference to the concerns that had come up at times since the Kansas City game. "He only had one M.E. [mental error] the entire game."

Kyle Boller had played well: 19-of-33, with four passes dropped, and his only interception caused by Clarence Moore pulling up going over the middle. "Clarence did that twice yesterday," David Shaw said. "I'll talk to him about it. It's the first time he's done it all season."

There was talk in the room that perhaps Moore and Sams were hitting "the rookie wall"— a common malady when players go from college football to the pros, where the intensity is higher and the season is longer. Sams had started the season at 188 pounds. He was now down to 179, perhaps confirming Gary Zauner's earlier concerns that he was wearing out. He hadn't dropped a ball from minicamp in April until November. Now he had dropped two punts in four weeks. They had survived the one against the Jets. They had not survived the one against the Bengals. There was also concern about Dan Wilcox, who had played in NFL Europe the previous spring before being signed by the Ravens. "He may have European [tired] legs at this point," Billick said. "We have to keep an eye on him."

Ethan Brooks had played his best game as a Raven, filling in for Orlando Brown. "Even if Zeus comes back, I'm not sure we aren't better off with Ethan playing at this point," Jim Colletto said.

Jamal Lewis might be ready to play this coming Sunday. The same was true for Deion Sanders. They would be as healthy as they had been at any time all season. The question hanging in the air was simple: was it too late?

Finally, Billick came to the point that was going to be most delicate. "Back end," he said, which was the terminology used to describe the secondary. Johnnie Lynn cleared his throat and dove in: "Will Demps had a solid game," he said, getting the good news out of the way early, "except for the one catch the tight end made on the last drive. Gary Baxter played well, but he made two key errors at the end. Corey Fuller did well but had two bad plays also. Chad [Williams] was good except for being the twelfth man on the field at the very end."

He was working his way up to where it was going to get tense. "Ed Reed tried to cover up for Chris as best he could. Chris just didn't produce at all. He made a bunch of mental errors."

Billick looked at Dennis Thurman. Lynn was new to the staff, having come to the Ravens after being Jim Fassel's defensive coordinator the previous year in New York. When defensive backs coach Donnie Henderson had been hired by the New York Jets as their defensive coordinator, Billick had hired Lynn. Thurman had been with the team three years and knew McAlister longer and better than Lynn. Now Billick turned to him, looking for answers. Thurman sighed and shook his head as if to say he had none.

"Until he got hurt [the shoulder injury in the Jets game] he was busting his ass," he said. "I think after he got the contract, especially, he was as happy as I've seen him. Since the injury he hasn't been the same player or the same person. He's not doing anything in practice. He's not competing. He gets beat, he just shrugs his shoulders. I couldn't believe he let Chad Johnson talk all that trash to him yesterday and never said a word. We have to show him the plays in this game where he just let himself get beat and say to him, 'Is this who you are?'"

Nolan and Billick had already had one conversation about McAlister earlier in the day, Nolan filling Billick in on what had happened at halftime. "You know, through all the ups and downs we've had with Chris, we've always said the important thing is that he likes football," Nolan said. "He always did his work and he really liked to play. Right now I'm not sure Chris likes anything."

They asked Newsome if there was anyone who might be able to sit down and talk to McAlister, to find out exactly what was bothering him. Newsome shook his head. "He listened to Donnie [Henderson] a little and he might listen to Earnest [Byner] every once in a while," he said. "With them gone, he's a loner around here."

"Even Ray and Ed don't feel like they can talk to him," Nolan added.

It was Billick who raised the most crucial question of all: "How much of this is about his lifestyle?" he asked.

Everyone in the building knew that McAlister liked to stay out late at night and that he liked to drink when he was out. Since the DUI stop the year before — the charges had been dropped, but McAlister admitted he had been drinking — he had been careful about having a driver whenever he went out.

Now, though, the question came up about whether his lifestyle had affected his performance on Sunday. There was even some question about whether he had gone out on Saturday night after the team meetings. That, according to McAlister, had never happened in six years.

Billick changed the subject. They discussed personnel changes that had to be made: Dave Zastudil should be ready to punt Sunday, but Nick Murphy would be kept on the fifty-three for the week, just in case. They might give Wilcox a week to rest, a move they could afford with Heap now healthy and Darnell Dinkins playing so well. Zauner wasn't thrilled with the idea because of how Wilcox was on special teams.

Quietly, Billick asked the scouts to excuse themselves. Newsome stayed, as did Steve Bisciotti, sitting in on his first Monday meeting since his surgery. He had listened silently throughout the McAlister discussion, waiting to see if anyone asked him what he thought should be done. Once the scouts were gone, Billick returned to the subject of McAlister. "We just made a huge commitment to this guy financially," he said. "He's a pivotal player for us. We need to figure out a way to get to him. If I thought motherfucking him would do it, that's what I'd do. But I'm sure if I did that, I'd lose him."

Newsome nodded his head in agreement. "Someone needs to talk to him about what happened yesterday," he said. "Because if he isn't embarrassed about it, then we've got a real problem."

"The problem is, he doesn't really trust anyone," O. J. Brigance said. "He honestly believes no one cares about him. When I tried to talk to him about his shoulder he said to me, 'You're just like the rest of them, you just want to use me.'"

Bisciotti finally spoke up. "What I'd really like to do is show Chris a tape of the last forty-five minutes," he said. "Show him twenty intelligent men sitting around trying to figure him out, trying to figure out how to get him to be the player he ought to be. I like investing in stable personalities. I can tell you guys from past experience that working with someone who has a victim mentality is almost impossible."

Matt Cavanaugh asked a question to the room: "Does it upset Chris that Ray and Ed get so much recognition?"

"Yup," Newsome said without hesitation.

"That's one reason he doesn't go to Ray's house on Thursday night," Thurman said. "That and the fact that he'd rather go out and party."

They went around some more. Billick instructed Nolan to treat his tape session with the defense that day as if it were training camp. "Correct, don't yell," he said. "Yelling isn't going to do any good at this point."

As they broke up, Bisciotti lingered to talk to Billick. "How would you feel if I take a shot at Chris?" he said.

Billick thought a moment. Normally, his instinctive answer would be no, that having a player called in by the owner wasn't a good idea. Now he nodded. "Why not?" he said. "Maybe you can be a different voice for him."

Billick gave them a pep talk on Monday afternoon. He pointed out that because Denver and Jacksonville had lost, they were right where they had been before Sunday's games. Of course, Denver had lost in San Diego (the Chargers were 9-3) and Jacksonville had lost to Pittsburgh, which was now 11-1. Neither team had blown a seventeen-point fourth-quarter lead at home.

"So, we have to go to Indianapolis and Pittsburgh and win," Billick said. "Anyone in this room who doesn't feel up to that challenge? Is there anyone in here who wants to point fingers right now? Anyone want to blame B.J.? Where would we be without B.J. this season? Anyone want to blame the DBs? How many times have they bailed us out? We aren't that kind of team. We never have been. Let's make sure we focus on what we have to do this week, nothing more, and then we'll let the rest take care of itself."

The players all knew the season was at a crisis point. They understood they had put themselves in a bad situation by letting the game get away on Sunday. They were angry and frustrated. "We aren't used to letting games get away like that," Mike Flynn said. "I think everyone's searching a little bit right now."

The defensive meeting, even with Nolan trying to correct, not yell, was tense. A number of the plays on the tape involved breakdowns, especially in the backfield in the fourth quarter. "Guys, you have to play the techniques we've taught you," Nolan said. "You all know what they are, you have to execute them, especially this time of year."

McAlister sat in his usual seat on the left side of the room, convinced that Nolan was talking to him. Certainly, several of the plays involved him. He was still angry about what had happened at halftime, and Thurman had told him that he should expect a call from Bisciotti, that there were concerns about his lifestyle and about how ready he had been to play on Sunday.

"I was *so* angry," he said. "I had a bad game, no doubt about it. That made, by my count, two bad games in six years. Was I the only one who played badly? I don't think so. It takes eleven guys for us to be good; it took eleven guys for us to be bad. I understand cornerbacks stand out — as heroes and as goats, it's part of the job. But I really felt like I was being made a goat."

When the meeting was over, McAlister headed for the parking lot. Corey Fuller chased him down there. Fuller's lifestyle was 180 degrees different from McAlister's. He didn't drink — never had — and he didn't go out late at night. But he was a cornerback and he knew what it felt like to be singled out after a bad game. Months later, McAlister still remembered the conversation almost word for word.

"I can tell you're pissed," Fuller said to McAlister.

"Damn right I am," McAlister said. "These guys are trying to blame me and me alone for what happened yesterday."

Fuller nodded. "That's exactly right, they are. You know why? Because they are paying you a *lot* of money and they made a commitment to you for a long time — which is what you told them you wanted them to do. For the money they're paying you, they don't expect you to play well some of the time, they expect you to play well all the time. They don't expect you to be ready two-thirds of the time or three-quarters of the time, they expect it a hundred percent of the time. And if we lose a game and you play bad and you've been out during the week, then you can expect them to blame you. You give them the chance to blame you by going out. If you don't go out and you play bad, it's one thing. If you go out — and you know as well as I do that they know when you're out — and you play good, it's not a problem. But if you play bad, it's a big problem."

McAlister listened to Fuller. He had always respected him, knew he had overcome a lot in his life and never made excuses for his mistakes. He had certainly had his battles with the coaches — specifically Nolan — during the season and yet he was telling him that he had set himself up for this by staying out late and coming to work on some mornings with alcohol on his breath. "You think people don't notice that?" he said. "Of course they do."

The two men stood in the darkened parking lot and talked for more than an hour. McAlister went home that night and did a good deal of thinking. It took a while, but he finally reached some conclusions. He had been angry at the team for not giving him a contract, and he had acted out at times because of that. Now, they *had* given him a contract. He had a responsibility to give them their money's worth. Plus, from a selfish standpoint, he wanted to be in the league for as long as possible. He certainly wasn't headed in that direction.

"I had spent most of two years being angry," he said. "I was angry because I didn't have a contract, and that led to what happened in San Diego. Then I was angry during the off-season and came to camp still angry. When they gave me the contract, I was happy. Then I got hurt and I was frustrated. Was I behaving as badly as they seemed to think I was? I don't think so. But Corey was right: if I did it all, which I did, I gave them a reason to single me out if I didn't play well. That's what I needed to make go away. The Chris McAlister who played in the Cincinnati game ceased to exist after Corey and I talked," he said. "He gave me a lot to think about. And I did think about it."

Little did the coaches, the scouts, or the owner know it, but the person who could get to McAlister had been found — in a place where they had never even thought about looking.

Ray Lewis was also searching. As the team's leader, he felt he had somehow let people down by not helping the defense find a way to stop the bleeding on Sunday. On Tuesday, the players' day off, he sat at home with his red spiral notebook in front of him. Lewis carries the notebook with him everywhere. When he thinks of something he wants to remember or hears something he thinks worth repeating, he writes it down in his notebook. Frequently, during the Saturday night Fellowship sessions, he would write at length in the notebook. Now he sat with his notebook, trying to think of something to say to his teammates that might get them back where they needed to be for the season's final weeks. He needed a theme. He started writing down his thoughts.

The word *life* came into his head. One of his many sayings in the locker room was "we're living our lives together."

He wrote down *living,* as in "we're living our lives together and making a living at the same time."

He stared at that for a while and then wrote down *instruments,* as in "we are instruments of God given a special gift to play football."

More staring and thinking. Then *free*, as in "we are still free to accomplish what we started out to accomplish this summer."

He knew now where he wanted to go. The last word he wrote down was *emotion*, which was "what we need in order to achieve what we want to achieve."

He had four words: Living-Instruments-Free-Emotion, or LIFE.

That was the message he delivered to the team early Wednesday morning before the weekly game-planning meetings began. He wanted to remind everyone that their future was still in their own hands if they didn't give in to the frustration they all felt. "It's all still out there for us if we stay together," he said. "Let's worry only about ourselves and what *we* think, not what anyone else thinks." He paused. "I've got one other four-letter word for you: *game*. This is a game, still a game. But it's a game we all play together. We can't win it unless we do."

That seemed to set a good tone for the week. They could make the case that this was a chance to start over again. They were healthy and they still believed that when they were healthy, they could beat anyone, anyplace. That included Indianapolis and Pittsburgh on the road. It would have to.

There was one new injury that caused some concern: Joe Maese. Outside the team, only the most hard-core fan would have any idea who Maese was. But he was a key component in the offense. He was the team's long snapper.

The notion of keeping someone on the roster strictly for the purpose of long snapping is a relatively new one in the NFL — and in football. For years most teams simply had their starting center snap the ball on placekicks and punts. But snapping a ball exactly eight yards to a kneeling holder or fourteen yards to a punter is a lot different skill from snapping it to a quarterback who is directly behind you. There was also the wear-and-tear problem: long snappers get hammered on every snap: because they have to take their eye off the man in front of them for a split second to make certain their snap is true, they inevitably get pummeled. The life of the long snapper was perhaps best described by Gary Zauner one night in a special teams meeting. Addressing Bart Scott, who often lined up against the other team's long snapper, he said, "Bart, if you hit the guy and knock him flat every single time, sooner or later he's going to make a mistake."

Not wanting their starting centers knocked flat ten to fifteen times a game and hoping to find someone who could get the ball back to their punter or holder consistently, coaches began looking for specialists. By the early 1990s almost every team in football had someone on the roster who was a long-snapping specialist. Occasionally he played another position. These days every team has someone on the roster whose only job is to long snap. The importance of the long snapper had never been more evident than in 2003, when the Giants' inability to get the ball snapped properly in kicking situations had cost them a playoff game against the San Francisco 49ers.

Maese had grown up in Phoenix, the eldest of Joe and Donna Maese's three children. He always wanted to play football, but his mother wouldn't let him, afraid that he would get hurt. "When I got to ninth grade, I just told her I was going to do it," he said.

Things weren't great at home in those days. According to his eldest son, Joe Maese Sr. was a drinker. "He was either the best guy in the world or the worst," Maese said. "It was sad. But it got to the point where it was a relief when he wasn't home. I was actually kind of glad when he and my mother split up."

That was during Joe's sophomore year in high school. He and his mom argued often after the split. It was only later, after Joe was out of college, that his mother told him that the tight rein she tried to keep on him was the result of concerns that he would follow in his father's footsteps and find trouble. During his senior year in high school, Joe moved out, finding a small apartment of his own. He supported himself by working as a bouncer in a local bar. By then he was long snapping for his high school football team, a job he had inherited as a junior when the team needed a new snapper. "I was terrible at it at first," he said. "Really bad. But I wanted to be good, so I really worked at it. By the end of the season, I was pretty good."

He was too small (six feet, 235 pounds) to be considered for a Division 1 scholarship as either a defensive lineman or a linebacker, and most schools weren't recruiting long snappers out of high school. He enrolled at Phoenix Community College, where he played on defense and became the team's long snapper. By his sophomore year, he was attracting attention from D-1 schools as a snapper — but no scholarship offers. He was majoring in fire science — he wants to be a firefighter someday and often goes on ride-alongs with fire departments — but he still wanted to pursue football. Arizona State's coaches told him they would give him a chance to make the team if he wanted to walk on. But the special teams coach at New Mexico made what sounded like a better offer: "They had a snapper, but they weren't that thrilled with him," Maese said. "He told me if I came there and beat the guy out and became the starter, they would scholarship me. I decided to take a chance even though it would cost more to go to school there than if I stayed in-state at ASU."

By the end of New Mexico's preseason training camp, Maese was the first-string snapper. But he didn't have a scholarship. "They said it was a numbers game," he said. "I was tempted to leave, but I was already enrolled in school and I wanted to play, so I stuck it out."

He never did get a scholarship, so he continued to work on the side to pay for his tuition. He dug ditches some of the time and continued working as a bouncer. When the coaches complained to him that they didn't like him working late hours as a bouncer, he told them, "Give me a scholarship and I won't need to work anymore."

By his senior season, he was attracting attention from pro scouts. The Ravens had just won the Super Bowl, but they needed a long snapper. They had used two different players in that role in 2000 and weren't convinced either one was a long-term solution. Ozzie Newsome has always believed that if you have a need, you should draft for it, especially if you think someone specific is the answer to that need. Maese's consistency impressed everyone in the organization. He was almost never off target with a snap. The Ravens drafted him in the sixth round in the 2001 draft — the only long snapper drafted that year — and he became their snapper from the first day of training camp. He had been the snapper since then, except for missing the last game of his rookie season with a knee injury.

Maese's only weakness as a snapper was a chronic back condition that occasionally flared up. This was hardly surprising for a man who made his living bending over a football, snapping it, and then getting hammered by a defensive lineman the instant he released the ball. Like a lot of specialists, Maese had a routine during games that he never violated. Anytime the Ravens had a third down, he would find a clear spot on the sideline, wipe his hands with a towel, bend over, and snap an imaginary ball between his legs. Then he would grab the towel again and either walk back to the bench if there was no kick or dry his hands once again, toss the towel on the ground, and trot onto the field to snap.

Now, though, Maese's back was sore and there was concern that it might go on him during the game on Sunday. The question was whether he could make it through the game. If he couldn't, the Ravens could be in trouble since there was no one else on the roster who could long snap.

Enter Mike Solwold.

Solwold was the long snapper who had been cut on the first day of training camp after recovering from a torn muscle in his chest, suffered during the first minicamp. "As soon as I told 'em I was healthy, they cut me," he said, laughing. "I guess they didn't want to wait for me to tear it again and get stuck with an injury settlement."

Solwold had no problem with business being business. In 2003 he had made the Ravens' practice squad as a backup tight end and as insurance at the long-snapper spot in case something happened to Maese. With three weeks left in the season, the New England Patriots offered him a chance to sign with them and be placed on the fifty-three-man roster. Solwold told the Ravens about the Patriots' offer. They made a counteroffer: stay with us and we'll put you on the fifty-three-man roster and guarantee you a spot there for the last three games of the season. That was an offer Solwold couldn't refuse. Even though he might have gone to the Super Bowl with the Patriots if he had stuck the rest of the season, he had no regrets about the decision.

"Three games on the fifty-three meant I'd be fully vested," he said. "Even though Joe was fine and I didn't get activated for any of the games, it got me vested. For someone like me, that's a big deal."

Solwold is part of that portion of the football-playing population that flies well under the radar of those who watch games on Sunday. His only appearances in the newspaper through the years had been in the agate-type portion of the sports page every day that reads, "Transactions." He had appeared in transactions frequently since graduating from the University of Wisconsin in 2000. There, he had been a backup tight end and the long snapper on back-to-back Rose Bowl teams while majoring in history. The life of Mike Solwold, professional football player, could be summed up by his appearances in "Transactions":

- Signed by the Minnesota Vikings as a rookie free agent, 8-25-01
- Waived by the Vikings, 8-27-01
- Claimed off waivers by the Dallas Cowboys, 8-28-01
- Waived by the Cowboys, 9-3-01
- Re-signed by the Cowboys, 11-14-01
- Waived by the Cowboys, 4-23-02
- Signed by the Tampa Bay Buccaneers, 5-6-02
- Placed on injured reserve (broken foot) by the Buccaneers, 10-1-02
- Contract with Buccaneers allowed to expire, 2-28-03
- Signed by the Baltimore Ravens, 6-9-03
- Waived by the Ravens, 8-25-03
- Signed to the Ravens' practice squad, 9-1-03
- Signed to the Ravens' active roster, 12-8-03
- Re-signed by the Ravens, 3-5-04
- Waived by the Ravens, 7-29-04

He had been with the Vikings just long enough as a rookie that he found himself standing next to Kory Stringer on the practice field on the day the massive offensive lineman collapsed and died. "I'll never forget that moment or that day," he said quietly. "Obviously I didn't really know Kory; he was a vet, I was a rookie. But I was standing with him when he went down. Your first thought was 'he's just dehydrated.' It was one of those brutally hot days. But when they took him away in the ambulance, it was frightening."

Gary Zauner — who would later play an important role in bringing Solwold to Baltimore — was the Vikings' special teams coach at the time. Late that night, when Stringer died, coaches made the rounds to players' rooms to tell them what had happened. "I think it was about four-thirty in the morning," Solwold said. "He knocked on the door and when I opened it, I knew before he said a word that Kory had died."

All of Solwold's wanderings had produced appearances in twelve NFL games: eight with Dallas in 2001, four with Tampa Bay in 2002. But Solwold had a Super Bowl ring because he had been on Tampa Bay's IR list when the Bucs won the Super Bowl in 2003. He also had started making plans for life after football. He had applied to graduate school for the fall of 2005. And yet football wasn't completely out of his blood, either. Soon after being cut by the Ravens during the summer, he had been walking through a mall when he spotted a lacrosse net in the window of a sporting goods store.

"The toughest thing about snapping is finding someone to snap to when you aren't on a team," he said. "The lacrosse net was six feet high and narrow. Perfect for me to snap into."

He had remained in the town house he had bought the previous spring a couple of miles from the Ravens' facility, working out to stay in shape should the phone ring. It hadn't until Friday, December 10, when George Kokinis called and asked if he could come to the Ravens' new facility the next day. There was some doubt, he said, about whether Maese could snap on Sunday.

Solwold drove over the next day and, after the team finished its Saturday walk-through, snapped to Dave Zastudil and Nick Murphy. In a bit of cruel irony, Murphy was helping to work out the player who would ultimately replace him on the roster. If Maese was healthy, Murphy would still be on the fifty-three for the Giants game as insurance for Zastudil. If Maese couldn't go, the Ravens would need a spot on the roster since Maese would simply be inactive for the game, not placed on the injured list.

With Kokinis and Gary Zauner watching, Solwold snapped for about thirty minutes. "It felt good," he said. "I was glad I had kept working. I wasn't nervous, I was doing something I knew I could do. When it was over, Coach Zauner said to me, 'You're it.'"

There was an if, though. If Maese's back felt okay on Sunday morning, he would dress. The Ravens signed Solwold to a contract on Saturday. He wouldn't know until Sunday morning if he would play under that contract or just watch.

Steve Bisciotti spent close to an hour with Chris McAlister on Thursday after practice. Rather than harp on McAlister's performance in the Bengals game, Bisciotti talked about living up to one's potential. "Why should it be automatic that Ray Lewis passes the leadership of this defense to Ed Reed?" he asked McAlister. "I'm not knocking Ed, believe me, but you should be right there with him. You have that kind of talent and, when you want to, the kind of personality that will make people want to follow you if you lead them."

He went on to tell him about the meeting Monday, the time spent on one subject — him — and the belief among the coaches that they were missing something because they hadn't been able to reach him with any consistency. "I didn't think it would help to beat him up again and tell him how frustrated everyone was with him," he said later. "I wanted him to maybe think of me as the guy on his side since he seems to think the coaches are out to get him."

Bisciotti tried to talk to McAlister as one imperfect human being to another. He told him that he liked to party as much as the next guy. "I stop drinking twice a year for a month, just to prove to myself that I can do it. I've got friends who can't do it, we all do. We're going to have guys on this team the next few years who aren't going to be perfect — like you and me. I need someone I can send them to, a player, not a coach, not an owner, a player who can say to them, 'Look, I've been there. I made mistakes and here's what I learned.' Who am I going to send them to: Todd Heap? You can be that person, Chris. You're a star and you should be a bigger star. Guys will look up to you and listen to you.'"

Bisciotti wrapped up the meeting by saying to McAlister: "Seven years from now [the length of his new contract] if you have just been a good player, or even a very good player, I'll feel as if I've failed and we've failed. And that would mean I invested a lot of money in you and made a mistake doing it. Here's my goal: when you give your induction speech for the Hall of Fame, I want you to mention my name."

McAlister listened. Bisciotti couldn't know it at the time, but he was preaching to the choir. "I had already decided by then that my partying days were over," he said. "I haven't seen the inside of a club since the night Corey and I talked. I understood Steve's message, but to a large extent I'd already gotten it."

Billick's message to the team wasn't nearly as complicated. He reverted to Al Davis-speak: Just win, baby.

"Don't play down to their level," he said on Saturday night. The Giants had lost five straight. "This is a struggling team, and we need to remind them why they're a struggling team right from the start. Let's not give them the idea that they have any chance to win this game."

Billick had decided prior to the game in New England to take a page from Belichick's book and have the team introduced all at once — on the road. "We'll let people boo all of us at the same time rather than individually," he said.

Kyle Boller and Anthony Wright had suggested to Matt Cavanaugh that they do the same thing at home. Cavanaugh said he would ask Billick about it. Billick shook his head. "Tell them maybe next year," he said. "We need that jump-start from the individual introductions, especially today."

It was the offense's turn to be introduced, and Billick thought that the last two players coming out of the tunnel, Heap and Jamal Lewis, would get the crowd going. On the surface, there was no reason to believe the Giants had any chance. But Billick had already been burned once by feeling too confident. He wasn't going to let that happen again. He might have been tighter on this Sunday morning than on any Sunday all season. When Kevin Byrne brought him the Giants' list of inactives, he smiled broadly when he saw that Mark Jones, a backup wide receiver, wasn't up. "He's got the kind of speed that can hurt us," he said. "That helps."

The Giants helped right from the opening kickoff. Derrick Ward took the kick, got hit by T. J. Slaughter, and coughed up the ball. Ed Hartwell jumped on it at the New York 27. "Come on, capitalize!" Billick screamed as the offense headed onto the field. "Get seven!" Like everyone else, Billick was getting a little tired of Stover kicking field goals instead of extra points.

It wasn't easy, but they got the seven. They needed help from referee Bill Carollo, who ruled Jamal Lewis down by contact on what appeared to be a fumble at the 12-yard line. On the next play, Boller found Clarence Moore in the back of the end zone for a 6–0 lead. The snapper on the extra point was Mike Solwold. Joe Maese's back had felt tight in the morning, and taking no chances, Billick and Zauner had activated Solwold. His snap was perfect, 7–0.

From there, they built the margin. Eli Manning, whom the Giants had ransomed a large chunk of their future to acquire on draft day in April, was making his fourth NFL start. He had no chance against the Ravens defense, and he got almost no help from the rest of his offense. Tiki Barber, the talented but occasionally stone-fingered running back, fumbled on the Giants' second possession, leading to a Stover field goal. A long drive by the offense in the second quarter, climaxed by Heap's first touchdown catch of the season, made it 17–0. The game would have been a complete rout if Boller hadn't been sacked on a blitz by Reggie Torbor and fumbled. Giants defensive end Osi Umenyiora scooped the ball up and raced 50 yards for a touchdown. The Ravens responded to that momentary glitch with ten more points before halftime: another Boller-to-Moore pass and a Stover field goal set up by an Ed Reed interception of Manning in the final seconds. It was 27–7 at the break. The Giants had 39 total yards in offense and four turnovers. Manning had completed five passes: three to his team-mates; two to the Ravens.

No one was feeling overconfident in the locker room after what had happened seven days earlier. Billick was concerned because Adalius Thomas and Terrell Suggs had spent time jawing with some of the Giants near the end of the half. "Don't let them draw you into anything," he said. "They're losers — don't get sucked in by them." He reminded them that the job wasn't done. The more telling message came from Deion Sanders, who walked from one defensive player to another, saying quietly, "It's the same situation as last week. Let's make sure we finish this time."

They finished. Stover kicked another field goal and Boller threw an-other touchdown pass to Heap in the third quarter to make it 37–7. Giants coach Tom Coughlin finally got poor Manning out midway through the fourth quarter, and Kurt Warner produced a consolation touchdown with fifteen seconds left to make the final score 37–14. It was an easy, dominat-ing victory, one that they absolutely had to have. If Manning ever became a star quarterback in the league, he would look back on this game as his low point: he had completed 4 of 18 passes for a total of 27 yards. By contrast, Boller had been superb, throwing four touchdown passes while completing 18 of 34 for 219 yards. The next night he would tell Fassel how badly he felt when he blew a read in the fourth quarter and threw the ball to the wrong receiver, missing a chance for a fifth touchdown pass.

"Look at how far you've come in a few weeks," Fassel told him. "You've gone from boos to cheers, and you've gone from talking about how bad your luck was on two of the interceptions against the Redskins to getting mad at yourself for not getting a fifth touchdown pass."

Boller was named the offensive player of the week in the NFC. Even so, there was a hollowness to the victory. They had beaten up on a very bad team with an overwhelmed rookie quarterback. The victory made them 8-5 and kept them tied with Denver, which had beaten the equally pathetic Dolphins, for the second wild-card spot. But it didn't change what was ahead the next two weeks: trips to Indianapolis and Pittsburgh. Billick may have summed up the feeling best during the Monday personnel meeting: "I feel a little like the guy who jumps off the thirty-story building and as he passes each floor on the way down, says, 'So far so good.'"

26

Almost Perfect

MIKE SOLWOLD'S COMEBACK with the Ravens lasted one day. On Monday afternoon, convinced Joe Maese would be ready to go the following Sunday in Indianapolis, the team cut him again.

He left with a smile on his face. "Hey, it was fun while it lasted," he said. "I knew going in, it was probably a one-day deal. I also know that the way this league works, I could be back on Wednesday."

In truth, that wasn't likely. Gary Zauner had found a long snapper who had recently been cut from the Jets' practice squad and could also help as a backup offensive lineman. The plan was to sign him for the practice squad. Still, Solwold had no regrets.

"Look, I know how this works," he said. "It's important to me that I had a good day because that may be my last memory of football. On our last punt, [Giants backup running back] Ron Dayne said to me, 'They told us to kill you on every play so you'd make a mistake and you didn't.' That made me feel good. I picked up a nice check [just under $27,000] for one day of work that wasn't work. I'm glad I showed people that I can still do this in case someone is looking for someone going into next year. I've got options."

He smiled and admitted the truth. "I've played football for seventeen years, since I was ten years old. Always loved it. I can retire and be fine with it. But I'd like to play for a little while longer."

In that sense, he was no different from anyone else.

Those who were not yet retired knew now that the next two weeks would almost undoubtedly decide the fate of their season. They could sit and do all the mathematical calculations they wanted to, but it was always going to come out the same: if they didn't beat Indianapolis or Pittsburgh, the regular-season finale at home against the Dolphins would almost certainly be the season finale, too. That wasn't the plan Billick had laid out for them in June or at any time since then.

"Get me rewrite," Phil Savage said, trying to find some humor in it all. "We've gone off script."

Savage was just one Raven employee whose name was being bandied about during the week. On Monday the Cleveland Browns had made official what had been rumored for weeks: Butch Davis was out as coach/general manager/god of all football operations. The Browns hadn't won since mid-October and, at 3-10, were headed for their worst season since they came into the league in 1999. Davis, citing exhaustion, resigned on Monday. By that evening Savage's name was being mentioned as the next general manager in Cleveland, and people were speculating that Mike Nolan might go along with him as coach.

"I lived in Cleveland once," Savage said when the team's young scouts Daniel Jeremiah, Chisom Opara, and Jeremiah Washburn teased him about the job over lunch. "I'm not sure I want to live there again."

Everyone knew that was a Nixonian nondenial denial, especially since Savage was smiling broadly when he said it.

Matt Cavanaugh wasn't denying anything. His name had popped up in the Pittsburgh newspapers in connection with the opening at his alma mater, created when Walt Harris decided to take the Stanford job. Dave Wannstedt, the former Miami Dolphins coach, like Cavanaugh a Pitt alum and Cavanaugh's onetime boss in Chicago, had been the first person mentioned, but Wannstedt had withdrawn from consideration. "I'd love the job," Cavanaugh said. "I'd like to be a head coach; it would be a place I know and I'm comfortable with." He paused and smiled. "And it would make things a lot easier for everyone around here."

Brian Billick knew that. Even though the team had just had its best offensive day of the season, everyone knew it was something of a mirage because of how awful the Giants were. He knew, especially after his preliminary meetings on the future with Steve Bisciotti, Dick Cass, and Ozzie Newsome, that he wasn't going to be able to rescue Cavanaugh again. In fact, Cavanaugh was pretty certain he didn't want to be rescued. "Sometimes you have to look in the mirror and say, 'It's time to move on,'" he said. "I know lightning might strike and we might explode the next few weeks, but that isn't likely. They took a lot of heat for keeping me last year. They'd take a lot more if they kept me again this year. There are times in life when change is the best thing for everybody. I don't lie awake at night, worrying about it, because I know I can coach and there will be a job out there for me. But I'd be lying if I said I wasn't aware of the pressure Brian's under or that I didn't hear what people say. Hell, I'm frustrated we haven't scored more points, too. There's no doubt in my mind it would be better for everyone if this worked out."

Pittsburgh athletic director Jeff Long had contacted Cavanaugh about getting together and had agreed to fly to Indianapolis on Saturday to meet with him. Billick told Cavanaugh that if he got the job and wanted to get started right away, he was welcome to go. He would take over play calling for the rest of the season if necessary. Billick wasn't at all concerned that the Pitt possibility would distract Cavanaugh. "Someone else maybe," he said. "Not Matt."

This was not a week when any distractions could be tolerated. Even though the Steelers, Patriots, and Eagles were all 12-1, there were some in the league who believed the Colts, at 10-3, might be playing the best football at that moment. Peyton Manning was a far cry from his little brother. He was now in his seventh year in the league and had shared the MVP award a year ago with Tennessee quarterback Steve McNair. He appeared to be a lock to win the award outright in 2004 because he was breaking records constantly, well on his way to setting an all-time record for touchdown passes in a season. He had a plethora of receivers to throw to, led by the all-world Marvin Harrison, Reggie Wayne, and ex-Raven Brandon Stokely. Since the Colts operated out of a no-huddle offense, it was tougher to get defensive personnel on and off the field. The no-huddle was something of a farce: it took Manning just as long to call the play at the line as it would have in the huddle, but it made it tougher for teams to figure out what formation the Colts were in because they appeared to be in constant motion while Manning was calling signals.

Billick was confident the defense could handle all the Colts would throw at it. "We react well to games like this," he said. "Plus, I think Mike [Nolan] has some ideas that will give them trouble."

They were about as healthy as an NFL team could hope to be in mid-December. Almost everyone in the building was feeling some kind of pain — that's the nature of an NFL season. Even those who don't actually have injuries are playing hurt by the fourteenth game. Deion Sanders had played against the Giants, but his foot still hurt enough that he was planning to take a shot before the Colts game. Billick had gotten Jamal Lewis in for eight carries, then took him out when the game became a rout, to save him for the Colts. Gary Baxter now had a shoulder injury to match the one Chris McAlister was still nursing. "There's no one in the secondary who doesn't have something hurting," Nolan reported during the Monday meeting.

There was also the issue of the artificial turf inside the RCA Dome. With Veterans Stadium's turf gone, the RCA Dome was now officially considered by players to have the worst playing surface in the league. It was hard on young, healthy legs, much less old, injured legs. They would have to watch everyone, but Sanders and Lewis in particular, very closely as the night wore on. And it would be night: this was the third and last ESPN Sunday night game on the Ravens' schedule. The 8:30 kickoff meant the team would get home between three and four o'clock in the morning. They would get off the plane either exhausted and thrilled or exhausted and desperate. The only thing certain was the exhausted part.

Billick's message to the team on Wednesday was twofold: First, foremost, don't worry about the circumstances they were in. There was no need to worry about the standings because if they played the kind of football he knew they could play, they would be exactly where they wanted to be when the playoffs began: playing.

"In the end it doesn't matter how you get in as long as you're in," he said. "We went to San Diego and won a year ago. Anybody in here afraid to go out there and play? Anyone in here who doesn't think we can beat Denver?"

Those were possible playoff matchups — both on the road. Part two of his talk was about the Colts, also a likely first-round opponent, until the very end. "Let me tell you about this team," he said. "They have a lot of impressive stats. They're good, really good. But they've beaten exactly one team — Minnesota — with a winning record. And I guarantee you they haven't faced anyone like us for a good long while."

That was the theme for the week. The Ravens now believed they were the Ravens again. The defense was banged up but healthy enough to play the way it was expected to. Boller had come a long way in a month and he now had everyone back: Lewis, Ogden, Heap. They had discovered a wide receiver who was a legitimate threat in Clarence Moore. Even Orlando Brown, who Billick had believed was done for the year, was going to play on Sunday. Only one player — Bart Scott, who had hurt his knee against the Giants — wasn't going to play and he was certain he would be ready for Pittsburgh the next week. "If it wasn't for that turf, I'd try it," he said. "But the doctors think it's too much risk."

In short, as difficult as the next two games were likely to be, the Ravens were as ready to play them as they could possibly be. "It also means we're out of excuses," Deion Sanders said in the locker room on Friday after practice. "We've had legitimate ones all year, right from the beginning. That's all over now. We find out who we are for real now."

They had believed all season that if they were healthy, there wasn't anyone in the league they couldn't play with. They felt as if they had gone into Philadelphia and New England playing with one hand tied behind their back because of injuries. Now both hands were free.

The trip to Indianapolis on Saturday took longer than expected because the plane hit headwinds. It was already dark and the temperature was in the teens — with the wind chill making it a lot colder — when they landed. But that wouldn't matter since they were playing indoors. The biggest challenge on Sunday would be killing time. Their three previous night games had been at home, meaning they could leave the hotel after morning meetings and go back to their houses. Now, they were in a hotel in downtown Indianapolis, with very little to do indoors and no one wanting to go outdoors.

Most of them watched football in the afternoon. One might think that every player in the NFL is a big football fan. That's not necessarily the case. Boller rarely watches football. "I look at enough tape, trying to learn, that when I have free time, I like to do other things" is his very reasoned explanation. When the Ravens returned from Philadelphia in October, the players knew that the Steelers and Patriots were playing in what was then a crucial game for them. Boller got into his car and turned on music. He was surprised when someone pulled up next to him in the parking garage and reported that the Steelers were winning.

If Boller had been watching on that Sunday afternoon, he would have been encouraged by the Broncos' loss in Kansas City, which dropped them to 8-6, but less than thrilled by Jacksonville's upset victory in Green Bay, which made the Jaguars 8-6. Buffalo also won, beating the Bengals, to raise its record to 8-6. The Ravens made the short bus ride to the stadium knowing that they once again had control over their own destiny. A victory would make them 9-5 and leave them alone in second place, one game behind the Jets, in the wild-card race. If they won out, they would be in the playoffs, regardless of what anyone else did. On the other hand, a loss would drop them into a four-way tie for the second wild card and everyone would start calculating tiebreakers that seemed to involve everything in the world, including the price of unleaded gas, in the formula.

The most remarkable ending of the day was in Detroit. With the Vikings hanging on for dear life to an NFC playoff spot, they found themselves in deep trouble against the Lions. Trailing, 28–21, in the final seconds, Detroit went the length of the field for what appeared to be a tieing touchdown, meaning the game would go into overtime. But Detroit kicker Jason Hanson never got a chance to kick the extra point. The snap was low and the holder couldn't get it down for Hanson to kick it. Long snappers get their name in the paper only when they make a mistake at a key moment. The snapper in this case was Don Muhlbach, who had been in training camp with the Ravens. He had been signed by the Lions a couple of weeks earlier. Watching on TV, Gary Zauner noticed on the replay that Muhlbach's head had come up just a tad prior to the snap. "I think that's what did it to him," he said. "I felt awful for the kid. He can snap in this league. I hope this doesn't ruin things for him."

It was ice-cold outside when the Ravens' buses pulled underneath the building formerly known as the Hoosier Dome, the temperature having dropped into single digits. Even inside, the place was cool, with an actual breeze blowing across the field. By any name, the dome has fewer seats for football than any stadium in the NFL: 57,240 is the capacity, and it is that much only because the Colts have put in three extra rows of seats so close to the field that the sidelines can be a dangerous place. Joe Maese, healthy again, almost became unhealthy a few minutes prior to kickoff when he went behind the bench to take a few practice snaps and almost got run over by the ESPN camera dolly as it whizzed past. When the Ravens asked the security people on the sideline if they could move the cheerleaders back so that Maese could have space to snap, they were told nothing could be done. Maese responded by snapping a ball off a security guard's head.

"Gee, I'm sorry," he said.

Everyone else was cracking up. In a thousand snaps Maese would never be that far off-line. In fact, he had snapped the ball exactly where he wanted to. The security guard decided to move the cheerleaders back a few steps so he could move back a few steps and get out of the line of fire.

The Colts and Ravens were, in an NFL sort of way, distant cousins. After all, if Robert Irsay hadn't moved the Colts from Baltimore to Indianapolis in 1984, the city would not have been available for the Browns. The Ravens had spent almost nine years in what had been the Colts' practice facility. The Colts were now negotiating for a new building to replace the dome. Jimmy Irsay, who had inherited the team from his late father, had made noises about moving to Los Angeles. It appeared that a deal to get Irsay and the Colts a new stadium was close to getting done, but it was not done yet.

Beyond the teams' city ties, Billick and Colts coach Tony Dungy had been coordinators together in Minnesota and were still friends. They talked easily during pregame while several of the Ravens had a brief reunion with Gerome Sapp, who had become a valued special teams player with the Colts after being cut by the Ravens during that painful second week of the season. The Colts were trying to lock down the third seed in the AFC behind the Steelers and Patriots. The next two weeks were as big to them as they were to the Ravens. After playing Baltimore, the Colts would host the San Diego Chargers. Since the Chargers had won in Cleveland that day (in the snow no less, an unheard-of feat for a warm-weather or indoor team), they would come to town with an 11-3 record. That meant the Colts had to win both this week and next to secure the third seed. The difference between the Colts and the Ravens was obvious: the Colts were playing for seeding, not for survival, and they would play their two key games at home.

Billick had made no bones all week about the fact that this was a big-time game in every way. He didn't talk at all about getting another chance in Pittsburgh if they lost this game. Everyone seemed to sense what was at stake and what was going to be needed. Ray Lewis paced up and down the small locker room, saying to anyone who would listen, "You have to run this race with all of your heart!" Stover, asked to do the prayer, said simply: "I just want to challenge everyone in this room to match the intensity of number fifty-two. If we do that, we can't lose the game." Those words were directed at his teammates. Then, after asking everyone to bow their heads, he said, "Lord, we come to pray before you as we have never prayed before."

The doctors were busy prior to the game. Jamal Lewis needed a shot in his ankle after pregame warm-ups. Deion Sanders needed one in his foot. Chris McAlister had forgotten about his weekly painkiller and had to be injected on the sideline just prior to kickoff.

Billick isn't very big on lengthy or eloquent pregame speeches. He usually stalks to the middle of the room and announces the captains and which unit is going to be introduced. At this point in the season he didn't need to do that. The captains were in place and the team was being introduced all at once. He then goes on to remind them about playing with emotion, not making mistakes, or letting the other team know right away which is the better team. This time, he stepped out of character. His voice was much softer than normal.

"Fellas, this game, this setting is what your whole life is about," he said. "This night is about why you do this. This is about celebrating the life you lead, the life we all lead. It's about more than just this season. All your lives, you've worked and sweated to play in a game like this. A game like this is about commitment. It's about passion. It's about being willing to give yourself up for the cause if you have to. This isn't about making the playoffs or not making the playoffs. It is about what is going to happen the next three hours out there on that field and how we will all feel about ourselves when it's over. If it were going to be easy, then nothing would be at stake.

"At times this year we've played with great emotion. At other times we've played smart. Tonight, we have to do both — for the entire game. I promise you it will be worth the effort."

As the players charged down the long hallway toward the field, Billick and Jim Fassel trailed them. For once, there was no chatter between them. Just a silent handshake.

*   *   *

The first half was full of all the emotion Billick had talked about. The Colts took Wade Richey's kickoff — Richey was up again because of Bart Scott's injury — and Manning promptly went to work. In four plays, he had moved his team from its own 28 to the Ravens' 9, and it looked like it might be a very long night. But then everything changed. After Edgerrin James had picked up 2 yards on first down, Manning should have been intercepted — twice. First Chad Williams had a golden chance in the end zone, but missed. Then Will Demps, darting in front of tight end Marcus Pollard, might have had an Ed Reed–like 100-yard touchdown return, except that he dropped the ball. The Colts settled for a Mike Vanderjagt field goal and it was 3–0.

The Ravens offense didn't exactly light things up, in the ensuing series. The most important play Boller made in the first quarter came when Jamal Lewis fumbled on the Ravens' first play from scrimmage. Before anyone else could make a move, Boller alertly dove on the ball, preventing what would have been a disastrous early turnover deep in Baltimore territory. The game became a punting duel between Dave Zastudil and Hunter Smith. With just under four minutes left, Manning completed a short pass over the middle to Reggie Wayne, and Ray Lewis and Marques Douglas combined to make the tackle. Lewis came up wincing. He took about three steps toward the sideline before his knees buckled and he went down, holding his right wrist, clearly in great pain. He had to be helped off, holding his wrist gingerly. Billick, hands on hips, stood and watched silently. He didn't need Andy Tucker or anyone else to tell him that it was a wrist injury. What he needed to know was how serious a wrist injury it was. The entire medical staff immediately surrounded Lewis as he sat on the bench.

While he was being attended to, the Ravens got the ball back and Jamal Lewis broke off his first big run in weeks, picking up 47 yards to move the ball to the Indianapolis 33. The offense stalled at that point — Lewis was stopped going up the middle on third-and-2 — but Stover came in to make a 42-yard field goal that tied the game early in the second quarter.

Remarkably, Lewis was back in the game for the next defensive series. The official announcement in the press box was that he had sprained his wrist. Only later, after an X-ray, would the doctors realize that the wrist was broken. Lewis told them he had no time for X-rays, he needed to play. They wrapped the wrist to immobilize it as much as possible and sent him back into the game. On the second play of the Colts' next series, he plugged the hole and slammed Edgerrin James down for no gain.

The defense was doing exactly what Billick and Nolan had hoped it would. Nolan had preached constant motion all week, telling his players not to stand still while Manning was lining his team up, because if they did, he would change the play based on where they were. The defenders kept bouncing around, and Manning looked confused at times, not quite sure where to throw the ball.

With the score tied at 3–3, the Ravens took over on their own 40 with 3:21 left. Boller immediately found Travis Taylor flying over the middle for a 33-yard pickup and a first down at the Colts' 27. Worst-case scenario, they were in field goal range. An incomplete pass to Darnell Dinkins and a 1-yard run by Lewis set up third-and-9. Boller dropped to pass — and never had a chance. Before he could even think about looking down-field, defensive end Dwight Freeney was on him. What was shocking to Boller — and everyone else — was that Freeney had gone past Jonathan Ogden to get to him. Ogden getting beaten, cleanly, by a defensive end on a pass rush was dog-bites-man stuff. Freeney is a superb pass rusher and is easily the Colts' best defensive player. The street that leads to the player entrance outside the dome is named Dwight Freeney Way. He had made a spin move and had gone around, or perhaps under, Ogden. At six-one, 268, Freeney is a relatively tiny defensive end and throughout the night he appeared to be getting under the six-nine Ogden. Boller deserved some credit for hanging on to the ball. Still, the sack took them out of field goal range.

"Miscommunication," Ogden said later. "I heard the wrong call and I didn't realize I had him until it was too late. The guy is quick."

Zastudil lofted a punt toward the Colts' end zone and B. J. Sams made a wonderful play, beating the ball down the field and downing it on the 1-yard line. This was one of those moments Billick had talked about to the defense after the New England game: the Colts were backed up, time was running out, and the defense had a chance to make something happen. Edgerrin James helped by pulling a Corey Dillon and running out of bounds on second down. A penalty helped, too. Then, on third-and-7, McAlister and Anthony Weaver combined to stop Harrison three yards short of the first down. Smith punted, his fifth of the half, unheard-of for the Colts, and Sams returned it 13 yards to midfield. They had fifty-one seconds and a time-out left to get on the board and gain some momentum for the second half.

Boller quickly picked up 11 yards on a pass to Chester Taylor, then spiked the ball to stop the clock with twenty-eight seconds to go. But before the Ravens could get off another play, Ogden was called for a false start. Clearly, Freeney's quickness had unnerved him and he started half a second too early. The ball moved back to the 44. The Ravens needed about 12 yards to give Stover a reasonable chance. There was still plenty of time. Boller threw for Clarence Moore over the middle. Moore was a step short of getting to it, causing Billick to scream, "Goddammit, Clarence!" He felt that Moore had run the pattern short, an unsettling reprise of the Cincinnati game. Third down. Boller again looked for Moore. Rushed, he overthrew him, and safety Mike Doss, peeling back, intercepted the ball at the 22. He weaved his way to the Ravens' 46.

Suddenly — stunningly — with thirteen seconds left, it was the Colts with a chance to score. Manning had two time-outs to play with. He needed only one. He quickly found Pollard over the middle, who was brought down on the 15 with five seconds left. Vanderjagt jogged on and made a 33-yard field goal with one second left, and instead of walking off the field with a lead, the Ravens walked off trailing, 6–3.

Fassel could see the steam coming out of Billick's ears as they walked toward the tunnel. "You told me before the season started to speak up, so I'm speaking up," he said. "This is not the time to go crazy on anybody."

Billick heard Fassel. He also knew that his defense was frustrated. Ahead of him in the tunnel, he could hear Ray Lewis saying, "Team football, we need to play team football."

He was reminding the rest of the defense that getting upset with the offense wouldn't do any good. The defense had played as well as it possibly could have hoped and still walked off the field trailing. Twice the offense had been set up in the final minutes to get at least three points, but it had ended up surrendering three points. That was tough to swallow. But they needed to swallow it and come back and play just as hard in the second half.

"Listen up, listen up," Billick said once they were inside the locker room. "We have got them playing our kind of football. Now we have to do the little things." He paused as if thinking if he should stop there. Later he would wish he had. But even with Fassel's calming voice in his ear, he couldn't control himself completely. "Clarence, I don't *ever* expect to see you short-arm a ball like that again. Understand?"

Everyone was wired during the break. Jim Colletto kept telling the offensive line that it had to make plays because "in a big-time game you have to make something happen, and this is a big-time game." Nolan couldn't ask for anything more from the defense. He simply pleaded with them to hang in there and keep doing what they were doing.

The third quarter wasn't all that different from the third quarter in New England. The offense stalled after picking up one first down. The Colts took over on their own 23 and promptly marched down the field, Manning mixing James's runs in with his short passes. On first down from the Ravens' 38, he threw a short pass to Wayne and it looked for a second as if Gary Baxter had wrested it away from him. But the official ruled it a catch for Wayne. Two plays later, on third-and-1, Manning play-faked to James, and McAlister, who had been superb up until that moment, bit on the fake. Harrison was wide-open at the goal line and glided in for the touchdown, making it 13–3 and, coincidentally, allowing Manning to tie Dan Marino's all-time record of 48 touchdown passes in a season.

The Ravens could have cared less about the record. All they knew was that they were ten points down. This time the offense responded. Boller quickly found Heap for a 24-yard pickup into Indy territory at the 46. Then he found Moore, who showed no signs of short-arming the ball, over the middle for 17 more yards and a first down at the 29. A pass to Jamal Lewis and then a run by him picked up another first down at the 17. If they could punch it in and cut the margin right back to three, it would be a ball game. But then, as had been the case so often all season, the offense bogged down. Lewis got 4 on first down to the 13, but then Boller threw incompletions to Heap and Chester Taylor. Fourth down. The consolation was that Stover's field goal, which would come from 31 yards, would get them within one score, at 13–6.

At that point in the year, Stover had missed one field goal — a 50-yarder — and had made 23 others. He was the closest thing the Ravens had to a sure thing. Stover, Zastudil, and Maese trotted out with 2:34 left in the quarter. Stover went through his usual routine, left arm in the air, shoulder down. He looked almost like a wooden soldier when he lined up and went through all this, but it worked. "If I do it the same way every time, I remember the same things every time," he said. "The important thing is to keep my head still and keep it down. If I do that, I'm pretty sure I'll make the kick."

This time something went wrong. The snap was good, the hold was good. But the kick never cleared the line of scrimmage. It was blocked, right in the middle of the line, by defensive tackle Larry Tripplett, who at six-two, 314, was not blessed with a great vertical leap. The immediate assumption on the sideline was that somebody had missed a block and let one of the Colts get too much penetration. Stover corrected that: "I messed up," he said. "I just kicked it low. My fault."

The ball caromed backward and was picked up as it bounced on the carpet by defensive back Von Hutchins. Dan Wilcox finally dragged him down on the Ravens' 31. You could feel the life go out of the Ravens' bench at that moment. If they couldn't count on Stover, could they count on the sun rising the next morning? On Tuesday following Monday? The offense not getting in the end zone was nothing new. Stover having a kick blocked — and it being his fault — was unheard-of.

"I've coached him for six years, I've never seen that happen," Billick said later. "Never seen it in a game, never seen it in practice. The guy is that good, that consistent. It's unfair to criticize him even for a second for turning human once in six years."

It didn't take the Colts long to capitalize. Manning completed passes to Stokley and Wayne to set up a first down at the Ravens' 7, then James needed two more carries to get into the end zone. Vanderjagt's extra point made it 20–3 with twenty-eight seconds left in the quarter. Exactly one quarter earlier, they had been at the Colts' 39 in a tie game, looking to take a halftime lead. Now they were three scores down with just a little more than a quarter to play. They finally managed to get into the end zone on the next series, Boller finding Heap from 13 yards out. One couldn't help but think how different the game might have felt if that touchdown had come the previous time the Ravens had been on the Colts' 13. This time it gave them a flicker of hope, down 20–10 with 12:50 still to play.

During the TV time-out prior to the kickoff, Ray Lewis called the defense together. "This is what makes a Super Bowl team," he said as they surrounded him. "If you want to be a Super Bowl team, you have to get this team three-and-out right now. There's no choice. Now or never."

They responded. James got one yard before Adalius Thomas slammed him down. Manning threw incomplete to Stokley. Then Baxter broke up a pass intended for Harrison. He came off holding his shoulder in obvious pain. "GB," said Lewis, who was playing in a fair bit of pain himself, "don't you even *think* about feeling pain. Not now."

They had gotten the Colts off the field three-and-out and used only a minute to do so. Now it was up to the offense. Sure enough, they began to move the ball. A Boller pass to Dinkins got them to the Colts' 41. Boller found Heap for 8 more. Then, scrambling to avoid a blitz, he found Heap again for a first down at the 15. Except that there was a flag. As often happens to linemen when a quarterback starts to scramble, Casey Rabach had turned upfield, thinking Boller would run, and had crossed the line of scrimmage, looking to block someone. When Boller threw the ball, that made him an illegal receiver. The play came back. Instead of first-and-10 at the 15, they had second-and-7 at the 38.

They never moved the ball another inch: Boller threw three incompletions, the last one on fourth down, a strike to Moore who couldn't hang on to the ball when Jason David hit him as the ball arrived. Billick had gone for the first down at that moment, understanding that giving the ball up without points at such a late stage was probably fatal.

The Colts then held the ball more than four minutes and even though the usually reliable Vanderjagt (perhaps out of solidarity with Stover) missed a 33-yard field goal at the end of the drive, the clock was now ticking toward four minutes. The Colts were in a prevent defense, giving up short passes. The Ravens took them. Boller got them to the Colts' 35 with a completion to Heap that wasn't called back with 1:46 to go. Again they bogged down in scoring territory. Again Billick went for it on fourth down, this time a fourth-and-3 at the 28, figuring the chances of Stover making a field goal and then getting the ball back on an onside kick and scoring a touchdown in 1:12 were close to zero. A touchdown, an onside kick, and a field goal was unlikely, but less unlikely.

It was all moot when Boller's pass intended for Travis Taylor was picked off by Cato June, who ran it all the way back to the Ravens' 4-yard line with fifty-nine seconds left. The crowd was screaming for Manning to throw the ball into the end zone and end the game by breaking Marino's record. Neither Manning nor Dungy wanted to do it that way. The game was over. There was no need to rub any salt into the Ravens' wound. Manning knelt twice as the crowd howled angrily.

"We'll see you again," Dungy said to Billick as they shook hands, trying to give his old friend a quick pep talk.

Billick put an arm around Dungy. "They're booing you," he said. "You're 11-3 and you just won a hell of a game and they're booing you. Your problem is you aren't an asshole like I am."

That was Billick's way of saying, "Thanks for having so much class."

Dungy's class and his pep talk couldn't make the loss any easier to take. They had done what Billick had asked: put themselves on the line and given everything they had. It had not been enough. In the locker room, Mike Nolan made a point of pausing during his postgame handshakes to spend an extra moment with McAlister. "Mac, you fought hard," he said softly. McAlister had been beaten on the first Colts touchdown. Other than that, he had been outstanding.

"Everybody listen to me for a minute," Billick said, as they knelt or sat, many of them in obvious pain. "All I can ask of you is that you do what you did tonight. I asked you for passion and you gave it to me. All you can ever ask for in this business is to play games that matter in December. You played in one tonight. We've got two more that are going to matter. You have got to hold on to this feeling and remember it's still out there for you. I know it doesn't feel that way right now, but it's still true.

"I'm proud of all of you. We still have a lot to hold on to. Let's not forget that."

Forgetting what had happened that night — and what could have happened — was going to be easier said than done.

They had two games left. Coming close in the next one would not be good enough. Their margin for error was now down to a round number: zero.

27

Crash

THERE WAS NO NEED for Brian Billick to show his players the schedule or the NFL standings on the Wednesday after the loss to the Colts. The team had the day off on Monday, after arriving home at 4 A.M. from Indianapolis. When they came back to work on Wednesday, everyone knew exactly what was going to be at stake on Sunday in Pittsburgh: the season.

A victory over the Steelers would make the Ravens 9-6 with only the Dolphins at home left on the schedule. No one was absolutely certain how the tiebreakers would shake out, because so many different teams could still finish 10-6, but there was a strong sense that 10-6 would get the job done. The Jets were still in the driver's seat in the wild-card race at 10-4. Then came the group at 8-6: the Ravens, Broncos, Bills, and Jaguars. Unless the Jets completely collapsed, only one of those four teams could make the playoffs.

Life would have been a lot simpler if the Ravens had been in the NFC instead of the AFC. The NFC was so weak that teams with records of 5-9 were still mathematically alive for the wild-card spots. In all likelihood, 8-8 would be good enough to make the playoffs in the NFC — and 7-9 was not out of the question. "That's just the way life works out sometimes," Billick said. "It doesn't do a bit of good to sit here and talk about how unfair it is. As my good friend Bill Parcells says, 'It is what it is.'"

What it was in Baltimore was Christmas week without too much joy to go around. The Christmas trees were lit up all over the building, but there wasn't a lot of caroling going on in the hallways. Everyone now knew that Ray Lewis had broken his wrist in the first quarter on Sunday night. He had played on gallantly the rest of the game and was planning to get a shot in the wrist on Sunday that would allow him to play. That would make him one of at least three players who would need pregame shots in order to get on the field. The others were Jamal Lewis and Deion Sanders. There wasn't any question about whether they would play. There wasn't any choice at this point in the season. Todd Heap was another story: he had reinjured his ankle playing on the turf in Indianapolis and was again having trouble walking. "If I can walk, I'll play," he said. "I'm not sure I'll be able to walk."

By Monday night, it appeared very possible — even likely — that Billick would be calling the plays in Pittsburgh. Matt Cavanaugh had met a second time with Pitt AD Jeff Long on Monday and had come away believing he was the front-runner for the job. The Pittsburgh newspapers had the same idea: they were reporting that Cavanaugh was likely to be named before the end of the week. Within the coaching staff the word was already circulating that Billick wanted Ron Turner, who had been fired as the head coach at Illinois, to succeed Cavanaugh at the end of the season.

The larger concern, of course, was the Steelers. Remarkably, they had not lost a game since that second-week loss in Baltimore back in September, a Sunday afternoon that now felt as if it had been a lifetime ago, not three months. Ben Roethlisberger was going to be the runaway choice for rookie of the year, and stories comparing him with Terry Bradshaw were starting to crop up. Jerome Bettis, benched at the start of the season in favor of newly acquired Duce Staley, had stepped in after Staley had been injured and played so well that Staley couldn't get back on the field. The Steelers had a chance to clinch home-field advantage throughout the playoffs with a win on Sunday. The Patriots had dropped a shocking Monday night game to the Dolphins in Miami and were now 12-2. That meant the best they could finish was 14-2. A Steelers victory over the Ravens would mean they could finish no worse than 14-2, and since they had beaten the Patriots head-to-head, they would get home field should the teams meet in the conference final. Given what it was like to play in Foxboro, that was undoubtedly just about as big a deal to the Steelers as a keeping-their-playoff-hopes-alive win would be to the Ravens.

What's more, the Steelers would want to show the Ravens, the world, and themselves that the one-sided Ravens victory in Baltimore had been a pre-Roethlisberger fluke and that there was good reason why they were 13-1 and the Ravens were 8-6. In short, it would be a long, grinding day in a very tough place to play. Heinz Field, named for the same company that had turned the "red zone" into a corporate promo, was such a hostile place for visitors that Steve Bisciotti had decided not to make the trip. "The last time I was up there, our box was right next to some very loud people," he said. "They all knew exactly where the visiting team's box was and every time they scored, they started banging on the walls. I figure if we win, I'll be so happy I won't mind being at home. And if we lose, I'll be very happy not to be there."

The team didn't have any such options. Not only did they have to make the trip, they had to make it on Christmas afternoon. Billick reminded them during the week that they would have all afternoon and evening on Christmas Eve with their families and Christmas morning, too. "Enjoy all of it," he said. "But when we get to Pittsburgh, be ready to get your heads back into playing the game."

As he often did late in the season, Billick adjusted his practice plans to take into account how bruised and hurt and tired the team was. Ray Lewis wasn't going to practice all week. Jamal Lewis, Sanders, and McAlister would be limited to light work. Todd Heap was held out of most practice work but insisted that he would play on Sunday, too. It was a tired, cranky group that reassembled on Wednesday. Jonathan Ogden was steaming after reading and hearing for two days that Dwight Freeney had "done a number on him."

"The guy's good, especially indoors on that turf," Ogden said. "The sack was a blown call. I thought I had the corner and at the last second I realized Freeney was unblocked and I couldn't get to him in time. Blown calls happen, but it looks like I got beat and I end up getting killed." He sighed. "I get paid a lot of money and I don't need people writing or saying every week that I'm great. But I do get tired sometimes of only seeing my name in the paper when people think I've screwed up. It gets old."

Knowing that his team was fragile both mentally and physically, Billick limited practice on Wednesday to little more than a walk-through of the plays they would be using in Pittsburgh. At this point in the season, there wasn't much to be accomplished by hitting in practice anyway. Billick's message Wednesday morning was about not giving up even though giving up might be understandable.

"What we can't do this week is give in to the circumstances," he said. "I know you're hurting physically. I know how disappointed you are about what happened in Indianapolis because I know you sold out to try to win that game. The easy thing to do now is just say, 'Hey, it's too tough this year, we caught too many bad breaks.' But we've never been like that. I know you guys are sick and tired of hearing me say this, but I'm gonna say it one more time because it's as true now as it was in July: it is still all out there for you. We win the next two Sundays, we'll be in the playoffs. I still haven't seen a team out there that we can't go on the road and beat. Anyone in here think that game on Sunday was unwinnable? I don't.'"

Later that day Ray Lewis walked through the locker room speaking to no one and everyone: "I pray we get to play in Indianapolis again," he kept saying. "I pray to God we get to go there again."

The week began to turn in the wrong direction on Thursday. The Pittsburgh newspapers were reporting that Dave Wannstedt's name had resurfaced in connection with the Pitt job. In fact, they reported, the job was his to turn down. Cavanaugh understood the thinking: Wannstedt was an established NFL head coach. He had been mildly successful in Chicago and very successful in Miami until the roof had fallen on his head beginning with the Ricky Williams retirement fiasco during the summer. He had been Pitt's first choice but had said no, undoubtedly because he had been hoping to get another shot in the NFL. But as the NFL season wound down, it was starting to look as if the number of coaching changes would be fewer than usual. Wannstedt had apparently called Jeff Long back and told him that he had reconsidered. Given that a local columnist in Pittsburgh had written on Tuesday that the hiring of Cavanaugh — or any of the other finalists — would be proof that the Pitt people undervalued the job, Wannstedt was something of a savior for Long; a big name with Pitt roots.

"If Dave wants it, it's his," Cavanaugh said on Thursday, clearly disappointed. "Believe me, I understand where they're coming from. I'd probably do the same thing if I were in their shoes."

Still, it hurt. Cavanaugh had started out as little more than an after-thought in the process, put on the list because he was a Pitt grad with an NFL pedigree. He had interviewed his way from afterthought to club-house leader only to have Wannstedt show up at the last possible minute to snatch the job away from him. On Friday, Pitt made it official, introducing Wannstedt as its new coach. By then, Billick had sent the players home for their Christmas celebrations. He had been pleased with their one full prac-tice of the week on Thursday, but Friday had been sloppy. "Christmas Eve," he said. "Their minds are elsewhere. Happens every year."

Billick and his family had their own Christmas traditions. After having dinner and exchanging presents, he and Kim and Aubree and Keegan went upstairs for the family's annual reading of *The Polar Express.*

"We started doing it when Aubree was two, and we've done it every year since then," Billick said. That was followed by Kim venturing outside to shake the leather bells on the windows to make them ring. It was a nice es-cape for Billick from the realities he would be facing the next day.

Given the time of year, they got lucky with the weather. It would be cold on Sunday, but there was no snow predicted and the biting wind that often cut through Heinz Field late in the season would be milder than it fre-quently was in December.

Saturday night's meetings were longer than usual. The only remnant left from Christmas was Gary Zauner's "Merry Christmas" message on the board in the front of the room. Right below it he had written, "Gotta stop #82," as if to make certain no one lingered on the Christmas message for too long. Zauner was referring to Antwaan Randle El, the Steelers' dan-gerous kick returner. Dave Zastudil would be asked to do a lot of direc-tional punting to keep Randle El near the sidelines.

In the defensive meeting, Nolan reviewed the keys to the game, most of them having to do with attitude and the need to impose their will on the Steelers. But he also reminded them about what to watch for with Roeth-lisberger: "He tends to eyeball one receiver," Nolan said. "If it doesn't work, he'll take off. We've got to contain him. He's not Mr. Nifty but he can elude people. Be aware of that."

Billick didn't often begin his Saturday night talks with any kind of film or video. He left that to the coordinators. But he was a movie buff and he had asked the video people to put together a cut from *Men of Honor,* specifically the scene where Robert De Niro orders the navy diver played by Cuba Gooding Jr. to take ten steps in full diving gear even though every step is so painful that he is almost in tears by the time he crosses the room.

The message across the bottom of the screen was what Billick wanted to get to: "No matter the situation, no matter the circumstance, determination will allow you to achieve your goals."

"I know you all had personal things to attend to this morning, that's why we didn't have a walk-through this morning," Billick said. "The challenge right now is to regroup and focus on what's ahead of us tomorrow. There are three things I want you all to think about:

"First, we all know what this game is about. These teams are built essentially the same way: physical defenses, run-oriented, play-action passes, and big plays with special teams. We know them, they know us.

"Second, it's clear-cut what's at stake here. We all know about the winloss situation. But it's more than that. We're playing the Pittsburgh Steelers and we know what that means, regardless of our record or theirs. We've set a mind-set and a tone the last two times we've played them. We took the ball back in September and went ninety yards, right down the field. We dictated to them from the start. Last week we dictated the nature of the game, we just didn't win. You must dictate your will on the game *again* tomorrow.

"Third, there are a couple of things we'd like to change in our season. We all know that. But even if those things were changed, it would not change anything about tomorrow. Sure, the business aspect is there. But even if it wasn't, even if we had home field through the playoffs locked up or we were already eliminated from the playoffs, it wouldn't change what this particular game is about."

He paused for a moment. "Think about why you do this. I know the obvious answers: money, fame, fortune, women, the physicality of it. But there's got to be more. A lot of you already have all that other stuff. So why? Why do guys come back from injuries, sometimes from retirement? Because this only lasts so long. The feeling we're all going to have on that field tomorrow is something none of us can hold on to forever. It's going to be gone someday. That's why the business aspect of the game has nothing to do with why we're playing the game. We're playing the game because of the way it will feel when we're out there tomorrow. Enjoy that feeling tomorrow because the number of opportunities we all have to feel that way is limited."

It was an eloquent talk, a good message going into a critical game. But a few minutes later, while the players were enjoying their post-meetings snack, Billick couldn't help but notice Ray Lewis sitting at a table with Andy Tucker and Leigh Ann Curl. They were telling him what kind of painkilling shots — it would take two, not one — they were going to give him to get him on the field the next day. No one understood what this game was about better than Ray Lewis. He would be playing it with one hand. Billick knew even Ray Lewis would have a tough time tackling Jerome Bettis with one hand.

Corey Fuller got the phone call from his fellow Florida State alumnus Derrick Brooks, now a star linebacker in Tampa Bay, on his cell phone during the short bus ride from the hotel to the stadium. Reggie White, the great defensive end for the Eagles, Packers, and Panthers, had died suddenly early that morning at the age of forty-three. The news spread quickly through the locker room.

There was no doubting Reggie White's greatness. He would be voted into the Hall of Fame the first year he was eligible. He had, in many ways, redefined the defensive end position. But he had become a very controversial figure late in his career. White was a lay minister, very outspoken on a number of subjects, including homosexuality. His views had drawn a great deal of scrutiny and criticism during his career and since his retirement. To most football players, though, and especially to devout African American players, he wasn't the least bit controversial: he was a hero. The news of his death on the morning after Christmas, a few hours before the most crucial game of the season, was both sobering and staggering. Ray Lewis sat in front of his locker for a long time with his headphones on, staring into space, saying over and over, "It all comes back to praying to Jesus."

Billick was saddened to hear the news but had little time to focus on it. He needed to know from the doctors if all the injured players who were going to receive shots could play. The more often one gets a painkilling shot, the more risk there is that it won't take. What's more, the pain when the shot wears off becomes more acute each time. The shot the doctors put into Deion Sanders's foot didn't take. "I feel like someone shot me," he said. "But I have to deal with it for a few hours."

Ray Lewis would get one shot that would get him through warm-ups, then a bigger one that, the doctors hoped, would last until the game was over. "If we do make the playoffs, there's a chance some of these guys won't be able to go," Leigh Ann Curl said. "There comes a point where you just can't keep giving them painkillers. They stop being effective."

They would cross that bridge — painfully — if and when they got to it. The only player on the inactive list who was injured was Bart Scott, whose knee hadn't improved as quickly as hoped. One surprise healthy scratch was Travis Taylor. Billick had decided during the week to go with Randy Hymes as the third wideout along with Clarence Moore and Kevin Johnson. "I just think Randy has more spring in his legs than Travis right now," he said.

He had told Taylor on Friday that he wouldn't be active on Sunday. This was a major blow for Taylor. He had known all year that his future with the Ravens was at stake, and he had been through yet another up-and-down year. There had been some spectacular catches and some spectacular drops — most notably the fourth-down play in Philadelphia. He had tried to play hurt when he shouldn't have in Cleveland and he had nursed nagging injuries all season. What's more, he and his wife, who had been married since Taylor's sophomore year at Florida and had three children, had separated and were headed for a divorce. Taylor was one of the friendliest men on the team, a truly gentle soul whom everyone liked. It had already been a difficult fall for him. Now, with the team playing its most important game of the year, he was inactive. To avoid embarrassment for Taylor — and questions for the coaches — the reason for his inactivity was announced as a combination of his being banged up and Hymes being fresher.

On Sunday morning Taylor had called Darren Sanders, the team's director of security, to tell him that he had to fly to Atlanta right away. His grandmother, he explained, was very sick. He never made the trip to the stadium with the team. His absence was, in many ways, symbolic. Deep down, everyone knew he wasn't going to be wearing a Ravens uniform anymore once the season was over. That didn't make anyone especially happy. Everyone liked Travis Taylor.

Even without a truly biting wind, it was a cold, blustery day. Heinz Field sits right on the banks of the Monongahela, right next to the spectacular new baseball stadium that opened in 2001. Wade Richey, who wasn't active for the game, sat on the heated bench during warm-ups and said with a smile, "You feel the cold more when you aren't playing. I better get warm now, because I'll feel guilty sitting here once the game starts. The guys playing need to keep warm."

Richey was another well-liked player whose future with the team was very much in doubt. If his self-confidence matched his leg strength, he would have been a Pro Bowler. But since his spectacular 21-of-23 (field goals) season in San Francisco in 1999, he had battled confidence problems much the way a golfer with the putting yips does. That was why he had been signed by the Ravens strictly to kick off. For this game, Matt Stover would kick off while Richey watched.

The locker room was as quiet during the final moments before kickoff as it had been all season. Part of that was Ray Lewis's absence. He was in the training room receiving his second shot. Billick's message wasn't much different from the night before. "Everyone up here tight, where you can all touch somebody," he said, pulling them together in what was the biggest locker room they had been in all season. "There should be no question in anybody's mind what the next three hours are about. This is the test you all live for. What you want won't come easy. You just have to give everything you have for three hours."

The game followed a familiar script. The Steelers scored on their first possession, going 80 yards in just five plays, Roethlisberger finishing the drive with a perfect 36-yard touchdown pass to Plaxico Burress. The Ravens answered right away with an eleven-play drive of their own, Kyle Boller setting up Jamal Lewis's 5-yard touchdown run with a 19-yard completion to Terry Jones. That made it 7-7. On the Steelers' next possession, Will Demps intercepted Roethlisberger on the first play at the Pittsburgh 45. The stadium, which had been wildly raucous at the start of the game and during the opening drive, was nearly silent. But the Ravens couldn't take advantage. On third-and-7 from the 25, with the field goal team readying itself for a Stover attempt on fourth down, Boller was blitzed, tried to get a pass off, and watched helplessly as it was deflected by linebacker James Harrison into the hands of Joey Porter.

The interception was about as painful as any that had occurred all season. To begin with, it wiped out a scoring chance. Beyond that, the interception was made by Porter, the same man who had pushed Heap over after he had been injured in the second game of the season. There was also the issue of Harrison, who was playing only because Kendrell Bell was injured. Harrison had been in the Ravens' early minicamp and had been released. Clearly, he remembered how that had felt.

In the coaches' box, Mike Nolan quietly seethed. To him, that series — pass, pass, pass — summed up everything that had been wrong with the offense all season. "Where was Jamal on that series?" he said later. "We get an interception, we have the ball in their territory, and he never touches the ball. Kyle's come a long way, but he is still the lowest-ranked quarterback in the league. I just don't think you go into Pittsburgh and ask him to beat the Steelers." Lewis had actually touched the ball twice on the series, but not enough to suit Nolan.

Nolan said nothing, of course, to Cavanaugh at that point. He had already had his blowup back in October and he wasn't going to repeat it. The tension between him and Cavanaugh and Billick had simmered since then. Cavanaugh and Nolan respected each other, but they were entirely different personalities: Nolan confrontational, Cavanaugh more likely to internalize frustration.

"I wish Matt had internalized *less,*" Billick said. "If Mike had done what he did in the Buffalo game when I was a coordinator, I'd have taken off the headset and said to him, 'There is no f —— way I need some defensive guy telling me what plays to call, now you shut the f —— up.' My guess is, Mike would have realized right then that he was wrong and he would have shut up. But that's just not Matt."

The Steelers pieced together another drive that ended in a 23-yard Jeff Reed field goal early in the second quarter. That was the end of the first-half scoring. The Steelers threatened again twice but came up empty, once when Terrell Suggs pressured Roethlisberger into an incompletion on a fourth-and-2 from the Ravens' 32 and once when Ed Reed jarred the ball loose from Randle El at the Ravens' 30 in the final minute and Demps came up with the loose ball. As a result, it was only 10–7 at halftime, even though the Steelers had more than 100 yards more offense than the Ravens did and hadn't punted the ball yet.

Billick talked bravely at halftime: "This is just the game we wanted," he said. Then, realizing he had said almost exactly the same thing in New England and Indianapolis at halftime, he added, "Now we have to finish it." Deep down, Billick sensed that his team was in trouble. Ray Lewis was playing gamely but was clearly in pain. The same was true of Sanders and McAlister — who had been beaten on the touchdown catch — and Heap. "How much have you got left?" he asked his players. "We're halfway through the three hours. But this is the hard part now. This is the part where you have to dig in and battle."

They knew all that. But they really didn't have that much fight left. As they walked back to the field there was very little of the usual yelling and catcalling or promising to do harm to the opponent. Lewis never said a word. He was saving what strength he had left.

The Steelers seemed to sense that the Ravens were on the ropes. They came out in the second half and put together a long, methodical drive, pounding away on the ground against a defense that wasn't accustomed to being pounded. After Roethlisberger opened the drive with a 7-yard completion to Hines Ward, the Steelers ran the ball on twelve consecutive plays. Bettis, all 260 pounds of him, hurtled through the line three straight times. Then Verron Haynes, normally the third-string running back (Staley was inactive for the game) came in and picked up 28 yards on four carries of his own. Back came Bettis to pick up 6 to the Ravens' 9. The defense tried to clamp down, forcing a fourth-and-1 from the 9. Steelers coach Bill Cowher didn't want a field goal, he sensed the kill. He went for it on fourth down and, unlike the first half when he had tried to throw the ball on a fourth down, he sent Roethlisberger, six foot four, 241 pounds, straight up the middle. He picked up 2 yards and the first down at the 7. Two more Bettis runs put the ball on the 2. Then Roethlisberger rolled left on play-action and found tight end Jerame Tuman wide-open in the back of the end zone for the touchdown.

Suggs nailed Roethlisberger after he released the pass and was hit with a roughing-the-passer penalty. Roethlisberger had to be helped off, but he had done a lot more damage to the Ravens than Suggs had done to him. The drive had taken 8:34, and the lead was now 17–7. Beyond that, the drive had taken all the swagger out of the defense. The Steelers had no fear of Lewis; they were running the ball right at him. If someone had suggested to the defense that anyone could run the ball twelve straight times on them on a single drive, he would have been laughed out of the room. But that was exactly what had happened.

The offense tried to answer. Boller completed two critical passes on the next drive, one to Kevin Johnson for 14 yards, one to Hymes for 22. That got them to the Steelers' 27. From there, they could pick up only one more yard, a familiar theme. Still, Stover's 44-yard field goal would at least cut the margin to 17–10 with more than a quarter to play.

Except that Stover missed, wide right. It was only his second actual miss — not counting the block — of the season and his first miss inside 50 yards. He had said prior to the game that the field, though essentially devoid of grass, wasn't as bad as he had thought it might be. But with the turf getting colder by the minute, he couldn't get into the ball solidly and he missed. Jeff Reed had better luck on the Steelers' next drive. After Roethlisberger completed two passes to get the ball to the Ravens' 28, Cowher decided not to take any more chances with him until and unless it was necessary and put Tommy Maddox into the game. It had been Suggs's sack of Maddox back in September that had made Roethlisberger the starter. Now, at least temporarily, Suggs had gotten Maddox back onto the field. Maddox was content to hand the ball to Bettis and Haynes until it was time for Reed to come in to kick a 40-yarder that made it 20–7.

The Ravens' season was now hanging by a thread. They had to score two touchdowns in under thirteen minutes — and hold the Steelers scoreless — or they would be virtually eliminated from the playoffs. Once again they were able to move into the opponent's territory. And again they couldn't finish the job. On fourth down from the Steelers' 34, Boller's pass was batted down by Harrison, playing the game of his life against the team that had cut him.

There were still seven minutes and forty-one seconds left, but the game was over. The Steelers again ran the ball right down the Ravens' throat. With Maddox in the game and the clock running, the Ravens knew the Steelers weren't going to throw the ball. They tried ganging up at the line, but it didn't matter. On third-and-8 from the Pittsburgh 37, Haynes ran straight up the middle and picked up 14 yards. Bettis then carried five times in a row while Billick spent his time-outs, trying to keep the game alive. Lewis was in on all four tackles, trying to tackle Bettis with one arm.

He needed help each time. On fourth-and-1 at the Ravens' 27, Bettis went up the middle one more time and picked up the first down. The Ravens were out of time-outs and out of hope. Maddox took a knee three straight times as the clock ran down.

At 3:58 P.M. on the day after Christmas, the Ravens hit the pavement after Billick's leap from the thirtieth-floor window. The crash was almost silent.

They were now 8-7, a record unthinkable before the season. The Broncos had already won the day before, and the Jaguars were about to win. The Bills were a virtual lock to win in San Francisco. That would put them behind three teams for the final wild-card spot. One might lose the next week, perhaps even two. But three? Just about impossible.

Billick stood in the middle of the locker room, hands on hips for a long while. Some of the players were slow to reach the locker room. Others were sitting in front of lockers, heads down. Everyone knew what had just happened. Billick was trying to gather himself, thinking about what to say. He knew this moment didn't call for telling them it was all still out there for them. It wasn't.

Finally, he called them up. They came slowly, tired, devastated, hurt. "There is nothing I can say right now to make anyone in here feel any better," Billick said quietly. "I know what a lot of you guys went through today, trying to play hurt. What we are probably facing now is the toughest kind of week there is in the NFL. We have to deal with it like men. Now we have to play for the love of the game. And we all have to take a good, long, hard look at how we got to be in this position."

A few minutes later Ray Lewis walked slowly into the training room to have the soft cast he had been wearing taken off for the plane ride home. His discomfort was so great that he could barely stand up. There were tears in his eyes as he sat on the training table. He was clearly in a great deal of pain.

And his wrist hurt like hell, too.

28

The Final Hours

NEVER IN THE NINE-YEAR HISTORY of the franchise had the Ravens faced a week like the final one of the 2004 regular season.

There had been years when they had been mathematically eliminated from the playoffs going into the final week, but those had been rebuilding years. This had not started out to be a rebuilding year. It had started out as a year when the goal had been to make it to the Super Bowl.

Billick and everyone else had put every ounce of energy they had into the season, and now, barring a miracle, it wasn't even going to produce the playoff trip Billick had believed was going to be there if they just showed up for sixteen weeks. Technically, they still had a chance, but it would take the three 9-6 teams all losing while the Ravens beat the Dolphins. Once Billick realized it was still mathematically possible to reach the postseason, he clung to that hope as if it were a lifeboat in the middle of the Atlantic Ocean.

"That has to be our approach this week," he told the coaches during the Monday meeting. "The mentality all week long has to be that we're playing for something."

Even as he said that, his mind was racing ahead. His questions to the position coaches that day were more about the future than about the present. What did Matt Cavanaugh think Kyle Boller needed to work on most during the off-season? (Footwork and self-confidence.) Did Jim Colletto think that Ethan Brooks or Orlando Brown could be effective for sixteen games at right tackle? (Maybe, but neither would ever be an especially good run blocker.) What would they need to do to convince Jamel White, who had proven to be another George Kokinis/Vince Newsome find, that he should stay in Baltimore even though there was no chance he would be a starting running back? (Love him up, explain his role.) If there was only enough money to sign either Dan Wilcox or Darnell Dinkins, which one did Wade Harman, their coach, prefer? (Wilcox did more things, but Harman wanted both back.) Did David Shaw think some of the problems Clarence Moore had experienced — especially going over the middle — in recent weeks were the result of having "rookie legs," or was it something in the kid? (Shaw said he believed it was rookie legs.) If Ed Hartwell signed some- where else, as was likely, did Mike Singletary think T. J. Slaughter was ready to start? (Yes, but he wasn't going to be Hartwell.) Did Rex Ryan think Dwan Edwards was going to be a factor on the defensive line at some point? (Yes, he was coachable and quick, he just hadn't been ready this season.)

There were short-term decisions to be made, but they would come later: Ray Lewis and Deion Sanders had played in considerable pain in Pitts- burgh; was it worth trying to get them on the field this week? "The way we might have to look at it is if we can get past this game without them, there's a better chance they'd be ready in another week if we had a playoff game," Billick said. The flip side was the danger of the message that would be sent to the players: we don't think much of Miami.

The Dolphins were coming in on a bit of a roll. They had won more games in December than the Ravens (two to one) and had upset the Patri- ots two weeks earlier. "Those were home games," Billick pointed out to the players at their Wednesday meeting. "Let's find out how they respond when we come out and get right after them the way we did the Giants. Their cars are running in the parking lot, they're ready to get out of here and go home. Let's make it not worth the effort to them early."

He had already thrown the schedule on the board one more time so they could see for themselves that they were still in the playoff race. "Fellas, these are the brutal facts," he said, reverting to the self-help book that had been the season's theme since June. "Pay attention to this for a minute be- cause what you're going to hear in here is a lot different than what you're going to hear away from here: we are still a part of all this. There are sixteen teams that aren't part of this, that have no chance. They play Sunday and go home — period. We aren't one of those teams. Do *not* eliminate your-

selves mentally and emotionally. Remember one thing: the difference between last season and this season right now is one game — *one* game. I
know it doesn't feel that way, but that's what it is. We've lost three road
games in the last month to teams that are a combined 39-6. Last year, the
last five teams we played had losing records. So, it's been a different kind of
challenge. So far we haven't been up to it. But we have one more chance.
Which is why this week boils down to one simple thing. He paused, then
clicked the button that put the words on the screen in bold red letters:

BEAT MIAMI

He went through what it would take to accomplish that and then
paused. He had been thinking for most of the morning about whether to
say what he was about to. He had decided there was really nothing to lose.

"I've talked to quite a few of you guys the last couple days," he said.
"Players and coaches. Every one of you has expressed frustration with
where we are and the wish that we had been a little better when we needed
to be. But not one guy — *not one guy* — has said to me, 'Coach, I haven't
done as well as I should. What can I do to be better?'

"Now, I love this room, I think you all know that. But that's what has
been missing. I know the want is there. I know all of you are hurt and I
know all of you have things going on in your lives with families and kids
and concerns about contracts. That's everyone, players and coaches. I understand all that; it is all legitimate. But this week I want all of you to do
one thing: think about how *I* can get better. Just worry about that for the
next few days and nothing else.

"As you sit here right now and listen to this, you're going to have one of
two thoughts:

"What poor SOB is he talking about?

"Or, why is he calling *me* out?

"The second one is better."

There was no way to avoid a tension-filled week. Everyone had to face the
inevitable questions about what had gone wrong. On Wednesday, Chris
McAlister stood in the middle of the locker room and said he didn't think

this team had been as close as previous teams. He wondered if perhaps some of it was the size of the new facility. "We're so spread out in here," he said. "Guys don't talk and hang out the way they did in the old place." He went on to add that he thought the team had become cliquish, which was a problem, too.

Billick didn't know whether to laugh or cry when he heard about McAlister's comments. On the one hand, it was borderline funny that McAlister, the team's ultimate loner, would suddenly be concerned about cliques and the team not being close enough. It was genuinely funny that anyone on the team would long for the old facility, which everyone had been crying to get out of for years. Billick dealt with that with humor: "If Chris McAlister would like to go dress in the old facility, we can probably arrange it," he told the media.

The part that wasn't funny was anyone's talking openly about the team not being close and being cliquish. Everyone knew this was a direct shot across Ray Lewis's bow: McAlister was not a part of Lewis's group and there were others in the room who also felt left out. On the other hand, everyone knew if the team had been 10-5 instead of 8-7, no one would be talking about cliques or worrying about who was left out and who wasn't.

"It's a chicken-and-egg thing," Billick said. "Did frustration in the locker room — or too big a locker room — cause us to be 8-7? Or is being 8-7 causing frustration in the locker room? My bet is that it's the latter. To some degree, if they weren't all a little bit pissed-off right now, I'd be worried. They should be pissed-off. We're all upset about what's happened. If we weren't, something would be wrong."

Billick was a lot more upset that night when two local TV reporters — Mark Viviano and Sage Steele — broke the story that Cavanaugh was going to be fired as soon as the season was over. This was hardly a shock to anyone — especially Cavanaugh — but given the delicate psyche of the entire building, the last thing Billick wanted was to deal with questions about the future of his coaching staff, especially its most controversial member, three days before the finale.

He was angry about the report, perhaps surprised that the story had been broken by two TV reporters, one of whom — Steele — worked part-time for Rave-TV, the team's in-house TV production group that had never asked her to back away from a story — past or present. Even so, Mike

Preston enjoyed pointing out on occasion how many members of the local media were on the Ravens' payroll. The Baltimore media wasn't the New York or Philadelphia media by any stretch, but it was certainly far less in the tank for the Ravens than the Washington media was for the Redskins. In Washington the Redskins were about to wrap up another 6-10 season — one that had started with many in the local media predicting a deep playoff run because of the return of Joe Gibbs — and yet there was very little criticism of Gibbs (the theory being that one year was too soon to make judgments on his return) or even of Dan Snyder, who was in year six of his reign of terror and mediocrity. Billick was aware of all that, and it may have been responsible for some of his frustration.

"The story is wrong," he told reporters the next day. "No decisions have been made about the coaching staff for next year. We'll deal with all of that, just as we do every year, whenever the season's over. Right now, our focus is on Miami."

In the strictest technical sense, Billick's comments were accurate. No one on the coaching staff had been talked to at that moment about his future, including Cavanaugh. No one in the brain trust had actually said the words "Matt Cavanaugh is fired," but that was because there was no need to. Everyone, Cavanaugh included, knew the change was coming, which was why everyone had hoped so ardently that Cavanaugh would get the Pittsburgh job.

Cavanaugh was neither surprised nor upset about the report of his demise. "I'd be lying if I said it didn't shake me up a little to be watching the news last night and see my face come up on the screen over the words 'Cavanaugh out,'" he said, laughing as he sat in his office after Thursday's practice. "I've known for a month this was coming. We've never been higher than twenty-eighth in offense all year. I know there are reasons for that, but in the end the reasons don't matter; the results matter. Brian and Ozzie and Steve can't keep me around for another off-season. They were subjected to ridicule for doing it last year when we'd won the division. Imagine what it would be like this year.

"I'm not concerned. What bothers me right now is that every day for the last month my ex-wife and my kids have called me to say, 'You okay? How you doing?' I love them for it, but it bothers me that they're spending that much time worrying about me. They've got better things to do. I'll find work."

He smiled. "I hear they give you free food if you work at Arby's. Sounds like a nice perk."

The McAlister and Cavanaugh stories combined to make for a less-than-collegial atmosphere in the building on Thursday. When the media were admitted to the locker room after practice, some of the players booed — half in jest, but half in earnest. Some players refused to talk. Others said they would talk, but only if questions were limited to the Dolphins. No one really wanted to talk about the Dolphins; the game had become almost an afterthought. Adalius Thomas, normally one of the most outgoing members of the team, yelled at several people who tried to ask non-Dolphins questions. The Ravens have always prided themselves on being a media-friendly team. Even in crises they have always made players available — at least once — to discuss their situations. Ray Lewis had talked to the media after Atlanta; Jamal Lewis had talked after his arrest, after his plea bargain, and after his suspension. This was a different kind of crisis, though, the kind that affected the entire locker room. Adalius Thomas yelling at people was a pretty clear indication that there was a good deal of frustration in the room.

Normally Billick would have been the calm in the storm. But he was so angry about the Cavanaugh reports that he wasn't any calmer than the players. "I knew this week wasn't going to be any fun," he said. "I guess I was right."

After what was likely to be their last real practice of the season on New Year's Eve, Billick made a point of telling the players to be careful that night. The last thing the team needed at this stage was someone getting arrested on a DUI — or, worse, being in an accident of some kind. "Remember, a lot of things can still happen, but only if we win this game," he said. "Tonight is amateur night on the roads. You guys know that." He smiled and a hint of the old humor returned. "We don't take part in amateur night — we're professionals, right?" For the first time all week, there were hints of smiles in the circle of players around Billick.

"Remember who you are, where you are, and who's watching you. Let's end the year on a good note and start the new one right."

They all nodded. No one was disappointed to see the old year end.

*   *   *

Billick's last words to his coaches on Monday had been simple: "Let's go coach 'em all up."

He had heeded his own words, trying to coach everyone up for the last week: players, front-office staff, and Rod Hairston. The biggest surprise of the week had come on Friday when McAlister had gone upstairs to see Newsome and then Billick. He told them both essentially the same thing: the old Chris McAlister was gone. He hoped they had noticed a change in him the past three weeks. He had done almost no drinking — a little wine on Sunday, maybe with dinner on Monday, but nothing after that and no clubbing, either. This was who he planned to be. "I'm going to be someone you can count on in the future," he said. "Not some of the time, all of the time."

Billick and Newsome were impressed, not only by what he said but by the fact that he had made a point to go to their offices and say them. "Of course, time will tell," Billick said. "But I think we both like what we're hearing right now."

As soon as Hairston began speaking during Saturday night Fellowship — which included a surprise first-time guest, Chris McAlister — it was clear that he and Billick had spent a little more time than their usual e-mail exchange discussing that night's sermon.

"Some of us are at a crossroads right now, aren't we?" Hairston began after Ray Lewis had said the opening prayer, thanking God "not for a New Year but for a new day."

"As we end one year, we wonder what the new one will bring. We worry about contracts, about where we'll be playing next year — will we play here? Will we play at all? Or, where will we be coaching?

"It's been a tough season for all of us, hasn't it? Sometimes desperation can lead to backbiting. Sometimes it can lead us to become eaters of one another. We have to be aware of that and not let it happen. Can I get an amen on that?"

"Amen."

Except for Lewis: "Wow!"

"There is no need to look back," Hairston continued. "Learn from the past, but don't go back there. We all want to be closer to God, but how do we get there?"

"You have to go through some things, don't you?" Lewis said from the back.

"Amen to that," Hairston said. "We have got to move on. You know, fellas, sometimes in trusting God, you have to take some risks. Sometimes you have to give God His due even when you aren't sure about what He's doing here on Earth. You have to trust that He's doing what He's doing for the right reasons even if they are not apparent to you right now!"

"Preach, Rev!" Lewis said, his right arm in the air, reminding everyone of the cast that was still there. He would not play the next day. Sanders and Heap would also sit out, as would Edwin Mulitalo, who had been injured in Pittsburgh. His injury meant that Mike Flynn would get the center position back, with Casey Rabach moving to left guard. If this were a playoff game or even a game in which a win would guarantee a playoff spot, the only one in the group who would not have played was Mulitalo. The rest, as in Pittsburgh, would have figured out a way to play.

Billick had canceled the usual meetings of the offense, defense, and special teams. He thought that going over tape one more time at this point was redundant. He wanted everyone in the same room and on the same page.

"You know, I spent the whole day today watching the bowl games," he said. "I loved it. I loved the joy of the college kids getting to play one more game even though none of them were playing for a national championship. [That game wouldn't be played until Tuesday.] None of the commentators out there seem to understand why we all play this game. It's for the joy of playing. It doesn't matter if it's the Super Bowl or the Slapdick Bowl, you play because you love to play.

"That's what tomorrow is. We've all given twenty-five weeks of our lives to this. Whatever's gonna happen at the end of the day is gonna happen. Let's all of us just go and play one more football game and enjoy being out there. Forget the circumstances, forget the future. I told you last week, this will end for all of us at some point. Don't miss a chance to play for the joy of playing. That's what tomorrow is. I'm not going to tell you it's anything more than that. But that should be plenty."

They headed to bed knowing that, for many of them, the next day would very possibly be the last time they played for the Ravens. Corey Fuller knew it might be his last day as a football player. The same was true for Cornell Brown and Kordell Stewart and Harold Morrow, all of whom had played the game for as long as they could remember. Players such as

Gary Baxter and Ed Hartwell and Casey Rabach would probably be faced with decisions about whether to take their shot at big money or stay with the Ravens for considerably less. All of them were at the peak of their career. This was their time to make the big money. All knew they would have to leave to do that.

Billick had opted not to discipline Travis Taylor for taking off in Pittsburgh without talking to any of the coaches. Taylor had let security director Darren Sanders know he was leaving and he had been told he was going to be inactive. But on a team where the inactive list had changed almost every Sunday just prior to its being submitted, he had put the team at risk by leaving. Billick had decided Taylor had been through enough. He was scheduled to be inactive again against the Dolphins. There was no doubt Sunday would be his last day as a Raven.

The morning was sunny and cold, though certainly not nearly as cold as one might have expected on the second day of the New Year. When Billick crossed the Hamburg Street bridge, the cheers that usually went up as the tailgaters spotted him were noticeably absent. "They're all just cold, Coach," Vernon Holley said.

Billick laughed. "Hey, at least they're not booing," he said. "I'm grateful for that."

The locker room was almost lively, the inactive players mingling with the active ones, a lot more conversation going on than normal. "It feels like the last day of summer camp," Jedd Fisch said. "Maybe loose will be good."

Long before most of the team arrived, Anthony Weaver, the defensive end from Notre Dame whose looks, sense of humor, and vocabulary had already landed him a TV job in town even though he still had many years to play, sat on the bench looking around at the empty stadium.

"I just can't believe this is almost surely our last game," he said. "I've thought about it and thought about it and I still can't fathom it. It just wasn't supposed to be this way." He paused, staring at the field for a moment. "Something happened in that Cincinnati game. We lost our aura of invincibility in that fourth quarter. We came back and played well in Indy, but it wasn't the same. We didn't have our swagger, and other teams saw us as vulnerable. We'll have to get that back next year." He laughed. "Listen to me talking about next year, with a game to play. I sound like a fan or something."

Or a broadcaster.

Mike Nolan didn't think the invincibility had been completely stripped by the disastrous fourth quarter against the Bengals. "We played as well as we can play the first half against the Colts," he said. "Being down 6–3 after the way we played at halftime really hurt. I think our guys lost something right there. Then Chris made the mistake on the play-action pass to Harrison. After that, it was over. We were hurt and tired and discouraged going into Pittsburgh."

Jim Fassel arrived in the locker room, armed, as was almost always the case these days, with a job rumor: "Cleveland's going to hire their general manager today or tomorrow," he said. "I think it may be [former Saints GM] Randy Mueller."

Billick was surprised. "That would leave Phil [Savage] out." He had heard from Newsome that Savage was the Browns' number one choice. Fassel was still hoping a head coaching job would open up for him, but it was looking more and more like a year with limited opportunities. The Dolphins had already hired Nick Saban as their next coach. (Interim head coach Jim Bates and his staff were all actively looking for jobs.) The Browns job was open, and rumor had it that San Francisco, Seattle, and New Orleans could open. Fassel's ear was to the ground at all times.

Zauner came in to tell Billick that Bart Scott's knee was still hurting and the doctors had recommended he not play. "Someone go tell Travis [Taylor] that he's up," Billick said.

There was one problem: Taylor wasn't in the locker room. Chad Steele, the public relations manager, found him eventually — upstairs in a box, planning to watch the game from there. He hustled downstairs and into uniform. He never set foot on the field. It was a sad ending to his career as a Raven.

The tone for the day may have been best summed up when the officials walked in for their 11:30 meeting with Billick. All season long, the officials had shown up in their stripes, ready to go to work. On this day, they were still in their street clothes.

Billick knew the intensity wasn't where he wanted it after warm-ups were over. "If I see anybody out there not playing with passion for the day and passion for the game, you're coming out, I promise you that," he said. "Celebrate being football players. Live for the day, for three more hours of joy."

Walking out of the locker room, Deion Sanders turned to Ray Lewis: "I don't know about you," he said. "But I have a feeling something's going to happen before this is over."

Lewis shook his head as if in disbelief. "That makes seven," he said. "Seven confirmations that I'm right. We're gonna play next week."

They started out as if they had forgotten the need to play this week. The Dolphins were down to Sage Rosenfels, their third-stringer, at quarterback. It was the first start of Rosenfels's career. On the first play of his first start, Rosenfels dropped back on a play-action fake, completely suckered Gary Baxter, and hit wide receiver Chris Chambers in stride going down the left sideline. The play was good for 76 yards and a touchdown, sixteen seconds into the game.

There were surprisingly few no-shows in the stands, given the circumstances. Most of the fans had just taken their seats when Chambers crossed the goal line. Many left those seats quickly to let the Ravens know how they felt about that play — and, no doubt, about the season.

The lightning-fast touchdown may have been a break for the Ravens because it seemed to wake everyone from their malaise. The offense quickly responded with a 64-yard drive that culminated on a shuffle pass from Boller to Terry Jones. Then the defense began to dig in. Billick had said several times that there was no reason for the Miami offense to gain "a single f—— yard." That goal wasn't going to be met, but the defense did begin to dominate. After a Stover field goal made it 10–7 early in the second quarter, Rosenfels dropped on a third-and-14 from his own 16 and tried, under pressure, to swing a short pass to running back Travis Minor. Jarret Johnson, in the game as part of the nickel package, made a spectacular play, leaping high to deflect the pass into the air. He then caught it, spun away from Rosenfels and Minor, and dove into the end zone for a touchdown. It might have been the most amazing play made by a Raven defensive player all season and it made the score 17–7. A late Stover field goal pushed the margin to 20–7 at halftime.

Throughout the first half, almost no one in the stadium knew what was happening in Buffalo, where the Bills were hosting the Steelers. A Buffalo victory would eliminate the Ravens. So would a Denver or Jacksonville victory, but those games didn't start until four o'clock. Billick had decided before the game that he didn't want anyone — players, coaches, or fans — focusing at all on what was happening in Buffalo. What the Bills did or did not do was irrelevant unless the Ravens won. He didn't want cheers or groans going up during plays or in between plays, and he didn't want the players studying the scoreboard for updates, instead of concentrating on the field.

So he told Kevin Byrne to keep the Buffalo-Pittsburgh score off the crawl that normally ran throughout the game at the bottom of the video boards at each end of the field. This created a problem for a good long while because it appeared that the only way to keep updates of the Buffalo-Pittsburgh game off the crawl was not to put anything up. Thus, midway through the second quarter, it appeared that none of the other one o'clock games had started. By halftime, the video staff had figured out a way to scroll the other scores without Buffalo-Pittsburgh. On the sideline, several people had BlackBerry handheld computers or cell phones that allowed them to get updated scores. When Billick wasn't looking, players would sidle over to those with the BlackBerrys and ask the score. Which meant that virtually everyone on the sideline knew the score as the game moved along.

Billick had predicted earlier in the week that, even in a meaningless game for the Steelers, Bill Cowher would not roll over for a team coached by Mike Mularkey, his onetime defensive coordinator. He was proven right. After trailing early, the Steelers had come back to take command of the game. Still, there was plenty of work to be done — in Baltimore and elsewhere.

Midway through the third quarter, the defense set up another touchdown. Ed Reed made his league-leading eighth interception of the season and almost produced his third touchdown, picking the ball off at the Miami 43 and weaving through traffic before finally being tripped up on the 2-yard line. Jamal Lewis scored on the next play and it was 27–7. But before everyone could start to relax, the special teams fell asleep at the wheel and Wes Welker took the ensuing kickoff back 95 yards to cut the margin to 27–14. All of a sudden, the Dolphins had life when they should have been thinking about the flight home. The offense did nothing, and the Dolphins promptly marched 90 yards for a touchdown that cut the lead to 27–21 with more than a quarter still left.

Clearly, the aura of invincibility wasn't what it had once been, especially with Lewis and Sanders in the role of cheerleaders.

The offense came back to produce a field goal as the third quarter ended to make the margin two scores again, at 30–21. The Dolphins, suddenly full of confidence, quickly moved right back down the field to the Ravens' 1-yard line. But on third down, Weaver picked off a Rosenfels pass in the flat, preventing the Dolphins from even getting a field goal that would have cut the margin to less than a touchdown.

A moment later came a play that was, in many ways, symbolic of the Ravens' season. A year earlier, backed up on their 3-yard line, there would have been little doubt about what was going to happen next. The quarterback — Boller or Anthony Wright — would have handed the ball to Jamal Lewis, the offensive line would have opened holes, and Lewis would have rammed the Ravens out of trouble. Now, though, the offensive line was a shadow of its former self and Lewis had heard the PA announcer congratulate him in the third quarter for going over 1,000 yards for the season — meaning he was exactly 1,000 yards shy of where he had been a year earlier. On first down, Boller handed the ball to Lewis, who tried to follow Jonathan Ogden and Rabach through a small hole on the left side. Fighting to pick up an extra yard or two, Lewis fumbled. The ball went flying backward toward the end zone, and a mad scramble ensued. If the Dolphins recovered for a touchdown, the lead would be down to 30–28 with more than ten minutes left and visions of the Cincinnati game would be dancing in everyone's head.

It seemed as if everyone in uniform was in the pile fighting for the ball. When the officials finally pulled everyone up from the ground, Kyle Boller was lying on top of it. He had dove backward the instant he saw Lewis lose control and had somehow beaten everyone to the ball and then hung on to it for dear life. It may have been Boller's most heroic play of the season. He had bailed out Lewis, he had bailed out the defense, he had bailed out his team when it was on the verge of a collapse against a 4-11 opponent that would have been humiliating — regardless of any playoff implications.

Instead of a touchdown, the Dolphins settled for a safety and the lead was 30–23. The defense found a second wind after that, not allowing the Dolphins inside the 40-yard line again. The offense took over with 3:29 left and, even with the Dolphins using their time-outs, managed to hold the ball until there were just forty-two seconds left. The Dolphins took possession for the final time on their own 28 with no time-outs left. On the last play of the season, Rosenfels completed a short pass to Bryan Gilmore, who lateraled to Chambers, trying to keep the ball alive. Chambers managed to get across the 40, but Chris McAlister came up to bring him down at the 44 before he could try to lateral again.

It was over: 30–23. It hadn't been easy and it hadn't exactly been the three hours of joy Billick had talked about — more like three hours and ten minutes in the dentist's chair without Novocain. But they had done their job for the day. With two minutes left in the game, Kevin Byrne had made the decision to let everyone know that the Steelers were about to beat the Bills, 29–24. That had elicited a cheer from the stands but little reaction on the sideline: most of the players already knew the score from the Black-Berry brigade.

Billick gathered them, full of life again, in the locker room one more time: "Two down, two to go," he said, referencing the Ravens' victory and the Bills' defeat, with the Broncos and Jaguars still to play. That drew a cheer. "Having fun yet?" he added.

"We'll meet at one o'clock tomorrow, regardless of what happens the next few hours. We'll either start to get ready for Indy [the Colts would be the opponent if the Ravens survived] or we'll deal with exit physicals and everything else that will need to be taken care of. For now, go home, turn on the TV, enjoy what you accomplished today, and dog-cuss those other teams."

Billick repeated that line a few minutes later to the media, saying he was going to pick up some Chinese food on the way home and spend a couple of hours being the biggest fan the Colts and Oakland Raiders had ever had. He had a big smile on his face when he walked back into his office. When he glanced up at the TV screen, the smile disappeared. The Broncos-Colts game was on and the first thing Billick saw was Jim Sorgi standing behind center for the Colts. Tony Dungy had talked about resting Peyton Manning in the game, which meant nothing to his team, but Billick had hoped he would play at least a half. The game was still in the first quarter and Sorgi was playing quarterback.

Billick sank into his chair, the smile gone.

"We're done," he said quietly.

Maybe Sorgi could produce enough points to win the game on a bad weather day in Denver?

"Nope," Billick said. "Mike [Shanahan] is not losing at home to Jim Sorgi with a playoff bid at stake."

Billick knew what he was talking about. The Broncos took control of the game in the second quarter and never looked back. Billick didn't even bother dog-cussing very much. It wasn't worth the effort. At 7:21 P.M. it became official: Broncos 33, Colts 14.

The Ravens were the last team officially eliminated from the playoffs. Twelve would move on. Twenty would begin thinking about next season on the next morning.

None of those twenty was more crushed than the Ravens. Their season was over. That was the last — and the most painful — brutal fact.

Epilogue

THINGS HAPPEN VERY FAST at the end of a football season, whether a team has just won the Super Bowl or has won the right to pick first in the draft. The Ravens had finished tied for tenth place overall in a thirty-two-team league, hardly a humiliating performance, especially given their injuries and their schedule, but none of that really mattered. Change would come swiftly.

"Injuries are a fact of life in football," Brian Billick said. "You can't use them as an excuse."

Billick made no excuses in his wrap-up press conference the day after the season ended. He readily called the season a disappointment without ifs, ands, or buts. They had started out with lofty goals, perhaps, in retrospect, goals that were a bit too lofty. Regardless, they had fallen well short. Now, he said, they would begin the self-examination that he hoped would lead to meeting some of those goals next season.

In truth, the self-examination had been under way for a month. By the time Billick met with the media on that Monday, Matt Cavanaugh was already cleaning out his office. There had been one glitch that morning when Billick and Cavanaugh sat down to talk. Billick didn't want to fire Cavanaugh because he didn't like the way it sounded, especially since he considered Cavanaugh a friend. Cavanaugh didn't want to resign. There was still enough of Youngstown in him that he didn't want anyone to think he had quit anything. They had finally agreed to "mutually agree" that Cavanaugh would leave. That done, they talked for another thirty minutes about both the past and the future. Billick was in an emotional mood when he met with his coaches soon after he finished talking to Cavanaugh.

He wasn't finished making changes. He had decided during the self-examination that the team needed a new offensive line coach. Like Cavanaugh, Jim Colletto had been with Billick since the beginning in Baltimore. There was no doubting his understanding of the game in general or offensive line play in particular. His players, who affectionately called him Crazy Jim because of his penchant for outbursts in the meeting room, liked him. But Billick believed that not getting any consideration for a coordinator job had soured Colletto. He had been a big-time college head coach (at Purdue) and now, at sixty, he understood that he wasn't likely to get a call when coordinator jobs opened. He talked about it often — too often, in Billick's mind. He knew that Chris Foerster, who had been the Dolphins' offensive coordinator, was looking for work. To him, that represented an opportunity: Foerster was younger, had coordinated, and would be a fresh voice for a line that would be rebuilt for 2005.

Cavanaugh knew what was coming. Billick had hoped Colletto might be offered a job someplace else, so he held off for a week before telling him he was making a change. Like all coaches, Colletto understood the nature of his profession. Even so, as he cleaned out his office, he said to a number of people: "Somedays this business isn't very fair."

No one would argue.

The first two weeks of the off-season were a whirlwind at 1 Winning Drive. Fassel's rumor about the Browns job had been wrong. Phil Savage interviewed with them on Monday, and on Thursday he was introduced as the new general manager. Everyone associated with the team was thrilled for him and believed the time had come for him to run his own ship. Ozzie Newsome and Savage had been together for fourteen years, and there was no doubt that life would be different without Savage walking the halls with his easy smile, his remarkable store of knowledge, and his soft Alabama accent. But front offices in football are like the teams themselves. Eric De-Costa and George Kokinis would each take over some of Savage's responsibilities. The Ravens would move on. Next Man Up applied to scouts, too.

Jim Fassel didn't get a head coaching job, or even an interview. In the end, only three jobs had opened: Miami, Cleveland, and San Francisco. All the other bubble coaches survived. Savage decided as a first-time general manager that he wanted a first-time head coach and hired Romeo Crennel, the Patriots' defensive coordinator. The 49ers, who had finished 2-14 and would have the first draft pick, also hired a defensive coordinator: Mike Nolan. All the years in football, first watching his father, then playing, then coaching, paid off for Nolan in his job interview. He was well prepared and was offered the job the day after he interviewed for it. Not surprisingly, one of his first acts was to hire Mike Singletary. Equally unsurprising, given Nolan's feelings about family, was his desire to honor his father by wearing a suit on the sidelines during games the way his dad had. That was a different time in the NFL. The league quickly told Nolan he couldn't wear a suit. Why? It wouldn't have an official league logo on it.

Nolan's departure meant that Billick had to hire two coordinators and a linebackers coach. The easiest part was defensive coordinator. A year earlier, when Rex Ryan had been approached by the Oakland Raiders about their coordinator job, Billick had promised him he would get Nolan's job whenever Nolan left. He kept that promise and hired veteran coach Clarence Brooks to replace Ryan. The change at linebackers was almost as easy: Billick moved Jeff FitzGerald into Singletary's job coaching the middle linebackers and promoted Mike Pettine to coach the outside linebackers. John Fassel was hired to take Pettine's spot as a defensive assistant.

John Fassel was the son of the new offensive coordinator. Billick had told people he would consider Jim Fassel for the offensive coordinator spot if he didn't get a head coaching job — if Fassel really wanted the job. The year spent as Kyle Boller's personal coach had been good for Fassel. It had allowed him to keep his hand in the game without putting in the killer hours he would have as a full-time coach. "When I finished the interviews with the Bills and the Redskins last year I realized I was lucky — and so were they — that I hadn't been hired," he said. "I was a dead man walking after seven years as a head coach in New York. I needed some kind of break."

That break had been the 2004 season. Fassel was now eager to coach again. If he couldn't be a head coach, coordinator was the next-best thing. The timing worked out well: Billick had interviewed both Ron Turner and ex–University of Washington coach Rick Neuheisel for the job while Fassel was still hoping for a head coaching chance. Turner had decided to go to Chicago, an easier move from the University of Illinois for his family. Billick had been prepared to offer Neuheisel the job as quarterbacks coach if Turner had taken the coordinator job, and Neuheisel, who had been fired at Washington because of his involvement in an NCAA tournament basketball pool, was more than willing to take it to get another chance to coach. When Turner went to Chicago and Fassel didn't get a job, Billick had the perfect setup: Fassel as coordinator, Neuheisel as quarterbacks coach. Neuheisel, a former UCLA quarterback and West Coast guy, would be a good fit with Kyle Boller. The quarterback's relationship with Fassel was already set in cement, meaning he should be in a perfect situation going into 2005.

In all, that meant there would be seven coaches in new roles in 2005. That sounded like a lot of change but really wasn't at all unusual in the NFL. There were changes on the scouting staff, too. Savage hired both T. J. McCreight and Chisom Opara in Cleveland. Newsome had known that Savage was planning to take McCreight with him but was surprised when Opara told him Savage had offered him a promotion and more money. Newsome didn't want to lose Opara: he was bright and hardworking and in just a year had shown great potential. But he wasn't going to jump him over more experienced scouts on the staff in salary or seniority. The system had to be honored.

There would be far more changes among those in uniform. As expected, Ed Hartwell (Atlanta), Casey Rabach (Washington), and Gary Baxter (Cleveland) were offered contracts the Ravens simply couldn't match because of salary-cap considerations. Several older players were quietly told that their services would no longer be required, Corey Fuller, Harold Morrow, Cornell Brown, Kordell Stewart, and Kevin Johnson among them. Phil Savage had been right about Johnson: he had been an ordinary receiver who had brought very little to the locker room and often complained about not having enough balls thrown to him even though he was rarely open. He found work in Detroit, signing a one-year contract with the Lions. By contrast, Stewart had become one of the most popular players on the team. He had done everything asked of him — including punting — and had never wavered in his support of Boller. After the final meeting broke up on the Monday after the season ended, Stewart hugged almost everyone in the room, knowing he wouldn't be back. Anthony Wright was expected to be healthy, and the Ravens, having lost Josh Harris to the Browns near the end of the season, would again draft a young quarterback in a late round for development purposes. Unlike some others, Stewart's presence would be missed.

Free agents Ethan Brooks and Wade Richey were not offered contracts, either, but the possibility remained that if they hadn't signed elsewhere when training camp began, they could be brought back. Brooks signed with the Jets in the spring. Both were solid citizens and had performed well at times. Newsome simply believed better players could be found to take their spots.

Sticking to his promise, Newsome was very active in the off-season market. A year after the T.O. caper, the Ravens finally found a free-agent wide receiver they thought could make a difference: Tennessee's Derrick Mason, a veteran with great speed who was more than happy to come to Baltimore. Knowing Baxter would be leaving, Newsome signed Samari Rolle, also a Tennessee free agent, to play cornerback. Dale Carter had been cleared by doctors to play and was hoping to return at the age of thirty-five. Newsome signed Keydrick Vincent to play right guard, handing him Bennie Anderson's spot. Anderson signed with Buffalo. Marques Douglas, who had traveled a long road from free agent out of Howard through being waived in both Baltimore and New Orleans through NFL Europe before finally becoming a starter, signed with Mike Nolan and the 49ers. Travis Taylor, knowing he would not be offered a contract by the Ravens, signed with Minnesota. The Ravens wanted Jamel White back, but Detroit offered far more money and he signed with the Lions.

The only true surprise was the departure of T. J. Slaughter. He had been penciled in as Ed Hartwell's replacement at linebacker, and Newsome had offered him a contract. Slaughter's agent kept insisting he should be paid more and Newsome kept saying just as insistently that was all he had to pay. While the negotiations — or, as Newsome would put it, the non-negotiations — were going on, Tommy Polley, a four-year veteran from St. Louis, came on the market. Newsome told Slaughter's agent that if he didn't accept the contract offered by the end of that week, he would offer Polley a contract. Apparently the agent didn't know Newsome very well because he decided to call his bluff. Newsome rarely bluffs. He signed Polley and left Slaughter looking for a new job.

Musa Smith's leg healed as well as the doctors had hoped, and he was hopeful that he would be on the field at 100 percent by the time training camp began. Trent Smith, whose injury had been far more complicated, was also hoping to be ready to come back — almost two years after his leg had been shattered. He was on the field in May for the early passing camps knowing he would face plenty of competition at tight end with Todd Heap, Terry Jones, Dan Wilcox, and Darnell Dinkins all on the preseason roster. The other players who had spent the season on injured reserve would also face uphill battles to make the team: Derek Abney would start off well behind the now-established B. J. Sams as a kick returner. Matt Zielinski had gone from long-shot free agent in the spring of 2004 to having a legitimate chance to make the practice squad before his early August injury. The coaches and scouts loved his strength and his attitude. He would certainly be given an opportunity to make the team.

Deion Sanders had surgery on his foot after the season was over and told the team he wanted to come back if his body felt up to it. Like Stewart, Sanders had been a more-than-welcome addition in spite of the injuries that had limited him to eight games. He had played well when healthy and had been an unofficial mentor to almost everyone on the team. His reputation as a great teammate had proven accurate. If he wanted to continue to wear his age as his number, it would not be a problem. Ray Walls, who had worn number 38 in 2004, was not re-signed and ended up in Arizona. Sanders signed up for one more year in June.

Chris McAlister spent more time in Baltimore during the off-season than he had at any time in his career. He also had postseason surgery on his foot and spent a lot of time in Baltimore rehabbing and then starting to get into shape for 2005. He got engaged and was insistent that he was a changed person. "I haven't even gone out during the off-season," he said. "I have six years left on my contract. I want to be here all six years." If he made the Hall of Fame, he said, Steve Bisciotti would definitely get a mention during his induction speech.

The Ravens would look considerably different in 2005 than in 2004. On the surface, the face of the franchise hadn't changed: Bisciotti, Cass, Newsome, and Billick as the leaders off the field; Ray Lewis, Jonathan Ogden, Ed Reed, Todd Heap, and Matt Stover the leaders on the field. But to those paying close attention, there had been considerable change. Kyle Boller was now considered by almost everyone in the organization to be an asset. If Billick decided to have an unofficial player council meeting at his house again, Boller would be included without any question. The offense belonged to him, and with the new receivers, there was little doubt in anyone's mind that he would become the quarterback they had believed he would when they made the trade to draft him in 2003. The defense still belonged to Lewis, but with Reed being named the NFL's Defensive Player of the Year, there was no doubt a transition — one everyone hoped would be a slow one — was beginning.

Unlike a year earlier, the Ravens did have a first-round pick in the draft (at twenty-two), and they used it on another receiver with speed: Mark Clayton from Oklahoma. In the second round they caught what they considered a huge break: getting linebacker Dan Cody. In November, Eric De-Costa had projected him as very possibly being the Ravens number one pick. To get him in the second round was, to Newsome and his staff, almost like getting two number one picks.

In all, fifteen of the fifty-three players who had sat in the auditorium on the Monday after the Dolphins game were gone by draft day. In early May, Peter Boulware, who had not been one of those fifty-three players because he was on the injured list, was cut after eight years with the team. The decision was a practical one: Boulware was thirty and had undergone knee surgery and foot surgery in a period of less than twelve months. Dan Cody was twenty-two and healthy. Boulware understood and said so publicly as he went off to look for a job. Football teams are not — cannot — be built on sentiment. Cody was Next Man Up.

Several more players would no doubt be gone by the time the team broke camp, and sadly, some would be injured in the spring and summer. As Billick had noted, injuries were a fact of life in football. So was change. There was, however, one constant: no one involved in the game, no matter how violent it was, no matter how insecure and pressure-filled it was, wanted to go home until the last possible moment.

Not at the end of a season. Not at the end of a career. They all lived, as Billick had reminded them, to play in those big games. Beyond that, to win them. They all wanted the pure joy they had felt that day in New Jersey when they had come from behind to beat the Jets in overtime. More than the money or the fame or the women or the glory, they played for that feeling.

Everyone on the Ravens agreed they hadn't had that feeling enough in 2004. With new players and new coaches, they would search for that feeling throughout 2005. And whether they found it or not in 2005, they would all want to try again in 2006. And keep on trying for as long as they possibly could.

Afterword: A Long Fall

OZZIE NEWSOME WAS as good as his word during the 2005 off-season. He had promised changes and they came swiftly.

There was no Terrell Owens available in free agency, but Derrick Mason, who had been a go-to receiver in Tennessee for eight years, was available. Without any of the fanfare attached to Owens, the Ravens signed Mason. They also used their first-round draft pick to take Mark Clayton, a tiny speedster out of Oklahoma. Kevin Johnson was long gone (signed by Detroit), proof that Phil Savage's draft-day objections a year ago had been correct.

Knowing that he couldn't afford to re-sign Ed Hartwell (who went to Atlanta for big money), Newsome signed Tommy Polley, a solid four-year starter with the St. Louis Rams. Newsome shored up the cornerback position by bringing in another free agent from Tennessee, Samari Rolle, an eight-year veteran who had been a seven-year starter with the Titans. Newsome also shored up the right side of the offensive line by adding Keydrick Vincent, who had started all sixteen games at right guard for the Steelers in 2004. The second-round draft pick was a pass-rushing linebacker, Dan Cody, a teammate of Clayton's at Oklahoma.

The way life works in the NFL, when a free agent is signed or a top player is drafted, it almost always means the departure of a veteran whose place he will take. Mason and Clayton would replace Johnson and Travis Taylor, who signed with the Minnesota Vikings. The arrival of Rolle meant the departure of Gary Baxter, who was signed by Phil Savage in

Cleveland. Vincent was signed to take Bennie Anderson's spot. Anderson signed with Buffalo. As expected, Cody was drafted to take Peter Boulware's spot after Boulware was released. One player the team didn't want to lose but couldn't keep was Casey Rabach, who had stepped in for Mike Flynn at center and proved himself to be a reliable starter. The team had already committed big money to Flynn, so signing Rabach to the kind of long-term contract he now commanded was out of the question. He ended up moving down I-95 to Washington. Marques Douglas, another free agent, ended up with Mike Nolan in San Francisco.

Corey Fuller was not invited back. Nor was Kordell Stewart. Joe Maese, the incumbent long snapper, was a surprise cut in camp, beaten out for his job by Matt Katula, a free-agent rookie from Wisconsin.

Deion Sanders decided to come back for one more year. All three players who had spent 2004 on injured reserve — Derek Abney, Matt Zielinski, and Trent Smith — were cut during training camp. Smith was a victim of a numbers game at tight end. His instinct during 2004 training camp that Dan Wilcox's emergence would ultimately hurt him had been correct. The signing of Darnell Dinkins during the season sealed his fate. As it turned out, Dinkins's presence would lead to Terry Jones's being cut in the fall of 2005 — five years after Brian Billick had mistakenly told him he was cut during his rookie training camp. Trent Smith was signed by San Francisco soon after being cut. Not surprisingly, the former Raven employees now in positions of power with other teams — Nolan in San Francisco, Savage in Cleveland — looked favorably on Ravens who became available, since they were known quantities.

Newsome and Billick believed they had plugged the holes that had sprung open during 2004. They were hoping that once Jamal Lewis's jail sentence was behind him, he would return to being the devastating big-play running back he had been in 2003. They hoped that Chris McAlister meant what he said about focusing more on playing and less on partying. They believed they had upgraded at key positions — wide receiver, the offensive line, linebacker, and cornerback. But everyone knew the critical question was likely to be the same as it had been in 2004: Kyle Boller. He had undoubtedly made strides in his second season. At times he had made big plays at big moments. At other times he had made critical mistakes. He was happy that Fassel would be his coordinator, and the upgrade at the wide receiver position was bound to help him. One of the overlooked factors in evaluating Boller's 2004 was the fact that he almost never found himself throwing to a wide-open receiver. The Ravens simply didn't have anyone on the team who could, in coaching vernacular, consistently achieve "separation."

The schedule certainly didn't do the team any favors. The opener would be against the Indianapolis Colts, a team many were picking to make the Super Bowl. There would be road games at Tennessee and Jacksonville and Denver along with Detroit and Chicago — games that looked winnable in preseason. The nondivision home games, in addition to the Colts matchup, were against the Jets — a playoff team in '04 — the Green Bay Packers, the Minnesota Vikings, and the Houston Texans, the closest thing anyone could find to a breather. Of course, in the NFL almost no game is a breather. Still, the beginning of training camp was upbeat. Dale Carter had recovered from his illness of a year ago and had been cleared to play, and Sanders was there from the beginning. There seemed to be fewer questions than a year earlier. There were no drug trials hanging over anyone's head. Steve Bisciotti had a full season under his belt as the owner, and no one was screaming for the head of the offensive coordinator.

It didn't take long for the all-is-well-in-Ravens-world scenario to begin crumbling. Dan Cody tore up his knee early in camp and departed for the season without playing a down. Peter Boulware was re-signed as a backup outside pass rusher. Jamal Lewis's play in the exhibition season was limited because he was still trying to work his way into football shape after his time in jail. Because he had been forced to spend time in a halfway house after being released, he had reported to camp late, having missed all of his normal off-season training and minicamp. The team insisted there was no need to panic, that Lewis didn't need that many preseason carries.

"All that matters," Billick kept saying, "is that he's ready on the night of September 11."

It was a chilling date for the NFL to begin Sunday play — exactly four years after the 9/11 massacre — but that was the way the calendar fell. The league decided that Colts-Ravens, having been a scintillating Sunday night game the previous December, was a perfect way to open its Sunday night schedule in September. The town was clearly ready for the game, the stadium rocking long before kickoff. Billick had encouraged the fans to be as loud as possible to try to make it difficult for Peyton Manning to call his plays at the line of scrimmage, and the fans responded by making the place as loud as anyone could remember.

The first half wasn't much different from the game the previous December in Indianapolis. Both defenses dominated. The Ravens certainly had chances. Down 3–0 after stopping an early Indianapolis drive inside the 10-yard line and forcing the Colts to settle for a field goal, the Ravens drove the other way, setting up what should have been a chip-shot 39-yard field goal for Matt Stover. Remarkably, Stover missed. That seemed to set an eerie tone. Before the half was over, four different Baltimore receivers had dropped passes. They hadn't failed to catch balls that were catchable, they out-and-out dropped balls that most Pop Warner League kids would have caught. Even Chris McAlister got into the act, stepping in front of a Manning pass on the goal line with 100 yards of open field in front of him — and dropping the ball.

The Colts opened the lead to 10–0. The Ravens got close enough for field goals twice more. Twice more, Stover missed. During the entire 2004 season, Stover had missed three field goals in thirty-two attempts. Now he had missed three attempts in one game. If Stover had been his normal self that night, the score would have been 10–9 early in the fourth quarter. Instead, the Colts were in control and the Ravens weren't on the scoreboard. Very little of that futility was Boller's fault. And yet, when he went down late in the third quarter in great pain, many of the fans cheered as he was helped off the field. Clearly, they weren't cheering his guts, they were cheering the fact that Anthony Wright was coming into the game.

Wright was no different from any backup quarterback in almost any NFL city: he was the most popular guy in town if the team wasn't winning. The Ravens had started 2004 with Super Bowl hopes and had finished 9-7. They had started this game with high hopes for the new season and they were getting shut out. Forget the drops and the missed field goals, someone had to be blamed. Matt Cavanaugh was gone. So Boller took the hit. The cheers, fans of his team happy that he was injured, hurt him. He was, after all, human.

On Wright's first drive, the Ravens got into field-goal position, setting up Stover's third miss. Naturally, the fans decided Wright was Johnny Unitas. Except that two series later Wright threw a pass that was intercepted and returned for a touchdown. Hold the Johnny U. talk. The final was an embarrassing 24–7, the Ravens scoring a token touchdown long after the game had been decided.

In a sense, the Colts game would turn out to be a microcosm of the season: it began with high hopes; it teased with great possibility at moments, and by the time it was over, the score looked bad and a key player was injured. Boller had torn a ligament in his big toe and would be out at least six weeks. Anthony Wright would get his chance. "Just once I'd like the chance to be a team's starting quarterback from January to January and see what I can do," he had said the previous season.

This wasn't January, it was September. But the job was now his, and if he played well, it would undoubtedly stay his. Wright had been good enough to take the team to the playoffs in 2003 when Boller had been injured midway through the ninth game of the season. That had been a different time: the AFC North was a weak division that year, with the Bengals still a joke, the Browns mediocre, and the Steelers having a rare off-year. Ray Lewis had been at his zenith, leading a defense almost as dominant as the Super Bowl defense.

The Ravens lost 25–10 at Tennessee in the season's second week, then managed a desultory win at home against the hapless New York Jets after the bye week. The Jets were down to their third-string quarterback by the time they hit Baltimore, having in a single game lost both Chad Pennington and Jay Fiedler for the entire season. Even so, the Ravens struggled to put them away because the offense couldn't get into the end zone until the fourth quarter. The final was 13–3. Hardly overwhelming. Still, a win was a win, and the Ravens had never been pretty winners, so the hope was that they were now headed in the right direction.

That proved to be false hope. A week later in Detroit, the Ravens suffered what might have been the most embarrassing loss in the team's ten-year history in Baltimore. Not only did they lose 35–17 to a mediocre Lions team but they came within one penalty of tying the all-time NFL record for penalties in a game — the record was twenty-two — eight of them being either personal fouls or misconduct penalties. The officiating in the game was *awful* and the Ravens had legitimate reasons to be frustrated by a number of calls. But that didn't explain players absolutely losing their cool on several occasions, a number of them at critical moments. As bad as the loss was, it was overshadowed by the public sense that the team was suffering a meltdown.

A win at home against the Browns calmed people down a bit, but Ed Reed suffered a serious ankle sprain in the second half, an injury that would knock him out for six weeks during the season's most crucial stretch. That did a great deal to stifle the joy that usually comes with a victory in the NFL. The offense scored a touchdown on the opening drive of the game, then failed to get into the end zone again. Fortunately the defense had enough going for it to hold on for a 16–7 win.

The team was 2-3, both victories at home against bad teams. The next three weeks would probably decide the direction the season would go in: a winnable game at Chicago, an extremely tough game in Pittsburgh, and a home game against the much-improved Bengals. Win two of three and get to the halfway mark at 4-4, at which point Boller would be ready to come back and anything could happen. Lose two of three and it would be an uphill climb. Lose all three . . . No one wanted to think about that.

Three weeks later they had no choice. The offense again failed to score a touchdown in a 10–6 loss in Chicago, a defeat that would look a lot more respectable at season's end when the Bears finished 12–4 and won the NFC Central thanks to their superb defense. This time it was Ray Lewis who was injured. He had tweaked a hamstring the previous week and had tried to play on it against the Bears — but quickly found out that he couldn't. As it turned out, his season was over. In truth, the Ravens' season was over too.

A week later, in their first performance AR (After Ray), the Ravens played their best game of the year in Pittsburgh on a Monday night, but the outcome was the same: a 20–19 loss. Then the Bengals came to town and controlled most of the game en route to a 21–9 victory. The team was 2-6, and barring a miracle, there would be no playoffs for a second straight season. By that point, no one was talking or thinking playoffs.

In fact, the talk in town had turned to whether Steve Bisciotti would fire Brian Billick. The media was full of speculation that Bisciotti would make such a move, but Bisciotti had no plans to fire his coach. To begin with, he's not the kind of owner who thinks one bad season makes a bad coach. Billick had been a very good coach for six seasons; he hadn't taken stupid pills during the 2005 off-season. Bisciotti knew two things for sure: If he fired Billick someone else would hire him in an instant. Plus, there was no one on the horizon who he believed was a better coach than Billick. Firing him for the sake of firing him or to appease fans or the media didn't make sense.

"I'm going to go stand next to Brian for a while," Bisciotti said before one home game. "It's symbolic, but I want people to understand he's still my guy — period."

Bisciotti also knew that Billick wasn't responsible for the injuries riddling the team or for the fact that Jamal Lewis looked like a shadow of his former self running the ball. Billick also wasn't the person who had drafted Boller, although in the eyes of most fans and media members, Boller was *his* responsibility. The fact was that the decision to draft Boller had been made by Ozzie Newsome and his scouting staff. Billick had been consulted, and he genuinely believed Boller could be a good NFL quarterback. Billick was going to defend him publicly, and he wasn't going to bring up the fact that Newsome had final say in the draft room.

If Boller's injury had proven one thing beyond a shadow of a doubt, it was that Anthony Wright wasn't the answer, just as firing Matt Cavanaugh had not been the answer. The team was better at wide receiver, especially with the addition of Derrick Mason. But the offensive line had gotten old: the hope that Orlando Brown had one year left had proven incorrect. Brown's back gave out on him nine games into the season and he didn't play again. Keydrick Vincent struggled to learn the system installed by Chris Foerster as the new O-line coach, and then, just as he was starting to grasp it, he hurt his thigh in the season's ninth week and was also gone for the rest of the year. Mike Flynn was solid at center, but Edwin Mulitalo looked a step slow at left guard. Jim Colletto's assessment of him in 2004 — "he's living the good life and not working like he used to" — was proving to be true.

Worst of all, Jonathan Ogden looked human at left tackle. He was still an all-pro, still better than just about anyone in the game, but he wasn't as dominant. On occasion, someone beat him to the outside. The holes for Lewis, so gaping in 2003 on the left side, just weren't there. Some people wondered if Ogden was upset because the team had decided to cut his younger brother Marcus, who had been signed to the practice squad in 2004. Ogden was upset about it, but the drop-off in his play probably had more to do with being thirty-one and having had ten years of NFL pounding than anything involving his brother.

The heart and soul of any football team is the offensive line. It had gone from being the Ravens' great strength in 2003 to a weakness in 2005. The running game wouldn't have been as good if Jamal Lewis had been completely healthy and hadn't spent most of the off-season in jail. Throw that in and the running game was a shadow of its former self. Boller's injury was a setback. Mark Clayton, the second-round draft pick, also got hurt and missed several games, slowing his development.

The defense, which had started the season looking rejuvenated, was beaten down by the inconsistency of the offense and injuries. There's not a defense in football that can afford to lose its two best players — especially when those two players are the last two defensive players of the year in the entire league.

The season spiraled. The losing streak reached four after an embarrassing 30–3 loss in Jacksonville, the game that marked Kyle Boller's return to the lineup. It was hardly an auspicious return. A week later a small ray of hope arrived in the form of a surprising and impressive 16–13 overtime victory over the Steelers. The happiness didn't last long. The Bengals hammered the Ravens in Cincinnati 42–29 on the Sunday after Thanksgiving, the offense coming to life when the game was already lost, the banged-up defense incapable of stopping Carson Palmer and his array of talented wide receivers.

Boller had some good moments after he came back, but also some bad ones. Billick had finally backed off from his "Kyle is our quarterback come hell or high water" stance by saying that the rest of the season was an audition for Boller. If he continued to improve and showed that he could be a consistent NFL quarterback, the team would go into 2006 with Boller as the starter. If not, there would be a need to bring someone else in to at least compete with him for the starting job.

The season played out in discouraging fashion, the only real highlight being a 48–3 demolition of the Green Bay Packers in the team's second Monday night game of the season. The Packers were having an even worse season than the Ravens, en route to a 4-12 finish, and had clearly quit on Coach Mike Sherman by the time they got to Baltimore. The Ravens took advantage. They then beat the Minnesota Vikings 30–23 on Christmas night to get to 6-9. One thing was apparent: the players who were still healthy had *not* quit on Billick. They were continuing to try hard even with nothing to play for.

Still, the finale was discouraging. The team jumped to an early 13–0 lead, then fell back into old habits: turnovers, missed chances, making a rookie quarterback look better than he should look. The result was a 20–16 come-from-ahead defeat, leaving the final record at 6-10 — Billick's worst as a head coach and the team's worst since 1998, the season before Billick arrived.

Bisciotti ended the speculation about Billick soon after the season ended, announcing his return at the season-wrap press conference. But in doing so he said publicly that he wanted Billick to change his style; that he wanted him to show more respect for the media (Billick had become very short and snappish in press conferences as the horrific season wore on) and in his approach to the players. A lot of people were surprised by Bisciotti's bluntness. That was Bisciotti, though: he didn't like putting himself out front very often, but when he did he spoke his mind. That meant he wasn't always politically correct, but it also meant people knew that when he said something, he meant it. No one working for Bisciotti would ever get a public vote of confidence one week and be fired the next.

As is always the case after a disastrous season, there were bound to be changes: Gary Zauner was gone, heading to Phoenix to work for Billick's old boss, Denny Green. As good as Zauner was at what he did, his often prickly relationship with other coaches and the scouting staff had become even more tense during 2005. It was a good move for both sides. Johnnie Lynn, Matt Simon, David Shaw, and Bennie Thompson were also gone soon after season's end. That meant — excluding strength coaches Jeff Friday and Paul Ricci — only Rex Ryan, Jedd Fisch, Jeff FitzGerald, Wade Harman, Mike Pettine, and Dennis Thurman — six of fifteen coaches — were left from the 2004 staff. None of them were in the same role they had played in 2004, and Jim Fassel, who had been Boller's personal coach though technically not on staff in 2004, was the offensive coordinator.

Player turnover would, of course, continue. By the time the Ravens assembled for their 2006 June minicamp, only twenty-four of the fifty-three players who had been on the roster for the final game of the 2004 season were still with the team.

Deion Sanders, who had managed to get through most of 2005 healthy, retired — although he never made a formal announcement. Chester Taylor signed a free-agent contract with Minnesota, and Darnell Dinkins landed in Cleveland. Alan Ricard, another injured player in 2005, wasn't re-signed. Will Demps signed a free-agent contract with the New York Jets, and Anthony Weaver signed with Houston. Dave Zastudil surprised everyone by signing with the Browns. "It was a chance to go home," he said. "If it had been any other team, I'd have turned it down." Kordell Stewart, who had been brought back briefly when Boller was hurt, retired. Anthony Wright signed with Cincinnati.

The biggest move didn't happen until June, when, after a lengthy and often heated negotiation, the Ravens traded a fourth-round pick to Tennessee for one-time MVP quarterback Steve McNair. The Titans had no choice but to let McNair go since he would have counted for $23 million against their salary cap in 2006 had he stayed with the team. They had made it clear McNair's days were numbered in April when they had taken Texas's Vince Young with the No. 3 pick in the draft.

Billick had already sat Boller down and explained to him that if the team got McNair it would be with the intention of starting him. McNair was thirty-three and he had been injury-prone, but, healthy, he was one of the best quarterbacks in football. Boller still had two years left on his Ravens contract, and playing behind an oft-injured twelve-year veteran, he would almost certainly see playing time. It was entirely possible that without having his every throw analyzed by everyone within a hundred miles of Baltimore, he might grow into the quarterback the team had believed he could become when he had been drafted.

There were other signings, too, most significantly Mike Anderson, a thousand-yard rusher in Denver, who was brought in to take Chester Taylor's place.

Edwin Mulitalo, read the riot act at the end of 2005, showed up at mini-camp in the best shape anyone had seen him in since 2003. Jamal Lewis, who had talked about leaving the team since his contract was up at the end of 2005, re-signed and would be able to return to his normal off-season conditioning program. He was still only twenty-eight years old and there was reason to believe his legs still had life in them. The No. 1 pick in the draft was Haloti Ngata, a massive six foot four, 340-pound defensive lineman from Oregon. The Ravens had the thirteenth pick in the first round; the Browns twelfth. Phil Savage persuaded Ozzie Newsome to give him a seventh-round pick to swap spots with him in order to get Ngata. No doubt Savage got a kick out of forcing his old boss to give him a pick to move up one spot.

Shortly after Ngata was taken, a radio interviewer asked Rex Ryan how he would be worked into the lineup. "Worked in?" Ryan shouted. "We didn't just take him with the twelfth pick in the draft to be worked in, we took him to *start*. He's a starter the day he gets here — end of story."

The person who had to be happiest about the arrival of Ngata was Ray Lewis. It had been a strange off-season for Lewis. He had spent a lot of time grumbling not-so-quietly about wanting a new contract — which wasn't going to happen. He had four years left on the contract he had signed in 2003, and he would be thirty-one when the 2006 season began. The Ravens were not going to destroy their cap by giving him a new contract — especially coming off a major injury.

Clearly displeased, Lewis did two off-season TV interviews that made the situation even worse. In one, he complained that the team had failed to sign defensive tackles like Tony Siragusa and Sam Adams, the two giants he had played behind in 2000, and that their absence — or the absence of similar size on the defensive line — had made it impossible for him to be the player he had once been. In the second interview he was asked about Bisciotti's decision to retain Billick. His answer was "No comment."

Those remarks, along with his seemingly detached attitude after his injury and his complaining — which everyone on the team knew about — over his contract, had put his unquestioned leadership of the team in jeopardy. If a coach can lose the locker room, so can a team captain. Lewis did the smart thing in May by showing up voluntarily for passing camp — which had been given another name by the NFL in order to give teams the right to close them to the media — and meeting with Billick and Newsome and his teammates. When he finally spoke to the media at minicamp in June, everything, according to Lewis, was wonderful. He'd been quoted out of context (tough to do on TV), and he and Billick had a very "peaceful relationship."

People would use many different words to describe Billick and Lewis. *Peaceful* wasn't likely to come up for either very quickly.

Still, there was reason to hope that 2006 would be different. A healthy McNair would be a huge plus, and the offensive line appeared to be improved — which was an absolute necessity. Lewis and Reed were both healthy and ready to go when camp began, as was Dan Cody, the No. 2 pick in 2005, who hadn't gotten to play at all during his rookie season. Mark Clayton had a year under his belt and, along with Mason and Heap, could be expected to give McNair plenty of targets. Matt Stover had recovered from his awful first game to have another stellar season and would be back as the placekicker for his ninety-fifth straight season. Okay, his sixteenth straight season.

The division would be difficult: the Browns had revamped, the Bengals had made the playoffs, and the Steelers were the Super Bowl champions. But as the weather turned hot in Baltimore and everyone began planning their trip out to Rte. 40 for another camp at McDaniel, complete with heat and lots of film study and rookie hazing, there was hope. In the NFL, August is always full of hope because history shows that while it is inevitable that players will be hurt and players will change teams and everyone will be searching for the Next Man Up, one other thing is equally certain: no one knows who will be the Next TEAM Up.

Acknowledgments

THROUGH THE YEARS, people have said many things about my books: some of them very nice, some of them not so nice. But one thing everyone has always been in agreement on is this: I write really long acknowledgments.

Well, to paraphrase something Ronald Reagan, one of Brian Billick's heroes, once said to Jimmy Carter, one of mine: here I go again.

As I mentioned in the introduction, the person who got me into the Ravens' front door was the man who owns the front door: Steve Bisciotti. In thanking Steve, I would be remiss if I didn't thank Maryland basketball coach Gary Williams, a longtime mutual friend who initially got me in touch with Bisciotti. Steve made an important point the first time we talked: the project couldn't work unless Ozzie Newsome and Brian Billick were comfortable with it. Brian was, and I know Ozzie did the very best he could to make himself comfortable. I'm grateful to Brian for so clearly understanding what I was trying to do and to Ozzie for putting up with me even when he found my presence discomfiting.

The list of others in the organization who were critical to making this book a reality is lengthy, but I have to begin with Kevin Byrne and Dick Cass. No one had more added to his workload because of me than Kevin but, at least in my presence, he was always patient and understanding and virtually all of my myriad requests were fulfilled early and often. Kevin would be the first to tell you much of that would not have occurred if not for his staff: Francine Lubera, Chad Steele, Marisol McMacken-Renner,

Susan Cole, Kenny Abrams, Melanie LeGrande, Adam Beasley, Jeff (the intern) Esposito, and Hillary Connelly.

Dick Cass walked into a new job and immediately found himself being peppered with questions about an organization he was trying to learn. Not only did he answer all the questions, he did so with great humor and never acted as if my constant presence was difficult in any way.

The coaches made me feel welcome almost from the start. I now count them as friends: Mike Nolan, Matt Cavanaugh, Gary Zauner, Bennie Thompson, Jim Fassel, Rex Ryan, Jeff FitzGerald, Mike Singletary, Johnnie Lynn, Dennis Thurman, Mike Pettine, Phil Zacharias, Matt Simon, Jim Colletto, Wade Harman, David Shaw, and the irrepressible Jedd Fisch. The strength coaches, Jeff Friday and Paul Ricci, even though they clearly recognized a hopeless case when they saw one, were great fun — especially on game days on the sidelines. I didn't spend as much time with Ozzie Newsome's staff as I did with the coaches, but they were also extremely patient and helpful. Thanks to Phil Savage, Eric DeCosta, George Kokinis, Vince Newsome, Ron Marciniak, Joe Douglas, Daniel Jeremiah, Jeremiah Washburn, Chisom Opara, and T. J. McCreight. Extra thanks to capologist Pat Moriarty, who tried to help me speak a language completely foreign to me.

Since I had to be dressed in some form of Ravens gear in order to be on the sidelines — yes, I got flagged by the NFL clothes Nazis — I needed constant help from Ed Carroll and Darin Kerns. Special thanks to Darin for finding me dry clothes for the trip home after the monsoon in Foxboro. All three trainers — Bill Tessendorf, Mark Smith, and Mark Teeples — helped me out, as did the team doctors, Andy Tucker, Leigh Ann Curl, and Alan Sokoloff, who dealt with all of my questions without once (noticeably) rolling their eyes. Jessie Markison, Ozzie Newsome's assistant, and I have been friends for longer than I can remember. Thanks also to Maria Scellini, Brian Billick's assistant. Operations director Bob Eller and his travel guru Joan Sieracki had enough to do without adding an outsider to their travel roster, but they did it and made my life very easy on the road.

Vernon Holley has, I think, forgiven me for outing him as a Democrat during one of our walks to the stadium with Brian Billick. His colleagues Darren Sanders, Ed Brown, Ken Welsh, Renee Crouell, and Darryl DeSousa all went out of their way to be gracious to me. Thanks also to Pam

Lund, Dennis Mannion, Baker Koppelman, Larry Rosen, Jeff Goering, Ross Hollebon, Bill Jankowski, Pattie Holtery, Jon Dube, Mark Bienvenu, Mark Burdett, Valerie Wideman, and Toni Lekas. Thanks also to Jeff Gersh for his weekly sidelines humor.

It was, I believe, a tough year for Art Modell and for David Modell as they adjusted to life as welcome visitors rather than the men in charge of the organization. Both went out of their way to be kind to me whenever our paths crossed.

Rod Hairston always made a point of making me feel welcome at his Fellowship meetings on Saturday nights and was good company during games. He didn't flinch when I had to ask some difficult questions about his role within the team.

Phil Hoffmann has taken the pictures for a number of books now and always makes the words better with his photos. And the words need plenty of help.

I work with a wonderful group of people in putting my books together. I start, as always, with Esther Newberg, who is not only the best agent on the planet but the fastest reader. My editor, Michael Pietsch, doesn't read as fast, but is a lot more patient. (We all have our strengths.) Together, they have spent a lot of years making my job not only possible but fun. Esther has now represented me on eighteen books (!!) and Michael has edited and published eleven of them. Both deserve a place in heaven for those efforts. Esther's staff took a hit when Andy Barzvi received a well-deserved promotion, but Kari Stuart has filled in well. Chris Earle is so good at what she does that both Esther and I turn to her often for advice, and when we're smart we follow that advice. We are both lucky to have her. So is her new husband, Sam. Michael and I are both fortunate that he has Stacey Brody and Zainab Zakari as his assistants. You wouldn't know it to talk to her, but Heather Fain is the modern-day Murphy Brown. She has never been able to keep an assistant for more than about fifteen minutes. It may have something to do with her collegiate background. Other than that, she is a talented and — note that this word comes up often in dealing with me — very patient publicist. Thanks, as always, to her boss, Heather Rizzo, and to Tom Campbell and Marlena Bittner. Holly Wilkinson will always be my PR person — whether she likes it or not.

Friends: always, I am happy to report, a lengthy list, although some would no doubt prefer to escape: Barbie Drum; Bob and Anne DeStefano; David and Linda Maraniss; Jackson Diehl and Jean Halperin; Lexie Verdon and Steve Barr; Tom and Jill Mickle; Jason and Shelley Crist; Bill and Jane Brill; Terry and Patti Hanson; Bob Zurfluh; Pete Teeley; Al Hunt; Bob Novak; Alex Cion; Phil Hocberg; Wayne Zell; Mike and David Sanders; Vivian Thompson; Bob Whitmore; Andy Dolich; Mary Carillo; Doug and Beth Doughty; David Teel; Beth (Shumaway) Brown; Beth Sherry-Downes; Erin Laissen; Bob Socci; Pete Van Poppel; Fran Davinney; Scott Strasemeier; Eric Ruden; Billy Stone; Mike Werteen; Chris Knoche (though he is a bitter man); Andrew Thompson; Joe Speed; Jack Hecker; the still and always great Dick Hall; Steve (Moose) Stirling; Jim and Tiffany Cantelupe; Derek and Christina Klein; Anthony and Kristen Noto; Roger Breslin; Jim Rome; Travis Rodgers; Jason Stewart; Tony Kornheiser (talk about bitter!); Michael Wilbon; Mark Maske; Ken Denlinger; Matt Rennie; Mike Purkey; Bob Edwards; Tom Goldman; Jeffrey Katz; Mark Schramm; Ken and Christina Lewis; Dick (Hoops) Weiss; Bob Ryan; Little Sandy Genelius; Jennifer Proud-Mearns; David Fay; Frank Hannigan; Mike Butz; Mike Davis; Mary Lopuszynski; Marty Caffey; Jerry Tarde; Mike O'Malley; Larry Dorman; Marsha Edwards; Jay and Natalie Edwards (politics aside); Len and Gwyn Edwards-Dieterle; Brian and Laurie Edwards; John Cutcher and Chris Edwards; Joe Valerio; Rob Cowan; Andy Kaplan; Chris Svenson, and Norbert Doyle, who has seen more football games than anyone I know. Special thanks to my orthopods: Eddie McDevitt, Bob Arciero, and Gus Mazzocca.

Then there are the groups. Swimmers: Jeff Roddin, John Craig, Mark Pugliese, Carole Kammel, Margot Pettijohn, Susan Williams, Amy Weiss, A. J. Block, Danny Pick, Warren Friedland, Marshall Greer, Tom Denes, Peter Ward, Doug Chestnut, Bob Hansen, Paul Doremus, the still-missed Penny Bates, and the ever-patient Mary Dowling. And the FWRH club: Clay Britt, Wally Dicks, and Michael Fell. Coral Springs in '06 everyone.

Basketball guys: Mike Krzyzewski, Gary Williams, Mike Brey, Tommy Amaker, Frank Sullivan, Rick Barnes, Roy Williams, Jim Calhoun, Phil Martelli, Doug Wojcik, Dave Odom, Jeff Jones, Jim Larranaga, Ralph Willard, Pat Flannery, Emmett Davis, Jim Crews, Billy Taylor, Fran O'Hanlon, Billy Lange, Jimmy Patsos, and Billy Hahn. Not to mention the still-legendary Howard Garfinkel and Tom Konchalski, who will always be the only honest man in the gym.

The China Doll Gang: Red Auerbach, Morgan Wootten, Hymie Perlo, Aubre Jones, Sam Jones, Rob Ades, Jack Kvancz, Joe McKeown, Stanley Copeland, Reid Collins, Arnie Heft, Pete Dowling, Bob Campbell, Chris (the Rookie) Wallace, Stanley Walker, Harry Huang, Herman Greenberg, Joe Greenberg, Alvin Miller, Johnny Auerbach, Stanley Walker, Charles Thornton, Bob Ferry, and, yes, George Solomon. Zang remains with us every Tuesday.

The Rio gang: Tate Armstrong, Mark Alarie, Clay (Lobster Boy) Buckley, and official secretary Terry Chili.

The Feinstein Advisory Board: Keith Drum, Frank Mastrandrea, Wes Seeley, and Dave Kindred. How they do it, I don't know. Then again, neither do they.

My family always comes last but, as I have said before, certainly not least: Jim and Arlene; Kacky, Stan, and Ann; Annie, Gregg, Rudy, Gus, and Harry; Jimmy and Brendan. Also: Dad and Marcia; Margaret, David, Ethan, and Ben; Bobby, Jennifer, Matthew, and Brian. Danny is now eleven and his latest hero is Bob Woodward. Excellent choice. Brigid is seven and her hero is Norma Rae. Mary Clare Gibbons Feinstein is older than both of them. *She* is my hero.

Index

About the Author

JOHN FEINSTEIN is the author of a dozen highly acclaimed best-sellers, including books on golf (*Caddy for Life, Open, The Majors, A Good Walk Spoiled*), basketball (*Last Dance, Let Me Tell You a Story, The Punch, The Last Amateurs, A Season on the Brink, A March to Madness*), football (*A Civil War: Army vs. Navy*), and other sports. He contributes to the *Washington Post*, writes a column for America Online, is a contributor to *Golf Digest*, and is a commentator on National Public Radio and Sporting News Radio. He lives in Potomac, Maryland, and Shelter Island, New York, with his wife and their two children.

John Feinstein on football

A Civil War
Army vs. Navy

"Feinstein knows how to get to the heart of the matter, and has done so once again. . . . *A Civil War* takes the reader into the locker rooms, hearts, souls, and minds of those coaches and players who constitute college football's purest rivalry."   — Bruce A. Nathan, Associated Press

Back Bay Books
Available wherever paperbacks are sold

John Feinstein on golf

Caddy for Life
The Bruce Edwards Story

"The emotionally charged story of Tom Watson's caddy of more than thirty years.... It's a modern morality tale centered on an oft-overlooked virtue: loyalty." — *Travel + Leisure Golf*

Open
Inside the Ropes at Bethpage Black

"Feinstein escorts us not only inside the ropes but behind the scenes.... Passion is what makes the U.S. Open more than just another tournament, and *Open* more than just another golf book." — Allen St. John, *Washington Post Book World*

Back Bay Books
Available wherever paperbacks are sold

The Majors
In Pursuit of Golf's Holy Grail

"If you want to know how touring pros think, on and off the course but particularly on the courses that are the crucibles of the majors, this is the book. . . . *The Majors* is another major triumph for John Feinstein."
— Dave Anderson, *New York Times Book Review*

A Good Walk Spoiled
Days and Nights on the PGA Tour

"*A Good Walk Spoiled* is as close as most people will get to understanding the guys they watch on TV each week hitting magnificent shots and missing meaningful putts. . . . Feinstein, as always, is observant, insightful, and amusing."
— *Golfweek*

Back Bay Books
Available wherever paperbacks are sold

The Punch
One Night, Two Lives, and the Fight That Changed Basketball Forever

"If you've seen the videotape, you've never forgotten the horror.... Now, thanks to John Feinstein, one of our finest sports journalists, NBA fans will better understand the fallout from what has simply become known as 'the punch.'" — Mark Luce, *San Francisco Chronicle*

The Last Amateurs
Playing for Glory and Honor
in Division I College Basketball

"Mr. Feinstein's strength, as always, is his access, and there are numerous behind-the-scenes anecdotes that keep the pages turning." — Larry Platt, *Wall Street Journal*

Back Bay Books
Available wherever paperbacks are sold

John Feinstein on basketball

A March to Madness
The View from the Floor
in the Atlantic Coast Conference

"A basketball junkie's nirvana."   — Charles Hirshberg, *Sports Illustrated*

Back Bay Books
Available wherever paperbacks are sold